Person to Person

PERSON TO PERSON

Positive Relationships Don't Just Happen

Second Edition

Sharon L. Hanna
Southeast Community College

Prentice Hall
Englewood Cliffs, New Jersey 07632

Library of Congress Cataloging-in-Publication Data

Hanna, Sharon L.
Person to person: positive relationships don't just happen / Sharon L. Hanna — 2nd ed.
p. cm.
Includes bibliographical references and index.
ISBN 0-13-226986-4
1. Interpersonal communication. 2. Self-actualization (Psychology) 3. Interpersonal relations. I. Title.
8F637.C45H32 1995
158'.2—dc20 94-31502
CIP

Editorial/production supervision: Jean Lapidus and Kurt Scherwatzky
Interior design: Jean Lapidus
Cover design: Wendy Alling Judy
Buyer: Tricia Kenny

A Simon & Schuster Company
Englewood Cliffs, New Jersey 07632

Printed in the United States of America

10 9 8 7 6 5 4 3 2 1

ISBN 0-13-226986-4

Prentice-Hall International (UK) Limited, London
Prentice-Hall of Australia Pty. Limited, Sydney
Prentice-Hall Canada, Inc., Toronto
Prentice-Hall Hispanoamericana, S.A., Mexico
Prentice-Hall of India Private Limited, New Delhi
Prentice-Hall of Japan, Inc., Tokyo
Simon & Schuster Asia Pte. Ltd., Singapore
Editora Prentice-Hall do Brasil, Ltda., Rio de Janeiro

To Bob Dinkel, my best friend and husband,
with whom I have grown in love and intimacy
and to whom I owe so much;

To my daughters, Lisa and Lyn Patterson,
and my stepsons, Jeff and Greg Dinkel,
who taught and gently guided me
into being both parent and friend;

To my parents, Lorane and Eldred Hanna,
whose love, support, and generosity were always there;

To wonderful family, friends,
and all those memorable human beings
I've connected with along the way,

and

To my students, those unique human beings,
who have touched and enriched my life.

CONTENTS

❧ PREFACE ❧

Person to Person: Positive Relationships Don't Just Happen is intended to encourage and guide you on a journey, first within yourself and then into the world of positive interactions and relationships. Ann Landers once wrote: "Life is peculiar. It waits until we flunk the course and then it teaches us the lesson." All of us will make mistakes during our lives; however, the fewer "courses we flunk," the better. This book, whether you read it for class or for personal reasons, can help you make wise choices and live a happier, more fulfilling life.

Building a positive relationship isn't an accident; each one requires understanding and effort. Relating with people is an art to be learned and practiced. Because the self is the foundation of all relationships, the goals of the first part of the book are self-discovery and self-satisfaction, with practical objectives of self-understanding and heightened self-esteem. Through interpersonal communication human beings interact and relate to one another. Thus, an essential part of human relations is learning how to communicate in a positive way—the objective of the second part of this book. Only after you have learned to love yourself and then develop effective communication skills is success in relationships probable. The last part of this book teaches about various interactions and all kinds of relationships. Career, love, marriage, and family are given special emphasis. The interaction skills presented throughout the book are useful in all walks of life and can help us live positively in a world of diversity.

Features of this book include objectives so that you know what is important, listings of resources for your use, and suggested readings marked in the References to encourage further exploration. I'm especially pleased about a new addition, REFLECTIONS AND APPLICATIONS, a separate section at the back of the book which you are encouraged to complete. The more you involve yourself, the more you will gain.

The book is written in an informal style for two reasons. First, I want it to be understandable and beneficial. Then I want you to get to know me as a human being, with thoughts and feelings similar to yours. Your enjoyment of the book is important, so I hope that the situations and examples will strike familiar chords with you.

I'm excited about this second edition, written three years since the original book. As mentioned, REFLECTIONS AND APPLICATIONS gives a stimulating "think-and-do" or hands-on learning dimension to the book. Also added are such important issues as sociological concepts related to self-development, learning disabilities, the "inner child" as a barrier to self-esteem, major depression, suicide, homosexuality and homophobia, diversity, multiculturism, dysfunctional families, and the important role of fathering. Updating and including more research was a fascinating experience. Such important health issues as AIDS, smoking, weight loss, and alcohol use focus on the latest available research. Reflecting more of a global perspective and multiculturism, studies conducted in other countries or those using diverse ethnic and racial groups are included. Critical thinking skills continue to be emphasized. The number of worthwhile books published since the first edition, while exciting, created a challenge. I wanted to share advice and insight from as many as possible so that they can serve as valuable resources for you.

My hope is that this book will become a cherished companion as you seek to understand yourself and unleash your own unique potential for building enriching relationships. The journey won't always be pleasurable. One 36-year-old student of mine, a Vietnam veteran and recovering alcoholic, wrote: "I had forgotten how much it takes to be a human being. This class has reminded me of that. At first I resisted because it hurt too much, but now I'm glad I let it sink in. It's been to my benefit."

At the end of the book you can be satisfied that you have become better educated about yourself and life. Hopefully, you will have a clear vision of what you want, a realistic idea of how to satisfy your goals, and the positive attitude and high self-esteem needed to achieve harmony and happiness. Inner direction and the realization that life has an ebb and flow can enable you to live life to its fullest with purpose and meaning and to reflect on your past while looking forward optimistically to continued growth and achievement.

If the book does for you what it has for others, I'll be delighted. One student credited the book for making her chosen path clearer. Another of my students once commented: "Thanks so much for my first real lessons about life. I'll never forget it. Now to put it all into practice . . . I can't wait!" I hope that you, too, will learn, grow, and benefit, and then put all you have gained into practice. Do experience joy along the way!

ACKNOWLEDGMENTS

Appreciation and praise are vital to positive human relationships. Although acknowledging by name everyone who has contributed to this book isn't possible, I want to express special thanks to the following people:

My husband and best friend Bob, who at times thought he had lost his wife (and then found her in the den in front of the computer) . . . for his deep love, affirmation, and encouragement, for the back rubs and hugs, for taking over so many responsibilities, and for always being "there" for me.

My family members and friends, whom I have continued to love although I did not spend enough time showing it . . . for their understanding.

The thousands of students and friends who have contributed to my personal growth as well as to this book by sharing their lives with me.

My deep appreciation also goes to the following people, who gave their time and talents behind the scenes:

Trish Reimer, who did research, updated the bibliography, proofread, and generally demonstrated excellence, always in her typically positive and delightful manner. And to her daughter Elizabeth, who waited to be born a week after the manuscript was completed!

Susan M. Dunn, reference specialist at Southeast Community College's Learning Resource Center, who diligently and cheerfully sought and found numerous requested books and articles. Her positive response was always, "I'll take care of it!"

John R. Bellefleur, Ph.D., Oakland Community College, Auburn Hill, Michigan, who responded to my request for input about the book with thoughtfulness and insight and whose ideas are incorporated in this second edition.

Teri Klahr and Ina Kelley, former students, who researched particular topics.

And to those whose work appears in the book: Greg Dinkel, photographer; Roberta Sward, artist; Ben Thomas, cartoonist; Bill Payne, drafter; and Susan Brasch, cover artist.

Copy reader Maria Caruso is to be commended, as are Kurt Scherwatzky and Eileen Smith for their production expertise.

I would like to thank the Prentice Hall reviewers: Professor Steven Stokes, Ricks College, Professor L. William Cheney, Community College of Rhode Island, and Professor Dewitt C. Davison, University of Toledo. Many of their ideas were incorporated.

And to the wonderful people at Prentice Hall: Heidi Freund, Senior Editor, Peter Janzow, Executive Editor, Marilyn Coco, Editorial Assistant, Production Editor Jean Lapidus, Lauren Ward, Executive Marketing Manager, and all the hardworking publisher's representatives who market this book. My questions and concerns were always addressed in the positive ways emphasized in *Person to Person: Positive Relationships Don't Just Happen*. At Prentice Hall they make positive relationships happen!

Sharon L. Hanna

Section One

Relating: Beginning with the Self

OBJECTIVES

After completing this section, you will be able to

- Define human relations and describe its main goals.
- Explain how people learn human relations skills.
- Describe the personal and professional benefits of human relations.
- Recognize that the employee characteristics desired by employers are those that are important in living a happy, satisfying life.
- Contrast personal and professional lives with those in the past.
- Realize that those who have desire can learn human relations skills.

If you want to live life fully, the journey begins within. Learning and applying human relations skills will lead you to healthy and satisfying person-to-person experiences.
—Sharon Hanna

Human beings need to belong and relate. Human development is a "story of learning to attach, to connect, to find ways of meeting one's complex needs for contact" (Josselson, 1992, p. 18). Personal growth and happiness are by-products of positive relationships. Because nobody is born knowing how to relate, interactive skills must be learned and cultivated.

Think of *human relations* as an ongoing interactive process that includes initiating, building, and enriching relationships with different people in a variety of situations. At times, it includes ending relationships. If the process goes well, we are likely to enjoy fulfilling lives. Positive human relations is an art.

How do positive relationships develop? The beginning of healthy relationships lies within the self. Only when you know and love yourself can you reach out positively to others.

Be gentle with yourself
Learn to love yourself,
forgive yourself.
For only as we have the right
attitude toward ourselves,
can we have the right attitude
toward others.

Author unknown

"Self-respect is the foundation of respect for others" (Branden, 1992, p. 15).

Individuals do not always understand the need to learn to relate.

> The expression on Rodney's face during his first human relations class ranged from a sneer to a glare. After class he came to me and said, "I just want you to know that I don't know why I have to take this class. I've been around the horn and seen everything, so I don't need it. What's more, I don't think it can be taught. You either have it, or you don't!" I was taken by surprise by his tirade; I thought that my introductory comments on the "why" of human relations training had been encouraging, if not inspiring. I told him that I hoped he would give the course a chance. Rodney, a defiant man in his late thirties, seemed to say, "I dare you to try to teach me anything."

Rodney's resistance was the greatest challenge in my teaching career. His comment that he had been "around the horn" implied that he already knew all about relating. He is not alone in this thinking. Others believe that experiencing life and just picking up ideas along the way is sufficient training in interacting. Is it? As an employer, would you hire an applicant for an important position who had learned only from trial and error in life's experiences?

The expectation that we learn about human relations simply by living has been challenged in recent years. Relationships do not usually conduct themselves in common sense ways; they are extremely complicated with many challenges and pitfalls (Duck, 1991) and demand careful management and skills.

Fortunately, formal training is now available. A logical place to learn is the edu-

Figure I-1

cational system. A few positive steps have been taken; however, more can be done. Carl Rogers (1972), a therapist who developed major psychological ideas about self-identity, wrote: "Sometimes I feel our education has as one of its major goals the bringing up of individuals to live in isolation cages" (p. 215). Leo Buscaglia (1982), one of the first to teach college classes about love and relationships, is critical of our current educational system, which proclaims the worthy goal of self-realization and then doesn't teach it. He asks: "How many classes did you ever have in your entire educational career that taught you about you?" (p. 71). How many have you had? Most people have had none.

The benefits to students are well documented. Research shows that self-esteem building and human skills training are related to enhanced academic performance (Baker, Beer, and Beer, 1991; Lecky, 1951; Rotheram, 1987). A school-based mediation program improved conflict management at home with a reported decline in frequency and intensity of sibling conflicts, less need for parental intervention, and improvement in communication (Gentry and Benenson, 1993).

Not many courses about self and relationships are offered because of an overloaded curriculum and lack of awareness of how valuable they can be. Even if such courses exist, they are usually not required. Think of people you know who could benefit from personal development and human relations courses. Would they voluntarily take them? One student said, "If only my husband would take this human relations course! But I couldn't drag him here!"

Until such courses are required, most people will continue to learn from experience and untrained "teachers." The home is the first learning environment; our ideas about self and relating to others are actually formed in the cradle. A sad truth is that families can be dysfunctional which means that many individuals learn negative patterns of interacting (Bradshaw, 1992). Humans learn in the following ways.

- Direct instruction ("Don't hit your sister")
- Modeling (watching a parent hit your sister—confusing if you've been told not to hit!)
- Experience (hitting someone and receiving encouragement or discouragement for doing so)

In addition to family members, we learn from friends, school experiences, the media, and other sources in the wider world. Love and marriage are depicted in movies; television soap operas serve as the basis for what many of us learn about relationships. What we learn is often neither helpful nor adequate. Having "been around the horn" just isn't enough.

The art of relating requires learning and practice. This book will help you gain insight into yourself and others, learn to communicate in a positive way, and discover how to develop healthy relationships. Take the time to appraise yourself using the first activity in REFLECTIONS AND APPLICATIONS. Even if you already interact in a positive way and enjoy fulfilling relationships, new human relations challenges will appear as you grow and change. And, as with any art, your present level of skill can be improved. If you are like most people, the experience will be unique!

What are the benefits of learning about self and relations? A basic one is *understanding of self and heightened self-esteem.* Rodney, the reluctant student, did not truly know or like himself, and his lack of self-worth created a fear of self-discovery. For every Rodney, however, there are dozens of others who eagerly anticipate the journey within. Most are pleasantly surprised with what they find. Karen, a young woman, wrote on a self-inventory:

> I've learned so much since I came back to school, but I never expected to learn about me. I never knew how much I was or how much I had the power to be. I never knew how interesting I was. I'm not so bad. I'm okay! No one ever taught me that.
>
> At first I was afraid to meet her . . .
> But you know
> The more I got to know her
> To accept and understand her
> The more I grew to love her.
> She is me.

Learning to relate can get you in touch with yourself and help you build feelings of self-worth.

Taking charge of your own life, being motivated to change, gaining insight into how to adjust, and learning coping strategies are other benefits. Have you ever heard anyone say, "I can't help it. I just can't change"? Some changes may be impossible, yet the self can be improved in a number of ways. The belief that you can change is a result of human relations training.

> I believe that wherever you are in life, and however you learned it, that if you want to learn it differently, anything that can be learned can be unlearned and relearned. So there's always hope and there's always wonder (Buscaglia, 1982, p. 66).

Usually, limits regarding change exist only in the mind.

Even when you want to change, you may still do nothing. The "how-to" component is missing. "All growth is a combination of insight and behavior change. Insight without change is frustrating" (Bloomfield and Felder, 1985, p. 19). Techniques for making desired changes can be learned and applied.

Human relations can also help you cope with stress and crisis. Feeling a heavy burden of guilt, a young student wrote:

> When my cousin was dying of leukemia, I didn't go to see her. I didn't think I could face it. Now she's dead, and I never told her how much I cared.

I tried to be comforting by reminding her that most of us have not been taught how to handle illness and death of loved ones.

A human relations course at my college has produced what could be called miracles. One case was Vernon, a 35-year-old, who reflected deep depression and low self-esteem on his first assignment. He wrote, "Sometimes I feel so totally worthless since I was injured and lost my job that I think my wife and kids would be better off without me." A few months later I was overjoyed to read on another paper:

> I'm beginning to love myself, not in a self-centered, conceited sort of way but that deep down, good kind of feeling that makes me glad I'm me. I'm ecstatic that this course was required. It has helped lift my veil of depression and allowed me an inner calm that has not been mine for some time.

He had learned to deal with crises and depression and, most important, how to change his thoughts about himself. His successes in college and his cheerful, positive attitude helped to create a changed person within a few months.

The ability to develop healthy relationships is essential and is a primary benefit of formal training regarding self and relationships. The quality of our relationships influences how productive and meaningful our lives turn out to be (D. Johnson, 1993). Today, adjustment and relating skills are more necessary than they were in the past. First, life is complicated in this mobile society. Coming into contact with greater numbers of people who are diverse demands finely tuned personal skills. Multicultural awareness and tolerance are expected. Male-female and family roles are more flexible. In a world where children were seen and not heard, communication skills weren't as necessary as they are now. When parents wish children were like "kids in the good old days," they forget that they do not act the way adults did in those "good old days" either. Neither children nor adults tend to be submissive and obedient today (Nelsen, 1987).

Years ago, social concerns such as divorce, teen suicide, drug use, and violence weren't occurring in the numbers they are today. For example, gunshots now cause one out of every four deaths among American teenagers, and the National Education Association reports that an estimated 100,000 students carry a gun to school (Hull, 1993). The leading causes of adolescent deaths are violent ones (Schachter, 1992). These demand special personal coping strategies.

Because we are afforded more choices than our ancestors were, decision-making skills are necessary. Change has always occurred; however, change years ago happened so slowly it almost went unnoticed. "There was a predictability about their lives. Now we can no longer say with any certainty what the next 10 years or even the next 1 year will bring, and the new roller coaster of change rolls faster and faster" (Helmstetter, 1991, p. 23). Finally, even if life stayed the same, simply because of longer life expectancy, humans experience many more interactions and relationships.

Both personal and professional relationships can be enriched as knowledge and skills are increased. Too often, married couples who don't know what to do about their problems either divorce or settle for less than a satisfying relationship. If people learn to relate, problems can be either avoided or solved. Remember Rodney? Toward the end of the course, he came into my office and announced, "I have to hand it to you. You've finally taught me something I can use. My wife and I have been having problems, and the stuff about fighting fair just might help." I was elated! Along with couple relationships, parenting is easier and more enjoyable after training. The probability of raising well adjusted children is higher if parents learn how. I am convinced that those who learn relationship skills will be better parents.

Possessing positive human relations skills will also be of great benefit in your career. Knowing yourself will assist you in choosing a satisfying career field; having a high level of self-esteem will help you get the job you want; having "people" skills will make you a valued employee. Employers often remark that they can teach technical skills, but they want the individuals they hire to come equipped with human relations expertise. Studies show that many of the people who have difficulty obtaining or holding a job or advancing to positions of greater responsibility possess the needed technical competence, but lack interpersonal competence (Reece and Brandt, 1993).

Employees are viewed as representatives of the employer. An owner of a fabricating company remarked, "I have a few employees I try to keep hidden from the public, and it's become increasingly difficult to do that." A truck-driving student announced, "I'm going into trucking because I just like to be alone." He learned quickly that he had chosen the wrong field. Unless you are training to be a hermit, ability to get along with people is a definite asset.

Generally, either personal or professional success will bring rewards in the other. Being satisfied with personal relationships will increase the likelihood of developing positive ones at work. Similarly, difficulty in one arena can lead to problems in the other. In research on home-to-work stress contagion, husbands were more likely than wives to bring their home stressors into the workplace, but both were affected by overloads and arguments at home (Bolger, et al., 1989). Those with rich personal lives tend to be more productive and satisfied with their work, according to *Psychology Today* (1993).

Another beneficial, and often overlooked, result of human relations training is *reduction in tragedy*. From 1986 to 1991, murders committed by teens 14 to 17 years old grew by 124 percent (Gibbs, 1993). Several of these tragic cases might not have occurred if individuals had learned to handle frustrations without hurting others. Two students in my human relations course lost their lives because others lashed out savagely. One was burned to death in a fire set by an angry stranger. Another was bludgeoned to death by two teenagers. Violence, suicide, alcoholism and other drug abuse, job failure, and poor academic performance are partly the result of not paying attention to relationships (Duck, 1991). Not all tragedy can be prevented, yet a dramatic decrease in the number of tragic incidents is possible.

The story of Rodney ends here. He called me at home one night after completion of the course. Obviously distraught, he said:

> I need to talk to you. I fell off the wagon and started drinking again today. I've just called my AA sponsor, and the only other person I want to talk to is you.

I continued to listen, and one point was especially poignant.

> I know now that if I had been raised differently and had understood myself better, I probably wouldn't be like this today. I could have used the human relations course years ago. In fact, I know now that I would have gotten a lot out of it back when I took it with you, but I was afraid and closed my mind to it. I wish I could take it again.

I have not heard from Rodney since and would love to have him take the course again. My sincere hope is that he has found a way to turn his life around. It was encouraging that he realized he could change. This was the necessary first step.

What Rodney indicated, *desire to learn and willingness to change* are all that one needs to improve human relations skills. You might question the necessity of other criteria. Don't you have to be physically attractive or smart to relate to others? Isn't it necessary to have an outgoing personality? The answer to each is no. Even though certain characteristics are advantageous, there are no physical, mental, or personality requirements beyond basic abilities as shown in these profiles:

- Alice, by society's standards, is considered homely. She had a lonely childhood and no boyfriends until after college. Yet, Alice's self-esteem is high, she is a sincere person with a strong compassion for others and is successful in her career.
- Verleen describes herself sometimes as a "chubbette." She handles it with humor, never as a drawback! Her ready wit makes her the center of attention in any group. She is generous and caring, a joy to be around. Those extra pounds are no obstacle.
- Bill has spent his entire 30 years in a wheelchair. He was born with cerebral palsy. Cheerful and friendly to everyone, he enjoys communicating. He is concerned about others and has a positive attitude.
- Chris is in his twenties; however, he has the mental ability of a much younger person. He was born with Down syndrome. His IQ is not high, yet his SQ (social quotient) would be hard to surpass! He is loving, congenial, and genuinely concerned about people and praised for his attitude and determination.

- Jan is introverted and prefers to be with just a few people at a time. She is not a party-goer. She is supportive to her friends, a great listener, polite, and fair-minded.

These individuals lack what might be considered the ideal "basics" for human relations; yet, they demonstrate positive behaviors. It may have been difficult for them to excel in "people" skills, yet each succeeded because of a desire to relate in a positive way. You, too, can learn, grow, and relish the joys and rewards of positive relationships. The process begins with you!

> *I am convinced that much human misery is rooted in ignorance of self and relationships.*
>
> —Teresa Adams

Figure I-2 Verleen, a delightful person who has learned to relate positively to others.

1

Knowing and Valuing Yourself

OBJECTIVES

After completing this chapter, you will be able to

- Explain the benefits of self-knowledge and understanding.
- Differentiate between the "I" and "me" of the self.
- Describe the four developmental areas of the self.
- Define attitude, compare a positive attitude and a negative one, and list benefits of a positive attitude.
- Relate the four developmental areas of the self to the others.
- Explain self-concept, self-esteem, and ideal self.
- Give reasons why high self-esteem is important.
- Explain the sources of self-concept.
- Discuss ways to build self-esteem.
- Use cognitive restructuring.
- Define self-fulfilling prophecy and recognize its existence in your own thinking.
- Define self-efficacy and discuss its implications.
- Raise your own self-esteem level.

The unexamined life is not worth living.

—Socrates

How would you reply to the question "Who are you?" An off-the-top-of-my-head answer is, "I am Sharon Hanna." Yet, you and I are much more than names, statuses, or even lists of descriptors. Each of us is a unique whole self, an integrated human being.

An early pioneer in understanding the self was George Herbert Mead, a sociologist. He believed that the process of social experience and activity shape what is called *the self.* "Selves can only exist in definite relationships to other selves" (Mead, 1934, p. 164). He divided the self into two components, the "me" consisting of the attitudes of others taken over into one's self and the "I" which is how we respond to the attitudes of others and includes thoughts and actions. From the "me," we know how to behave at a funeral or in a classroom. Your "I" could decide to violate a norm and behave in a bizarre way at a funeral or, hopefully not, in my classroom!

Psychologists, too, have a keen interest in the self. The humanistic approach focuses on a complete, or holistic, view of self. The emphasis of humanistic psychology is not selfishness but self-discovery, self-awareness, and self-fulfillment. A humanistic goal is to help people become fully functioning and achieve their full potential and, thus, have more to give to others.

Although learning about the self can be fascinating, reluctance to seek insight is common. Initial pain may be the price one pays. I encourage anyone who is hesitant to press on as the rewards are many, and as the process continues, the discomfort becomes less painful. "The greatest joy in life is to know oneself from the inside out. Such knowledge enables us to know another and be known" (Adams, 1987, p. 1). Among the markers of maturity are accurate self-insight and understanding (Heath, 1991). However, self-discovery isn't a quick study nor one that is ever finished. "The self is a vast continent whose exploration we can never complete" (Branden, 1983, p. 173).

YOUR DEVELOPMENTAL AREAS

Recognizing that the self is whole, experts in the human development field identify areas of change over a lifespan. These parts are typically studied in child development courses. Well-known child-development specialist Burton White (1975), in his book *The First Three Years of Life*, pays special attention to four of these parts: physical, mental or intellectual, emotional, and social. Let's take the self apart and concentrate on one area at a time, with the assurance that it (and we) will come together again!

Physical Self

The physical area of the self includes appearance and condition of body. Characteristics such as race, sex, hair texture, natural hair and eye color, bone structure, height, and size of feet are either determined or greatly influenced by heredity. Others such as hues of complexion, weight, hair style, and muscle tone are within our control. Accepting what cannot be changed is wise. For example, your age was determined by others—your parents. It does no good to bemoan the fact that one is 20 years old, or 30, or—for some the worst of all—40! Each of us will age—as long as we are alive! Viewing the aging process as depressing, which is common in this society, is setting yourself up for despair. Similarly, wishing to be another sex or race or 4 inches taller is self-defeating.

Recognizing the positive changes you can make, however, is exciting. Try to think of any possible physical improvement. Most say that they would like to exercise for conditioning or weight loss or both. Exercise has additional benefits including bolstering our immune systems. In one study inactive women who began walking 45 minutes a day, 5 days a week, got half as many colds as women who didn't exercise (Laliberte, 1993).

Figure 1-1

Sedentary men with diabetes are three times more likely to die than active men (*Prevention*, 1993). The cardiovascular system benefits from just 30 minutes a day of moderate activity such as yard work and walking (Painton, 1993). The key is to find something you enjoy doing. Later chapters give other reasons to become more physically active. Reasons for not exercising are easy to find. "I can't afford to join a health club right now" or "I don't have time" are among the most common. In Chapter 3 you will see how excuses can block happiness. Be honest with yourself. If you sincerely want to exercise, you can. In fact, keeping to a regular exercise program is a statement of personal power (Ryan and Travis, 1991). Carve out the time needed and then walk, jog, swim, or exercise at home! Other improvement possibilities are a new hair cut or style, fingernail growth, better nutrition—any number of possibilities. Wellness, which is excellent health, is emphasized throughout this book with specific areas covered in Chapter 5.

A strong point could be made that Americans pay too much attention to one part of the physical self: the outer shell. Women work hard to achieve certain standards of beauty. How one looks can become an obsession and often leads to undue emphasis on the female body. Another point is that women are less apt to consider what feels comfortable. It is doubtful that men would ever squeeze their feet into pointed-toed, high-heeled shoes just to look good.

Achieving the "thin look" can become all-important, and most females are dissatisfied. A study of female adolescents found that over 54 percent rated themselves as too fat; yet, only 17 percent were overweight (Page, 1991). It is sad that we put such a high premium on weight especially when health isn't even the reason! Being considerably over one's ideal weight can be a health hazard so a deliberate attempt to achieve a fit body is positive. Losing weight healthfully is covered in Chapter 5. Reasons for resisting are usually psychological. A young woman wrote:

> My weight has been my protection from people.
> It's a shield I could hide behind and feel safe.
> I have noticed cracks in that shield recently, and I am finding the will to change.

Recently, men have felt pressured to achieve a "look." Steroids are used for purely cosmetic reasons. In a study of high schoolers, a third of those who took steroids wanted to acquire a muscular look (Toufexis, 1989). Sadly, this carries risks including irritability, hostility, and mood swings. While the effects vary among individuals, anger, distractibility, violent feelings, insomnia, confusion, forgetfulness, and headaches are possible (Sealock, 1993). Steroid users often develop mood disorders that may be accompanied by violent or aggressive behavior (*The Menninger Letter*, 1994b). The desire to be muscular certainly isn't worth the price especially since other ways to achieve that look are available.

Both male and female Caucasians in the American society have "bought into" the belief that a tan look is attractive and necessary in spite of conclusive research on skin cancer. The incidence of melanoma, a serious form of cancer, has increased about 4 percent every year since 1973. The encouraging news is that the share of those who avoid tans is higher than those who seek them (Waldrop, 1993). Awareness does help, and a change in this particular standard of attractiveness would be most welcomed.

Overemphasizing a person's appearance is unfortunate and can limit possibilities. If you judge others only on "looks," you could be led into unhealthy relationships as well as miss out on other wonderful opportunities. Check your appraisal of your physical self and decide to make wholesome and realistic improvements. Looking as attractive as possible can be an enjoyable expression of how we feel about ourselves. It becomes a problem when we believe that how we look is a yardstick for our value as a person (Bepko and Kreston, 1990).

Mental Self

The mental and or intellectual self is fascinating. Learning abilities, thought-processing patterns as well as beliefs and attitude are facets of this important area of the self. Cognitive (thought) development occurs throughout one's life.

Mental abilities. How mentally able are you? Tests have been developed to measure intelligence and aptitude. What intelligence means and how to assess it are controversial issues. For years *intelligence* was considered to be a capacity or potential that every human being possesses to some extent. Recently, attempts have been made to change this definition. Howard Gardner (1983), professor of education at Harvard, defines intelligence as the ability to solve problems or create products that are valued within one or more cultural settings. He proposes that human beings have *multiple intelligences*. In addition to language and mathematical competence, he includes music, spatial relationships (perceiving the world accurately and being able to re-create or transform parts of that world), bodily kinesthetic (using the body and handling objects skillfully), and two intelligences clearly in the realm of human relations: interpersonal (getting along with others) and intrapersonal (empathy and insight). He contends that a narrow scholastic definition of intelligence causes most children to think they are stupid even though they have valuable abilities. Other researchers note that nonacademic abilities (everyday competence, problem solving, social competence, and display of curiosity) are as important as what has been considered intelligence (Rodin et al., 1990). Intelligence is often gauged by intelligence quotient (IQ) tests. Whatever IQ tests measure, researchers believe that heredity is 50 to 70 percent responsible (Franklin, 1989). Educators probably used an IQ score as an indicator of your level of ability and potential mainly in language and mathematics.

Caution is advised in interpreting test scores. Low achievement can be caused not by lack of intelligence but by test anxiety or *learning disabilities*, a group of related and often overlapping conditions that lead to low achievement by people who have the potential to do much better (Smith, 1991). Most with learning disabilities are quite talented and bright; however, this does not show up in traditional schooling. Fortunately, the educational system has recognized that not everyone learns the same and has found ways to diagnose and then help those who learn differently. Reading books such as *Succeeding Against the Odds* (Smith, 1991) and seeking help from a specialist can make all the difference in the world. "College students with learning disabilities who ask a lot of questions and seek support are more likely to graduate than those who don't" (p. 268). By learning to learn differently, those with learning disabilities can realize their potential. Most important is degree of motivation. Grades in school are frequently a reflection of how much effort a person is willing to make. Whatever your measured degree of intelligence or your style of learning, you choose how to use it.

Learning readiness and strategies. Willingness and eagerness to learn are valuable traits, and employers view them as assets. Curiosity about a number of subjects can result in a well-rounded person who is both interested and interesting. Neurolinguistic programming (NLP), as an educational process, encourages curiosity.

> Consider making everything into an introductory seminar, in the sense that you never learn so much that you miss what else there is to know. All too often, people forget how to not know (Bandler, 1985, p. 157).

You may be surprised to realize that being confused can set the stage for learning. Questioning is usually positive even though it may be considered negative. Students confess that they are afraid to ask questions citing situations in which they were put down or laughed at because they did so. This is unfortunate. What is often the case in an average classroom is that only the teacher asks questions. In one study 40 questions were asked *and answered* by the teacher during a class period (*Adult Perspective*, 1992). As an instructor, I will, if necessary, "play a waiting game!" If you are reluctant to ask a question, examine why and try to overcome the hesitancy. Questions can be asked orally or silently as you read and listen. Try to regard questions as an indication of some knowledge and a desire to learn that will broaden your ability to think.

How do you learn most easily? Individuals typically learn from their experiences so actual hands-on learning is desirable. *Experiential learning*, as these experiences are called, is effective. For example, you may have been instructed verbally on how to set a videocassette recorder. Wouldn't it have been better to have actually gone through the motions, as well?

Thought processing is an integral part of life. As you read this book, you will see how important thoughts are. "All our distinctively human accomplishments are the reflections of our ability to think" (Branden, 1987, p. 27). Each person develops methods of processing information and acquires a number of beliefs. These ideas are beneficial only if they aren't so rigid that they limit a person's ability to discover, think, and learn.

Critical and creative thinking. How much have your ever thought about thinking? Where did you learn to think? Or were you ever taught actual thinking skills? *Thinking* is the ability to activate and then pursue mental activity in any number of situations. For years our education system presumed that if students were reasonably intelligent, they were able to think and didn't need training. Educators only gave information and told students about ideas. The same practices exist today and do not encourage thinking.

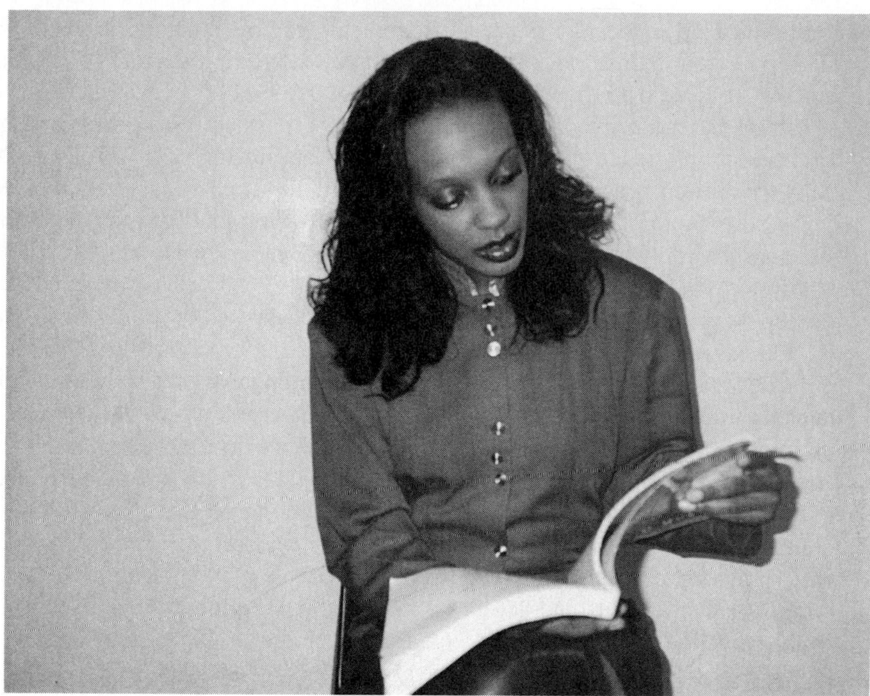

Figure 1-2 Reading is a favorite way to develop mentally.

> The emphasis on standardized test scores encourages teachers to toss chunks of predigested knowledge to students to be copied into notebooks, memorized, and reproduced on demand for the exam. No wonder that most young people see "real" education as: "Don't confuse me with questions. Just give me the answers to copy—and tell me when the test is" (Janko, March, 1989, p. 544).

Too often, only memorization skills are needed, and those who have difficulty memorizing don't do well. Ability to think is rarely assessed. The course of education often follows this path: (1) a teacher (a big pitcher) pours into little pitchers (students), (2) on examinations, the little pitchers pour back into the big pitcher, (3) the little pitchers (students) have nothing left to use!

> Much of our educational system is geared toward teaching people the one right answer. By the time the average person finishes college, he or she will have taken over 2600 tests, quizzes, and exams. Thus, the "right answer" approach becomes deeply ingrained in our thinking. This may be fine for some mathematical problems where there is only one right answer. The difficulty is that most of life doesn't present itself in this way. Life is ambiguous; there are many right answers—all depending on what you are looking for. But if you think there is only one right answer, then you will stop looking as soon as you find one (von Oech, 1983, p. 21).

Being "right" or certain stops us from being curious, and curiosity is the basis of learning.

Taking nothing for granted is one aspect of *critical thinking*. Do you believe everything you read or hear? If so, you aren't using critical thinking. Do you "dig" deeper, challenge assumptions, and examine the logic of differing points? If so, you are thinking! Try to develop a "working knowledge" of material by thinking, talking, and actually using what has been read or presented. A study revealed that students of high and average mental abilities profited from learning critical thinking skills (Gadzella et al., 1989). Another showed that problem solving and creativity could be taught (Boyle et al., 1991).

You employ *creative thinking* when you think about ideas in different ways and generate a variety of solutions to problems. In fact, brilliance has been defined as the ability to look at old things in new ways (Zois, 1992). The basis of creativity is mental flexibility. When you realize that there's no particular reason to do things the way they have always been done, creative thinking is set in motion (von Oech, 1986). Try creative thinking and come up with different uses for common objects such as a brick. A problem that isn't too difficult (although you may be surprised how many times individuals don't seem to be able to solve it) is that it's 7:30 in the morning, and your car won't start. You have a class in 1 hour. What can you do? Creative thinking is liberating!

Why are different types of thinking so important? First, new facts and opinions bombard us. Every day we decide which conclusions to accept, which to reject, and which to withhold judgment on (Browne and Keeley, 1990). Too often, people depend upon so-called experts and accept all that they see and hear. This, in turn, causes what could be called "brain death" or, at least, a decrease in the active use of the mind. "As far as your brain is concerned, it's clearly a case of 'use it or lose it' " (Benson, 1987, p. 35). And learning to use it in critical and creative ways is excellent mental exercise!

I recall a middle-aged student who approached me the last day of a sociology course. He said, "Well, I don't know for sure how much I've learned, but all of it really taught me to think." I told him that learning how to think was the most valuable lesson of all. Limiting yourself by lack of curiosity, fear of questioning, and lack of confidence is a waste of human potential. As you read this book and participate in discussions, use your wonderful mind to ask questions, present alternative ideas, and generate thoughts! Be like Carolyn, a middle-aged student, who wrote: "My mind has been resting on a shelf for too long, and now it's ready to apply its power!"

Attitude. Part of the mental self is *attitude*, a word defined broadly as an overall approach to life, the "way you look at your whole environment" (Chapman, 1993 p. 21). In referring to the future, the words optimistic and pessimistic are used. Optimists who have positive thoughts about the future were identified in a study as being generally healthier and enjoying greater successes (Myers, 1992). Optimistic patients do

Figure 1-3

better because they believe a positive change is probable while pessimists seem less likely to change any unhealthy habits (Goleman, 1991b). In contrasting the two words humorously, think of optimists as being "sure they'll never die or if they do die, they'll wake up to the glory of heaven, while pessimists are sure that they won't live much longer, and that if they wake up in heaven, they won't like it" (Chance, 1988a, p. 18). Optimists and pessimists who have the same experiences interpret them differently.

Some people have been "attituded" excessively, with such common statements as "Your attitude stinks," "If you'd only improve your attitude," or "You've got an attitude" so I sometimes hesitate to introduce the subject to my classes. However, the effect of attitude on the self is so powerful that it cannot be disregarded because of the word's overuse.

> If you can create and keep a positive attitude toward your job, your company, and life in general, you should not only move up the ladder of success quickly and gracefully, you should also be a happier person. If you are unable to do this, you may find many doors closed to you on the job, and your personal life less than exciting (Chapman, 1993, p. 20).

Attitude is described as positive or negative; it usually varies between these two extremes. A positive attitude is not equivalent to a "Pollyanna" way of looking at life. That is, you can still have a positive attitude and realize that life is not absolutely wonderful all of the time. Being positive means that you look on the brighter side of events, that you are more "up" than "down," and that you usually feel responsible and in control of yourself. Positive people are generally energetic, motivated, and alert.

With a negative attitude the world almost always appears bleak, a "down" feeling is apparent, and blaming and excuse making are common. Think of someone you know whose attitude is negative. Any of these descriptions may come to your mind: fault finding, irresponsible, lazy, apathetic, complaining, or gloomy. An individual who fits this description is likely to be avoided by others. "Misery may love company, but company doesn't love misery" (Myers, 1992, p. 20).

Employers want employees with positive attitudes. The answers to "why" they do could be found in the preceding paragraph.

> Attitudes are caught more than they are taught. Both negative and positive attitudes are transmitted on the job. A persistently negative attitude, like the rotten apple in the barrel, can spoil the positive attitudes of others. It is very difficult to maintain a high level of productivity while working next to a person with a negative attitude (Chapman, 1993, p. 23).

Attitudes are truly contagious!

In specific situations, employees can especially benefit from positive attitudes. Pretend you are a supervisor. You have two employees who have a disagreement, and they come to talk to you. Jim is a positive person, and he rarely complains. Jean's attitude is generally negative, and this is not the first gripe she has brought to you. The two tell different versions of the same event. Which one will you believe? Even if Jean's version is accurate, the odds are that Jim's story will carry more weight!

A positive attitude is highly desirable beyond the workplace as well. Ask athletic coaches, teachers, and others who work with people about the advantages of a positive attitude. Positive individuals are better competitors and give up less easily; they try harder in the classroom and use their mistakes to improve; they are enjoyable people, and interactions with them are more productive. Think about individuals you know. Don't you prefer to be around those who are more "up" than "down"? An outstanding example of a positive attitude maintained against all odds was Mike, a student who wrote as a description of himself: "I have a slight health problem-cystic fibrosis, but I don't let it get me down." Cystic fibrosis is much more than a *slight* health problem; however, Mike has never let it change his marvelous attitude.

Examine your way of approaching life. You have an opportunity to rate your attitude in REFLECTIONS AND APPLICATIONS and compare it with what others think. Remember that attitude is always a choice; the key is to change both thoughts and behaviors. The book *Learned Optimism* (Seligman, 1990) is an excellent guide with ideas on how to become more positive. Coursework can also help. I was delighted when a student wrote on a paper, "After only two human relations classes, I have a better attitude about life!"

A positive attitude is a major component in what is called the *power of thought*. Norman Cousins (1979, 1983, 1989) told remarkable stories of his recoveries from a serious illness and a heart attack and of research he was involved with at UCLA. All indicated that mental attitude can influence the course of diseases. "Intense determination and hope can have a physiological effect" (Cousins, 1989, p. 12). Researchers are studying the mind-body connection in health-related matters and discovering how to use the mind to improve performance and conquer pain. "Just as belief or attitude may cause pain, our mental processes can also reduce or eliminate painful sensations" (Benson, 1987, p. 84). In this book you will learn more about the power of the mind and how to change your thoughts.

Emotional Self

A third part of the self is emotional which is composed of feelings and ways of expressing them. Human beings are often unaware of their emotions. For example, when asked, "What are you feeling right now?" a common answer is, "I don't know." Each of us is emotional; that is, we experience emotions which color our lives. Personal expressions of feelings vary considerably. Because of its importance, Chapter 4 is devoted to the subject of the emotional self.

Social Self

"How do you get along with other people?" This question relates to your social self. The *statuses*—positions you have—and *roles*—behaviors practiced in those statuses, your relationships, and how you behave socially are vital to your well-being. Humans

Figure 1-4

Figure 1-5

require interactions with others in order to be loved and to learn to love. Sociologists point out that we must have social exchanges in order to learn to be human. "One has to be a member of a community to be a self" (Mead, 1934, p. 162). Nobody can survive in a vacuum!

A primary objective of this book is to guide you in the development of relationships. A beginning step is to understand how you have socially developed. Personality, covered in Chapter 2, plays a major role in the social aspects of life.

YOUR WHOLE SELF

Fortunately, you aren't like Humpty-Dumpty who couldn't be put back together again! The parts comprise a whole, and examining your integrated self is fascinating. "Every baby born into this world is a living question mark. The first question asked is about self: Who am I?" (Powell, 1976, p. 47). Humans continue to search for the answer. By discovering and valuing your own self-identity, you can have a positive relationship with yourself.

Coming together, or integration of the self, is illustrated in Fig. 1-6. The arrows indicate that the parts are interrelated, and they influence each other both negatively and positively. Can you remember a time when you were not feeling well physically? What were you like mentally, emotionally, socially? Even if you didn't realize it, you were probably diminished in the other areas, too. The good news, which has already been mentioned, is that a positive spillover also occurs. Attitude can make a positive difference in the physical, emotional, and social parts of life. Studies indicate how important it is to pay attention to a patient's emotional distress and social support along with the physical. A 1990 Stanford University study revealed that women with advanced breast cancer who were in support groups lived twice as long as others (Goleman, 1991). Medical research showed that depression produces profound physiological changes and can adversely affect the body. On the other hand, a decline in depression as well as determination and purpose can activate forces within the immune system setting the stage for improvement (Cousins, 1989).

Improving yourself physically, mentally, emotionally, or socially will create benefits in the other developmental areas. Pat, a young woman who for years felt inferior and was depressed and shy, lost weight and had her hair cut and styled. She reported how much better she felt emotionally and described a definite improvement in her social relationships. The connections among the four aspects are exciting and have been the focus of several research studies. "Medical researchers are discovering connections between the belief system and the healing system. They are discovering the way all the body's systems are interconnected" (Cousins, 1991, p. 84).

The first activity in REFLECTIONS AND APPLICATIONS gives you an opportunity to describe yourself in all areas. Checking to see that you are balanced in the four

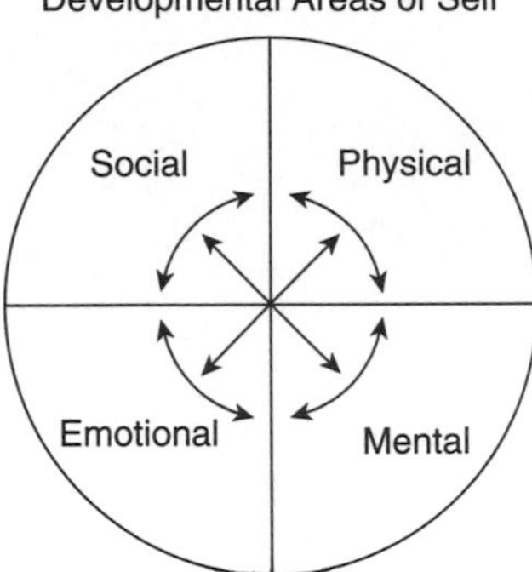

Figure 1-6

areas is also important. Some people devote a great deal of time and energy to their mental self and exclude their social development. Others build their bodies and are a stranger to their feelings. Jack was happy-go-lucky and sociable. He left home to attend college. Within a year he was depressed, and he sought counseling. He had been concentrating on social activities and found himself failing in school and feeling physically ill; he slept minimally, his diet was poor, and he drank excessive amounts of alcohol. He learned the hard way that he was an integrated being.

YOUR PICTURE OF SELF: SELF-CONCEPT

An individual's collection of thoughts describes the self.

> The most important psychologic discovery of this century is the discovery of the self-image. Whether we realize it or not, each of us carries about with us a mental blueprint or picture of ourselves. This self-image is a conception of "the sort of person I am" (Maltz, 1960, p. 2).

How this self develops is of interest to both sociologists and psychologists. Of utmost influence is the *generalized other* which Mead (1934) described as the organized community or social group. Thinking of the attitude of the whole community gives you a concept of the generalized other. Have you ever thought, "I can't do that. What would *they* think?" If "they" doesn't refer to specific persons and means a collective attitude, you are tapping into the generalized other which guides our behaviors and development of self.

All of the ideas you have gleaned about yourself make up what is called the *self-concept*. Included are descriptors of yourself in all areas, an ideal self, and the sense of self-worth or self-esteem you possess. Using the key word "like," this may help to conceptualize self-concept. Think of it as: (1) what I'm like, (2) what I'd like to be like, (3) how much I like what I'm like.

Carl Rogers (1961) was one of the first to write about self-concept and how it develops. As a psychotherapist, Rogers worked with clients as they struggled with crises. At the heart of most problems was a search for self. Fulfillment of self means that one is basically positive, open to experience, trustful of his or her own thoughts and feelings, self-valuative rather than at the mercy of others' approval, and willing to be a process rather than a product. Rogers was optimistic about human potential and believed that the search for self is ongoing.

Figure 1-7

Your current self description and your *ideal self*, the image of what you would like to be, may be similar or quite different. Because of external standards, you may have an unrealistic ideal. If so, that image is more hurtful than helpful. Amy described herself as a little overweight, short, red-haired, average in intelligence, not artistically talented, impulsive, talkative with friends, shy with strangers, and unhappy much of the time. Her ideal self, she was quick to describe, was slim, at least 5 feet 6 inches tall, brilliant, artistic, always in control, less talkative with friends, friendly and outgoing with strangers, always happy, and not red-headed. Decide which descriptors of her ideal can help her improve and which would just be hurtful. As was mentioned earlier, knowing what you can change and what you cannot is valuable. Amy has formulated an ideal self that, in some respects, is not possible.

Also important is to realize that achieving one's ideal self is not a requirement for high self-esteem nor happiness. Instead, if your ideal is reached, set your sights even higher. People who think they have reached the ideal can be annoying as they try to fool themselves and others. "Most people who seem to have it all together are pretty much fake" (Nathanson, 1992, p. 202). Try thinking of this image as your *possible self*, rather than ideal self. Then, use it to discover ways to improve in realistic ways remembering that you are involved in a lifelong process of striving for betterment.

YOUR OWN EVALUATION: SELF-ESTEEM

A critical part of self-concept is the value that we place on ourselves known as *self-esteem* or self-worth. Whether you perceive yourself to be competent to cope with life's challenges and to be deserving of happiness is a reflection of your self-esteem (Branden, 1992). Esteem can be thought of as a point on a scale ranging from very low to very high; it goes beyond acceptance of self and is virtually self-love.

You may be thinking, "Love myself? That's selfish!" This notion was disputed by Fromm (1956) who asserted that a selfish person does not possess true self-love. His belief that self-love is necessary in order to love others is now widely accepted. In fact, self-love and love of others may be indistinguishable (Peck, 1978). If you are a loving individual and care about yourself, then you can be of value to others.

Can you think too highly of yourself? What is the difference between self-love and vanity or conceit? Vain individuals do not truly love themselves; instead, they love an image of themselves which is usually mere appearance (Halberstam, 1993). Self-inflation is a sign of self-doubt. A person whose self-esteem is low may try to mask inadequate feelings with a false show of pride (May, 1953). Genuine love for self is a feeling of worth and dignity. Branden (1983) makes a sensible point: "No one would ask, 'Is it possible to enjoy too high a level of physical health?' Health is an unqualified desirable. So is positive self-esteem" (p. 15).

Self-esteem is of utmost importance. One of our primary needs as humans is to feel worthwhile (Glasser, 1965; Maslow, 1968). Self-worth is essential to mental health (Peck, 1978) and the most valuable psychological possession of a human being (Powell, 1976). A Gallup poll of thousands found 89 percent believing that self-esteem was important in motivating a person to work hard and succeed (Adler, 1992). From my work with thousands of students of all ages, I am convinced that the vital ingredient of a satisfying life, in and out of the classroom, is a positive reflection of self.

Effects of Self-Esteem

What specific areas of life are affected by self-esteem? A quick and wise response would be, "All areas."

Academic success. Some of the earliest self-worth experiments were carried out by Lecky (1951). He showed that performance changed when a student's self-image was altered. Studies have found a significant positive correlation between self-esteem, grade-point average, and positive classroom behavior (Baker et al., 1991; Rotheram, 1987). Students identified as gifted were found to have adequate self-esteem (Pearson and Beer, 1990). In terms of potential academic performance, a student's IQ score may not be as important as the self-esteem rating. "Self-confidence permits a child to perform; whereas brilliance may be trapped in low self-esteem" (Briggs, 1970, p. 270). Although individuals with low self-esteem can achieve, they will be less effective and creative than they could be and "crippled in ability to find joy in achievements" (Branden, 1992, p. 10).

Emotions and behaviors. Happiness and high self-esteem are positively related (Joubert, 1990) while low self-esteem, loneliness, and depression, which can cause one to question life's meaning, often go hand-in-hand (Jackson and Cochran, 1991; Kernis et al., 1991; Workman and Beer, 1989). In a study, the 29 percent of high school students who had thought about suicide were more likely to have lower self-esteem along with poorer quality friendships and a history of more stressful life events. "Life has little purpose if one's self lacks value or merit" (Robertson and Simons, 1989, p. 135).

A study of college students related low self-esteem to unhappiness, fatigue, and withdrawal (Epstein, 1976). Connections between depression and low self-esteem have been found (Hymes and Akiyama, 1991; Myers, 1992); raising self-esteem may alleviate depressed feelings (*The Menninger Letter*, 1994a). Shyness and self-esteem are also related (Zimbardo, 1977). Calling self-esteem the "mainspring that slates every child for success or failure," Briggs (1970) describes how self-worth influences human relations, productivity, creativity, and stability. "Self-esteem is the armor that protects kids from the dragons of life: drugs, alcohol, delinquency, and unhealthy relationships" (McKay and Fanning, 1987, p. 226). A search for markers of happiness found that self-esteem definitely mattered. "When the going gets tough, those with strong feelings of self-worth keep going" (Myers, 1992, p. 108).

Self-improvement and choices. Self-esteem enables us to assess ourselves realistically and to make desirable changes. In fact, the greater the number of choices and decisions we face, the more urgent our need is for self-esteem (Branden, 1992).

A benefit to those with high self-esteem is the ability to recognize self-improvement possibilities and the tendency to view criticism as constructive. They do not interpret a "no" as an assault or a rejection; instead, they usually learn from mistakes and have more energy to begin anew. Both Lisa and Sue were criticized by their track coach for not pacing themselves over a long race. Lisa accepted the criticism and changed her pattern. Sue, whose self-esteem was below average at the time, became disheartened and quit the team. Individuals with healthy self-worth are likely to view difficulty as a challenge, choose wisely, and engage in positive personal growth.

Evidence of the powerful impact of self-esteem is beautifully demonstrated in two poems written by a delightful student. Lorena's self-esteem was rising when she started the human relations course, and as she put it, "The class was the 'icing on the cake'!" What Lorena achieved was finding her true self.

A Little Girl in Grown-up Clothes

A little girl in grown-up clothes
Sitting here in this world unknown.
No one knows how much I feel
I think that this world is fake, unreal.
The wind sweeps by, the rain may fall
What's it all matter, when you feel so small.
I look at myself, I can't explain what I see
I want to be someone, I want to be me.
I try so hard to reach so high
Then I look again and ask myself why.
I want to conquer mountains too high to climb
Seems these days I don't have the time.
I tell myself I know it's there
Yet I can't find it, someone show me where.
A little girl in grown-up clothes
It's just a disguise, and no one knows.

—Lorena Lutz, 1980

To My Teacher: Who Helped the Little Girl Blossom and Grow

A little girl in grown-up clothes
Learning to understand "myselfs" unknown.
Learning to like the way I feel
Knowing I'm important, I have meaning, I'm real!
The wind sweeps by, I watch the rain fall
Isn't it wonderful to find joy in it all?
I look at myself, and I like what I see
I'm special, I'm happy, I'm proud to be me.
I'm not perfect, I can always try

I've learned to set goals but not too high.
Happiness isn't found in a mountain you can climb
It is right inside me, something I've learned to find.
A little girl who's learning to "grow."
I can throw away my disguises
*For now I **want** to let myself show.*

—Lorena Lutz, 1990

Relationships. Friendships and love relationships thrive in the presence of high self-esteem. Feeling liked and loved by others isn't possible until you believe you deserve it. A study of 524 college students indicated that a combination of low self-esteem, depression, and reassurance seeking put males at higher risk of rejection by roommates (Joiner et al., 1992). How you treat others is related to self-worth. "You will do unto others as you do unto yourself" (Briggs, 1977, p. 4). High self-esteem encourages us to seek out others and to develop healthy relationships enhanced by caring, democratic behaviors. "We are more inclined to treat others with respect, benevolence, good will, and fairness since we do not perceive them as a threat" (Branden, 1992, p. 15). According to Maslow (1968), the best helpers of others are those who feel positive about themselves. "So often the sick or inadequate person, trying to help, does harm instead" (p. iii). One of my students, Debra, expressed a benefit of self-love beautifully, "My self-nurturance is my gift of love to others."

Long-term relationships are more likely to succeed if both people feel self-love. Falling in love is easy; sustaining love over time requires high self-esteem. Parenting is one of the most critical responsibilities in life. A classic study found that parents with high levels of self-esteem have a better chance of raising children with high levels of self-worth (Coopersmith, 1967). Relationships built on high levels of self-esteem are more likely to be nourishing rather than toxic (Branden, 1992). When you love yourself, you are not going to deliberately hurt yourself or anyone else (Hay, 1991).

Career success. What about career possibilities? A job seeker with high self-esteem will almost always achieve better interview ratings and receive more job offers than those with low self-esteem. On the job, high levels of ambition and achievement are consequences of self-esteem. Because employees' work will reflect the degree of their own self-worth, employers seek applicants who value themselves. As one advances, self-worth continues to pay off. Managers with high self-esteem have less trouble giving up control and delegating. Qualities such as innovation, personal responsibility, self-management, and self-direction are all by-products of high self-esteem (Branden, 1992). "In the workplace self-esteem is a survival requirement" (p. 77).

Pride in what is produced comes from pride in self. For example, my income is from teaching. I would be paid the same salary regardless of how well I taught. It is self-esteem, not the money, that motivates me to strive for excellence. "You will succeed in life only to the extent that you care about yourself" (Helmstetter, 1991, p. 196). The following profile hopefully either sounds like you or will become a worthy goal.

> High self-esteemers feel self-confident. This makes them eager to get involved wholeheartedly, to express themselves. It gives them courage to stand up for their convictions. They are not isolated nor loners. They can take criticism, tolerate frustration, and are not threatened by failure. They tend to be physically healthy, enjoy life, and have a positive outlook. They are not critical of themselves although they are realistically aware of both their strengths and their shortcomings (Briggs, 1970, pp. 14–15).

Clearly, self-esteem influences all aspects of life; in fact, it is the foundation upon which happiness and well-being are built. Psychological well-being is either undermined or enhanced by the level of one's self-esteem (Brodzinsky et al., 1992). "Of all the judgments that we pass in life, none is as important as the one we pass on ourselves, for that judgment touches the very center of our existence" (Branden, 1983, p. 1).

SOURCES OF SELF-CONCEPT AND ESTEEM

Human beings are not born with self-identity or esteem. Both are developed throughout life, and neither is static. You have learned who you are and how worthy you feel from internalized messages and a variety of experiences. Four broad contributors to self-esteem can be identified: (1) social interaction, (2) social information, (3) social comparison, and (4) self-observation (Baron, 1985).

Social Interaction and Social Information

The first two categories have to do with relationships. How people reacted and treated you in social interactions and their valuative comments about you have had much influence, and they still do. An early, well-researched study found that the quality of the relationships between children and significant adults in their lives laid the foundation for self-love (Coopersmith, 1967).

Babies and young children are especially vulnerable in terms of the actions of others; parents usually serve as the most significant influences. Children learn they are lovable by being treated as if they are special. A tragic price of low self-worth or worse is paid if there is lack of warmth, love, care, and attention. The parents' child-raising style during the first 3 or 4 years determines the child's beginning level of self-esteem (McKay and Fanning, 1987). An essential parenting behavior is holding a baby in a loving way.

> The infant must be adequately held to exist as a self. Babies sometimes fall, of course. It is important that arms are available to pick the baby up again. Babies become calm when they feel held again, when they feel the enclosure of the arms around (Josselson, 1992, p. 30).

Parenting effects remain influential throughout a child's life. Perceived parental rejection is significantly related to low self-esteem in adolescents (Robertson and Simons, 1989). A detrimental parental message is that a child is not good enough. Sometimes the messages are blatantly negative such as, "You'll never amount to anything," or "What did I do wrong to deserve you?" Without a doubt, these do grave damage. Others are more subtle or underlying and are still injurious.

"Can't you ever do something different with your hair?"

"When I was your age, I had a full-time job and still got good grades in school."

"I wish you'd try out for the play instead of spending so much time with music. That's such a waste of time."

"You could do a lot better if you'd just ever try."

Several of my students have identified the last message as common. "No matter what grade I brought home, short of 100 percent or A+, my dad told me I could have done better," a troubled young woman shared. Can you think of similar messages you received? The underlying theme is that something is missing or wrong.

Parents' opinions usually continue to have an impact after a young adult leaves home. A 25-year-old confessed:

> I don't know why I care what my parents think of me anymore. Most of what they did was criticize me, and that's what they still do. But I care so much, it hurts. I'm still trying to be the way they want me to be.

Opinions of other family members are also important. Students often mention siblings who teased and ridiculed them, and they cite these experiences as having led to diminished self-worth. "I am convinced that there are no genes to carry the feeling of worth. It is learned. And the family is where it is learned" (Satir, 1972, p. 24).

Joyce, a middle-aged student, remembered her childhood and a negative family environment. She wrote of feeling clumsy, skinny, and not as smart as her siblings. Those feelings came from her own parents. "My dad said until the day he died that I

Figure 1-8

was the clumsiest kid he had. When Mom made clothes for me, she said I was so straight that nothing fit me. They both told me I should do better in school because the other kids did." Sadly, she could not recall any positive messages. In fact, she said that any pride in accomplishment was frowned upon. Her parents thought that pride was the same as bragging.

When Joyce was 40, she finally came to grips with her feelings of low self-esteem. The pain resurfaced when she prepared a childhood analysis for extra credit. She told me, "I didn't want to do the paper, and I did want to. I knew I didn't have to. But something kept pulling me to do it. I realize now I needed to unload some more, and I felt better afterwards." As a postscript to the paper, she wrote: "This has been a painful experience for me. Lots of feelings that I didn't want to deal with came back. Not one of us kids came out of that family with anything but low self-esteem." Today Joyce feels positive about herself. I smiled as I read: "I am respected by my classmates, I am a good person, and I will make a success out of despair." And she has! Another student Linda optimistically wrote:

> A self-esteem tip that hit home with me was not to belittle or label your children negatively which is what happened to me. Unfortunately, my own parents' self-esteem was negative, and it was passed on to me. *But cycles can be broken, and this one is already beginning to crumble.*

Incidentally, self-esteem can also be damaged by neglect (Hopson and Hopson, 1990).

In addition to family contributions, interactions with and information from others were important to you as a child, and they continue to make a difference now. Think back to school experiences and relationships with teachers and peers. For some, school is a nightmare. I remember a junior-high teacher who delivered a daily assault of put-downs to a timid boy. "Can't you write any neater than that?" "Hurry up. You're so slow!" "That's a dumb question." One day he announced that the lowest grade in the class was Gary's-as usual! Several students followed the teacher's lead, and Gary became the object of many cruel tricks and insults. That Gary survived is remarkable; the damage to his self-esteem is hard to imagine.

Children learn to tease others usually because of physical appearance. Children who are teased about size, shape, or any aspect of their bodies experience a feeling of shame (Bradshaw, 1992). In adulthood, victims of teasing can suffer from high levels of dissatisfaction with their bodies which impacts on self-esteem and depression levels (Blakeslee, 1991).

As a warning, Ellen Rosenberg, an author of *Growing Up Feeling Good*, told an audience of teachers, "Self-esteem may not be a separate subject in school curriculums, but children's self-esteem is being chipped away or built up at every minute at school or elsewhere." If educators understood this, fewer children, like Gary, will suffer. Also, the question could be asked, "Why aren't we making 'How to Build Self-esteem' a separate course in our schools?"

Once self-esteem is high, input from others is less influential. Nevertheless, students remind me how rewarding it is when instructors praise their work, and I, too, relish favorable comments. One way to assess whether a relationship is healthy is to ask if it enhances feelings of self-worth. We may be secure, yet replenishment is invaluable! The self-concept inventory in REFLECTIONS AND APPLICATIONS gives you a chance to receive input from others and compare it with your own self-concept.

Social Comparison

How often do you compare yourself to others? Social comparison is a powerful source of ideas about self. People tend to measure themselves against others, and these comparisons are frequently related to physical appearance and popularity.

Sadly, research reveals that African-American children have an especially difficult time with self-esteem because the pro-white message is so powerful. In 1985 black children were asked to select either a white or black doll; 65 percent preferred white dolls, about the same percentage as in a 1947 experiment. One child explained, "Black is dirty" (White, 1993, p. 48). To avert the possibility of children believing they are inferior, books have been written to help black parents and others build self-esteem in children who face an additional extra comparison obstacle (Comer and Poussaint, 1992; Hopson and Hopson, 1990).

Any *minority*, a group lacking power within a society, faces similar challenges. "Homophobia, a fear or hatred of lesbian women and gay men, is so interwoven in society that lesbian and gay youth face especially difficult struggles for self-esteem, emotional security, and a sense of a caring community" (Whitlock, 1989, p. 1). Even though homophobia is rooted in ignorance and untruths, it does immeasurable damage to individuals. Gay and lesbian students are oppressed by name-calling, physical violence, and perhaps worst of all, myths about who they are and what they can be (Elze, 1992).

Any difference can be either ridiculed or looked at with positiveness. Aspects of self, when affirmed rather than condemned, bolster self-esteem. A study of high school and college students showed that a positive self-concept was related to identification with both one's own culture and the mainstream. *Multiculturism*, appreciation for everyone's "roots," coupled with pride in the culture of society yields the highest rewards (Phinney et al., 1992). Hopefully, this pride in self and society will be every child's birthright. Then comparisons will no longer hurt.

When I ask my students how many were compared to their siblings, almost every hand goes up. Generally, they acknowledge that the comparisons weren't motivating or helpful and could be harmful. One young man realized why he harbored negative feelings about his older brother: "I was never as good as Scott. He was better-looking, smarter, and athletic. I was nicer, but that didn't seem to matter to Dad." Any comparison can diminish your uniqueness if you try to be someone you are not. Keep in mind that someone better-looking, smarter, friendlier, or more popular likely exists somewhere so what difference does it make? Comparisons are helpful only if you learn constructively from them.

Do you realize that it's possible to compare yourself to a person who does not exist—your ideal self? If your self-description and ideal self are quite different, self-esteem will be low. You may be underestimating your current self or harboring an unattainable self-fantasy. Perfectionism is having an inflated ideal self. Perfectionists believe that they must set the highest performance standards or be second-rate. They have perfect ideal selves, and then no matter what, they aren't good enough. The first step in increasing self-esteem is to create a realistic ideal or possible self. After therapy, clients of Rogers (1961) described themselves in significantly more positive ways, they were less demanding, and their ideal selves were more attainable. Examine your ideal and use it as a friendly guide, not as an enemy.

Self-Observation

The fourth category, self-observation, comes from your own feelings, thoughts, and actions. You have an awareness of your behavior as well as your feelings and thoughts about it. Picture two young children on a playground. Terri successfully climbs the ladder of the slide and glides down. Sheryl stands at the bottom, fearful of the ascent. After working up the courage to mount the steps, she sits frozen at the top and begins to cry. Terri comes to her rescue by sitting behind her and helping her down. Can you see how Terri and Sheryl created different self-images?

Adults continue to be self-observant. Mike and Brett are newly hired firefighters. Brett has been involved in two heroic rescues. Mike has spent most of his on-duty time cleaning the station, playing cards, and keeping in shape. He has participated in a few minor fire calls and is feeling frustrated. In the two situations Terri and Brett have enhanced their self-esteem because they succeeded with a challenge. Sheryl and Mike, on the other hand, have pictures of themselves as failures or underachievers. Self-observation becomes increasingly important as you mature. Are you aware of yourself? What are you doing with what you observe? At this point in your life, you have a great deal of control over your level of self-esteem.

Anything that influences your evaluation of self is worth examining. Of utmost

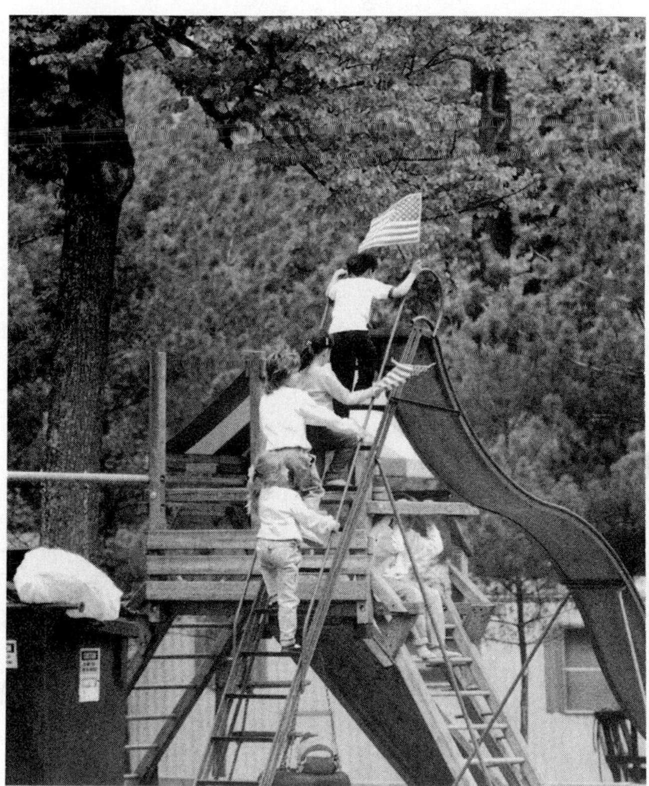

Figure 1-9 Fun on a slide can build self-esteem.

significance are the thoughts that create your own reality. Consider two young men who are insulted by a co-worker. Tim thinks, "I must be a hard person to work with if that's what he thinks of me." Greg's thoughts are: "I don't know what his problem is. He must be having a bad day." How will the two thoughts differ in their effect on self-esteem? Do you see how powerful your thoughts are? "It's not the events of our lives that shape us, but our beliefs as to what those events mean" (Robbins, 1991, p. 73).

Realization of the impact of thinking makes a difference. Before I became aware of how powerful internalized thoughts were, I could be my own worst enemy. An honors English class in creative writing was a devastating experience. Although I had been warned that the professor was overly critical, her unfavorable written comments diminished my desire to write. My final grade was satisfactory, not as high as I wanted; my confidence was at a low ebb. I believed that because she hadn't been impressed, I must not have any ability. I finally was able to ask myself, "How much value do I want to place on one person's opinion? If I want to write, and if I believe in myself, I can do it." It's sad that talent and ability are wasted because people have not been taught to assess a situation and develop different thoughts. Take charge of your thoughts and avoid letting others determine your destiny.

BUILDING AND STRENGTHENING SELF-ESTEEM

If early influences contributed to a moderately high to high level of self-esteem, you are fortunate. Use the rating scale in the self-concept inventory in REFLECTIONS AND APPLICATIONS to measure your level of self-esteem. For those with healthy levels, self-esteem strengthening is a wise investment. If yours is low, you can do much to change it! Beginning to realize your sense of worth is a vitalizing experience. "You literally uncover the hidden jewel of your own value" (McKay and Fanning, 1987, p. 83).

Healing Past Hurts

One day Teri, one of my outstanding students, came to see me. In her forthright manner, she said, "Sharon, your suggestions on developing self-esteem are great, but I don't think they will work for anyone who feels terribly wounded. They wouldn't have worked for me years ago." Our discussion clarified why individuals may engage in self-sabotage or handicapping. Over the years I had experienced frustrations and disappointments working with some people because they would not take even the basic steps to build self-esteem and appeared destined to hurt themselves. At fault could be the *inner child*, made up of feelings, memories, and experiences from childhood (Chopich and Paul, 1990; Whitfield, 1987). Pain comes from an inner critic made up of judgments from others (Stone and Stone, 1993) which is "like a dragon that keeps growing heads as long as you do not deal with it" (p. 5).

Many, especially those who grew up in troubled families, are in serious psychological pain (Whitfield, 1987). A wounded inner child can come from severe childhood trauma, lack of healthy love, neglect, or persistent eroding of self-worth. The result is toxic shame which means having shame as an identity—to "believe that one's being is flawed, that one is defective as a human being" (Bradshaw, 1988, p. vii). The wounds manifest themselves in repression of emotion, lack of assertiveness, self-sabotage, a feeling of powerlessness, codependency, eating disorders, drug abuse, inability to form healthy relationships, and, certainly, low self-esteem coupled with hopelessness.

How do you know that the inner child needs to be healed? Clues can be found in the previous paragraph, and, perhaps, the following portions from Teri's story will help.

> I have personally experienced the inner torment, mental confusion, and negative physical results of a damaged and hurting inner child. The physical manifestation took the form of obesity. I did manage to muddle through 26 years by creating a facade, a "face" to the world. My weight was a problem and didn't match the facade so I lost about 90 pounds. Now to the outside world I had it all! But there was something wrong inside. I was miserable, wasn't "together," and was lonely and hurting even though I was a wife and a mother. I was so good at hiding my real self that I didn't know myself nor recognize my feelings. I divorced and then dealt with my mother's illness and death. The one coping skill I had was to ignore my feelings, and I was left very vulnerable. My second marriage was a dreadful descent into my husband's world of alcoholism, drug addiction, and domestic violence. The day he literally picked me up and flung me through our sliding glass door I realized I needed intense professional help. A first realization was that I'd always "been there" for a multitude of people, but no one had been there for me.

Teri's story had a wonderful ending which turned into a new beginning for her. Her therapist suggested that she read *Healing Your Aloneness* (Chopich and Paul, 1990) and then she began her inner child work.

> My inner child began to heal. The effects of all those years of frustration, ineffective coping skills, inner pain, mental confusion, and unhappiness began to fade away. The main therapy strategies of imaging, journaling, self talk, thought-blocking, and affirmations combined to bring about a wondrous change. I began to establish personal boundaries, I demanded respect for myself as a person, and I respected other's boundaries, too. I built my self-esteem. Life is now fun, challenging, and easier. I make positive choices and look upon each new experience as a challenge and opportunity to learn and grow.

Another obstacle in building self-esteem may be unfamiliarity with secure feelings. Jenni wrote in a class journal: "I think sometimes I'm afraid to feel good about myself—to not be insecure. It sounds so odd, but it's almost like letting go of something you know so well and for so long for something you have never known." Paul expressed it as "just too afraid to feel good." An intriguing theory of self-verification is that individuals with low self-esteem may long for praise yet have a strong desire to preserve their self-concept even if it is a negative one (Bower, 1992).

Another major stumbling block in terms of self-esteem is extreme depression. Many depressed people actually seek out a steady stream of disapproving comments from others (Bower, 1992). Because they lack the willpower to build self-esteem, the depression must be lifted before elevating the self. Ways to do this are covered in Chapter 4.

Finally, you can set the stage for building self-esteem by recognizing what has been called an *Achilles Heel*, a "weakness, insecurity, or vulnerability that regularly trips us up" (Bloomfield and Felder, 1985, p. 2). The irony is that the real Achilles had only three inches of weakness in his whole body which became his downfall. Similarly, one weakness can become the sole measure of self-worth. This, invariably, sets people up for defeat before they even start.

If you think you might be in need of healing, if feeling positive seems strange, if you are severely depressed, or if you allow weaknesses to "trip you up," seek counseling, read any of the books cited in this section, and then take steps to change your life. You deserve it! As Debra, a vibrant student, expressed it, "I found that a decision that you are *for* yourself is the beginning of an entirely different life."

Living Consciously

Living consciously is basic to building self-esteem. Thousands of times a day people choose the level of consciousness at which they will function (Branden, 1987). Living in a mental fog, even partially, limits potential for self-love. You can choose how you want to function. The choice may be between habitual drug use and alertness, or between fatigue and getting enough sleep. Lack of alertness is related to inattention, mistakes, and falling asleep on the job, in class, or behind the wheel. Less than 5 hours of sleep dramatically reduces alertness (Moore-Ede, 1993). The visibly alive, bright-eyed students I see each day have made a wise choice and are completing the first step toward building high self-esteem. Others are severely limiting themselves.

Concentration on Strengths

The next step is to concentrate on your strengths. What do you like about yourself? Even the simplest positive quality is an important one. Do you listen well? Do you have a nice smile? Are you considerate? What are your talents? Make a list of strengths and post it where you will notice it—on your walls, refrigerator door, and mirrors. Positive statements about self are called *affirmations*. Easy to use, affirmations are powerful tools. State them as if something is already happening (Jeffers, 1987). Some general examples are: "I am worthwhile," "I deserve happiness." More specific ones would reflect unique positive aspects such as, "I am kind." Repeating these frequently helps empower the self.

A woman working on self-esteem started each day by repeating three positive statements to herself and ended the day with three different ones. She reported a positive outcome: "I've become a much better friend to myself." In addition to writing, reading, and thinking affirmatively, you can visualize yourself in a positive light.

There is a tendency to key in on weaknesses and become bogged down. All of us have drawbacks. As a basis for lasting change, the key is to keep our sights on the positive characteristics and appreciate ourselves exactly as we are, including our weak spots (Bloomfield and Felder, 1985). Focusing on your potential, not on limitations, is a way to build self-confidence and self-esteem.

Demonstration of Strengths

Demonstrating strengths is even more affirming. Whatever you already do well, do! If you have musical talent, join a performing group. If you're a whiz in the kitchen, bake a cake for someone else. Accept any compliments, and don't put yourself down if your attempts don't yield perfect results. Contributing to worthwhile causes can be a tremendous definite boost to self-esteem. Tina volunteered to accompany elderly people on shopping trips. Brad became involved in both a political campaign and an environmental clean-up project. Each reported heightened feelings of self-worth. One of the surest ways to sustain a change in self is by helping someone else. Being selfless at times will strengthen the self (Chellis, 1992). Giving to others is a gift to yourself!

Making Positive Changes

Making constructive changes improves your present self and ensures future well-being. Make an attainable, yet challenging, ideal-self list. Then choose an improvement area and set up an action plan. Chapter 5 suggests ways to achieve a goal. Express the change in a positive way. Say, "I will become assertive" rather than, "I don't want to be passive." Being against weakens while being *for* empowers (Dyer, 1992). Also, emphasize self-directed action. Instead of, "I hope I improve my grades," think and say, "I am studying so I can improve my grades." Think, "When I lose weight, I will feel better," not "*If* I lose weight" (Canfield and Siccone, 1993).

Allowing yourself to make mistakes along the way is healthy. High self-esteem does not mean that you never make errors. Rather, it means that regardless of mistakes, you accept yourself as a worthy human being. "Feeling good about yourself is not something you do after all mistakes have been corrected; it's something you do in spite of mistakes" (McKay and Fanning, 1987, p. 124). Instead of berating yourself, use your mistakes as helpful information and change your course of action. Of utmost importance is to give yourself many "hurrahs" along the way!

Seeking Positive Relationships

Building self-esteem is easier with the help of positive, supportive people. Those with low self-worth tend to surround themselves with others who feel inferior. Pam, a young woman with low self-esteem, said she was bothered by a friend who was critical. I advised her to seek new relationships with individuals who feel positive about themselves. These people don't need to put others down, and modeling after them is beneficial.

Changing Thoughts

Let's continue the esteem-building process by taking a closer look at what is called *cognitive restructuring* or thought changing. Tuning in to your *self-talk*, your thoughts about self, is the first step. "The practice of self-love begins with your mind. You must learn to control your thinking" (Dyer, 1976, p. 54). And learning to listen to ourselves is a way of learning to love ourselves just as listening to others is a powerful form of love (Borysenko, 1990). What do you think about yourself—your appearance, your behavior, your impact on others? Your self-talk can be pictured as an accumulation of drops of water that becomes either a clear, unpolluted body of water or a toxic one. The self-talk sets up the mental atmosphere in which we operate (Hay, 1991). Do you hear critical remarks? To decrease the criticisms, follow a suggestion of Glasser's (1984): "I live by a helpful little motto, 'I won't criticize myself—there are more than enough people willing to do this for me' " (p. 165).

Most of us find it virtually impossible to eliminate all negative thoughts. Reframing or restructuring a self-critical thought is useful, however. Try using these cognitive restructuring steps.

1. Identify untruths, exaggerations, or belittlements such as: "I'm a terrible person," "Nobody will ever love me," "I can't talk to people," "I'm a failure."
2. Substitute the truth. Tell what actually happened or what brought out the original thought.
   "I lied to her about missing class," "Mary told me she doesn't love me," "I went to a party and didn't talk to anyone," "I didn't pass that course."
3. Challenge your original thoughts using this formula: "Just because (<u>the truth as identified in Step 2</u>) doesn't mean (<u>the untruth, exaggeration, or belittlement in Step 1</u>). "Just because I lied to her about missing class doesn't mean I'm a terrible person."
   Try using the formula in Step 3 with the other untruths given as examples in Step 1 and the truths in Step 2.
   Debate your original negative thought in the same way you would talk to anyone who expresses unrealistic ideas.
4. End your self-talk with affirmations. Relate to the specific situation or use general ones.
   "I will tell the truth in the future," "I have more positive qualities than negative ones," "I'm fine," "I'm doing okay," "I'm doing a good job," "I'm in control of my life," "I'm important," "I like me."

If you don't succeed in switching to positive self-talk using these steps, try a cognitive technique called *thought-stopping*. Mentally, you can say any of the following loudly, clearly, and angrily: "Stop thinking this way!" "This is unrealistic. I won't think it!" "This is garbage I heard when I was little. Quit it!" or just "STOP IT!"

Evaluating Sources

Analyzing how your self-esteem developed can be quite helpful. All of us have been criticized or put down. Instead of accepting negative assessments from others at face value, you might ask, "Why did they say (or do) that? Could it have been because they felt inferior or lacked self-esteem? Were they taking their frustrations out on me? Is it because they thought that teasing me would make themselves the center of attention? Were they just being hateful?" Put-downs and attacks on people are often caused by others' self-defenses.

Another possibility is that they were doing what they thought would help or was "right." Parents raise children with the resources they possess, and they almost never intend to harm their offspring. If you understand that your parents probably did the best they could do within their limitations, you can free yourself of damage to self-esteem. Finding the true reason for an irrational feeling can break the spell it has (Steinem, 1993). Research has shown that, except perhaps for extreme parental deprivation, early learning and patterns of being can be changed by later experiences (Parkeret et al., 1992). Extreme cases can be helped with therapy.

The helpful book *Making Peace with Your Parents* (Bloomfield and Felder, 1983) gives reasons and methods for releasing resentments. "Holding on to our past resentments toward parents robs us of our current peace of mind and our ability to experience satisfaction in our here-and-now relationships" (pp. 21–22). Relieved of resentments, you can put the past behind and take responsibility for your own self-esteem. I love the simple, true statement, "You make up your adulthood" (Spezzano, 1992, p. 17).

Perhaps you weren't criticized by external sources, yet your self-esteem has suffered because you think you have disappointed someone. Troy "kicked himself" often about his career choice. "My folks want me to go to law school, and they think I'm crazy for deciding to be a teacher. Last week Dad said that my decision showed that I'm afraid to use all my abilities, and he's disappointed. I'm at the point of believing him." Children often feel forced to live according to their parents' expectations and to reach for unrealistic standards of excellence.

Can you think of some areas in which you didn't measure up? A frequent one is tidiness. Some parents demand perfection in bed-making, cleaning, and organization of belongings. "No matter how hard I tried, I couldn't make my bed to please my mother," said Janet, "so I finally quit trying. It's only been recently that I can challenge the importance of being perfect at bed-making!" Breaking away from other's expectations is liberating. "If your life is a continual assessment of whether or not you please others, you are having your buttons pushed from behind" (Satir, 1978, p. 90). Caring what others think about us can be beneficial; however, decreased self-esteem is the price for trying to be only what someone else wants. Similarly, taking responsibility for ourselves is affirming. This is covered more in Chapter 3.

We weren't born with self-esteem; low self-worth is the result of deficient learning (Kiley, 1989). Rather than blame others for where we are now, we can overcome the past and build and strengthen self-esteem in the present. Help is readily available in excellent books and articles. Those cited in this chapter are listed in the references section at the end of the book. One basic question has to do with whether you are as kind and supportive to yourself as you are to a good friend. If you aren't, why not become your own best friend?

YOUR FRIEND OR FOE: SELF-FULFILLING PROPHECY

Predicting the future is usually the work of astrologers or those who claim to be prophets. In reality, each of us predicts what will be, and we also make it come true. A *self-fulfilling prophecy* is a thought or expectation that helps bring about a predicted event or behavior which then strengthens the original thought. Prophecies can be imposed by one person on another or self-imposed (Adler and Towne, 1993).

For example, a youngster who is labeled a brat is likely to believe and, thus, become one. I remember my first year of teaching. Jimmy, a sixth grader, suffered from an eye disease. I received the message from other teachers that I could not expect him to do what other students did, neither in quantity nor in quality. However, as a novice teacher, I had optimistic thoughts. I asked Jimmy how he felt. "Do you want me to treat you like the others and expect you to handle it?" He said that he did. He and I spent hours after school; his own determination made the difference. He left sixth grade with average grades, and the next fall strutted into my classroom with a beautiful smile on his face. "Guess what?" he said. "I made the honor roll in junior high!" Jimmy provided a wonderful lesson. What one believes can become reality. We fulfill our own prophecies either after internalizing those from others or by creating our own.

Relationship Between Thoughts and Behaviors

Behaviors reflect thoughts. Let's say that you think of yourself as shy. Shyness means being afraid of people (Zimbardo, 1977). Listen to your self-talk:

> I'm a shy person. I've always been that way. I was born shy. And because I am, I don't like to be around people. I can't talk to them, and I'm always uncomfortable. I will go through the rest of my life being shy, and that's it.

Powerful thinking, right? A friend (you have one even though you're shy!) invites you to a party. What is your reaction?

> I don't want to go. I never have a good time at parties. I'm shy, so I can't look at people or talk to them. I'd just have a terrible time because I'm the way I am.

In this case your friend persuades you to attend the party. "I know I won't have any fun because I'm shy," you tell yourself. How will you act at the party? You stand next to the wall away from the others and you look up, down, at the wall. You appear unapproachable and don't smile because shy people act this way! After a miserable evening, a strong confirming thought surfaces:

> See, I knew I wouldn't have any fun. Nobody talked to me, and I couldn't talk to them. I never enjoy myself at parties because I'm shy.

As illustrated in Fig. 1-10, this type of self-fulfilling prophecy becomes a vicious circle. A thought about self is carried out in behavior, which then brings about an even stronger confirming thought. You, the shy person, have fulfilled your own prophecy. If the descriptor is a positive one which increases your self-esteem, the self-fulfilling prophecy is a friend. Too often, though, our thoughts are limiting and serve as our enemies.

Self-fulfilling prophecies are powerful. A story is told of two brothers, one who was alcoholic and one who hardly drank liquor. A psychologist wondered why they differed. One brother said that because his father was an alcoholic, he had become one, too. His self-fulfilling prophecy told him that he would drink because of his father. The other explained that because his father was an alcoholic, he learned the horrors of the habit and decided to abstain (Branden, 1983). Clearly, two people with the same background are capable of formulating opposite prophecies with different outcomes and, thus, create their own unique realities.

Changing a Self-Fulfilling Prophecy

In describing a theory of personality called self-consistency, Lecky (1951) pointed out that students with behavior problems had a negative concept of themselves, and they behaved according to their conceptions. He succeeded with students by helping them change their self-image. I learned the power of self-perception from Jimmy who produced in spite of his visual limitations because he believed he could. Examination of self-fulfilling prophecies is valuable. If you want to change any of yours, two avenues are possible. Lecky, and the many psychologists who emphasize cognitive changes, would tell you to change your thoughts. Learning theorists would have you alter your behavior. I recommend, as do many in the cognitive-behavioral area, changing both.

Let's go back to the example of shyness. An unrealistic thought would be, "I am no longer shy." However, you could use cognitive restructuring and think, "Just because I've been shy in the past doesn't mean I have to continue. I don't like it, and I am going to change." One authority on shyness says that you are shy if you think you are (Zim-

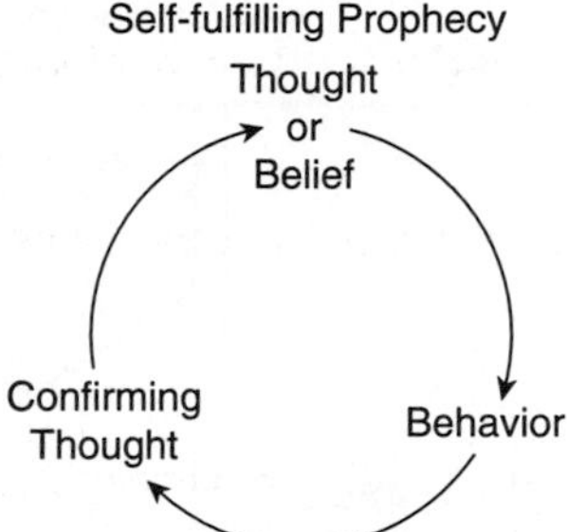

Figure 1-10

bardo, 1977). Empowered with a different belief, you can attend another party and change your behavior. As difficult as it may be, you position yourself near people. A next step would be to look at others with an open expression. You might even smile! If you are not approached, you can muster your courage and go up to someone and say hello. In almost all cases, the person you approach will respond positively. At that point you have broken out of the vicious circle.

With success, new ways of behaving become easier. In one research study, 80 percent of the people said they were once shy. Only half described themselves as presently shy (Zimbardo, 1977). This finding can inspire change. If others can change, so can you.

For a class self-improvement project, a female student decided to try to lose weight. She didn't lose as much as she wanted; however, what she learned was invaluable. She recalled how painful her self-fulfilling prophecy had been.

> I felt so insecure when, as a teenager, my parents nagged me about my weight. I felt I was being judged because I was fat so I wouldn't give people the chance to reject me; I rejected them first. It was a perfect example of a self-fulfilling prophecy. I mourn all the friendships I missed out on. With the help of this course I see that when most people look at me, they see *me*, not an overweight person, and when I look at them, I see them as they are and not just as individuals who could hurt my feelings. I also have learned that people are not going to love me more if I get thin and that my problems are not because of my weight.

Examining all of your self-prophecies is wise. As a way to strengthen self-esteem, keep the ones that are friends; work on the foes!

> *The greatest discovery in our generation is that human beings, by changing the inner attitudes of their minds, can change the outer aspects of their lives.*
>
> —William James

YOUR PERSONAL CAPABILITY: SELF-EFFICACY

Whether you have the confidence to even begin a self-improvement project will depend upon what has been identified and defined by Bandura (1977) as *self-efficacy*, "the conviction that one can successfully execute the behavior required to produce the outcomes" (p. 79). In other words, it is a sense of capability or competence. Notice the difference between thinking, "I can handle it," rather than, "There isn't anything I can do about

For Better or For Worse® **by Lynn Johnston**

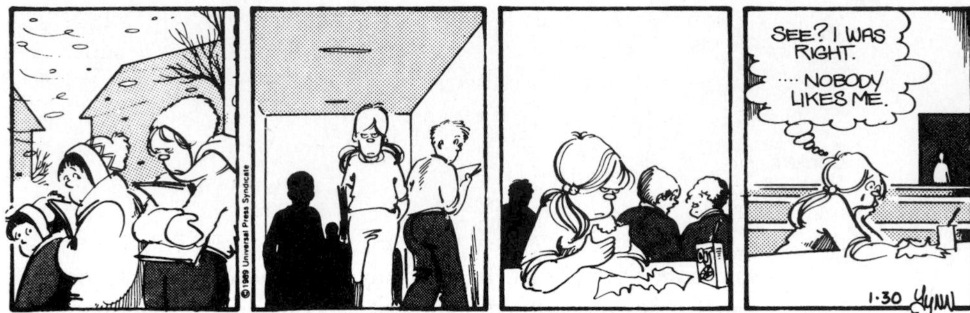

Figure 1-11 Copyright 1989 Universal Press Syndicate. Reprinted by permission. All rights reserved.

this." You may remember the story of the little engine who succeeded by saying, "I think I can, I think I can." People who possess self-efficacy think they can.

Self-efficacy pertains to a particular event or task. How you assess your capability in a specific situation influences success in several ways. First, you are more likely to attempt a particular task if you think you can do it. Second, if you expect a positive outcome, you will exert more effort, and, finally, you will persist much longer. Success is then likely to occur. "Perceived incompetence is a real barrier to growth and performance" (Spezzano, 1992, p. 134).

A person's self-efficacy is related to attitude and self-esteem. In fact, self-efficacy and self-respect are the dual pillars of self-esteem (Branden, 1992). Self-efficacy and self-esteem are positively related so that each strengthens the other (Wyatt, 1990). Which comes first doesn't matter. A book for teachers on developing students' self-esteem points out that addressing both sides is powerful. "The most powerful approach is to create an ever-expanding upward spiral of self-esteem and self-efficacy" (Canfield and Siccone, 1993, p. 109). Of interest is that self-efficacy can also be increased by exercise (McAuley et al., 1991).

A cycle of self-competence is taught by Professor John R. Bellefleur, Ph.D. Taking a reasonable risk comes first. The act of risking motivates us to work to find a solution. A solution, found and tested, gives a sense of competence followed by self-respect and self-confidence. Then our greater capacity to risk increases our capacity to grow and develop self-esteem. Self-efficacy motivates us to take sound risks, and success encourages us to risk again.

Results of Self-Efficacy

Studies have been extensive and show that self-efficacy can improve outcome. Positive results in the treatment of arthritis, heart disease, and phobias have been noted (McLeod, 1986). In a study of men infected with the virus that causes AIDS, those who actively coped were better able to resist the disease (Smith, 1989a). Increased self-efficacy helped people with phobias cope with stress, and their immune systems were also enhanced (Wiedenfeld et al., 1990). Cancer patients who developed an "I-can attitude" used a strong will to live and blazing determination to decrease depression and enhance their immune systems (Cousins, 1989).

Studies showed that self-efficacy activated participation in physical fitness programs (Bezjak and Lee, 1990), seemed to motivate and lead to more positive feelings during exercise (McAuley and Courneya, 1992; McAuley et al., 1991), was found to help alcoholics resist relapse (Rychtarik et al., 1992), acted as a buffer protecting high school students from external influences to smoke (Stacy et al., 1992), and improved the outcome for those trying to quit smoking (Garcia et al., 1990). In a study of college undergraduates, self-efficacy was found to be significantly related to academic performance and to self-set academic grade goals (Wood and Locke, 1987). A Canadian study found that self-efficacy was positively related to students' cognitive performance and that teachers were quite influential in its increase (Bouffard-Bouchard, 1990).

Some caution is in order. In one study, self-efficacy that was too high seemed to lead to complacency about the difficulty of smoking cessation so that those with moderate self-efficacy fared better than either the ones with high or low levels (Haaga and Stewart, 1992). Also, if others perceive your level of over-all self-efficacy to be high, they may not think you need any help. After my surgery for cancer in 1985, my husband and I participated in a two-week program to learn to deal with emotions and thoughts about the disease. I realized then that because I appeared to be capable and strong, others were less likely to provide support. Admitting that I didn't want to always handle things without help encouraged necessary support. We all need to lean at times!

Think of times in your life when your own self-efficacy has motivated you. Has a lack of self-efficacy ever hindered you? Take the opportunity to describe self-efficacy and one of your self-fulfilling prophecies in REFLECTIONS AND APPLICATIONS. Developing affirmative prophecies, self-efficacy, and self-esteem is wise. Each enhances the others.

SUMMARY

Awareness of self is at the heart of human relations, and understanding is an ongoing process. Each of the four developmental areas (physical, mental, emotional, and social) influences the other, and all four together form an integrated, whole self.

Sociologists explain the development of the self and the evolvement of the "I" and "me." Psychologists are interested in the self-concept, a collective view of self including self-description, ideal self, and self-esteem. Ideal self is an image of what one wants to be like and is most helpful when it is realistic and becomes a possible self. Self-esteem is the value placed on self.

Self-concept and self-esteem develop through feedback and interactions with others and through your own observations and judgments. Self-esteem can be enhanced through a variety of methods. Changing the way you think is a sound first step. Sometimes, steps to heal psychological pain and depression are needed.

Self-fulfilling prophecies can be helpful or damaging. They can be examined, evaluated, and changed. Self-efficacy is the sense of competence one has in a given situation. Many studies have shown that self-efficacy is related to well-being and success in life.

I am convinced that the crucial factor in what happens both inside people and between people is the picture of individual worth that each person carries around.

—Virginia Satir

RESOURCES

- Learning Disabilities Association of America, (LDA), 4156 Library Road, Pittsburgh, PA 15234, (412) 341-1515
- Parents and Friends of Lesbians and Gays (PFLAG), P. O. Box 27605, Washington, D. C. 20038
- Counselors in educational institutions can help with learning disabilities as well as personal problems.
- Self-esteem classes are often offered through wellness centers at hospitals, social service agencies, colleges, and organizations. "Women Who Love Too Much" support groups and other codependency workshops are offered through social service agencies.

❧ 2 ❧

Understanding Yourself Throughout the Life Span

OBJECTIVES

After completing this chapter, you will be able to

- Discuss what is meant by and known about personality.
- Describe the three psychological theories of personality development and explain how socialization influences behavior.
- Explain Erikson's psychosocial theory of human development and relate it to your life.
- Discuss transactional analysis and use your understanding of ego states, life positions, scripts, and strokes.
- Understand personality typing and describe eight preferences.
- Distinguish between extraversion and introversion and note advantages and disadvantages of each.
- Accept personality differences in a positive way.
- Define gender role and discuss its influences.
- Summarize how gender role is learned.
- Identify disadvantages of stereotypic gender roles for both sexes.
- Define androgyny and describe its potential benefits.
- Contrast assertiveness with aggression and nonassertiveness.
- Recognize that growth and positive changes are possible using a variety of methods.
- Understand yourself and others better.

When one is a stranger to oneself, then one is estranged from others, too.

—Anne Morrow Lindbergh

Do you know yourself? Even though self-understanding deserves attention throughout life, people may simply neglect to think deeply about themselves, or they actively resist doing so. The effort to develop relating skills begins with understanding a most fascinating subject: the self! So, to resist self-analysis is to block affirmative relationships. In Chapter 1 you were asked to think about yourself and your sense of self-worth. From this chapter you will be able to gain deeper self-understanding and develop strategies to make desired changes.

PERSONALITY: THE UNIQUE YOU

Begin to describe yourself. If you are like many people, you begin with physical descriptors. Some people have difficulty going further. *Personality* is the "unique you" that consists of characteristics or traits related to ways of thinking, feeling, and behaving. The combination of all these qualities is possessed only by you and is usually apparent to others. Most psychologists agree that personality gives an individual a separate identity and that a pattern of consistency over time is the norm. Have you ever heard someone say, "She has no personality"? This usually means that the person is extremely reserved or dull. The personality may not be projected, but one does exist!

DEVELOPMENT OF PERSONALITY

With a perfect memory, you could describe the numerous experiences that have influenced your personality. Even that would not tell the entire story. Studies on identical twins reveal that approximately 50 percent of similarities in personality are based on heredity or genetic influences (Eysenck, 1990; Tellegen et al., 1988). An analysis of several studies shows a high genetic correlation (Plomin and Nesselroade, 1990). Extraversion and conformity seem to be at least 60 percent genetic, while heredity accounts for only 33 percent of intimacy, defined as a preference for emotional closeness (Wellborn, 1987). Agreeableness or "niceness" appears to be mostly a result of environment or learning (Franklin, 1989). In one study adopted children tended to change over a 10-year period in the direction of genetic parents' personality although changes as a result of individual experiences were also found (Loehlin et al., 1990). Personality development is the result of both heredity and environment, according to a study of twins (Chipuer et al., 1993). "Genes aren't the sole ingredient of the personality soup; they are merely the well-seasoned stock" (Franklin, 1989, p. 41).

Questions arise about differences in the personalities of siblings. I've heard parents ask, "How can they be so different? We raised them the same." First, raising children the same isn't possible nor advisable. Sibling dissimilarities aren't surprising when one considers birth order, spacing, gender, age differences, physical and mental abilities and preferences, genetics, and the realm of human experiences (Bower, 1992; Hoffman, 1991). Even for brothers and sisters, heredity and environment are different.

Three general approaches or theories of personality development are presented in most introductory psychology courses. The pioneer in personality development was Sigmund Freud, the father of *psychoanalysis*. His theories dealt with early childhood influences, the role of the unconscious, psychosexual stages, and a structure of the personality made up of three parts (id, super ego, and ego). Psychodynamic theorists continue to contribute significantly to the ongoing study of personality, emphasizing the influence of the unconscious on personality development and human behaviors.

A second approach, made up of *behaviorism and social learning*, focuses on environmental influences and observational learning in shaping human behavior. B. F. Skinner, who experimented with operant conditioning, maintains that personality develops in response to stimuli in the environment. Rewards and punishments strengthen and weaken behavior (Skinner, 1953; 1987). An influential social learning theorist, Albert Bandura (1977), credits modeling as a strong influence on personality. If you think that you act just like one of your parents, observational learning undoubtedly played a part. Behaviorism and social learning are useful in helping to understand personality and in devising practical ways to make desired changes using behavior modification principles.

Humanism is the third major approach to personality. Emphasis on the development of the self-concept and individual choices in improving personality are central points. Carl Rogers (1961), a leader in the field of humanism, identified major characteristics of healthy personal growth: openness to experience, freedom and responsibility, and trust in the self. Developing one's full potential is an ideal goal. Ideas from all approaches are helpful in understanding yourself. Because humanism focuses on choices and self-control, several of its ideas are emphasized throughout this book as are behavior modification methods and several of the newer cognitive techniques.

Sociologists, too, are interested in personality development. They emphasize *socialization*, a process of learning in which we are prepared to behave according to the requirements of our society. Various sources or *agents of socialization* such as family, schools, religion, and the media teach the culture and, in doing so, encourage us to form basic qualities. We learn to follow *norms*, those behaviors expected of us as contributing members of society.

Both psychology and sociology recognize that personality is influenced by the interaction between *nature* and *nurture* meaning that both heredity and environment contribute. In addition, both psychological and sociological conditions have an impact on personality. In REFLECTIONS AND APPLICATIONS you can describe your own personality and compare it to family members. Undoubtedly, you are the product of both nature and nurture!

STAGES OF LIFE

Personality develops in a series of stages, according to Erikson, an influential theorist in the fields of both psychology and human development. He emphasized social interactions and the influence of social development on personality and believed that personality formation continued throughout one's lifetime.

Erikson (1963) described eight psychosocial stages of the life span. His basic premise was that a significant task or need presented itself at each stage, and, ideally, is completed or satisfied. If it is not, the outcome is detrimental. The stages build on one another; if one task is not successfully completed, it will be impossible, or at least quite difficult, to master the next stage. Think of a set of blocks and imagine trying to build a tower. Maybe the first block isn't on a solid surface. Or maybe the second block is not centrally placed, so the tower falters a bit. Another poorly placed block will surely cause the blocks to topple. Just as the tower can be rebuilt at any point, a person can later work through a missing stage.

The stages are related to chronological ages throughout the life span, yet variance of age is possible. A recent 22-year study provided considerable support for Erikson's theory and showed an increasingly favorable resolution of stages based on prior successful completion. The researchers suggested that all psychosocial issues could reach ascendancy at any particular time. They also cautioned that the stages not be regarded as a set prescription for development as exposure to historical, social, and cultural realities could affect order and time (Whitbourne et al., 1992).

Other researchers using Erikson's model identified specific adoption-related tasks and wrote a book *Being Adopted: The Lifelong Search for Self* (Brodzinsky et al., 1992). One male student told me that it was the most helpful book he had ever read in his search to understand himself. Knowing Erikson's theory can help identify your developmental stage as well as show you how to assist others in completing developmental tasks.

Stage One (First Year of Life): *Trust versus Mistrust*

A newborn needs to feel secure in the environment. Trust develops when a baby is loved. What are the behaviors that demonstrate love? Parents or other primary caregivers who respond to the baby's needs and express caring by holding and touching are helping the baby develop trust. The opposite is a stressful, unpredictable, and unloving environment. This leads to a strong sense of mistrust.

> When security and trust are present, we begin to develop an interpersonal bond, a bridge of mutuality, crucial for the development of self-worth. The only way a child has of developing a sense of self is through a relationship with another. We are "we" before we are "I" (Bradshaw, 1988 p. 5).

Holding during this stage is of utmost importance. "Based on early good-enough holding, children reach out for experience with the expectation that the world will not let them fall" (Josselson, 1992, p. 33). If trust does not develop, all stages after that will be almost impossible to successfully complete. According to pediatric expert William Sears, M.D., a baby requires a great deal of loving physical contact which leads to a secure and dependent feeling before she or he can become independent (Lingston, 1992).

> Jason cried often, and his parents believed that they would "spoil" him if they responded. Jason was frequently left to cry. When he was only a few months old, a sitter began to spank him for crying and when he didn't respond to what she said. Jason became detached and mistrustful of people.

Stage Two (Second Year of Life): *Autonomy versus Shame and Doubt*

A typical 2-year-old is learning about independence. The toddler has developed a measure of control over the environment, and a show of assertiveness is common. The "terrible twos" are normal! Yet parents who don't realize this often respond with force and a suppression of any attempt at autonomy. A constant barrage of "no," "you can't do that," and "you're naughty" will lead to the opposite of autonomy: shame and doubt.

> Kristen was a clinging toddler. Her mother bragged about how much the little girl depended upon her. She was so attached to her mother that she cried whenever she was

left with a relative or sitter, and she had difficulty starting kindergarten. An interesting addendum to this story is that when Kristen was 13 years old, her parents divorced, and she chose to live with her father. She had finally achieved independence from her mother!

Stage Three (Third to Fourth Year of Life): *Initiative versus Guilt*

When a child begins and then proceeds with an activity or uses creativity, initiative is developed. Children at this stage often have their first experience with a nursery school or day care center. Wise parents will check to see what the facility does to encourage this developmental task. For example, beware of perfect art work; it is probably the product of the staff, not the children. Children who are criticized or deprived of opportunities to do for themselves learn to feel guilty.

Tony was a curious child who enjoyed trying new things. His mother was a perfectionist who wanted the house to be immaculate. She seldom let him to do anything that might make a mess. He also liked to put on his own clothes and button his coat but was rarely allowed to do so. "I'm in a hurry. Let me do it for you," his mother would say. Tony learned to lie about any creative activities. He felt guilty about this, yet it was easier.

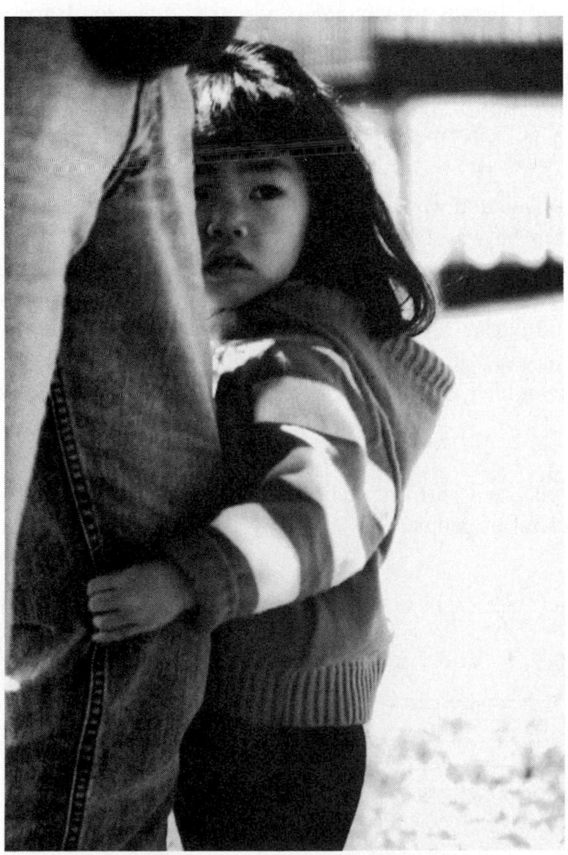

Figure 2-1 Life can be fearful as a young child develops autonomy.

Stage Four (Elementary School Age): *Industry versus Inferiority*

Children want to develop skills and carry out tasks during this stage. They like to help. They may even beg to stay after school to assist the teacher! Boys and girls at this stage are ready for household chores, paper routes, and various projects. Think of the eager Girl Scout selling cookies at your front door. Encouragement and praise for trying are important.

> Jodi wanted to help her dad with yard work. She was 8 years old and so enthusiastic. Her dad was in a hurry and worried that she might get underfoot and hurt herself. He told her to go inside and watch television. Seven years later Jodi was lying in front of the television when her dad asked her to help him outside. She said she didn't want to miss her favorite program. "When you were young, you wanted to help, and now that you're old enough, you won't. I don't understand." No, Dad didn't understand!

Stage Five (Adolescence): *Identity versus Ego Diffusion*

The critical task of this stage is to determine one's central identity. The adolescent is beginning to sort this out, and in the process, will "try on many hats." Extremely influential is the peer group. This can be an exasperating time for both the adolescent and the parents as separation begins to occur. For adoptees, the search for identity may be especially complicated (Brodzinsky et al., 1992). Adolescence is a risk-taking time, and the trauma of this stage is influenced by the success with which earlier stages were completed. Can you think of some "crazy" things you did during these important years? Each of us was searching for self.

> Chris had been a passive child who seemed to change dramatically during puberty. His parents divorced when he was 14, and he and his mother moved to a different city. Chris started running around with a gang who had a reputation for drug use. He became surly and quiet. When he was home—which wasn't often—he stayed in his room and played loud music. Inwardly, he struggled with mixed feelings of rebellion versus love for his mother. He felt conflicted and wasn't sure who he really was. He lacked a firm *identity* which includes accurate self-insight and understanding as well

Figure 2-2

as the ability to accept as well as reject others' views of self, to affirm self-worth independently of others' valuations, and to direct and control self-growth (Heath, 1991).

Stage Six (Young Adulthood): *Intimacy versus Isolation*

After a sense of identity—a task which may or may not be completed during adolescence—an individual is ready for intimacy. This task is to develop a close, meaningful relationship with another person while continuing to feel inwardly secure. In most societies this type of relationship leads to marriage. Research shows that adolescent marriage is associated with marital instability (Teti and Lamb, 1989), and teenagers are more likely to divorce (Sweet and Bumpass, 1987). Erikson's theory can explain why. "Adolescent marriage may disrupt the ability of adolescents to resolve crises of intimacy and identity formation, and may thus lead to problems in the formation and maintenance of intimate relationships" (Teti and Lamb, 1989, p. 209). Tammy wrote about what stage of life she was in: "I married too young and never developed my own identity. I had children while I was still a child myself. Instead of growing and learning about myself, I became "Mommy" and nothing else. My divorce has brought me to college. I need to learn professional skills and, most importantly, about myself. Losing a husband is hard, but finding myself is wonderful."

> Eric was 19 years old when he entered the U.S. Army. He had been struggling with identity questions for years. He had not successfully completed several of the earlier psychosocial stages, and his adolescence was troubled. The army was helping him find who he really was. He received orders to go overseas, which prompted a threat from his 17-year-old girlfriend. "Marry me so I can go with you, or I won't be here when you return." Against the wishes of family, Eric and Teresa married. They had numerous disagreements and power struggles. Their relationship was a classic example of a union between two people who hadn't completed the identity stage and weren't ready for intimacy. Within a year they divorced. In actuality, this freed them to discover who they were.

Many individuals remain within a marriage for years unable to achieve intimacy; instead, they feel isolated. Linda, an excellent student, recalled that the identity stage was especially difficult for her. She had come shakily through the earlier stages feeling inferior for being "the kid with red hair, freckles, buck teeth, and used clothes." She used alcohol and drugs excessively, engaged in promiscuous sex, had a horrible relationship with her mother, and quit school at 16. She got married at 17 and ended up in a disastrous marriage. Several years later she "woke up" and realized that she wanted to grow. Counseling and college helped her discover who she truly was, and, as she puts it, "I'm rebuilding my block tower, it's going well, and I feel great!" I can verify that she is doing a superb job.

Stage Seven (Middle Age): *Generativity versus Stagnation*

Looking beyond one's self rather than remaining inwardly focused is one way to describe this stage. Erikson viewed it as a desire to guide the next generation, and he included productivity and creativity as helpful behaviors. Many people devote time to their children during this stage; others are involved with careers and causes. For most, this stage includes the time when children leave home which can result in what is called the "empty nest syndrome." If generativity were pursued beyond self and family, this sense of emptiness would likely diminish.

> Margaret's marriage was an unhappy one. She tried to compensate by devoting her time and energy to her two children. She worked a few hours a day out of necessity at a job she didn't like. After her younger daughter was married, Margaret lapsed into a severe depression; she felt worthless. She became preoccupied with her health and was frequently ill.

Stage Eight (Older Age): *Integrity versus Despair*

The last stage of life is one of acceptance and satisfaction. If all the preceding stages have been successfully completed, Erikson (1963) wrote that "the fruit of these seven stages may gradually ripen" (p. 268). Older people often spend time reflecting on life; contentment and peace are possible if the memories are meaningful and fulfilling.

> Harvey, a 70-year-old man, had periods of irritability and bitter nostalgia. He often spoke of what he wished he had done and of how life had cheated him. He had retired from a long career as an insurance salesman and had developed no hobbies. He spent many hours alone watching television.

Each of the foregoing examples described unsuccessful completion of the developmental task or need. In most cases, the difficulty occurred because of problems with prior stages. If you understand Erikson's theory, you will be able to figure out why each person experienced hardship.

Think about your life up to this point. Answer the questions about your developmental stages in REFLECTIONS AND APPLICATIONS. Keep in mind that you can now concentrate on any of the undeveloped tasks. Even if you successfully completed each, one stage may need to be reworked. For example, what could happen that would cause a person to lose a sense of identity? Any dramatic change may necessitate a new search for one's identity. Familiarity with the psychosocial stages is like a road map for your life as long as you realize there may be detours. This book can help you discover what is missing and give you the tools to fully develop your personality.

Personality development is fascinating. The unfolding of the life span can be viewed from many perspectives. Whether you are looking at your past, present, or future, an understanding of development ideas and awareness of stages can be beneficial.

CHALLENGES TO DEVELOPMENT

Personality development can encounter challenges. As mentioned in Chapter 1, a dysfunctional family experience and the presence of a severe "inner critic" can hinder positive growth. Low self-esteem and depression can block substantial progress at any stage.

Of particular challenge to a segment of the population is sexual orientation. The American society is predominantly heterosexual. The numbers have varied over time, and figures of homosexuality range from a little over 2 percent to 10 percent of the population (Crispell, 1993). What causes homosexuality has not been determined. The latest studies point to a genetic or hereditary base (Henry, 1993; Pool, 1993). Most lesbian women and gay men begin to realize their homosexuality during or shortly after puberty although hints of it may have been there earlier.

When homosexuals discover this uniqueness, a tremendous struggle begins. Most feel forced to hide an important part of themselves out of fear. They feel "different" and in this homophobic society are condemned solely on the basis of sexual orientation. They learn that they are seen as somehow less than human in a world that fears and despises them (Whitlock, 1989). Obviously, this is a major challenge to achieving a strong sense of identity and in building self-esteem.

> Facing almost universal condemnation, most homosexual young people strive at all costs to hide who they are. The fear of being found out pervades everything they do and say. Many withdraw from family and friends (Stoddard, 1993).

Fear and intolerance of homosexuals strain family relationships by restricting communication among them and loosening the very ties that bind (Blumefeld, 1992). We are told that disclosure of ourselves can lead to self-understanding and acceptance. Yet telling parents about homosexuality can create great turmoil and hurt feelings. Risk of negative reactions by parents is of major concern, and parents' reactions have an important impact on self-esteem even into adulthood (Cain, 1991). Mike, a young male student, talked candidly with me about his pain at keeping his homosexuality hidden from his parents. "I think they suspect because they make remarks. Dad said once, 'If I ever found out you were queer, I'd kill you.' It really hurts to not be able to be who I am with people I love."

Being *who I am* is vital to living a happy, satisfying life, and it is tragic that individuals are deprived of this right. Most people do not realize that homosexuality, just like heterosexuality, is not just a matter of sexual relationships. Just as heterosexuals are attracted to a special person to share deepest thoughts and feelings, to have fun with, and to devote time and energy to, so are homosexuals. Lesbians, as diverse among themselves as female heterosexuals are, share one commonality: they prefer women not only sexually but as partners (Faderman, 1991).

Not being free to be *who you are* creates feelings of being closeted, unhappy, furtive, and guilt ridden, as if you are living a lie (Miller, 1989). Because homosexuality is not a choice, forcing anyone to live a life of denial is cruel. One young man explained that homosexuality is not a choice any more than race or sex and added, "Think about it folks, with homophobia, AIDS, discrimination, hate crimes, what sensible teenager would make a choice like that?" (Minton, 1993). During a discussion of homosexuality one student suggested that being homosexual may not be a choice, but acting on it was. She thought a homosexual *should not* act like one. My response was a simple question: "Would you want to be told you couldn't act on your heterosexuality?"

Extreme courage is required of homosexuals if they want to live open and truthful lives. One such person is Amy who wrote me a wonderful and motivating note at the end of a human relations course concerning the first edition of this book.

> I think your book is wonderful; what you say is true and very helpful. As I read it though, I notice that it is very heterosexually focused as are most textbooks. I have been forced to switch things around to make them apply to me. Can you imagine how it feels to read and read and never see yourself in words? I had such a hard time dealing with my sexuality when I was younger. I thought I was the only one who was having these feelings, and I found nothing to validate that what I was feeling even existed. I remem-

> ber my feelings the first time I read a book that dealt with a homosexual relationship. It was only a brief mention, but my feelings were so intense, I almost cried. I know that human relationships are all basically the same, yet I think there are enough differences to at least warrant a mention. I think if nongay people had to read chapter after chapter about relationships from a gay point of view, they would have a hard time relating. I don't want to sound as if I'm jumping on my soapbox, but I get so frustrated at never being validated or placed first. I know you are a very open-minded and understanding person, and I also know you are in a tough position, but I would like you to at least give thought to what I've said. Maybe sometime in the future you can make a difference to someone like me who wanted to kill myself because I never had any positive reinforcement or situations I could relate to about the way I was feeling. Thanks. I feel lucky that I am able to be comfortable in sharing my thoughts with you.

As I read those words, tears came to my eyes as I decided to try to help someone else. After assuring her that she would see herself in the second edition, I asked permission to use her note. I hope Amy's words will touch you, as well.

PERSONALITY OVER A LIFETIME

What will you be like in 20 or 30 years? Obviously, you do not know for sure. Stage theories say that your personality will be influenced by successful or unsuccessful development along the way. Variation seems likely. However, researchers who study personality generally agree that stability and consistency over time is common (Block, 1981; Costa and McCrae, 1980; Livson, 1976, Myers, 1992). Individual traits can be changed while alienation, degree of morale, and feelings of satisfaction can vary greatly. Anxiety levels, eagerness for novel experiences, and friendliness change little over a lifespan. People who are dogmatic and closed to experience early in life tend to remain so. Research found no increase in irritability as people age which strikes another blow to one of the stereotypes about aging (Goleman, 1987).

One of the reasons that class reunions are enjoyable to me is the familiarity of people from years past. When someone inevitably says, "Sharon, you haven't changed a bit," I know they aren't talking about my appearance. My personality is what is familiar. Certain small changes are inevitable, and a gentle personality transition occurs for most. Occasionally at reunions, a classmate returns who seems to have a new, dramatically changed personality. Remember Gary from Chapter 1 who was berated by a junior high teacher? During high school he was quiet and somewhat odd. At our twenty-fifth reunion, he was outgoing, confident, and demonstrative, a totally different person. Knowing about personality consistency, I was amazed. When I talked with him, he confided: "I think this was the real 'me' back then, and I just couldn't let it come out. I felt that I needed a cocoon around me then, and I don't now." This satisfied my curiosity about what seemed to be his personality change. I did experience some sadness, though, as I thought about individuals who feel a need to wrap their personalities in cocoons.

UNDERSTANDING THROUGH TRANSACTIONAL ANALYSIS

Transactional analysis (TA) makes it possible to comprehend why people would feel compelled to hide their true personalities. Described as a system for understanding human behavior and a personality theory, it provides insight into self-awareness and personal growth (Clarkson, 1992).

Eric Berne, a psychiatrist who developed TA, used it to help his clients understand themselves and change their lives. The general public learned about the theory and methods when the book *I'm OK, You're OK* (Harris, 1969) became a best-seller. Several other books that describe practical applications have been published, and seminars and classes have been organized around the TA format. The current major current focus has shifted to Europe with an emphasis on human freedom and autonomy (Clarkson, 1992). This section will describe the basics of TA and show how to use them in your own life.

Ego States

Basic to TA are *ego states* which are states of mind and related patterns of behavior (Clarkson, 1992). Serving as the model for ego states was Freud's personality structure of id, ego, and superego. Berne's names for them are related to actual life figures, and personality consists of all three.

Impulsive, spontaneous, emotional, and creative are words that describe the *child ego state.* It was so named because this part is childlike (like a child between the ages of 2 and 5, according to Berne). Think of the child as a pleasure seeker doing what feels good. In the child are "the countless, grand 'a-ha' experiences and feelings of delight" (Harris, 1969, p. 27). People of all ages have a child ego state, although it varies in how noticeable and freely expressive it is. Your "child" is the part of you that loves and hates, feels exhilarated or completely miserable, relishes ice cream and pizza, laughs and cries, and can enjoy life. Imagine a wild colt with no restraints. A person's "child" could resemble one.

The child ego state did not develop freely, however. As soon as you were able to understand parental figures in the environment, another ego state began to develop. This part consists of verbal and nonverbal messages you received. Think of it as a collection of recordings in the brain that function as a conscience. This ego state contains rights and wrongs, "shoulds," "oughts," and strong ideas of what to do and not to do.

The messages poured in during your early years and were largely unedited; that is, you didn't question or reject them (Harris, 1969). And no matter how old you are, you continue to receive directive messages that can sound like commands. They are recorded and automatically play back in your mind. Or you have a visual image of a nonverbal message. A good example came from Lisa: "When my mother was watching television, she usually ignored me when I'd ask her a question. As a kid, I'd always feel as if I'd done something wrong. And when I'm ignored today, I tend to feel that way, too." Because so many of these messages came from actual parents, this is called the *parent ego state.*

The "parent" is "replete with opinions, judgments, values, and attitudes of two major types: nurturing and controlling; the latter is sometimes called prejudicial parent or critical parent" (Woollams and Brown, 1979, p. 21). Think of these two types as trying to reach the same goal by different avenues. The *nurturing "parent"* is protective and sounds concerned, while the *controlling "parent"* demands and overpowers. For example, a message from the nurturing "parent" would be, "Now, honey, you want to grow up to be big and strong so eat your peas," while the controlling "parent" would say, "Eat those peas or else!"

Remember that the messages originally came from an external source and are now internalized. A partial list of some hilarious messages contributed by students over the years follows. Can you think of any of your own that strike you as ridiculous?

- Benjamin Franklin took a bath every day of his life, and he was never sick!
- Lift your feet off the floor of the car when you cross over railroad tracks.
- Swallowed gum will stick to your spine, and you won't be able to stand up straight!
- If you stick your toe in the shower drain, you'll slip through and disappear!
- Nice girls don't wear red fingernail polish or pierce their ears.
- Masturbation will cause blindness.
- Clean the house before you leave in case of a fire.

Incidentally, wise and useful "parent" messages also exist!

Often, when you are in your parent ego state, you feel, think, and act like one of your own parents. If this has not yet happened, you will probably have the experience of saying something to one of your own children that has a familiar ring to it. Ironically, it is often exactly what you vowed you would never say! Even though "parent" messages affect your parenting behavior, you can—and ideally will—parent from all ego states.

Before we discuss the third ego state, imagine this scenario. It's 7:00 on a cool, rainy morning. The alarm clock rings, and you hit the snooze button. You feel warm and happy lying in bed, and your child ego state is enjoying it immensely. "Ohhh, to just stay here and sleep, skip class. This feels so good," it says. Then another voice penetrates your relaxed state. "Get up! You shouldn't miss school! Don't be so lazy!" It sounds like Mom or Dad, but it isn't because you don't live at home anymore. You're hearing your own parent ego state. What a dilemma—the struggle between "child" and "parent" continues in your mind.

How fortunate that you have another ego state that can enter the picture at this point. "Let me think—I haven't missed that class yet, and I remember the instructor saying there was going to be a film. I could watch that at another time. I haven't been getting enough rest lately. I think I will sleep this morning" which is one possible resolution. A second one is, "I've missed that class several times, and I don't think it's wise to be absent that much. Besides, the lecture is always full of important material! I think I'll go to class." Other creative solutions—which I hesitate to mention—are possible from this ego state: sleeping in for a while and going to class late, going to class and leaving early to head back home to bed, or going to one class and skipping another.

This part of the personality thinks and is able to logically and objectively analyze. It sees alternatives and acts as a decision maker using facts in a cool, calm way. The name *adult ego state* is quite appropriate as is calling it the executive of personality (Clarkson, 1992). Like a computer, the "adult" gathers information from the three sources of "parent," "child," and stored "adult" data as well as new evidence in the present (Harris, 1969). The "adult" can find either the "child" feelings or the "parent" messages appropriate and allow them to prevail. Also possible is to strike a balance between the two or gather additional information and make an original decision. The "adult" begins to develop at about 10 months of age (Harris, 1969). The infant begins to have control over the environment, and choices are then possible!

Each ego state has its positive and negative qualities. The "child" is exuberant, enjoys life, and readily expresses affection; yet, it also can be depressed, fearful, wounded, and defeated. The "parent" has useful knowledge and reacts quickly. How fortunate we are that our parent ego state tells us to look both ways before crossing streets. Unfortunately, the "parent" contains some outdated and negative information, can be close-minded, and passes on potentially damaging messages. The "adult" is a necessity in most situations; however, it can be programmed with detrimental or inaccurate information.

A well-adjusted individual uses all three ego states. In some cases, an ego state is more powerful and overwhelms or contaminates the others. An overpowering "child" is what Kushner (1986) cautioned against: "Fun can be the dessert of our lives but never its main course. It can be a very welcome change of pace from the things we do every day, but should it ever become what we do every day, we will find it too frivolous a base to build a life on" (pp. 69–70).

Which of the three ego states is dominant in the following examples?

Joan is aloof and reserved. She does well at her accounting job and finds it easy to analyze data. She is a calm person who rarely shows emotions.

Kim is a 12-year-old who has strong convictions about many subjects. She tends to be domineering and judgmental.

Paul is a twinkly eyed 80-year-old. He enjoyed a raft trip down a rushing river as a way of celebrating the event. He is witty, enthusiastic, and readily shows his feelings. However, he often acts on impulse and can be moody.

If you named "adult" for Joan, "parent" for Kim, and "child" for Paul, you are correct. An imbalance can occur regardless of age. Even a 4-year-old can exhibit an expanded "parent."

How well developed are your ego states? Do you have a healthy, happy "child"? Do you ever act on impulse? When were you last spontaneous? Can you wonder and dream? Do you truly feel your emotions, and do you express them? When did you last really laugh? Are you a hugger; do you enjoy being hugged?

Leo Buscaglia, who is widely known as a big hugger, encourages people to "let down their hair" and be a little crazy once in a while. He tells of coming home from Wisconsin on a late-night flight. He carried gifts he couldn't check in as luggage: a large pumpkin, leaves (which he loves), cheese, and homemade bread. When airborne, he impulsively spread the gifts across several seats and pushed the call button. The tired flight attendant was quite surprised and, amazingly, re-energized by the craziness. She called the other attendants; they brought wine and had a party! A potentially boring flight was special because of someone's "child." A class viewed a videotape of Buscaglia in which he talked of his passion for leaves. One autumn day, a student told me he wished he could give all his raked leaves to Leo Buscaglia. Spontaneously, I said, "Let's do it!" We collected beautiful Nebraska leaves (the prairie state really has them!) and mailed them in a large cardboard box with love to Leo. His thank-you note reflected his joy at our craziness. One student, however, asked in a bewildered voice, "Why would we send him leaves?" I patiently explained as I wondered about her "child."

Some do not notice that they are not using their child ego state until it is too late. An 85-year-old reflected on life.

> If I had my life to live over again, I'd dare to make more mistakes next time. I'd relax. I would limber up. I would be sillier than I have been this trip. I would take more chances. I would take more trips. I would climb more mountains and swim more rivers. I would eat more ice cream and less beans. I would perhaps have more actual troubles, but I'd have fewer imaginary ones. You see, I'm one of those people who lived seriously and sanely hour after hour, day after day. Oh, I've had my moments, and if I had

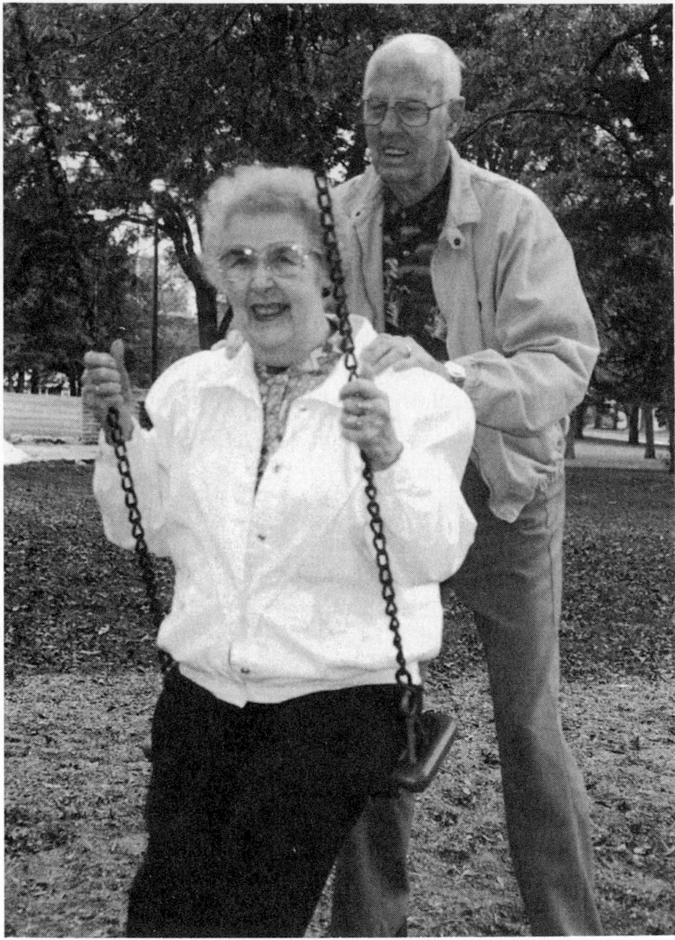

Figure 2-3 The child ego state can be alive and well at any age!

> it to do over again, I'd have more of them. In fact, I'd try to have nothing else, just moments, one after another, instead of living so many years ahead of each day. I've been one of those people who never went anywhere without a thermometer, a hot water bottle, a raincoat, and a parachute. If I had to do it again, I'd travel lighter. If I had my life to live over, I'd start barefoot earlier in the spring and stay that way later in the fall. I'd go to more dances. I'd ride more merry-go-rounds. I would pick more daisies (Walker and Brokaw, 1992, p. 327).

Think of all the "parent" messages that restricted her "child." Can you think of any "child" wants and wishes you are denying yourself? How free is your "child"? If you were 85 years old, what would you wish for yourself? What can you do about it now? Remember, an 85-year-old doesn't have life to live over, and neither will you.

Another problem lies with inconsistent messages. Did you have a parental figure who said one thing and did just the opposite? Did anyone say, "Don't drink and drive," and then proceed to do exactly that, or, "Religion is important, so go to Sunday School" yet who rarely went to church, or a significant person who maintained, "All people are equal," then said, "I don't welcome one of those people in this house"? A sad "parent" message is, "Do as I say, not as I do."

"Parent" messages can be retrieved by thinking about why you do what you do, why you have certain beliefs and ideas, and where they came from originally. A major task of healthy adulthood is to process "parent" messages through the adult ego state. Some will be retained, modified, and many will be eliminated. Getting rid of extremely harmful and hateful messages is highly recommended. Buscaglia (1982) reveals that he has been more involved in unlearning than in learning during various stages of his life. "I'm having to unlearn all the garbage that people have laid upon me" (p. 147). That "garbage" consists of "parent" messages. With each discarded piece he becomes freer. As you process messages through your "adult," you become more your own person. Use REFLECTIONS AND APPLICATIONS to describe your ego states.

Recognizing your own ego states can be beneficial in making decisions. Jack is a 36-year-old factory worker who quit high school to marry and get a job. He realizes he is going nowhere with a career and is considering quitting and going back to school. Of value to Jack would be awareness of the role of each ego state. His "parent" has such messages as "A man is supposed to support his family," "You're too old to go back to school," "Everyone will think you're dodging responsibility." The "child" in him is frightened by risk yet somewhat excited at the prospect of a new experience. Jack will benefit from "plugging into" his adult ego state. This ego state will gather more information about costs, management of the family's financial situation, and benefits compared to losses. A goal of TA is to encourage freedom of choice—the freedom to change (Harris, 1969). This can happen if you, like Jack, become aware of each ego state and use your "adult" in the decision process.

Life Positions

The book title *I'm OK, You're OK* (Harris, 1969) came from the preferred life position in the TA framework. A *life position* can be thought of as a perspective on the world based on feelings about self and others. Berne (1962) identified four positions. The preferred, or healthy, position, I'm OK, you're OK, is based on equality and positiveness. In one's initial approach to people and situations, hope and optimism are present. "Persons in this position are winners. They reflect an optimistic and healthy outlook on life and freely relate with others" (Woollams and Brown, 1979, p. 107). This position requires self-love and esteem. The "I'm OK" belief is followed by tolerance, equality, and acceptance of others.

The I'm not OK, you're OK position is not unusual. In fact, some consider it to be the most common one (Woollams and Brown, 1979). Self-esteem is low; the individual feels inferior. "I'm unworthy, and everyone else has it together" would be a typical thought. These people appear defeated; they usually have difficulty accepting compliments or communicating positive self-talk.

Several years ago a man by the name of Patrick Sherrill committed a violent crime; he killed several co-workers and then himself. The headline read, "Gunman Hated the World and Himself." This is a dramatic example of the position I'm not OK, you're not OK. The position reflects an extremely negative, pessimistic attitude. These people seem to hate themselves and the world. They can behave in various ways, and most are not criminals. Some retreat from the world and become loners, and others simply give up and just manage to survive. The frightening ones are those like Pat Sherrill who take out their self-hatred on others. Sometimes, identifying this position is difficult because those who occupy it may came across as cocky and self-assured. Beneath this "I'm something" facade, however, is probably an "I'm not OK" person.

An annoying and potentially damaging position is I'm OK, you're not OK. People in this position feel superior to others. They show it in annoying ways by maintaining that they are always right, judging or patronizing others, and telling others what to do.

What position are you occupying? The question is frequently asked, "Can you be in more than one?" You may have characteristics that fit more than one position; however, view yourself in a general way. What orientation do you usually take toward others and the world? If it's not **I'm OK, you're OK**, decide to work toward it!

Life Script

Think of a script for a play. A life script is similar. The TA framework does not suggest that your life is predetermined or that you simply read lines and play a role. However, it is influential. A *script* is an ongoing program, developed in early childhood under parental influence, that directs behavior (Berne, 1972).

Unless you become aware of your life script, you may be playing it out without realizing it. Those self-fulfilling prophecies are compelling directions within your script. Julie could be counted on to be late to class. She explained:

> I'm late to everything, including work. I've always been this way. Mom told me I wasn't organized, and Dad said I had no concept of time. My friends just expect me to be late and wouldn't believe it if I were ever on time. I'm just a flake.

Julie played the part of the always-late, disorganized "flake," and she played it well.

Does Julie have to continue playing this part? The TA framework provides a technique called *script analysis*. An individual first becomes aware of thoughts and behaviors and then decides to take different courses of action. Julie did not have to continue in her role, but the decision to change had to be hers. After college she landed a job. A few months later she was fired; you guessed it—chronic tardiness. She rationalized that it wasn't her dream job anyway. Within a short period of time she was hired as a fashion buyer-an ideal position for her! When she was warned about lateness during her first evaluation session, she made an attempt to be on time, yet it was short lived. Losing that job was depressing for Julie, yet it proved to be the jolt she needed. She resolved to change her script, and with the help of a counselor, set up a behavior modification program. She rewarded herself for each on-time experience and relished the praise of others. The always-late, disorganized Julie is rarely seen any more, and part of her new script is, "I can make positive changes if I really want to!" She proved what Nathaniel Branden (1992) wrote, "We need never be the prisoner of yesterday's choices" (p. 73).

Scripts are based on the past. Even though you cannot change your past, learning from past experiences is invaluable. Ask yourself, "Is my past illuminating my present or contaminating it?" (Satir, 1976). The present is where change is possible, and you can rewrite your future script if you choose to do so. Can you think of some changes you would like to make in your script? Taking charge of your own life and destiny isn't necessarily easy, but being your own script-writer is very rewarding!

We are not prisoners of the past. We are pioneers of an exciting future.

—John Powell

Strokes

"I enjoy having you in class." "I like you." "You did a great job." These phrases, along with a smile, a hug, and a friendly wave, are special verbal or nonverbal behaviors called *strokes*. Usually, these feel good to the receiver; if so, they are positive strokes. Negative strokes do not feel good and are generally meant to be hurtful. Think of some negative verbal and nonverbal strokes. (See Table 2-1 for examples of each type.) Strokes are necessary for human survival (Steiner, 1974). "All people need emotional strokes for a healthy well-balanced life" (Ryan and Travis, 1991, p. 86).

Strokes can be conditional (based on certain behaviors or conditions) or unconditional (given simply because the receiver is alive). A mother commented, "I realize that I've been giving positive strokes but only under set conditions. I decided to tell my son that I appreciated him simply for being here—to stroke his person." She had realized the beauty of unconditional strokes!

Can you add others to the lists in Table 2-1?

Teachers would benefit from considering the type of strokes they give. Praise usually depends on teacher-approved behavior or performance. Yet, encouragement and recognition of a student's contributions and growth is a powerful boost to self-esteem. Saying, "I enjoy having you in my class," enhances self-worth.

Even young children appreciate the nature of strokes. When director of an early childhood center, I used the program "TA for Tots." Positive strokes were called "warm fuzzies," while negative ones were "cold pricklies." The children soon recognized how much more comfortable the atmosphere was when "warm fuzzies" were being given and received. A few times a week we had a "warm fuzzy" circle. The children gave and received positive strokes. In the beginning, several were hesitant—an indication that "warm fuzzies" weren't too familiar to them. Gradually, they became comfortable. Verbal strokes seemed easier, and few nonverbal strokes had been given until one interesting circle. Danny was a spontaneous and expressive boy with a healthy child ego state. Tim was reserved and unexpressive. On this particular day, when it was Danny's turn, he did something out of the ordinary. He gave Tim a big hug and kiss on the cheek. The others seemed embarrassed, and I quickly said, "I really like that 'warm fuzzy.' I'd like to see more of those!" Because young children look upon teachers as a final authority,

TABLE 2-1 Strokes

Verbal Positive	Verbal Negative
"I love you."	"I don't like you."
"I like your smile."	"Get lost!"
"You're a great employee."	"You're lazy."
"Hello, how are you?"	"You look awful!"
Nonverbal Positive	**Nonverbal Negative**
A pat on the back	A shake of the fist
A wink (if it feels good!)	A hit or a slap
A back rub	A frown
A special card or gift	Inattention
A hug or kiss	Laughter at someone

they reacted in a positive way—all except Tim. I was saddened that this boy, at the age of only 4, recoiled from his friend's gesture. For whatever reason his script included, "I don't want to be touched." During the course of the year he became more open to expressiveness. That was years ago. I wonder how Tim is today and whether he changed his script.

Strokes, or lack of them, influence scripts and life positions. An all too common scenario goes like this: A child makes the bed and completes assigned tasks each day, but receives no recognition, no positive stroke. One day the bed is not made! What happens? A negative stroke is delivered immediately: "You're irresponsible and lazy!" This scenario is played out frequently in the home, at school, and even at work. Even though evidence shows that positive strokes are powerful motivators, negatives are more common.

When people don't receive positive strokes, they tend to settle for negative ones. "Taking negative strokes is like drinking polluted water; extreme need will cause us to overlook the harmful qualities of what we require to survive" (Steiner, 1974, p. 127). A child who is misbehaving or an adolescent who "acts out" may be deprived of positive strokes and willing to settle for any kind. One student remarked that we give pets more pats than we do human beings. Buscaglia (1982) writes of laws against hugging in public! Positive strokes can be lacking in marriages. One young married female wrote:

> Sometimes I feel as if I'm dying of lack of attention. We've been married only 5 years, and the only time he touches me is in bed. I haven't heard a positive word from him for a long time. I feel so dried up and starved for affection, and I don't know what to do.

I suggested she start by asking for positive strokes and see what happens.

In your life, monitor the strokes you receive and record them in the personality activity in REFLECTIONS AND APPLICATIONS. Ask, "Whom do I receive them from? What kind are they? Under what conditions do I receive them? What do I want?" Also, become aware of the strokes you give by asking the same questions. My husband and I tried a stroke-monitoring experiment with the four children in our household, keeping track of numbers and types of strokes given and received. The one who was receiving the fewest positives and the most negatives from us was, in turn, sending the same back. At that time he was also "acting out" more than the others. We can all influence

Figure 2-4 Copyright 1981 Universal Press Syndicate. Printed by permission. All rights reserved.

the quality of our own lives and of those around us by increasing the number of positive strokes and decreasing the number of negative ones.

The TA framework has much to offer. Only the basics have been presented here. If you want to learn more, read any of the identified selections cited. Transactional Analysis can be used to enrich your life.

WHAT IS YOUR PERSONALITY LIKE?

Craig is miserable at work. He enjoys being around people, yet his job demands that he analyze data in a back office. Connie is frustrated in a certain classroom situation. The instructor doesn't seem to be organized, and the class discussions focus more on possibilities than on realities. Rich and Jamie had been so happy when they first married. Three years later, they both feel dissatisfied. Rich doesn't like the way Jamie seems to make irrational decisions, and she finds him too analytical and inconsiderate of others' feelings.

An understanding of personality types could help each of these individuals. Psychological typing categorizes several related personality traits. Carl Jung (1923), a pioneer in psychological typing, believed that behavioral differences are based on the ways people prefer to approach life (Jung, 1968). Based on Jung's typology with some of their own refinements, Isabel Myers and her mother, Katharine C. Briggs, developed the Myers-Briggs Type Indicator (MBTI). It achieved widespread acceptance in the 1970s and has remained a popular instrument. Its application in education, business, the artistic world, and in decision-making processes of businesses have been extensive and well received, according to a review of research (Murray, 1990). Intended for use with "well" people, the indicator focuses on positive aspects. You can use it to make decisions about education, career, marriage, and parenting, to gain personal insight, and to learn how to work with others.

The book *Gifts Differing* (Myers, 1980b) describes personality preferences as well as ways in which people can use their own strengths and understand the differences of others.

> All too often, others with whom we come in contact do not reason as we reason, or do not value the things we value, or are not interested in what interests us. The merit of the theory is that it enables us to expect specific personality differences in particular people and to cope with the people and the differences in a constructive way (Myers, 1980b, p. 1).

Even though people are more similar than dissimilar, differences provide zest and interest in relationships (Malone and Malone 1987).

Personality Types

Following is a brief summary of the four pairs of personality types. The MBTI will show your preference for one or the other.

- **Extraversion–Introversion** (type E or I)
  Relates to an inward or outward orientation and to life energy sources. (Note: The spelling extraversion is used in this book to correspond to the MBTI. The spelling extroversion is also common.)

- **Sensing–Intuition** (type S or N)
  Pertains to the preferred ways of taking in information.
- **Thinking–Feeling** (type T or F)
  Indicates whether one prefers to use thought or personal values in decision-making and judgments.
- **Judgment–Perception** (type J or P)
  Includes the processes of dealing with the outer world.

Understanding their meanings and knowing that we don't have absolute preferences are important. A common misconception is that an extraversion preference means being totally extraverted. Instead, most of us are both extraverted and introverted, yet in differing degrees.

The meanings of extraversion and introversion are typically misunderstood. Unfortunately, this confusion has led to an assumption that a person needs to be extraverted in order to be successful and happy. "Western culture seems to sanction the outgoing, sociable, and gregarious temperament. As a consequence, introverts are often the ugly ducklings in a society where the majority enjoy sociability" (Keirsey and Bates, 1978, p. 16). I have had several students confess that they wished they were extraverted. I rarely hear individuals express a desire for introversion and believe that this is because of a misunderstanding of the two.

In fact, most of the words commonly used as synonyms for extraverted such as friendly, outgoing, caring, and open are positive. However, these are not replacement words for extraverted. And while introversion is often identified with such descriptors as shy, lonely, uncaring, and snobbish, these do not define introversion. This inaccuracy is unfair, and a true understanding of type can correct these misconceptions.

Let's look at what these types really are. Think in terms of life energy or force. What charges your battery? If your preference is *extraversion*, you get much of this force from external sources, including other people, and you probably project energy outward. *Extraverted* does mean outgoing—having an outward orientation and a preference to operate in the outer world of people and things. If there were such a word as "ingoing," it would describe an introverted preference well. *Introversion* means an inner orientation and having an interest in the inner world of concepts and ideas. The source of energy is within and from solitary experiences. Thus, those with a preference for introversion can re-energize themselves and don't rely on external stimuli. In fact, interaction drains their energy, and they need to spend time recharging themselves.

People who prefer extraversion will usually behave in a friendly fashion, and they appear to be open. They are not necessarily any more emotional, caring, or loving. Those with an introversion preference will generally be more reserved in a social setting, and they do not usually seek out others. This does not mean that they are uncaring, snobbish, lonely, or shy. They are often skilled in working with people; however, their preference is for smaller numbers and an opportunity to know the people well. People who are described as shy, lonely, and uncaring are lacking in social skills and may be either introverted or extraverted.

Another difference, noted by Jeanne and Birk Adams, coordinators for a chapter of the Association of Psychological Types, is that extraverts will usually respond more quickly than introverts. Introverts think about what they are going to say; extraverts tend to think out loud. In fact, extraverts commonly talk their thoughts! If you often "put your foot in your mouth," extraversion could be a partial reason. However, talkativeness is not necessarily an exclusive characteristic of either. Because introverts prefer smaller groups, you could be sitting next to a person on a bus or airplane who talks and talks in a one-on-one situation and be surprised to know he or she has an introverted preference. Similarly, in my classroom introverts may participate often and surprise their classmates when personality types are identified.

Both types have advantages. Extraverts frequently report greater happiness and satisfaction with life. Reasons could be the experience of more potentially positive interactions, ease with affectionate behaviors, more acceptance by society, and greater social support (Myers, 1992). Extraverts initiate social exchange more easily; in fact, they are usually eager to do so. Would it surprise you, though, to know that extraverts can behave in a shy manner? *Shyness* is timidity in a social situation. As an extravert, I have felt and acted shyly at some social activities because I didn't feel at ease or wasn't in the mood to talk. The dissatisfaction I felt after the event came from not using my extraverted preference. If I were an introvert, I probably wouldn't have been bothered. That leads to one distinct advantage for introverts. They don't require social exchange and can get along just fine alone for long periods of time. In addition, introverts are often thought of as sincere people and good listeners even though they may be neither. Can you think of other advantages for each type?

What about disadvantages? Extraverts can be overwhelming in social interactions and be seen as obnoxious loud-mouths. If they are extreme in their extraversion, others may see them as superficial or phony. Another potential problem for an extravert was expressed by Jodi in a class one day:

> I'm quite extraverted, but there are still times when I am quiet. If that happens around friends, they act upset with me and ask, "What's wrong with you anyway?" I find it hard to have any quiet time when I'm around others. They expect me to be the life of the party.

In contrast, introverts are criticized for their lack of conversation and what is often interpreted as aloofness. They may be perceived as uncaring or uninterested. If an extreme introvert does go to a party, the stay will likely be short. The accusation of "party pooper" is inaccurate; in actuality, the party "pooped" the introvert (Keirsey and Bates, 1978). How might a person with an extraverted preference (E) and one with an introverted preference (I) seem to each other? Without understanding their differences, an "E" can seem shallow to an "I," and an "I" may seem withdrawn to an "E." After a program I gave on preferences, a woman in her 60s approached me and laughingly asked, "Where were you 3 years ago when I got divorced? I thought I was married to a 'dud,' someone who just didn't know how to have fun. Now I realize he was just introverted which to me seemed terrible. This could have saved my marriage!"

Extraversion and introversion were looked upon as valuable opposites by Carl Jung. He believed that most individuals use both types but not with equal ease (Myers, 1980a). The U.S. population consists of about 70 percent extraverts and 30 percent introverts (Jeffries, 1991). The most important points are that both extraversion and introversion include positive behaviors and advantages, and we have preferences in varying degrees for both. Later in the book these two preferences will be examined in relation to career satisfaction and marital choice.

Each preference is important, and if their meanings are not clarified, confusion and misunderstanding are probable. The other three pairs of preferences can be understood as follows:

- When you want to find out something, your preference may be sensing (S) or gathering facts through the senses. "You tend to be realistic, practical, observant, and good at remembering a great number of facts and working with them" (Myers, 1980a, p. 2). If you like intuition (N) better, "you tend to value imagination and inspirations, and to be good at new ideas, projects, and problem-solving" (Myers, 1980a, p. 2). In perceiving reality differently, sensors are concrete and attuned to details, and intuitives are visionary and ablaze with possibilities and ideas. Any successful business needs people with both preferences. When working on a task, sensors prefer a systematic step-by-step procedure and don't seem to be bothered by repetition. Intuitives often devise their own methods, will work on several steps or projects at once, and prefer variety. An intuitive preference gets restless with "sameness" and tries to modify life while appreciating new and different experiences (Hirsch and Kummerow, 1989).

Can you see how these preferences can affect job satisfaction? About 70 percent in the United States are sensing while 30 percent are intuitive (Jeffries, 1991).

- Once you have found what you want to know, you may have a decision to make. If your preference is for thinking (T), you will predict the logical results of your actions and decide impersonally. The other way to decide is through feeling (F). You will consider anything that matters or is important to you or to other people (logic is not required) and decide according to personal values (Myers, 1980a). Those who have a clear thinking preference view emotions as more of a problem than as part of a solution (Keating, 1984). This person can be oblivious to other people's feelings, while the opposite (a strong feeling person) can "bend over backward" to avoid hurting anyone. Either can become a problem. Both preferences can care a great deal about people and believe that their decisions are based on the "right" motives. Caring from a "T" is more apt to be sympathy and from the "F" empathy (Jeffries, 1991). The two preferences can clash or complement each other. Clashing is probably more common.

A crucial difference between a "T" and "F" which isn't easily bridged is how issues are perceived. A "T" prefers to deal with them in a detached manner outside of self. "It's as if the process took place in a bubble out in the air while the 'F' takes that same bubble and tucks it inside and thinks in terms of I, me, we, you, us" (Jeffries, 1991, p. 90). Even though in the United States the population seems to be about 50 percent of each, within the feeling preference, 60 to 66 percent are females; within the thinking preference, 60 to 66 percent are males (Jeffries, 1991).

- The descriptors judging (J) or perceptive (P) refer to your attitude toward the outer world. Judgment means that you prefer living in a "planned, decided, orderly way, wanting to regulate life and control it" (Myers, 1980a, p. 6). Planning and preparation are typical behaviors. A judging person seeks closure and prefers to reach a decision or judgment quickly. If instead you like living in a "flexible, spontaneous way, wanting to understand life and adapt to it," (Myers, 1980a, p. 6), your preference is perception. You often "go with the flow" and prefer to delay closure and continue perceiving. Key words are organization for the judging preference and adaptability for perceivers (Jeffries, 1991).

I laughed when I read a comment written by Paul, a strong judger. "I like the idea of someone throwing me a surprise party, but I want to be prepared for it." He also wrote, "I live by my planner. I take it everywhere, even parties." In contrast to Paul, a perceiver probably wouldn't have a planner or be like Kari who said, "I bought a calendar diary but just don't bother to use it!" In the workplace, colleagues of these two extremes can have difficulty getting along. The judging person would probably view the perceptive individual as disorganized or flighty, while the perceptive one could become frustrated with a perception of an overly organized and inflexible co-worker. Keep in mind what judging means. I remember one student who was upset to discover he was a "J." He said, "I'm not a judgmental person!" I quickly assured him that "J" doesn't mean that. Judgers (55%) and perceivers (45%) seem to be fairly split throughout the population of the United States (Jeffries, 1991). I appreciate both in the classroom. Judgers remind me of due dates, time, and schedules, and perceivers readily adjust to any deviation!

Think about which of the preferences in each of the four categories sounds like you and then elaborate on these in REFLECTIONS AND APPLICATIONS. The combination of the four choices becomes what is called *psychological type*. Remember that being an "ENFP" doesn't mean you don't have and won't use the other preferences of "ISTJ."

The preferences paired reflect decision-making styles.

- Sensing thinking (ST) focuses on verifiable facts then makes judgments by impersonally evaluating the facts. Decisions are usually practical and matter-of-fact.
- Sensing feeling (SF) focuses on verifiable facts then makes decisions by weighing values and considering others. Decisions tend to be sympathetic and friendly.
- Intuition thinking (NT) prefers a variety of possible solutions then selects by impersonal analysis. Decisions are likely to be logical and ingenious.
- Intuitive feeling (NF) recognizes a wide range of possible solutions and decides by weighing values and considering others. Decisions are generally enthusiastic and insightful.

A study showed that job applications are geared toward those with sensing and thinking preferences (ST) as they are detail-oriented, require short answers, and don't provide room to expand. One might question if such applications could restrict the balance of personality types within an organization (Hai et al., 1986).

A college library or counseling service may have a version of the MBTI you can take or you may have an opportunity in a class or workshop. The book *Please Understand Me* (Keirsey and Bates, 1978) offers a questionnaire that yields scores in the four categories. Remember that with any measurement, the results may vary for a number of reasons. Taking the test more than once and being honest in answering the questions will give you a more reliable profile. The indicator identifies a preferred trait and is not intended to exclude other possibilities. For example, you may have a strong preference for using your right hand, yet you can also use your left. Personality typing indicates your strengths (Hirsh, 1985), and in some situations, you are wise to use the lesser preference. The extent of difference between the two will influence your degree of ease in various personal and professional situations. If the two preferences are close, you probably are comfortable using either one. Remember that this is not intended to pigeonhole people nor arm them with excuses for certain behaviors (i.e., "I can't help that I'm disorganized. I'm a 'P'!" to which I would respond, "You also have a 'J' preference into which you can shift"). Reading books on the subject will give further ideas for using this understanding in career, marriage, parenting, and leadership situations.

Can you recognize how personality was creating hardships for the individuals in the examples at the beginning of this section? Craig is extraverted, and his job doesn't allow him to be in contact with people. Connie is more sensing, while her instructor appears to be intuitive. The marriage is in trouble because Rich, who has a thinking preference, and Jamie, who prefers feeling, don't understand each other. Knowing more about your personality can help you make wiser choices and maximize your potential. By understanding your own personality type and that of others, you can draw on your strengths and appreciate and grow from the differing gifts of others. Remaining open to and understanding differences leads to enrichment.

GENDER ROLE: INFLUENCES ON YOUR LIFE

How would your life be different if you had been born the opposite sex? This may be difficult to imagine and, possibly, even distasteful. Once when I asked students to react to this, I received a quick, loud response from a 37-year-old man: "It makes me sick to think about it!" His reply demonstrated an attitude I was planning to later discuss with the class and made a salient point more dramatically than I could have.

Male and Female Differences

Over a period of several years, I have asked more than 1800 students the question, "How would your life be different if you had been born the opposite sex?" An interesting pattern has emerged. Following are the categories most often mentioned, with a general explanation of the differences imagined by the men and women.

Career choice. This area was by far the most commonly mentioned. When considering being raised male, women would have made a different career choice, had an earlier pursuit of career, put more emphasis on career, and realized a definite increase in financial assets. Some felt they would be more restricted: "I would have been forced to take over the family farm or business." Men indicated that, as women, they would either have a different, stereotypic female career, slow advancement, or no career at all! "I'd be more sheltered and let others take care of me" and "I'd just go out and trap a rich guy!" were two male observations. One man said, "Maybe I'd really go radical and be a doctor!"

Education. Women said they would have gone to college earlier, finished earlier, attended a more prestigious college, and planned their education based on future earning power. One woman said, "I would have been forced to achieve more from my education all the way through because I'd need it to earn a living." Men mentioned not going to college, and a few said they wouldn't have been able to afford further education.

Sports and other activities. Although opportunities in women's athletics have increased as a result of legislation in the 1970s, women still reported that they would have participated more and been involved in a wider variety of sports. Men, conversely, said that they would have been less involved. One outstanding female basketball player remarked, "I may have taken a shot at playing professionally. As a female, there isn't much of an opportunity for that." Another woman said that, as a boy, she would not have been a cheerleader. A distinct difference was mechanical. Women were sure that they would know more about automobiles and other machines. And a young man said, "As a female I wouldn't know anything about a car. I would just expect a man to handle it!"

Household tasks. A definite sex difference was clear in this category. Men, if raised female, would do more housework and cooking and no outside chores. Women would move out of the kitchen and into the garage and yard. Most women said that they would be paid more for allowances. One man stated, "I'd be getting only 10 cents for washing dishes instead of a dollar for mowing the yard!"

Marriage and child raising. Several women said that they would have married later or not at all if they had been men. The men envisioned being married, having the role of housewife, and being the primary parent. One male reply was, "I'd probably have married young, been married two or three times, have lots of kids, and be looking again for someone to support us!" "If male, I wouldn't have custody of my children," said a young woman.

Self-esteem and self-efficacy. Both sexes viewed women as placing a lower value on themselves and having less confidence. An older female student said that she would have had higher self-esteem earlier in life and wouldn't have wasted her talent for so long. Another woman reported that her family had favored boys: "Boys are very special, and they know it." However, a disadvantage to men was also noted. A woman said, "I'd be under a lot more pressure and have more stress. I'd probably die younger thinking I had to handle everything."

Independence and assertiveness. Both sexes perceived men as more independent, self-sufficient, assertive, and in control of their lives. One woman said, "I'd have more 'guts.' " Two other comments from women were, "I wouldn't be taken advantage of" and "My needs would come first." A disabled woman said, "I would have a harder time being handicapped; as a female, it's easier to ask for help."

Emotions. The stereotype of men as unemotional, unfeeling, and in control came through repeatedly. Both sexes mentioned that being female meant being more sensitive, aware of feeling, and expressive. One man said, "I wouldn't have gotten spanked for crying when I was young." Women were seen as shyer and more fearful by both sexes.

Turn back to the personality activity in REFLECTIONS AND APPLICATIONS and answer the questions about differences in your life related to gender role. You may be surprised that your life, too, would have been different.

Gender-Role Stereotypes

The replies to this question reveal a great deal about sex-role perceptions and the limitations created by stereotypes. A *stereotype* is a preconceived idea or belief, often a generalization, about an identifiable group. Stereotypical expectations and behaviors have influenced your life and continue to do so. Some of these are so subtle that they go unnoticed and yet have an impact.

If a woman has difficulty imagining any difference in her life, I ask, "Do you plan to marry?" Most say they do. "Will he take your name?" I have yet to hear a "yes" to that question because males in the American society are not expected to change their names. Most individuals haven't given the question much thought; after they do, this gender difference is apparent. Interestingly, the idea that names would even be "up for discussion" seems radical to some. Some don't even know that it is legal in all states for a woman to keep her birth name (NOW Legal Defense and Education Fund and Cherow-O'Leary, 1987). A study of college students (Scheuble and Johnson, 1993) found that most females (81.6%) planned to change their name while 7 percent planned to hyphenate. Not one man was going to make *any* change in his name. Among those who believed that a woman should *always* change her name were 32 percent of males and 5.1 percent of females. Finding it acceptable for a woman to keep her family name were 91.8 percent of women and 57 percent of men. The main reasons given for maintaining a name were professional purposes and to keep a family name alive.

Name changing was the subject in a sociology class. Impatiently, a young man asked, "What's the big deal anyway? It's just a name." Yet, when asked, "Then would you take your wife's name?" he quickly shook his head and said a definite, "NO." Another student interjected, "Then it *is* a big deal, isn't it?" Calling the name problem for married women a clumsy mess, Lance Morrow (1993) identified choices: (1) keep your family name, (2) take the husband's last name, (3) use three names or hyphenate two last names, or (4) use unmarried name in most professional matters and husband's names in domestic ones. The author noted: "Most men, if they were to wake up one morning and find themselves transformed into married women, would (rather huffily) choose Option No. 1," (p. 76). Incidentally, even when women hyphenate, men usually do not.

Gloria Steinem (1992) comments on the path from "Mrs. John Smith" to "Mary Smith" to perhaps "Mary Jones" as becoming independent much like slaves became free and gradually assumed different names from their masters. An interesting discussion of name changing can be found in the book *Sex and Gender* (Doyle, 1985). Included are choices and suggestions for solving any name-changing difficulties from "Taking Your Own Name" (Lilly, 1984). One can seriously question whether the sexes are equal until couples seriously consider which name to retain.

Other subtle differences are in the areas of finding an intimate partner and physical attractiveness. Women pay far more attention to both. Romance novel readers are 98.99 percent women, and advertising for beauty products and fashion occupies about 90 percent of full-page ad space in at least a dozen of best-selling women's magazines (Farrell, 1986). I wanted to see if things had changed since Farrell wrote *Why Men Are the Way They Are* in 1986 in which he contended that magazines for teenage girls have almost no articles on career success and financial independence while concentrating on beauty and dating. In 1994, the same was true. In fact, I found *no* articles on anything except how to be beautiful and attract boys!

Gender-Role Development

Studies of male-female differences have been numerous in the last 20 years. A classic in the field (Maccoby and Jacklin, 1974), addressed both actual and perceived differences between men and women and encouraged researchers to explore gender, an aspect of self that had been virtually ignored. Gender or sex-role development is now covered in most introductory psychology and sociology courses and is frequently offered as a separate course in colleges and universities. *Gender* refers to social and psychological traits associated with masculinity and femininity which are socially and culturally determined (Popenoe, 1993). It differs from the category of sex which refers to biological differences. *Gender identity* is an individual's emotional and intellectual awareness of being either male or female while *gender role* consists of personality characteristics, attitudes, and behaviors determined by society (Hendrick and Hendrick, 1992).

Generally, explanations of gender differences focus on learning. Sociologists believe that socialization is a main cause (Macionis, 1994; Popenoe, 1993) and that gender is a product of social conditioning and circumstances. Psychologists tend to acknowledge that few actual psychological differences exist and credit learning experiences as being strong enough to counteract most biological inclinations (Plotnik, 1993; Rathus, 1993). Studies (Hyde et al., 1990; Hyde and Linn, 1988) that show almost no general cognitive differences between the sexes add strength to the theory that differences are learned. "Former differences in intellectual skills such as mathematical, verbal, and spatial abilities have gradually vanished or are too trivial to matter" (Tavris, 1992, p. 288). Differences resulting from social and cultural expectations tend to fade if individuals aren't bound by gender.

Gender roles are shaped by observational learning, modeling, identification, and socialization. An example of the latter would be two young children with skinned knees. Both begin to cry. Janie is hugged and consoled, while Johnny is scolded for not being brave. Learning theory emphasizes rewards, punishments, encouragements, and discouragements humans receive. I once asked a young man in class what his parents' reactions would have been if he had come home and announced that he was going to try out for cheerleading. "Mom would have been embarrassed and disappointed; Dad would have killed me!" was his honest reply.

The tasks and activities of young children play an important role. One student said her brother's one household task was to take out garbage. "My mother even cleaned his room, and now his wife does it!" Humorous or pathetic? Studies show that a mother's sex-typed attitudes and behaviors led to the same in children as early as age 3 (Fagot et al., 1992), that daughters' gender roles were significantly influenced by their mothers' behaviors (Arditti et al., 1991), and that children of mothers engaged in nonstereotypic occupations had fewer stereotypic vocational interests (Barak et al., 1991). Clearly, parental influence is of utmost importance.

The field of cognitive psychology emphasizes thoughts and processing of information. Young children begin to make distinctions between what is masculine and feminine and then act upon these distinctions. Years ago, I worked in a preschool language-development program and knew little about gender roles. One of the activities involved categorizing toys into a boys' and girls' pile. Almost every child by the age of 3 could do so without hesitation. This grouping carried over into their actual activities. Seldom did a little boy venture into the play kitchen, and then it was usually to ask what was for dinner! Have things changed? A study in Canada traced the development of first-born children until age 2. Parents, especially mothers, selected stereotypic toys for their children; the ones for boys required more active play. The researchers concluded that changes that would provide equal opportunities for girls and boys during their early development are not occurring quickly enough (Pomerleau et al., 1990). Even later, the norms are recognizable as one person described:

> At school dances the girls made the decorations, but the boys got on the ladders to put them up. At the actual event, boys were expected to risk rejection when they requested a dance while the girls waited and tried to look appealing! At church it was only women who worked in the kitchen.

Disadvantages of Stereotypic Gender Roles

No matter how gender role developed, your personality, behavior, and aspirations have been influenced by it. Of value now is to become aware of what you think about your own gender role and that of the opposite sex. How have your perceptions influenced expectations of yourself and your behaviors? How do they affect your relationships? Are you stereotypic or not?

Conforming to sex-role stereotypes has several disadvantages. Both men and women suffer from a rigid perception of roles. As evidenced by the responses of my students, men are generally regarded in a more positive light by both sexes. Thus, many women may behave like the weaker sex and feel inferior. A study of 1607 adolescents (whites and blacks) revealed that stereotypically traditional girls were more likely to begin having sexual intercourse earlier than those who were nontraditional (Foshee and Bauman, 1992). It seems girls were seeking self-worth by being sexual. The book *Reviving Ophelia* (Pipher, 1994) is an excellent wake-up call regarding adolescent females and our "girl-poisoning culture."

> Girls today are much more oppressed. They face incredible pressures to be beautiful and sophisticated, which in junior high means using chemicals and being sexual. America today limits girls' development, truncates their wholeness and leaves many of them traumatized (p. 12).

Cases of wasted female talents are evident at all ages. Skills are not used because of lack of confidence or reluctance to move beyond the stereotype. A bright young woman in one of my classes disclosed that she had always wanted to become a physician. She was settling for a career as a medical assistant, she said, because her fiancé was in school too, and she needed to work to help pay his tuition. "He doesn't really want me to go to medical school," she reported. This reluctance to develop a self-supporting career puts women at risk during each stage of life. At retirement women typically don't have their own pension. If they do, it is typically less than half of a man's because women tend to work for a shorter time and earn less money (Schwartz, 1993). The *feminization of poverty*, covered in most sociology books, is a tragic result of relying on someone else to take care of me, as women have traditionally done. Even when women excel, they have found it difficult to achieve top positions. Fewer than half a dozen women have reached the chief executive post at America's 500 largest corporations (Greenwald, 1993). "The beauty-focused woman who depends on men to 'tow my car,' 'pick up my packages,' and 'pay for the dates' pays a high price for her dependence on men and becomes less happy the older she gets" (Farrell, 1986, p. 76).

Men, too, have suffered. Pressures to achieve and to be the primary "breadwinner" have caused undue stress. In a tragic situation in Lincoln, Nebraska, a middle-aged man killed his family and himself. He had been depressed because of his financial difficulties and what he perceived as his inability to support his family. "Men pay dearly for the privilege of dominating" (Keen, 1991, p. 42).

The pressure of high expectations takes its toll on health. Although the exact cause is unclear, men have shorter life expectancies. A woman can expect to live about seven years longer than a man (Inlander and Hodge, 1992). Stereotypic men seem to be at a higher risk. One reason men suffer more from physical decline may be because of viewing health-giving behaviors as feminine and not something a "real" man will worry about (Goldberg, 1979). Do you know men who resist help until their symptoms or pain are acute? "The blueprint for masculinity is a blueprint for self-destruction" (Farrell, p. 17).

Men are also restricted and limited. They feel forced, in certain situations, to behave, not as they want to, but to satisfy the stereotype. They can be forced into unsatisfying careers and deprived of certain activities for fear of ridicule. One man said that he was an excellent volleyball player and would have liked to have been on the high school team. "It never went beyond a secret desire. Volleyball was considered a girl's sport, and I would have been the laughingstock of the school."

In addition, men generally are not raised to be nurturing and expressive, which can deprive them of close relationships with other men and even with their own children. Men do not learn a language for expressing feelings; instead, men learn a language for achievement and competitiveness (Pasick, 1992). One woman shared her greatest wish as wanting to be close to her dad and to have him verbalize and show his love. "He keeps saying that he just can't show it. He doesn't know how because men aren't like that."

As long as stereotypic differences are emphasized, equality isn't possible. Interestingly, even being pampered and allowed to go first as "ladies" traditionally are isn't conducive to equal rights and treatment. Even viewing the sexes as extreme opposites is an enemy of equality. Because men have long been dominant, what is considered masculine is viewed as worthy. By contrast, feminine traits are devalued. For example, women who develop stereotypic masculine personality traits such as independence are praised; not so for men who reflect the softer feminine side of nurturance and warmth. Consequently, women are either considered deficient or at an advantage by demonstrating stereotypic masculine personality traits.

Recently, men have become targets of negative stereotyping and "male bashing." One young man commented, "It's considered out-of-line to put women down but really funny to degrade men." A common theme is that men are unable to feel and not compassionate nor warm enough. "Many men today feel blamed, demeaned, and attacked—involved in a night battle in a jungle against an unseen foe" (Keen, 1991, p. 6). While "turning the tables" may please some, prejudice against men is self-defeating for women just as male chauvinism diminishes men (Cowan and Kinder, 1985). William Pollack, author and faculty member of Harvard Medical School, stated, "The stereotype of men as bad without any virtuous pieces is not right. It's time to stop arguing about which is the better half and to look for what is good in both" (Rios, 1993, p. 6).

Does it seem reasonable to continue sex stereotyping? The answer would seem to be a resounding no. Not only are there definite disadvantages to both women and men, stereotyping isn't logical. "Assigning people to roles because of their sex makes no more sense than assigning them to play positions on a baseball team based on their shoe size" (Worchel and Shebilske, 1989, p. 352). Because bipolarity and stereotyping ultimately hurt everyone, what is fair and reasonable is to proclaim and live our *humanity*.

Benefits of Androgyny

Androgyny, a blend of positive masculine and feminine personality traits, allows us to be free as human beings. Androgynous (from andro, male, and gyne, female) behavior allows for flexibility. Being able to respond to the demands of a situation is more practical than the restrictive behaviors of a stereotype. Early studies indicated that stereotypically feminine women were limited by being less independent and assertive than masculine men or androgynous individuals. Masculine men were less playful, warm, and responsive than feminine women or androgynous people. Stereotypic individuals resisted behaving differently even though they would have benefited. In contrast, androgynous men and women coped more effectively with diverse situations (Bem, 1975).

Later studies show that androgynous people generally feel happier and handle stress better (Shaw, 1982), manage anger in healthier ways (Kopper and Epperson, 1991), have a stronger sense of their own identity and are more able to form intimate, sharing relationships than stereotypic individuals (Schiedel and Marcia, 1985). Self-disclosure that leads to closer relationships is more likely with androgynous individuals (Shaffer et al., 1992). Those who were androgynous scored higher on verbal expressions of love and nonmaterial evidence of love and were more tolerant of their loved ones' faults and more likely to express their feelings than feminine or masculine individuals (Coleman and Ganong, 1985). "It is not macho men and feminine women who make the best lovers, at least not as love is measured in this study" (p. 174).

Reduced levels of intimate aggression and abuse were found among androgynous men (Boye-Beaman et al., 1993). In another study female college students viewed androgynous men as more likable, adaptive, moral, conscientious, and reliable (Cramer et al., 1991). A study of middle-aged men who were successful and fulfilled identified their most noticeable personality strengths as androgyny and maturity. Their wives, too, were androgynous (Heath, 1991).

A scale was developed by Sandra Bem (1974) to measure psychological androgyny. She challenged the idea that a person has to be either masculine or feminine in personality traits and behaviors and suggested that strongly sex-typed individuals might be seriously limited. A female student described her own path to androgyny.

> Self-doubt came from years of my mother's coaching: "Stephanie, get a job in a hospital so you can marry a doctor or Stephanie, become a stewardess so you can find a pilot to marry, or Stephanie, put on your make-up because your looks are all that count." My response today: Well, MOM, I'm going to be the doctor or the pilot. I'm not going to watch others achieve while I sit on the sidelines and put on make-up!

Becoming aware of how stereotypic or androgynous you are is the first step in deciding to make positive changes. Check to see how androgynous you are by responding to the personality questions in REFLECTIONS AND APPLICATIONS. "We are all pioneers in this era of loosening and changing gender definitions to fit human needs rather than to reinforce masculine and feminine stereotypes. It is both an exciting and a threatening time." (Goldberg, 1979, p. 275).

Figure 2-5

POSITIVE CHANGE AND GROWTH

Awareness of self followed by a sincere desire to change are the forerunners of personal growth. Electing to improve in one area will likely affect the whole self. Gender role changes influence several aspects of life. If a woman is stereotypic feminine, she will be passive and meek. Women who fully accept the traditional feminine gender role are likely to believe that they are to be dominated. They lack assertiveness and because they don't say what they need and want, are often frustrated. Low self-esteem is typically the result. "Every time we fail to speak up, we lose a little more regard for ourselves" (Pennebaker, 1992, p. 73).

Rebecca was a middle-aged woman who fits this description. A stereotypic male, by contrast, will probably be aggressive. Rebecca's husband, Jerry, behaved in a tough, somewhat threatening manner and controlled the family. He lost respect for Rebecca because she was so submissive. Recent studies found that when wives were only agreeable and compliant, the marriages suffered (Gottman, 1991). Rebecca, too, was becoming frustrated with Jerry and their relationship.

Becoming Assertive

After seriously considering divorce and obtaining marital counseling, Jerry and Rebecca became interested in what they felt could save their marriage: *assertiveness*. This learned set of behaviors includes maintaining one's legitimate rights, choosing for self, and expressing genuine thoughts and feelings in nonthreatening ways.

> Assertive behavior promotes equality in human relationships, enabling us to act in our own best interests, to stand up for ourselves without undue anxiety, to express honest feelings comfortably, to exercise personal rights without denying the rights of others (Alberti and Emmons, 1986, p. 7).

Each partner would need to change in order to improve the marriage. Let's see how Jerry and Rebecca did so using several different techniques. If becoming assertive is one of your goals, you can use them, as well.

First, they employed thought changing, an idea from cognitive therapy. Rebecca's thoughts were: "Just because I've been passive and unassertive doesn't mean I must continue to be. I know that my relationships would be more positive and I'd feel better about myself if I stood up for myself and expressed my genuine thoughts and feelings." In Jerry's mind was: "I'm causing problems for myself at home and work by coming on too strong. I know it won't be easy because I've been like this all my life, but I want to become less aggressive without becoming weak and powerless." Every day they demonstrated self-efficacy by thinking, "I can change!" They challenged their old ideas about male-female roles and their stereotypic behaviors. They filled their minds with new thoughts.

One of these was that each partner controlled his or her own life. An understanding of control theory (Glasser, 1984) helped them see that changing both the thinking and doing components of their behavior was important. Recognizing that control of what they did would profoundly influence other components of thinking and feeling, they worked hard to do things differently. Jerry lowered his tone of voice, counted to ten before reacting, and deliberately encouraged decision making on Rebecca's part. He found his thoughts and feelings about her changing. He acted similarly at work and enjoyed the praise he received. Rebecca spoke louder and began to be more decisive in important situations. She began to think of herself as a confident person, and her feelings of helplessness decreased. Both learned to communicate in assertive ways. As they began to act differently, it became difficult to remember their old thoughts and feelings.

They drew upon social learning theory and selected a person they wanted to emulate and used modeling techniques. They kept track of successful attempts to become assertive and rewarded each other. The two talked about their childhood and adolescence and thought about why they behaved as they did. Rebecca recalled several messages, some she hadn't been aware of before, that gave her the self-image of the weak, submissive woman. "I remember my mother telling me that a man loved a woman only if she let him be the boss." Jerry's messages had been mixed. His father had been browbeaten by his mother and somewhat passive at work. In high school Jerry had associated with a crowd of stereotypic boys who acted tough and made fun of any boy they considered to be a sissy. Jerry and Rebecca were becoming aware of unresolved issues and conflicts identified in psychodynamic theory. They were analyzing their scripts and understanding all the "parent" messages they had received.

Writing an analysis of self-concepts was enlightening. They included how they presently saw themselves, and how they would like to be, and then they rated their self-esteem. They repeated this exercise monthly. The humanistic approach assured them that they could make positive choices in their lives. They experienced what Maslow (1968) predicted for humanistic psychology: action and consequences that can help generate a new way of life.

They read books about assertiveness and discussed the differences among assertive, nonassertive, and aggressive behavior. Instead of denying the self and allowing the other to control and always choose (nonassertive and passive) or enhancing the self at another's expense and trying to control and choose for others (aggressive), each worked toward assertiveness. They developed specific behaviors of: using affirmations of purpose and intent (focusing one's mind on a positive desire or outcome), taking responsibility for self (expressing clearly what is wanted), limit-setting (letting others know where one "draws the line,"), and expressing both positive and negative feelings ("I like it when you . . . ," "I resent it when you . . . "). They used nonverbal assertive behavior including full and direct eye contact, appropriate facial expressions (firm or pleased, for example), confident body stance, calm and controlled body movements, even and calm tone of voice, and moderate rate and volume. "Body language can speak more powerfully than words" (Bower and Bower, 1991, p. 1988).

In addition to these behaviors, they practiced open, assertive ways to verbalize thoughts and feelings covered in Chapter Seven. To overcome intimidating fears related to embarrassment and rejection, Rebecca began using a simple technique (Butler, 1992). Whenever she caught herself thinking, "What if he gets upset when I state my opinion," she changed it to, "So what if he gets upset" or "What if I answer a question in a group, and someone laughs," to "So what if I state my opinion in a group, and someone laughs." Adding the "so" sapped the strength of the first fearful thought. They reminded themselves often that "there aren't any naturally assertive persons, only those who have learned to behave as they do. And it's never too late for you to begin the same process" (Alberti and Emmons, 1975, p. 28). Their efforts met with success as they enriched their marriage and enhanced themselves!

Check your own assertive behavior by responding on the personality activity in REFLECTIONS AND APPLICATIONS. Assertiveness may not be one of your needed changes, although professionals agree that because no one is born assertive, almost everyone can benefit from skills training. Assertiveness is related to self-esteem, and lack of assertiveness erodes self-worth (Ryan and Travis, 1991). Certain personality preferences may have an advantage in that assertiveness is related to extraversion in women and the thinking preference on the MBTI for both women and men (Tucker, 1991). However, any personality type can become assertive.

The path is not necessarily an easy one. As a person becomes assertive, others may resent and feel offended by this "new" individual especially if they have been somehow served by your nonassertiveness (Mastrich and Birnes, 1990). Jen confided to me that she had made an assertive comment to her father which led to a major confrontation. She was ready to give up. I encouraged her not to quit and to be assertive in situations where success is likely. Then she could "tackle" her dad when she feels quite confident!

Whatever you desire, within reasonable parameters, can be accomplished. Understanding what you are all about, how you developed to this point, and what you can do to improve can turn a desire into reality. The choice is yours!

SUMMARY

The self is a fascinating subject. Having a strong sense of your self-identity and realizing that you can choose to bring about changes are conducive to personal growth. The core of self is your personality—the unique combination of qualities and behaviors that only you possess.

Your personality has been influenced by both heredity and environment. Major theories in both psychology and sociology explain personality development. Erikson linked personality to social development and identified eight psychosocial stages. Personality is relatively stable over the life span, although changes in specific traits are common.

The TA framework can help to understand yourself, others, and your interactions. Three ego states compose the personality. The four life positions are perspectives on life, with the preferred I'm OK, you're OK seen as a healthy orientation. Your script is a personal design of life. Strokes are positive or negative, verbal or nonverbal behaviors. The types of strokes you received influenced your script and life position.

To understand your personality you can use the MBTI. It gives a reading of your preferences in four areas. One of these deals with extraversion and introversion, which are important in social interaction. Understanding the other three areas related to gathering information, making decisions, and dealing with the world and combining the four into a personality type can be enlightening and useful in all aspects of life.

A perception of your gender role and how you view the opposite sex are valuable. Generally, masculine and feminine traits are learned as part of one's culture. Gender role influences personality, behavior, and expectations. Stereotypic behaviors are disadvantageous for both sexes while androgyny has positive effects.

People experience personal growth through positive changes. Using many different techniques, you can alter your thoughts, behaviors, and feelings. Assertiveness is a set of learned behaviors which can improve self and relationships. If a sincere desire to change is present, human beings can choose from many strategies and embark on an exciting journey of self-improvement and life enrichment.

The art of being is the art of knowing ourselves, of accepting and existing in harmony with ourselves, and of living out, in action, the highest possibilities of our nature.

—Nathaniel Branden

3

Achieving Happiness and Satisfaction

OBJECTIVES

After completing this chapter, you will be able to

- Discuss the problems of defining happiness and satisfaction.
- Describe need theories related to satisfaction.
- Explain how expectations can be obstacles to happiness and change your expectations to realistic ones.
- Tell why dependency on external sources of happiness is inadvisable.
- Identify and act on ways to create your own happiness.
- Differentiate between an excuse and a reason and realize that excuses do not promote long-term happiness.
- Reduce the uses of the words can't, couldn't, should, and shouldn't in your thinking and speaking.
- Be positive, use alternative thinking, and act on desired changes.
- Concentrate on the present and enjoy life's pleasures more.
- Appreciate more fully what is positive in your life.
- Recognize the joy of giving.
- Realize that you can create happiness by developing healthy relationships.

Happiness is having a sense of self—not a feeling of being perfect but of being good enough and knowing that you are in the process of growth, of being, of achieving levels of joy. It's a wonderful contentment and acceptance of who and what you are and a knowledge that the world and life are full of wondrous adventures and possibilities.

—Leo Buscaglia

THE QUEST FOR HAPPINESS AND SATISFACTION

What do human beings desire and seek? Some replies are health, wealth, relationships, success, and love. Each is a probable avenue to happiness and self-satisfaction. The quest for happiness is universal. "Happiness is native to the human mind and its physical machine. We think better, perform better, feel better, and are healthier when we are happy" (Maltz, 1960, p. 95). A study found that, in general, happy people are strikingly energetic, decisive, flexible, creative, sociable, and more trusting, loving, and responsive than unhappy people. They can tolerate more frustration, are more lenient, forgiving, willing to help those in need, and able to fight off disease. They are also less likely to be abusive. Happiness is good for self and society (Myers, 1992).

As valuable as happiness is, not much is done to help people learn to be happy. Don, a troubled 19-year-old, wrote in a paper, "I've spent a large part of my life in mental health facilities. The personnel there teach us that we have problems but don't direct us the right way. They prevent suicides, but don't give reasons to live." Our brief class discussion on happiness was definitely not enough for Don. His fully clothed body was found in his apartment a few weeks after the term ended. The cause of death was not a homicide, just unknown. What appeared to be a suicide is another tragic reminder that more can be done to teach people to live happy, satisfying lives.

But what is happiness? How does one become and stay happy? These important questions are easy to ask; the more significant answers are difficult. This entire book provides insight. Specifically, this chapter will provide a basic overview of the concepts of happiness and satisfaction and will suggest ways to achieve them.

WHAT IS HAPPINESS?

A starting point in any search is to know what is being sought. Defining happiness is difficult for several reasons. First, each of us is unique, so what happiness is for one may not be so for another. Mary found satisfaction in creating beautiful paintings in art class. Beth was unhappy trying to achieve even average work in the same class. Each has a slightly different path to follow.

Another difficulty is that happiness, like trust and love, is intangible. It can't be seen, heard, or touched. Abstract words are difficult to define. A simple way is to think of happiness as the feeling you have when things are going the way you want them to go, and unhappiness is when things are not going the way you want (Narciso and Burkett, 1975). Determining exactly what happiness is for ourselves frees us to be unique. However, for the purpose of clarity, think of *happiness* as a general sense of well-being that can range from contentment to ecstasy.

SATISFACTION OF NEEDS

Related to happiness is satisfaction. Satisfaction can precede or follow the emotion of happiness and almost always accompanies it. One way of looking at either is to equate them with the fulfillment of needs. For example, "If you spent a long time without water in the desert, you would feel that you were the happiest person in the world if you found an oasis. Even the word ecstasy might not adequately describe your feelings as you took

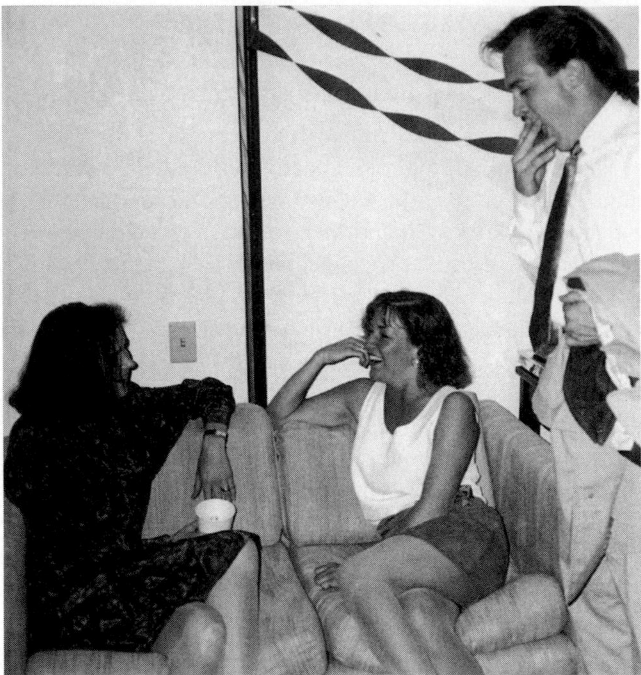

Figure 3-1 What is enjoyable for one may be boring for another.

your first sip of water" (Williams and Long, 1983, p. 339). After thirst has been quenched, extreme happiness will probably not persist; then a higher need will take precedence.

Hierarchy of Needs

Maslow's (1968) *hierarchy of needs* has become a standard in outlining human motivation. He identified five levels of needs. The first four are: survival, safety, love and belongingness, and self-esteem. An individual may achieve satisfaction by fulfilling a need at each stage. The highest and most difficult to attain is the fifth level of self-actualization. Individuals do not even work at this stage until the previous four stages are completed.

Self-actualized people share special characteristics, which will be identified in this chapter and elsewhere in the text. To Maslow, *self-actualization* meant achieving one's full potential, fulfilling a mission, possessing fuller knowledge of and accepting one's self, and feeling unified or integrated. The process of self-actualization will vary from one person to another; yet, all self-actualizers share a desire to become all they are capable of becoming (Schott, 1992). Maslow described self-actualization as full humanness and believed that few achieved it, only a fraction of 1 percent of the population (Hoffman, 1992). However, many could be striving toward that pinnacle. A no-limit person is what Dyer (1980) calls an individual at this level of existence. Both men agree that fulfillment of needs is a process of growth that can lead to happiness and satisfaction.

Basic Human Needs

Needs have also been identified by Glasser (1984), as follows:

The need to survive and reproduce
The need to belong—to love, share, and cooperate
The need for power
The need for freedom
The need for fun

In a speech, Glasser mentioned that people could be happy if they spent their time and energy working on fulfilling these needs instead of choosing to be miserable. A hunger for strokes is also a need that can be extremely motivating (Clarkson, 1992). The relationship of self-satisfaction to fulfillment of needs is sensible. That happiness would follow is logical. Quite often, the quest for one leads to the other.

OBSTACLES IN THE QUEST

In the pursuit of happiness several obstacles can hinder a person. Before you can create happiness and become satisfied, eliminating the barriers is essential.

Unrealistic Expectations

Expectations often set up a roadblock. Far too many people expect happiness to just happen. "They don't see it's something they have to do. People will go to a lot of trouble to learn French or physics or how to operate a car, but they won't be bothered learning how to operate themselves" (Newman and Berkowitz, 1974, p. 21). Those who view happiness as a "given" are seldom happy because rarely does the emotion just happen.

Others have opposite expectations and believe that they can't be happy or don't deserve to be. To them, happiness is not possible. Dan, a young man, had suffered many disappointments, and he believed that he never had any luck, good things just didn't happen to him, and happiness was for others. What would you predict for him? Dan succeeded in fulfilling his own prophecy, as discussed in Chapter 1. Happiness is neither automatic and easy nor impossible and overly difficult to achieve. Expectations at either extreme are an obstacle.

Another unrealistic expectation is that we will be, or even need to be, happy all the time. Life is just not like that. All around are possibilities for happiness and satisfaction, yet life is not just a "bowl of cherries!" It seems sensible to accept what is called the *10-80-10 spectrum*: Life is spontaneously wonderful and deliriously happy 10 percent of the time and another 10 percent is extremely difficult, tragic, and miserable. It's hard to sustain either dejection or elation (Myers, 1992). The remaining 80 percent of life is what you make it. "It rains every day of your vacation, but you have a terrific time in spite of the weather" (Bloomfield and Felder, 1985, p. 153). Check your own "happiness pulse" in the Chapter 3 activity in REFLECTIONS AND APPLICATIONS.

The realization that all people go through unhappy times can help us accept trials and tribulations and appreciate the many positives in life. In fact, unhappiness can be a forerunner to happiness. Buscaglia (1982) is a firm believer in the value of unhappiness: "Joy is a great teacher, but so is despair" (p. 74). A widow in a workshop on coping with crisis shared her personal experience with the participants and me.

> My husband died 18 months ago. I loved him, and I miss him. It was painful. However, a few months ago I realized that I felt reborn. While married, I didn't take classes or use talents outside the home. I've been doing so lately; from my loss has come happiness.

Accepting pain and allowing the reality of unhappiness to contribute to learning and growth translate into long-term happiness.

Searching Outside of Self

Where is happiness found? How can satisfaction be achieved? Too often people engage in a frantic, fruitless search for these elusive feelings, usually in the wrong places. Looking outside of ourselves is common. What are some external sources? A partial list includes: material possessions, money, a certain person, a job, marriage, a baby, drugs, the weather, activities, and even a day of the week (maybe Friday?).

How often have you had the thought that a particular person or a specific thing could make you happy? This belief carries grave risks. One of these risks has to do with dependency. Relying on an external source for happiness puts control of your life outside yourself. If externals make you happy, they can also make you unhappy. And expecting happiness from things or others often means that we do little about our own happiness except just depend.

We further risk losing happiness by putting all our happiness "eggs in one basket." Reliance upon only one source is dangerous, and dependency upon a person is a mistake. "If you expect another person to make you happy, you'll be endlessly disappointed" (Peck, 1978, p. 105). Julie believed that her fiancé made her happy. She was devastated when he broke their engagement, and she believed she could never be happy again. She became severely depressed because she did not recognize other potential sources of happiness. One day she tragically ended her life because she believed in one person as an external producer of happiness. This sad story illustrates the importance of being responsible for one's own happiness.

People may equate a certain achievement with happiness. While satisfaction and temporary happiness accompany a successful experience, the achievement is not the answer.

> We constantly tell ourselves such things as, "If I could just go back to school and acquire more knowledge—perhaps get a master's degree—then I will be happy." But are people with master's degrees or Ph.D.'s any happier than the rest of us? It is beautiful to acquire knowledge, but it is misleading to expect it to bring us peace, love, and happiness (Keyes, 1975, p. 5).

Another problem is that this "mad search" is unending. Happiness is always at the next turn or over the hill ahead. The pursuit then becomes the purpose of life. Those who seek money to make them happy, once one plateau is reached, will simply want more and continue the endless quest. "No one seems to arrive. We all are so busy chasing after external objects of one kind of another that we have no time left for enjoying our lives" (Dyer, 1980, p. 17). Even though finding satisfaction outside ourselves is impossible, unhappy people persist in trying to do so.

Advertisers, because they realize that people desire happiness and have a tendency to look for it externally, use it to sell products. Thumb through any magazine or watch television commercials; an ad may show the merits of a product, but what is enticing is the subtle message that the product will bring happiness. Alcoholic beverages are sold almost exclusively with this theme. Picture the scene: A group of young people are playing volleyball on the beach with a cooler of ice cold beer near at hand. The play is often interrupted for one guzzle after another. Each beer seems to increase their skill level—amazing! They seem ecstatic. What is the message? Drink beer and be happy. The tragic side of alcohol abuse will never be shown in the product's advertisement and usually the taste is not the point. The sales pitch is concentrated on satisfaction and happiness for the consumer.

The same could be said for new clothes, cars, and other material goods. Even toilet bowl cleaners have happy users! Research shows that the relationship between consumption of products and personal happiness is weak. Neither is happiness associated with age, nationality, having children or siblings or not, nor money (Myers, 1992). People living in the 1990s are on the average four and a half times richer than their great-grandparents were at the turn of the century, and they certainly aren't four and a half times happier (Durning, 1993). Poor people who struggle merely to survive typically are less joyful and more stress-ridden; however, having more than enough provides little additional boost (Myers, 1992). "People at the top are not happier" (Brim, 1992, p. 47).

Advertisements also try to persuade parents to buy products to make their children happy. This is potentially damaging. Because children learn from parents, the message that happiness comes from things is perpetuated. "We are raising the next generation of frustrated consumers (who may face house prices double or triple what they are today) on a steady diet of television ads. Most children have fantasies of desire long before they

Figure 3-2

have fantasies of achievement" (Spezzano, 1992, p. 170). Also, by relying on a happiness-producing product to entertain, parents may deprive their children of valuable personal attention and meaningful parent-child interaction.

Although the media and general public have many ways of creating the illusion that happiness is out there "somewhere" and can be sought and bought, the belief is a fallacy. You don't become happy by pursuing happiness. "It is always a by-product, never a primary goal. Happiness is a butterfly—the more you chase it, the more it flies away from you and hides" (Kushner, 1986, p. 23).

A review of studies on happiness show that characteristics of age, gender, race, income, and education combined explain only about 10 to 15 percent of variation in happiness. Most of the differences between people are the result of individual actions (Brim, 1992). For example, people of all ages who continue to use their brains are happier. Older people who keep mentally active are most likely to maintain their intellectual abilities and to be generally happier and better adjusted than those who don't (Kolata, 1991a). Assess your own degree of happiness in "Happiness-It's Up to Me!" in REFLECTIONS AND APPLICATIONS remembering that the source is not outside waiting to be discovered. *Potential happiness is inside waiting to be created.*

CREATION OF HAPPINESS AND WELL-BEING

Creating an inner reservoir of happiness is something only you can do. If you build a base of internal happiness, more can then be derived from externals. Otherwise, the positive feeling is fleeting. This reservoir can be called "inner joy," which is a power source—not something that happens to you but something you create (Bloomfield and Kory, 1980).

A fine-line difference exists between someone or something making you happy and your using externals to increase a personal store of internal happiness. For example, with self-satisfaction and a general sense of well being, becoming happier because of another person, material possessions, and the like is possible. However, *they do not make you happy*. How, then, can a person create this reservoir and add to it? No magic formula exists, and no one way is right for everyone. Nevertheless, suggestions and guidelines can point the way. Ten keys to happiness are recommended by the American Psychiatric Association.

1. Experience love and friendship.
2. Develop a sense of self-esteem.
3. Seek accomplishments and the ability to enjoy them.
4. Develop an attitude of openness and trust.
5. Appreciate the joys of day-to-day living.
6. Be fair and kind to others.
7. Contribute to the well-being of others.
8. Have fun in your life.
9. Learn to cope with anxiety, stress, grief, and disillusionment.
10. Develop a philosophy or system of belief.

You create your own happiness. Consider the suggestions in this chapter and the rest of the book as building blocks and steps you can put into action.

Develop Self-Esteem and an Optimistic Attitude

A basic recommendation is to know yourself well. This will enable you to determine what happiness and unhappiness mean to you. "Nothing is more destructive to the human spirit and to personal happiness than never quite knowing who you really are, what you really want, and what you were put here on earth to accomplish" (Bloomfield and Kory, 1980, p. 3). Developing self-esteem, as discussed in Chapter 1, is essential. Happiness and success are possible only to the extent that you believe that you deserve to be happy and successful. Generally, people with low self-esteem put themselves into situations that perpetuate unhappiness. Most women who are abused suffer from low self-esteem and are not happy; yet, they tend to go from one abusive relationship to another. "If we care little for ourselves, we are likely to end up as someone's doormat" (Buscaglia, 1992, p. 285). Women with critically low self-esteem, who do not believe that they deserve to be happy, and who tend to depend on others for their sense of self-worth have been referred to as "women who love too much" (Norwood, 1985). They believe that they must earn the right to enjoy life.

Mary Hollins, an insightful student whose self-esteem had been low, shared some of her writing with me.

> To listen to others' reassurance of your self-worth is positive. But when practiced by your own tongue, you begin to blend the fine qualities of self-love, respect, and rebirth. You cannot live for or be another person. The joy and the happiness is to know, accept, and grow, becoming uniquely you.

Mary made a conscious effort to build her self-esteem as can each of us. Closely related to self-esteem is an optimistic attitude. Unhappy feelings follow a pessimistic way of thinking. Those who learn what Seligman (1990) calls *flexible optimism* are not only happier but have limitless possibilities in all aspects of life.

Have Realistic Expectations

People who create happiness have a realistic self-appraisal and accept their true potential. They do not live their lives at one extreme, where they require perfection, or at the other extreme, allow themselves to "just get by." A student, for example, would be unrealistic to expect all top grades if she or he were not capable of them. Yet, the thought "Just so I pass," if a person can do better, is self-defeating. In the first case, failure and unhappiness could result; in the latter, not giving oneself the opportunity to feel proud and satisfied isn't a way to happiness. "It is well to challenge ourselves with dreams of what we would like to be, but it is wiser to stay within the realistic realm of who we are" (Buscaglia, 1992, p. 285).

Neither is the deadly "perfectionist trap" conducive to happiness. Wanting to do well is one thing; thinking that one must be perfect is another. A perfectionist is someone who thinks that anything short of perfection in performance is unacceptable (Hendlin, 1992). Often, the obsession with perfection stops us from trying and robs us of potentially rewarding activities. Jane strongly believed that she had to be a perfect golfer. She took lessons and became quite skilled. Then one day she "whiffed." Having missed the ball completely, she knew she wasn't going to play a flawless game. She left the course and decided that she was through with golf! She gave up hours of potential pleasure because she couldn't be perfect. Her case is an exaggerated one, yet many persons who participate in sports do not truly enjoy themselves unless they are performing almost perfectly. The happiness comes not from playing but only from superb performance.

Perfectionistic people frequently avoid challenges and do not comprehend the value of failure. Perfectionists do not welcome mistakes as sources of learning, and this deprives them of helpful information. "The dream of perfection turns mistakes from warnings into sins" (McKay and Fanning, 1987, p. 125). Perfectionists seem to believe that mistake-free living is not only possible, but absolutely necessary (Mallinger and DeWyze, 1992).

Even if a person accepts a challenge, perfection can reap hollow rewards. How many are like Beth, who earned 96 percent on an examination and wasn't satisfied because she thought she should have done better? Perfectionists don't feel at ease with the world and tend to focus on other people's imperfections so they also have difficulty enjoying relationships (Mallinger and DeWyze, 1992). Most people with addictions talk about being burdened by perfectionism. They see what's wrong, not what's right, don't allow for mistakes or failures, find it hard to relax, and don't enjoy accomplishments (Daley, 1991). Perfectionism creates or aggravates common physical and psychological problems and illnesses. Perfectionists take on more than their fair share of guilt (Hendlin, 1992). According to research, perfectionists are most likely to become depressed (*The Menninger Letter*, 1993b).

An example from baseball could free you from insisting upon perfection. Neither players nor fans expect perfect hitting over an entire season. In fact, a batting average of .400 (four hits out of ten times at the plate) is outstanding and quite rare. Yet, do we accept a less-than-perfect performance in aspects of our lives? Liberating words are expressed by Newman and Berkowitz (1974).

> Perfection is not for human beings. A perfect person, whatever that would be, would be unbearable. Judging yourself by superhuman standards is another way of mistreating yourself, and a good excuse for giving up (pp. 82–83).

Instead of perfectionism, why not make excellence a standard for performance? Then you can accept a less-than-perfect performance without feeling inadequate. Satisfaction and pride can be derived from a good-enough performance which frees you to be motivated by joy and challenge rather than driven by fear of failure (Hendlin, 1992).

Tasha talked one day about what she had learned about perfection.

> I've been struggling with perfection for a long time. I didn't think I was a perfectionist, but now I realize I am. I want to be perfect at school, as a mother, at work, and in my recovery program. I've been putting a lot of high expectations on myself. I'm beginning to see it's unrealistic to try to be perfect. All I have to do is try to do as well as I can.

How do perfectionistic expectations develop? They are learned from the media and from other people. Family members, especially parents, are often proponents of perfectionism. Were you raised with the idea that you must "be the best" in something—maybe the best scholar, the best football player? Being the best is almost impossible. Unfortunately, people obsessed with this idea set themselves up for certain heartache.

More common is to receive the message, "Whatever you choose to do, do your very best." Does that sound familiar? Most of us heard it from parents, school personnel, coaches, and friends who had well-meant intentions. Allow yourself to challenge this belief. Think of at least five of your *statuses*, social positions you occupy such as student, employee, parent, son or daughter, friend. What you do within that status is your *role*. In order to do your very best, what is required of you in any one status? Time, energy, effort, commitment, and determination certainly are necessary. Is it possible, then, to do the very best you can in all statuses at the same time? Buying into the belief of having to be the best in all we do and then kicking ourselves when we do not succeed leads to unhappiness. Fully enjoying what you are achieving is impossible if you're carrying around the guilt from not performing the best in everything. Nobody has or can have unlimited power. "Limitation is our essential nature. Grave problems result from refusing to accept our limits" (Bradshaw, 1988, p. 4).

Janet was a full-time student, mother, wife, friend, member of her original family, and church member. She didn't seem to be satisfied with anything in her life as she kept thinking, "I must be the best student I can be, the best mother, wife, friend, family member, and church member." One day she came to an important realization. "It's not realistic for me to expect to be the best in each of these. Right now being a student is primary, and I think I can still do a better-than-average job as mother and wife. I'll just put the others on the 'back-burner' and learn to feel okay about that." She freed herself to be happy. This liberation is difficult for those of us who have been led to believe that we must excel in all endeavors.

In *The Sky's the Limit*, Dyer (1980) writes of being the best.

> You were weaned on being a superachiever and never permitted yourself the luxury of just enjoying an activity; instead you were told to always do your best at everything, even though this kind of mentality leads to ulcers, depression, and self-reproach (p. 334).

As long as this "be-the-best" belief persists, happiness is not possible. Instead, happiness can be created, as Janet did, by prioritizing your statuses and deciding that you will do the best you can in each one under the circumstances. Creating happiness means looking for challenges that are right for you and then working at the right level of manageable difficulty (Brim, 1992).

Neither perfectionism nor striving toward other unrealistic goals was indicated when successful and fulfilled people were studied. The core strengths of their personalities were: caring, sense of humor, compassion, honesty, integrity, openness, undefensiveness, tolerance, acceptance of others' quirks and failings, dedication, and commitment to fulfilling chosen roles. Interestingly, not one principal strength of their personalities is directly measured by academic grades and aptitude test scores (Heath, 1991). Nor are any of these strengths directly taught to most people.

At the extreme opposite of overly high self-expectations are those who are apathetic about life and accomplishments. They seem to lack self-pride and any hint of motivation. For whatever reason they have little direction and seldom make attempts to achieve. They pretend that they are happy just getting by, and perhaps they feel as happy as they want to be. Sadly, they may be depriving themselves of the potential for much greater life satisfaction.

> *Do not be timid and squeamish about your actions. All life is an experiment. The more experiments that you make the better. What if you are a little coarse, and get your coat soiled or torn? What if you do fall, and get fairly rolled in the dirt once or twice? Up again. Never be afraid of a tumble.*
>
> —Ralph Waldo Emerson

Initiate Activity and Pleasure

Satisfaction eludes many people because they do not take the initiative in bringing about pleasure. They play a waiting game. It's as if they believe that there is a "happiness godmother" who will invite them to participate in life. Conversely, those who create happiness realize that there is much they can do for their own well-being. Happy people are active in life. They know what can add pleasure to their lives, and they go for it. They are willing to take risks. Carolyn, a middle-aged woman who was just starting college, wrote, "I've been taught to take a 'better safe than sorry' approach to life. I'm now throwing that safety role out the window and taking chances. It's really invigorating!" The fully alive person asks, "How can I enjoy this person, place, situation, or challenge?" This requires a positive, creative mental attitude.

How alive do you feel? How often do you seize the moment and create delight? "Mentally healthy people keep a vital forward thrust through life until death" (Adams, 1987, p. 198). In contrast, noninitiators are inactive and wait for a "bolt of happiness" to strike them. They put someone else in charge.

> Most of us do not 'sculpt' our lives. We accept what comes our way, then we gripe about it. Many of us spend our lives waiting—waiting for the perfect mate, waiting for the perfect job, waiting for perfect friends to come along (Jeffers, 1987, p. 63).

Julie was a divorcée who talked about her desire for a social life. On Monday mornings she would usually say, "I had a boring weekend. I wanted to go out, but nobody called. After you're divorced, couples don't want you around, you know, so I sat home. I could not call them." Gladys, a widow, said, "I get so tired of sitting home, and I wish my family would come visit more often and take me places." Julie and Gladys are not inca-

Figure 3-3

pacitated; they just do not initiate. You may want to look at pleasure in your life and ask what you are doing to bring it about.

> *For those of you wondering what to do while waiting for your prince to come, I say; "Enjoy the frog!"*
>
> —Ric Masten

Refrain from Excuse Making and Take Responsibility

Excuse making, a common way of not taking responsibility for one's own happiness, can create dissatisfaction and unhappiness. In order to avoid the harmful excuse-making habit, it helps to recognize the difference between an excuse and a reason. A *reason* is a statement of fact usually offered with acceptance of responsibility and control. An *excuse* can consist of facts; however, responsibility for behavior is lacking. Instead, an excuse usually includes a "that should get me off the hook" presumption.

Fraudulent excuse making, in a study of college students, was common. Personal and family illnesses were the two most common fraudulent excuses. Men and those with GPAs under 3.00 were more likely to invent and use excuses (Caron et al., 1992). As an instructor I have heard almost every excuse! One of my favorites was, "My dog 'diddled' on my paper, and that's why I'm not handing it in on time." This was clearly an excuse; a reason, on the other hand, would have been, "I left my paper on the floor, and my dog 'diddled' on it. I realize it's late, and I'll take the responsibility for it." Stating reasons and then verbalizing your responsibility is like a breath of fresh air!

An excuse-making example about a patient who had cut her wrists in a suicide attempt is told by Peck (1978).

> She was a military wife living in Okinawa. She said she couldn't stand the island and planned eventually to kill herself. Her hatred of Okinawa came from not having any friends and being alone. Why haven't you made friends, she was asked. Because none of her neighbors spoke English. Why not go to the American housing area or to the wives' club and make friends? Oh, her husband had to drive their only car to work; she couldn't possibly take him to work and keep the car because of its stick shift. The next obvious question was why she didn't learn to drive a stick-shift car. Her quick answer (from someone who had just said that she was planning suicide) was that it was ridiculous for her to learn to drive on such terrible roads; after all, she might have an accident and be killed.

Can you see how she didn't feel responsible for her own unhappiness? Instead, she lacked any control over her plight. Any positive change would probably not be forthcoming.

Excuses limit choices. Contrasting excuses with reasons is helpful in distinguishing between the two. For example:

I couldn't go visit him because it was raining.	versus	I didn't go visit him. I don't like to drive in the rain so I decided not to go.
I didn't have time to study.	versus	I didn't take the time to study. I chose to use my time to do other things.

Lack of time, as used in the second example, is a common excuse. When I remind students that they really did have time to complete a paper or study for an exam, I can get indignant protests. There wasn't *any* time, I hear. How much time do we literally have? The answer is that each of us has 24 hours in every day-long period, 8760 hours each year. In reality, we do have time; we just may not have time left over. "We always have time, if we but use it aright (sic)," said the German poet and dramatist Johann Wolfgang Goethe, who died in 1832. This is still true today.

When we persist in thinking that we don't have time, it really does seem to be nonexistent. Potentially satisfying experiences can be delayed or never accomplished. Melissa insisted that she wanted to exercise regularly, but she just didn't have time. So she didn't exercise. One day she decided to awaken earlier and exercise. She found time that had actually always been there!

Another common excuse that is a definite obstacle to happiness is age. "I'm too old for that" is a phrase that, if recognized as an excuse, can be eliminated. When I exercise, I sometimes feel winded. It's tempting to think, "I'm just too old for this." My preferred thought is, "I'm just not in shape yet!" The beauty of thinking the latter is that I can change my physical condition and stamina; my age is unchangeable.

Certain obstacles exist if you have some type of disability. Having an artificial eye has been challenging for me, and using it as an excuse is occasionally tempting. I recall trying to do so once when planning a tennis match with my older daughter Lisa. She showed up with a patch over her eye and proceeded to win the set and remind me of the senselessness of excuse-making! In a beautiful book *Flying Without Wings* (Beisser, 1989), the author encourages people to see beyond any limitations.

> Even though I am severely physically disabled, the feeling of well-being that I sometimes have now is just as intense as it was when I was called healthy. I seem to have no illness when I am unaware of what limits me and can see only the horizons I aim for (p. 27).

Sources for excuses are bountiful. Passage of time, people, the weather, a car, and even the dog can be at fault. Another convenient scapegoat is an emotion. Have you ever thought or said something like, "I was so angry that I just had to scream at him like that," "I was so frustrated that I couldn't help breaking the plate"? Ask yourself what part of that statement is true. You were angry (even so angry) and frustrated; the rest is inaccurate. You did not *have to* scream or break a plate. A young woman said, "I was so depressed, I couldn't go to work." Have you ever gone to work or to classes when you were depressed? Obviously, she could have gone to work, but she did not. Taking control of her life would mean thinking, "I was depressed, and I chose (or decided) not to go to work." Then she is free in the future to be depressed and go to work if she chooses. Certainly, emotions are important influences in our lives; however, they do not have to control or justify behavior. "I couldn't help it" usually means "I didn't help it."

Blaming outside forces takes away freedom and power. "This class is boring," someone might say, and then the class or the instructor is at fault. This blaming could prevent a person from ever enjoying the class because the responsibility is elsewhere. Don complained that he was unable to study for a test because his roommate was talking on the phone. He blamed his roommate for his poor test score. Who was actually responsible for his score? As long as Don continues to blame others, he will be at their mercy and will be unable to change his life. Responsibility gives us the power to make changes. When people learn to recognize their choices and take them, they can create their own lives (Chellis, 1992; Hay, 1991).

An *inner locus of control*, or the belief that you are in control of your life, is psychologically healthy. The opposite, a perception that external factors control one's life is related to a lack of hopefulness (Brackney and Westman, 1992). Both Japanese and American students had higher levels of depression when they perceived lower levels of control (Hymes and Akiyama, 1991). Conversely, an inner locus of control empowers individuals (Spezzano, 1992). "There should be a course taught from first grade through college called locus-of-control management" (p. 30). Along with helping to create happiness, perceived control is emotionally calming (Rodin et al., 1990). When elderly people in a nursing home were encouraged to take more control over their lives, 93 percent of them became more alert and happier (Rodin, 1986). People who are happy have a belief that they control their own destinies (Myers, 1992).

Excuses are like antacids; they can bring temporary relief but do not contribute to long-term happiness. Excuses decrease self-control and dim feelings of success. For example, how can you feel proud about a high grade if you don't take responsibility for the low ones? Cammie shared a belief of hers which emphasized inner locus of control and taking responsibility for self.

> I believe that the road you choose to travel is yours to maintain. You need to keep the weeds down and the trash picked up and the path in top condition. Your travels will be safer, less worrisome, and enjoyable. Then you can reward yourself for a well-maintained "Life Highway."

Even though it may be temporarily upsetting to realize that you have created some misery for yourself, this realization is your biggest blessing. "If you know you can create your own misery, it stands to reason that you can also create your own joy" (Jeffers, 1987, p. 51). Shedding defenses is liberating even though the avoided feelings may be temporarily painful (Zois, 1992). Happy individuals welcome control over their lives. Ultimately, excuses prevent present happiness and block potential well-being.

Change Can't and Couldn't Thinking

Excuses frequently include the words can't or couldn't. People think and verbalize in these terms. Have you ever said or heard this common expression: "I couldn't get up this morning!" Really? Picture what would be necessary for this to be true. Perhaps you were lying there in a full-body cast? Usually the person means "I didn't get up because I decided not to," "I had a hard time getting up," or "I didn't want to get up." Sometimes the use of can't or couldn't is just a matter of semantics; at times, potential happiness is threatened. Analyze can't and couldn't messages, and then challenge them. What might a person miss by thinking and then behaving accordingly?

> I know I can't ski.
> I can't talk to people.
> I couldn't ask her to go to the party with me.

Do you see how limiting such thinking is? Most people use only about 10 percent of their potential (Powell, 1976), and can't and couldn't are frequently at fault. How often are they true? Think of as many literal uses of the words as you can, and you'll discover that the words are correctly used in only a few instances such as, "I can't fly like a bird." Even if you can't do something now, in most cases, you could do it eventually if you wanted to! A wise decision would be to stop using the negative words unless they are entirely accurate. "Adulthood is the time for doing what you can and not talking about what you can't" (Spezzano, 1992, p. 20).

Obviously, life has circumstances or external forces (Buscaglia, 1982) that cannot be changed. You can't control the weather, many tragedies, and other people's behavior. You are, however, in charge of internal forces which are your reactions and future actions regarding these uncontrollable events. Thus, learn to distinguish between external and internal forces so that you aren't thinking *can't* when you actually have control. A feeling of control is associated with positive stress management (Kobasa, 1979), hopefulness (Brackney and Westman, 1992), and resolution of grief (Campbell et al., 1991).

Can't may be a cover-up for fear. Other times a can't is wishful thinking. A student wrote on an evaluation form, "I liked this class. I wish I could have put more into it." She *could* have put more into it. Replacing the word could with would means she can be more involved in future classes and have a happier experience. How frequently do you say, "I can't," or "I couldn't"? To create happiness, you eliminate as many as possible and think, "Yes, I can."

Rethink Should and Shouldn't

Closely related to can't and couldn't are should and shouldn't. Perhaps you are not feeling happy or satisfied about what you do because you think in these ways.

I should study more.
I should visit my grandparents more often.
I should work harder at my job.
I should exercise more.
I should lose weight.
I shouldn't waste time.

Figure 3-4

I shouldn't ever be late.

I shouldn't ever get angry.

What emotions are likely to follow a should when it is not acted upon? What feelings do you have when you think shouldn't and do it anyway? Guilt, frustration, or anger are common responses, and these emotions go hand in hand with unhappiness.

"Shoulditis" is what Briggs (1977) calls this. She points out that "should-ought-must-have to" messages lower self-esteem and lead to unhappiness. Also, a should simply doesn't sound like fun. When someone says, "We should go to lunch" or "We should get together," does it sound inviting? Wouldn't it be more positive to hear, "I'd like for us to go to lunch" or "I want us to get together"? Part of being fully alive is to enjoy activities and want to participate rather than think you have to. Other words that are like should are: must, have to, need to, and ought. They, too, are best avoided.

You are likely to be happier if, whenever possible, you replace these words with want or don't want. If should or a similar word is accurate because the task isn't something you want to do, think about the results or outcome. You may not want to study, yet you do want better grades. If you honestly don't relish doing the task and you don't want the outcome, either finish it anyway or get rid of the thought and move on with enjoyable living! When a student says to me, "I have to leave class early to go to a doctor's appointment," I reply, "Remember that you don't *have* to. You want to and have decided to leave, and it's fine." This change of words helps to chalk up another step toward creating happiness!

Concentrate on Positives

Can't, couldn't, should, shouldn't are used in negative self-talk. Additionally, personal put-downs are nonproductive and obstacles to happiness. Some types of negative thoughts are obvious. "I'm no good." "I can't do anything right." "I can't make friends." "I'm not attractive." A most devastating example of negative self-talk is, "I can't change."

Describing a codependent person's negative self-talk, Beattie (1987) writes:

> We don't like the way we look. We can't stand our bodies. We think we're stupid, incompetent, untalented, and, in many cases, unlovable. We think our thoughts are wrong and inappropriate, our feelings are wrong and inappropriate. We believe we're not important, and even if our feelings aren't wrong, we think they don't matter. We have never come to grips with ourselves, and we look at ourselves not through rose-colored glasses but through a dirty, brownish-gray film (p. 109).

More potentially dangerous than blatantly negative examples, perhaps, are thoughts such as, "She's smarter than I am," "My brother was more athletic, and everyone liked him," "I wish I were prettier," or "I could have done better or more." Because they are subtle, you may not even recognize their damage. Any time you use a qualifier and think or say, "I'm *only* a kid," "I didn't do *much* in high school," or "I've *just* had work experience on a farm," you are taking away from your sense of self-worth and well-being. Many job applicants make the mistake of emphasizing what they lack and unwittingly lower their chances of getting the job.

People who engage in negative self-talk and see the worst in everyone and everything seem addicted to negativity and can be called "negaholics." Those who suffer from negaholism limit their own abilities, convince themselves that they can't have what they want, and sabotage their wishes, desires, and dreams (Carter-Scott, 1989). They also dampen the spirits of others.

If you truly want happiness, learn to challenge negative self-talk. Qualifying thoughts and comments even emerge after a positive. "Even when I feel proud, I qualify it by thinking that we were so busy at work that anyone could have made as many sales as I did," said a clerk. After recognizing this, she began to challenge such thoughts by telling herself, "Even though we were busy, I don't know that anyone else could have done as well as I did. I made the sales, and that's great!" Whenever you hear yourself saying something like, "I was just lucky to get a good grade," rephrase the thought and eliminate the qualifier. Thought-stopping, explained in Chapter 1, can be useful here.

Thinking and speaking negatively about yourself lowers self-esteem and leads to unhappiness. What about other negativism? Interestingly, the use of what are called "bummer" words (Buscaglia, 1982) can depress your spirits. Try saying these words aloud.

no	sick	bleak
not	gloomy	worthless
negative	dumb	hate
never	bad	wrong
ugly	bored	awful

Did you notice any change in your feelings? Most people become aware of how depressing both the sounds and the images of the words are. Depressing, by the way, is a "bummer" word. Now do the same thing with this list.

yes	well	great
cheerful	fun	wow
super	smart	love
laugh	good	excited
right	able	alive

Just by using different words, you may be able to change your mood. In describing people who excelled, Helmstetter (1991) reported that the words people used such as anticipation, choice, creativity, and achievement were literally creating successes or failure. Imagine going through life thinking and verbalizing in "bummer" language. Instead, think differently and increase the number of positive words you use. Thinking and talking about your beliefs about happiness and success will help you actually achieve them. "Mental energy directs physical energy" (Dyer, 1989, p. 192).

After you rid yourself of negatives, remarkable things can happen. When you employ positive self-talk, your mental image will focus more often on what is positive about yourself, what you can do, and what you have done well. Most important, you will know that you can change if you want. You will no longer put yourself second or third in all aspects of life. If someone is truly better looking or more talented, you can acknowledge this as a reality yet understand that it is only as important as you make it. Concentrating on your own positives means that you aren't second rate at all.

Why would anyone use negative self-talk instead of positive? Such a person might have had well-meaning parents who didn't want their children to seem conceited or vain. They might have encouraged them, instead, to be modest and not to think too highly of themselves. For an unfortunate few, it's the result of direct put-downs that they have internalized. Negaholism is frequently handed down from generation to generation (Carter-Scott, 1989). Julie spoke of her mother's emphasis on negatives. "I was excited about a piece of pottery I had finished and told my mom to come see it. She walked in, and the first thing she said was that the table where I had placed it needed dusting!"

Seek Alternatives

An important part of the thinking process, and essential for achieving happiness and satisfaction, is the ability to recognize alternatives. "Locked-in" thinking can be depressing as it limits you to only one way of viewing life.

Not being able to think of alternatives can be more than depressing; it can be tragic. The story is told of a woman who is waiting for a phone call from her boyfriend, Buster. The call does not come, and, in despair, she kills herself (Buscaglia, 1982). This tragic and desperate behavior, as in most suicides, is the result of an inability to think of any possible alternative. In contrast, my students suggest several. First, they let Buster off the hook by giving reasons for his not calling. A unique one is that he hadn't paid his phone bill and found that his line was dead. If, in fact, Buster no longer loves the woman, alternatives are still possible. "Find a better Buster!" is a common recommendation. "Maybe the truly mentally healthy individual is the one who has the most alternatives, the most viable alternatives," (Buscaglia, 1982, p. 108). Remember that any problem has more than one solution.

The happiest people are those who don't limit their choices. Being confident that you can solve your problems by thinking of several options is a sign of maturity and strength. Critical and creative thinking skills, discussed in Chapter 1, emphasize unlocking people's minds, seeing a multitude of possibilities, and then exploring alternatives. The dimension of thought has no limits (Dyer, 1989).

Choices are more difficult for some people. Because of our original socioeconomic status and upbringing, the concept of choice may not be easily grasped, or basic decision-making skills may be lacking. In addition, life delivers some devastating blows, and we may feel trapped by circumstances. Society can be instrumental in providing training and resources related to coping. In this book, the ability to choose is emphasized.

Take Positive Action

Seeing alternatives and choosing aren't effective if you don't act. In fact, understanding what to do and then not doing anything can be stressful. A frustrated student came to me one day after reading several self-help books. She said, "I'm so upset because now I know what to do, but I'm not doing it!" I reminded her that human beings are not perfect, helped her plan some action steps, and encouraged her to continue to strive to make desired changes. To maintain mental fitness individuals must be willing to take action and be responsible for their actions (Zois, 1992). Not acting can have dire results. "It costs far more not to change than to change. The alternative to change is stagnation. To stagnate is to die while still breathing" (Adams, 1987, p. 206).

Looking for what can be done in any circumstance is happiness producing, and you can be proud of any positive action. Jan is unhappy about her sloppy roommate. What can she do about it? If she does nothing, is she pursuing happiness? Jan can start with the easiest possible solution and act on it. If it doesn't work, she can go to the next one. If she exhausts all the alternatives, she still has a choice. She can accept what she has not been able to change, or she can remove herself from the depressing situation. Wasting precious time and energy bemoaning your plight in life is draining and not conducive to happiness. Instead, do something constructive, learn from mistakes, and avoid negative situations in the future. Then pat yourself on the back for taking action and enjoy the energizing feelings from taking even a small step! The happiest people are those who have been able to take whatever cards they've been dealt and turn them into a winning hand (Swartz, 1993).

> *Life is in your hands. You can select joy if you want or you can find despair everywhere you look. Kanzantazkis says, "You have your brush and colors. You paint paradise, and then in you go."*
>
> —Leo Buscaglia

Avoid Chronic Procrastination

Procrastinating or putting off behavior changes could deprive you of a more positive future. Procrastination, which is covered more fully in Chapter 5, surprisingly can be used in a creative way. You could, for example, choose to postpone a tedious task in order to engage in a pleasurable activity. Or, as pointed out by Burka and Yuen (1983), you might decide to put something off because it's low on your priority list or because you want to allow time to make a thoughtful decision. In that case, "delay is an ally" (p. 5).

Chronic procrastination is the habit of postponing behavior, and it blocks happiness. If you want and plan to complete a task, putting it off delays the happiness of achievement and creates stress in the meantime. Check your behavior in this regard. If you have a pattern of procrastination, do something about it now!

Live in the Present

When are you living your life? This may sound like a senseless question yet asking it is sensible! Do you harbor thoughts such as, "I'll be happy when I graduate" or "I can't wait until I get to move away from home and be on my own"? Describing this type of thinking as *futurizing*, Dyer (1980) calls it "the most destructive of habits" (p. 19). Maltz (1960) describes many of his unhappy patients as living their lives on the deferred payment plan as they wait for a future event to bring them happiness.

In the book *Making Peace with Yourself* (Bloomfield and Felder, 1985), a chapter is devoted to "I'll be happy when." It is interesting that many of the events are opposites (when I get married, when I get divorced; when I have children, when the children leave home). All are excellent examples of, "The grass is always greener on the other side of the fence!"

People who defer happiness miss the "now;" they are grabbing for the brass ring on the merry-go-round that is always just out of their reach. "Many of us live the first half of our lives postponing satisfaction and the last half with regrets. Fulfillment seems always to be just over the hill" (Bloomfield and Felder, 1985, p. 147). When I hear people say, "I can't wait until the weekend," I often reply, "I hope you can, and I certainly hope you enjoy each minute from now until then!" Too many people seem to be focused on endings—the end of the week, the end of the day, the end of the school term.

Are you happy only when looking forward to an ending? Happy, satisfied people can honestly say that beginnings, too, bring delight, and that the ongoing process of living *now* creates happiness. "Learning to live in the present and appreciate the ongoing flow of life, rather than being caught in the goal-oriented future, brings a powerful realization of the immediacy and joy that are possible in our lives" (Hendlin, 1992, p. xxii).

Another habit is one I somewhat jokingly call *pasturizing*—mentally living in the past. "If only I had married John instead of Jim" and "I wish I had started college right out of high school instead of later" are examples of wishful thinking that destroy opportunities for present happiness. People who converse only about memories and past accomplishments or problems in the past are also not living in the "here and now."

Well-adjusted people accept and appreciate the past and can enjoy nostalgia. Wise, healthy individuals use the past as a series of vast learning experiences to make their present more rewarding. Happy people plan for their future and anticipate to a certain extent, yet they keep focused in the present. In his public appearances and books, Leo Buscaglia (1982) dramatically emphasizes this point.

> The only reality is the now. Yesterday is gone, and there's nothing you can do about it. It's good because it brought you to where you are right now. It isn't real any more. And tomorrow? Tomorrow is a wonderful thing to dream about, but it isn't real. And if you spend your time dreaming about yesterday and tomorrow, you're going to miss what's happening to you and me right now (p. 75).

A *self-actualized person*, as described by Maslow, fully experiences life in the present. Obviously, the present may be quite unpleasant, and you will, at times, hope tomorrow comes quickly. Nevertheless, if you make a habit of living elsewhere, you'll realize too late that you haven't really lived. Focusing on life as a journey, not a destination, is helpful.

Recognize that "now" is the only time you ever really have. An example I wish I didn't have available to use is that of Lynn Hansen, a student who was the daughter of a couple from my home town. She graduated from college and began her career full of excitement and hope. That same month a malignant brain tumor was discovered and removed. Lynn survived the delicate surgery and the cancer treatment and spent several months in a rehabilitation center. When I visited, I was impressed with her positive attitude and hope for the future. Nine months after the tumor was found, Lynn was buried in the local cemetery, leaving behind many who loved her—a terrible loss. Nobody is guaranteed a future. It's a depressing thought, but one that can keep us focused. Happiness must be practiced in the present. A consolation is that Lynn experienced happiness in the "now" of her short life. "It's too late for yesterday and too soon for tomorrow" (Buscaglia, 1992, p. 189).

Enjoy Life's Pleasures

"Stop and smell the roses." What a delightful idea! How often do you do it? "Roses" can be anything as long as pleasure is felt, and sensory delights are everywhere. Do you see sunsets? Do you feel awe when viewing nature's treasures? Do you smell the scents of spring or fall? Do you marvel at a snowflake? Do you hear the delightful songs of birds? Maslow (1968) wrote of *peak experiences*, brief moments of extreme pleasure which are characteristic of a *self-actualizing person*. Often, these come from the simpler pleasures of life. "Fully alive people are aware of the thorns but concentrate on the roses" (Powell, 1976, p. 57). Any activity that directly stimulates the senses in pleasurable ways increases positive feelings (Braiker, 1988).

Why wouldn't people take the time to marvel at life? "I'm too busy. I don't have time" is a common excuse. Ask yourself when will you have time and when will you not be busy? "If we wait for everything we want accomplished to be completed before we celebrate, we will miss the party of life" (Pearsall, 1988, p. 61). "But I have to clean the house" and "I can't stand it if the yard isn't in good shape" are detriments to enjoyment (unless you enjoy cleaning the house and doing yard work, that is!).

When you decide to more fully enjoy life's pleasures with the least expenditure of time, consider what Clarke Metcalf, a talented, creative former student, called *awareness enhancement* which means to seek out and marvel at bits of beauty everywhere. He wrote of "architectural gingerbread on buildings, custom fence designs, and the little girl in the bright pink dress standing beside the rusty brick schoolhouse." He expressed that we live among deliberate and accidental beauties that can be delightful *if we are aware*. Joys are missed when we are rushing through life. Wonder, related to joy, is an "opening attitude—an awareness that there is more to life than one has as yet fathomed, an experience of new vistas in life to be explored" (May, 1953). Another feature of a *self-actualized person* is openness to new experiences, necessary if one is to experience wonder. Buscaglia

Figure 3-5 Taking time to enjoy the beauty of nature.

(1982) speaks of joy as "songful, and laughing, and dancing all along the way" (p. 84). The very words sound fantastic. Be sure to experience wonder and joy—over and over!

One of the most treasured memories in my teaching career is of a lovely 29-year-old woman named Dawne. The single mother of two children, she had a great desire to better herself and make a happy life for her family, and she was thrilled that she had returned to school. She was bright, articulate, and enthusiastic—a joy to teach. One spring she brought her completed final examination to my desk and said, "Sharon, all quarter we've been talking about hugs, and I want to give you one!" That was so like her. I happily agreed, and we embraced warmly. It was the beginning of the summer break, and as Dawne walked out of the room, she reminded me to "practice what I preach" and enjoy my few weeks of vacation. She smiled and was gone. The next day she and her daughter were killed in a car-train accident—a horrible, unexplainable tragedy. As I grieved, I remembered that last loving encounter and the poignancy of what she wrote to me at the end of her test: "Now remember, Sharon, to stop and smell the roses." Whenever I forget to do so, I think of Dawne, a lovely person who followed her own advice so well. Ways of creating happiness by "smelling roses" are everywhere. Don't miss them!

> *Mini-vacations of the spirit—truly noticing the seasonal variations, observing children at play, hearing the chirping of birds, smelling the air after a cleansing rain, patting a dog—are precious interludes. They replenish us and are ours to enjoy if we only go slower on our journey through life.*
>
> —Sharon Hanna

Count Your Blessings

One day in class a student remarked, "Sometimes it helps when I stop and think of what isn't wrong with me and then I feel grateful." Too often, we forget how fortunate we are. Think right now of how many blessings you have. Are you healthy? The absence of health can breed misery (Myers, 1992). Can you see and hear? Consider what life would be like without one or more of our senses. Do you have loving relationships? In the process of creating happiness, it can help to experience an occasional reminder of how bad things could be and be reminded of our blessings (Myers, 1992). Equally affirming is to keep in mind that "for every act of unkindness, there are a million kind acts, a network of good" (Dyer, 1992, p. 255).

Give to Life

Life is full of wonder and beautiful experiences; happy people take in as much as possible. They also give back to life. People who are truly happy don't pursue happiness; they become happy by living a life that has meaning (Kushner, 1986). Self-centered people tend to be unhappy while those who contribute are creating happiness and developing a positive legacy that will remain after they have died. Key behaviors of a *self-actualizing person* are reaching beyond self and contributing to the greater good of humankind. Joy comes from giving, not getting; from contributing, not acquiring (Dyer, 1992).

Giving to life doesn't necessarily mean great works. You can create satisfaction by doing worthwhile and purposeful deeds. Possibilities are all around. When was the last time you visited someone you knew in the hospital or a nursing home? Have you recently volunteered to help in a worthy cause? Have you taken the time to do a favor for anyone? When did you last send a "just thinking about you" card or note? Have you even smiled at someone recently? Buscaglia (1982) underscores this point, "Every day you take from the ground, you take from the air, you take from the beauty—what are you giving back?" (p. 82). Even the smallest gesture can do wonders for another, and, in return, for you.

Giving to others enhances self-esteem and builds happiness (Myers, 1992). The peak experiences in life where the highest forms of joy, love, and inner peace are found come from reaching out and helping others (Jampolsky and Cirincione, 1990). Being altruistic and assisting others can even result in a healthier immune system (Pearsall, 1988). Giving is a way of enhancing your own well-being. A major reason for enhancing self-esteem is to have something to offer. We can only give what we possess, and the more we have, the greater our capacity to give. "You cannot give away what you don't have. If you don't have love, harmony, and peace within, then you simply can't contribute these" (Dyer, 1992, p. 257). I was delighted that Linda and Kathy, two former students who after raising their own self-esteem, wanted to help improve the lives of others. They started a mentoring and support group for women trying to improve their lives through education called New Horizons. Another student, Paul, formed Voices, a support group for males who were sexually abused as children. "Each of us can make a difference. We can choose to live a life in which we can say, when we die, that the world is a better place for our having been here" (Jampolsky, 1990, p. 5).

Develop Nourishing, Rewarding Relationships

A primary objective of this book is to help you learn to develop positive relationships. Their value in the creation of happiness is unquestionable. Unhappiness is directly related to shyness and loneliness. A study found that lonely and shy individuals tended to be unhappy while happy college students were neither lonely nor shy (Booth et al., 1992). Maslow (1968) identified love and belongingness as a need of human beings. A *self-actualizing person* feels kinship and involvement with humankind and is able to develop intimate relationships with friends. Love, belonging, and affection are essential to well-being. Unfortunately, the two primary sources of happiness, social relations and leisure, frequently "take a back seat" as people strive to succeed and build income (Durning, 1993). You are wise not to let this happen in your life.

In the creation of happiness what really does matter is our success at relating to others. Would you want to be remembered for your punctuality and success at earning money, or because of your loving relationships? Most would agree that what really matters are the heart connections, the love we share with others (Jampolsky, 1990). Adams (1987) notes that "intimacy demands the highest risk but yields the richest reward" (p. 119). Many of the guidelines presented in this book can help you develop nourishing relationships. Self-satisfaction and happiness are the rewards.

SUMMARY

The search for happiness and well-being is an ongoing one. Not knowing what happiness and satisfaction are, having unrealistic expectations, and looking for happiness outside of self are three obstacles. To overcome them, you are wise to learn and broaden your concepts about happiness and satisfaction.

Having realistic expectations about happiness is wise. Realizing that unhappiness is a part of life is realistic and can help you appreciate your happiness even more. Happy people learn from their misfortunes and grow from adversity. They know that happiness does not magically come from external sources. One must be happy inside; if not, all the outside sources in the world will bring only temporary happiness at best.

Happiness is within reach, yet it does not automatically fall into anyone's lap. Initiative and effort are necessary. A reservoir of internal happiness must be created. Externals then can add to what is already there. Happy people become happier from outside sources; unhappy people continue to seek in vain.

Creating happiness means developing a high degree of self-worth, a positive attitude, and an inner locus of control. Happy people rarely use excuses and negative words. They look for possibilities, not limitations. Happy people see alternatives in life. Negative self-talk is avoided, as is chronic procrastination. Individuals who create their own happiness are active and do what is best for them. They do not *futurize* or *pasturize*. They make good use of the past and strive for a happy future, yet they live in the present. Happy people are seekers in life who enjoy discoveries and simple pleasures. They stop to "smell roses" and count their blessings. Because they are truly happy within, they tend to reach out and provide happiness for others. Satisfied, happy people are nourished and rewarded by positive relationships. See how you create happiness by doing the happiness exercise in REFLECTIONS AND APPLICATIONS. The reservoir of happiness and satisfaction within is bountiful and unlimited; happy people replenish theirs often by living life to its fullest.

Alas for those who never sing but die with all their music in them.
—Oliver Wendell Holmes

Figure 3-6 A headstone of a young man who is still alive. Think about all you've read so far and speculate about the meaning of this headstone (photo courtesy of Greg L. Baker).

4

Developing Emotional Well-Being

OBJECTIVES

After completing this chapter, you will be able to

- Define emotion and explain some of the complexities.
- Describe three components of an emotion.
- Name at least six different emotions.
- Realize that emotions are an important part of the self.
- Describe ways in which emotion can be expressed.
- Name and describe influences on emotional expression.
- Relate the transactional analysis ego states to emotional expression.
- List benefits of expression in each of the four developmental areas.
- Realize that you can become more demonstrative.
- Vent emotions such as anger in appropriate ways.
- Describe ways to change your feelings.
- Use rational-emotive therapy to change what you feel.
- Use control theory to change aspects of your behavior.
- Define stress and stressors and explain how important they are.
- List possible effects of stress.
- Explain the theory of the mind-body connection.
- Name sources of stress.
- Describe and use various means of handling stress.
- Identify types of crises.
- Describe and use coping methods.

Emotions can be viewed as the spice of life; they give our lives character and pizazz.
—Stephen Worchel and Wayne Shebilske

A letter arrives congratulating you on a scholarship that will pay a full year's college expenses. Your supervisor refuses to give you a day off to attend a good friend's wedding. You and a family member disagree, and your reasonable suggestions are being misinterpreted. A co-worker has spread some untrue stories about you, and other employees have been avoiding you. An automobile coming toward you seems to be out of control. What do these situations have in common? All can be antecedents to an emotion. Each event is likely to be associated with a feeling.

Emotions make up a most interesting and important developmental area of self. Human beings are emotional, and our feelings both enrich and disturb our lives. "All feelings are human. They bring texture, color, and sensitivity to life. Without feelings, we would be robots. Your feelings show your current temperature" (Satir, 1988, p. 45). Feelings enhance personal experiences and influence and enrich relationships. If you stop to consider how drab life would be without emotions, you will begin to grasp their value.

Because emotions are so important, one would think that the field of psychology would have discovered all that is possible to know about them. Far from it! The complexity of the emotional self has generated differences of opinion, and much is still to be learned. Despite their complexity, a knowledge of emotions develops dramatically between birth and adulthood (Shaver et al., 1987). Children are able, for example, to name an emotion being expressed in pictures, and older children can often predict what emotion will occur in a particular situation. Even with general knowledge, the perplexity and confusion of emotions frequently create problems in individual lives and within relationships.

Check yourself to see how puzzling elements of your emotional self can be. First, are you in touch with your feelings? Sometimes you may have difficulty deciding whether a state of being is an emotion or some other aspect of self. For example, when you say you feel confused, you are identifying a mental lack of understanding, not an emotion. "I feel tired" is a physical description. Can you identify what emotion you are experiencing at any given time? Most people have difficulty in this area and will typically reply that they feel fine, good or bad rather than labeling a specific emotion. Can you pinpoint the reason for your feelings? Several emotions are *situational* which means preceded by an event. Others seemingly come from *out of the blue*, and the cause is not apparent.

How accurate are your predictions of emotions? Do you know how you will feel under certain circumstances? Mary was shocked to discover on her wedding day that she suddenly felt sad. She loved Matt and wanted to marry him. What would cause her to feel sorrow? Finally, can you tell what emotion is being experienced by observing behavior? Picture this scene. Three individuals are waiting in line to go on a thriller ride at an amusement park. All three are smiling, laughing, rubbing their hands together, and pacing. What are their emotions? Possibly, one person could be excited and full of anticipation, another could be mildly anxious, and the third could be terrified!

Were you able to predict what feelings would probably be present in the examples at the beginning of the chapter? The emotions of joy, disappointment, frustration, anger, and fear come readily to mind and, in most cases, would be accurate predictions. As you will discover, however, these particular feelings do not have to occur; you may respond with different emotions depending on several factors. Even though several believe that the physiology and expression of emotion are universal and biologically based (Ekman, 1992; Hatfield and Rapson, 1990; Plutchik and Plutchik, 1990), "the historical era in which people live, the cultural and social groups to which they belong, and the type of family in which they are raised, insure that, in part, the language of emotion that they speak must be their own" (Hatfield and Rapson, 1990, p. 12). For example, a study showed Japanese students to be generally more depressed than their American counterparts and also less self-serving (Hymes and Akiyama, 1991).

This chapter will clarify the mysterious emotional self. You will become more familiar with what an emotion is, how feelings can be expressed, their effects, how to change what you feel and cope with emotional crises, and, most important, how you can enhance your life through deeper emotional awareness and understanding. Developing emotional well-being is an exciting challenge!

CHARACTERISTICS AND IDENTIFICATION OF EMOTIONS

What is emotion and how do you differentiate among feelings, thoughts, physical characteristics, and behaviors? How do you know what you are feeling? The answers to these questions are not easy and reflect a variety of ideas from different psychological theories. An *emotion* can be described as a complex chain of events triggered by certain stimuli. These events involve cognitive interpretations, feeling states, physiological changes, impulses to action, and displays of behavior (Plutchik and Plutchik, 1990). When considering emotions, we are usually referring only to the pleasant or unpleasant feeling states although emotions are generally more complex (Hatfield and Rapson, 1990). Examination of three components of emotion provides insight. Later in this chapter the cognitive component will be discussed.

Physiological arousal. One component is *physiological arousal or response* also known as affect (Nathanson, 1992). Reactions to an emotion include the activities of the nervous system, various glands, and organs within the body. If you are frightened, your glands secrete hormones into your blood stream causing your heart rate to quicken and your pupils to enlarge. Other responses will also occur. You may or may not be aware of these changes; although when frightened, you usually are. In some cases, the reactions are observable. Have you ever blushed in an embarrassing situation? The redness of your face was caused by what was going on inside your body. Many of these responses can be measured by instruments such as medical monitoring devices and biofeedback equipment.

Awareness. A second component is *awareness* of an emotion or the feeling state. This is the presence or experience of emotion—the sensation itself. For example, you may say, "I'm happy." How do you know you are happy? What clues do you have? You may be aware that a physiological change is taking place, and you identify this as a feeling (Nathanson, 1992). Or you may not recognize the affect and still be aware of a happy feeling. You have learned to associate your sensation with the label of "happy." A person will often do more than just give a label. "I feel like I have knots in my stomach," "My blood was boiling," or "Chills ran up and down my spine" are attempts to describe the feeling and may be descriptive of the physiological reaction. Or, you may be unaware of a present emotion.

Expression. The third component is *expression*. How do you show happiness? Sadness? Fear? Anger? Expressions are observable verbal or nonverbal behaviors. Sometimes the expression of emotion is confused with the feeling state itself. For example, when asked to identify an emotion, someone may answer, "Crying." Do you see that crying is expression, not the emotion? In the following, see if you can identify the three components.

> Joan continued to cry. She had received a letter telling about the death of a close friend in a distant city. She was shocked and extremely sad. She felt numb and shook her head in disbelief. "Why did this happen?" she asked her husband. He reassuringly took her hand in his and noticed how cold it felt. Joan gulped and said, "I feel almost dead inside, too."

Physiologically, her hand temperature reflected a reaction to the shock. Her numbness was probably the result of physiological changes as well. The feeling of sadness and her description of feeling almost dead inside were reflections of what she was experiencing—the awareness. Her expressions or behaviors were crying, shaking her head, talking, and gulping.

All three components are not necessarily present in every emotional situation. Have you ever felt sad and not showed it? Expression is missing more often than the other two. Conversely, according to the major theories of emotion, physiological arousal is always present. You may not be aware of what is actually happening or be able to identify the emotion; however, your body does react. Which of the three, then, is most controllable? Even though you may hear someone say, "I was so angry I just had to scream," the person could have controlled the behavior. Expression is the one component over which we have the most control. Later in this chapter you will read about ways to regulate physiological responses as well.

Researchers, in an attempt to clarify the emotional self, have identified and categorized possible feelings. One model distinguishes eight basic emotions of fear, surprise, sadness, disgust, anger, anticipation, joy, and acceptance (Plutchik, 1980). From a study in which introductory psychology students first identified words as emotions then put together ones with similar meanings, six major clusters emerged (Shaver et al., 1987). These were love, joy, surprise, anger, sadness, and fear (see Fig. 4-1). The researchers pointed out that some emotions are blends or combinations; sympathy, for example, can be a mixture of sadness and love. Several of these emotions will be discussed throughout this chapter. Other sections of the book focus on feelings of joy and love.

Helpful in identifying emotions is to know that they can vary in intensity. For example, you may be mildly annoyed if a friend is 5 minutes late meeting you for lunch,

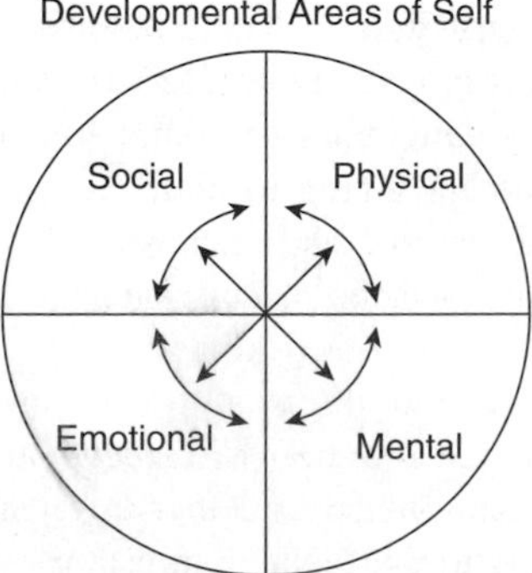

Figure 4-1

upset after a half hour, and outraged when you discover that she or he has deliberately "stood you up" because of a preference to have lunch with someone else. The underlying emotion is anger. Almost every feeling has a wide range (Nathanson, 1992; Plutchik, 1980).

Regardless of how emotions are described and categorized, the realization that they are an integral part of you is basic to self-understanding. Human beings cannot escape having emotions and experiencing physiological arousal. Because expression of emotions, the behavioral component, influences relationships to such an extent, it deserves special attention.

EXPRESSION OF FEELINGS

Laura dramatically explained, "I'm an emotional person. I cry at weddings, funerals, movies—you name it. I let people know when I'm mad or happy. I'm demonstrative, sometimes to a fault. But that's just the way I am." In contrast, Barbara said, "I'm a controlled person. I don't let others know what's going on inside of me. I never show anger or sorrow and rarely my pleasant feelings either. But that's just the way I am." Is it just the way Laura and Barbara are? Opinions and theories vary. Expressiveness likely has a genetic base (Ekman, 1992; Hatfield and Rapson, 1990; Plutchik and Plutchik, 1990), yet because our emotional socialization and experiences are different, much of "if, what, and how" we express has been learned.

Emotions are expressed in various ways. For what reason would you suspect that another person is upset? Verbal expression is one possibility: "I'm upset because you borrowed my book and didn't return it right away." Or, the words could be less direct and might even belittle or deny the feeling: "I just don't understand why some people do things like that, but I guess it's really nothing." Other possibilities are profanity or hostile insults. One of the problems with verbal expressions is that people may not accurately state what they are feeling. Perhaps the person doesn't really know, feels embarrassed, or simply doesn't want to reveal. Individuals may worry about hurting someone's feelings. Generally, we have not been trained to express our emotions assertively.

Nonverbal expressions of emotion are more common. Individuals knowingly or unknowingly reveal many feelings through what is called body language. Facial expressions, changes in voice, behaviors such as laughing and crying, and posture offer glimpses into the emotional self. "We may stand erect when proud, droop in shame, adopt a 'fighting stance,' jut the head forward in anger or disgust, and cringe in fear" (Nathanson, 1992, p. 55). It is best to be cautious, however, when you try to interpret others' nonverbal expressions. For example, why does a person cry? An obvious answer is because of sadness. Can you think of other emotions that may result in crying? How about disappointment or hurt? Or anger and happiness? Even at a wedding, interpretations can be inaccurate. Mark shed a tear at his daughter's wedding. Monica, the mother of the bride, sniffled into a handkerchief. Another young woman sobbed. Mark's tears were the result of pride and happiness. Monica was sad and somewhat regretful that her daughter was old enough to be married. What about the young woman? She had once been engaged to the groom and was feeling resentful and jealous!

Facial expressions have long been considered the key to feelings (Nathanson, 1992). Facially, happiness seems to be the easiest emotion to detect while surprise is most difficult. Children have difficulty recognizing anger and fear in facial expressions (Kestenbaum, 1992). Evidence suggests that certain facial expressions communicate similar meanings across different cultures (Ekman, 1992). Although this implies a biological basis for feelings, learning and cultural influences play significant roles. For example, Italians are more likely to let their faces show emotion (Zajonc, 1990). Emotion can usually be disguised, however. You may have heard the expression "It's written all over your face." Yet, aren't you able to mask your true feelings? Interpretations based only on facial expression can be inaccurate. "Facial expressions are imperfect communicators of emotional states. Connections between emotions and facial expressions are subject to many disrupting influences. Facial expressions are only one aspect" (Plutchik, 1980, p. 268).

Figure 4-2 Joy.

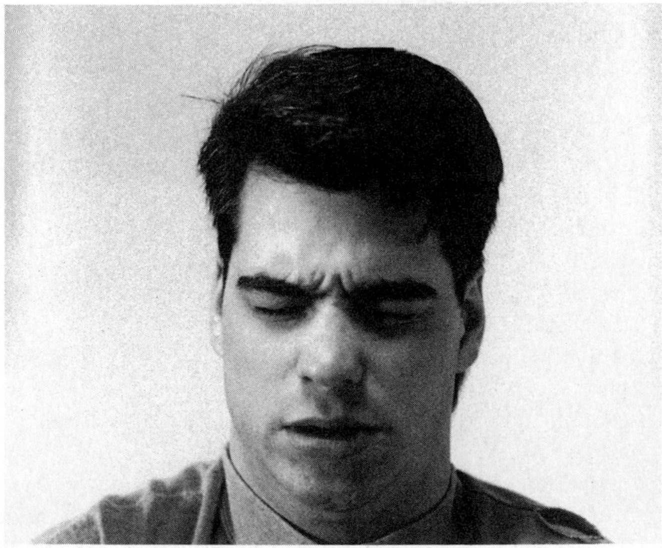

Figure 4-3 Sadness.

Figure 4-4 Anger.

Figure 4-5 Fear.

Influences on Emotional Expression

How and what did you learn to express? Two ways we learn about expressing are direct instruction and modeling. Think of some messages about emotions and how to show them. A partial list follows:

Keep a stiff upper lip.
Don't be a crybaby.
She's too emotional.
Cheer up.
Others have it worse than you.
Don't wear your heart on your sleeve.
Big boys don't cry.
Don't be a 'fraidy cat.
You'll get over it in time.
Cool it.
Shut up or I'll give you something to cry about!

Do you see a common theme among them? "Keep your feelings to yourself" is the underlying message. A sociologist might explain this in terms of the "I" wanting to express and the "me" restricting emotional expression.

Each society teaches emotional expression. The American cultural message has generally been one of emotional nonexpressiveness. Control of emotion is invariably equated to keeping feelings to oneself instead of choosing how to express them. The strong, silent type is heralded as a hero. Even in extremely sad situations, you may hear someone being praised for being "strong," which means that grief isn't being shown. Emotional crippling—being afraid to feel, afraid to express, and afraid to have others feel toward one—is a norm for many (Rubin, 1969).

Men are given the "don't express" message more often and more clearly than women. As pointed out in Chapter 2, a definite gender difference exists. Men and women, in general, have different ways of expressing emotions along with preferences for ones they feel comfortable showing. In their closest relationships, women claim to experience more total emotion than men do (Berscheid et al., 1989). The American society is in a transitional stage, and differences are not as extreme as they were in the past. Nevertheless, they still exist, and men typically show fewer feelings than do women. "The emotions are there, but the admonitions against expressing them have progressively caused them to be blocked out of consciousness. As a boy, the message he received was clear: Feelings are taboo" (Goldberg, 1979, p. 19).

If you were asked to identify emotions that men are allowed or encouraged to feel more than others, what would they be? Over the years the typical first response in my classes has been anger. Table 4-1 shows some examples of stereotypic differences in encouragement and allowance for women and men.

If you were asked to list emotions that are discouraged or not allowed, a switch of columns indicating opposite expectations for men and women would suffice. For example, women traditionally have been discouraged from awareness and expression of anger, and labels such as "shrew" and "nag" condemn women who get angry. Conversely, there is no unflattering word for a man who vents anger (Lerner, 1985). *Fear*, an emotional response to a perceived threat or danger, is customarily handled quite differently by women than by men. Women are allowed to be afraid of spiders, mice, the dark, and strange noises. Can you picture the reactions if a man demonstrated the same fears?

Feedback is a powerful force in learning emotional expression, and women and men are given different messages. Female college students were more responsive to films that evoked sad or fearful feelings while males were happier than females when the positive films were viewed (Berenbaum and Rotter, 1992). A study of community college students revealed that females were more confident expressing vulnerable feelings of sadness and fear as well as love and affection while males were more secure in expressing anger (Blier and Blier-Wilson, 1989). Even though there is no difference between men and women in the existence and intensity of emotion, expression is gender-related. "To the extent that women are encouraged to talk about their emotions, men are in general expected to remain controlled and silent about theirs" (Tavris, 1992, p. 263).

These gender differences can create problems. The benefits of expressiveness, which will be covered in the next section, are generally not experienced by men. In the past, men paid a price if they dared to show even overwhelming feelings. For example, when Senator Edmund Muskie, the leading candidate in the 1972 Democratic presidential primaries, expressed his displeasure with a newspaper publisher in an indignant and tearful outburst, he was chastised in the press. His genuine expressions of feelings, especially the tears, were considered signs of unmanliness and weakness. This incident seemed to be a major contributing factor in his unsuccessful bid for the nomination (Naifeh and Smith, 1984; Rubin, 1973).

Innocent people may pay a price, too. When legitimate fears aren't expressed or acted upon, other individuals can suffer. An account of an airline crash in Washington, D.C., during a blizzard illustrates this. Judging from the tape-recorded conversations of the crew, the pilots' attitudes about the buildup of ice on the wings of the airplane was casual. They didn't mention any concern to the control tower, and with what seemed like an air of bravado, decided to just "go for it." The jet slammed into a bridge and plunged into the Potomac River, killing 72 passengers, 4 passing motorists, and the pilots (*Time*, February 15, 1982). How tragic that individuals not wanting to display even legitimate fear frequently take unnecessary risks with their own and others' lives.

Lack of expressiveness causes relationships to suffer. Ironically, when women are asked to identify characteristics they would like in a man, they mention ability to express emotions such as fear and sadness. "I wish he would just cry sometimes," one young woman said. On the other hand, men can be confused about the expressiveness of women and feel frustrated when they are accused of not understanding. When women

TABLE 4-1 Emotional Expression and Gender Role

Encouragement and Allowance	
Men	**Women**
Anger	Sadness, depression
Bravery	Fear
	Hurt
	Love, affection
	Worry, anxiety
	Disappointment

and men are raised differently in the area of emotional expressiveness, confusion and misunderstanding are bound to exist.

Regardless of a person's sex, the family is likely the most powerful source of emotional learning. Which sounds more like a description of your family?

- Almost no emotions are expressed. The children observe parents who are controlled. The parents rarely touch each other or the children or express warm, loving feelings. Neither do they display anger or frustration. Relationships are rather businesslike.
- Some emotions are encouraged. The parents show love and warmth occasionally. They show anger at times; however, the children are scolded if they behave angrily. A common command is, "Go to your room and don't come out until you're over it." Children are not supposed to cry often or loudly, and praise is given for being brave and strong.
- Several emotions are acted upon. Parents let the children know when they are angry, frustrated, disappointed, depressed, and hurt. The children react with displays of negative feelings. Almost no expressions of warmth and affection are present.
- All emotions are present. Parents express their feelings and let the children do so. The household is emotionally charged, and many hurtful behaviors can be observed. For example, a verbal or physical assault almost always follows anger.
- Emotional expression is encouraged. Parents try to model constructive ways of dealing with feelings. Open communication allows for discussion of present emotions as well as possible ways of expressing future ones. When a person hurts others with a behavioral expression, an apology is given with acknowledgment of the mistake.

Figure 4-6

Variations of the five models are possible. If your family sounds like the last one, you are fortunate and rare. Most families either repress emotional expression or allow hurtful behaviors. Few make the attempt to model and teach constructive emotional expression.

The degree and means of emotional expression are influenced not only by the family, but by ethnic, religious, and peer groups. Cultural differences in emotional expression are common (Nathanson, 1992), and societies develop their own ways of blending and expressing them (Gallois, 1993). A Central American student expressed amazement during the discussion of gender role differences. "In my culture the men are usually the expressive ones, and women are expected to be more controlled," she said. People from Mediterranean and Latin nations are generally more expressive than those from Nordic and Oriental cultures. Anglo-Nordic norms, which are followed in the United States, prohibit tender physical contact among males and restrict public displays of affection (Zimbardo, 1977). Also, some religious groups show more emotion in their services, while others are cold and staid.

From childhood through adolescence, the influence of your *peers* (others of a similar age) is strong in both happy and sad settings. A peer group may demonstrate warmth and affection by touching, or they may be more reserved. At funerals young people may openly cry and hug each other in support, or they can be uncomfortable with displays of sorrow. Numerous sources which give similar or diverse messages are influential in emotional expression. If you had models of expressiveness that encouraged constructive behaviors and you were generally accepted and praised for showing feelings, your emotional self is likely to be healthy. Use "Emotional Monitoring and Learning" in REFLECTIONS AND APPLICATIONS to gain insight.

The transactional analysis (TA) framework covered in Chapter 2 can be used to better understand emotional expression. The child ego state is the home of all emotions, the feeling part of your personality. Your parent ego state contains messages telling you to express or not to express. The adult ego state is unemotional yet plays a role in the emotional self. Your "adult" may decide to permit or deny emotional reactions of the "child." Later in this chapter you will learn how to change what you feel in which the "adult" plays a major role.

Any difficulty in expressing could be the result of your social role or a fear of disclosing. Certain people believe that they must be controlled in their professional positions, and they become almost emotionally sterile. For example, until recently physicians generally elected to remain emotionally aloof. Bernie Siegel (1986), a surgeon, changed his traditional style of emotional detachment and encourages other physicians to do so, also. "Because I was hurting, I withdrew when patients needed me most. We need to be taught a rational concern which allows the expression of feelings without impairing the ability to make decisions" (p. 14).

Another reason for not expressing has to do with protection. If you have been hurt as a result of expressing, you may have built a wall around your emotions. Neil told another firefighter how apprehensive he felt at an accident scene. The fire captain heard about it and cautioned Neil about his feeling. Neil was embarrassed and angry with the other firefighter and resolved to keep future emotions hidden. Dave expressed his love for Janet only a few days before she told him she was going to marry someone else. His hurt led to a layer of defensive inexpressiveness.

A major barrier is equating self-control with emotional repression. If you believe that any show of feeling means you are weak and not in control, you will probably repress rather than express. "I know people who are as afraid of being openly emotional as many people are of the dark. Love, joy, and rage frighten them because they feel out of control" (Kushner, 1986, p. 107). It would help to substitute a different belief: *showing feelings requires strength, and expressing doesn't mean lack of control.* In fact, control could be defined as deciding whether, when, and how to express. Andrew, a man not used to expressing his feelings, heard a rumor at work that he had been passed over for promotion. He seethed all morning, then stormed into his supervisor's office and announced loudly that he was quitting, and walked out. He stopped to pick up his mail and found a memo congratulating him on his promotion. His display of emotion was not only inappropriate, but disastrous. Sometimes, you are wise to wait before venting a feeling. A well-adjusted person can choose to express, can select from any number of responses depending upon the situation, or can decide not to show a particular feeling.

Even if an emotion is not shown, having an outlet is wise. Anger, for example, can be put down but not out. "I never get angry," said a middle-aged woman in my class. What she meant and eventually said was that she didn't show her anger. As Rubin (1969) describes it, her anger went into a slush fund. If you feel limited in this regard, the rest of the chapter can help you release the emotions your body is experiencing and enjoy the benefits of being emotionally expressive.

Constructive behaviors can be developed at an early age or learned later. Sadly, most of us were not exposed to the full range of possibilities. I ask students how and what they were taught about expression and receive fairly predictable responses. A common one is, "You have no right to feel that way!" Instead, we have every right to feel what we feel and then express it in an appropriate way. Healthy messages would be that all feelings are acceptable and that any way of expressing that is not intended to hurt would be allowed. Helpful suggestions can be ordinary or creative. Mary shared an idea with the class. "I keep egg cartons. When my children are upset, I encourage them to 'punch the pouches.' It's a great way for them to work through the feeling." We need more helpful parents like this!

BENEFITS OF CONSTRUCTIVE EXPRESSION

Constructive emotional expression can be thought of as a way of behaving that provides a healthy, nonhurtful outlet for feelings. A person can learn, model, and teach positive expressive behaviors and reap many benefits. Do you remember the four developmental areas? Each is enhanced by emotional expression.

Physical self. In recent years the link between physical health and emotional expression has been strengthened. On the positive side is evidence that such expressive behaviors as hugging, laughing, and crying are health producing. Any type of positive touch, including hugging, can raise hemoglobin levels. This vital part of the blood carries supplies of oxygen to all organs of the body. Touch stimulates the production of chemicals in the brain that feed blood, muscle, tissue, nerve cells, glands, hormones, and organs (Colton, 1983). According to Herbert Lingren, family life specialist at the University of Nebraska, regular hugging can cure harmful depression and stimulate a stronger will to live. Hugging, he says, eases tension, fights insomnia, and provides a wholesome alternative to unhealthy habits such as alcohol and drug abuse.

In an engaging book, Keating (1983) maintains that stimulation by touch is necessary for physical and emotional well-being. Therapeutic touch is now recognized as a valuable tool in healing and is often a part of training for nurses and other medical personnel. In both the toucher and the touched, physiological changes take place. Hugging is a special type of touch that can contribute to healing and health at all ages. "Holding contains the invisible threads that tie us to our existence. From the first moments of our life to the last, we need to be held or we fall" (Josselson, 1992, p. 29).

Laughing has received attention as a physical tonic for human beings. When people laugh, muscle tension is relieved. Huffing and puffing from laughter has been equated to physical exercise. Laughter can also help a person let go of anxiety, fear, hostility, anger, and embarrassment (Long, 1987). Believing that laughter contributed to his miraculous recovery from what was thought to be an irreversible, crippling disease, Norman Cousins (1979) describes laughter as a form of inner jogging and a behavior that creates a mood in which other positive emotions can more easily function. "Laughter helps make it possible for good things to happen" (p. 146). Infection in his body was measured before and after a few minutes of robust laughing. The amazing results showed a decrease in inflammation that held up over time. The retreat of pain meant an increase in mobility that helped his healing. Years later when much more had been learned about the biology of the brain, Cousins (1989) speculated that laughter had

Figure 4-7 A hug is healthful and feels so good!

helped to activate the release of endorphins, neurotransmitters in the body that act as pain killers. His research and that of others indicate a relationship between laughter and the immune system (Cousins, 1991). A study in Canada found links between laughter and improved immune function, cardiovascular tone, and pain endurance (Pennebaker, 1991). Cousins (1991) cautioned not to substitute laughter for medical care but use it to bring forth love, hope, festivity, determination, will to live, and purpose. "The positive emotions can be no less effective in bolstering the immune system than the negative emotions are in weakening it" (p. 91). And laughing has a way of bringing forth those positive feelings.

The most wasted of days is that during which one has not laughed.

—Sebastian Chamfort

Crying has long been a way of releasing feelings. Surveys showed that 85 percent of women and 73 percent of men reported feeling psychologically and physically better after crying. Fascinating research also reveals that the chemical composition of emotional tears differs from that of irritant ones (induced with freshly cut onions). Thus,

Figure 4-8 When did you last really laugh? Make it a habit!

shedding tears may be a way of ridding the body of substances that build up in response to stress. Crying for emotional reasons appears to be healthful, and suppressing tears may make people feel physically and psychologically worse (Leatx and Stolar, 1993; Levoy, 1988).

In the American society, men are typically ridiculed for crying and discouraged from doing so. According to research, women cry five times as often as men, and when they do, their tears are more frequently flowing. Men's tend to well up in the eye and not overflow, and they also can stop crying more easily than women. Men, more than women, may have to actually give themselves permission to cry (Brzowsky, 1984).

> A good healthy cry can be a sign of maturity. We've got it all wrong if we still believe that crying is a sign of weakness. Real weakness is in not allowing ourselves access to the emotions expressed through tears (Buscaglia, 1992, p. 280).

The restrictions can be prevented from the beginning. If you have input into a young boy's life, avoid the common message "Don't cry" or "Boys don't cry."

Men are also given less freedom to hug than women are. Watch men interacting with others. A study of travelers in the Kansas City International Airport revealed that women greeted other women physically with mutual lip kisses, embraces, and held each other for relatively long periods, while men just shook hands (Marsh, 1988). Only in recent years have genuine hugs been exchanged between men, particularly in sports settings. Perhaps as we learn more about the benefits of hugging, laughing, and crying, all human beings will become freer in their expressions.

Is lack of expressiveness linked to health problems? Research has focused on this question. About one in six people could be described as a repressor, according to Daniel Weinberger, a psychologist at Stanford University. Their calm is bought at a price—a higher risk for asthma, high blood pressure, and overall ill health (Goleman, 1988). Repressed emotions can damage your body, and even though you may try to keep them hidden, you will probably fail. "Any emotion that is repressed will eventually seek manifestation. What you resist emotionally, persists" (Ellsworth, 1988, p. 77). Are you aware of times when your repressed emotions seemed to play havoc with your physical condition? Anxiety often leads to headaches and stomach distress. I love John Powell's (1969) quote, "When I repress my emotions, my stomach keeps score" (p. 155).

Some serious diseases appear to have an emotional link. A study of 1000 male medical students conducted at the Johns Hopkins University School of Medicine found that a group named the "loner cluster," those who felt lonely and faced the world with bland, unemotional exteriors, had the highest incidence of cancer. They were 16 times more likely to develop the disease than the most cancer-free group, the "acting out/emotional cluster." The trait common to most of those with the higher cancer rates was a tendency to hide real feelings, particularly negative ones (Smith, 1988).

Another elaborately designed study indicates that hopelessness and repressed emotions are related to cancer (Fischman, 1988). The type of personality ascribed to a cancer-prone individual combines two major features: an inability to express emotions such as anger, fear, and anxiety and an inability to cope with stress with a tendency to feel hopelessness, helplessness, and finally depression (Eysenck, 1988). While research on the relationship between emotions and the body is inconclusive, several studies suggest that expression has positive outcomes (Cousins, 1989).

Mental self. Not recognizing or experiencing what you are feeling can cloud your thinking. Greg was considering a job change and a move to another city when his fiancée ended their engagement. Even though he showed little emotional reaction, his thinking abilities seemed impaired; he was confused and indecisive. He talked to a friend of his who was a counselor. With a great deal of encouragement, he began to talk about feelings of shock, hurt, and anger. The breakthrough in his seemingly blocked mental state came after an intense session of physically working out his feelings. After beating on a stack of large pillows with a tennis racket, he felt absolutely cleansed of negative feelings. "It was a cathartic experience, and I felt as if a weight was lifted from my body. It's hard to really describe." His reward was renewed ability to think about himself and his life. "As feelings are experienced, the mind clears" (Branden, 1983, p. 155).

Emotional distress can have an effect on mental performance. The underlying concerns that come from negative thinking before a test seem to affect outcome more than either academic skills or degree of self-efficacy (Smith et al., 1990). Can you remember a time when your feelings hindered the ability to use your brain? Expressing an emotion can lead the way to resolving a mental block. Test anxiety is a good example. Betty found that if she vented her feelings before an examination, she could think in a calmer, more organized manner.

Social self. "Communication of feelings is the bridge between two people upon which relationships are built" (Adams, 1987, p. 122). If you want to develop close relationships, being able to express feelings is a necessity. Two robotic persons may not notice how colorless their relationship is. When one robotic person interacts with a fully functioning emotional being, neither feels fulfilled. And the emotional individual is apt to be frustrated. The closest, healthiest, and most meaningful relationships are between two emotionally expressive individuals.

Think of emotional expression in relationships as a positive circular effect as illustrated in Fig. 4-9. As you feel and express genuine feelings, you learn about yourself. Others get to know who you truly are and are apt to appreciate knowing a whole person. Then, it is likely that they will feel free to share feelings with you leading to close relationships. Both empathy and supportiveness are enhanced by genuine emotional expression.

The price of not expressing can be high. If demonstrating affection is difficult, people tend to refrain from doing so. They usually think they will show their caring some day. A letter to Ann Landers from No Name, No City, No State is quite moving.

> A few weeks ago I kissed my son for the first time and told him I loved him. Unfortunately he did not know it because he was dead. He had shot himself. The greatest regret of my life is that I kept my son at arm's length. I believed it was unmanly for males to show affection for one another. I treated my son the way my father treated me and I realize now what a terrible mistake it was. Please tell your male readers who were raised by "macho" dads that it is cruel to withhold affection from their sons. I will never recover from my ignorance and stupidity.

On a positive note, a study of fathers and preadolescent sons showed that intimate and nurturing types of touch were a frequent and important part of their relationship (Salt, 1991).

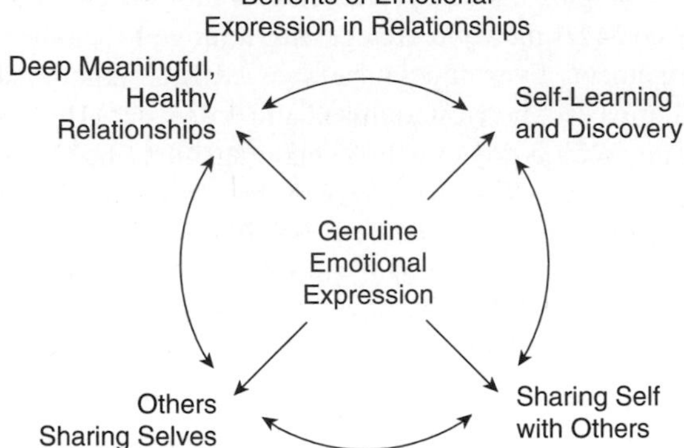

Figure 4-9

An advantage for societies and their inhabitants was suggested from a survey of primitive cultures. The peaceful ones were inhabited by adults who hugged their children; the ones who treated their children coldly produced brutal, violent adults (Bloom, 1989). A longitudinal study showed that adults who had been treated with warmth and demonstrated affection as children enjoyed happier and more well-adjusted lives (Franz et al., 1991).

Even expressing unpleasant feelings can create a closer feeling. In closest relationships, even though positive emotions outnumbered them, negative emotions were frequently expressed as well (Berscheid et al., 1989). When my husband talks about the closeness between himself and my two daughters (his stepchildren), he gives credit to honest emotional expression. "We had some verbal battles where anger was genuinely expressed," he says. "After we had let off steam, we talked and shared positive feelings and really got to know each other." Relationships with unexpressive individuals aren't deep or close, and they are usually weak. Expressing your feelings gives nourishment to relationships.

Emotional self. Expressing your feelings makes the emotional self healthier. Margaret felt resentful because she thought her mother favored her sister Janet. She bottled up this feeling for years and found herself becoming angry and even hostile. One day she told Janet a lie about their mother and then suffered from guilt. She became deeply depressed and went for counseling. After a period of time, she realized that the initial resentful feeling had led to several others. She decided to express in writing her true feelings to her mother and sister and acknowledge the lie she had told. The three of them came together and leveled with each other. They honestly expressed their emotions, and the feeling was one of relief. "I felt as if the clouds had lifted, and my only regret is that I didn't do it sooner," said Margaret.

Emotional relief is not possible if you have a bagful of stuffed feelings. Expressing one emotion often reveals the presence of another. During a cancer coping session, Marian went through a process that stripped away one emotion after another. She began by expressing depression, which was covering fear. Underneath all this was intense anger. She had been feeling emotionally drained; after the expressive experience, she was energized.

Expressing emotions is essential for healing psychological wounds such as the "inner child" discussed in Chapter 1.

> A critical part of healing our wounded children and recovering our lost vitality is unloading the emotions that are hidden in our bag. Remember that the contents of the bag have been composting, getting wilder and wilder. Anger stuffed in the bag becomes rage. Fear stuck in the bag becomes panic. Sadness stuck in the bag becomes paralyzing grief or emotional numbness. Expect that you will relive very powerful emotions as you begin your healing. This is not craziness; it is the beginning of sanity. But it is painful. There is no way to avoid facing the pain that is still locked inside (Borysenko, 1990, p. 71).

Getting emotional relief is important. In addition, becoming more expressive enriches all your emotions. In describing what he calls "super joy," Pearsall (1988) writes, "The risk to super joy is that too many people have too much control of their emotions" (p. 105). Repression inhibits all feelings, even joyful ones.

Being honest in your expressions helps you feel authentic. This leads to pride and enhanced self-esteem. Individuals who do not express can feel phony, frustrated, and depressed. Resentment is a typical one to repress and especially damaging. Resentments are like "tiny emotional abscesses—pockets of venomous feelings that never disappear" (Bloomfield and Felder, 1983, p. 21). Even when one has awareness of resentment, expressing it is difficult. "It's easier to keep quiet," said one woman. After she was encouraged to let her resentment be known in a nonthreatening way, she admitted, "I feel so relieved now. Keeping a lid on resentment was causing me frustration and unhappiness. Being assertive has made all the difference in how I feel about myself." In all developmental areas, positive growth is a benefit of genuine emotional expression. True sharing of feelings leads to heightened self-esteem and a healthier life style.

DEMONSTRATION OF FEELINGS

"I realize that I could benefit from becoming more expressive, but how do I go about it?" is a common, important question. As with any change, the primary step is a desire to do so. Giving yourself permission is often the biggest hurdle. Telling yourself, "I want to express my feelings more, and I'm going to try," begins the process. Being determined, yet patient, is good advice. Just as you couldn't expect to lose 30 pounds in a short period of time, you won't become expressive overnight. We can, however, act ourselves into a new way of thinking and think ourselves into a new way of acting. "We may be products of the past but are also architects of our future" (Myers, 1992, p. 122). Concentrated effort is required, and you can expect to feel uncomfortable at first.

If you aren't what I call a naturally warm, demonstrative person, use your adult ego state in permitting the "child" to act. Joyce had a life-threatening accident from which she recovered. She decided that she wanted to become more affectionate and demonstrative. She told her husband, children, and friends, "I want to give and receive more hugs and pats on the back." She actually had to tell herself in the beginning, "Go give Tom a hug," and she kept track of how many she gave and received. Anyone in the family could request a hug. They treated it as somewhat of a game until they found that hugging had become second nature.

I cherish a note from a student of mine. She wrote: "Sharon, I am so thrilled to tell you about this. Yesterday, I hugged my grandma and for the very first time told her I loved her. She looked so surprised, and tears came to her eyes. She seemed to like it. I didn't think I could just go do that, but, thanks to your class, I got up my nerve!" I smiled as I thought to myself that hugging hadn't been one of my typical behaviors until I began to teach about human relationships, and now others were learning from me. Affection can also be expressed in words, writing, gifts, favors, helpful behaviors, and just by listening.

Other emotions, too, may require your permission. Few people have received constructive modeling or advice on expressing anger and sorrow (discussed in a later section on coping with crisis). Recognizing that repressing either or both can result in physical problems may motivate you to learn how to express. *Anger* is a universal response in which a person is aware of being in or feeling a state of displeasure (Rubin, 1969). The awareness component of anger is not uncommon. Anger exists for a reason, is a signal worth listening to, and deserves respect and attention (Lerner, 1985). Anger is often related to powerlessness and a perceived lack of control (Strachan and Dutton, 1992).

Understandably, anger and love occur in the same relationships. "Where there is intense love there is also the opportunity for intense anger" (Bloomfield and Felder, 1983, p. 51). Expressed anger can actually demonstrate that you care enough to tell—that you care enough to want a change for the better (Rubin, 1969). However, chronic anger in a relationship is a message. Finding out what you are really angry about is essential (Lerner, 1985).

Although being angry usually doesn't cause problems, not expressing anger constructively will. "Anger can't be suppressed without self-damage," (Bloomfield and Kory, 1980, p. 232). Health problems, as we have noted, are related to unresolved anger. *The Angry Book* (Rubin, 1969) points out the many "assorted poisons" related to repressed anger: anxiety, guilt, depression, overeating, high blood pressure, self-imposed starvation, sleep problems, psychosomatic illnesses, obsessions, and compulsions. He also identifies a serious side effect of what he calls "freezing" your anger.

> Freezing never works on anger exclusively. It always affects all our emotions, including love. We cannot feel with a frozen finger, and we cannot feel with frozen emotions (p. 44).

Teresa Adams (1987), a therapist, author, and friend of mine, writes: "In every divorce, the mishandling of anger is a major cause of the failure of a marriage" (p. 151). Continually stuffing your anger is a way of mishandling it.

Because repressed anger is destructive and hostilely expressed anger is harmful, the issue becomes one of discovering healthy ways to express. Brainstorming sessions in my classes have produced many possibilities. Following is a partial list.

Walk, jog, swim, engage in any type of physical exercise.

Hit a pillow, punch a punching bag or stuffed object.

Talk, scream (in a private place), write angry thoughts, cry.

Clean house, pull weeds.

Have an imaginary conversation with the source of your anger.

Two methods that have worked well for me are the tennis racket pounding described earlier and hurling glass jars and bottles into large collection bins for recycling. A physical act seems to be especially relieving. Thought changing, covered in the next section, can be helpful but is usually not enough. A suggested guideline is to make the expression cathartic—that is, an expression that physically releases the pent-up feeling. How do you know when you have released enough? The sensation of anger will no longer be there.

If you are angry with an individual, if at all possible, let him or her know. "Just blowing off steam often doesn't result in relief because it doesn't take into account the person you are angry with. If the object of the grievance is not confronted, it matters little whether the anger is kept in or let out" (Gordon, 1988a, p. 47). The key is assertiveness and the use of positive communication techniques covered in later chapters rather than unbridled expressions of sheer anger.

Making anger constructive begins with recognizing the source of your anger. Is it coming from old hurts or is it current? "Anger that stems from emotional slush is almost always destructive" (Bloomfield and Kory, 1980, p. 215). Also, believing that others make you angry and not feeling in control of your feelings makes you unable to create your own joy. Taking pride in yourself means that you don't just respond; instead, you decide. Responding to hate with hate, or anger with anger, is not because of what was directed your way; it's because of what's inside of you (Dyer, 1992).

Letting go of anger is rewarding; setting a goal to express all emotions in healthy ways is wise. If you become aware of the problems associated with repression and the benefits of expressiveness, the next steps become obvious. Select behaviors that seem to fit you and even experiment with some that at first seem uncomfortable. I'll never forget the first time I used the tennis racket technique. I used all kinds of self-talk to force myself to engage in what seemed like childish behavior. Because it worked so well, I've become a strong advocate. Continue to practice your new expressive actions and monitor yourself to see how you're doing. Have you hugged anyone recently? When was the last time you really laughed? What did you do or not do the last time you felt angry? What could you have done? Are you allowing any tears?

Keep in mind what most people do not realize: suppressing any emotion will affect total expressiveness. "I believe you feel either all your feelings or eventually none at all. You cannot select which you will feel and which you won't. You simply can't have one feeling without the other. Negate anger and you must also negate love" (Rubin, 1969, p. 187). The emotional health of individuals determines the atmosphere of any setting. In an emotionally healthy climate all feelings are not labeled good or bad, and all are given ample play and freedom.

> This atmosphere says, "It is all right to feel love, and it is all right to feel anger. It is all right to express love, and it is all right to express anger. Your feelings are welcome here, and we would like to know what they are. You are loved and accepted and safe with all your feelings. You needn't stifle any of them to please us" (Rubin, 1969, pp. 21–22).

How liberating and positive such a climate would be!

A rich, satisfying life is possible only with involvement of all parts of the self. "Devaluing feelings is a direct link to devaluing self" (Satir, 1988, p. 24). Your emotional self is a fascinating and vital developmental area. Empowering the child ego state by feeling and demonstrating all emotions enhances and enriches your existence.

CHANGING WHAT YOU FEEL

Experiencing and sharing your feelings are beneficial. Being an emotional being, however, does not mean that you are at the mercy of your feelings. Having the ability to change what you feel is an extremely useful and significant way of taking charge of your life.

The Power of Your Thoughts

The relationship between thoughts and emotions has received a great deal of attention. Cognitive psychologists believe that a person's thoughts about an event determine the particular emotion (Beck, 1976; Burns, 1989; Lazarus, 1966). "Your emotions result entirely from the way you look at things. If your understanding is accurate, your emotions will be normal" (Burns, 1980a, p. 29). A *cognition* is a thought, and negative or inaccurate thinking patterns actually cause unpleasant emotions (Burns, 1989). Similarly, thoughts can create pleasant emotions or relieve unpleasant ones. For example, pretend that you are driving a car and are stopped at a red light. The instant the light turns green, you hear a horn honking behind you. Do you feel surprised, concerned, angry, annoyed, or calm? Whether you realize it or not, how you feel depends on your thought about the honking, not the event itself. "Oh, I wonder who is honking at me. Maybe it's someone I know" would elicit surprise and possibly even delight. "The person must have an emergency to be in such a hurry" is a thought that could result in concern. "How dare anyone honk at me! I know what a green light means" would spark anger or annoyance. "Somebody likes to use their horn. I'm glad I'm not that stressed," you think and then feel nothing but calmness. "Your thoughts create your physical reality" (Dyer, 1992, p. 253).

What you think and feel then guides your behavior. You may turn around, scowl, and shake your fist—or worse. Or you may turn around, smile, and wave or choose to do nothing. You have the choice. Perceptions cause our emotions and influence our behavior (Powell, 1976). Realizing that thoughts or beliefs are instrumental in emotional responses is an important step in learning how to change what you feel. Sadness and depression result from thoughts of loss, frustration comes from unfulfilled expectations, anxiety and panic follow thoughts of danger, and anger is usually the outcome of perceptions of unfairness (Burns, 1989). Cognitive therapy trains people to change the way they interpret and look at things so that they can experience different emotions, feel better, and act more productively.

Rational-emotive therapy. One of the best known and applicable cognitive systems, rational-emotive therapy, or RET, was developed by Albert Ellis (1984). It shows how emotions and behaviors stem from thoughts or beliefs and also identifies common irrational beliefs. The approach uses the letters "ABC."

A stands for *activating* event, situation, or experience.

B represents *beliefs* or thoughts about the activating event.

C means *consequences* (emotions, further thoughts, and behaviors).

Let's put RET into practice. You receive a failing grade on your first college examination. This is the activating event (A). Your initial belief or thought (B): "That's it. This proves I can't handle college-level coursework. I might as well quit right now." Can you see that at this point your thought is irrational? With these thoughts your emotions would probably be disappointment and frustration. Further consequences could include additional feelings of depression and hopelessness, continued dead-ended, despairing thoughts and behaviors followed by actions to quit school (C).

RET teaches that a change in belief will change the consequences. Remember the cognitive restructuring formula from Chapter 1? Consider this alternative, "Just because I received a failing grade on the first exam doesn't mean I can't handle college-level work. I didn't perform as well as I wanted to; however, one grade does not mean I will fail this course." You have now eliminated the irrational thought. How would the consequences be different? Your initial emotion may still be disappointment, yet you would then feel hopeful, your thoughts would be more positive and directed to doing what you could to improve, and your behavior would be different. You would not quit school on the basis of one examination grade!

Cognitive techniques work best for those who have the ability to reflect on their own thoughts. Individuals with a thinking preference in decision-making may have an advantage over feeling types. However, if you are inclined to "think with your heart," you can especially benefit from the use of RET. It can be helpful in daily situations as well as in treating emotional challenges. Be patient, as using your adult ego state, or "shifting into your 'T,' " as I like to call it, does require practice. See if you can use RET in REFLECTIONS AND APPLICATIONS, the activity for Chapter 4.

RET is not useful when your thoughts are rational and suitable to the occasion. It is not desirable to change appropriate positive emotions—in essence, creating unpleasant ones by thought changing. For example, Mike had been invited to go out of town for the weekend with friends. His original thought was, "It was neat that they asked me, and it sounds like a good time." His feelings were anticipation, excitement, and happiness. Later he found himself thinking, "I wonder why they asked me. I'll bet they needed another car, and I have a nice one." Do you see how quickly his feelings would then change? Be careful that you don't replace pleasant, realistic thoughts with unpleasant, irrational ones.

Neurolinguistic programming. A fascinating way of using our brain's power is based on specific elements of mental pictures, sounds, or other sensations that can be changed in order to increase or decrease the intensity of experience (Robbins, 1991). The way the brain sorts and codes sensory experiences influences emotions. *Neurolinguistic programming*, often referred to as NLP, can help you change "human software"—how you think and respond (Bandler, 1985). You can alter your mental pictures in terms of brightness, color, clarity, and size. As you change the picture, your feelings follow suit. NLP also can modify emotions by changing concentration. This example is used by one of the first to write about NLP:

> Once I asked a man how he depressed himself and he said, "Well, like if I go out to my car and find there's a flat tire."
> "Well, that is an annoyance, but it doesn't seem like enough to get depressed. How do you make that really depressing?"

> "I say to myself, 'It's always like this,' and then I see a whole lot of pictures of the other times that my car broke down."
> I know that for every time his car didn't work, there were probably three hundred times that it worked perfectly. But he doesn't think of them at the moment. If I can get him to think of all those other times that his car worked fine, he won't be depressed (Bandler, 1985, p. 27).

In addition to changing emotions, NLP has applications in several other aspects of life such as career success and goal achievement.

The Power of Your Behavior

Closely related to RET is *reality therapy* developed by William Glasser. A basic premise is that in order for people to take responsibility for themselves and learn to fulfill their needs, rational thought and behavior are necessary (Glasser, 1965). As in the cognitive theories, the ability to think of several possibilities is invaluable. Glasser (1984) has also taught and written about *control theory*, which describes behavior as four components: doing, thinking, feeling, and physiology. In the earlier example of failing your first examination, control theory would say you are depressing yourself. If you want to feel different, first change your behaviors. Instead of moping around, you can choose to socialize with friends, go to a movie, or do whatever is pleasurable. You can alter your thinking, too, as suggested before; however, more emphasis is placed on behavioral changing.

> Because we always have control over the doing component of our behavior, if we markedly change that component, we cannot avoid changing the thinking, feeling, and physiological components as well. The more we get involved in an active doing behavior that is markedly different from what we are doing when choosing a misery, the more we will also change what we think, feel, and experience from our bodies (Glasser, 1984, p. 50).

Have you ever whistled or hummed cheerily and then recognized a slight mood elevation? If so, you were using basic control theory.

A fascinating idea from studies conducted by Paul Ekman is that facial expressions may change feelings. People imitated facial expressions associated with fear, anger, and disgust without being told about specific emotions. They then experienced the feeling that their faces showed (Nechas, 1985). Later studies showed that facial expressions are related to different patterns of brain activity. A particular type of smile, one in which the eye muscles are active, was related to enjoyment and reports of positive emotions (Ekman et al., 1990). Simple experiments in my classes indicate that happy facial expressions and positive behaviors can pleasantly affect feelings. Try putting on a happy face and see what happens!

Cognitive and behavioral techniques can be used effectively to change most emotions including minor depression or a "down" feeling. In a Gallup survey of 1000 women (ages 18 to 54), 93 percent had experienced low moods commonly because of too many demands on their time. Several reported that the "blues" resulted from the stress of trying to be everything to everybody (Braiker, 1988). If you recall the part in Chapter 3 about unrealistic expectations and multiple statuses, you might advise these women to change their thoughts and quit trying to be all things to everyone!

If you experience this "blue mood" once in awhile, use any of the ideas for creating happiness covered in Chapter 3 plus thought and behavior changing. When the women in the Gallup survey were asked what helped, they mentioned exercise, reading, putting their minds on work, meditating, and praying. Sleeping and drinking alcohol were the least effective helps (Braiker, 1988). A technique called mental rewiring could also be useful. Instead of thinking, "I just can't help the way I feel," you think, "The feeling is here, and I can control what I do about it" (Braiker, 1988). Then do something! Your health will probably benefit. A study showed that antibody response of the immune system was lower on days with high negative moods and higher when the feelings were positive (Stone et al., 1987). We really do have control over those brief occasional "bouts with the blues" as we do other emotional states. An underlying theme of this book is that human beings have numerous choices, one of which is learning to use various techniques to change your emotions.

SEEKING PROFESSIONAL HELP

Certain emotions do not lend themselves exclusively to self-help. A common one is *major or clinical depression*, a medical disorder that affects thoughts, feelings, physical health, and behaviors. It is characterized by a depressed mood most of the day, nearly every day for at least 2 weeks or loss of interest and pleasure in things one used to enjoy. Other symptoms are: diminished ability to think or concentrate, feelings of worthlessness or guilt, thoughts of death or suicide, increase or decrease in appetite or weight, insomnia or sleeping too much, and loss of energy (U.S. Department of Health and Human Services, 1993).

Millions of Americans suffer from severe depressive episodes. Many do little or nothing to alleviate their pain even though treatments are usually very successful. "Even in cases where a depression is quite severe, medications used in conjunction with psychotherapy generally boast a success rate between 75 and 85 percent. They can and do work" (Podell, 1992, p. 150). Sadly, only 20 percent receive the help they need (DePaulo and Ablow, 1989). Even though people can and do struggle through repeated episodes, early treatment is important. It can keep the depression from becoming more severe and chronic, as the more incidents one has, the greater the chance to have others (Elmer-Dewitt, 1992; Leshner, 1992; U.S. Department of Health and Human Services, 1993). If depression is untreated, its chances of returning can run almost as high as 90 percent (Podell, 1992). Another sound reason for seeking help is that successful treatment resolves other problems, as well (Dowling, 1991).

Important to realize are the possible causes of depression. One is *seasonal affective disorder* (SAD) which stems from lack of sunlight and is usually experienced only in the fall and winter. An easy solution, light therapy, is quite effective (Kamberg, 1989). Recent strong evidence suggests a biological or genetic base in many cases of clinical depression (DePaulo and Ablow, 1989; Fieve, 1989; Kamberg, 1989; Leshner, 1992; Papolos and Papolos, 1987; Podell, 1992; U.S. Department of Health and Human Services, 1993). If the cause is biochemical, drug therapy is needed. Indicated in studies are the value of drug treatment and psychotherapy together (Reynolds, 1992), the use of antidepressant medication in mildly depressed people (Stewart et al., 1992), and lithium being added to the therapy of adolescents already using imipramine (Strober et al., 1992). For severe depression, studies show that medicine is very effective (U.S. Department of Health and Human Services, 1993). Most carefully designed antidepressant drug

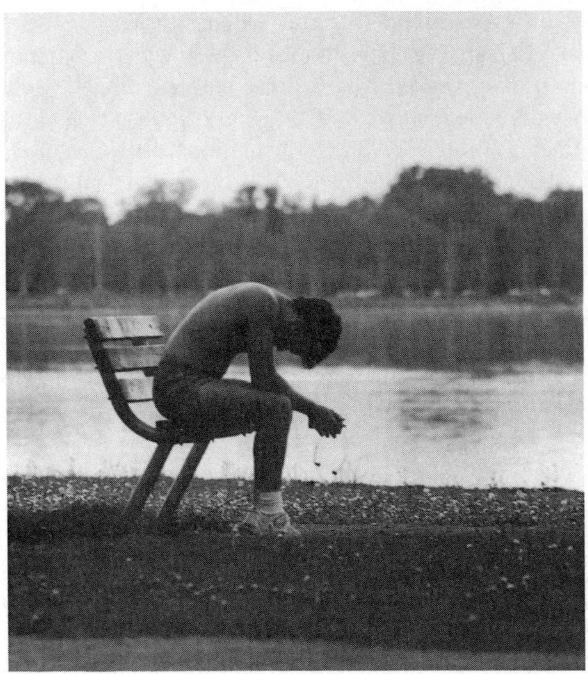

Figure 4-10 Severe depression can be difficult and dangerous.

studies with all forms of depression show that up to 75 percent improve substantially within 2 to 6 weeks of drug treatment (Fieve, 1989).

"But I don't want to use drugs" is a common protest. It can help to realize that the proper prescription of an antidepressant merely restores the functioning of the brain to normal. The medications "fix" what's in need of repair and do not create something artificial or unnatural (Podell, 1992). Antidepressant medicines are not addictive or habit forming (Dowling, 1991; U.S. Department of Health and Human Services, 1993); however, taking the one best suited for a particular patient and diagnosis in the correct dosage is essential (Leshner, 1992). Being cautious in selecting an experienced psychiatrist or, ideally, a psychopharmacologist whose specialty is drug therapy is critical (Dowling, 1991; Papolos and Papolos, 1987). "Prescribing psychiatric medications is an art as well as a science" (Podell, 1992, p. 149). The results of successful drug therapy seem like miracles. "I feel like a completely new person," said Mark, as he walked confidently into my classroom. Cognitive therapy, discussed earlier, is used successfully to treat depression (Burns, 1989) either along with drug therapy or alone if the cause is not biochemical.

Not only is clinical depression a dreadful feeling that impinges severely on quality of life, it can produce profound physiological change and adversely affect the biochemical balances of the body. Decline in depression was accompanied by an increase in certain immune cells in a study of patients with melanoma cancer (Cousins, 1989). According to Margaret Kemeny, Ph.D. at UCLA, chronic depression has negative biological consequences such as vulnerability to heart attacks and other kinds of diseases (Moyers, 1993).

Another compelling reason for seeking professional help is that suicide is often an answer for a severely depressed person. The suicide rate for 15- to 24-year-olds has tripled in the last 30 years (Beattie, 1991; Becker-Fritz and Barbee, 1993; Fieve, 1989; Papolos and Papolos, 1987) and is now the second leading cause of death for that age group (DePaulo and Ablow, 1989). Someone commits suicide every 17.3 minutes (Beattie, 1991), and every day in the United States 1000 young people attempt suicide. Most at risk are white males 15 to 19 years of age (Fieve, 1989). About 80 percent of adolescent suicides occur when the individual is depressed (Fieve, 1989). Drug abuse is also related to suicide (Depaulo and Ablow, 1989). A study showed that depression and alcohol dependency were significantly related as were depression and low self-esteem (Reed and Greenwald, 1991). Because the two major factors in suicide attempts are depression and drug and alcohol use (Smolin and Guinan, 1993), treatment needs are obvious and require professional help. An excellent book I would like to see in the hands of anyone even remotely considering suicide is *A Reason to Live* (Beattie, 1991). The book gives many ways to feel in control of life again, suggestions of options to suicide, and numerous resources.

One strategy that some of my students have shared with me is to imagine how devastating your death would be to someone with whom you are not angry and for whom you care deeply, such as a grandparent. "Anytime the idea came into my mind, I saw my grandma's face and knew I would never do that to her," said one young man. Remember if you ever consider suicide: "Keep it a question. It's not really an answer" (Colgrove, Bloomfield, and McWilliams, 1991, p. 69).

Even if suicide is not attempted, depression can hurt more than the one person. The book *Contagious Emotions: Staying Well When Your Loved One Is Depressed* (Podell, 1992) describes how other individuals and relationships are adversely affected. Depression, he says, can be masked by emotions such as anger and behaviors that reflect hostility. Also symptomatic of a depressive disorder are belittling humor, needling, and biting chronic sarcasm. Substance abuse is a sign as well as a contributor. His book suggests how you can help both the depressed person and yourself.

Ideally, a depressed person will seek help. However, because lack of motivation or energy is usually a symptom, this may not happen. An estimated 80 percent who commit suicide do, however, give clear warning signals (Becker-Fritz and Barbee, 1993). If you know someone who has any of the depression symptoms, drastic changes in his or her behaviors, or talks about death or suicide, do all you can to get them to a professional. You might take the educational approach and point out that the brain, like any organ, can get sick or, if necessary, use confrontation.

Selecting a professional can begin with a licensed or certified counselor or therapist (trained in psychology or social work) or a physician who knows enough about depression to refer the person to a specialist in mood disorders (psychiatrist or psychopharmocologist). Or, one can get references from hospitals, universities, or professional associations (see resource section at end of chapter). A therapist's expertise in diagnosing and treating depression is most important (Podell, 1992). Most experts recommend that a client have a positive feeling about the doctor and that counseling be a part of the total treatment (Elmer-Dewitt, 1992). "Good psychotherapy enhances the treatment of mood problems; people should never be treated with drugs alone" (Burns, 1989, p. 42).

Hopefully, the stigma attached to drug therapies will be eliminated and the future will be bright for those who suffer from major depression as well as their families and friends. "When medication can ameliorate the symptoms of a chemical imbalance, why should we be made to feel that taking it is somehow irresponsible? Do we condemn those with hypertension for their dependence on medications that lower blood pressure?"

(Dowling, 1991, p. 25). After Vincent Foster, deputy White House counsel, committed suicide, columnist Donald Kaul (1993) emphasized how primitive we still are about depression and how difficult it is for a person to seek help.

> Vince Foster was, by all reports, a fine man. His tragedy is not merely personal, however. It is a tragedy in which we all share in direct proportion to our refusal to confront the ultimate truth about mental illness. It can happen to anyone (p. 18).

And, in most cases, it can also be successfully treated.

MANAGING STRESS EFFECTIVELY

Stress, although not an emotion, is closely related to the subject of emotion and deserves much attention. *Stress*, according to the "father of stress research," Hans Selye (1974), is the nonspecific response of the body to any demand made upon it. Stress is what the human body experiences when a person perceives a demand to adjust. Emotions such as anger, anxiety, and depression can precede or follow stress as both causes and effects.

Stress has been intensely studied for years and much has been discovered, yet questions remain. One point is clear: stress cannot be avoided. *Stressors*, the conditions that cause stress, are numerous and never ending. Instead of life being a bowl of cherries, one could say that life is a bowl of stressors!

Effects of Stress

Stress that is either not handled or mishandled is related to numerous problems. Poor health conditions like the ones linked to suppressed emotions can result from unhealthy stress management. "Stress may be the greatest single contributor to illness in the industrialized world" (Eliot and Breo, 1984, p. 14).

> Stress is now known to be a major contributor, either directly or indirectly, to coronary heart disease, cancer, lung ailments, accidental injuries, cirrhosis of the liver, and suicide—six of the leading causes of death in the United States. Stress also plays a role in aggravating such conditions as multiple sclerosis, diabetes, genital herpes, and even trench mouth. According to the American Academy of Family Physicians, two thirds of the office visits to family doctors are prompted by stress-related symptoms (Wallis, 1983, p. 48).

Conditions ranging from headaches to poor sexual performance can have a stress link. Irritable bowel syndrome (IBS), which afflicts mostly women under the age of 35, is associated with anxiety, a tendency to suppress negative emotions, and ineffective ways of dealing with stress (Adessa, 1989). Chronic stress may lead to illnesses like heart disease (Moyers, 1993). How can stress be involved in such diverse physical conditions? Under stress, the heart, lungs, and nervous system plus other bodily functions work harder. Most important, stress appears to weaken immune systems so we are susceptible to all health problems (Morris, 1993; Moyers, 1993).

The other three areas of self can also suffer. Mismanaged stress contributes to relationship or social problems, emotional distress, and severe mental challenges. Stress is associated with decreased grade point averages (Felsten and Wilcox, 1992). Not surprisingly, various stressors seemed to make parents more irritable, critical, and punitive which led to an increased likelihood of the children developing behavior problems (Webster-Stratton, 1990). In the work environment, stress takes a heavy toll. Symptoms related to stress such as absenteeism, company medical expenses, and lost productivity can definitely have a stress connection.

Even with its potentially high cost, stress is not necessarily negative. A certain amount of stress can be motivating and healthful. Equate stress to the strings on a violin. If they are stretched tightly, the tone of the violin is sharp; too loose and the sound is flat and lifeless. Either way beautiful music is an impossibility. The key is to adjust the strings to a desirable degree of tightness. Similarly, individuals can benefit from knowing how much and what type of stress is good for them. Each person is different. For example, you may be one who feels quite relaxed sitting in a boat all day fishing. Another person would be bored and actually experience stress engaging in the same activity.

Stress that is good for you is called *eustress*. One's attitude about an experience is what determines whether the stress is a eustress or not (Selye, 1978). All human beings need some stress in order to flourish. "Stress is the spice of life. Who would enjoy a life of no runs, no hits, no errors?" (Selye, 1974, p. 85).

How do you know when your level of stress is unhealthy? There will be clues. Are you experiencing frequent headaches, stomach distress, minor aches and pains, muscle tension, or fatigue for no apparent reason? Do you feel uneasy, tense, or irritable? Are you having difficulty sleeping or concentrating? Even apathy may be a sign. "Your body, mind, and spirit will send you their distress signals. Be aware. Listen to yourself" (Tubesing, 1981, p. 5). Learning about stress—what is an optimal level for you and how to handle it in a positive way—is a "must" in terms of self and relationships.

Sources of Stress

What are the stressors in your life? Most of us have long lists. Some deny that they have stress; this means they are either unaware of what stress actually is or they try to ignore its existence.

Stress has a myriad of sources which researchers have uncovered. One of the first studies was conducted by Holmes and Rahe (1967). Their subjects identified major changes in their lives. Each event was then given a value based on its magnitude or effect. The top five stress-producing events then were (1) death of spouse, (2) divorce, (3) marital separation, (4) jail term, and (5) death of close family member. I jokingly ask my students how they could avoid the top three. Not getting married would seem to do it! Both positive and negative events if they prompted some type of coping or adaptive behavior were stressful. The study indicated that when too many events happen in succession, the strain can produce unhealthy effects. "Too many stress points in too short a time, especially without relief and relaxation, will jeopardize our health" (Albrecht, 1979, p. 102).

Another study (Lazarus, 1981) dealt with minor irritants, or the hassles of everyday life. Viewed as ongoing stressors, these are often left unattended because they occur so often and are seemingly routine. Jan was annoyed by a tiny squeak everyday as she drove to work. She kept telling herself that some day she would get it fixed. That some day never seemed to come until she realized that her irritation at work and at home might be related to the annoyance she experienced each day. "The petty annoyances, frustrations, and unpleasant surprises that plague us every day may add up to more grief than life's major stressful events" (Lazarus, 1981, p. 58). What everyday hassles bother you? What are you doing about them? If your answer is "nothing," the accumulative effects of stress may be harmful.

Stressors are either external or internal. *External stressors* are those that come from outside of self. Other people, events beyond your control, and the environment deliver daily doses of stress. Can you name some? *Internal stressors* are those we create. Irrational thoughts, unrealistic expectations, inability to express emotions, and unnecessary worry fall into this category. Especially troublesome is the stereotypic feminine gender role of passivity which leads to worrying without taking any action. Some even feel guilty when they don't worry which adds to their emotional pressure (Handly et al., 1990). "Worry makes fools of us all. It controls our lives and leaves us with empty hearts and missed experiences" (Buscaglia, 1992, p. 184). Worry is a learned response perpetuated by the following myths (Goulding and Goulding, 1989).

Worrying keeps your worries from coming true;
Other people make you worry;
Events make you worry;
If you love or care, you worry;
If you are human, you worry.

The reality is that if you are a worrier, you manufacture stress. And you have a lot of company. A study showed that college students worried during much of each day. Aca-

Figure 4-11

demic success was the most common reason with social relationships, health, finances, and career also mentioned (Vasey and Borkovec, 1992).

People have a hard time differentiating between worries and concerns. The difference lies in your ability to do something about potential disasters. Concern leads to action while worry arises from feelings of powerlessness. Sorting out real concerns from the mass of imaginative and insignificant worries is a worthy challenge. Ninety percent of what we worry about never happens (Buscaglia, 1992). "Worry never robs tomorrow of its sorrow; it only saps today of its joy" (Buscaglia, 1992, p. 182).

Two practical books *Not to Worry*! (Goulding and Goulding, 1989) and *Why Women Worry and How to Stop* (Handly et al., 1990) describe methods that can free you from unnecessary anxiety and reduce the impact of this internal stressor. Some quick tips are to change "what if" to "so what if," set aside 30 minutes to really worry and refuse to do so at other times, keep a worry journal so that the thoughts are put on paper, and definitely *act* on your worry or use thought-stopping and quit dwelling on it.

Other internal stressors come from overloading yourself, having unrealistic expectations, taking on too much, neglecting your physical health, and even living a boring life. Negative self-talk creates stress. The list goes on and on. An awareness of the sources can enable you to analyze, possibly decrease the numbers, and reduce the impact of stressors.

Taking Charge of Stress

The subject of handling stress is well covered in a variety of books and articles, and the number of suggestions is mind-boggling. Yet, many people still do nothing about stress.

Perhaps you are one of the fortunate people who already has what is called *psychological hardiness* (Kobasa, 1979). In a classic study of middle and upper level executives who had experienced high degrees of stressful life events, the differences between those who became ill and those who did not were noted. Those who stayed well shared personality characteristics of hardiness: strong commitment to self and various areas of life, a sense of meaningfulness or purpose, the attitude that change was challenging and vigorous, and an internal locus of control. David Felten, M.D., Ph.D., has identified lack of control in any situation as a factor in a diminished immune system (Moyers, 1993). If the descriptors of hardiness don't sound like you, consider what you can do to become hardier!

When faced with an immediate, apparent stressor, you can choose among three direct coping methods: *confrontation, compromise*, and *withdrawal* (Morris, 1993). This means you choose to either face the problem directly, negotiate and usually yield somewhat, or stay away from the stressor. Withdrawal may involve getting out of a stressful relationship or getting rid of other people's problems and returning them to their rightful owners. Regardless of whether a stressor is apparent, you are wise to employ a regular stress-management routine which protects you from the effects of those daily stressors that are not always evident. Several practical stress-reducing suggestions and elaborations follow. The challenge is to put them into regular practice.

- Whenever possible, reduce or wisely schedule major life events. For example, don't begin college, start a job, move, get married, quit college, and get divorced in the same year!

- Prioritize hassles in your life. Take action to eliminate or reduce the most annoying ones. If a messy desk is bothering you, take the time to clean it. Carry extra keys in case you lock one inside the car or house.
- Challenge worrisome or anxiety provoking thoughts. Don't be afraid to seek information. When faced with physical pain or another symptom, don't ignore it if you have the slightest worry. And ask questions so that you feel in control. Learn techniques to eliminate unnecessary worry and anxiety.
- Use cognitive techniques to change stress-producing thoughts. Much unnecessary stress is manufactured by the ideas we have. Try asking, "What's the worst thing that can happen here?" Many times the worst isn't so awful. Or, if you think that saying no isn't a nice thing to do, change your thinking to, "Nice has nothing to do with this."
- Develop a decision-making process and use your thinking preference. Don't be hasty, yet remember that "staying on the fence too long" is stressful.
- If you feel frustrated or worried, ask yourself what you can do about it. Either act or let go of the feeling. Be realistic about what is possible.
- Say no and stick with it if you truly don't want to do something. Pent-up resentment is stressful.
- Learn to manage your time constructively and to schedule well enough so you aren't rushing through life. Make time for relaxing, pleasurable activities. If you are a workaholic or a person who is always in a hurry, attempt to change. Add variety to your daily routine. Slow down and smell some roses.
- Escape from stressors periodically. Physical and mental changes of scene offer temporary respite.
- Express your feelings and begin to communicate and share more with others.
- Find a reliable support system. Write in a journal or diary. Studies confirm the value of expressing stressful thoughts to others or getting them down on paper (Pennebaker, 1991).
- Have a good relieving cry. Find someone to hug and a pet to love.
- Develop a healthy degree of self-efficacy and an internal locus of control.
- Schedule pleasurable activities and engage in them often. Laugh and enjoy life. Engage in an enjoyable hobby or diversion. Don't take most things so seriously.
- Breathe deeply and frequently into the diaphragm. Slow, regular, and deep breaths, characteristic of abdominal breathing, are associated with physical calm (Eliot and Breo, 1984). See directions in REFLECTIONS AND APPLICATIONS.
- Keep your body well rested, nourished with nutritious food and water, and in the best possible health.
- Raise your self-esteem level. According to Lazarus (1966), low self-esteem is related to reactions to stress.
- Engage in a type of regular exercise. Select something you enjoy and stick with it, or try something new.
- Use a deep-relaxation technique and learn biofeedback.

Along with deep breathing, the last two are among my favorite methods. Exercise has become a popular antidote for stress, and the benefits have been confirmed (Cooper, 1982; Fuenning, 1981; Leatz and Stolar, 1993). Female high school students with stress from moving or a romantic breakup who did not exercise reported high levels of illness and discomfort, while those with similar stressors who had exercised regularly suffered from much less illness (Fischman, 1988).

Exercise offers other stress-reducing benefits such as relief of depression, reduction in the risk of heart disease and infection, an increase in the level of high-density lipoprotein (HDL), or "good" cholesterol, possible prevention of cancer, improvement in quality of sleep, and slowing of the aging process (Koontz, 1988). Another is a more pleasing appearance. When asked to identify the everyday hassles in life, middle-aged people listed weight as their main concern (Lazarus, 1981). Doesn't it seem likely that exercise would do much to alleviate this problem, thus reducing stress? Even if you don't engage in a full-scale aerobic exercise program, try walking, an activity that has earned much praise for its stress-reducing benefits. A longitudinal study of nearly 17,000 Harvard University alumni showed that stress symptoms decreased among subjects who were physically active. In addition, risk of death among male participants who walked 9 or more miles a week was 21 percent lower than for those who walked less than 3 miles (Elmer-DeWitt, 1986). Enthusiastic walkers talk as much about the relaxation benefits as they do the physical benefits. Nothing keeps most people from becoming more physically active except their own thoughts. You have the power to change yours. Take those extra 10 minutes over a lunch period and walk. A medical examination before you begin any strenuous program is suggested. If reduction in stress and other listed benefits are not motivational enough, consider that you can feel better, have more energy, and save money on medical bills. The time spent exercising could be the wisest investment you'll ever make.

"Give me an hour of your time because what I want to show you could make all the difference in the world," said Andrea Sime, a friend of mine and a biofeedback and stress-management specialist. She suggested this after learning that I was facing surgery for removal of what would, in all probability, be a cancerous eye tumor. I gave her the hour, and I am tremendously grateful to her for introducing me to biofeedback and deep-relaxation techniques and teaching me that I can change my physiological reactions to stress.

Progressive relaxation is one method of *deep relaxation* which is:

> a profoundly restful condition in which one feels physically relaxed, somewhat detached from the immediate environment, and usually to some extent even from body sensations. It involves a feeling of voluntary and comfortable abandonment of one's conscious control and stewardship over major body functions—a distinctly passive attitude in which one simply turns over control of the body to its own built-in "autopilot" (Albrecht, 1979, p. 191).

Why would one want to do this? Besides a wonderful feeling, as Andrea describes it, deep relaxation allows the body to become balanced, or homeostatic, and, thus, work as it is intended to. This may explain why relaxation is the most powerful proven behavioral therapy to reduce high blood pressure without drugs (Eliot and Breo, 1984).

One of the first to enlighten society about protection from "overstress" was Herbert Benson (1975), a physician and associate professor of medicine at the Harvard Medical School. He taught and wrote about the relaxation response and since then has added what he calls the principle of the maximum mind with noteworthy results. The use of these techniques led to a significant increase in examination grades. Elementary school students who used meditation, relaxation techniques, and concentration scored higher on standard achievement tests. Their increased calmness reduced their levels of anxiety and stress and increased their learning skills (Benson, 1987). Another study using a meditation technique successfully reduced symptoms of anxiety and panic (Kabat-Zinn et al., 1992).

In addition to progressive relaxation and meditation, methods that produce similar results are self-hypnosis, yoga, guided imagery, and autogenic training. "Individuals remain awake and alert and remember all that occurs; there are no mystical and magical words, symbols, or phrases. The control of and responsibility for the person is ultimately in his or her own hands" (Miller, 1978, p. 3). Patience is beneficial. "Relaxation and meditation are perhaps especially difficult for Americans. Our constant mental diet of advertising, noise, violence, and media stimulation makes it very difficult to endure even a few minutes of inactivity and quiet" (Siegel, 1986, p. 148). Being taught, then employing a technique for only about 15 to 20 minutes on a regular basis can produce astonishing results. Most people report feeling buoyant, energetic, exuberant, optimistic, cheerful, and kindlier (Albrecht, 1979). The effects of stress on the body seem remarkably diminished.

Relaxation exercises are frequently used in *biofeedback training*; a person learns to regulate physiological responses such as muscle tension, peripheral skin temperature, and heart rate. Through the use of monitoring equipment, an individual becomes aware of changes within the body and then discovers how to control the changes using relaxation. In addition to lowering stress reactions, biofeedback has been used successfully to treat hypertension, heart arrhythmia, epilepsy, chronic pain, tension, migraine headaches (Runck, 1980), and irritable bowel syndrome (Adessa, 1989).

> In biofeedback research we are beginning to see that almost any internal process that can be monitored and fed back (so that a person can see what is happening inside his or her body) can be controlled, at least to some extent consciously (Norris and Porter, 1987, p. x).

If an organic basis for an ailment has been ruled out, a strong recommendation is to see a biofeedback specialist.

Mind-Body Connection

Could healthy stress management lead to better health? A mind-body model suggests that the type of stress that lends itself to depression and despair can set the stage for cancer growth. A research team (Simonton, Matthews-Simonton, and Creighton, 1978) used psychological interventions with medically incurable patients and noted that a number of them improved and were living longer and better lives. This finding led the team to propose a mind-body model of recovery. Psychological intervention (relaxation, visualization techniques, and perception-changing) reduced stress, decreased feelings of depression, and helped patients feel more hopeful. This made cancer regression possible. Witnessing and being personally involved with these techniques at the Cancer Education and Support Center in Menlo Park, California was a fascinating and affirming experience for my husband and me. We discovered that relaxation, meditation, and optimism do boost healing powers (Myers, 1992).

A number of authors have written about the mind-body connection. "There is an undeniable, even if somewhat mysterious, interaction of body and mind. Anxiety can precipitate an attack of asthma. I am personally convinced that health is basically an inner attitude" (Powell, 1976, p. 61). Others have demonstrated miraculous recoveries (Cousins, 1979, 1983; Norris and Porter, 1987). The link between stress, attitude, emotions, and the immune system is being confirmed by research (Cousins, 1989). Some remain skeptical, and ongoing studies are carefully scrutinizing the impact on the immune system of stress, emotions, thoughts, and psychological hardiness.

Several recommendations in this book—having a positive attitude, taking responsibility for self, developing an inner locus of control, expressing emotions constructively, building self-esteem and self-efficacy, and changing irrational, negative thoughts—are related to the mind-body connection and to stress reduction. Stress will be a part of your life; by learning about it and taking charge, you can make a positive difference in your health and well-being.

COPING WITH CRISIS

My sister-in-law sounded numb when she called at 3:30 in the morning. "Steven was killed in an automobile accident about midnight. A drunk driver going over 80 miles an hour on the wrong side of the highway hit his car head-on." I managed to gasp, "Oh, no" as a jolt of disbelief and horror hit. Steve, my beloved 22-year-old nephew, was dead. The grieving began at that moment, and years later the sorrow remains, diminished somewhat by time, coping strategies, and beautiful memories.

The death of a loved one is a profound tragedy. Losing a child is the ultimate crisis. Not only is there a loss of a precious life, but a young person's death seems so unfair and unthinkable. It was supposedly Albert Camus who explained: "The order of nature is reversed. Children are supposed to bury their parents" (Stearns, 1984, p. 15). A child's death is not only the pain of losing a person; it means a loss of parents' dreams, a part of themselves, and a part of their future (Davis, 1991). A child's death is "like having part of ourselves sliced away" (Sanders, 1992, p. 120).

Steven's tragic death began a series of crises for my family. Within a little over a year I underwent cancer surgery and was fitted with an artificial eye, my 16-year-old daughter experienced a prolonged illness and surgery as a result of a rare blood disorder, and my father died unexpectedly. I was beginning to believe what I had read on a greeting card: "Into every life some rain must fall" and on the inside: "followed by large hail and damaging winds." On a positive note, these crises led to personal learning and can now provide hope, encouragement, and suggested coping strategies to you.

The Path of Life

"Life is difficult," writes Peck (1978, p. 15). "The farther one travels on the journey of life, the more births one will experience, and therefore the more deaths—the more joy and the more pain" (p. 75). As an introduction to my human relations course, I draw on the chalkboard a line depicting life. What do you think it looks like? It's not a straight line, nor is it vertical or horizontal, and neither does it go up for a period of years (maybe 39?) and then head downhill. The "dip 'n doo" line, as I call it, goes up and down like a series of peaks and valleys. The drawing reveals the certainty of change. "Life, at its best, is a flowing, changing process in which nothing is fixed. When life is richest and most rewarding, it is a flowing process" (Rogers, 1961, p. 27). Life has both positive and negative experiences from which we can't escape. "Life for me is like an ocean, with waves sometimes high, sometimes low, sometimes smooth, sometimes rough" (Satir, 1978, p. 91).

What can the line teach? The word *choice* comes readily to mind. All of us will spend time in the valleys, and it's important to remember that you aren't helpless at that time. What are your choices? One is to make the situation worse. Tragedy can become more tragic because of one's thoughts or actions, or both. Kurt was badly injured in an accident. He had not used alcohol much before; now its effects seemed to lessen the hurt. He was frequently verbally abusive to his family. His actions hurt both himself and those he loved. Another possibility is to remain stagnant, do little, and maybe wallow in self-pity. The thought, "There's nothing I can do about this" is common. The best choice is to gather your resources and strength and begin to ascend from the valley. Recognizing the pattern of the lifeline reminds you that dips eventually curve upward.

Another relevant point has to do with learning. Joyful and peaceful times are too often unappreciated. "I look back on those days before I was ill and kick myself for not enjoying them more," reported a cancer patient. "Now I am grateful for each minute of life." Because we often take the peaks for granted, generally, less learning is experienced there. Valuable lessons are learned in the trenches, the dips of life. In one study, 85 percent of those who had been ill or in an accident indicated positive long-term effects (Lauer and Lauer, 1988). The variety of life's experiences adds depth and meaning to existence. "A full life will be full of pain. But the only alternative is not to live fully or not to live at all" (Peck, 1978, p. 133). Crises can be traumatic, yet the possibility of positive growth offers a beacon of hope.

> *Sometimes when the bottom falls out of our lives, we are set free. Loss can make artists of us all as we weave new patterns into the fabric of our lives.*
>
> —Charles Stephen

Kinds of Crises

Exactly what constitutes a crisis? What kinds of crises are possible? Any unexpected negative or positive event that dramatically changes your life is a *crisis*. Categories of crises include: new meaningful relationships, interpersonal and personal problems, social transitions (i.e., moving and travel), crucial decisions, and changes in philosophy. Women in a study reported a much higher percentage of interpersonal crises while men were twice as likely to mention crucial decisions (Lauer and Lauer, 1988).

Loss is commonly experienced in a crisis. Examples of these are: rape, chronic illness, the birth of a disabled child, and loss of a job, personal possessions, or a dream. Because the emotions and thoughts associated with loss are painful, coping will probably be more difficult. How long is the path to recovery, how much time will it take, are open to question.

> The length of time required for moving through a crisis depends largely on the circumstances. When a significant loss has us in its grip, a minimum of six months to a year is usually required for healing. Some aspects of the process continue into the second year. Resolution may not come until even later (Stearns, 1984, p. 19).

When a crisis of loss isn't resolved or healed, problems can emerge later. "Unresolved grief haunts us" (Kennedy, 1991, p. 12).

How to Cope

The coping mechanisms that will be most effective in a situation depend on the nature of the crisis. Some require less emotional, mental, and physical challenges than do others. Whenever a loss is involved, the following coping behaviors make the going easier, perhaps faster, and increase the possibility for growth.

Feel your feelings. An emotional response is inevitable in any crisis. Keep in mind that suppressed feelings can cause unwanted problems and almost never help the situation. You may be reluctant to express, especially if the feeling is an uncomfortable one for you. Depression is one of my least favorites. Going through an unwanted divorce was depressing, and the accompanying feelings of hopelessness and helplessness made it worse. Wanting to appear strong, I seldom let anyone see how I felt and even believed that I was doing a good job denying my feelings to myself. Knowing what I do now, I'm convinced that my body wasn't fooled.

> Any emotion that is repressed will eventually seek manifestation at a later date. What you resist emotionally, persists. And by experiencing the emotion I don't mean you need to act out the emotion. Simply feel the emotion fully (Ellsworth, 1988, p. 77).

Feeling the emotion goes beyond naming or talking about it. During my first cancer-center session I eagerly volunteered to be the first to tell my story. The leader stopped me after a few minutes and asked, "How did you *feel* about losing your eye?" I glibly put names to the feelings: anxious, sad. When she pressed me to actually feel what I felt, I found myself resisting. She said, "I don't think you have really dealt with that loss." To my surprise, I felt the tears coming. She asked me why losing an eye was so sad. Without thinking, I blurted out, "Because I have always been complimented on my blue eyes. My husband said it was one of the first things he noticed about me, and now one is gone." Both my husband and I cried then-a welcome release and a sure sign that until then we hadn't truly experienced the pain of the loss.

> Lean gently into your pain. You won't find it bottomless. Let yourself be with the pain. When it is at its worst and you feel it all, you're already starting to heal (Bloomfield and Kory, 1980, p. 268).

Release feelings. In any crisis, emotional expression is extremely therapeutic. Crying, deep breathing, hugging, and other types of touch are appropriate behaviors intended to relieve tension. Being touched is reassuring. I remember the horrible night I was told that there was a 98 percent probability that my eye tumor was cancerous. Crying was a welcome release; being held by my husband got me through the night.

The relaxation techniques described earlier can be quite soothing. Some audiotapes are designed to help people release feelings and then move on with their lives by accepting changes. Another possibility is to keep a journal. Writing your thoughts and feelings is relieving. I remember keeping a journal during several crises and feeling a release as the feelings seemed to move from inside me onto the paper. Often, when thoughts are put on paper, a person can begin to see "form in the chaos" (Kennedy, 1991, p. 29).

Another benefit may not be so obvious. One Sunday I wrote about my pleasant feelings and positive attitude. I noticed that on the previous Sunday I had been quite depressed. I thought, "It's hard to believe I felt that down." I was left with the assurance that more positives lay ahead.

Research supports the benefits of writing about problems. College graduates were asked to write for 20 minutes on 4 consecutive days about either superficial topics or traumatic events they hadn't shared with anyone. Amazingly, the blood samples of those who wrote about highly personal and upsetting experiences showed evidence of an enhanced immune response more than did the samples taken from the others. Even after 6 weeks, students who wrote about traumatic events continued to demonstrate the greatest improvement in health (Moss, 1988). In another study, disclosing severe traumas led to health benefits (Greenberg and Stone, 1992).

Take charge of your thoughts. Your thoughts can help or hurt. The cognitive techniques are especially beneficial. Be aware of what you are thinking during a crisis. Is it realistic? If not, remember that you can change it. In both crises of divorce and cancer, I set out to find evidence to support positive thoughts. I found books about and living examples of people who had survived those experiences, and I filled my mind with hope. At times, discrediting someone else's opinion is necessary. One day I heard someone say, "The weeds in my yard are like a cancer. They just spread and spread, and there's absolutely nothing you can do about it." I said to myself, "Oh, yes, there are many things you can do about cancer." Thought stopping becomes a lifesaver. When a dreary, anxiety-provoking thought appears, tell yourself to stop and replace it with a positive one.

Acceptance of reality and realization of what you cannot change are healthy. "My husband no longer loves me and wants a divorce," "My child is addicted to drugs," "I have a serious disease," "My mother is dead," "I lost my leg in a farm accident" are difficult to think about, yet, as facts, they need to be acknowledged so they can be dealt with. Denial is usually a first reaction, and it helps absorb the shock. After a time, denial is unhealthy. After the pain has been experienced, the next step may be to ask a challenging question. I remember standing in front of a mirror one morning and saying, "OK, you are going to be divorced. What are you going to do now?" The statement freed me to move on with my life, and the question forced me to take action. Recognizing and then acting upon what you can do will make any crisis easier to bear.

Become educated. Educating yourself about any topic related to the crisis can make a positive difference. Libraries and bookstores contain many resources on coping and offer positive examples of those who "have gone before you." Decide how much you want to know, ask questions, and reframe your thinking in a positive direction. It's important to note, though, that too much obsession isn't advisable. Thinking and talking only about your crisis is not only unhealthy, it is likely to "turn off" others.

Seek support. Isolating yourself for a long period of time during any crisis is not a good idea because, more than ever, support is necessary. Family and friends can be comforting and helpful; however, they may need guidance. Letting them know what you need and want as well as what you don't want is wise. A woman in a cancer support session reported that her family had descended upon her when they learned of her diagnosis. They were overly helpful and refused to let her do anything even though she could. Without understanding, they were contributing to her helpless, out-of-control feelings. She decided to tell them to stop doing certain things for her because helplessness and lack of control could make her condition worse. The book *The Healing Family* (Simonton, 1984) is an excellent resource for families dealing with illness. The author writes: "So often family members, even those with the best intentions, give the wrong kind of support, which sometimes hurts more than it helps" (p. 2). Friends and family can be asked to carry out tasks, talk, listen, touch, or just be there. Tell them what you want.

Support groups made up of others who have had similar crises are an invaluable source of help. Mutual-help groups that empower an individual to cope can strengthen self-esteem. If you have any reservations about seeking support, you are probably equating it with being weak. Instead, believe that you *deserve* help and that you are showing internal strength by seeking and responding to external support (Chellis, 1992). An immediate benefit is the realization that you are not "different" and weren't singled out for this particular hardship. Education and a safe place to vent feelings are necessary ingredients of worthwhile groups. "Support groups are especially life affirming. Each member becomes a symbol of hope" (Lagrand, 1991, p. 217). A partial listing is given at the end of this and other chapters. Most telephone directories list support groups in a special section, or you can check with directory assistance. You may need courage to pick up the phone or attend a meeting, yet the benefits almost always outweigh any initial discomfort. "Buried feelings fester. Shared feelings enrich and lead to growth and healing" (Smolin and Guinan, 1993, p. 164).

Professional help is frequently needed, and you don't have to be feeling desperate to seek it. Any one of several reasons could motivate you. You may not be receiving needed support from family, friends, and groups. Therapy could move you along faster in a healing process. Seeking help is not an indication of illness; it's a sign of having the strength and determination to care well for ourselves (Stearns, 1984, p. 137). Think of therapy as a way of clearing up confusions, encouraging a sense of self-worth, and an avenue toward growing and changing, a kind of "emotional penicillin" (LeShan, 1990).

Words of caution about selecting a counselor are in order. Be as careful as you would in choosing any medical specialist. Don't just pick a name out of the yellow pages. Use suggestions given in the earlier discussion about depression. Ask people for recommendations. Feel free to interview a few counselors and find out their level of expertise, their degree of familiarity with your particular crisis, and, most important, how much rapport you have with them. Then, if you aren't satisfied with the counselor, find another one.

Be extra kind to yourself. Taking good care of yourself is good advice any time; during a crisis, it is of utmost importance. Some studies show that widows and widowers have a higher mortality rate than their married counterparts and that the possibility of the survivor's dying increases significantly following the death of a spouse. Neglect of the survivor's own health may be a factor (Kaprio et al., 1987). If unresolved stress does affect one physically, it stands to reason that during periods of unusual strain, our bodies will suffer. Eating well even if you don't feel like it, exercising, and getting plenty of rest become even more important. Rest is the number one prescription for any physical or emotional injury (Bloomfield and Kory, 1980). You can also pamper yourself without feeling guilty. Those ice cream cones I ate during my cancer surgery recovery I deserved!

Stay active and set goals. Even though a crisis generally depresses your system so that motivation is lacking, activity is a reassuring measure. Even simple tasks such as showering, brushing your teeth, and making coffee can be energizing. Pleasurable activities divert your thinking temporarily and convince you that life can still be enjoyed. A change of scene is especially refreshing. A few months after my first husband asked for a divorce, my daughters and I traveled to San Jose, California, to visit my sister. The trip itself and the time I spent there bolstered my spirits immensely. I thought, "There's a big world out here just waiting for me to explore, and it's filled with beautiful people and enjoyable activities."

Sometimes a death opens doors. As a 54-year-old widow, Bernice decided to attend college and acquire career skills. She discovered a new person within herself and thoroughly enjoyed her learning experiences. Others become involved in volunteer work, refresh their talents, learn skills, and acquire new hobbies and interests. Setting goals goes hand in hand with optimism. If you set a goal, you are saying that you can move beyond the crisis, your thinking becomes more directed, you are acting upon life rather than being acted upon, and you are sending positive messages to your body. Goals stimulate feelings of hope and anticipation and are a reinvestment in life. Delaying major decisions, however, is wise as your judgment will probably be clouded for awhile. Ways of setting goals, beneficial in all aspects of life, are covered in Chapter 5.

Death: The Ultimate Crisis

Any crisis is challenging; however, the death of a loved one is identified as most stressful (Holmes and Rahe, 1967). This could be because death is often so unexplainable and includes other losses, as well. Judy Mize, a dear friend whose husband died unexpectedly, expressed it so well. "It's so hard. Relationships don't die with death. I still have a relationship with Paul; yet, Paul isn't here to have a relationship with." Rita, a widowed student, reflected:

> I have come to realize there are many more losses tied to John's death. I lost my husband, my life-time partner, my best friend, and my son's father. Resulting losses from his death included leaving my job and moving from Virginia. I felt I had lost myself along with John. The "me" that was, was no more. She was gone forever.

Death is a universal crisis because all of us, unless we die before every other person we care about, will face this loss. "One out of one dies. Nothing, no one, lives forever. All things end at some point" (Sims, 1985, p. 1). Because death is considered such a taboo subject, most people try to avoid it in their thinking and talking. Unfortunately, this avoidance means that coping strategies are not being developed.

> Americans tend to have a negative attitude about grieving, feeling that it is something we should get over with as soon as possible. Grief, whether our own or that of someone in our social or business life, is an inconvenience, an interruption in our hectic schedules. We harbor many misconceptions about the grief process and scarcely comprehend or appreciate its value and purpose (Vail, 1982, p. 52).

Grief is an emotional, physical, spiritual, and intellectual response to loss (Edwards, 1989) and the way to heal from pain. Even though grief is the hardest work we will ever have to do, we must "go through to get through" (Edwards, 1989, p. 16). How long the process takes isn't certain. In one study, 92.4 percent of the participants reported a duration of 1 year or more (Vickio et al., 1990). A low spot for many comes at 6 months (Farberow et al., 1992). Knowledge of and an active involvement in the grief process can prepare you for and reduce the pain of the most stressful experience of all. "The pain of mourning is a horrible thing, but it is the only door through which healing can begin" (Donnelley, 1987, p. 44).

Stages of grief. The pioneer of death and dying research, Elisabeth Kübler-Ross (1969) identified five stages associated with final acceptance of death: denial, anger, bargaining, depression, and acceptance. Her stage theory has led to a closer look at the grieving process. Others have suggested similar processes (Ginsburg, 1987; James and Cherry, 1988; Sanders, 1992; Tubesing, 1981). The basic theme is that grieving is a series of somewhat predictable thoughts, feelings, and behaviors that are subject to individual differences.

Each stage has its challenges and its usefulness. Denial, the instant shock and disbelief in the face of tragedy, is initially a protector. Judy, after the sudden and unexpected death of her husband Paul, said, "I am so grateful for the denial part." Anger, even if incomprehensible at the time, may allow a bereaved person to vent deep feelings. And depression, which is so unpleasant, can indicate that one is approaching the acceptance stage.

Understanding the basic stages can help you see where you are in the process and why you feel as you do. A student read a book about dealing with death for a class project. Her comment was, "Until now I didn't understand what I went through when my mother died. It was over a year ago, and the book still helped me see that it's normal to feel what I do." A college classmate of mine hinted at the stage process in a lovely book she wrote for her two children before her untimely death in 1976.

> When you are very close to someone who dies, there will be sadness. You won't be sharing your life with that person anymore. Sadness hurts. You may feel as though a big hole has been torn in your life. And there will probably be feelings of loneliness as you remember the good times you had with the person you loved. Sometimes it takes a very long time for the sadness to melt away, but slowly you will begin to remember important shared times without the hurt tugging at your memories (Potter, 1979, p. 12).

Do you ever get over the death of a loved one? Most experts say that you don't. You do, however, arrive at an acceptance stage when you can look back with an altered feeling.

> The rainbow hues of your grief—the red-yellow anguish, the blue-green questions, the purple confidence—are woven permanently into the tapestry of your life. Grief invariably leads to new strengths. When you allow yourself to experience fully the subtle gradations of its colors and textures, grief adds to your personal richness and depth (Tubesing, 1981, p. 57).

Thinking only in terms of stages has some disadvantages. People can get discouraged if they believe they should progress in a certain order and time frame. More helpful is to think of the process as a "fluid experience of a variety of emotions with one underlying theme: coming to terms with the loss" (Davis, 1991, p. 13).

Behaviors of grief. Has anyone said to you, "Don't grieve when I'm gone. I don't want you to cry about my death"? Although the remark was well meant, the person isn't doing you a favor. Expressing your sorrow is in your best interests. You may think as a young mother did, "Crying may be good for me, but my children have lost a father, and I have to be strong for them." As mentioned before, we would be better served by getting rid of the equation between strength and hiding our feelings. Most experts would agree that a good thing a widowed mother could do for her children would be to model grieving behaviors and share her sorrow. Widowed individuals in southern Germany who did not grieve had problems with psychological adjustment (Stroebe and Stroebe, 1991). To grieve means that you care, that you loved the person who has died. "Grief is the price we pay for love. Though death comes, love will never go away" (Sims, 1985, p. 6).

A new understanding of grief is emerging from research. As a culture, we have handled grief badly. Even though crying is what is expected in a tragic situation, some do all they can to hold back the tears. Others seem to have tear ducts that are closed. If we learned to withhold tears, we can also give ourselves permission to let them come. Knowing the benefits of crying, each of us could help ourselves by unlearning and relearning.

Grief can be tremendously unsettling. Many times death is irrational, illogical, and crazy so a reaction which can feel like the "crazies" is normal (Donnelley, 1987). "Significant emotional loss is an abnormal event in a person's life, and there is no normal way to react to an abnormal event" (James and Cherry, 1988, p. 11). Anxiety and depression are common emotions (Sable, 1991), and the reactive depression may be accompanied by the same symptoms as experienced in chemical depressions (Fieve, 1989).

Even though grief is painful, like death, it is a part of life. Experiencing all of life means that you and I will grieve.

> I don't like being hurt. I don't really enjoy experiencing pain. But I believe that I become less of a human being if I learn the art of detachment so well that I can experience the death of a friend or relative and not be emotionally affected by it. To be alive is to feel pain, and to hide from pain is to make yourself less alive (Kushner, 1986, p. 89).

Grief research has shown gender differences in the process. Men and women share equal feelings of pain and grief, yet women seem to use their social support system while many men either do not have one or don't use it. Women reported receiving more support in their grieving for any type of death (Farberow et al., 1992). In a study about death of a marriage partner, widowers were more likely to feel lonely and depressed and were less willing to discuss their feelings. During times when husbands and wives need each other's support, the differences can cause problems. A high percentage of marriages break up after pregnancy losses (Cole, 1988). Of benefit would be to learn from each other. Men then could connect more with others and be more expressive, and women could become more decisive, independent, and task-oriented as they put their lives back together. "It would seem what matters most is not who suffers more but how we can learn to help one another to suffer less" (p. 61).

Other differences have to do with cause of death. Suicides appear to be the most difficult. Survivors of suicide report low levels of social support (Wagner and Calhoun, 1992), significantly lower than that for natural death survivors (Farberow et al., 1992) or more variability in support (Thompson and Range, 1993). In addition to depression, guilt is the most intense emotion for parents. They first blame themselves than another (Smolin and Guinan, 1993). After a child's suicide, 92 percent of parents experienced guilt, and 34 percent reported it as the most distressing aspect (Miles and Demi, 1992).

A disturbing study of adolescents revealed that friendship with a suicide attempter was a marker of vulnerability to emotional problems and, perhaps, suicide itself (Hazell and Lewin, 1993). This reminded me of a student's deep anxiety when she said, "I feel so guilty and depressed about his death from suicide, I've thought about just doing it myself." After listening to her distress, I was relieved that I could recommend some excellent books and resources (see References). Because there was so little about those left behind, two authors wrote a book in which they point out that for every suicide about 7 to 10 others are intimately affected. Immediately finding a therapist who is an excellent listener is strongly recommended. It can also help parents to keep in mind that they can do a thousand things for a child but perhaps not a thousand and one (Lukas and Seiden, 1987).

Research supplies several answers to what helps during a grieving process including: hardiness, covered earlier as a protection against stress (Campbell et al., 1991), involvement of people and emotional support (Lund and Caserta, 1992; Vickio et al., 1990), and memorial contributions, especially those that further medical research (Euster, 1991). "It's as if his life had even more meaning," is how one person expressed it. Feeling a need to talk to others about the death of their child was acknowledged by 89 percent of parents who were surveyed (Ponzetti, 1992). Silence only increases pain. A creative suggestion is to go through a short, focused period each day when you give full attention to your grief in a "sanctuary," a special place you set aside for that purpose (Kennedy, 1991). Equally important is a recommendation to give the mind a mini-vacation from pain by concentrating on something else in the landscape of life (Edwards, 1989).

Writing about the deceased is therapeutic. After my nephew's death, I asked anyone who knew him to contribute letters describing memorable times, poems, and tributes to a booklet in his memory. One classmate, in praising Steve's lust for life, his caring, giving ways, and his accomplishments, offered solace with: *The donation of life, more than the duration, is significant; length of one's life is less important than the beauty of one's life.* I completed the project a year after his death, experiencing further emotional release because of it, and at the end wrote:

> Because of Steve, we have all loved, cried, shared, and grown. Our lives are all the better for his having lived. I continue to grieve because Steve deserves each tear I shed.

Writing a tribute to the person who has died can serve a dual purpose. Amy Sheil, a student, used an original poem to release her feelings and extol her father after he died.

I Love You, Dad

Theodore Alan Sheil was my Father.
I think he was the greatest man
to ever be on this earth.
He was kind, considerate and he always
wanted to do things for other people.
I want, more and more, to be like him
in almost every way.
I wish he was here now
to see what I am doing with my life.
Sometimes I feel cheated,

I didn't get to know him
as long as everybody else did.
The time I did know him was very special to me.
He got struck with a horrible illness called cancer.
He was very strong, and this was probably
the time when I learned the most I could
about how special he was and also how strong.
I tried to be there for him
as much as I could, but it scared me
to think of losing him,
so I ran away from it.
All I did was try to have fun with my friends
and try to still be there for him some of the time.
I do have so many good memories of him and of the family,
but it seems so empty now without him.
It's like a part of the family
died with him.
I thought he was so handsome and so special.
I thought he would never die.
It's unfair to Mom, too.
They were married for a long time
and they still acted like
they were on their honeymoon.
So much in love.
I hope I have a marriage like that one day;
at least they gave me a good example.
Now, my thoughts are all jumbled
But I want to put my feelings on paper,
so I can read this years from now
and know how I felt in my 18th year of life.

During the final work on this edition, the father of a friend of my daughter's since grade school died suddenly. Susan Brown's beautiful poem touched all of us at his funeral.

He Wasn't Plain Vanilla

A man of many stories
As you know
He loved to tell them.
Now, reflecting on his life
I remember a story he loved
About who he was
through my eight-year-old eyes
after a visit to the ice cream store:
"I'm sure glad you're not a plain vanilla dad,"
I said to him.
But he already knew.
Because he loved tucking us in at night,
Teaching us to sail,
Making cheesy scrambled eggs on weekends
Taking us to movies, the zoo, and the ranch.
He never got tired of playing "Bet You Can't Make Us Laugh, Dad"

And he always won.
He passed on his love of music, cooking, learning,
and people of all kinds.
Never did we come
or go
without kisses and hugs.
He was not a plain vanilla dad.

He was not a plain vanilla friend.
Always had a joke
Or two, or three.
He loved to make folks laugh.
His house was always open
to his friends
for a movie, a boat ride,
his cooking, or a talk,
And often, all of the above.

He was not a plain vanilla man.
To his family and friends
He gave a lifetime of love
And his stories are ours
Through which he lives on.
His spirit
His flavor in our lives
Anything—but plain vanilla.

I hope Susan, Amy, and all of us who have grieved remember:

> We never lose the people we love, even to death. They continue to participate in every act, thought, and decision we make. Their love leaves an indelible imprint in our memories. Memories make us immortal (Buscaglia, 1992, p. 230).

Other creative talents such as composing a song or just singing one in memory or tribute, painting, sculpting, or drawing are all ways of releasing. A tragedy can result in worthwhile actions, and becoming involved in a cause related to the death is an excellent idea. Mothers Against Drunk Driving (MADD), an organization that has made a significant difference, was started by a woman whose daughter was killed by a drunk driver. My nephew Steve's death launched a campaign at Bowling Green State University called "Never Again" to combat drunk driving. Grief can be channeled into positive energy. To gain insight into stress, crisis, and coping in your life, use the Chapter 4 activity in REFLECTIONS AND APPLICATIONS.

Practical tips for helping yourself through grief can be found in any of the books cited in this chapter. At some point—and only the grieving person can decide when that point has been reached—moving on with life is essential. "Life still offers us many opportunities if we but permit ourselves to be an open channel" (Ward, 1989, p. 17). At that time you may be able to see that death can be a teacher and help us appreciate each other, ourselves, and life itself. Realizing that death will occur can increase awareness of the importance of living life abundantly and the wonder of each moment. Adolescents who experienced the death of a peer reported that they became closer to other friends, shared feelings more freely, took time to tell people that they cared, wore their seat belts, spent more time with and became closer to family, joined Students Against Drunk Drivers (SADD), and decreased or stopped use of alcohol (Schachter, 1992). "An awareness of death increases my appreciation of the preciousness of life. The glory of life is inseparable from the fact that it is finite" (Branden, 1983, p. 200).

> *Life—a lovely, lively flame dancing inside us. At death, the dancing stops. But the special feeling for the person we loved never stops.*
>
> —Linda Lytle Potter

Coping with any kind of crisis is challenging. We have received little training in this regard. Learning coping behaviors before they are necessary is a sound idea. The realization that life's richness consists of both joy and sorrow, both triumph and tragedy, is basic to learning to cope. Viewing crises as possibilities for growth diminishes their negative impact.

SUMMARY

The emotional self is interesting, complicated, and challenging, and confusion is common. An emotion has three components: awareness, physiological arousal, and expression. Researchers have been helpful in identifying and categorizing emotions. The behavioral component, expression of feelings, is the most controllable of the three. Expression is learned from a variety of sources. The American society is generally less expressive than others. Men, especially, receive restrictive messages.

All four developmental areas are strengthened by constructive emotional expression; self-esteem is also bolstered. Relationships thrive on open, honest, and constructive expression. For many, demonstration of feelings is not easy yet can be developed.

You can change emotions by altering your thoughts and behaviors through rational-emotive therapy, neurolinguistic programming, and control theory. This is beneficial when emotions are unpleasant and causing harm. In clinical depression, therapy is highly recommended. Suicide is the tragic outcome of many cases of deep depression.

Stress cannot be avoided and can be harmful. Stressors can be externally caused by major life events and everyday hassles outside our control or by internal factors. Stress that is good for you is called eustress. Research into the mind-body connection has shed new light on the importance of dealing positively with stress and has opened pathways to a holistic approach to health and healing. Daily management of stress is viewed as essential for optimal health and well-being.

Crises of any kind create stress and can wreak havoc on the emotional self. Loss is a common thread in most crises. Specific strategies can lessen the impact and help you resolve the crisis faster, reduce thc harmful effects, and use the situation for positive growth. Death, which affects everyone, is the ultimate crisis. Grief, while not welcome, is necessary on the road to recovery. The death of a person you care about is a dreadfully painful experience. You can cope and, in some cases, use the tragic event to improve your own life and make needed changes in society.

> *The full and free experience and expression of all our feelings are necessary for personal peace and meaningful relationships.*
>
> —John Powell

RESOURCES

- Human Service Directories (included in most telephone directories) will list agencies and support groups dealing with almost all situations.
- National Self-Help Clearinghouse, 25 W. 43rd St., Room 620, New York, NY 10036, (212) 642-2944 (listing of self-help groups)
- Emotions Anonymous, P.O. Box 4245, St. Paul, MN (for anyone wanting to learn to deal with emotions)
- Recovery, Inc., 802 N. Dearborn, Chicago, IL (for symptoms of nervousness/stress)
- Depressives Anonymous: Recovery from Depression, 329 E. 62nd St., New York, NY 10021, (212) 689-2600
- Suicide Prevention Hotline, 1-800-333-4444 or 1-800-882-3386
- American Psychiatric Association, 1400 K St. NW, Washington, DC 20005, (202) 682-6000
- American Psychological Association, 750 First St. NE, Washington, DC 20002-4242, (202) 336-5700
- National Association of Social Workers, 750 First St. NE, Washington, DC 20002, (202) 408-8600
- The National Institute of Mental Health, 5600 Fishers Lane, Rockville, MD 20857, (202) 955-7600
- National Depressive and Manic-Depressive Association, 730 North Franklin Street, Suite 501, Chicago, IL 60610, (312) 642-7243
- The Hudson Center for Brief Therapy, 11926 Arbor St., Omaha, NE 68144, (402) 330-1144
- The Menninger Clinic, P.O. Box 829, Topeka, KS 66601-0829 (mental health)
- Cancer Education and Support Center, 1035 Pine Street, Menlo Park, CA 94025, (415) 327-6166 (cancer support and education programs)
- Compassionate Friends, P.O. Box 1347, Oak Brook, IL, (312) 323-5010 (for bereaved parents)
- Rainbows for All God's Children, 111 Tower Road, Schaumburg, IL (for children and adults who have experienced death, divorce, separation, or abandonment)
- Widowed Persons Service, 1901 K St. N.W., Washington, DC, (202) 728-4370 (for widowed of all ages)
- Heartbeat, 2015 Devon St., Colorado Springs, CO 80909, (719) 596-2575 (for survivors of suicides)

5

Assessing Values, Wants, and Goals

OBJECTIVES

After completing this chapter, you will be able to

- Define values and list sources.
- Describe how the ego states can be involved in values.
- Explain why it is wise to evaluate your own values.
- Discuss Kohlberg's theory of moral development.
- Identify and give examples of the three methods and influences in receiving and learning values as described in value programming analysis.
- Explain the decade theory of values development and relate it to at least two decades.
- Name and describe two ways of transmitting values and tell why they are not recommended. Discuss recommended ways to impart values.
- Describe and give examples of reasons for a change in adult values.
- Differentiate between healthy and unhealthy values.
- Identify several choices in life that require decision-making abilities and a sense of values.
- Relate the three ego states to goals.
- Ask questions to check the likelihood of achieving a goal.
- Achieve your goals by using goal-completion criteria.
- Free yourself from chronic procrastination.

All values, when pushed too far, become demonic and destructive. Beliefs not examined, as the life not examined, are hardly worth having. Values held thoughtlessly are without substance.

—Charles Stephen

Would you lie to a friend?

Would you withhold hurtful information from a loved one?

Would you break a law?

Have you exceeded the speed limit?

If under age, would you drink alcohol? (Note that the last two are law-breaking behaviors!)

How much time do you spend with family members?

Do you want high grades?

If a cashier gave you too much change, would you say anything?

How often do you do favors for friends?

Your answers reflect *values* which are qualities, conditions, and standards that are desirable, worthy, and important. You may also name people, relationships, objects, and mental states as values because you hold them in esteem. Values coincide with beliefs about what is "good" and "just" and motivate us to act (Lewis, 1990).

Values are directly related to the kind of person you are and will be, goals and aspirations, behaviors, and to the quality of your relationships. Even though choices, decisions, and courses of action are based upon them, rarely are values examined. You may know your values; do you also know how they came to be and how they may change? Are your behaviors in harmony with what you value? This chapter will offer insight and suggest ways to clarify your values. Values, wants, and goals are related; the last part of the chapter explains how to get what you want out of life.

ORIGIN OF YOUR VALUES

You and I were not born with a set of values. They were given to us; we learned what was important. Remember "parent" messages from transactional analysis? Most values originate as verbal or nonverbal messages from others. Families play a dominant role, and other agents of socialization and institutions in society such as peers, schools, religion, government, and the media contribute. We learn the values of our culture through socialization.

Parents' values determine both the outcomes they want for their children and their parenting behaviors. Those who value conformity are apt to want good manners, neatness, cleanliness, actions that reflect how a boy or girl should behave, and obedience to parents, and insist that their children follow strict rules. On the other hand, parents who want self-directed and independent children will use a different parenting style. A study showed that these parents were higher in education and occupational self-direction and status and wanted children to have good sense, sound judgment, an interest in how things happen, responsibility, and consideration of others (Spade, 1991). Your values will affect your parenting behaviors just as your parents' values influenced how you were raised and what kind of person you are today.

Although some people and groups oppose discussion of morality in the classroom, schools in recent years have been encouraged to teach values. Many have successful projects that teach cooperation and character building, and support for moral education is growing (Smith, 1989b). Even if no programs exist, teachers, counselors, and coaches are influential. A powerful source of values is the media. Messages from television programs and advertisements bombard us. An example is a value on youth. Is it any wonder that, unlike other societies, the American society devalues aging? In addition, your own experiences have influenced your values and will continue to do so. For example, if you frequently seek and receive the support of friends, you likely place a high premium on friendship. If you have been hurt by dishonesty, you probably value honesty.

The parent ego state in TA has an important role in values. "Parent" messages did and continue to tell you what is of value. "A dollar saved is a dollar earned," "I owe all my success to always having been early," "Take your vitamins," and "Work hard and play later" are examples of value-laden messages. If, as a child, your parents buckled your seat belt and then fastened theirs, you received a subtle "this-is-important" message. Conflicting ideas can come from "parent" messages. "Our family values human equality and goodwill toward all people," you may have been taught. Then you come home with a new friend of a different race and receive a different message. Little wonder that you were sometimes confused.

The parent ego state now serves as a conscience and will admonish you when you act against your values. To Judith, religion was an important value, as it had been for her family. One week she was exhausted from a full schedule of work and classes; she overslept and missed the worship service. She could hear the inner voice chastising her for sinning. A powerful parent ego state can be a stern critic. A more balanced "parent" gives helpful advice about values. Even though conscience is generally thought to be the negative voice of tradition speaking within, a constrictor of one's activities, there are positive aspects of conscience—using it to tap wisdom and insight within. Conscience can be a guide to enlarged experience (May, 1953).

What is the role of the child ego state? Interestingly, different functions are possible. It can motivate you to enthusiastically behave according to your values. The "child" feels proud when your values and actions are in harmony and guilty when they are not. Because the "child" seeks and enjoys pleasure, tempting you to disregard a value is another possibility. Sexual morals can be sorely tested by the passionate "child."

The adult ego state has a major role in values clarification. On the road to becoming your own person, your "adult" questions current values embedded in the "parent," looks at alternatives, and makes valuative decisions based on your own thinking processes. Why is it important to question your present values? Let's assume that many of your values reflect those of your parents. Their values were possibly acquired from questionable sources and definitely developed during an earlier time in different environments and situations. Because personal values direct your life and could possibly influence the next generation, taking a critical look at them is advisable.

> Maybe one of the kindest things we can do for ourselves at this moment is to take a look at everything we believe in and ask ourselves if it really fits or is it something that we were told should fit. Is it a carryover from the past that we have accepted without any critical investigation? (Satir, 1978, p. 113).

Values become truly your own only when "parent" value messages have been processed through your "adult" and accepted. How do you know when this occurs? A way to check is to ask yourself, "Why do I believe or value this?" Henry, at age 75, attends mass every week without fail. One of his grandchildren asked him why he went to church even when he wasn't feeling well. He replied, "You're supposed to, so I do." Henry's value on religion and church attendance is based in his "parent." His wife, Helen, goes to church regularly, and she explains, "I value my religion and enjoy going to mass because I feel spiritually fulfilled afterward. I can miss and feel fine, too; however, I prefer to attend." Do you see the difference? Helen's is an "adult" value. When values become yours, they feel comfortable and are easier to act upon.

Going through a valuative process can be challenging, and people typically experience discomfort when confronted with possible change. If values were given to you by someone whose support is important, any deviation is difficult. Processing, however, is in your best interest. "Neither pride nor self-esteem can be supported by the pursuit of second-hand values that do not reflect who we really are" (Branden, 1992, p. 41). New thoughts and beliefs expand your horizons and encourage you to become your own person.

Values and morals are closely related. Morals are related to rightness or wrongness and are more specific than values. Just as personality and other areas of self develop in stages, so do values and morals. Because values and morals essentially guide your life, you can benefit from knowing how they evolved.

MORAL DEVELOPMENT STAGES

Research on values focuses on the way people think, not necessarily on how they behave. Moral judgment, or a sense of right and wrong, was traced by Kohlberg (1963), who presented short stories with moral dilemmas to individuals and then asked them what they thought the characters should do. Kohlberg was more interested in the reasoning behind the answers. One of his classic stories follows.

> In Europe, a woman was near death from a special kind of cancer. There was one drug that the doctors thought might save her. It was a form of radium that a druggist in the same town had recently discovered. The drug was expensive to make, but the druggist was charging ten times what the drug cost him to make. The sick woman's husband, Heinz, went to everyone he knew to borrow money, but he could only get together $1,000, which is half of what it cost. He told the druggist that his wife was dying, and asked him to sell it cheaper or let him pay later. But the druggist said, "No, I discovered the drug, and I am going to make money from it." So Heinz got desperate and broke into the man's store to steal the drug for his wife.

Consider how you would respond to questions such as, "Was Heinz justified in stealing the drug? Why?" "Should the druggist have been charging that much? Why?" "Which is worse—to steal or to let a loved one die? Why?" The *why* is the key.

The results led Kohlberg to identify three levels of moral development, each composed of two stages. The first level is *preconventional*, when rewards and punishments are most impressive. This is obvious in ideas expressed by young children: "I won't take her toy because the teacher will send me to the 'time-out' area." *Conventional* is the second level; individuals at this level conform because of social disapproval from peers or authorities, especially. "I'll take her book because the other kids think it's funny to tease her." Many adults are still at the conventional level. "I laughed at the racist joke because I wanted to be a part of the group" is an example of this kind of thinking. Authority is respected, and a law is a law and should be obeyed. Research shows that most people never progress beyond the conventional level (Conger and Peterson, 1984).

The highest level, *postconventional*, is based on moral principles. Those at the first stage of this level follow democratically accepted laws. They generally behave according to societal rules, yet are capable of seeing the arbitrary nature of laws. If they see a law as unfair, they usually work to change it. At the highest stage, which few people reach, individual principles take precedence; universal ethical ideas can supersede a law. Mahatma Gandhi and Martin Luther King were individuals who followed their own consciences and defied laws that they considered unjust.

RECEIVING AND LEARNING VALUES

During personal presentations and in the videotape "What You Are Is What You Were When," Dr. Morris E. Massey points out various methods and influences at different age periods. He calls this value programming analysis. Think about your own life as you look at Table 5-1 and read about his ideas.

The first stage is similar to both the psychodynamic and humanistic theories of personality and self-concept development in emphasizing the importance of early childhood. Transactional analysis, too, points out the power of "parent" messages during these years. Values programming analysis calls the earliest method of receiving values *imprinting*. Think of making an imprint of your foot in wet sand or imprinting a design on a shirt. Imprinting of values means that little children do almost no editing and receive values as absolutes.

You may be thinking of a 2-year-old who balks at what you say. "Eat your vegetables. They're good for you," a parent says. "No," is the typical reply, "I hate vegetables." Is the child rejecting the idea? Follow that child next door or to the day care center and listen as others are told, "You're supposed to eat your vegetables. They're good for you. My daddy says so." The message registered. Do you know people who eat everything on their plate even if they aren't hungry? Ask them why, and the response may be, "I was told to do it. I've done it all my life. You're supposed to." They're hanging onto a powerful early idea.

Little children are open to the values of people they trust and love. Think about this when you choose caregivers outside your family. Of all considerations, one of the most significant is the values they can instill. I smile when I remember the years I worked with preschool children. They looked upon me as almost a supreme being. "Teacher says—that's why" was a frequent comment. You may not remember exactly the time, but try to recall values messages that you received during that early period of life. "Our first map is usually made up of the one right way" (Satir, 1978, p. 112).

The second stage features a *modeling* method. The family remains influential; however, the child is looking outward, away from home. The role models could be older children, teachers, and local sports leaders; however, the primary influence comes

TABLE 5-1 Receiving and Learning Values

Chronological age (approximate)	Method	Influence (who/what is most influential)
1–6	Imprinting	Family, especially parents and significant caregivers
7–12	Modeling	"Heroes" and "stars," usually those in the media
13–19	Socialization	Peers

through the media. Because of the popularity of television, this stage may begin earlier than age 7 and overlap with the first. The principal role models are those in the movie and television industries and the sports world.

In 1982, Sydney J. Harris, a columnist, wrote about these models. He described a study in which 2000 eighth-grade American students were asked to name their top 30 heroes—the people they most admired and would want to be like when they grew up. Their leading role model was the screen actor Burt Reynolds, followed by entertainers and actors Richard Pryor, Alan Alda, Steve Martin, Robert Redford, and the late John Belushi, who died from complications of a drug overdose. All 30 were entertainers or sports figures, and only five women—all actresses or pop singers—were named, even though half the children polled were girls. Harris wrote the column because he was concerned that not one of the thirty had made a humanitarian contribution to the world (although some had been involved in worthy causes). He said, "Our heroes and heroines are not people who have done big things, but people who have Made It Big" (p. 6).

In a survey replicating Harris's, Trish Reimer and I asked the same question of 193 fifth and sixth graders in Lincoln Public Schools in 1993. Interestingly, even though they named most often athletes (54) and entertainers (23) for a total of 77, family members were listed by 60 children. Mothers were first with 19 and fathers close behind at 13. Others were siblings, grandparents, and aunts. Of the "stars," Michael Jordan with 15 responses was the most highly regarded individual. Reasons given were: (1) He's the best basketball player, (2) He can jump high, (3) He is rich and famous. Whitney Houston was named most often of the entertainers because (1) She sings so good, (2) She's beautiful.

Some of the answers given for admiring parents are worth savoring.

My dad because he is strong, he likes kids, he likes cars, he makes a lot of money. I really like him.

My mother because she is good with kids, has a great job, is creative, and has a good future planned out for me. She supports my family when we need help.

My dad because he knows math real well.

My mom because she is pretty and nice, and anybody that meets her becomes her friend. She knows how to have fun, and I love her very much.

My dad because he is such a good family man, a great lawn mower, and a real nice guy and the BEST DAD!

My mom because she's honest, nice, and fun to be with.

My grandfather because he's loyal, kind, caring, loving, trustworthy, reliable, a great man, and my grandfather. I love him deeply, and I'm thankful to have him.

Don't these answers leave you a warm feeling that the world is in fine shape with this future generation?

The survey indicates that children continue to be enamored with "stars." As a parent, I watched my children go through idolization phases, and I recall a few of my own. My philosophy was usually, "This, too, will pass," as the various posters showed up on walls and bulletin boards. And it always did, even though the star-struck stage sometimes continued into high school days. Can you remember some of your own idols from the preteen years? What did they represent, and how much influence did they have?

"Everyone else is doing it so I want to do it too" typifies the next method called *socialization*. The stock answer from generations of parents is, "If everyone else jumped off a cliff (or bridge), would you do it too?" Frankly, a teenager might! The adolescent period is a time of searching for an identity. Feeling a part of the group is critical and probably started before the teenage years. The *peer group*, those of your approximate age with whom you identify, has great influence. The peer environment, in one study, was found to be a crucial factor in adolescent smoking behavior (van Roosmalen and McDaniel, 1992). Other interesting research showed that black youths perceived less peer pressure and reported a lower need for peer approval than did whites (Giordano et al., 1993).

Regardless of race, adolescence can be a frightening, stressful time for both teenagers and parents. The young person will likely experiment with "in-vogue" behaviors and attitudes. If the peer group reflects most of the parents' values, this period can be relatively easy. Usually, though, at least some parental values are challenged. Parents can make this an easier time by being understanding and flexible. If the request is reasonable, parents who say emphatically, "I don't care what anyone else does. You aren't going to, and that is that," are setting the stage for added problems. Expecting a teenager to uphold all parental values and ideas if they are opposite those of a normal peer group is asking for supreme sacrifices and potential damage to self-esteem and the sense of belonging. According to at least two experts (Steinberg and Levine, 1990), adolescents generally choose friends whose values, attitudes, tastes, and families are similar to their own. They rarely go "bad" because of their friends.

Figure 5-1 Adolescents searching for an identity will seek to "fit in" with their peers.

Teenagers can help by understanding themselves and their parents and by being reasonable. Parental values are not necessarily wrong just because of their ownership, and rebelling just for the sake of being a rebel is neither mature nor healthy. Open communication and democratic discipline techniques (covered in later chapters) can make a major difference during this challenging time. Adolescents are more likely to make wise choices if they have parents who practice the values-development techniques described later in this chapter.

Societal influences are also part of value programming analysis. According to the theory, children at about the age of 10 become aware of events in the world and begin to incorporate these into their values systems; societal events continue to influence values throughout life. I refer to this as a *decade theory* because the framework is built around 10-year periods. Table 5-2 outlines one decade and one event.

Think about events during and since your 10-year-old decade. Do you recognize how they have affected you? Looking at various decades will also help you understand why people of other ages have dissimilar viewpoints. "Now I know why my grandmother does some of the crazy things she does!" exclaimed one student. Her grandmother might say the same about her granddaughter if she knew about the decade theory.

Comparing specific decades is interesting. For example, the major event of the 1940s was World War II. People who were 10 years old and older then are usually patriotic and, in many cases, fairly definite about right and wrong. The war demanded a united national effort, and almost all United States citizens had no question about the justness of their cause. Quite the opposite is true of the 1960s and 1970s, when the Vietnam conflict and the Civil Rights Movement split the nation followed by a sense of disillusionment resulting from the Watergate scandal and the resignation of President Richard Nixon. Thinking more in "gray" than in "black-and-white" and doubting the absolute rightness of a country or philosophy are more characteristic of individuals influenced by those decades.

What about 10-year-olds today? How might current events influence their values? The various conflicts throughout the world, unexplained violence, AIDS, advanced technology, divorce and remarriages, minority issues, and equal rights are only a few of the concerns with potentially powerful effects. Because the world is figuratively at their fingertips due to mobility and the media, few happenings escape the minds of young people today. One can be pessimistic about the problems or look at the challenges as opportunities.

Young people have several alternatives. They can "cop out" and value only their

TABLE 5-2 Decade Theory of Values Development

Birth decade	10-year-old decade	Significant events	Influence on values
1920s	1930s	The Great Depression	Conservation of money and resources Strong work ethic Government seen as an aid to the citizens

self-interests, or they can decide to take action and do what they can to solve societal problems. "We can become fatalistic and not allow ourselves to plan for our future, or we can continue living in the moment while designing a future, even if we do so with some anxiety" (Corey, 1986, p. 351). Being actively involved in society is as important today as it ever was, and this appears to be happening. Teenagers in 1992 were less materialistic and more concerned about social issues such as AIDS, drunk driving, drug abuse, and the environment than in 1988, according to a poll by Teenage Research Unlimited. A wise course for each of us is to value the moment because the future is unsure and then take action to make the tomorrows better.

Giving or Transmitting Values

Values are passed from one generation to another. The principal characters in this action are parents. How did your parents convey their values? As a parent, how will you (or how are you) transmitting yours? Traditionally, adults have used two distinctly different ways of imparting values, neither of which is recommended.

Moralizing is the direct, although sometimes subtle, transmission of the adults' values to young people (Simon et al., 1991). Based on the assumption that the adult has experienced life and knows best, moralizing is telling others to believe and value what the moralizer believes and values. Moralizers have powerful parent ego states. Delivery of values can vary. The "controlling parent" states definitely what is of value and how life should be lived. "A well-paying job is important, so go out and find one" is the command. The "nurturing parent" delivers essentially the same message in a different manner: "Now, honey, you know how nice it is to live comfortably, so you really need to find a well-paying job." Indirect messages are also possible: "I'll bet John's parents are really proud of him. He got a well-paying job last week."

Moralizing is common. Parents, teachers, ministers, priests, rabbis, and administrators are among those who use direct, commanding statements to tell others what is important. Even friends can moralize: "Barb, you really should break up with Kent. He isn't going to amount to anything, and you wouldn't want to have his children." As common as it is, moralizing doesn't work effectively and usually generates resentment on the part of the recipient. Why?

One reason is that each of us is unique, and moralizing takes away individuality. What is good for one person may not be for another. As the decade theory shows, people are influenced by timely events at different times in history. What might have been a worthy value for a grandparent or parent may not fit today's world. Another problem is that a moralizer may have questionable values. Can you think of someone who loudly champions some questionable viewpoints?

A point of confusion for a child is the variety of moralizing messages. Parents say one thing, teachers may say another, and the media may offer a third. Furthermore, the words and behaviors of a single moralizer may not mesh, so that a young person is left hearing and seeing two different things. "Do as I say and not as I do" is a common refrain of moralizers because they often have a hard time living up to their words.

Reactions to moralizing provide added reasons why moralizing isn't recommended. People exposed to moralizing can rebel, or they might be passive and obedient individuals who follow strong leaders and commands. Easily recruited into cults are victims of moralizing. Their biggest handicap is an inability to think for themselves and make their own decisions. "I think that's been my problem for years," said a 30-year-old student. "My mother always told me what to do; I didn't make decisions for myself. My

Figure 5-2

mother is dead, and I have a hard time trying to decide what to do about most things." In contrast, I enjoyed what a female student wrote, "I think that some people believe I need to rely on my family because they are all I have now. I have news for them—I have ME, and that sounds good!"

The opposite means of transmitting values is by a *laissez-faire*, or *hands-off*, method (Simon et al., 1991). The young person is left to discover values without leadership or guidance. Permissiveness is the parenting style, and the child is left to run rampant. "Go out and find your own way" is the message. For what reasons isn't this recommended? Simply put, children need guidance. Young people do not want adults to run their lives; yet, most do want and need help (Simon et al., 1991).

Recommendations for Values Development

What does work? The following suggestions are likely to lead to the development of worthy values and specific behaviors that enable an individual to make life-enhancing decisions.

Set a positive example. The message of "Do as I say, not as I do" is nonsense. People are more influenced by behavior than words. Modeling the values you want to see is extremely important. This means that if you want someone to value health, first examine your own health habits. If you think honesty is important, check to see how you exemplify honesty. "If we do not believe in violence, an action is to turn off the TV set when violence starts, or change channels. Leave books around if you value reading and read," (Harris and Harris, 1985, p. 264).

Children will be exposed to numerous models; however, parents are most influential. If you are a kind, considerate person, others can learn the value of loving behaviors. If you are in school pursuing a degree, realize that you are transmitting a powerful message to young people that education and dedication to a goal are of value.

Encourage the values you think are important. Offer praise when someone demonstrates one of your values. *Positive reinforcement*, presenting a pleasant stimulus that increases a certain response or behavior, is not used nearly as much as it could be. Instead of waiting to criticize when others don't measure up, give credit or praise when they do. "I'm proud of you for telling your teacher the truth," "I like it when you share your possessions," and, in the workplace, "I appreciate your loyalty to the company" are powerful motivators. Give rewards to show your approval. Even though you may simply expect others to behave morally, showing appreciation doesn't hurt.

Teach and guide. Instead of teaching and guiding, moralizers tell individuals what to value—a much less effective technique. Teaching opportunities regularly present themselves. For example, watch a television show with children and then discuss situations that require moral reasoning and judgments. Ask questions and encourage them to express their opinions. "The lyrics of that song are immoral, and I won't let you listen to it," says a moralizer. A teacher or guide would ask, "What do you think about those lyrics? Do you see any potential harm from listening to them? What do they say to you? What do they say to younger children?" You can eventually express your own opinions *after* encouraging an open, free discussion.

You can do the same when decisions are to be made. Children will be exposed to choices. Giving options to younger ones and explaining why other choices are not allowed is instructive. With adolescents, rather than telling them what to do, you can discuss the situation and then guide them toward understanding the values you think are important. They may persist in different ideas, yet your chances as a teacher and guide are better than as a moralizer. At times you may feel compelled to try to prevent certain behaviors by children; however, do so only after you have been open to their opinions.

> Children need limits. They need guidelines. They need them for their security, and they need them for their survival. One can teach with respect, or one can teach with intimidation. One can speak to a child's intelligence or to his or her fear of punishment. One can offer a child reasonable choices within sane and comprehensible ground rules, or one can lay down the law, as is done in the army (Branden, 1983, p. 136).

At times, stand back and let a person's own experiences teach. Can you remember learning from your mistakes? Consequences of behavior are among the best teachers in the world. As difficult as it may be for a loving parent, "letting the chips fall" can lead to effective results. Ellen was slow and nonchalant about getting ready for school. After weeks of begging and nagging Ellen to be ready, her parents, who took turns driving her to school, left the house one morning at 8:00. Ellen walked to school in a rainstorm, was quite late, and suffered the consequences. The problem was solved because Ellen had discovered firsthand the value of punctuality. If she had not gone to school, other consequences would teach a lesson. Most individuals are influenced by consequences.

Instill a value of self. Of all the values a parent can inspire in a child, the most important is the value placed on self. Already covered in Chapter 1, the importance of self-esteem cannot be overemphasized. Although most students acknowledge this, "self" rarely appears when they are asked to identify their five top values while friends, family, and others are listed by almost everyone. You may need to remind yourself often that it is necessary to value yourself before you can value anyone else. The *self-actual-*

ized person develops a value system based on acceptance of self, others, and nature (Schott, 1992). "Self-esteem is one of the most powerful forces in the universe. Self-esteem leads to joy, to productivity, to intimacy. That's why I advocate a value system that promotes self-esteem. Self-esteem is like faith: it can move mountains!" (Burns, 1989, p. 115).

Cheri, a student in her late thirties, wrote about her values.

> When I was younger, I devoted my time and energy to my family and home. I got lost somewhere in the shuffle. My insistence on working outside the home has helped me to grow. I like myself more than I did in those earlier years. My education has always been a dream, and it took a lot of courage for me to return to school. I know now that I'll always be in pursuit of knowledge. What I'm learning is helping to open my eyes to new ideas. I feel like a little bird that has just begun to stretch its wings. Everything I am learning and all the new people I am coming in contact with are the wind beneath my wings.

Valuing herself made this possible. Another student, Deborah, mentioned that she had valued others before herself for most of her life. After elevating her self-esteem, she said that she still valued her family; however, now she valued and relied on herself even more. This allowed her to "be there" for her parents and siblings as they had been for her.

Encourage a value on thinking for self. Critical and creative thinking require a questioning mind. Parents too often stifle children's questions either because they don't want to answer or because they just don't like being questioned. Children who are fearful about questioning a parent grow into adulthood afraid to ask which interferes with learning and their ability to make wise decisions. Often, parents react negatively when a child disagrees with their opinion. Rather than rigidity in thinking, a realization that life is full of many rights and numerous ways of thinking, not of absolute sets of right-wrong, is beneficial. "Things are not usually all good or all bad, all right or all wrong. Life is just not that simple. The answers and solutions we seek usually lie somewhere between the opposites" (Buscaglia, 1992, p. 9). Parents and others who care are wise if they stimulate and encourage the use of a child's adult ego state so that she or he learns about choices and constructive ways of making decisions.

Influences on Adult Values

After adolescence, according to values programming analysis, values are established. They could remain similar throughout adulthood, yet most people's values will change. What are some general influences on values during the rest of your life?

Major life change. Just as stress is related to a major life event and change, so is an analysis of values. Beginning in the early twenties and continuing throughout life, any *significant life change* has the potential to alter your values. At age 23, Joe valued health, sports, and bodybuilding. One summer day he was riding his motorcycle and had a terrible accident. He was left paralyzed from the waist down and confined to a wheelchair. After soul-searching and values analysis, he altered his emphasis on sports and bodybuilding so that he could participate, yet in a different way. Other values became important, and he began to help individuals with special needs.

An accident or injury is one type of major change. Others are the birth of a child, loss of a job, divorce, or death of a loved one—any of the crises discussed in Chapter 4. A change can motivate you to develop worthier values. Julie was an adolescent, unmarried mother. She candidly talked about how her values had changed.

> At sixteen I valued friends and good times. I partied a lot and didn't care much about school or working. I just wanted to have fun. After Jason was born, I changed my whole way of thinking. Because of him, I realized how important it is to take care of my health, get some education, and learn to support us. I'm a new person, and I like who I am.

Mental unrest. The second general way in which values can change is *mental unrest*. Exposure to new ideas can cause you to think more deeply about your beliefs. You may question them and change your mind. Added knowledge can come in a formal learning experience. Tony took a sociology class and became aware of different ideas regarding equal rights. Kelly began to question her strict religious upbringing after studying philosophy and religion in college. In informal ways, too, you can learn. Reading a book, talking with people who have different beliefs, traveling, and watching tele-

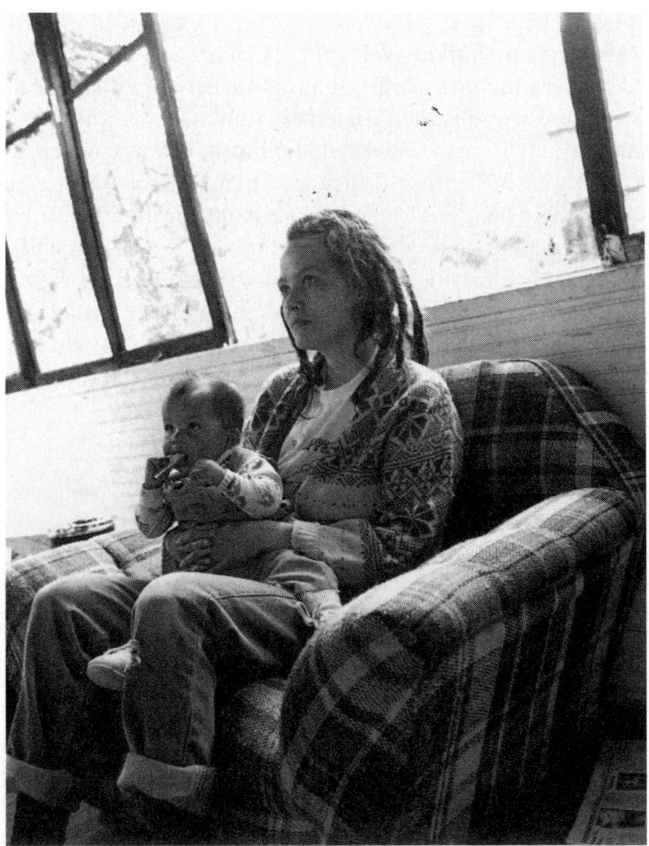

Figure 5-3 Having a baby is likely to change one's values.

vision are some of the ways you glean new information. Having a closed mind to new ideas will make learning less likely; however, most people are open enough to at least wonder.

Changes in needs. As your *needs change*, values will probably be altered. Most of us have a strong need to belong and have the approval of others so throughout life, we adjust our values somewhat to conform. Values also can vary as statuses and roles change. A new business owner is likely to adjust values and think differently than she did as an employee.

Commonly, one value will take precedence over another. If you have always valued socializing and then you find that you have a health problem requiring long-term rest, you will probably put your own condition ahead of the need to go out with friends.

> Many people mistakenly feel that favoring one value over another is tantamount to a rejection of the other. This is not true. You are as deeply committed to the other value as before; you have simply acknowledged hierarchy (Porat, 1988, p. 144).

Healthy values criteria. The likelihood that you will experience a major change, mental unrest, and different needs during a lifetime is extremely high. For this reason, *flexibility* is necessary. Having a strong value system does not mean upholding the same ones throughout a lifetime. Instead, a strong system includes the ability to process and evaluate. Well-adjusted people understand that they may discard, modify, add, and change values themselves or their ranking.

Sherri, who had valued marriage, traditional suburban life, and a lovely home, found her life dramatically changed when her husband divorced her. She was no longer married, was no longer a part of traditional, couple-oriented suburban life, and was unable to make house payments. Flexibility allowed her to change her priorities and to develop new values in order to survive. Independence, education, and career emerged as high values.

Lack of flexibility has definite drawbacks. Inflexible values tend to make individuals judgmental.

> The more we adhere to any system, the more this belonging will be limited to others who believe as we do. We even see our children as "bad" if they don't follow "our" way (Glasser, 1984, p. 85).

Close human relationships have been threatened and even destroyed by people's unwillingness to adjust their thinking. Inflexibility and certainty can also stifle learning.

> When we think we are absolutely right, we stop seeking new information. To be right is to be certain, and to be certain stops us from being curious. Curiosity and wonder are at the heart of all learning. The feeling of absolute certainty and righteousness causes us to stop seeking and to stop learning (Bradshaw, 1988, p. 8).

Practicing flexibility rather than rigidity seems justified.

Other criteria can indicate whether your values are healthy or unhealthy (McKay and Fanning, 1987). *Healthy values are owned.* You are not living by someone else's values. Ask yourself why you chose the career field you did. Why did you marry, or why will you marry? Usually, until a careful analysis is done, people are unaware of how their behavior might be based on someone else's "should."

Healthy values are realistic and promote behavior that leads to positive outcomes. Acting on unrealistic values means acting on principle no matter what pain resulted. For example, one student of mine had written on an assignment, "I don't believe in divorce no matter what." I posed some questions to her such as, "Even if you were being abused? Even if your children were being abused? Even if the person became a despicable individual who was involved in all kinds of unethical behavior?" She thought and then replied, "I hadn't even considered those possibilities, and in those cases, I certainly wouldn't hold fast to that value."

Finally, *healthy values are life-enhancing* rather than life-restricting. An example of a life-restricting value would be to esteem another person in such a way that you allow him or her to rule your life. "I won't go back to school because he wants me to stay home" is life-restricting. Conversely, life-enhancing values encourage you to do what is nourishing (McKay and Fanning, 1987).

Restrictive, rigid values destroy freedom. An adoption of what I call a broad-based approach to values has been beneficial in my life. This means that rather than having pat answers to all moral dilemmas, I use an evaluative approach. I ask questions such as, "Are the behaviors I choose likely to harm others or myself? What are the probable consequences? If pain is a possible side effect, does the outcome warrant it?" Critical thinking about values is healthy.

Also helpful is to consider each dilemma on its own merits. A value on human life may mean that capital punishment is always wrong, but could there be justifiable cases? If you believe that life begins at conception, a value on human life translates into an anti-abortion belief. Could any situation warrant an abortion? For example, a news story told of a 12-year-old girl who had been raped and was pregnant. Carrying the baby meant a 50:50 chance of death for both her and the fetus. The girl's mother, because of her religious views, forbade an abortion—an absolute stance. What do you think about this particular situation? "Although it takes more effort, you will be more in control of your life if you evaluate each situation at the time you encounter it rather than rely too much on any value system" (Glasser, 1984, p. 85).

Values are personal, and you may be more comfortable with absolutes. If you are, at least, consider options. After evaluating and processing, individuals are more capable of acting in their own best interest. Having your own realistic, life-enhancing, and flexible values sets the stage for a workable value system and helps you accept different ways of thinking. To gain insight into your values development, do the Chapter 5 activity in REFLECTIONS AND APPLICATIONS.

CHOICES AND DECISIONS

A workable, healthy value system frees you to make your own choices and decisions. Almost every human being values freedom. Ironically, individuals will shy away from what personal freedom offers-an abundance of choices and the probability of changing a belief. Mental unrest isn't pleasant for most. Some people are frightened by freedom and personal responsibility. "They may yearn for the 'rules,' the absolutes, the 'rigid ancient law' which relieves us of 'this fearful burden of free choice' " (May, 1953, p. 221). When individuals face being renounced by others, they can be fearful and hesitant in standing by their own convictions. Conformity may seem easier; usually, though, it demands a high price.

Choices in Life

Think of all the choices you have already made and all that lie ahead. Your decisions greatly influence the quality of your life. Several choices involve health. How important is your health? For most, it is of highest priority. Yet, many admit they don't practice health-enhancing behaviors, and several even pursue unhealthy life styles, especially during high school and college years. You may take your health for granted. Disregard for health has ramifications for the future. Former governor of Colorado Richard D. Lamm stated:

> The single most important factor determining our quality of life is our health, and the single most important factor affecting our health is the degree to which we as individuals are willing to take responsibility for our own diets and exercise, no matter what age we are at the present time (Carlson and Seiden, 1988).

Valuing health is an important first step in staying healthy. A study of 3045 Navy personnel indicated that the value placed on health predicted specific health behaviors and the general practice of wellness (Abood and Conway, 1992). The self-concept inventory in REFLECTIONS AND APPLICATIONS asks about values. Was health one of yours?

How do you define health? For many, being healthy means being free of disease, yet is that all there is to it? Included in today's definition of *health* is a general feeling of physical and mental well-being. Inner peace is even seen as an important ingredient (Jampolsky and Cirincione, 1990). A concept called *positive wellness* is described by Bloomfield and Kory (1978) in a book about holistic health. According to them, you have achieved positive wellness if the following characteristics describe you (pp. 20–21).

- trim and physically fit
- full of energy, vigorous, rarely tired
- free of minor complaints (such as indigestion, constipation, headaches, insomnia)
- alert, able to concentrate, clearheaded
- radiant, with clear skin, glossy hair, and sparkling eyes
- active and creative
- able to relax easily, free of worry and anxiety
- self-assured, confident, optimistic
- satisfied with work and the direction of your life
- able to assert yourself, stand up for your rights
- satisfied with your sexual relationships
- free of destructive health habits, particularly smoking, overeating, and excessive drinking
- fulfilled and at peace with yourself

Sounds ideal, doesn't it? Even though few people possess every characteristic, wellness is possible; the closer you come to it, the higher your chance for a fulfilling life. A study identified good health as a predictor and marker of happiness. People in good physical health consistently succeeded in more areas of living than those in poor health (Myers, 1992). Try thinking of the body as a machine. Unfortunately, most people use the machine too hard or not hard enough; many throw junk into it resulting in an inappropriate fuel mixture (Bortz, 1991).

That doesn't have to be your choice, however. Improvements in the direction of wellness built on a foundation of self-responsibility, self-esteem, and self-empowerment can be accomplished in small steps. A book suggesting 32 simple steps or processes is *Wellness: Small Changes You Can Use to Make a Big Difference* (Ryan and Travis, 1991). These changes then will "have a ripple effect because of the inter-dependence" (p. 2). One of the tips in the book is to remember that water is essential to balanced health and to drink at least eight big glasses per day. Why not go get a glass right now? An excellent way to achieve wellness is to engage in more physical activity which influences us physically, mentally, emotionally, and socially. One medical doctor believes that exercise is more important than the other two tenets of health, nutrition and rest. Yet, he maintains that most of us eat enough or too much, get enough rest, but definitely do not exercise enough (Bortz, 1991).

> Movement is a sign of life. Seriously inhibit movement of limbs and organs, and you encourage illness. Stop motion altogether and you are dead. Allow yourself to move as fully as possible (Ryan and Travis, 1991, p. 68).

A unique suggestion is to learn to be comfortable with silence which is really learning to be comfortable alone with yourself. In this noise-infested world, spending time in silence is a healthy habit. Try it, and if you're uncomfortable, keep trying!

One way to motivate yourself to adopt a healthier life style is to keep abreast of research and be informed on health issues. Then if you truly value yourself, you can make wise choices. I'm amazed whenever I ask students any questions about nutrition. Except for what advertisers and others tell them, most are woefully "in the dark." Ask yourself how healthy you want to be and how best you can achieve that level of health. You will make several health and wellness choices on a regular basis. Educating yourself can make the decisions easier.

Smoking cigarettes. If you smoke, you inhale several potentially dangerous substances, including the most potent cancer-causing substances known as carcinogens (Laszlo, 1987). Research leaves no doubt that smoking is extremely unhealthy, and a survey found that 88.4 percent of adults believed that smoking was harmful to health. The adverse effects of lung cancer, emphysema, and heart disease were identified in that order (Brownson et al., 1992). In spite of awareness, the number of smokers in the United States increased from 25 percent in 1992 to 30 percent in 1993, according to a survey by *Prevention* magazine (*Lincoln Journal*, June 24, 1993).

The known risks are high and the future for a smoker is bleak. About 250 million people living in the developed nations will die because of smoking, and they will die an average 23 years sooner than people who do not smoke (*The Economist*, 1992). Tobacco use is the most prevalent cause of death before old age (Peto et al., 1992) and a significant predictor of hospital stays and death (Kaplan et al., 1992). Heavy smokers are significantly more likely than nonsmokers to die of cancer and heart disease (Gorman, 1988), to contract myeloid leukemia (*Time*, 1993a), have cardiovascular problems (Fackelmann, 1990), be depressed, and at a higher risk for suicide (Hemenway et al., 1993).

Smoking poses specific risks for women in cases of acute pelvic inflammatory disease (Scholes et al., 1992) and diabetes (Rimm et al., 1993). Pregnant women are well-advised to quit because smoking decreases blood flow to the fetus and increases carbon monoxide in the blood. As a result, heavy smoking during pregnancy increases the risk of stillbirths, premature births, and low weight babies (Barr et al., 1990). A study of about 56,000 Canadian women showed a strong association between smoking and miscarriage (Armstrong et al., 1992).

As employers become more aware of the relationship between health and cigarette smoking, smokers may find it difficult to get jobs. A division of Dow Chemical found that smokers averaged 5.5 more days of absence each year and took more days of disability leave. The annual medical tab for smokers is $50 billion with half the money spent on hospitalization alone (*Time*, 1994).

Motivation to quit may stem from other reasons. A psychology student said, "I've heard it all, and nothing has jolted me to quit smoking until you mentioned that study on wrinkling. That did it!" She was referring to research which found that heavy smokers were nearly five times more likely to show excessive skin wrinkling than nonsmokers (*Prevention*, 1991). If health and physical appearance aren't motivating enough, maybe money will talk. With increasing costs of cigarettes, several have decided that the money saved is worth it. And cigarettes aren't the total cost. Smokers spend more on cold remedies, health care, and life insurance. Tobacco addiction is a major economic handicap (Tobias, 1992).

Think how much value you place on the longevity and quality of your life. Having severe emphysema is definitely not a quality way of life. If you are a smoker and want to quit, arm yourself with as much data as you can about the ill effects and possible repercussions of smoking. Smoking is a matter of free choice; that choice, scientists say, means choosing to take years off life expectancy (Laszlo, 1987).

Because passive, or secondary, smoke has been linked to health problems, a person might choose to quit because of someone else such as a child. A review of studies concluded that children of smokers suffer more bronchitis, pneumonia, and other respiratory illnesses, and a study in the *New England Journal of Medicine* said that parents who smoke may raise the risk of their children getting lung cancer when they grow up (*Lincoln Journal*, September 6, 1990). Children aren't the only potential victims. Nonsmoking spouses of smokers as well as other adults exposed to smoke over a number of years face a greater risk of death from cardiovascular disease (Humble et al., 1990) and lung cancer (Brownson et al., 1992; Gibbs, 1988). A woman who lives with a moderate smoker has a 30 percent higher risk; with a heavy smoker, the increased risk is 80 percent. Those exposed at work have a 39 percent higher one (*University of California at Berkeley Wellness Letter*, 1994). According to other research, the blood platelets of nonsmokers who breathe air laced with cigarette smoke, even for short periods of time, become sticky which can help form clots (Fackelmann, 1990). As many as 53,000 deaths each year may be attributable to passive smoke; as such it is the third leading preventable cause of death (*Lincoln Journal*, January 10, 1991). With regard to health, nonsmokers have choices to make. Opting not to breathe someone else's smoke may require assertive behavior. Whether you smoke or not, you have choices, and the value you place on health will undoubtedly affect your decisions.

If you are a smoker, you can demonstrate consideration by checking with nonsmokers about smoking and then understanding and accepting their wishes. One student commented that she didn't understand the complaints because, as a nondrinker, she didn't object to alcohol use in her presence. She was quick, however, to recognize the difference between unwanted smoke *in the air* and alcohol in another's body. Your choice to quit smoking may well be the best health decision you will ever make. Because thousands have quit, you can, too!

Drinking alcohol. Alcohol, the most widely used and abused drug in many societies, has wreaked havoc on health and personal lives. From 10 to 15 percent of Americans are afflicted with alcoholism (*The Menninger Letter*, 1993a). Alcohol abuse is frequently at the root of domestic violence, child abuse and neglect, crime, lost productivity, chemical dependency, and fatal accidents and injuries. Alcohol can harm the body, lead to a psychological and physical dependency, and increase one's level of stress (Cole et al., 1990). In excess, alcohol and other drugs are "truly the crutch that cripples" (Eliot and Breo, 1984, p. 200). The innocent suffer, too. Each year about 73,000 babies and young children are affected by their mother's use of alcohol during pregnancy. They may be born with fetal alcohol syndrome (FAS) or suffer from less-severe effects such as learning impairments or hyperactivity (Newman and Buka, 1991).

Although drinking among college students has been described as harmless and to-be-expected, the Center on Addiction and Substance Abuse at Columbia University released alarming statistics (*Lincoln Journal*, June 7, 1994).

- The average student imbibes 34 gallons of beer, wine, or liquor a year. The total spent each year is $5.5 billion.
- One student in 12 has at least 16 drinks a week.
- White men drink far more than any other group averaging 9+ drinks a week—twice the rate of white women. Black men consume 3.6 drinks per week and black women only one.
- The percentage of women who drink to get drunk has more than tripled in the past 15 years and is now at 35 percent.
- Ninety percent of campus rapes occur when either the assailant, the victim, or both used alcohol.
- At least one out of five college students abandons safe sex practice when drunk.
- Sixty percent of college women who acquire sexually transmitted diseases including AIDS were drunk at the time.

Hopefully, awareness of the problem will lead to decreased emphasis on using alcohol excessively. Binge drinking, according to the report, is no longer harmless; instead, it is a major problem. For social drinkers, especially those who "binge" on weekends, more drinking can lead to lack of enthusiasm, poor appetites, inability to sleep, and feelings of hopelessness and depression (Tyler, 1988).

Children of alcoholics, as many as 28 to 34 million Americans (The *Menninger Letter*, 1993), are wise to be aware of a serious statistic: "They are three to four times more likely to become alcoholics than their peers are" (Chollar, 1988). Caucasian men seem to be at greater risk than Caucasian women and Hispanic men and women. Important to note is that the men's risk was still in the normal range (Harman and Arbona, 1991). This indicates that although heredity may play a part, environmental influences are powerful, and many raised in alcoholic families make healthy choices.

Alarming are the figures revealing that first drinking usually occurs at age 13. Of 11,631 high school students in the United States, Puerto Rico, and the Virgin Islands, 88 percent had consumed alcohol (*The Journal of the American Medical Association*, 1991). Other reports indicate that 9 out of 10 teenagers have experimented with alcohol (*Tufts University Diet and Nutrition Letter*, 1992). Besides health and relationship repercussions, social consequences of alcohol abuse among young people include traffic deaths, academic difficulties, and acts of violence (Elson, 1991).

How effectively do parental values influence children's alcohol use? A study by the Council on Alcoholism and Drugs in Lincoln, Nebraska, showed that even though 94 percent of parents disapproved, 86 percent of teenagers reported drinking alcohol. What parents believe does not stop an adolescent from experimenting with alcohol. Remember the peer influence during adolescence? Teenagers in one study seemed to "hang out" with others whose substance use or nonuse was similar to theirs (Kafka and London, 1991).

Although the adverse effects of alcohol, when used lightly or in moderation, are not as clear as those of other mind-altering drugs, wise choices are more likely to be made by those who are informed and don't try to fool themselves into thinking that no harm can come to them. All of us know that irresponsible drinking has many disquieting effects. A person may not be an actual alcoholic, yet still have a problem. My definition of a "problem drinker" is anyone who causes problems because of drinking. If an individual becomes extremely obnoxious, abusive, hurtful, it's time to modify habits.

The potentially devastating effects of drinking and driving are unquestionable. The number of deaths due to alcohol-related traffic accidents in 3 years will roughly equal the number of Americans killed in a decade of fighting in Vietnam (Turrisi and Jaccard, 1991). Alcohol-related highway deaths are the number-one killer of persons between the ages of 15 and 24, and about 65 out of every 100 persons in the United States will be in an alcohol-related crash during their lives, according to statistics from the National Highway Traffic Safety Administration. If you have not been affected by someone's death from a drunk-driving incident, you are lucky. Keep in mind that you or someone you love could be.

Kristi went home one weekend during her first quarter of college. She made an unwise decision and rode with a friend who had been drinking. For months after their tragic accident, Kristi lay almost completely paralyzed in a hospital. A year later she has some mobility; however, her life has been tragically changed. In another situation, Scott came to tell me that he was quitting school. "I'm going into a treatment program to get control of my drinking," he said. "I was the drunk driver who hit and killed the pedestrian last weekend. I'll be facing criminal charges, too, and I'm really scared." Sue tearfully told a class about an accident in which a drunk driver hit a crowd of pedestrians. Her sister is now paralyzed.

Remember these stories and others when you consider getting behind the wheel of a car after drinking or riding with a driver who has been drinking. Make a conscious decision that you will not combine drinking and driving, program your mind when completely sober, and then let others know of your decision. This is important because drinking can diminish moral maturity and judgment. In a study, certain "wrong" behaviors were identified by people; the more they drank, things changed as they were swayed by habit, convenience, and the behavioral clues of others (Denton and Krebs, 1990). On the positive side, among 1250 adults polled by Princeton Survey Research Associates, only 17 percent said they sometimes drive after drinking, down from 28 percent a decade ago (*Lincoln Journal*, June 24, 1993). Be assertive about refusing to allow others to drive drunk. Alcohol use numbs thinking processes. Accept that it will.

Your personal support for and involvement in organizations such as Mothers Against Drunk Driving (MADD) and Students Against Drunk Driving (SADD) can show that you act on your values and will help decrease the number of tragedies. Candy Lightner started MADD in 1980 after her daughter was killed by a drunk driver. By 1985, that same driver had been arrested six times for drunk driving, and in one accident injured another young girl. Lightner says, "We've kicked a few pebbles, we'll turn a few stones, and eventually we'll start an avalanche" (Lee, 1985, p. 77). Most of the strides against drunk driving are the results of efforts by MADD and other activist groups.

For those who are addicted to alcohol or even have problems with its use, support groups such as Alcoholics Anonymous are available in most communities, and treatment programs are offered by most hospitals. Some programs use cognitive techniques and self-esteem building as their foundation. Because individuals are unique, no one program works for all. People are advised to try a different one if there is no improvement. Having an attitude of cautious optimism is important (Blau, 1991). Believing that shame is the core and fuel of all addictions, Bradshaw (1988) thinks counseling is necessary. Learning about the long-term effects of all drugs is the first step in taking control of your own use. Then, if you continue to have a problem, seek help for yourself and for all those who care about you.

Losing weight. Another health issue, as well as one of physical attractiveness, has to do with weight. A survey by *Prevention* magazine revealed that 65 percent of American adults are overweight which is higher than anytime in the last decade (*Lincoln Journal*, June 24, 1993). The Nurses' Health Study (Lincoln Journal, March, 1990) blames overweight for 40 percent of all heart disease among women. Being at a healthy weight cuts your risk of heart attack by 35 to 55 percent and greatly reduces the possibilities of diabetes and breast cancer, and you'll feel much better (Delaney, 1993b).

Being trim and physically fit come from wise choices regarding nutrition and exercise. Just deciding to diet isn't the best choice. People who do this often end up in repeated cycles of weight loss and gain. This "yo-yo dieting" is not only unhealthy; it doesn't work. The emphasis today is on using sound nutritional practices and physical activity to decrease body fat and increase metabolic rate. Foods lower in fat are advisable keeping in mind that the body needs some fat. Americans, however, consume more than twice the fat that Japanese and Chinese citizens do. Higher breast cancer rates and fattier bodies are the result (Bricklin, 1993a). Eating more fiber, whole grains, legumes, fresh fruits, and vegetables is the key.

Because most people will consider weight loss at some time in their lives, education is a practical idea. Food provides energy so when the body is deprived of food, energy level is low and metabolism slows down so you don't burn off fat nearly as efficiently. In fact, one weight-loss theory says to keep your metabolism rate normal by eating at least as much as your body requires at rest (Kaplan, 1993). Breakfast, by the way, is your "metabolism wake-up call and kicks it into a calories-burning mode. If you don't eat in the morning, you may ultimately burn fewer calories" (Delaney, 1993a, p. 65).

Weight loss comes from taking in fewer calories than you burn off; any form of physical activity burns calories. One choice is walking which is easy for most people. Physical activity, along with better nutrition, does away with the traditional idea of dieting and becomes a way of life. In fact, scientists at Tufts University compared people who cut back on calories to those who maintained their regular diet and also exercised. The exercise group lost 16 pounds more without cutting out calories (Bricklin, 1993b).

> A sensible approach to weight loss includes a plan that you can weave into your life style. Good diets emphasize changes in what you eat, how and when you eat, and physical activity. Low-calorie diets (fewer than 800 calories per day) should not be undertaken without medical supervision. Quick-fix diets with magic foods, devices, or pills will probably lead to rapid weight losses, but they will be followed by even faster regain. The body just wasn't designed to be a yo-yo (Brownell, 1988, p. 23).

Learning all you can about weight loss and making it part of a total wellness program is the answer to a challenge faced by many Americans. Later in this chapter are action steps to weight loss.

Engaging in sexual activities. Sexual behavior in today's society can pose a dire health risk. "People are literally dying because they contracted AIDS through sexual activity" (Rathus and Boughn, 1993). AIDS, acquired immune deficiency syndrome, should be a household word. First identified in 1981, it is caused by HIV, human immunodeficiency virus. In 1981, fewer than 100 people in the United States had died from AIDS. By the end of 1991, 202,000 cases and more than 130,000 deaths had been reported (Rathus and Boughn, 1993). AIDS is the number one killer of men in 64 U.S. cities (*Lincoln Journal*, June 16, 1993).

Different age groups and both sexes are at risk. Adolescent sexual behavior is of grave concern. About 20 percent of all AIDS patients are under 30 years of age. An incubation period of about 8 years or more means that many were infected as teenagers (Gibbs, 1993). The growth of AIDS cases among people 15 to 24 years of age has increased 77 percent in 2 years. Worldwide, 50 percent of those infected with the virus became infected between the ages of 15 and 24. The disease itself comes later. "The new face of AIDS is going to be a young face—and girls more than boys—will be more at risk" (*Lincoln Journal*, June 6, 1993, p. 3A).

Lack of education and concern about AIDS is evident. Studies show that college students enrolled in a course on AIDS had a relatively low level of concern about casual sex and transmission of the virus (Strauss et al., 1992) and AIDS was not an issue of personal concern to the majority of college students (Gray and Saracino, 1991). Not surprisingly, safer sex practices correlated with assertiveness in one study, and women took the lead in insisting upon precautions (Yesmont, 1992). College women in a 1989 study didn't seem to be concerned and were as sexually active, had about as many sex partners, and engaged in as many varied forms of sexual behavior as their predecessors did in 1975 and 1986 before the high awareness of AIDS. The only difference was an increased use of condoms; however, these were used by only 41 percent (*Parade*, May 6, 1990). In another study, only 60 percent of 1326 adolescents were aware that using a condom might prevent transmission of the disease. Nearly 25 percent believed AIDS was curable (Hersch, 1988).

One can only wonder whether adults are any more enlightened. Accurate information is available, and anyone who values health will seek it. An excellent resource is *AIDS—What Every Student Needs to Know* (Rathus and Boughn, 1993). It contains information about and recommended ways to avoid AIDS and other sexually transmitted diseases as well as sound advice concerning rape and assertiveness in sexual situations. Required reading would be an excellent idea. AIDS is not curable; it is preventable. One recommendation is to avoid multiple sexual partners; yet, a survey revealed that among sexually active teenage girls, 61 percent have had multiple partners (Gibbs, 1993). On a positive note, education does work as demonstrated in a program where substantial improvement in AIDS knowledge led to a reduction in risky behavior (McCusker et al., 1992).

Education about AIDS can also help to change people's attitudes and feelings about victims of the disease. Blaming a certain group of people for a disease is ridiculous. For example, decades ago polio was a serious, often fatal disease. Polio, like AIDS, was caused by a virus. Who were its victims? For the most part, they were children. Wouldn't it have been ridiculous to harbor and voice such thoughts as, "Those children caused polio," "We should just get rid of all those kids, and that'd take care of polio," and "They deserve what they're getting"? Yet these are the exact thoughts and feelings that uneducated people have about victims of AIDS who, initially, were mostly homosexual men and intravenous drug users. Today, AIDS is every group's potential disease.

Regardless of AIDS and other sexually transmitted diseases, sexual activity among unmarried individuals remains high. Among all adults, 80 percent of women and 90 percent of men now engage in premarital intercourse (Rosellini, 1992). By the time they are 20, 75 percent of young Americans have had sexual intercourse (Gibbs, 1993), and the activity occurs at increasingly younger ages. About one quarter of boys and 10 percent of girls are sexually experienced by the age of 15, according to the Alan Guttmacher Institute (*Lincoln Journal*, June 7, 1994). In Japan, only 6 percent of boys and 4 percent of girls have engaged in sexual intercourse by age 15 (Gibbs, 1993). One could ask if American youth are any better off for all their experience.

The societal messages in the United States are confused and confusing to young people. At the same time they are being told to just abstain, they are bombarded with about 14,000 sexual encounters from television alone. The stereotypic gender double standard messages exist. While 60 percent of parents tell their daughters to remain chaste until marriage, less than half tell their sons the same. More than two thirds of the teens agree that a boy who has sex enhances his reputation while a girl's suffers. When teenagers were asked why kids they know have sex, 63 percent of the girls compared to 50 percent of the boys said they were in love while 65 percent of the girls and only 35 percent of the boys said they were pressured from those they were dating. Incidentally, the main reason given by both sexes was curiosity and desire to experiment (Gibbs, 1993). The experimentation can be deadly.

The outcome in terms of disease and unplanned pregnancies is quite troublesome. An estimated 12 million persons in the United States acquire a sexually transmitted infection each year. One fourth of all teenagers contract a sexually transmitted disease (Gibbs, 1993). As for birth control, in one survey nearly 40 percent of teenagers reported using it only sometimes or never (Gibbs, 1993) although another more optimistic report showed that about 70 percent of sexually active teens use contraceptives (*Lincoln Journal*, June 7, 1994). Regardless, about one million adolescents in the United States become pregnant every year (Ketterlinus et al., 1991; *Lincoln Journal*, June 7, 1994), and about 24 percent of all births are out of wedlock (Furstenberg and Cherlin, 1991). The costs in terms of health and well-being are high. Hardships for young mothers include discontinued education and reduced employment opportunities leading to social service dependence, unstable marriages, repeated child births, increased health and developmental risks to the children, and a greater likelihood that these "children of children" will repeat the cycle and become teen parents themselves.

The answers to the problems that result from irresponsible sexual activity are not simple, and few are forthcoming. Parents today are more likely to talk with their children about sex, and more people recognize the need for sex education. Could it also help to teach young people how to make responsible decisions based on healthy values? All through life, decisions about sexual behavior will be required. Choosing wisely is essential to well-being and, perhaps, a matter of life or death.

Growing older. Earlier in this chapter, the societal emphasis on youth was mentioned. Too many have bought into the media message that extols the virtues of youth. Old age is not considered of value and, in fact, is actually looked down on and thought of as a dreary wasteland. Attacking what she calls the mystique of age, Betty Friedan (1993) contends that almost all media images of older people are bleak. Consider the absurdity of such an attitude. As long as you live, you age. If you don't want to grow old, you will have to die young. Does that make sense? If aging continues to be viewed as negative, anyone who remains alive is heading for depression and despair. "The main problem represented by advancing age may well be connected to negative expectations" (Cousins, 1989, p. 245). More often, it's the fear of being old and infirm that keeps us from being old and healthy (Bortz, 1991). As one who is aging and enjoying almost every minute of it, I would like to share Tubesing's (1981) description:

> Growing older is not a downhill process from 17 to 70. It's an unfolding, like the maturing of a rose. The bud holds a promise in its tightly formed compactness but has not yet achieved its full beauty. As the process continues, each new layer of petals unfolding adds depth and significance to the flower. So also with you. Your potential unfolds as you age. In the bud of life, only a portion of your loveliness shows. Your potential is revealed in the unfolding process. Each stage reveals new beauty. Each stage brings fuller life. Each stage allows a more complete expression of your inner self (p. 50).

Getting rid of stereotypes about aging and old people would be beneficial to individuals and society, as a whole. "After we have broken the stereotypes of what older people cannot do, there is a floodgate of opportunity opening for us all" (Bortz, 1991, p. 283). Medical research verifies that age by itself does not automatically diminish brain power (Cousins, 1989). As many as 20 percent of the elderly lose *none* of their mental faculties (Kolata, 1991b). Only 15 percent of people over age 65 suffer serious mental impairment, and half of those are due to Alzheimer's disease (Tavris, 1989).

A 1968 study showed that 70-year-old men who engaged in regular exercise were able to match the reflexes of an average 40-year-old (Michaels, 1983). Much of the physical decline is caused from not remaining active. A fit person of 70 has the same oxygen-carrying capacity as an unfit person of 30 (Bortz, 1991). And the immune functions of healthy, elderly persons compare favorably with those of far younger people (Cousins, 1989). A final blow to the "woe-is-me" stereotype comes from a survey of 1200 individuals 100 years of age and older. Reporting themselves to be in good to excellent health were 82 percent, 75 percent were fully mobile, and 30 percent were still doing some work (Bortz, 1991).

In addition to changing our picture of old age, we can realize that there are advantages to aging besides the obvious one of continuing to be alive! For most people, stress declines because of fewer daily hassles and upheavals, short-term illnesses are not common, and frustrations are less because of added realism. Many report newfound sources of pleasure (Myers, 1992). Leisure time, which most young people crave, is usually more plentiful. The successful completion of Erikson's seven preceding stages leads to an old age of fulfillment and the achievement of integrity. For certain individuals, self-actualization has been achieved or is close.

Research provides insight into how to age positively and how to be a happy old person. Wise choices help to bring about a high quality of life throughout the lifespan so taking care of yourself while still young is important. Having purpose in life and meaningful activities throughout life make the difference. This was demonstrated in research at Baylor College of Medicine. A group of healthy older people were studied for 4 years over which time one third continued to hold a job, another third retired yet remained mentally and physically active, and the other third were inactive. Basically, they sat at home and did nothing. Scores of IQ were taken at the beginning when all were normal for their age and again after 4 years. The inactive people had less blood flowing to their brains and did significantly worse on the tests (Kolata, 1991b). It's truly a case of use it or lose it, and this is a choice. "Old age is a habit that a busy person doesn't have time for" (Bortz, 1991, p. 271).

Mental and physical activity and stimulation are essential. The brain responds actively to stimulation and weakens with disuse (Bortz, 1991; LeShan, 1990; Montagu, 1990). In fact, much of what we call aging is merely a case of disuse. "A mind at rest tends to remain at rest" (Bortz, 1991, p. 207). Growing evidence shows that a mind challenged by reading, paid or volunteer work, or an engrossing hobby will remain vigorous and able to learn and create (Kolata, 1991b). Increasingly, researchers believe that the mental changes commonly attributed to aging are due to illness (Kolata, 1991a).

Keeping an active sense of curiosity and a love for learning are highly recommended. Many adults stop any conscious efforts to learn early in their adulthood which is sad. We can remain youthful throughout life if we learn to act more like a child: imaginative, curious, playful, open-minded, flexible, humorous, energetic, honest, and eager to learn (Montagu, 1990). Keeping a sense of humor will make the rough spots much

Figure 5-4 Couple having the time of their lives prepare for take-off in their Piper Cub (printed by permission of Lincoln Journal).

easier. A wonderful book of humor and sage advice with a title that sets the tone is *It's Better to Be Over the Hill Than Under It* (LeShan, 1990).

Physical activity is a "must" as the body wasn't meant to be immobile. A person can expect to live 2.15 years longer if 2000 calories are spent per week in active activity (Bortz, 1991). The more you don't walk, the less you will be able to walk so it's important to keep moving (LeShan, 1990). What is tragic is to stagnate, to pull away from activities, and to allow negative thoughts to prevail. "When we retire from life, life retires from us" (Bortz, 1991, p. 320). Withdrawing from the mainstream of life, doing nothing, is as detrimental to happiness at age 80 as it is at age 18. Growing older is tragic when it represents the only form of growth. If you continue to value yourself throughout life, you will value aging because to age is to live. "It's not how old you are; it is how you are old" (Bortz, 1991, p. 112).

> *The 50-year-old who stopped growing at 20 will spend a lot of time wishing that he or she was 20 again. Aging, like a hand-me-down shirt, won't fit unless we grow into it.*
>
> —Bob Resz

Other choices reflect how much you care about yourself. What types of food do you eat? Do you get enough rest? Are you usually a careful person? Do you expose your body to a dangerous amount of sun? Do you practice stress management? Are you giving your body enough physical activity and your brain adequate stimulation? Your answers to these questions affect your present and future health. We will never be perfect; however, improvement in well-being is worth pursuing.

Making Responsible Decisions

Choices set the stage for decisions. Decision making means to select one alternative from various possible courses of thought or action. Because change is involved, decision making is usually stressful, and some people resist or have difficulty making decisions. Keep in mind that indecision, or not making a decision, is a decision. Seeking closure too early may be problematic; however, at some point, decisiveness is in order. Knowing how to make any decision has value in reducing stress and putting you in charge of your life. Those who make wise choices are prepared with increased knowledge and level of understanding (Beach, 1993).

Understanding your personality type helps to know your strengths and weaknesses in making decisions. In some cases, you may want to call upon others who are strong in your weaker area. For example, because Monica's personality preference was "feeling," she had difficulty keeping her personal values detached from some business decisions. A colleague with "thinking" strength offered additional logic to the process. Yet, the different preferences may annoy one another. Those with a judging preference are apt to make decisions fairly quickly while perceivers enjoy keeping options open and will change their minds more easily. A person who leans toward both intuition and perceiving will have numerous ideas and possibilities and not make a final choice which can be interpreted by others as stalling or being wishy-washy.

Six steps in decision making can be spelled out with the acronym ACTION (Halloran and Benton, 1987). See Fig. 5-5.

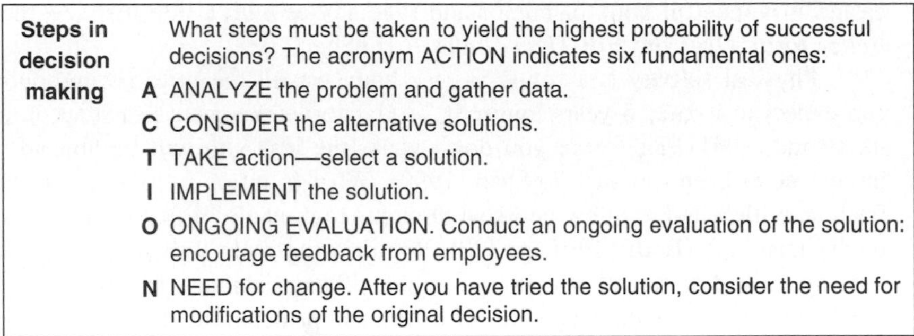
Steps in decision making What steps must be taken to yield the highest probability of successful decisions? The acronym ACTION indicates six fundamental ones:

- **A** ANALYZE the problem and gather data.
- **C** CONSIDER the alternative solutions.
- **T** TAKE action—select a solution.
- **I** IMPLEMENT the solution.
- **O** ONGOING EVALUATION. Conduct an ongoing evaluation of the solution: encourage feedback from employees.
- **N** NEED for change. After you have tried the solution, consider the need for modifications of the original decision.

Figure 5-5 From Halloran and Benton, Applied Human Relations (1987), p. 372, Prentice Hall.

Any decision has a risk factor. You could be wrong! What could be helpful is to remember that for most decisions, there is no absolute right and wrong. "There are merely different courses of action with varying consequences" (Bloomfield and Kory, 1980). When a mistake is made, you are wise, however, to accept it and keep in mind that they are necessary in any learning process. If you're not failing occasionally, you may not be taking any risks and charting new territory. "Rather than fearing mistakes, you need to welcome them. Mistakes are information about what works and what doesn't" (McKay and Fanning, 1987, p. 125). A healthy way of accepting mistakes is to see them as errors which can be corrected. Learning when to correct, not trying to avoid all mistakes, then becomes the key to success in life (Jeffers, 1987). You won't want to make mistakes on purpose; however, do regard them as valuable insight.

Decision making deserves attention and study. As with other life skills, you have probably received little formal training in how to evaluate choices and make decisions. Because we must make so many decisions in life, an essential choice is necessary: Do you want to take charge of life or let life be in charge of you?

WANTS AND GOALS

Chuck stifled a yawn in the career planning class. "Today we're going to discuss and set goals," the instructor had just announced. Several other students looked bored. Chuck thought, "If I've heard this once, I've heard it a thousand times. I'm only 20, and I'm already sick of hearing about goals. Isn't there a new way to approach this?"

Chuck would be pleased to know that there is. Using the ego states from TA can change the traditional ways of thinking about goals. Did you receive messages about goals from your parents, teachers, and counselors? The idea of even having goals was originally a "parent" message from somewhere: "You should have goals." "You'll never amount to anything without goals." A student in a career development class put it so well: "When I got out of high school, all I knew was that I had to get 'there,' wherever 'there' was, and it didn't sound like fun." Although their importance is realized, goals may seem tedious.

Even the language underlying most goals is "parent." How many of these sound familiar? "I should lose weight." "I ought to be on time." "I must get a job." Is it surprising that so many goals are not achieved or even acted upon? Restricting them to the parent ego state makes them boring and dreadfully task laden. No wonder only 13 percent of the population set goals on a serious basis (Breidenbach, 1989). How many actually succeed could be considerably less.

After identifying the role of "parent," Harris and Harris (1985) wisely recommend that getting the child ego state involved makes a positive difference. A first step is to allow yourself to dream; let the "child" out without restrictions from "parent" or "adult." Get rid of the "parent" language and let the wants flow! An activity in REFLECTIONS AND APPLICATIONS directs you in this enjoyable fantasy. A want is fun and spontaneous. The emotion within the "child" is motivating and energizing.

An employer speaking to a career development class said, "Human beings will if they want to and won't if they don't. I want employees who want to work and will be enthusiastic about it." Motivation toward what is pleasant is more powerful than any other kind. Using pleasant feelings to move toward what you want instead of away from what you don't want works well in goal achievement as well as everyday behavior (Bandler, 1985). Thinking about what motivates you is worthwhile, and you might be asked about this in a job interview. Some are motivated by money, and others need to be "pushed" by others. Neither of these is the most positive answer. If you are one who is motivated by the thrill of accomplishment or the pride of achievement, you're ahead of the rest. Self-motivation for worthy purposes is commendable.

How does the adult ego state get involved in goal achievement? Remember that the "adult" is the thinker that processes information and makes decisions. Your "adult" can look at your wants, determine how realistic they are, put them into order of importance, and then direct you in the process of achieving. The "adult" also helps in evaluating your goals and in changing them, if necessary. A goal may not be achievable so the "adult" adapts and selects an alternative.

The healthiest goals enhance personal growth. What you become as you work toward a goal is a primary consideration. Goal achievement and high self-esteem are directly related. Adolescents with some career goals had significantly higher self-esteem than those without any idea of what they wanted (Chiu, 1990). In Norway, success-oriented high school students perceived goals as shorter term, planned to initiate preparation earlier, and planned to devote more time to goals than did failure-oriented individuals (Havari, 1991). "Goal fulfillment is essential to life. Without purpose, life is meaningless" (Porat, 1988, p. 159).

Achieving Your Wants

A want is anything that is desired. Turning a want into an achieved goal is much easier after the "adult" has decided on its importance and the "child" remains enthusiastic. Even when a goal is determined and desired, you can create obstacles if you don't ask specific questions based on goal criteria (Walker and Brokaw, 1992).

- *Is the goal mine and not someone else's*? Can you think of some examples of trying to live another person's goal? Do you know anyone who is in college pursuing a degree only because a parent wants it? A characteristic of *self-actualization*, the pinnacle of human achievement, is to make growth choices rather than fear choices. Values based on what someone else wants are usually based on fear.
- *Is the goal in accord with my values*? Because values are powerful motivators, you will find the path difficult if you don't feel in harmony with what you believe.

- *Is the goal a priority of mine*? Goal overload is suffered by people who don't recognize honest human limitations. Can you achieve high grades, work full time in order to advance in your career, be an outstanding parent, build a successful marriage, develop close friendships, and serve as an organization's leader at the same time? The key is to concentrate on what you specifically want at any given time.
- *Is the goal realistic*? Sometimes the answers are obvious. Trying to lose 25 pounds in one week is not realistic. You could want too much or be shortchanging yourself. What is wise is to look for challenges that are right for you-for what you can effectively manage (Brim, 1992).
- *Is the goal specific*? A common problem is to have a vague goal such as, "I want to be rich," "I want to travel," or "I want to be thin." Identify how rich you want to be, where you want to travel, and how thin you want to be. Then add a "by when" date to each.

If you can answer yes to each of the questions, you are ready to move ahead with enthusiasm. A goal shapes the plan, the plan sets the action, and the action achieves a result. Successful completion means that a goal is thought out, planned out, written out, and carried out (Helmstetter, 1991).

Write the goal. Of benefit is to put your specific goal in writing and post it where you will look at it daily. Goals that are floating around in your head stand little chance of being acted upon. Jackie wrote, "I want to send out ten resumes and cover letters during the month of October" and tacked it to her bulletin board above her desk. She also wrote little notes in the form of questions and placed them in other strategic spots—on the bathroom mirror, on the refrigerator door, and inside her briefcase: "What about the resumes?" "How many resumes have you sent so far?" "RESUMES?"

Identify specific action steps. A main reason a goal remains only a goal and is never achieved, despite the best intentions, is that even a realistic goal can seem overwhelming. The first way to change this is to pinpoint, or set goals with realistic numbers attached (Schmidt, 1976). Instead of, "I want to quit smoking by the end of January," you would say, "I want to decrease my cigarette smoking to one pack a day by January 15." One pack a day can be measured so you can see whether you succeed. Pinpointing helps you to break your goal into specific action steps with time deadlines attached to each. This practice is what is described as "making mole hills out of mountains" (Schmidt, 1976, p. 11).

Action is the key word. Action is choice in motion; it turns a good plan into accomplishment (Helmstetter, 1991). For a goal-setting activity in one of my classes, losing weight is a popular choice. Over and over I read, "I will lose 2 pounds by October 7," "2 more by October 14," and "2 more by October 21." In big letters I write, "HOW?" Do you see that describing exactly what you will and won't do is essential? A first action step is to find out how much you weigh. Then note the following specific action steps:

- I will walk 2 miles each day starting October 1.
- I will buy a calorie-counter on October 1.
- I will learn how to calculate healthy levels of fat intake by October 1.

- I will decrease my intake of calories to 1400 and my fat intake to 40 grams or less per day beginning October 2.
- I will not skip any meals and will try to spread my intake of food throughout the day beginning October 2.
- I will eat four servings each of fresh fruits and vegetables a day beginning October 2.
- I will decrease my intake of cola to two cans a week beginning October 2.
- I will eat a dessert only once a week beginning October 2.
- I will write down everything I eat or drink beginning October 2.

The chance of successfully achieving the desired weight loss with a pinpointed plan is much higher than it would be with the typical, "I should lose weight" or "I'm going on a diet next week." Being specific about each step is the difference. For example, instead of just, "I will exercise daily," write down exactly what and how many exercises you will do for how long and when. Then you will know whether you have accomplished what you intended.

Another advantage of having small steps is that you can acknowledge each minor success which converts into the energy to continue. "That good feeling of accomplishment you get every time you complete a small piece of the task will sustain you through a lot of drudgery" (Bandler, 1985, p. 79). What if you don't succeed with one action step? Check to see whether it's realistic. You can then decide whether to change it. A temporary problem with one step won't defeat you unless you let it. A worthwhile goal now is to do the activities related to getting what you want in REFLECTIONS AND APPLICATIONS. *Self-actualized individuals*, according to Maslow, do not live by the memory of past accomplishments. Instead, they strive toward new goals with first-rate efforts.

> *Either you let your life slip away by not doing the things you want to do, or you get up and do them.*
>
> —Roger von Oech

Defeat procrastination. After all systems are "go," do you act? Or is procrastination a formidable enemy? Putting things off once in a while is no cause for alarm and, as pointed out in Chapter 3, can even be in your best interest. But if the habit of procrastination keeps you from getting what you want, rid yourself of it. This necessity usually becomes more pronounced. "The demands and responsibilities of adult life are much greater, and procrastination begins to feel more like a prison than a game. Yet it can be very difficult to break free" (Burka and Yuen, 1983, p. 15).

Despite the difficulty, when the consequences of procrastination are faced, most people want to change. Consider the costs (LeBoeuf, 1979).

- *Waste of the present:* I'll do it tomorrow, but tomorrow may not come.
- *An unfulfilled life:* Today won't count for anything if nothing is accomplished.
- *Boredom:* Life can become dull and flat when filled with things undone.
- *Anxiety:* Working under pressure at the last minute is a stressor.
- *Impotent goals:* Goals not acted upon are like hot air, one "I'm gonna" after another with no results.

- *Unsolved problems:* A constant plague of these is like vermin, one breeding another and another.
- *Continuous frustration:* Not getting any "wants" becomes disheartening.
- *Poor health:* Putting off taking care of self or maintaining safety can be harmful.
- *A mediocre career:* Delay and inaction lead to nonproductivity, and even though most procrastinators claim that they will be different at work, the habit lingers.
- *A life of indecision:* Becoming a slave to the future instead of the master of it is a heavy price.
- *Fatigue:* Putting things off takes energy.

Studies show that compulsive procrastinators tended to sabotage themselves more, have lower self-esteem, greater self-consciousness (Ferrari, 1991), and high test anxiety (Milgram et al., 1992). Doesn't all this sound dreadful? Anyone who wants to live a happy life would adopt the worthy goal of defeating procrastination.

Individuals procrastinate for different reasons. Discovering why you procrastinate can help you find another way to satisfy your need or to decide whether the reason is worth the costs. Is it because the task seems overwhelming or unpleasant? Then break it into those smaller action steps described earlier. This puts an end to initial procrastination and motivates you to take the second step. Unpleasant tasks can be evaluated. How important is this? How bad will it be if I don't do it? What are the rewards? For example, cleaning toilet bowls is not high on most people's lists of desirable tasks. Next time you are faced with the chore, apply the three questions. If you honestly decide that cleaning the toilet is unimportant, that it won't be so bad left undone, and that the rewards aren't worth the effort at the time, you aren't procrastinating!

Is procrastination an excuse for a poor performance? If so, this is like trying to make two wrongs into a right. Most students who leave major projects to the last minute do poorly. Ironically, a number of them will say, "I didn't do well because I ran out of time," and they will expect to be excused because of lack of time. As discussed in Chapter 3, you and I do have time, and running out means mismanagement of it. Another procrastinating message about time is, "I'll do it when I have more time." We will never have more time, and allowing too many demands on your time leads to pressure. "Most people would gladly become less tense and rushed-if only they had the time" (Bloomfield and Felder, 1985, p. 103). Procrastinators are often time-wasters who don't use small time segments. "The weekend flew by, and I didn't accomplish anything" is a common remark. In most cases, things did get accomplished; however, a true procrastinator may be speaking the truth. Small scraps of time can become significant. Cutting out just 20 minutes of wasted time a day gains you a whole year by the time you're 70 (Tubesing, 1981). Even though enjoyable activities are important, too often, people who say they don't have time are actually using a great deal of it for enjoyment. You might consider keeping a weekly account of how your time is actually spent and then learning time management.

Do you use procrastination to gain sympathy? Donna played the "poor-me" game to explain why things didn't get done. "I wanted to be a good mother and take the kids to the zoo, but too many other things came up" and "I have more things to do than most, and I can't afford to take time for myself" were some of her pleas for sympathy. When a friend told her that she was tired of hearing all her tales of woe, Donna maturely took a look at herself and decided to end the game.

Are you defending against blows to self-esteem by putting things off? In a study, compulsive female procrastinators tended to be anxious individuals who actively avoided evaluative information. Both sexes viewed self-worth solely on how well they did on a particular task so they delayed task completion (Ferrari, 1991). "I didn't get it done" may be a cover-up for "I was afraid it wouldn't be good enough." Perfectionists tend to procrastinate for this reason.

> A perfectionist requires that he or she accomplish unattainable goals without risking failure. Some are too fearful even to risk achievement because of the uncertainty about outcomes (Adams, 1987, p. 180).

Several books on procrastination and time management can help you learn to make better use of time. Raising self-esteem and getting rid of perfectionistic attitudes are also recommended. One way to raise self-esteem and decrease procrastination at the same time is to complete a task and then praise and reward yourself for doing so. In the final stage of achieving what you want, making a commitment of time, energy, and efforts is imperative. Commitment coupled with enthusiasm is an unbeatable combination.

> *Enthusiasm is one of the most powerful engines of success. When you do a thing, do it with all your might. Put your whole soul into it. Stamp it with your own personality. Be active, be energetic, be enthusiastic and faithful, and you will accomplish your objective. Nothing great was ever achieved without enthusiasm.*
>
> —Ralph Waldo Emerson

SUMMARY

Values are top priorities in life—qualities, conditions, and standards that are desirable, worthy, and important to individuals. They motivate behavior and affect all aspects of life. Assessing what you value and why you do are important in self-understanding and achieving your own identity; this is a lifelong process. Values originate from external sources. The three ego states play principal roles in values development and implementation. Morals are standards reflecting right and wrong. Your morals and values develop in stages.

The ways in which values are received can be traced by values programming analysis. Imprinting, modeling, and socialization are three methods of receiving values from different influences. Societal events in various decades also affect values. Values are transmitted by parents and other authority figures. Two methods, moralizing and laissez-faire (or hands-off), are not recommended because of their ineffectiveness and potential problematic results. Several other methods are more likely to produce well-adjusted individuals capable of making healthy decisions.

During adulthood, values may alter because of a major life change, mental unrest, and a change in needs. Flexibility and ability to adjust are encouraged. Other characteristics of healthy values are ownership, realism, and life-enhancement. Restrictive and absolute values can destroy individual freedom of choice. Freedom to make choices is of value. Life is full of choices. In areas of health, drug use and abuse, weight maintenance, aging, sexuality, career, and relationships, you have alternatives. Being educated is important.

Making responsible decisions is a learned process, and decision making models are useful. Valuing what can be learned from mistakes helps us to accept and benefit from them. Getting what you want isn't easy. Goals based on wants are more likely to be achieved. Questions can be asked to check a goal for possibility of success. Then, putting a goal into action is necessary. Chronic procrastination is to be avoided. Effective time management improves many aspects of life. In the final analysis, commitment to achievement is the key.

To think, to judge, to choose our values, is to be individuated, to create a distinct, personal identity.

—Nathaniel Branden

RESOURCES

- AIDS Hotline, 800-342-AIDS (2437)
- National Council on Alcoholism Hotline, 800-622-2255
- Center for Substance Abuse Treatment Hotline, 800-662-4357
- Al-anon Family Group Headquarters, Inc., P. O. Box 862, Midtown Station, New York, NY 10018, (212) 302-7240 (for those with a friend or relative who has an alcohol problem)
- National Association for Children of Alcoholics, 31582 Coast Highway, Suite B, South Laguna, CA 92677, (714) 499-3889
- Smokenders, 1430 E. Indian School Road, Suite 102, Phoenix, AZ 85014, (602) 248-0374
- Overeaters Anonymous, P. O. Box 92870, Los Angeles, CA 90009, (310) 542-8363

Section Two

Communication: The Key to Relationships

OBJECTIVES

After completing this section, you will be able to

- Define communication and describe its process.
- Discuss the importance of communication.
- Explain how and where people learn to communicate.
- List ways in which family communication could be improved.
- Give reasons for formal training in interpersonal communication.
- Describe characteristics helpful in being a positive communicator.

I see communication as a huge umbrella that covers and affects all that goes on between human beings—the largest single factor determining kinds of relationships and individual happenings in the world.

—Virginia Satir

"We don't communicate," was the couple's agreed-upon answer when asked why they wanted a divorce. "Oh, but you do," was the surprising reply from the marriage counselor. The couple did not realize that whenever two people occupy the same environment, communication is taking place. Although people can stop talking, they continue to communicate with bodily appearances, mannerisms, personal actions, and facial expressions. An accurate reason for wanting a divorce is, "We don't communicate well" or "The way we communicate has caused problems and damage."

Whether intentional or not, communication influences all relationships. Without communication, interaction would not occur. In fact, communication can be described as interaction (van Oosting, 1992). A more complete definition is *a complex process of mutually exchanging messages between two or more individuals which can enable them to function, learn, share, and grow*. Models of communication are not simple diagrams. Within exchanges, people are continually sending, receiving, and reacting to each other. *Creating and sharing a meaning* is the main purpose of interpersonal communication. Both the sender and receiver are responsible for clarity. When different meanings come from messages, the outcome can be negative. Poor communication is filled with disparate meanings. "But that's not what I meant" is far too common. What is worse is not being aware that you have been misunderstood. Experts believe that as much as 70 percent of our communications efforts are probably misinterpreted, misunderstood, rejected, disliked, or distorted (Donaldson and Scannell, 1986). Communication is as diverse and mysterious as those who engage in interaction (Van Oosting, 1992).

The importance of clear, positive communication cannot be overemphasized. Research indicates that communication is the foundation for all relationships and the primary cause of their success or failure. Ineffective or faulty communication is at the root of most interpersonal difficulties. Conversely, effective communication is necessary to develop and maintain any positive interpersonal relationship (Okun, 1992).

Being able to communicate effectively benefits you in everyday situations, in a job search, in the advancement of your career, and in all types of relationships. When you think of your friendships, doesn't communication strike you as an essential component? It is highly unlikely that you will remain friends with someone with whom you have difficulty communicating. Between patient and physician, full communication is indispensable because communication can be as important to healing as medicine (Cousins, 1989). One study showed that inadequate communication was a major source of stress for caregivers and other health care workers (Riordan and Saltzer, 1992). On the other hand, communication was found to serve a critical role in reducing or moderating the experience of burnout (Miller et al., 1990) and to increase the level of trust between supervisors and their employees. "Trust is strongly dependent on the ability to communicate clearly" (*Menninger Letter*, 1994c).

Most of the communication research has focused on couples. Leo Buscaglia (1984) conducted a study in which he asked couples about problems and strengthening factors in their relationships. The same factor was identified as being both the most problematic and the most strengthening. Not surprising, it was communication. More than 85 percent of the hundreds of respondents said that the most essential quality for a lasting relationship was the ability to communicate (Buscaglia, 1992).

A group of women and men were asked to list the three most important factors necessary for a good marriage. Communication was named by 81 percent of the 90 respondents ahead of love and friendship. Studies conducted by a colleague and myself indicated that positive communication contributed to the strength of the stepfamily (Hanna and Knaub, 1981; Knaub, Hanna, and Stinnett, 1984). When stepchildren were asked to identify areas of concern, communication was frequently mentioned (Knaub and Hanna, 1984). One girl offered this response to an open-ended question: "The worst thing about my stepfamily is that my stepfather thinks he's always right and we're always wrong—what he says goes" (p. 87). She suggested that he listen and show a willingness to compromise, two important ingredients in positive communication.

Couples and families have overcome extraordinary hardships with effective communication. Read any book on relationship success, talk to counselors and other experts, and ask the couples themselves; the powerful influence of communication will be evident. "An effective communication model is perhaps the most important element in secure and lasting marriages" (Gordon, 1988b, p. 46).

> *Human communication is the most awesome force in the world. It can be directly responsible for peace or war, love or hate. Communication is unavoidable, and our communication skills are directly related to the quality of life we experience.*
>
> —Jacquelyn Carr

Human beings are not born knowing how to communicate. In fact, it is an acquired skill, not a natural byproduct of people coming together (Buscaglia, 1992). Realizing how important communication skills are, one could assume that they would be taught as systematically as other valuable behaviors. Are they? How did you learn to communicate? Were you taught by trained professionals? For almost everyone, the answers are that learning was by observation, modeling, and feedback, and that the teaching came from untrained individuals.

> All communication is learned. Every baby who comes into this world comes only with raw materials—no self-concept, no experience of interacting with others, and no experience in dealing with the world. Babies learn all these things through communication with the people who are in charge of them from birth on. By the time we reach the age of five, we probably have had a billion experiences in sharing communication. Unless something powerful changes our conclusions, that early learning becomes the foundation for the rest of our lives (Satir, 1988, p. 52).

Patterns of communication in many families are poor, and, in all families, communication can be improved.

A survey of psychology students at Southeast Community College assessed family communication. Through questionnaires, 145 students rated communication on a 5-point scale ranging from excellent to poor, first within the family as a whole, and then separately with their fathers and mothers. The results were interesting.

- Almost 50 percent rated overall family communication as good or excellent. About 20 percent placed it below satisfactory, and 30 percent rated it as satisfactory.
- A definite difference between fathers and mothers was noted. 35 percent said their fathers needed improvement compared with 14 percent for mothers. Excellent were 28 percent of the mothers and only 8 percent of the fathers.

If males are not raised to be communicative, they will be less capable in this regard as parents—another sad outcome of gender-role stereotypic training. Even though more students rated the quality of communication as satisfactory or above, several comments to an open-ended question indicated how much better it could have been. These responses can serve as suggestions.

- Set aside time to talk and listen. Be sure that communication takes place daily. This may seem like an unnecessary suggestion, since families are expected to talk. Statistics show, however, that a mother on a typical workday spends 11 minutes in focused conversation with her children, and the father spends just 8 minutes (Cutler, 1989).
- Talk about everything, not just gripes and problems. Include as many or more positive subjects than negative ones.

- Allow and encourage everyone to talk. Consider all points of view and don't judge.
- Be sincerely interested and show this by actively listening.
- Ask questions, especially those that require more than a one-word answer: not, "How was school today?" but, "What class did you like (or not like) today and for what reason?"
- Be open, honest, and flexible when you communicate.

Openness of family communication was associated with family cohesion and satisfaction with the family relationship in a sample of 174 junior high students (Papini et al., 1990). Open communication is covered in Chapter 7. Another important aspect of positive communication is a supportive climate in which the sender of a message feels free, safe, comfortable, and accepted (Wolvin and Coakley, 1988). If communication skills are left to amateurs who learned from untrained people, is it any wonder that communication difficulties are plentiful?

> Effective communication makes life work. But where can you learn it? Parents are often dismal role models. Schools are busy teaching French and trigonometry. Communication skills have been known and available for years. They can and should be taught right along with the three R's (McKay et al., 1983, p. 8).

When verbal exchange is taking place, what exactly is happening? Speaking and listening are two necessary parts of the process. Nonverbal behaviors accompany both. A communication interaction is a circular process in which a message is sent verbally and nonverbally; the message is received and interpreted, and verbal and nonverbal feedback is usually sent; the sender reacts to the feedback. The people in the exchange are simultaneously sending and receiving messages, and the interaction occurs within a social context.

Do you see how complex the communication process is? Skills that can be learned are beneficial in ensuring that a common meaning is shared. If you've followed the suggestions offered in this book, you have a head start on becoming an excellent communicator. The positive attitudes and behaviors needed in communication are those practiced by well-adjusted individuals with high self-esteem. Several are especially important in the communication process.

- A life position of I'm OK, you're OK is at the heart of positive communication. Participants have high self-esteem, and they treat each other with respect.

Figure II-1 Reprinted with permission of King Features Syndicate.

- Honesty in communication means authenticity. Communicators do not play games, mislead, and try to manipulate each other. Knowing that another person will be "up front" with you creates a positive atmosphere for communication.
- Openness is a necessity if you want to communicate positively with others. A closed person who isn't interested in learning and growing is a poor interpersonal communication candidate. You are likely to be enjoyed as a conversationalist if you are open.
- Willingness to share means that you are able and willing to disclose about yourself and to express your ideas. Listening is a valuable skill; however, if you only listen, you aren't completely participating in an exchange.
- Expressiveness has been praised in terms of health and well-being. Willingness and ability to show your feelings also helps you to be a better communicator.
- Appropriateness relates to the content of a message. An effective speaker, through awareness, knows what is suitable to say and what is not. Do you know people who talk about topics in an inappropriate setting or who dwell on unsuitable subjects?
- Flexibility is needed in positive communication. Being closed-minded is detrimental to a give-and-take communication process.
- A sense of humor, while not a necessity, separates good communicators from excellent ones. Having a sense of humor does not mean telling one joke after another. Instead, you see humor in life, add a witty spark to conversations, don't take yourself too seriously, and appreciate others' humor. Judicious humor is not sarcastic; instead, you perceive the ludicrous, comical, and absurd in life and express it without bitterness (Cocola and Matthews, 1992).

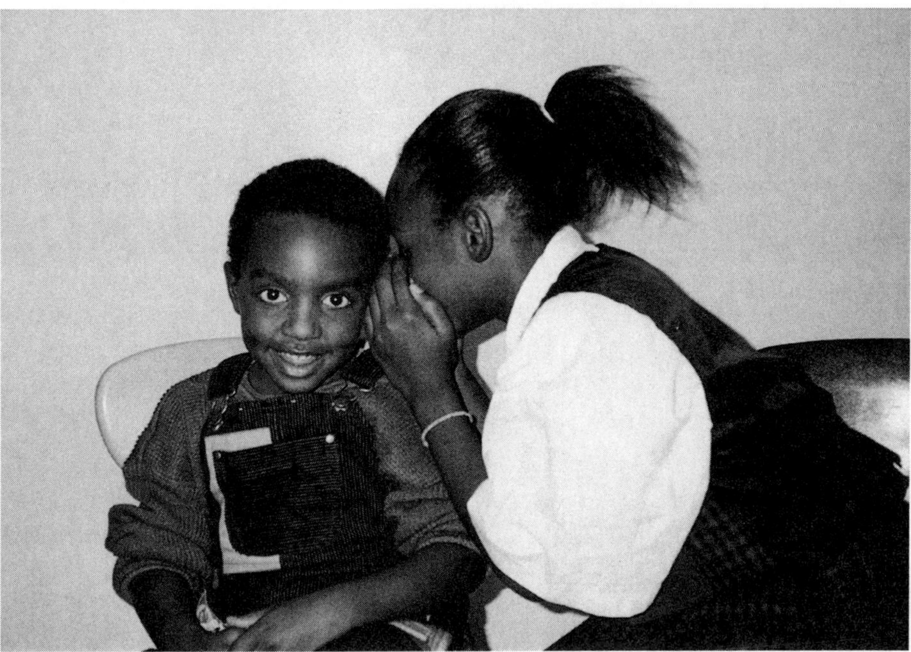

Figure II-2 Communication can be a joyous experience.

- Understanding and the ability to interpret are needed in order to achieve a shared meaning. Being a critical thinker with the ability to process and see alternatives can solve communication problems caused by locked-in thinking.

Healthy communication is gratifying to the participants. During an exchange, each may experience frustration; however, the gratification often comes with the outcome. The outcome *could* be a realization that you misunderstood the other. If you learn from mistakes, you can still feel satisfied. Rewards of affirmation, understanding, and intimacy are viable products of healthy communication.

> *If you and I can honestly tell each other who we are, what we think, judge, feel, value, love, honor, and esteem, hate, fear, desire, hope for, believe in and are committed to, then and then only can each of us grow.*
>
> —John Powell

6

Becoming a Positive Listener

OBJECTIVES

After completing this chapter, you will be able to

- Define listening and recognize what is involved.
- Differentiate between hearing and listening.
- Give reasons why listening is important.
- Identify barriers to positive listening.
- Understand the importance of body language and verbal responses.
- Describe negative listening behaviors.
- Name and give examples of the types of listening.
- Become a better listener!

Listening is the most profound ingredient of communication. Listening is a hallmark of loving another.

—Teresa Adams

The day care director spoke to an excited group: "Children, you need to listen to your teachers and me." The bright-eyed children nodded their agreement. They had heard about listening at home and knew that it was expected. If we could follow each child from that time until adulthood, we would find that a few had somehow learned to listen well, several had an average skill level, and others were poor listeners. They were told to listen yet not instructed in how. What we so often fail to realize is that good listeners are made, not born (Ryan and Travis, 1991).

LISTENING AS AN ART

Listening is not a given. Instead, listening well is an art. Positive listening is made up of skills; each is learned and can be improved. *Listening* is an active process of attending, receiving auditory stimuli, interpreting, and then providing feedback. Understanding comes from both an accurate interpretation of the content as well as nonverbal clues. Listening is active because if you are good at it, you are not passive.

When you are hearing noises or sounds, you can be inactive. *Hearing* is using the auditory sense to take in a message. Listening includes not only hearing but interpretation and feedback, too. When you listen positively, you are attentive, involved, stimulated, and animated. The next time you are in the listener's role ask yourself, "Am I truly listening? Do I give the impression that I am?"

The Why of Listening

Listening has purpose. You may listen for any of these reasons.

Enjoyment—Of particular pleasure are the times spent in enjoyable listening. Examples are daily conversations at work and home, the radio, television, and movies.

Information—You receive information by listening. Students in the classroom listen primarily for this reason. You also get information from the media and in conversations. Enjoyment and information listening can coincide; often, the best listening situations are those that include both. Isn't a classroom more interesting when you are engaged in informational and enjoyable listening?

Help—Relationships supply support, and you will receive and provide help by listening. Relationships thrive on a positive listening environment.

Whatever the purpose, positive listening in relationships helps you to develop a full understanding of another person's situation, concern, or point of view (Miller et al., 1988).

The Importance of Listening

Listening is basic to learning, and people who cannot hear must employ other means to receive messages. Because listening is the first language skill developed by those who hear, all other skills are dependent upon it. Yet, in school listening is the most neglected of all the language arts skills (Wolvin and Coakley, 1988). How much of communication consists of listening? Of communication activities engaged in by college students, listening consumes the most time. Figure 6-1 shows the results of a study on college students (Barker et al., 1980). When you consider the amount of time college students spend listening in classrooms alone, the results are not surprising. If you want to succeed in academics, good listening is a "must!"

The workplace, too, demands good listening skills. Initially, you will receive information and directions during the job interview. An applicant with a hearing impairment said, "People who can hear have such an advantage, and they don't even realize it." Demonstrating good listening skills to get a job is only the beginning because learning

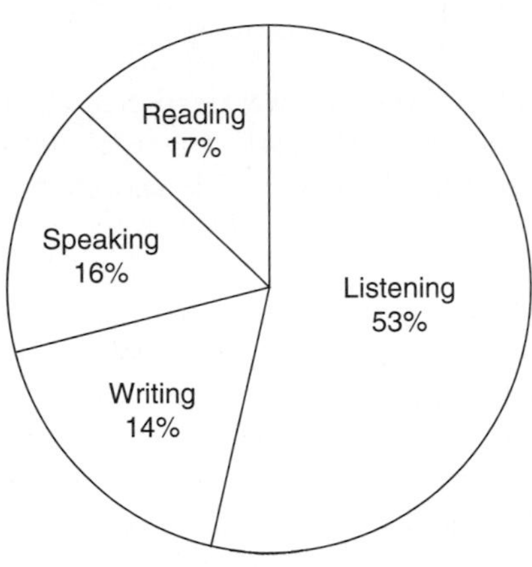

Figure 6-1 Time spent in listening.

comes from listening, not talking (Wolvin and Coakley, 1988). Besides helping employees learn required technical skills, positive listening builds satisfactory customer relations, and enriches work relationships. Unfortunately, listening is often a neglected tool even among managers (Kurtz, 1991). Inefficient or poor listening becomes costly to both businesses and consumers.

Listening creates and improves personal relationships. Being a good listener is a frequently mentioned characteristic of a cherished friend. A person who has difficulty listening may be avoided by others. Satisfying communication in marriage requires excellent listening skills.

> Since true listening is love in action, nowhere is it more appropriate than in marriage. Yet most couples never truly listen to each other. Consequently, when couples come for counseling or therapy, a major task is to teach them how to listen (Peck, 1978, p. 128).

A common complaint in families is that nobody listens. Parents lament that their children don't listen to them (usually because the child has not completed a task or followed a command), and children complain that their parents don't listen. Listening is a sign of affirmation. When family members truly listen, they contribute to one another's self-esteem. When they don't, the interpretation is frequently negative. One of the common comments of students in the survey described earlier was that true listening was missing in their families. The art of listening is the single skill necessary for establishing loving relationships (Jampolsky and Cirincione, 1990).

If you are a parent, you undoubtedly realize that total listening whenever a young child talks is virtually impossible and impractical, especially if she or he is talkative. However, even a small amount of time devoted to true listening yields invaluable rewards. One of the most rewarding rituals my husband and I established even before we became a stepfamily was to have an evening out with each of the four children. Once a week, we two adults went out with one child for dinner, and the focus of attention was on the child. One evening I started to chat with my husband about a business matter, and my 8-year-old daughter, Lyn, assertively said, "Hey, remember that this is my time." She and the others, when it was their turn, came ready to talk, and we truly listened. I treasure those precious evenings when we learned and shared so much.

How and Where Listening Is Learned

When you entered school, if you could hear, you were expected to know how to listen. Listening skills activities may be included as a part of a class; however, a specific course on how to listen is a rare offering even today. The executive director of a banking association commented:

> I spent years in school learning about history, math, and science. In my career I spend most of my time communicating, much of which is listening. How much training did I get in listening? None. If they taught it, I missed it.

He probably didn't miss it; the skills just weren't taught. A business executive spends roughly 1 hour of the day reading, 2 hours talking, and 8 hours listening. Yet in school, most time is spent learning to read, a smaller amount learning to speak, and almost no time learning to listen (Peck, 1978). If you are like most, you'll need to learn the art of truly listening. "Most of us are poor listeners if we actually listen at all. But there is hope because listening is learned. Love is a perfect impetus for working at that art" (Buscaglia, 1992, p. 167).

BARRIERS IN THE LISTENING PROCESS

If you are planning a trip by automobile, you can make it more pleasant by knowing about any road construction, poor weather conditions, or detours along the way. Then you can avoid them or at least be prepared to face the delays. Recognizing barriers in the listening process is necessary if you are to avoid or decrease their negative effects.

Preoccupation or Lack of Interest

A major obstacle is preoccupation or lack of interest. All too often, when one person is talking, the other is thinking her or his own thoughts, impatiently waiting for a chance to talk, or silently thinking about a rebuttal. When two people talk but nobody listens, both individuals feel lonely and misunderstood (Love and Robinson, 1990). If you aren't interested in what a speaker has to offer, you will probably not want to listen. You have at least three choices. You may listen anyway and attempt to develop an interest. You might pretend to listen, or you can be honest and tell the person you aren't interested. The decision would be based on the situation and your feelings at the time.

Besides disinterest, preoccupation can be caused by other factors. Have you ever said or heard someone say, "I can do more than one thing at a time, so I can listen to you while I'm reading the newspaper (or watching television)"? People can do more than one thing at a time; however, they aren't doing any with complete concentration. Full attention is required if you are going to do your best listening. "Careful listening, your total presence, is a precious gift you can give. It's a gift that communicates care and concern" (Miller et al., 1979, p. 66). Chronic preoccupation is sure to deaden a relationship. A study designed to predict marital success identified a pattern of listening called stonewalling, a behavior in which the listener presented a stone wall to the speaker, not moving the face very much, avoiding eye contact, holding the neck rigid, and not using any listening response. Husbands used this more than wives, and over time it led to marital dissatisfaction (Gottman, 1991).

Environmental Factors

The environment can provide barriers. Noise detracts, and even with the best intentions, listening is difficult in the middle of an explosion of sounds. Have you ever tried to communicate when a television set is turned on somewhere in the room? Even if nobody is actively watching, or even if the sound is turned off, the set attracts attention. The visual distractions are just as bothersome as auditory ones. Temperature and lack of air flow can also be distracting. The extent of listening I can expect from students is directly related to the climate of the classroom. Important listening situations deserve an environment free of distractions.

Psychological Filter

Of prime importance in the listening process is the listener's psychological filter, which is composed of preconceived ideas, moods, assumptions, labels, stereotypes, past experiences, emotions, hopes, memories, and even degree of self-esteem. We form impressions of a speaker quickly, and our filters influence what those impressions are. The older we get, the more clogged this filter can be (Walker and Brokaw, 1992). Attitudes predispose us to respond positively or negatively. For example, if you know that you do not agree with a speaker and there will be no opportunity to respond, the chance of your listening deeply is probably slight. Also, a negative self-fulfilling prophecy may keep you from even trying to listen. John commented that he has been told so often by teachers and parents that he is a poor listener, he believes it and continues the inactive listening behaviors he developed early in life.

As selective listeners, we can hear about half of what is said and filter out anything we consider unimportant (Buscaglia, 1992). Obviously, we can miss important and

HERMAN®
"I really look forward to your visits."

Figure 6-2 Copyright 1986 Universal Press Syndicate. Reprinted by permission. All rights reserved.

interesting information. Just as a homeowner checks a furnace filter periodically, examining your psychological filter is a good idea. You may not be able to entirely eliminate it, yet being aware of clogging elements and discarding whatever you can will help you become a better listener.

Rate Differences

The differences between speaking and thinking rates can create another obstacle. Figures vary; regardless, a person talks at a slower rate than the listener thinks. The average rate of speech is about 125 to 175 words a minute while the brain can think at the rate of 500 to 1000 words a minute. This means that you, as a listener, are ahead of the speaker! You might think of a car traveling 55 miles an hour left hopelessly behind by a jet going 550 miles an hour (Donaldson and Scannell, 1986). The span of time can hinder your continued concentration, and the mind can meander. Positive listeners remain focused.

Negative Intentions

Although they may not realize it, listeners can have negative intentions. Persuasive listeners, described by Miller and colleagues (1988), want to lead the conversation. They listen briefly and then jump to conclusions, interrupt to disagree, give advice, and attempt to impose their perspective or solution on the speaker. They want to persuade the other to see it their way, so they don't truly listen; instead, they are thinking about and rehearsing what they will say. Because of this, they frequently interrupt.

Other negative intentions are listening to gain an advantage or to "win," to devise a way to manipulate another, to use the information in a harmful way (as in the case of gossip), or to feign an interest that doesn't exist. Just as insincere or phony talkers eventually reveal their true colors, listeners with negative intentions generally end up losers in human relationships.

IMPROVING LISTENING BEHAVIORS

Eliminating any of the barriers sets up a positive listening atmosphere. Then, being aware of your own behaviors, improving your skills, and becoming active will lead to positive listening.

Attentive Body Position

Do you appear to be listening? The way you position yourself in relation to the speaker makes a difference. Being a comfortable distance apart is basic. Physical space zones are covered in Chapter 7. Being on the same level sets the tone for the interchange because if one stands and the other sits, the person seated can feel at a disadvantage. Facing the speaker is essential. Turning your body away carries a message of disinterest and lessens your involvement, while facing the speaker squarely and leaning slightly forward demonstrates attentiveness.

Adopting an open, attentive posture indicates interest, openness, and involvement. Sitting with legs and arms crossed, slouching, and leaning away from the speaker give negative impressions. Instead, you can sit with hands at your sides or on your lap. In situations such as a job interview, you appear more professional if you keep your feet together on the floor. A slumped posture may be comfortable, yet if you are truly interested, your body usually reflects it by an upright position. Having attentive posture does not mean being rigid and tense. A relaxed position of openness and attentiveness is ideal.

Positive Eye Contact

Maintaining eye contact in the American society is a must. In fact, conversation usually doesn't even start until eye contact is made. A person who does not look at you or who often avoids eye contact can cause discomfort. Employers will likely have negative impressions of applicants who don't keep their eyes on the interviewer. Poor eye contact may be interpreted as a lack of confidence or as indicative of dishonesty or lying. Knowledge of culture is important as a student from the Middle East commented that direct eye contact is discouraged in his society. In other societies looking down rather than at the speaker is respectful.

Knowing how important eye contact can be and being able to actually maintain it may be altogether different. A student said, "Sharon, I hope in your book you will do more than just say, 'Have good eye contact.' I already know that, but how?" First, realize that eye contact is almost never a direct meeting between sets of eyes. You don't have to look squarely into a speaker's eyes and can focus anywhere on the face, including the nose, mouth, or ear. As long as you are at least 18 inches away from the speaker, the person usually can't tell that you aren't maintaining exact eye contact.

A recommendation is to look at the speaker's face for roughly three quarters of the time, in glances lasting from 1 to 7 seconds. A speaker will look at a listener for less than half the time, and these intermittent glances rarely last for more than a second (Marsh, 1988). In a job interview, paying attention, maintaining direct eye contact most

Figure 6-3 Body language can reveal a great deal.

of the time, and periodically looking away or above or below the interviewer's eyes is appropriate. Staring is definitely not recommended. Knowing that you can look elsewhere and keeping a relaxed frame of mind make it easier to maintain eye contact.

Facial Expression

Feedback is delivered to a great extent by changes in facial expression. A "poker face" is helpful in a card game; it is generally useless, and often demeaning, in the listening process. A positive listener reacts to what is being said by registering any thinking and feeling responses. A smile, a frown, or a look of bewilderment or surprise are just a few of the expressions your face can make. Actually, about 20,000 different facial expressions are possible (Carl, 1980). Changing your facial expression isn't that difficult! Look into a mirror and actually practice changing your expressions. Joel said, "I know it's important to smile, but I hate the way my teeth look." He finally decided that getting his teeth fixed was worth the price he had been paying in decreased relationship skills.

Head and Body Movements

One of my favorite listening behaviors is nodding the head. An affirmative nod shows the speaker not only that you have heard but also that you agree. A nod can motivate and energize a speaker. "Nodders" are worth their weight in gold! Even a side-to-side nod indicating confusion or disagreement can be helpful if the objective is to arrive at shared meaning.

Nodding can be developed. You may want to tell yourself to do so until the behavior becomes natural. Since it is possible to nod too much, be sure to use the movement moderately and when appropriate. Other body movements such as tilting the head to one side or shrugging the shoulders also provide feedback to the speaker.

Touching

Depending on your relationship with the speaker, listening can be improved by an appropriate touch. One day a student came in to talk about a personal conflict and was having difficulty expressing herself. I reached over and touched her hand, and the words poured out. My touch had evidently reassured her so she could speak freely.

Research on touching indicates that the arm is a neutral or nonvulnerable area and generally accessible to others. Vulnerable areas are comfortably touched only by intimates. Even though touching can serve as a positive listening behavior, being appropriate is important. Touching is covered more in Chapter 9.

Verbal Responses

Listening is usually a nonverbal activity; however, verbal responses are also included in positive listening. These can vary from a simple "Oh" or "Hmm" to "I see" or "That sounds interesting." You can, however, use too many responses and literally interrupt the speaker's flow. "Really," "I know," or "I understand" stated after each comment is distracting and annoying. A question that encourages the speaker to continue is an excellent response. Some possibilities are: "How do you feel about that?" "What are your alternatives?" "What kind of advice are you getting?" "What happened next?" "Can you tell me more about what happened?" If you are an attentive listener, your question will not move the conversation away from the point. Note the difference in these two examples.

1. SPEAKER: I'm upset with my supervisor. She scheduled me to work this weekend after I told her I wanted the time off.

   LISTENER: Did she just get mixed up?
2. SPEAKER: I'm upset with my supervisor. She scheduled me to work this weekend after I told her I wanted the time off.

   LISTENER: Well, did you hear about Joe getting fired?

Open questions requiring more than a simple yes or no answer are preferred because they are encouraging and move the conversation forward. You are telling the speaker, "What you are saying is of interest, and I want to hear more."

Verbal responses can involve more than short reactions or questions. *Paraphrasing* is restating in your own words what you think the speaker said. Here is an example of paraphrasing.

SPEAKER: My kids have been driving me crazy.

LISTENER: It sounds like you are really bothered by them.

When you paraphrase, you don't add to the message; instead, you are repeating the meaning you received. The response shows that you received the message and want to be sure the meaning is shared. You can use such lead-ins as, "It sounds like," "In other words," "You mean that," "What I hear you saying is," or "Let me make sure I understand what you mean." Paraphrasing may seem clumsy at first; yet, once you find and practice a few phrases that sound natural, using them will become easier.

The benefits of paraphrasing are worth the initial discomfort. First, people appreciate that they were heard. Paraphrasing can stop anger from escalating and cool a crisis situation, decrease misinterpretation because errors can be corrected immediately, and aid in remembering what was said. Paraphrasing can work beautifully with children, who often just want to know that their message was received. For example, picture a 4-year-old girl who tearfully tells you that an older brother has yelled at her. "It sounds like you didn't like him to yell at you" is the parent's paraphrase. That is usually all that is required. In most cases, the child will nod and return to whatever she was doing.

Clarifying goes just a little further than paraphrasing. You not only restate; you also ask questions to get more information and background. Your questions are genuine attempts to ensure that the two of you are sharing the same meaning. By paraphrasing and clarifying, you can create a shared meaning. In doing so, you improve both the exchange and the relationship. Listen. Paraphrase, Verify. When we follow this simple 1-2-3 procedure, we automatically deepen our level of trust and intimacy which makes everyone a winner (Love and Robinson, 1990). Try to use "echoing," a technique in which you listen for the speaker's intent, then verbalize back to show understanding and acceptance even if you don't agree (Cocola and Matthews, 1992).

Expressing an understanding of the speaker's emotions is particularly helpful. Jason tells Nancy that he is "down in the dumps." She says, "You sound really depressed." Jason can then think about her impression. He may respond, "I'm not really that unhappy," or he can say, "Yes, I am really down." When the listener provides an idea of the feeling that is sensed, the speaker receives valuable information. The speaker may also feel free to elaborate further about the feeling and even express other emotions. A listener who echoes a feeling is essentially saying, "I'm here for you."

Feedback, the last step in the listening process, comes after other listening behaviors. *Feedback* is responding with what you, as the listener, think, feel, or sense. You may still be clarifying with questions such as, "Is this what you meant?" or "Is this the way you feel?" Feedback can also provide information about the effect of the message. You eventually respond with your perspective or point of view. Important rules govern feedback (McKay et al., 1983).

- Feedback must be immediate.
- Feedback must be honest. Give your true reaction and do so in a nonhurtful way. Avoid beginning your response with the word you. Instead of "You would be crazy to take a job for that kind of pay," say "I think you'd be wise to consider how satisfied you'll be with that pay."
- Feedback must be supportive. Whatever you say does not put the speaker down. If the person entrusted you with thoughts and feelings, handle them and the individual with care.

Feedback is more accurate if you have paid attention to the speaker's nonverbal behavior, voice, and words. For example, my stepson Greg responded to my question of where he was going with, "Over to my friend's house for a while." I noticed his facial expression, which appeared hostile. My thought was that he really didn't like me, and I was glad I clarified by asking him whether I had done something to offend him. He looked genuinely surprised and said, "No. What makes you think that?" I gave him feedback by describing what I thought his face was saying and how I felt. He laughed and said, "I probably looked mad because I was thinking about my car's empty gas tank!"

The meaning of voice quality can be confusing to a listener, and again, feedback is appropriate. Judy said to her friend, "I'm just fine. I don't need any help." The words said one thing, and her weak, quivering voice revealed another meaning. Her friend responded by telling of her concern and doubt that everything was fine. Usually, the quality of voice is more honest; however, a good listener will check to make sure.

Are you surprised by the number and complexity of listening behaviors? Can you see why listening is considered active and animated? Good listening is not for the lazy.

Elimination of Negative Listening Behaviors

Knowing what to do is essential; knowing *what not to do* is equally important. The opposites or extremes of the behaviors just described are obvious negatives. In addition, an inappropriate facial expression can be unsettling. For example, have you ever tried to describe a serious incident to a listener who is slightly grinning?

Interrupting, unfortunately, is common and is one of the surest signs that a person isn't truly listening. Individuals who enjoy talking have more difficulty with this bothersome behavior. One study found that male and masculine-oriented individuals of either sex interrupted most often (Campbell et al., 1992). Families composed of outgoing, talkative members can have frustrating scenes. My brother Dave once commented about an unusually boisterous exchange among our family members, "Sometimes being in this family is like being in an echo chamber!" He was absolutely correct!

Interrupting can be a part of another disaster in listening: a two-way conversation. A conversation starts. Instead of remaining attentive, the listener begins to speak about a different topic. The speaker can either stop, continue with the original topic, or switch to accommodate the interrupter. If the speaker stays with the first topic, a two-way conversation results and shared meaning is completely lost.

Figure 6-4

Certain listening gestures and sounds can bother the speaker and create a negative communication climate. Several are identified by Ernst (1973).

- cheek puffing and corners of mouth going down,
- "basket hands," with finger tips touching and then moving open and closed,
- foot-swishing, in which the foot and ankle move from side to side,
- eye rolling,
- shoulder shrugging to indicate an I-don't-care attitude,
- head nodding if done rapidly several times in succession,

- corners of the mouth pulling back,
- leg bouncing up and down at high speed,
- index finger extended and moving from side to side in a scolding manner,
- drumming the feet or fingers or thumping the hand or arm,
- a "tsk"ing sound made by the tongue or sighing.

Students in my classes have added a few of their own in role-playing activities such as loud gum chewing, yawning, and knuckle-cracking. Can you identify the negative messages these behaviors might communicate? If you recognize any of the behaviors in yourself, try to eliminate or at least decrease them.

TYPES OF LISTENING

All listening is not the same, even though the active listening behaviors described earlier are essential ingredients in all positive communication exchanges. Different types of listening are most effective in certain situations.

Empathic Listening

Empathy-being able to put yourself in another's place and see and hear from that person's perspective-is a quality to be treasured. *Empathic listening* means that you try to become aware of the speaker's feelings and to feel similarly. You not only understand what the speaker is feeling; you actually feel the emotion. Empathy is easier when the other's thoughts are also understood even if you disagree with them. A comment such as, "I can see why you feel (or think) that way" makes an exchange more pleasant and positive.

Because emotional expression is beneficial, an empathic listener has a worthwhile role. As was pointed out in Chapter 4, people can have difficulty verbalizing feelings. A safe, comfortable climate for communication encourages expression, and an empathic listener sets the tone. Listening in depth and with empathy makes it easier to effectively help others. A therapist who is attentive and concerned will listen beyond the words (S. Jackson, 1992). Suggestions related to empathic listening include (1) step into another's shoes, (2) aim to discover, not reconfirm what you think you already know, and (3) listen for the concern and love instead of reacting to just the words (Cocola and Matthews, 1992). For example, when a mother says, "I wish you just weren't so busy," she may sound critical and angry; however, she could be feeling disappointed, hurt, and sad. An empathic listener is likely to recognize the difference or probe to discover the underlying emotions.

A communication empathy scale, proposed by Messina (1982), is a good way to check your empathic listening. Pretend that a friend has just told you that he has lost his job. Following are descriptions of four levels and examples of responses:

Level 1: Listener misses both the facts and the feeling-"Let's go get a bite to eat."

Level 2: Listener grasps facts but misses the feeling-"It's too bad you lost your job, but something else will come up."

Level 3: Listener understands the facts and realizes that the speaker has a feeling but isn't empathic enough to be correct about which one-"It's too bad you lost your job. I'll bet you're really mad."

Level 4: Listener correctly understands both-"I realize that losing a job is a bad deal. It sounds like you're upset and depressed about it, and I can see why."

The fourth level is a worthy goal. Notice that the use of the word "but" in Level 2 seems to negate the speaker's situation.

Empathic listeners express empathy by tone of voice and body language. In addition, they can use short verbal responses. Some listeners are quick to say, "I know just how you feel"; such a response is not recommended. Even though you empathize, you do not know just how another feels. A better response would be, "I have a strong sense of how you feel." Can you detect the use of empathic listening in the following?

JEANNE: I was trying to lead the group discussion, and she kept interrupting. I felt like she thought that I wasn't handling it right.

BRENDA: It sounds like you were in a difficult spot.

JEANNE: I'll say. I tried to politely tell her to quit distracting us, but she kept doing it.

BRENDA: I would have been frustrated.

JEANNE: I was really frustrated, and by the time the evening was over, I was ready to scream.

BRENDA: I can almost feel what you were going through. It sounds like it kept building up until you were really angry.

JEANNE: That's right.

Note that Brenda expressed the sense of frustration and then picked up on the escalation to anger. The "I can almost feel" phrase is much more honest than, "I know exactly how you feel."

Empathic listening is desirable in most exchanges. Once in a while, however, you can better serve the speaker by being objective. If the person is "in a rut" or demonstrating inappropriate feelings, first express your understanding. Then, because empathizing would validate the person's inappropriate emotional reaction, use feedback to express your true reaction in a nonthreatening way.

Receptive Listening

All listening is receptive; however, truly *receptive listening* is a specific type with certain restrictions placed on responses. In some cases, silence is best if accompanied by appropriate nonverbal behaviors. Perhaps, it is no coincidence that "silent" and "listen" contain the same letters (Wolvin and Coakley, 1988). When using receptive listening, you will do the following.

Listen without interrupting. As mentioned earlier, people interrupt, and nothing except preventing an injury justifies it. Keep silent, and if you do interrupt, apologize and let the speaker continue.

Listen without judging or "putting down." People seem to have great difficulty keeping critical, judgmental, and admonishing reactions to themselves.

SPEAKER: I decided to call him yesterday.

LISTENER: You did what?

SPEAKER: I called him just to talk.

LISTENER: That's crazy. You know better than that.

What do you think the speaker's reaction would be? Most people would react defensively and, usually, the interaction would end on a negative note. Note the following improvement.

SPEAKER: I decided to call him yesterday.

LISTENER: Oh, you called him?

SPEAKER: I just wanted to talk.

LISTENER: How did it go?

Listening openly is not easy and requires patience. Later, in the feedback stage, the listener can express any concerns and reservations. Being judgmental will only cut off further communication.

One reason that individuals don't express their feelings is that judgments are frequently leveled at emotions. "How could you be angry about that?" "That's stupid," "I wouldn't have let that bother me," or one of the worst, "You have no right to feel that way," are almost sure to prevent further disclosures of emotion. Ironically, judging can be so ingrained that we tend to use it even in simple exchanges. Have you ever told someone you enjoyed a movie and received the immediate response, "Oh, I don't see how anyone could like something like that?" In Chapter 7 you will learn ways to voice an opinion that doesn't sound like a judgment.

Listen without one-upping. When I present this in class, the reactions clearly indicate how common this response is. "One-uppers" have a definite intent: to tell their own story, which is more dramatic, more interesting, better, or worse than yours.

SPEAKER: I went fishing yesterday and caught two bass. I—

LISTENER: (interrupting) That's nothing! I caught six last week.

SPEAKER: I've been really depressed because my favorite aunt died a few days ago.

LISTENER: I know just how you feel. My grandmother died a few months ago, and I'm still trying to get over it. She was such a wonderful person, and we all loved her. Why, just before she died, she was helping my cousins settle an argument. (Story would continue!)

SPEAKER: I'm really excited. We're leaving for Mexico next week.

LISTENER: You're going to Mexico? I'm going to Europe. I'll be in England a few days, then on to Scotland, then to France. I'll be gone for at least four weeks then . . .

Incidentally, students were amused when two students were role-playing the last conversation, After the listener stopped, the speaker said loudly, "And I hope your plane goes down!" The laughter indicated that any of us would probably harbor similar thoughts!

Do you recognize anyone, even yourself, as a "one-upper"? You probably won't be able to entirely avoid responding in this way; however, awareness can eliminate or decrease most of its use. Remember to not jump in too quickly and sound as if your story is better. If you slip, acknowledge that you took over the conversation and lead the speaker back to the original story.

Listen without problem solving. Caring individuals have difficulty with this one. They want to be helpful, so they are quick with advice not realizing that it often stops the exchange prematurely. Either the MBTI personality preferences of feeling or thinking can respond too quickly. Thinkers do so because they enjoy problem solving, and it's logical to do so as quickly as possible. Feelers can experience so much empathy, they just feel compelled to help.

SPEAKER: I'm having trouble communicating with my parents.
LISTENER: I can suggest several good books for you to read.

SPEAKER: I'm upset about my relationship with him.
LISTENER: I think you should just call it quits.

Can you see how the quick response can end the exchange or steer it in another direction? A better response would be to paraphrase or express understanding of feeling when appropriate or show that you are receptive just by body language. In most cases, the speaker has more to express either verbally, nonverbally, or both.

I was reminded of the importance of listening without attempting to problem solve when one of my students stayed after class. She looked sad, and I asked her how her life was going. She replied, "Just terrible. I've been sick, and now my husband has started drinking again." I stifled a strong urge to tell her about support groups for families of alcoholics and books she could read. Instead my facial expression was one of concern. I said, "Oh," and because she looked so forlorn, I put my arms around her. She started to cry, and we stood there for about 2 minutes while she sobbed. Afterwards, we talked, and I eventually made some suggestions. If I had responded immediately with my well-meaning advice, the opportunity for her to release stress and genuine emotion would have been lost.

Receptive listening means that you remain in the listening role longer and don't jump in too soon. Think of it as keeping an invisible piece of tape over your mouth for awhile. Show encouragement nonverbally or with short, inviting responses.

Directive Listening

This type of listening is more controlling than either empathic or receptive. Asking questions is the key technique. Five different types of questions can be used; they are listed here in the order of most to least effective (Miller et al., 1988).

Figure 6-5 Positive listening is an art.

Open questions: These usually begin with who, what, where, when, or how, but not why. Open questions allow the speaker choices.

Multiple questions: These ask for more than one answer at a time. They flood the speaker, and the questioner often doesn't get the desired information. For example, a job interviewer who asks, "What are your strengths and weaknesses and how might you improve?" is unlikely to get complete responses in each area.

Closed questions: These are questions that can be simply answered with one or two words. In some cases, you offer two choices, yet the response is still limited.

Leading questions: These are designed to get a certain response. For example, "Don't you think you'd be wise to check the benefits they're offering?" is a disguised way of telling the other person what to do.

"Why" questions: Reactions of defensiveness and tension are typical when confronted with "why?" Instead of using "why," try: "How did you go about making that decision?" or "What information did you have to point you in that direction?" or "What reasons did you have for that choice?"

Directive listening is appropriate when there is a need to resolve issues efficiently or make decisions quickly. Job interviews, other business exchanges, and consultations employ directive listening. And, at times parents feel a need to use it, as well! Knowing how to direct conversations with effective questions is a practical skill.

Listening is of great significance in the communication process. Take the opportunity to check your own listening on a scale in REFLECTIONS AND APPLICATIONS. Then use positive listening to create an open communication climate that leads to healthy relationships.

When I ask you to listen to me and you
start giving advice,
you have not done what I asked.
When I ask you to listen to me and you
begin to tell me why
I shouldn't feel that way, you are
trampling on my feelings.
When I ask you to listen to me and you
feel you have to do
something to solve my problems, you
have failed me,
strange
as that may seem.
So please, just listen and hear me.
And if you want to talk,
wait a few minutes for your turn and
I promise I'll listen
to you.

Author Unknown

SUMMARY

Listening is an active process of attending, receiving, and interpreting auditory stimuli then providing feedback. Listening well includes observing and interpreting nonverbal behaviors and reacting to a speaker. Listening goes beyond hearing because it involves interpretation and responding. Listening is an art; the skills can be learned and improved. Individuals listen for various reasons. Three purposes for listening are to enjoy, to become informed, and to help. A goal of listening is to share a common meaning with another person.

Positive listening cannot be overemphasized. In work situations, friendships, and family relationships, listening is the key to healthy interactions. Parents and children often find that poor listening creates problems. As important as listening is, almost everyone learned to do it informally. Little, if any, formal instruction is offered in school curriculums. Becoming a positive listener is an individual's responsibility.

General barriers to listening are preoccupation, environmental factors, psychological filters, rate difference between speaking and thinking, and negative intentions. Improvement means eliminating barriers and demonstrating positive nonverbal and verbal behaviors. Paraphrasing, clarifying, expressing an understanding of feeling, and delivering feedback are important skills. Negative listening behaviors can be identified and eliminated.

All listening is active. Specific types of listening include empathic, receptive, and directive. The rewards from learning and practicing positive listening are well worth the time and effort.

How easy it is to say, "I'm listening." How hard it can be to practice the art of positive listening. Yet, the rewards are well worth the difficulty.

—Sharon Hanna

7

Improving Communication: How to Send Messages

OBJECTIVES

After completing this chapter, you will be able to

- Explain the importance of how messages are delivered.
- Contrast the open and closed styles of verbalizing.
- Discuss the benefits of open communication.
- Define, describe, and give examples of three types of closed verbalization.
- Recognize dogmatic, commando, and grandiose wording.
- Use "I" statements, tentative words and phrases, and qualifiers to change the closed style to an open one.
- List and describe dimensions of effective expression.
- Recognize metamessages.
- Reduce the number of fillers in your speech.
- Provide an explanation and description of paralanguage.
- Define body language and describe three aspects of it.
- Give examples of the functions of body language.
- Realize the importance of both paralanguage and body language.
- Be an open, effective communicator.

The "how" of communication is as meaningful as the "what."

—Sharon Hanna

Speaking is of primary importance in the communication process. Of course, it is possible to send information without talking. People who are unable to speak can learn to send messages proficiently, and most people can get a point across without verbalizing. Most of us, though, verbalize when we send information. What is said, obviously, has great importance and will be covered in Chapter 8. However, the manner and method of delivery, often considered of secondary importance, deserve special attention. This chapter will focus on improvement of how messages are delivered both verbally and nonverbally. Specifically covered will be openness, effectiveness, paralanguage, and body language.

STYLES OF VERBALIZING

Have you ever thought about the way you deliver your thoughts, feelings, and needs? *Style* refers to how you verbalize. Communication styles can be identified and changed. A particular style influences how the speaker comes across and usually elicits a certain response.

Pretend you are the listener in the following conversations and assess each one in terms of your reactions:

1. People in this neighborhood just don't care about their property. They let their houses run down, and their yards are a disaster. You'd think they'd never heard of a lawn mower! Anyone who owns property should keep it up or just move to an apartment and let someone else do it for them!
2. I've noticed in the last few months that the houses in the neighborhood look shabbier than they used to. And I haven't seen anyone mow a yard for at least a week. I'm frustrated by it because I take pride in my property and believe that it's considerate to keep my house in good condition.

Essentially, the same message was delivered. Yet, if you are like most people, your reaction to each would have been different. In the first one, the speaker used a *closed style* of verbalizing. This means that the comments were definite and left little opportunity for a reasonable response. The closed style, because of its absoluteness, finality, forcefulness, and all-inclusive/exclusive language, stifles positive exchange. A student once commented about a friend, "I cannot win his kind of conversation, so I just keep my mouth shut." The closed style fosters a negative communication climate. Opinions stated as inflexible truths invariably close the door to healthy communication.

In the second example the *open style* is used, and discussion is encouraged. Note that a point of view is stated in a flexible manner. Because the expressed ideas sound open, they invite a reasonable, positive response. A study of early adolescents showed that their perceptions of the openness of family communication was related to how much and what they disclosed (Papini et al., 1990). Open communicators are refreshing! Others appreciate their receptiveness and want to converse with them. Rather than offending or "turning others off," open communicators attract people and are more likely to develop and maintain healthy relationships.

Changing the Closed Style to Open Communication

Awareness of the closed style and recognition of its use is the first step in becoming an open communicator. Then, simple re-wording guidelines change the closed to an open style. Following are descriptions of three types of closed communication and ways to change to the open style.

1. Dogmatic—"definitely definite," rigid, absolute, and inflexible. When verbalizing, a dogmatic communicator sounds like the final authority and essentially *expresses opinion as fact*. Here are some dogmatic statements:

"The weather is lousy" or "It's a beautiful day today."
"Valentino's has the best pizza in the world" or "Valentino's has the worst pizza in the world."
"He has been a very poor president" or "He has been an excellent president."
"Religion is necessary for a happy life" or "It isn't necessary to be religious to be happy."

How a comment is stated, not its content, makes it dogmatic. In each example, *opinion is stated as fact or truth.*

Using "I" statements. The basic technique of open style communication is to rid yourself of dogmatic comments by the use of "I" statements. Because you are speaking for yourself, "I" statements are also regarded as assertive language. "I" statements empower individuals (Canfield and Siccone, 1993). I was pleased to discover that in sign language, "I" statements are effectively utilized, too.

"I" statements can be divided into two categories. The first group consists of phrases known as actual "I" statements. The word "I" is said first or begins a phrase used elsewhere in the sentence (see Table 7-1). The "I" statements in the first column are used to offer ideas or opinions while the others state preferences, wants, and feelings.

A common error is to use "I know" for "I think" such as "I know students do better in smaller classes." The speaker does not *know* this, and "I know" is not considered an "I" statement. When a fact is being stated, then "know" is correct.

The second category is made up of phrases that give an "I" meaning. These, too, demonstrate that the speaker's opinions do not necessarily take precedence over others (see Table 7-2).

TABLE 7-1 Actual "I" Statements

I think	I like	I want
I believe	I consider	I feel
I feel that	I prefer	I am or was

Note: An opposite could be made of each by inserting don't or another appropriate word.

TABLE 7-2 Phrases Conveying "I" Meaning

In my opinion	In my way of thinking
As far as I'm concerned	My thoughts are
It seems to me	To me it appears

Following are rewordings of the dogmatic statements on page 201:

"I like (or don't like) the weather."
"As far as I'm concerned, Valentino's has the best (or worst) pizza in the world."
"I think he has been a poor (or excellent) president."
"In my opinion, religion is necessary (or not necessary) for happy life."

Remember that "I" statements are not necessary in all verbalizations. When you express facts, they certainly aren't. My dad, who died at the age of 77, expressed many of his opinions in a dogmatic way. I suggested that others would react much more positively to him if he used "I" statements. He "leaped" into this in his usual enthusiastic fashion, and it was as if the three words "in my opinion" gave him freedom to say anything. In his zeal, he used the phrase frequently. One day he came into the house and said, "It's raining outside," and then, looking directly at me, added, "In my opinion." I hurriedly explained that when expressing a fact, "I" statements aren't necessary! Also, simple dogmatic observations such as "It's a beautiful day" are hardly ever considered offensive.

To become an open communicator, listen for your dogmatic statements and then concentrate on using "I" statements. A world of difference exists, *in my opinion*, between saying, "College just doesn't prepare you for the real world" and, "It seems to me that college experiences rarely reflect what actually goes on in the world." Remember that you affirm yourself when you own and express opinions in an open style.

The second type of closed communication adds another dimension.

2. Commando—forcing, pressuring. This category includes words and phrases such as "should," "have to," "must," "ought," and "need to" which leave little, if any, opportunity for alternatives. Note the authoritarian, commanding nature of these statements:

"You should get a job."
"They must learn to work before they play."
"She has to listen better."
"You had better take my advice."

Consider how you react to forcing words, especially when they are preceded by the word "you." Defensively? In a study, adolescents rated accusatory "you" statements as more aversive and likely to evoke stronger antagonistic response inclinations than assertive "I" statements. Using "you" with angry messages especially increased hostile responses and reactions. Parents were cautioned that "you" statements are much more likely to provoke resistance and rebellion (Kubany et al., 1992). When people speak in a commando way, reactions of defiance, resentment, or passivity are possible; none would appear to be healthy and positive. The commando type is usually expressed dogmatically as well, which obviously makes such statements sound even more closed. This style may remind you of moralizing, which was discussed in Chapter 5. Moralizers make use of commando-type words.

Being tentative and flexible. When the "commando" type has been used, first check to see whether the statement is also dogmatic. If so, create an "I" statement, and then replace the forcing part with a flexible and tentative phrase. See Table 7-3 for examples.

TABLE 7-3 Some Tentative Phrases

It would be a good idea if
He or she, they, or you could benefit from
It could be helpful if
You might want to consider
It seems important that
He or she, they, or you might be wise to
It could be beneficial

Following are changes in the commando statements on page 202:

"I think it would be a good idea for you to get a job."
"As far as I'm concerned, getting work done before play is important."
"I believe she would benefit from listening better."
"It seems to me that my advice could be helpful to you."

The forcing words "should," "must," "has to," and "had better" were replaced with tentative phrases, and "I" statements were used. The same point is made in a less demanding way.

The third type can be fun to identify and important to eliminate.

3. Grandiose—exaggerated, all-inclusive or all-exclusive, and often dramatic. The use of this type can lead to inaccuracy or a distortion of the facts. Following are examples of grandiose words and statements in which they are expressed:

everyone–no one
everybody–nobody
all–none
always–never
everything–nothing–anything
only
every

"All kids today are disrespectful."
"He doesn't do anything except lie around."
"The only way to become skilled in word processing is to take a class."
"Nobody cares."
"Every time I wash my car, it rains."

One of my favorites is the comment "This is the worst climate in the world—no doubt about it!" Isn't it likely that many people from all over the world would make the same statement about their climates? Note that grandiose statements are almost always (not always) dogmatic, also.

A statement that contains grandiose words is usually inaccurate. How often is "always" correct? Be careful you don't answer that with "never!" Not only can the literal meanings be incorrect, but the words are often emotionally laden and tend to harm rather than enlighten (Satir, 1976). At one time I was suggesting the possible elimination of the words "always" and "never" from the language until Ed, a good friend, reminded me of their accuracy in certain statements. He noted that the Pope is always Catholic and never Jewish! I quickly agreed!

In most cases, grandiose words are used only for their dramatic effect; yet, exaggeration and absolutes set up an atmosphere of helplessness and despair (Canfield and Siccone, 1993). And because they usually create an inaccurate statement, the point can be lost. I have often cautioned parents not to say to a child, "Your room is always a mess" or "You never clean your room." Why? The child can clean once in a 5-year period and prove that you are wrong!

Listening to others as well as to yourself for examples of the grandiose style can actually be fun. Keeping a sense of humor, one can challenge the obvious inaccuracy of such comments. Try inwardly responding with the suggestions in parentheses when you hear these types of statements:

"All men are that way." (All? Really?)

"You never do anything right." (Surely once in a while the person does!)

"All he does is eat." (That's all he does? Amazing!)

"I'm always late." (Not even once on time?)

Depending on your relationship with the grandiose speaker, you may be able to verbalize these questions. When students say, "There was *no* way I could have come to class," I try to *humorously* challenge them! Awareness is the first step toward improvement.

Adding or replacing with qualifiers. To correct the "grandiose" type, an "I" statement may be needed to get rid of dogmatism. Then replace or modify the grandiose word with a qualifier (see Table 7-4).

For example, if "always" or "never" has been used, check for accuracy. Is the word correct? If not, select a qualifier that does not change the meaning to any extent. In the statement "She's never on time," what word could be used to qualify "never?" Some possibilities are "rarely," or "hardly ever" as replacements or adding "almost" in front of "never" as a modifier. Be careful that you don't change the meaning to any great extent. For example, if you are rewording "Everyone is so rude," the meaning would be significantly changed if you replaced "everyone" (the grandiose word) with "someone." Instead, use "many people" or add "almost" to "everyone." Some possible open statements are, "I've noticed that she is rarely on time," and, "It seems to me that most people are rude."

TABLE 7-4 Words Useful as Qualifiers

Almost	rarely	infrequently	frequently
Nearly	often	hardly ever	some
Many	most	several	quite a few
Few	seldom	possibly	sometimes
Usually	generally	probably	in general

Using qualifiers makes statements accurate and less hurtful. A young man said that his father repeatedly told him, "You'll never amount to anything." "Never" and "anything" felt like arrows accentuating the attack on his self-esteem. Qualifiers decrease the sting of a critical remark. Again, compare the statements that follow with the ones given in the description of the grandiose type on page 203.

"In my opinion, many kids today are disrespectful."

"It seems to me that he spends a lot of time lying around and doing very little."

"I found that taking a class in word processing really improved my skill, and I would recommend it."

"I feel as if most people don't care."

"It seems that it usually rains after I wash the car."

These reworded statements are accurate, less dramatic, and open. Note that each is an "I" statement.

All three types of the closed style set up obstacles to honest interactions. Either they stop communication or if exchange does take place, disagreement or combativeness is apt to be the reaction. Statements that contain all three types aren't unusual. In a book written for teenagers in stepfamilies (Getzoff and McClenahan, 1984), closed communication, called *aggressive language*, is related to responses of defensiveness, attack, or resentment. None solves a problem. Read the following and note how each contains all three.

"Politicians should tell the truth, and they never do."

"You ought to spend your money only for what you need."

"Students need to study hard to get good grades."

How well did you do? All are dogmatic because they express opinion as fact. Did you find the forcing words (should, ought, and need to)? In addition, politicians and students

Figure 7-1

with an implied "all," and the word "only" are grandiose. Don't these reworded statements sound open and positive?

"I believe that the majority of politicians rarely tell the truth, and I think it would be much better if they did."

"It seems like a good idea to me to buy what you need first."

"I think that most students who study hard can get good grades."

Open communication is worth the time and effort spent in developing the techniques (a dogmatic statement, by the way; however, these are sometimes permitted in textbooks)! The first step in making positive changes is a desire to become an open communicator. The second requires listening to your usual style. Then, recognizing the three closed types, rewording mentally, and restating aloud will complete the process. Accomplishment comes from practice and more practice! To help, REFLECTIONS AND APPLICATIONS asks you to identify and rewrite closed statements. Eventually, open communication will become easy and natural.

BECOMING AN EFFECTIVE COMMUNICATOR

In addition to using an open style, you can improve communication by expressing yourself effectively. This can be accomplished by paying attention to certain guidelines (McKay et al., 1983).

Directness

Being direct means stating what you want to say. You don't assume that others know what you are thinking or feeling, and you don't hint. People, often those with a feeling personality preference, may not say what they mean because they don't want to offend others, not because they lack conviction. Yet, indirectness can lead to deeper hurt. Lack of directness also results from indecisiveness, shyness, and nonassertiveness. For example, since her parents' divorce, Jane had spent 2 months each summer visiting her dad. One summer she didn't want to stay the full time, yet she was concerned about hurting his feelings. Because she wasn't direct with her dad, she stayed and felt resentful causing their relationship to become distant. This hurt both individuals.

Not having your ideas or feelings known or being misinterpreted are prices you can pay for indirectness. Also, "beating around the bush" doesn't strengthen self-esteem or create happiness and can be annoying to others and harmful to relationships. "We cannot hear what the other is not saying; and, sometimes, when we finally do, it's too late" (Buscaglia, 1992, p. 152). A message worth sending deserves to be delivered directly.

Immediacy

Waiting too long to express can be ineffective and also lead to frustration and resentment. More effective messages are often immediate ones. For example, imagine a passenger in an automobile who delays saying anything about the recklessness and speed of the driver even though he or she feels a great deal of anxiety. Because nothing was said, a tragic accident could occur. Similarly, individuals may hesitate to deal with conflict and make matters worse. Gauging each situation for the ideal degree of immediacy is recommended.

Clarity

Basic to effectiveness is delivering a clear message. Individuals who use ambiguities such as, "I feel funny" or, "There's something wrong" aren't being clear.

A person might ask a question when a statement would be more effective. For example, "Why don't you try harder?" would be much clearer as a statement: "I've noticed you haven't been turning in as many projects of high quality lately, and I'd like you to try harder." My husband reminds me to be clear whenever I ask, "Are you planning to get yourself more coffee?" He responds, "Does that mean you would like me to get you some?" Sheepishly, I realize that I'm being neither clear nor direct. Simple requests may be harmless; however, lack of clarity and confusion can lead to serious problems in relationships. For example, what does "I'll call you later" mean? It could be fifteen minutes in one person's mind and one week in another's. A message received that is not the same as the intended message is the foundation of errors, misunderstandings, and strained relationships (Alessandra and Hunsaker, 1993).

A problem with clarity comes when someone says one thing and indicates another with body language. "I'm listening!" she says as she continues to write a letter. How do you know which to believe? "A message clearly given that is clearly received is a rare and beautiful phenomenon" (Adams, 1987, p. 135).

Straightforwardness

Ineffective communicators may disguise their intentions and be actually dishonest in their expressions. Being straight means being honest and being careful not to disguise information or intention.

Using hidden meaning is common and potentially damaging. *A metamessage* is defined as "a second level which communicates the speaker's attitudes and feelings" (McKay et al., p. 72). The true meaning is not openly expressed and instead is given by accenting a word, changing the tone of voice, or commenting in suggestive ways. For example, if a person says, "*Obviously*, you're right," the real meaning probably is, "You act like you're always right." Note the following metamessages and the possible intended meanings:

"She must have really been an interesting conversationalist."
(Meaning: I was hurt that you spent so much time talking to her and avoiding me.)
"It's great that you can wear that style. I'd look too fat in it!"
(Meaning: I don't like that dress, and I think it makes you look fatter.)

Instead of using a metamessage, be straightforward and honest. If you want attention, state what you need. If hurt or misinterpretation could result, remaining silent may be the better choice. Being straight or keeping quiet may be difficult; however, the alternative is to be deceitful by speaking in veiled terms. In the next chapter you will learn how to respond to metamessages effectively; you undoubtedly know someone who uses them!

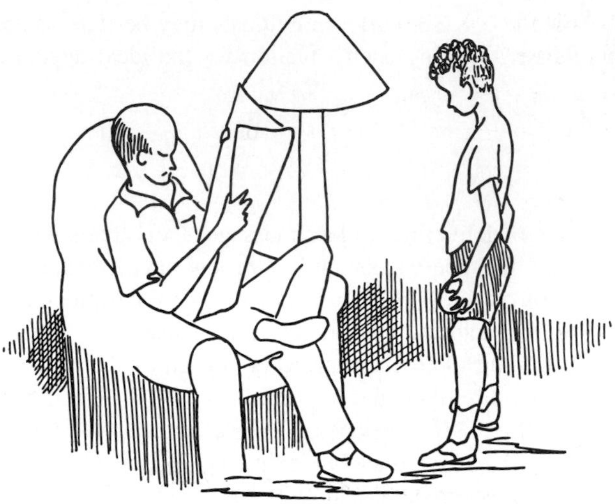

Figure 7-2

Supportiveness

Effectiveness is not enhanced by hurting someone or trying to appear superior. Supportive communicators don't use derogatory labels. Other nonsupportive techniques are using sarcasm, calling attention to past errors and problems, comparing others unfavorably, attacking in a judgmental way, and delivering threats. Effective communicators are not out to prove points or win; instead, they want to be supportive and promote understanding and good will.

Efficiency

Finally, effective communication is damaged by meandering and using fillers or too much detail; an efficient speaker is appreciated. What creates a barrier in the following?

> "Well, you know—I go to college—you know—and—a—it's been a good experience—you know. I've really—you know—learned a lot—you know—and I think you—uh—oughta—well basically—you know—try it!"

Is there any doubt? The filler "you know" is heard in all walks of life from the playground to the corporation board room. A *filler* is a word, phrase, or sound used for no reason except to replace silence. Other common ones are "basically," and saying "right?" after every statement such as: "I went to the movies last night—right? There was this guy there—right? And he struck up a conversation with me—right?" An odd one that I used a few times is "Believe you me" at the beginning of a statement. One day a student asked me what it meant to which I replied, "I have no idea," as I vowed to rid myself of that habit. How many other fillers can you identify? An effective communicator eliminates fillers. A speech class can do wonders in this regard. Another idea is to ask someone else to "catch you" using the filler.

An efficient speaker reaches the point so that the listeners aren't frustrated or bored. For example, let's listen to Mary and John tell about their vacation.

MARY: We left last Monday morning.

JOHN: No, it was after lunch.

MARY: No, it was morning because it was before the mail came.

JOHN: Well, go on, but I know it was afternoon.

MARY: We stopped for lunch in Platte City—or was it North Platte? I think it was North Platte. Do you remember, John?

JOHN: No, but I know we left after lunch.

If you're smiling, this probably reminds you of someone. The story lasts a long time! Efficiency is most appreciated at this point.

Effective communicating is an art and takes practice. To achieve your purpose, follow the guidelines of effective expression and use open communication. In the process, positive interactions have a better opportunity to develop.

PARALANGUAGE AND BODY LANGUAGE

The "how" of communicating is greatly influenced by other factors. In fact, about 93 percent of an expression is conveyed by vocal changes and nonverbal behaviors, and not by the words alone (Mehrabian, 1968; 1981). Becoming aware of paralanguage and body language and learning to use yours effectively are valuable tools in communication.

Using Paralanguage

An important part of verbalizing is *paralanguage* which consists of the variations in the human voice with the exception of the words themselves (Vargas, 1986). Of the 93 percent nonverbal part of an expression, 38 percent consists of paralanguage. Paralanguage has several components.

Rhythm. When emphasis or accent is placed on different words, rhythm varies. For example, in the phrase, "It seems to me," if you accent *seems*, you are giving the impression of openness; if you emphasize *me*, you have defeated that purpose.

Inflection. Inflection is a change in the pitch. When you phrase a question, you may change inflection to indicate that a response is desired. Note the dramatic example of rhythm and inflection variation that changes the meaning of the same series of words.

Am <u>I</u> in love!

<u>Am</u> I in love?

Inflection can be used in a negative way to convey sarcasm and criticism. For example, "You said <u>that</u>" can sound critical. Robert Frost, the famous poet, put it clearly, "There are tones of voice that mean more than words." Listening to your own voice variations and, at times, recording yourself can be very helpful. You may be expressing more than you realize!

Volume. The loudness or softness of speech changes meaning. In specific situations volume adds meaning and drama. A lesson taught to me in college comes to mind.

A professor told a group of aspiring teachers that in order to get the attention of noisy students, we should whisper; this, she contended, would quiet them faster than a loud voice. I can honestly report that whispering has worked for me—and then again, it has not! It depended on the group of students and the specific situation. Regardless of its effectiveness in quieting others, varying the volume of expression can add interest and meaning to your speech.

Pitch. Low and high describe pitch. In normal conversation, positive communicators will vary their pitch purposefully. And in certain circumstances, pitch seems to have a mind of its own! Have you ever been embarrassed because of the upward change in your voice? Johnny's voice was becoming the lowered voice of a young man, and he was pleased. He mustered up the courage to ask a special girl to a party and was mortified when his voice seemed to go up two octaves! Depression or physical fatigue can create a lower voice. Expressions take on a different meaning simply because of pitch.

Speed. The rate at which one speaks makes a difference in the degree of understanding as well as the interest level of the receiver. People who talk quite fast are often misunderstood, or they tend to overwhelm the listener—think of the stereotype of the fast-talking salesperson! In contrast, a slow speaker can easily put others to sleep or create a great deal of frustration! Again, variety and appropriateness are important.

Articulation. "What did you say?" The question is often asked because of poor articulation. A speaker mumbled and was not understood. Enunciation, or distinct pronunciation, is a necessary element in delivering a clear message; however, you can overenunciate and give an unfavorable impression. If problems exist in this area, awareness and practice can be beneficial.

Effects of Paralanguage

Paralanguage, whether adding positiveness or negativeness, is an important dimension in communication. It adds meaning to what you say and makes you a more interesting speaker. Because of paralanguage you can seem insensitive or be hurtful. At times, certain paralanguage usages have struck me as demeaning. You probably will (or already do) engage in conversation with elderly people in a work or personal setting. Varying the paralanguage can result in a condescending or patronizing manner. Speaking softly and slowly and articulating dramatically, as if the receiver were incapable of understanding, in many cases is unnecessary and serves to diminish the self-esteem of the elderly person. I was delighted one day when an older friend of mine told a young receptionist, "I am quite capable of understanding you if you speak to me exactly as you did to the last patient!" You may not be made aware of this habit as the receptionist was; thus, it's up to you to become more aware of how you sound to others.

Understanding Body Language

Body language consists of all nonverbal communication and may make up as much as 55 percent of the meaning of a message (Mehrabian, 1968; 1981). Realizing its impact is extremely valuable. Think of times when what was expressed by body language carried more impact than the person's words. Misinterpretation is common. For example, Steve was surprised and dismayed when his wife Melissa frowned, tossed her head, and turned away. "Why are you mad?" he asked. "Mad? I just remembered a phone call I was going to make," was her reply.

Importance of body language. Nonverbal behaviors can express emotions, communicate messages, and control human beings; both individual preferences and cultural influences are involved (Scheflen, 1972). Because body language conveys more than half the meaning to most messages, its influence is immense. Body language is also used in what is called *presentation of self*, the attempt to present ourselves to others so they will see us as we wish to be seen (Goffman, 1959). Think of appearing capable your first day of work or sociable at a party. How many ways can you communicate these traits through body language? Jason came to an interview in a nice-looking dark gray suit, white shirt, and a fashionable necktie. From his polished shoes to his neatly combed hair, he looked the part. He smiled confidently, looked directly into the interviewer's eyes, and responded to the outstretched hand with a firm handshake. He was off to an excellent start!

Nonverbal behaviors play another part in indicating aspects of personality. We could be considered rude if we don't look at a speaker or if we stare too fixedly (Duck, 1991). Aggressive, timid, shy, and confident are all personality traits that may be assigned to individuals because of their body language. Experts on interpersonal communication recognize how functional body language is in emphasizing, changing, or erasing a verbal message. Those skilled in sign language certainly understand the power of body language. The impression you make and the ones you receive, as well as the health of your relationships, are greatly influenced by nonverbal behaviors.

Interpretation of body language. Entire textbooks have been written on the subject of body language. The science of body language is called *kinesics* (Fast, 1970). After learning about body language, you may realize as one student of mine did, "I never thought about it like that. I've become much more aware of how I may appear to others." If you are in the presence of others right now, ask yourself, "What impression am I giving with my body language?"

Each of us has individual patterns of behavior that carry meanings as well as those common to a particular society. Ask an individual from another country to identify some gestures. You may be surprised to know that the same one carries different meanings.

Even within a society, body language differs. Fascinating studies have revealed different nonverbal behaviors related to gender. Video tapes of people from second grade through college were analyzed. At every age females sat closer and looked at each other more directly while males sat at angles and looked at each other less often. Males anchored their gazes elsewhere and occasionally glanced at each other (Tannen, 1990). I am happy to say that most males in my classes maintain excellent eye contact!

Some caution regarding body language is recommended because a few simplistic interpretations have emerged. One seminar leader tried to convince participants that all behaviors carry deep psychological meanings. When he said that stirring an iced drink with the tip of one's finger always has a sexual meaning, I reacted with nonverbal behavior—a shake of my head, which meant "I don't agree!" As he added more examples, I realized that he was interpreting in an imaginative way. Most body language is learned and then develops into habits (Scheflen, 1972). Stirring an iced drink with the finger usually comes more from convenience or habit than from deep sexual longings.

Figure 7-3 What nonverbal message is being communicated?

Videotape can be used to see how you appear to others. As students in a career development class watch themselves during a mock interview, the amazed reactions are predictable: "I didn't know I did that," "Do I really look like that?" "I'm going to have to sit on my hands," "I sure looked a lot more confident than I felt." If you have an opportunity to see yourself as others do, take advantage of a unique learning experience. "You will see what other people see or hear. It is sometimes a jolting experience. This jolt is a cheap price to pay for more satisfying outcomes for yourself" (Satir, 1976). Good communicators know how important body language is, realize what they are expressing nonverbally, and seek consistency between what they say and what messages their bodies are sending. Three areas of body language can be monitored and analyzed.

Body movements. Facial expressions, eye contact, gestures, and other body parts can vary immensely while verbalizing. A positive description of one's face is "animated." I once asked my class how they could tell that I enjoyed teaching (expecting to get a reply related to a particular comment I had made earlier). One student quickly replied, "It shows all over your face during class." What a compliment!

How often have you "read" someone's eyes? They, too, are capable of expression. The eyes have been called 'the mirror of the soul,' and an "evil eye" was something you didn't want to receive (Duck, 1991). Contending that the eyes are "physiological dead ends and not really capable of expressing emotion in themselves" (p. 138), Fast (1970) explains that expression is actually transmitted "by length of glance, by opening of eyelids, by squinting, and by a dozen little manipulations of the skin and eyes" (p. 139). In other words, the eye by itself doesn't create expression. Yet, some eyes do seem to dance and sparkle while others look vacant or like lumps of coal.

Even less expressive eyes can be a positive factor if the person maintains direct eye contact, at least in the American society. Not doing so causes others to sometimes doubt the words and to feel uncomfortable. Talking about intimate topics is not enough; it must be stage-managed correctly. You must attend to the person and the person's face especially (Duck, 1991). In other societies, direct eye contact is not necessarily viewed as positive. Good eye contact is generally more difficult when speaking than it is when listening, and women seem to have an advantage as they tend to look more at another person for longer periods of time and to register more facial expressions than men (Richmond et al., 1991).

Gestures which are movements of the hands and arms can transmit meaning and bring forth a response. Students in my sociology classes identify a variety of gestures as symbols of a culture. Differences in their meanings from society to society are common and well-worth learning if you plan to travel in other countries. If you have taken a public speaking class, you were taught the importance of gestures. As helpful as they can be, gestures can be overdone, as in the case of people who "talk with their hands." Or, gestures can express negativism. Think about how you react to a finger pointed at you to emphasize a statement. Defensive or resentful? These are common reactions even though the "pointer" may just be doing so from habit. Males have greater displays of dominant gestures while females are usually more submissive (Richmond et al., 1991). Clearly, these behaviors are learned. In your gestures, aim for the "happy medium" between enough movement to add spice and emphasis and too much motion which detracts, and avoid potentially annoying ones.

Body position. Another element of body language has to do with how you sit or stand. Position, or posture, creates an impression. Postures of agreement, disagreement, interest, boredom, respect, affection, dominance, and harmony are possible. "How you hold your body can reveal feelings about events—how interested you are—and about people—how much you like them. It can show whether you agree with an idea, and it can help you to take your place in a hierarchy" (Bull, 1988, p. 57). Positioning yourself at a different eye level than another is not recommended. Try sitting and carrying on a serious conversation with another person who is standing. "I don't like it at all" is a common comment. A tall young man in a stepfamily success class my husband and I were teaching said, "I've never had kids, and my fiancee's little boy acts scared of me." My husband suggested that he get down to the 3-year-old's eye level the next time he talked with him. "Wow!" he said the next week, "What a difference that made."

Closed positions include crossed arms and legs, the head turned slightly away, and a slouched posture. Open positions are achieved by just the opposite. A relaxed position, as opposed to a rigid, tense one, generally creates a positive climate for communication. The situation will influence body position. Your position when conversing with a friend in a home setting will usually differ from your posture during a job interview. In the classroom, others, including the professor, assess students' body position. How would you describe yours? In all situations, appearing open and interested is positive.

Spatial relationships. Where you position yourself in terms of distance from another is the focus of spatial relationships. Four distinct zones have been identified (Hall, 1969).

Intimate (actually touching-18 inches apart)
Personal (1 1/2 feet to 4 feet apart)
Social (4 feet to 12 feet apart)
Public (12 feet or more apart)

Individuals vary in their personal-space preferences. Generally, a closer proximity indicates a more intimate relationship. For most people conversations within the personal zone are comfortable. The social zone is used more in business or other formal interactions.

People can communicate an attitude or emotion simply by the amount of personal space they afford another. Standing close to someone could imply invasion or domination or could signify dependence. Keeping your distance may indicate disinterest, discomfort, or dislike. Being aware of the appropriate physical space distances and placing yourself accordingly are advantageous behaviors.

Are you recognizing that communication is complicated? Its many dimensions can be somewhat overwhelming, yet awareness of all aspects of communication is needed

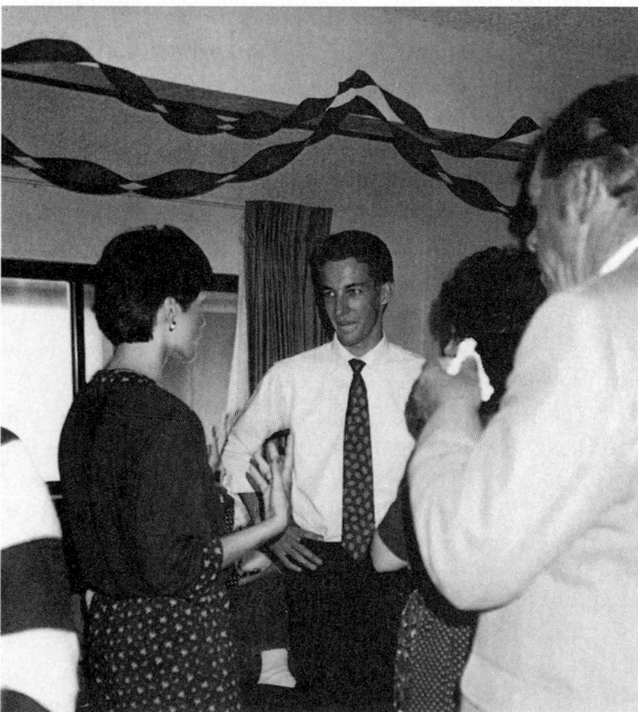

Figure 7-4 People usually feel comfortable conversing within the personal spatial zone.

to understand and improve interactions and relationships. Remember that you learned how to communicate, and you can unlearn and relearn.

SUMMARY

The "how" of verbalizing is an area not often analyzed. People commonly express their ideas and feelings in a closed style using dogmatic, commando, or grandiose expressions instead of being open, flexible, and accurate. Open communication consists of "I" statements and tentative words and phrases and qualifiers. Because this style is likely to result in positive relationships, developing the skills is a worthy goal. You can also become an effective communicator. Being direct, timely, clear, straightforward, supportive, and efficient are beneficial.

Paralanguage adds depth and meaning to expressions and can convey a positive or negative tone. The old adage, "It's not what you say, but how you say it" has a great deal of merit. Body language, the nonverbal behaviors related to movement, position, and spatial relationships, is of utmost importance in the communication process. An activity in REFLECTIONS AND APPLICATIONS lets you work with both paralanguage and body language.

Such elements as verbalizing styles, effectiveness, paralanguage, and body language can be analyzed and then modified until a desired skill level is reached. Be patient. Positive communication techniques, in the beginning, can be awkward and difficult. Start listening to yourself and others, and, if necessary, reword, add, subtract, and modify in an attempt to improve. Clear, effective, and open verbalization, combined with positive uses of paralanguage and body language, are rewarding human relations skills.

> *Positive communicators lift us by their warmth; their eyes light up in response to us, showing their openness. They refresh our spirit, making us glad to be around them. Negative communicators repel us and arouse feelings of uneasiness within us. We feel lonely, shut out or attacked around them. Even if they are in our families, we want to avoid negative persons because they zap our energy.*
>
> —Teresa Adams

8

Improving Communication: What to Say

OBJECTIVES

After completing this chapter, you will be able to

- Discuss how people verbalize on different levels.
- Name and give examples of the four levels of self-disclosure.
- Recognize appropriateness of self-disclosure.
- Describe benefits of healthy self-disclosure.
- Give and receive compliments in a positive way.
- Explain perception and ways in which perceptual errors can be made.
- Use perception checking and the awareness wheel.
- Respond positively to criticism, metamessages, and bothersome language patterns.
- Improve the quality of what you say.

Only if we honestly reveal ourselves, can we truly know and appreciate each other.
—Sharon Hanna

"Yackity-yack, yackity-yack" is a recurring phrase in a light, popular song of years ago. *Content* consists of the words and sentences uttered during the communication process. "Yackity-yack" refers to mindless chatter and idle comments that comprise the content of many conversations. However, content also includes words that go down in history such as President John F. Kennedy's famous lines, "Ask not what your country can do for you—ask what you can do for your country." Examining what you say and finding positive ways of expressing yourself will help you become a better communicator which leads to healthy relationships.

WHAT YOU TALK ABOUT

Think of all the topics you cover during the day. "What time is it?" "Good morning," "How are you?" "Nice day, isn't it?" "I got a speeding ticket on the way to work!" "I don't like greasy food," "I'm feeling depressed," "I think that employees deserve more input into company policy," and "Your new car is neat" are just a few pieces of possible conversation. Although some comments lack depth and may even be trivial, to talk with others is important.

Levels of Content

Categorization of content is useful. Five levels identified by Powell (1969) are related to an individual's willingness to share parts of the self. The levels are listed here in order of least revealing to deepest sharing.

Cliché conversation. This is made up of superficial and conventional comments such as "How are you?" and the predictable response of "Fine," "What do you think of the weather today?" "Nice party," and "Have a nice day." Sometimes called cocktail-party talk, this is usually safe with no sharing of self. This type serves its purpose, however, and life would be dreary without it.

Reporting the facts about others. Just a step above a cliché is a comment about a neighbor, friend, co-worker, or family member. Whether positive or negative, nothing is revealed about the speaker except that she or he can talk about other people.

My ideas and judgments. This is riskier because the speaker reveals thoughts and opinions. Fearing rejection, the usual pattern is to say only so much and retreat if any adverse reaction is noted.

My feelings (emotions) or "gut level." Because of emotional repression and lack of understanding, this level is difficult for most. Verbalizing what is felt, however, is essential if one is to live as an authentic human being.

Peak communication. Openness, honesty, and complete willingness to share occur at this level. For most, this level is achieved only with close friends and loved ones. Sadly, too often what would seem to be a close relationship lacks this level of communication.

Content organized on these levels is used by excellent communicators in appropriate situations and in reasonable amounts. For example, people who discuss only the weather or similar superficial topics, those who spend an unreasonable amount of time at any level, or individuals who use the deepest levels with mere acquaintances are not effective communicators. Disclosing either not enough or too much to almost everyone in the social environment often indicates psychological problems. Well-adjusted individuals generally disclose deeply to close friends and family members and appropriately reveal themselves to others.

Awareness of Content

The words we use reveal a great deal about our attitudes and personalities and directly influence the effect we make on others. A positive communicator recognizes how content can alter interactions and change relationships and wants to avoid potential pitfalls in the communication process. Specific areas of possible difficulty follow.

Semantics. A major common problem is a difference in *semantics*, the meaning of words. In a career development class, I noticed a puzzled and disturbed look on the face of a Vietnamese man as I talked about the need to sell yourself in order to get a job. Later, he told me, "Selling myself is bad." Understandably, he had literally interpreted the word "sell." After I explained another meaning, he was reassured and said, "Yes, that's good."

Even if people share the same native language, misunderstanding can occur. As individuals exchange messages, the likelihood of attaching all the same meanings is doubtful. Abstract words such as "trust" can be especially difficult. Expressing yourself as clearly as possible, stating your own meaning, then using examples that are concrete or describe behaviors will decrease the opportunities for semantics problems. Feedback by listeners (discussed in Chapter 6) is helpful in this regard. "If verbal communication is to be reasonably clear, both the sender of a message and the receiver have the responsibility to make it so" (Satir, 1983, p. 88).

Dialect. Related to semantics is *dialect*, any form of speech that differs from the standard including distinct pronunciations, unique meanings, and different words altogether. Dialect often reflects differences in region and culture. I was amazed when I lived in the East that they didn't know what I meant when I mentioned "pop" (Coca-Cola). "The word 'pop' appears on Midwest menus," I hastened to explain. Differences in dialect can be interesting and fun and only disconcerting when some people insist that their way of speaking is the only way. Being aware of and accepting differences, adjusting, and seeking to understand and be understood are positive behaviors.

Bias-free language. Awareness is necessary in order to avoid the use of biased language. Sensitive people do not want to offend, and in the career area, using biased language will keep you from being hired or could get you fired. Certain examples related to race, religion, gender, disabilities, and ethnic background are obvious. For example, derogatory labels such as "broad," "retard," "nigger," "honky," "spick," or "fag," and words that historically are demeaning such as "boy," "colored folks," "little woman," "deaf and dumb," "poor white trash," "illegitimate child," are degrading and are to be avoided.

People may use biased words because they forget or are unaware of the meanings attached to words. As a teacher of a sixth-grade class years ago, I responded to a comment about a "colored" kid by asking the young boy, "What color of kid do you mean?" He looked surprised then said, "Hey, that's right—we're all colored."

One of the challenges in being free of biased speech is that meanings change over the years. Sexual-equality consciousness has challenged language that denotes male dominance. For years the use of male pronouns and other words has both openly and in subtle ways delivered messages of superiority and exclusion. A study supported the idea that the generic "he" results in a disproportionate number of male images, and even when he or she was used, most participants comprehended the sex of the person as male

(Gastil, 1990). Additionally, when "he" is used to refer to everyone, an underlying message is that males are regarded more highly. Other examples of undermining females that are less obvious and, in many cases, said with no overt sexist intention are referring to a woman as "honey," or "sweetie" and to women as "girls" or "gals." A group of professional men referred to as "boys" or "guys" is seldom heard. Keep in mind that it is easy to ask "sweeties" to bring coffee and work overtime, and neither "girls" nor "boys" may receive raises or promotions. "Sexist language contains the message of inequality in many forms. Sexist communication tends to elevate males and debase females" (Gerlach and Hart, 1992, pp. 50–51).

Nonsexist language is now taught and its use encouraged in classrooms, the work environment, and within the mainstream of society. For example, the word chairman is more appropriately chairperson or chair, and because women have established nontraditional careers, firemen and policemen are now firefighters and police officers. Fair-minded men recognize that they wouldn't like it if things were reversed and are positive about elimination of outdated sexist speech. In fact, sexist language can be used against men, too. In one study, the 60 participants were not sensitive to sexism in language toward men even though they were so toward women (Hale et al., 1990). Participants in another study were told a story about an employee stealing from the company and were asked what the supervisor should do. Most of them used male pronouns in referring to both the supervisor and the thief. Those who used sexist pronouns were more traditional in their gender role perceptions (McMinn et al., 1990). Since anyone can suffer from biased language, eliminating it is in order.

One difficulty in sensitivity is that individuals have various preferences and attach personal meanings to words. You may not know, for example, whether to refer to a person as a Black or as African-American or as a White or as Caucasian. The wisest choice is to ask the person what she or he prefers. College students sometimes struggle with what to call an instructor or professor and wonder whether one title is better than another. For example, at my community college, some women instructors prefer "Mrs. Smith," while others are irritated with the "Mrs." title, even if married. Still others solve the problem by telling students to address them by a first name. An interesting piece of awareness is that when two people interact with one using a first name and the other the surname, an unequal relationship is generated (Butler, 1992). This is why I prefer a mutual first-name basis with students. Your best course of action is to let others know your preferences and to ask about theirs. A person who is skilled in human relations will keep abreast of new developments and will be sensitive to all human beings.

Emotion-packed phrases. Inadvertently, you may use what are called emotion-packed phrases (Walker and Brokaw, 1992). These are groups of words usually delivered as lead-ins to statements that carry an emotional punch. Some of these follow.

After all I've done for you
How dare you
When I was your age
You'd better listen
You should know better
After you've worked here as long as I have
You're so ungrateful
I'll tell you

Note that many emotion-packed phrases begin with "you" and can easily be reworded. Listen to yourself and to others. How many such phrases do you hear? They can "turn off" the listener or sidetrack a positive exchange, so try to eliminate as many as you can.

Disclaimers. These expressions are ways of denying or not taking responsibility for something that has been said or is hinted. A common one is, "Not to change the subject, but." The speaker has said that the intention is not to change the subject; however he or she will do so anyway! Confusing? Instead, why not say, "I'm going to change the subject," or "I'd like to change the subject for the moment." Disclaimers may seem easier and less offensive; however, the other conversation participants can become annoyed or resentful of the indirectness of the disclaimer.

The key word in disclaimers is "but," which is a way of saying yes and no in the same sentence (Satir, 1976). Examples are:

I love you, but I wish you would take better care of yourself.

I'm sick, but don't worry about me.

You can go, but I want you home early.

These statements will frequently leave the listener feeling uneasy, uncomfortable, frustrated, and confused. A definite improvement in the foregoing statements is to substitute the word "and" for "but" (Satir, 1976). Another example of a disclaimer is the "just in jest" remark. If there is any negative reaction to a comment such as, "You're so slow a turtle could get there faster," the disclaimer is, "Just kidding." The reaction is justifiably one of annoyance.

Vagueness in language. Clarity in communication suffers when vague words are used. Pronouns (words used in place of names, places, and things) can obscure meaning such as, "*They* say too much sun is bad for you." Verbs that describe action can also be misleading. Some have more than one meaning, and others are vague and subject to several interpretations. For example, "You aren't listening" doesn't describe or specify exactly what the person is doing or not doing.

Using observable behavioral words can eliminate confusion. Describing specific happenings and behaviors clarifies the message. For example, a parent says to a child, "I want you to respect me." What does that mean? Instead, a parent can describe what is meant by respect such as "I don't want you to use profanity in front of me." Some ambiguity is bound to occur; however, the less veiled your statements are, the more likely you are to be understood. Being specific and descriptive and speaking for yourself are ways to prevent vagueness and probable misinterpretations.

Slang, colloquialisms, and vulgarity. Slang terms are those that are popular or in vogue at a given time. They are usually interesting and fun to use yet become a problem if they are misinterpreted or overused. A job interviewer wrote on an evaluation form: "I don't like the company referred to as 'you guys'" as in, "What kind of product do 'you guys' manufacture?" Incidentally, the applicant did not get the job. Monitor your own use and be aware that slang can cause problems.

Colloquialisms are informal folksy words or phrases. They can be quaint and add color to expressions, yet can also be overused and misunderstood. An added problem with some colloquialisms is possibly creating an unfavorable impression in the listener's mind. For example, in the Midwest, the word "yes," is commonly replaced with "yeah."

Figure 8-1

In formal situations such as a job interview "yeah" sounds unprofessional. Others include "nope," "ya don't say," "no kiddin'?" and "how ya doing?"

Vulgarity and the use of swear words have become commonplace. Relying too heavily on substandard expressions can leave others wondering about the extent of the speaker's vocabulary. Also, swearing and crudeness do affect people's sensitivities and can be offensive. A wise human relations course of action is to limit your use of vulgar and profane expressions or eliminate them entirely. Keep in mind that patterns of expression are difficult to change from one situation to another. An applicant was embarrassed during an interview when he said, "People who don't give a damn annoy me." He later said, "I swear a lot, but I was sure I could control it during a job interview." He learned the hard way that positive language patterns, like all skills, require daily use.

Vocabulary and grammar. Building your vocabulary and learning and practicing accepted grammar are extremely valuable. People who are limited in either or both are likely to express themselves poorly. In certain situations, their self-esteem will suffer as a result. I remember a period of time when my daughters and stepsons were in school and proper grammar was not "cool." As a parent and a teacher, I managed to endure "ain't" and "he don't," and even "it don't make no difference," coming from the mouths of intelligent human beings! We purists were competing against the lyrics of music and words uttered by role models of the time.

Although perfection in language skills isn't necessary, effective communication goes hand in hand with ability to speak a language acceptably. If your vocabulary or grammar skills are poor, you can take advantage of courses or use self-study resources to improve. Also, you might consider a brush-up course in writing skills as well. Using the best of the language, you will be a better communicator.

REVEALING YOURSELF: SELF-DISCLOSURE

Self-disclosure is defined as making the self known; you reveal yourself so that others can know and understand you. Individuals disclose verbally and nonverbally. This section will focus on verbal self-disclosure.

Self-Disclosure Findings

The earliest research on self-disclosure revealed that women disclosed more than men. Unmarried participants revealed more to their mothers than to fathers, male friends, or female friends, while married individuals shared more with their partners. Another study found that nursing students who were most disclosing to parents and friends were better at establishing close relationships with patients. In addition, they earned better grades in nursing school than did low disclosers. Patients who self-disclosed seemed to fare better, as well (Jourard, 1971).

Self-disclosure continues to be the focus of studies. One showed that it is related to age in that older elementary students disclosed more than younger ones (Rotenberg and Chase, 1992). Children in another study were more likely to disclose about emotions if they thought their parents were open and their families close (Papini et al., 1990). Individuals who knew themselves better disclosed more than those who did not (Reno and Kenny, 1992); females with high self-esteem more likely disclosed especially to males (Dolgin et al., 1991). Even though women generally have been higher disclosers than men, the sex difference in one study was so small that the researchers concluded it was time to stop perpetuating the myth that one sex is more likely to disclose (Dindia and Allen, 1992).

Degrees of Self-Disclosure

Just as all kinds of content can be organized into levels, self-disclosure also has its degrees. Identified by Glaser (1986), the following indicates what is disclosed.

Basic data refer to biographical and demographic information. I'm 22 years old. I was born in Denver, Colorado. I'm attending college in Ames, Iowa. I live in an apartment.

Preferences are likes and dislikes, pleasures, and displeasures, what one would rather do or not do. I like pizza. I enjoyed going back to Colorado this summer. I'd rather attend a small college. I don't like having two roommates. I love summer.

Beliefs consist of thoughts, opinions, and attitudes. I believe that young adulthood is a challenging time of life. I think that small colleges offer more individualized attention. In my opinion, educators aren't paid enough.

Feelings are disclosures about emotions. I'm proud to be in college. I feel sad when I think about moving to a new city. I was scared when I heard about the accident.

These degrees are arranged in order of least to most difficult to disclose, in general (see Fig. 8-2). For a number of people or in certain situations, beliefs may be more difficult to disclose than feelings. In most cases, basic data is risk-free and relatively easy to reveal. Even though preferences can usually be disclosed with little risk, some people will challenge you. For example, have you ever told someone that you liked a certain kind of food and had them reply, "That stuff? How could you like it?" Arguing over

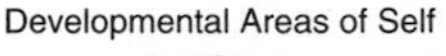

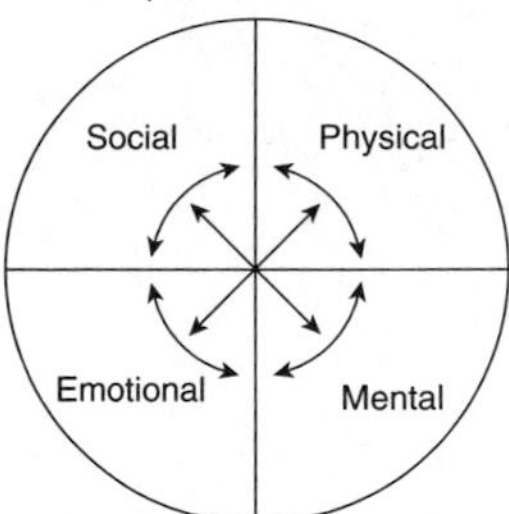

preferences seems trivial and unnecessary, yet you will find some who seem to have difficulty accepting differences even about preferences.

Beliefs and feelings do include a degree of risk and indicate a deeper level of disclosure. Thoughts and opinions, as pointed out in Chapter 7, are often verbalized in the closed style which leads to confrontation. If the open style were used, beliefs would likely be more acceptable and, consequently, easier to reveal. Emotions can be hidden from others for a variety of reasons. As discussed in Chapter 4, expression of feelings is beneficial. "None of us who value our relationships can afford to retreat from communication on an emotional level" (Branden and Branden, 1982, p. 66). Using sixth graders in video-taped conversations, Tannen (1990) discovered that in a 20-minute period, boys covered about 55 different topics while girls spent almost all the time talking about problems they were having with another friend. When asked to talk about what happened last night, girls talked about family problems, and boys discussed television programs. Generally, boys talked about things, activities, and opinions while girls concentrated on friends, friendships, and feelings. Boys' reluctance to disclose can be potentially dangerous. In a survey, it was found that boys were far less likely than girls to tell someone that they had been sexually harassed with only 27 percent of boys telling anyone, not even a friend (American Association of University Women, 1993).

Regardless of gender differences, all relationships benefit from self-disclosure. The levels can be useful in checking out how open you are. Do this in the Chapter 8 activity (REFLECTIONS AND APPLICATIONS). Do others reveal all degrees to you? If they don't, do you know the reason? The depth of self-disclosure is generally an accurate reflection of the closeness of two people.

Awareness and Sharing

The Johari awareness model (Figure 8-3) represents a total person in relation to other persons. (Johari, interestingly, is a combination of Joe and Harry, the first names of its two developers.) The divisions or quadrants are based on awareness of behavior, feelings, and motivation (Luft, 1969). An explanation follows.

Quadrant 1
(open) refers to what is known to self and to others.

Quadrant 2
(blind) refers to what is unknown to self, but known to others.

Quadrant 3
(hidden) refers to what is known to self, but unknown to others.

Quadrant 4
(unknown) refers to what is unknown to self or to others.

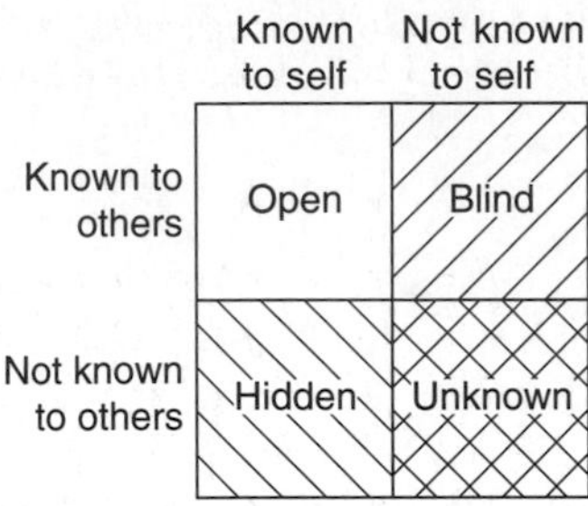

Figure 8-3 Johari awareness window. From *Of Human Interaction* by Joseph Luft, with permission of Mayfield Publishing Co., copyright 1969 by the National Press.

Although the model shows equal-sized quadrants, or windowpanes, each will actually vary in size because of individual differences, as a result of particular situations, or simply because of experiences over time. For example, you may be an open person, so your quadrant 1 would be much larger than that of a friend who is rather private. If you are in a situation with strangers, you may choose to reveal little, which means that quadrant 3 is larger. Finally, people change because of experiences. You may develop an annoying habit of which you are unaware yet others are; thus, the blind quadrant becomes larger. A change in any quadrant affects the other three. For example, if you reveal a feeling to a friend for the first time, quadrant 3 will decrease while quadrant 1 increases.

The open quadrant is the basis for interaction and exchange. Called a "window raised on the world, the smaller the first quadrant, the poorer the communication" (Luft, 1969, p. 14). Increasing the open quadrant by disclosing more is the key to developing close relationships.

Balance in self-disclosing is healthy. Even though having a large open quadrant can improve communication, you can be too open, overly talkative, and inappropriate. Keeping some things to yourself is healthy. Potentially hurtful or embarrassing is a huge blind windowpane which means that others will know you better than you do yourself. For example, Jerry consistently behaved as if he were spending his last dime. His wife joked about his fumbling for his wallet whenever the bill was delivered to the table. He was oblivious to what was obvious to his family and friends. One day a friend's remark registered, and Jerry realized how his behavior appeared to others. He was embarrassed and hurt; however, his awareness allowed him to change. In any disclosing conversation, risk is involved; however, the benefits of self-disclosure almost always outweigh any jeopardy.

Benefits of Self-Disclosure

Dean frowns at Sue when she says, "I wish you'd share more of yourself with me." "Why?" he asks. If Sue is well informed, she will be able to explain the benefits of self-disclosure. One reward has to do with knowing and understanding yourself. As you disclose aloud to another, you learn more about yourself. Each self-disclosing statement brightens the light of self-understanding. As you reveal, you feel more honest, authentic, and validated. "This is who I am" can be an exhilarating feeling. Self-disclosing is usually a self-esteem builder.

Other benefits are related to the emotional, mental, and social selves. Sharing can be relieving. Stress and certain emotions can be managed positively by self-disclosure. Julie described a change.

> I was negative, and now I'm positive. I think it's because I'm being more open and honest. I'm willing to share my 'real' self now. I'm glad because people now are starting to look at me from the inside to the outside.

Talking to others about disturbing aspects of life is relieving. Divulging thoughts and feelings to others can be psychologically healthy (Pennebaker, 1991).

Building close relationships is also an outcome of self-revelation. In fact, achieving intimacy is impossible without disclosure of self. A longitudinal study showed that the amount of overall disclosure was the best predictor of whether a romantic couple remained together (Sprecher, 1987). Self-disclosure makes relationships interesting. Think how boring life would be if people conversed only on basic data and preference levels. When content is confined to superficial topics, individuals can easily run out of things to talk about. Revealing yourself to another indicates that you trust, respect, and care about that person. Disclosing affirms the other by saying, "I care enough about you to share my personal self."

In terms of health, a self-discloser seems to benefit. Inhibiting one's thoughts and feelings gradually undermines the immune function, the action of the heart and vascular system, and even the biochemical workings of the brain and nervous system. Not disclosing has been linked to the severity of asthma, diabetes, anorexia nervosa, and even pain thresholds. In an experiment high self-disclosers showed significant drops in blood pressure compared to low disclosers. The difference in terms of health among adults who had suffered from early childhood traumas was related to whether or not the trauma had been disclosed. If not disclosed, it seemed to adversely affect adult health (Pennebaker, 1991). Silence can lead to sickness, and one effective way of handling stress is to verbalize about our thoughts and feelings.

Finally, when people self-disclose, the communication process is improved. Individuals are better able to understand and provide feedback to each other and create an

For Better or For Worse **by Lynn Johnston**

Figure 8-4 Copyright 1982 Universal Press Syndicate. Reprinted with permission. All rights reserved.

open, accepting environment. Self-disclosure is usually reciprocated. One study showed a correlation between what persons are willing to disclose and what others reveal to them (Jourard, 1971). The openness of one person can begin a sharing process that creates a close relationship.

Obstacles to Self-Disclosure

Even if Sue convinces Dean that the benefits are well worth his consideration, he still may resist self-disclosing or find it difficult. He has a great deal of company in this regard. Why? When I ask students why anyone would withhold beliefs and feelings, the most common reason is fear: "I'm afraid that others will laugh at what I believe." "I was hurt before when I revealed how I felt, and I'm not going to let that happen again." "I told another student how proud I was of my final grade, and she put me down for bragging." The fears could be of ridicule, embarrassment, conflict, or pain. The threat of rejection is frightening, and actual rejection is quite painful. "But, if I tell you who I am, you may not like who I am, and it is all I have" (Powell, 1969, p. 20).

Most people receive "parent" messages telling them to be close-mouthed. "Don't let others know about your financial situation," "Your sex life should be private," "You shouldn't let them know all that personal stuff," "It's not polite to talk about yourself so much," and "What would the neighbors think if they knew?" are common "parent" messages. Thus, many of us grow up believing that silence is golden, and it's often easier to keep quiet. Culture has an effect on self-disclosure. In Japan, for example, disclosure of feelings is thought to be inappropriate and self-indulgent while information about family, status, and social position is entirely suitable to disclose (Duck, 1991). A person's personality can also be a factor. Studies on identical twins suggest that inhibition or keeping things to oneself is about 30 to 50 percent genetic (Pennebaker, 1991). This doesn't mean that opening up is impossible; for some, however, it will be more difficult.

The type of disclosure could restrict some. Only when what was revealed was considered to be either positive or non-intimate did research participants expect it to be well-received (Goodpaster and Hewitt, 1992). In another study, *interpersonal trust*, defined as the expectancy that another's word or promise could be relied upon, was associated with self-disclosure (Steel, 1991). Obviously, after trust is developed, two people are more likely to disclose.

Self-disclosure, like all communication skills, is not taught or even encouraged in many cases. Because of lack of instruction in how to verbalize beliefs and feelings, attempts are often unaccepted or lead to disagreement. "I told him about my religious beliefs, and he came back with arguments" and "I let her know she hurt me, and she took it personally and got mad" are only two of many such examples. Regardless of the possible obstacles, rewards far outweigh costs.

Steps to Positive Self-Disclosure

Before you disclose, you might consider each of the following:

Is my level of disclosure appropriate in this situation?

Do I trust the person to whom I'm disclosing?

For what reason am I self-disclosing? Is it a positive or worthy one, or am I being manipulative, petty, or cruel?

Are the risks worth my disclosure? What can be gained versus lost by this revelation? Will my disclosure place an unreasonable burden on another person?

Is this the most opportune time and place to self-disclose? Is the atmosphere conducive to a positive interchange?

Positive answers to these questions give you a "green light." Then you can give attention to how you self-disclose.

The use of "I" statements is highly recommended. As we noted in Chapter 7, the open style lends itself to positiveness. Body language in harmony with the verbal message is important. Stating that you think open communication is important while maintaining a closed body position is confusing. Being clear, specific, and descriptive are invaluable. Vague disclosures may be worse than none at all. Telling too much over a long period of time may turn a listener off. After disclosing, be ready to accept feedback and keep the exchange open.

COMPLIMENTS: GIVING AND RECEIVING

Compliments can be like breaths of fresh air. *Compliments* are verbal positive strokes-comments of admiration and praise. People give and receive compliments, yet they may not be aware of the variations and the benefits.

Compliments can initiate a relationship. On his first day at work, Bill was complimented by Rick, a co-worker. The expression of praise started a conversation. The next day Bill asked Rick for some advice. After a few weeks the two were socializing with each other. Compliments definitely enhance relationships and build a bond between individuals. Expressions of admiration and praise establish a positive climate for communication.

Giving Compliments

Are you a compliment-giver? Opportunities for expressions of admiration and praise are plentiful; too often, such opportunities are overlooked. Stinginess in compliment giving may be the result of reluctance to praise, a tendency to take others for granted, or an inability to recognize a situation in which a compliment would be appropriate. Hesitation can come from shyness, embarrassment, or concern about how the compliment will be received. If you have any difficulty, consider how valuable a compliment can be.

Jennifer related that she had been depressed and had decided to quit school. Then she was complimented about her class participation by an instructor and praised by another student for her note-taking abilities. "Those compliments were like a tonic to me," she said. "I had lost faith in myself, and all at once it was restored. I changed my mind about quitting school." Research verifies the value of compliments. In therapy situations compliments empowered and motivated clients (Wall et al., 1989).

Compliment-giving guidelines. Raise your awareness level to the point that you notice praiseworthy situations. Although it may not be readily apparent, everyone has a positive quality. Don't confine your compliments to people you know. A clerk in the department store, a taxi cab driver, a waiter or waitress, a cashier, a person who gives you directions, and a person behind the voice on the phone are candidates for compliments. Being sincere is important. Phoniness and insincere flattery are likely to be detected and will be disturbing. If you don't truly admire something, you are better off saying nothing.

Vary the reasons for your compliments. People usually compliment others on the basis of appearance. Certainly, people appreciate a new hairstyle, attractive clothes, and loss of weight being noticed. However, you can also compliment on other praiseworthy qualities and behaviors. "I enjoyed your comments in class," "I thought your work on the project was terrific," "I admire your positive attitude," and "I love your laugh," are generally greatly appreciated by recipients.

When you compliment, check to see that your words, paralanguage, and body language are saying the same thing. Without meaning to do so, you can express a genuine compliment in a tone of voice that sounds negating. Beware of giving "back-handed" compliments. These are comments that start out sounding positive and end with a sting, a question, or a rider that implies they aren't wholly true. Many of them are metamessages as described in Chapter 7. Some examples are: "You drew a beautiful picture for a change," "I can't believe your room is clean," "I like you no matter what they say," and "How did you manage to throw such a great party?" Can you see why these need to be reworded or are better left unsaid?

A positive behavior is to be a third party compliment giver. For example, what can you do if you hear a positive comment about another person? Passing it on to that individual is almost as good as giving it originally. You can also add to it. For example, "I heard Matt tell Craig that you're a great bowler. I can see why he thinks so. You did a terrific job of picking up that spare."

Thinking about yourself as a compliment giver and realizing the benefits of these positive comments can encourage you to increase both their number and their variety. You might want to set a goal of doing so. Your acquaintances, friends, and family members will benefit right along with you.

Receiving Compliments

"I enjoy giving compliments, but I feel funny getting them," was Al's honest comment. How do you react to a compliment? The comment is, "I really like your suit." Do any of the following responses sound like you?

"This old thing? I've had it for years."

"Oh, it's so wrinkled. I look like I've slept in it."

"I hate it. I just pulled it out because everything else was dirty."

"Your taste in clothes is slipping."

"Really?" (while wrinkling your nose)

Consider some of the possible responses to this compliment: "Wow, you really did well on the exam!"

"I could have done better."

"It was just luck."

"The test was easy. Anyone could have done well."

"You're just trying to make me feel good."

Rejecting or denying compliments is common, and the potential for damage is extensive. A compliment rejection is essentially an insult. It's as if the positive comment is hurled back into the face of the giver. A rejecting or denying response is hurtful and can bring negative results. Once rejected, a giver will be reluctant to deliver more compliments. A relationship can be harmed because one individual did not graciously receive what was offered. Also, the positive effects for the receiver are negated. People with low self-esteem are often guilty of this practice and so do not benefit from a sincere comment of praise. Finally, the communication climate can become negative. Imagine a black cloud settling in because the compliment giver feels diminished.

How to receive. Receiving a compliment in a positive way is simple. A "thank you" is enough. If you want to add more, some possibilities are "Thank you; I really appreciate that," "Thank you; I've been feeling a little down, and you helped," and "Thank you; I did spend a lot of time on the project."

If you honestly don't agree with the comment, you can choose to keep quiet or you can mention it without denying or rejecting the compliment. Say, for example, that you really don't like the suit you are wearing, and you receive a compliment. A possible honest response is, "Thank you. I had my doubts about it, and it's nice to know that you think it looks good." Sometimes, you may wonder about returning a compliment with a compliment. For example, in response to "I like your suit," someone could say, "I like your outfit, too." If the response is sincere, no harm will result from a mutual admiration exchange. You might first thank the giver for the compliment and then say, "I'm not just returning one compliment for another. I like your outfit, too," or even, "Thank you. You beat me this time because I was just thinking that I like your outfit."

CHECKING YOUR PERCEPTION

Picture a person standing on the roof of a house with arms waving in front of the face and over the head. Three people from across the street look at the scene. Later, each tells about the incident.

Mary to her husband: "This guy was acting really crazy. He was on top of the house and waving his arms like he was trying to scare someone."

Tom to his children: "A man was trying to get my attention by waving his arms at me. I thought he was in trouble, so I came into the house and called 911. I haven't found out yet what was going on."

Ed to a friend: "I didn't have my glasses on, but it looked like a woman up on the roof who was ready to jump. She was yelling really loud, too."

Each person offered her or his perception of a situation which was inaccurate or incomplete.

What is perception and how does it affect the communication process? *Perception* is a mental process of creating meaning from sensory data. We receive stimuli (sensory data) through our senses; a message is carried to the brain which then acts to organize and interpret the data. At times you won't even be aware of the process. In perceiving, our brains are like computers. Once "turned on," we take in data through the senses of sight, sound, smell, taste, and touch. The perception process begins when sensations are received (like raw data being fed into a computer) and continues as the brain quickly interprets. It tries to make sense out of the sensory data (as a computer computes) and attaches meaning to the input.

In interpersonal relationships we receive most information from seeing and hearing, although touching and smelling can also be involved. An individual's perception affects communication and all other aspects of human relationships. If perception were always accurate, several interpersonal difficulties could be avoided. But is it? At the beginning of this section, three people described the same experience differently. Because of uniqueness, no two people's perceptions are ever exactly the same. "No two pairs of eyes see things in the same way. Our differences in perception begin with this basic and astonishing fact" (Harrison and Bramson, 1982, p. 6).

Effects on Perception

Perception is affected by such factors as background, self-esteem, personality, and values, as well as age, sex, physical condition, and mental health.

> Whether you were an orphan or a rabbi's son, whether A's came easy or you had to labor for a D+, you form a model of the world that fits your experience. You don't experience the world directly. You experience your subjective representation of it. What you see, hear, and feel is converted into a thought or an interpretation. Your "idea" of the world becomes your reality (McKay et al., 1983, p. 97).

Expectations greatly affect perception. For example, read the beginning of the nursery rhyme in these boxes.

Jack and Jill went up the the hill	To fetch a a pail of water

Look carefully at the nursery rhyme again and ask yourself how you read it. If you read it as written here, you used *the* twice in the first box and *a* two times in the second. If you read it as you expected it to be (without the extra words), don't be surprised. *Expectations* do influence what you actually see and act upon.

How does this relate to perception of human beings? If you expect to see or hear a certain thing, that may well be your sensory data. A custodian, who was cleaning an office, was facing a window. An office manager came in, sat at her desk, and after awhile, said, "You're really working late. I'll bet your girlfriend or wife doesn't like that very much." To her surprise, a female voice replied, "Actually, it's my husband who minds!" Expecting custodians to be male led to incorrect sensory input.

In addition, the senses and their abilities to gather accurate information differ from one person to the next. If you don't have perfect vision, and especially if you need corrective lenses, you can probably identify with Ed's problem of not seeing clearly enough to determine the sex of the person on the roof in the earlier scenario. He also erred in thinking that the person was getting ready to jump and in hearing yells. Or did he? Could the others who told of a man waving his arms have been mistaken? Knowing that Ed's vision was limited makes that unlikely. Even though well-adjusted people are generally capable of receiving accurate sensory data, that is not a guarantee. Talk to a police officer investigating an accident scene!

Even if the sensory data is correct, what about comprehension? Have you ever been misinterpreted? Have you misinterpreted another person? The potential for errors is enormous. In fact, misperception causes much of the conflict and difficulties in relationships. Others may not mean what we thought they said. "Nothing is more deeply disquieting than a conversation gone awry—to say something and have it taken to mean something else" (Tannen, 1986, p. 19). As an example, imagine the following scenario.

> You are in the cafeteria at school or work, and a friend who is usually outgoing walks past your table. She glances at you and then turns away.

You saw what she did, so the sensory data is correct. Recognize, however, that another person might have "seen" it differently. Next is your interpretation. Think of as many possibilities as you can—such "whys" as:

> She's mad at me.
> She didn't really see me or recognize me.
> She just doesn't want to talk right now.
> She's preoccupied with a problem.
> She's stuck-up.

Which is correct? One cannot know at this point, and a person skilled in communication and human relations will want to clarify it.

A first step is to be aware that you don't *know* for sure. Even though evidence points to one interpretation more than another, the human experience is full of inconsistencies.

Figure 8-5

Using Perception Checking

When you have any doubts about your perception, a communication technique called *perception checking* can be helpful. This process involves describing the specific sensory data you have received and the interpretations you are making about that data (Glaser, 1986). You use it because your perception may be inaccurate. In cases in which you have no doubts, the technique would be senseless. For example, if someone walks up to you, says, "I don't like you," and punches you in the face, you are receiving a clear message!

Perception checking includes three steps. The first one describes your sensory data, what you have actually seen and heard or, in some cases, smelled, tasted, or touched. What's important is to be specific and descriptive. The second step gives an interpretation of the sensations. What did they mean to you? The third step checks out or asks a question to check the accuracy of both. Ideally, "I" statements are used in the first two steps, while the third step is framed as a question. Note the following language possibilities.

1. *Give sensory data:* I noticed, saw, observed, heard, overheard, tasted, smelled, touched. Be sure to describe in behavioral terms. Exactly what did you see or hear? Include who, when, and where, if possible.
2. *Give interpretation:* I thought, it seemed to me, to me it appeared, I took that to mean, I believe, that led me to believe or think. Interpretation tells the meaning you have attached to the sensations and, at this point, is delivered tentatively. Don't say, "I wonder if." State in a positive way what you *think*.
3. *Check both sensory data and interpretation:* Is that right? Am I correct? Is that how it is or was? Note that the question is checking only the accuracy of your perception. At this point you are not asking whether the person wants to talk, needs help, or the like; nor do you offer to give help yet.

One phrase or question will probably sound more natural to you than another. Or, all of the language may seem awkward at first. With use, you will become comfortable with it.

In differentiating between sensory data and interpretation, think of a courtroom scene. On the witness stand, a person is allowed to give only the facts, or sensory data: "I *saw* the suspect get into a red car and drive away." If a witness begins to add interpretation such as, "I *thought* that he had come out of the bank and was probably fleeing from a robbery," a good attorney will object. Interpretation is not allowed as evidence.

Let's go back to the situation where your outgoing female friend has glanced at you and then looked away. Using perception checking, you could say:

1. "In the cafeteria this noon when you walked past my table, I saw you glance at me and then look away."
2. "It appears that you were upset for some reason."
3. "Am I right?"

The friend can then confirm, modify, or deny either your sensory data or your interpretation or both.

You may be wondering why going through all three steps is important. Let's consider some other possibilities. What's wrong with just asking, "Why?" For example, one could ask, "Why did you look away when you walked by me?" or "Why are you mad at me?" In both cases, you are assuming that your perception is accurate, and it may not be. Also, how do you react to most "why" questions? Generally, people are "put on the spot" and feel defensive when asked the "why" of their behavior. Another reason to avoid "why" questions is that people frequently do not know why, yet they feel compelled to respond, which leads to frustration. Also, many of us were raised with "why" questions that were not asked to find out the real answer. As one young man commented in class, "Whenever my folks asked 'why,' I knew they didn't approve of whatever I had done, and I was going to hear about it."

Another way to begin a discussion with the friend is what many people do, and it goes like this: "You're mad at me, aren't you?" or "You don't like me any more, I guess." An even worse approach would be, "You ignored me, and I *know* you are mad at me." These examples leave out all sensory data and leap directly to conclusions. Instead of checking, you have already made an interpretation, concluded that you are correct, and now the friend is being told the reason for her behavior. Note that the sentences begin with the word "you," which is threatening in itself, and they are all assumptions based on sensory data that has not been communicated. In many cases, people just assume that what they thought is true, may become upset, and not say anything. "I'll treat her just like she treated me" is their way of handling the situation. Too often, relationships suffer because people do not openly share their perceptions.

Perception checking is direct and honest. Unless you are speaking to a troubled person, perception checking will be nonthreatening. The goal is to clarify a situation, and, in most cases, the person will respond in such a way that this is possible. Positive human relationships result when individuals are willing to check both sensory data and interpretation when their perceptions may be inaccurate.

USING THE AWARENESS WHEEL

Perception checking clarifies sensory data and interpretation. You and the relationship can benefit from sharing even more. Besides sensing and thinking, you also experience feeling, wanting, and doing. Although you may be unaware of them, five key pieces of information are present in a given situation (Miller et al., 1988).

Recognizing Five Dimensions of Awareness

The awareness wheel can be used to help you first become aware of yourself and others and then as a guide in sharing what is experienced. The five dimensions are described as follows.

Sensations: Verbal and nonverbal input from people's actions as well as subtleties of what you see, hear, smell, taste, and touch.

Thoughts: The meaning, interpretation, or conclusions from the sensory data. Thoughts are subjective and not objective truths. Interpretations are not "the way things are." They are the way you put your world together-the way you make sense out of data. What is real for you counts; however, others may see and hear the same data and come to very different conclusions.

Feelings: Emotional responses, which are important to share in most interpersonal relationships. Being able to connect with your feelings is invaluable when communicating.

Wants: Intentions, desires, and wishes for yourself, for others, and for your relationship together. These are mini-plans and hopes.

Actions: Behaviors consisting of past, present, and future actions. These are, or will be, observable, and they indicate commitment.

Confusion between wants and future actions is common. The difference is that intentions do not carry a definite commitment to act and are only desires, wants, and wishes. Future actions are disclosures about what you will do. You may also share what you have done or are presently doing in the specific situation.

Verbalizing the Five Dimensions

Becoming aware of the five dimensions in any interaction is important. Expressing these to another person indicates a willingness to reveal what you know about yourself. Like perception checking, using the awareness wheel is a disclosure of yourself. Using "I" statements is important. Following is a way to use the awareness wheel in the same situation of the friend in the cafeteria.

(Sensing)	This noon as you walked by my table in the cafeteria, I saw you glance at me and then look away.
(Thinking)	It seemed to me that you were upset.
(Feeling)	I'm concerned about this.
(Wanting)	I'd like to straighten this out.
(Acting)	In fact, I asked Michele if she knew if something was wrong. She didn't so I'm checking it out with you.

You probably won't want to express each dimension in exactly the same way or order presented here. One advantage of the awareness wheel is that you can begin with any dimension and word each one in a way that is comfortable for you. For example,

> I'm concerned because I noticed that you looked away from me when you walked by my table in the cafeteria this noon. I was sure you had seen me, and it led me to think that you're upset with me. In fact, I even asked Michele if she knew if you were upset and she didn't. I'd like to straighten this out, and I have time to talk about it right now if you do.

If you're thinking that this is too involved and will be time consuming, ask yourself how worthwhile clarity and a nonthreatening communication climate are. Partial awareness is a major problem in the communication process.

> We must never assume that we are fully aware of what we communicate to someone else. The job of achieving understanding and insight into mental processes of others is much more difficult and the situation more serious than most of us care to admit (Hall, 1973, p. 29).

The awareness wheel can help you discover any areas of self-*un*awareness. For example, you may be able to communicate four dimensions and recognize that your feelings are not clear-even to you. Sorting out the missing elements is particularly helpful because when key parts of awareness are not expressed, disappointment, frustration, and even anger can result. Because something is lacking, misunderstanding can develop. In fact, a major source of unhealthy conflict is lack of complete disclosure.

My introduction to the awareness wheel came when my husband and I participated in a series of Couples Communication classes early in our relationship. Since then we have taken trainer workshops. If you can participate in Couples Communication, take advantage of a tremendous opportunity to enrich your relationships. We credit the program with many of the successes enjoyed in our marriage and stepfamily. Learning the skills initially was the easiest part; putting them into practice was, and still is, the most difficult. Usually, it helps to announce that you want to share your awareness and would like the other to do so too. The awareness wheel is not a tool that you will use in every situation; however, when used, a positive outcome is likely.

DELIVERING CRITICISM

A life in which criticism is unnecessary may sound wonderful; however, such an ideal world does not exist. Because you will undoubtedly deliver criticism, learning how to do so in a constructive, positive way is valuable. A first step is to ask yourself the reason for criticizing. Is it justifiable? Is it potentially beneficial? Destructive criticism which is meant to put down, punish, or manipulate is damaging to relationships (Bloomfield and Felder, 1985). Constructive criticism, on the other hand, is "supportive and empowering with a commitment to a positive outcome" (p. 83). If you believe that you can be constructive, you will feel more confident and can present a concerned attitude.

Preparing yourself by thinking about what you will say, and even rehearsing it, is highly recommended. Picking a suitable time and place, if possible, is also a good idea. Be aware of body language and paralanguage. Assertiveness is important. When you deliver a critical remark, use "I" statements. "You" statements will most likely elicit a defensive, combative response. Directing attention specifically and descriptively to behavior or a situation you don't like is more acceptable than being critical of the person. Using perception checking or the awareness wheel is an effective way to deliver criticism, and a receptive response is more likely. Other recommendations are to sound concerned and warm, be brief, open to the other person's thoughts and feelings, willing to hear the other person's point of view, patient, and committed to a positive outcome (Bloomfield and Felder, 1985). Another suggestion has been called the "Mary Poppins rule" (Levine, 1988). Based on the idea that a "a spoonful of sugar helps the medicine go down," the aim is to make the criticism more acceptable by prefacing the criticism with a sincere compliment. For example, "Professor Martin, I enjoy your lectures a lot; however, I don't think that the examination policies are as fair as they could be." Using the person's name, also, can be affirming. Note this criticism given to a sloppy roommate.

> Rhonda, I really like you and have had a lot of fun living with you. I am frustrated about one thing, and that's how messy this apartment has been lately. I've cleaned the kitchen for the last four days, and I've noticed that your clothes have been left all over the living room. I think that maybe you've been so busy you just haven't noticed. I

don't want this to become a big problem between us, which is why I decided to mention it.

Unless Rhonda is an extremely defensive person, this criticism will not offend and will usually get desired results. If it doesn't, you can at least be satisfied that you have expressed in an open, nonthreatening way.

EFFECTIVE RESPONSES

Self-disclosing, perception checking, using the awareness wheel, and delivering criticism initiate an interchange between you and another person. You will also receive information and then respond. What you say in response to comments from others is generally as important as any initial expression.

Understanding Criticism

Criticism is almost impossible to avoid and can be difficult to receive. If constructive and delivered in a nonthreatening manner, it is easier to handle; however, a sizable number of critical statements are made negatively and for reasons that are not evident. Of benefit is to know who criticizes and why.

Sources of criticism. Critical remarks are delivered by family members, friends, co-workers, supervisors, and mere acquaintances. The source influences the initial response. According to a survey in *Psychology Today* (1989), people most resent criticism from a spouse's parents. Following closely behind in-laws are the spouses themselves. Criticism from a subordinate at work ranks third. Men are more resentful than women of criticism from their children. Resentment is also predictable when parents criticize adult children (especially when using a style from years before).

What might be helpful is to realize that criticism is a common by-product of closeness and that, in most cases, the critic does care for you (Tannen, 1986). Also, criticism if given and received in a positive way can actually help a relationship.

Reasons for criticism. You can be criticized for any number of reasons. The critic's motives may be to help you or to hurt you. If you know common reasons for criticism, you may be able to avoid them or at least understand the "why" of the critic. Behavioral types who tend to draw criticism are described by Bright (1988).

1. Poor organizers, who annoy and inconvenience others
2. Agreement breakers, who don't keep commitments nor follow through on tasks
3. Go-getters, who take on so much that they have difficulty completing tasks and therefore produce sloppy work
4. Opinion seekers, who ask for advice and then don't make decisions
5. Quick-draw criticizers, who complain about and find fault with everything and everyone
6. Ostriches, who miss or ignore what is going on
7. Reassurance seekers, who air their faults and seem to want only sympathy or who ask an opinion and then become upset with an honest, critical remark

8. Social norm violators, who do anything to get attention and go against the "flow"
9. Fuzzy trappers, who either don't express or don't clarify expectations and then become annoyed when others don't do what they expect

If you recognize yourself in the list, you probably deserve some criticism. You, like most people, are probably unjustifiably criticized as well. Whether the criticism is deserved or not, a response determines, to a great extent, the course of the exchange and possibly the relationship itself.

Inappropriate Responses to Criticism

Eliminating ineffective or negative responses can clear the way for responses that work in your behalf. In general, individuals respond either aggressively or passively, or a combination of the two. An aggressive method is one of counterattack. A person feels wronged, justifiably or not, then lashes out at the perceived attacker. The criticism may be stopped for the moment; however, the aggression is resented, and the situation is only worsened. In the workplace, an aggressive response will probably get you fired. Consistently responding in an aggressive fashion is a mark of low self-esteem, and counterattacking sets the stage for even more criticism, followed by lowered self-worth (McKay and Fanning, 1987).

Passive responses are ones that agree, apologize, and acquiesce; they can be delivered verbally or nonverbally. Silence is often a form of surrendering to criticism. If you are a "peace-at-any-price" person, passivity and withdrawing may seem inviting. Nevertheless, the potential damage to your physical and psychological well-being is seldom worth the price. Meek receivers of criticism also invite further attacks, and self-esteem can suffer.

A combination of the two occurs when an individual responds passively and then acts aggressively at a later time: "Yes dear, I know I have neglected paying the bills, and I'll make sure it doesn't happen again," is the initial agreeable response. The bills get paid, and two checks are returned from the bank for insufficient funds. The person who was criticized either purposefully or unconsciously may have found a way to "get back" at the critic. Because this behavior is essentially manipulative and indirect, a relationship can be badly damaged.

In addition to these general styles of responses, denying or defending are possible (Heldmann, 1988). Excuse making is a far-too-common response. Usually, the criticized person recognizes that the criticism is appropriate yet still finds it difficult to accept. "Yes, but" is an irritating response. Blaming other people or externals is a continuation of excuse making and makes an individual appear immature and irresponsible.

Positive Responses to Criticism

If your goals are to maintain or increase your self-esteem level, preserve or improve the relationship, and make the situation better for yourself, positive responses to criticism are the key. "The effective way to respond to criticism is to use an assertive style. It doesn't attack, surrender to, or sabotage the critic. It disarms the critic" (McKay and Fanning, 1987, p. 150). The key is to not overreact and make matters worse. Positive responses can be learned and rehearsed. Two general ones, related to the level of agreement, follow a practical sequence of steps.

Agreement with criticism. Even if you realize that the criticism is justified, you can still feel somewhat defensive and hurt. Hence, you may respond in a way that will make the situation worse for you. Instead, follow these steps using "I" statements.

1. Agree with the criticism, using such phrases as "I realize," "I agree," "I know," and "I understand."
2. Optional: State the reason briefly and be sure your reason is fact, not excuse. (The reason this step is optional is that you may not want to tell the "why.")
3. State what you plan to do to prevent future occurrences or what you propose will solve the problem.

Pretend you have been late for work for the past few days, and your supervisor has criticized you. As mentioned before, a common reaction is to make an excuse or blame. Refrain from either! Instead, use a response that is refreshing and much more likely to bring about positive results.

1. I know I've been late, and I can understand your concern.
2. I've had several frustrating problems with my car (optional).
3. I'm taking it in to be fixed tonight, and I plan to be careful about my punctuality in the future.

Or, if you don't want to mention your car at all, skip step 2, and in the third step just say, "I will correct this problem in the future." Dramatically promising that you will *never* be late again is unwise because you might.

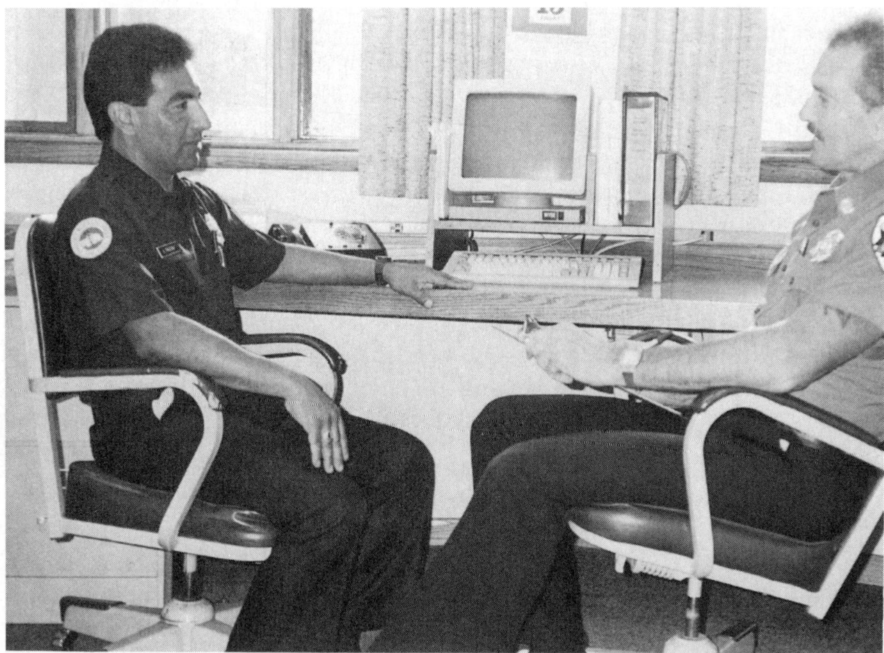

Figure 8-6 During a performance evaluation, a fire captain and a firefighter engage in positive criticism.

You can also agree with part of the criticism. You might understand the person's interpretation and want to clarify. For example, if your supervisor said, "You seem to have lost interest in doing a good job," you can respond, "I can see why you would think that because I have been late the past few days. I want to assure you that I haven't lost interest. My being late is due to other factors which I plan to correct."

In certain instances, humor can be used to defuse the situation. Care must be taken so that the criticism is not rejected and the remark doesn't appear to be offered as an excuse. When Senator Bob Kerrey of Nebraska was running for Congress, a loud critical voice from the audience said, "I don't know why I should vote for you. During one whole year when you were governor, I don't remember anything you did except entertain that actress, Debra Winger." Kerrey smiled, rubbed the side of his head, and replied, "I know what you mean. Sometimes I don't remember much else about that year either." The crowd broke into laughter, including the critic, and what could have become a negative situation, didn't.

Not understanding the criticism. Frequently, criticism is vague, and you honestly don't understand what the person means. Emotionally, this is difficult to handle. A temptation is to defend even if you don't know the reason for the criticism. Resist the temptation! The following response technique, using "I" statements, is particularly helpful.

1. State your lack of understanding with phrases such as, "I don't understand why you think that," "I'm confused as to why you said that," "I don't know why you have that impression."
2. Tell the person what you need to increase your level of understanding with such phrases as, "I'd like you to explain to me why you think that way," "I'd appreciate your telling me what I've done or not done to lead you to think that," or "I would like to know what you are basing that on."

Now the critic is in the responding position. You have been honest and politely requested what you want while giving yourself time to calm down if needed. You wait for the explanation, which usually gives you enough information to respond specifically. Interestingly, if the critic had used either perception checking or the awareness wheel in the first place, you likely wouldn't need added information. What is usually missing in vague criticism is sensory data.

To illustrate this response, pretend a co-worker has said to you, "You don't like to work with me anymore." You have no idea why she believes this because she has not given you her sensory input. You can say:

1. I don't know why you think I don't like to work with you.
2. I'd appreciate your telling me what has caused you to think that.

You now wait for the answer, which should enable you to respond specifically to what sensory data led to her interpretation which she has poorly stated as fact. Then you can deal with concrete descriptive material.

Surprisingly, the person may not be able to provide what you have requested. The response may be, "Well, I don't really know. I just don't think you do." This is frustrating; however you are wise to continue to behave positively. You can question the person by asking whether you have said or done something. Key questions you can use are: "Can you give me some examples?" "Exactly what happened?" "Can you specifically describe what I did?" In some cases, you may have an idea of the reason for their criticism and can guess. Be careful about this, however. Say, for example, you ask the co-worker, "Is it because I told the supervisor that you hadn't finished your share of the project before you left yesterday?" If you aren't certain that this is known by the co-worker, you will be in for a surprise when she says, "No, I didn't know you did that, and now I'm really upset!" If you have probed and still haven't received any pertinent sensory data, you can conclude by saying, "I don't feel that way; however, until you can give me some specifics, I'm not able to offer more than that."

Not agreeing with the criticism. Emotionally, the most difficult situation to deal with is one in which you disagree with the criticism. The person has given you sensory data either initially or after you have requested clarification, and you do not agree. A positive response is still the best one.

1. State your disagreement: "I don't agree," "I guess we don't agree on this," or "I don't see it the way you do." Be sure that you are expressing this in a nonthreatening way keeping your voice calm. Usually, a quick "I disagree" sounds aggressive, so it is better avoided.
2. Either use your own sensory data to give reasons for your disagreement or simply conclude the conversation. Your choice will depend upon what is at stake, what chances you think you have of coming to some sort of an agreement, and other extenuating factors such as fatigue levels and time constraints. You can suggest a future discussion as well as an acknowledgment that disagreement isn't always negative.

Two other tactics may be helpful. "Fogging" suggested in the book *When I Say No, I Feel Guilty* is a method of neither agreeing nor disagreeing with criticism. Instead, you simply acknowledge it and let it go. For example, a parent says to you, "Your apartment (or house) is such a mess, I don't know how you stand to live here." You can reply, "Yes, it is a mess," or "I guess it is. It *is* amazing how I stand it." Other "fogging" phrases are: "You *may* be right" and "That could be true." If you feel strongly about the criticism, "fogging" isn't advisable. However, in many situations, criticism can be like "water off a duck's back" if you allow it to be.

The other technique is to delay. If you are completely surprised by the criticism and, especially, if your reaction is anger, you can express your confusion or surprise and state that you want to think about it for awhile. A good response is, "I'm not sure how to reply. I'm going to think about it, and then I'll get back to you."

> By backing up for a moment to examine our feelings, rather than simply reacting from panic, we can most effectively sort out and respond to the realities of the critical message (Butler, 1992, p. 165).

Positive responses to criticism are sensible and not difficult to learn. They lead to a feeling of enhanced self-esteem and of being in control and serve to move relationships in a positive direction. Definitely, check your skills in the communication exercise in REFLECTIONS AND APPLICATIONS and then strive for positive changes.

Responding to Metamessages

Metamessages, comments with a double-level meaning, were discussed in Chapter 7. Metamessages are usually hidden criticisms, yet they may not be. Recipients of such messages cannot be sure until they check. To cope with a metamessage, first repeat the message in your own mind while you figure out what you think it means. The second step is to state what you think the person is saying and ask whether you are correct (McKay et al., 1983). For example, imagine that your mother says, "You are *so* busy these days." The emphasis on "so" creates a metamessage. The statement means more than just that you are busy.

During your processing, compute what you think was meant and include any feelings, too. Is concern about your welfare being expressed, or does your mother mean that you don't spend enough time with her? Whichever you decide, state it clearly and tentatively: "I wonder if you're worried about me" or "It seems to me that you don't think I'm spending enough time with you." In essence, you guess at the meaning of the metamessage. You can phrase it as a question such as, "Do you mean that I'm not spending enough time with you?"

You will frequently find that the metamessage giver is reluctant to be direct and will continue to hedge. You can decide to encourage further disclosure by repeating or rephrasing your response. Adding specifics will help. In the situation with your mother, you can say, "When you accented the word "so," it led me to believe that you were concerned about something." Or, you can state that the emphasis on the word led you to believe she was feeling hurt (or whatever emotion you detected).

If you commonly receive critical metamessages from the same person, you can try, "Are you saying that" for awhile and try to get the critic to be direct. If this doesn't work, it may be best to use perception checking or the awareness wheel and let the individual know exactly how this practice is affecting you and the relationship. Another choice is simply to ignore it; however, realize that a relationship based on openness and positiveness is then in jeopardy.

Responding to Offensive Language Patterns

Being able to respond assertively to offensive language patterns (discussed earlier in this chapter) is a worthwhile human relations skill. "I hate it when people make bigoted remarks. I just don't know what to say," said one individual. Overuses of profanity, biased language, slang, emotion-packed phrases, disclaimers, and vagueness can be handled in one of the following ways.

Assertively state your opinion; in doing so, you set limits.

"I don't appreciate profanity."
"I don't listen to those kinds of jokes."
"I prefer that words like that not be used."
"I don't like to hear others put down."

Tell how you feel.

"I feel resentful when you start your sentence with 'Let me tell you.' "
"I get frustrated when you make frequent references to 'when I was your age.' "

"I'm hurt by those kinds of comments."

Politely challenge with a question.

"Can you clarify that?"
"Is that your opinion or is it based on research?"
"Who are 'they'?" (helpful when someone begins with "They say or said").

Suggest another alternative.

"I would like you to be more exact."
"I'd like to suggest that you use 'and' instead of 'but' when you say that."
"I'd prefer that you didn't say, 'You have no right to feel that way.' I do have a right to my feelings."
"I'd like to talk about something else."

Too often, individuals simply react and respond with whatever happens to come to mind not realizing what impact their response has on both the communication climate and the interaction. Being prepared with positive responses is an important part of communicating and deserves attention.

Handling Verbal Abuse

When a person is told over time in subtle and not-so-subtle ways that his or her perceptions and feelings are wrong, the challenge is learning to respond to *verbal abuse*. This type of abuse doesn't leave physical evidence; however, it is just as painful, and recovery takes much longer (Evans, 1992). Prolonged verbal abuse is "damaging to the spirit and takes away joy and vitality" (p. 43).

The first step is awareness that verbal abuse is taking place. The book *The Verbally Abusive Relationship: How to Recognize It and How to Respond* (Evans, 1992) describes possible characteristics of an abuser and 14 different types, some of which may surprise you. One not often recognized is verbal abuse disguised as a joke. This kind of abuse, not done in jest, "cuts to the quick, touches the most sensitive areas, and leaves the abuser with a look of triumph" (Evans, 1992, p. 85). Some examples are, "You couldn't find your way out of a paper sack," "You'd lose your head if it wasn't attached," "What can I expect from a blonde?" The abuser makes a disparaging remark and if challenged, will often accuse the "victim" of having no sense of humor. Common is a comment, "I was just kidding. Can't you take it?"

Any verbal abuse tactic requires assertive responses. Allowing yourself to be verbally abused is belittling and will lead to more unhappiness in the future. After recognizing a pattern of verbal abuse, you can start to set limits not by threatening but by stating a fact: "I will not accept jokes that put me down or belittle me." The abuser may not honor your limits and then you have other choices. Finding a supportive counselor and asking the abuser to go with you is one possibility. If you decide that the abuse isn't going to end, you are well advised to end the relationship. Handling the abuse with positive, assertive responses may not be the only step you take; however, it is the beginning of finding the respect you deserve.

Learning effective and positive responses to criticism, metamessages, offensive language, and verbal abuse prepares you for situations that are often emotionally charged. Without forethought and preparedness, individuals either don't verbally respond, or they lash out aggressively and defensively. Neither course of action will lead to feelings of self-worth or improved relationships. An extremely important question is to ask yourself: "Do I want to make things better or worse for myself?" The wise choice, obviously, is in the affirmative. Making things better (either for self, the relationship, or for both) requires thinking ahead and deciding how you will respond. The suggested response techniques can serve as useful guides.

As covered in this chapter, learning about all content along with practicing can greatly improve what you say. Many people, after gaining awareness of content, say, "I didn't realize so much was involved. I used to just open my mouth and talk. Now I think about it first!" Awkwardness is to be expected initially. Do you recall learning to ride a bicycle, to water ski, or to type? Your first attempts probably felt clumsy, and you may have thought that you would never learn. If you persisted, it was likely you wondered how it could have been so difficult. Learning communication skills is similar. After exposure and practice, less intense thinking is needed, the skills become quite natural, and you will wonder at your initial lack of ability.

You are now ready to complete the communication exercises in REFLECTION AND APPLICATIONS. If you do well on the ones from Chapters 7 and 8, you deserve a pat on the back. Keep in mind that content does make a definite difference in all interactions and especially in close relationships, and you influence the course of a relationship by what you say.

SUMMARY

Content consists of verbalized words and sentences. What you talk about can be organized into levels ranging from superficial chit-chat to deep, intimate communication. People who can converse on all levels in appropriate situations and in sensible amounts possess positive verbalizing abilities.

Awareness of content and its influence on communication can help you avoid some common pitfalls. Self-disclosure means revealing about yourself. It can be organized into degrees or levels that move from basic data through preferences to beliefs and feelings. Individuals vary in their willingness and ability to self-disclose. Appropriate self-disclosing carries personal and professional benefits. Despite known advantages, an individual may not self-disclose because of obstacles that, with awareness and determination, can be avoided. After deciding to disclose, a positive communicator uses "I" statements and body language to match the verbal message, and the message is clear, direct, and specific.

Compliments are verbal positive strokes that praise and affirm another person. Increasing the number of sincere compliments you give, doing so in positive ways, and receiving compliments graciously are means of improving your relationships.

Perception, which includes taking in sensory data then interpreting its meaning, is a process intrinsic to human beings. Individuals can err in the accuracy of either the initial input or the meaning they attach to it. Techniques such as perception checking and the awareness wheel aid in understanding and clarifying one's awareness. Effective responses are usually as important as initial comments. Understanding criticism and learning positive responses to it, metamessages, and offensive language patterns are beneficial human relations skills. Handling verbal abuse assertively, which is especially challenging, is necessary in building healthy human relationships.

Improvement in communication is possible, and you can earn the regard of others for being a positive communicator. As with any art, interpersonal communication requires attention and practice.

It is certain that a relationship will be only as good as its communication.

—John Powell

RESOURCES

Interpersonal Communication Programs, 7201 South Broadway, Littleton, CO 80122, (800) 328-5099

Section Three

Positive Relationships: The Ultimate Achievement

OBJECTIVES

After reading this section you will be able to

- Explain why your own relationships are important.
- Describe loneliness and what the research shows.
- Give examples of how relationships can be beneficial.

Relationships with others lie at the very core of human existence.

—Ellen Berscheid and Letitia Peplau

You have learned about the foundation of positive relationships. Understanding and love of self along with interpersonal communication skills provide the groundwork. Interacting is the beginning of relationship building.

We, as individuals, would not have developed a "self" unless we had experienced relationships, according to sociological theory (Mead, 1934). Each of us became what we know as our "self" through relations with others. As we move through life, others continue to contribute toward our development.

Our exploration of human relations as a process continues with a look at the benefits of relationships. Why bother relating to others? One reason is pleasure. Enjoyment of life is a worthy goal, and relationships contribute a great deal. Jointly participating in activities and just being together are major reasons. Even brief encounters with people can be interesting and stimulating. "I don't think hermits have much fun, and loners look sad," a student said when I asked this question in class.

Another young man answered, "To avoid loneliness, which is a bummer." His description was accurate. A social stigma is attached to lonely persons; they are perceived as less liked, less preferred as a friend, rated as more passive and weaker as well as less attractive, less sincere, and not as well adjusted (Lau and Gruen, 1992). Lonely females in late adolescence were found to be at a higher degree of alcoholism risk (Page and Cole, 1991). "Acute loneliness is a terrorizing pain" (Rokach, 1990, p. 41). Loneliness, even in crowded societies, is not uncommon. When a group of Americans was asked whether at any recent time they had felt lonely or remote from others, about 25 percent said that they had (Perlman, 1988). Research about loneliness has provided much insight. *Loneliness* as defined in one study is "a feeling of being alone and disconnected or alienated from positive persons, places, or things" (Woodward, 1988, p. 4). Loneliness can be short term, or it may last a long time. Although people can feel alone at any age, adolescence, surprisingly, has been found to be the phase of life when loneliness is greatest (Woodward, 1988). However, young children are also lonely. When asked, nearly all kindergarten and first grade children seemed to understand loneliness, and over 10 percent expressed lonely feelings. Understandably, poorly accepted children experienced the most (Cassidy and Asher, 1992). Children in both Australia and the United States had similar levels of loneliness again related to being less accepted, having fewer friends, and their own withdrawing behaviors (Renshaw and Brown, 1992). A study of 8634 African-Americans, Mexican-Americans, and Caucasian-Americans found loneliness more common among late adolescence and young adults than the elderly. The strongest predictor of loneliness was marital status with separated, divorced, and widowed showing the highest levels. Income and educational attainment were also associated with loneliness (Page and Cole, 1991).

The first year of college is a vulnerable time. Both Japanese and American students away from home had high loneliness scores with Japanese youth somewhat higher (Pearl et al., 1990). Similar cultural differences were evident in a comparison between Korean and American college students in their own countries with Korean students being lonelier (Simmons et al., 1991). Women more than men answer in the affirmative when asked whether they are lonely. Interestingly, on more subtle measures of loneliness, men have higher scores (Marsh, 1988). In another study, elderly men were lonelier than women (Mullins and Mushel, 1992).

Can people be lonely in the presence of others? The answer is a resounding yes, and at these times, the feeling can be even more pervasive and dreadful. Julie commented, "You can be in the center of a crowd and be dreadfully lonely." Rita, whose husband had left her, said, "I have periods of loneliness now, but it's nothing compared to how lonely I felt when he was sitting in the same room with me." In fact, *living together loneliness* (LTL), the result of a perceived discrepancy between expected and achieved contact, has been identified (Kiley, 1989). Perhaps more than one fourth of married people, the majority of them females, suffer from LTL. Men, too, suffer from this loneliness; however, they seem to have more difficulty admitting it. If unattended, this type of loneliness will eventually take its toll on physical health.

Can anything be done about loneliness? After admitting that you are lonely, it is wise to take a good look at yourself. "Because loneliness is more involved with the inside world than the outside, we must look inward for help with loneliness. We must depend on ourselves" (Woodward, 1988, p. 94). A difference between people who feel lonely and those who don't is self-esteem. "Finding someone to love is not the solution. The solution is learning to love yourself" (Burns, 1985a, p. 25).

If you experience loneliness on a regular basis, do something about it. Cognitive restructuring is important because thoughts create reality. Behavioral techniques are also helpful. Think of what you have done during lonely times. Engaging in enjoyable activities is a common way of coping; however, the relief may be temporary. A good idea is to call or visit someone; yet, people who have been lonely for some time often feel reluctant to reach out. Nevertheless, if loneliness is to be conquered, the risk is necessary. Ways to create happiness suggested in Chapter 3 can alleviate loneliness. One of the easiest ways to prevent or end loneliness and to feel a sense of belonging is to find a group that needs you, and these groups are everywhere. Participants or members are wanted, so you will be welcomed. Any number of volunteer, personal interest, and support groups exist in communities. If getting involved doesn't interest you or if you lack the willpower to take the first step, you would be wise to seek counseling.

Diminished loneliness is related to satisfaction with friendships, not just to increased contacts. Mistakenly, lonely high school and college students may believe that they just need to get out and do things with large numbers of people. Instead, the time could be better spent deepening and enriching their relationships. A study on coping with loneliness revealed strategies that did not help such as addictive behaviors, avoidance of the problem, and self-induced isolation. What did help were professional intervention and support, reflective solitude, and social contact (Rokach, 1990).

The recognition that all people experience loneliness at some time can be helpful.

> There is no complete escape from loneliness. It is part of being born, of being human, of living, of loving, of dying. Perhaps there shouldn't be a complete escape. Why would anyone want to be deprived completely of an emotion? To experience the emotions of passion, happiness, grief, love and loneliness is part of living, part of being human (Woodward, 1988, p. 85).

Few cases of loneliness persist if the individual tries to live differently. Stimulation from companionship and fun is within the reach of any lonely person.

Important other reasons for having relationships are apparent. We look to those with whom we have relationships for favors, help, advice, and support. "My car didn't start, so my neighbor gave me a ride to work," "My buddy loaned me money until payday," "She offered to let me stay with her until I find a place," and "When I moved, I called everyone I knew to help" are typical descriptions of relationships.

Support is a major benefit of relationships. Positive relationships provide psychological support and help individuals cope with life. Being able to share stress, emotional challenges, and problems with someone else decreases their impact. When interviewees in a study were asked to describe their most important relationships, the word "there" kept being used. "She is always *there* for me," "I can count on him to be *there*." Consistently, "thereness" seemed to be the key element in the "why" of their relationships (Josselson, 1992).

The necessity for emotional support struck me a few years ago as I waited for a surgeon to report on my daughter after major surgery. Trying to relieve stress, I wrote my thoughts at that time. These shakily written notes are in my journal.

> Waiting for surgeon and looking around the waiting room and seeing family and friends who have given so much support—my husband, my daughter Lisa, my parents who haven't been in good health themselves, two close friends, and my former husband, who must be as worried as I am. Along with the risk and the pain involved in human relationships is the beauty of emotional support. By reaching out and touching each other, people do so much for each other.

Just like a song says, "We all need somebody to lean on." "If I didn't have friends, I'd have given up a long time ago" is how some people feel. Do you remember a time when you didn't have anybody near to call upon? If so, you know how reassuring relationships can be.

Having a *confidant*, a significantly close personal friend with whom one can safely share one's deepest concerns and joys, has been found to be related to higher levels of well being, satisfaction, and lowered distress among widows (DiGiulio, 1989). A study of 9000 people found that being married had virtually no effect on life expectancy; however, having at least one close relationship did. Older people who had a confidant lived longer than those who didn't (Belsky, 1988). "Close relationships help people weather life's slings and arrows and may even reduce our chances of getting physically ill" (p. 73). By becoming involved in life around them and not dwelling on themselves, older people are more likely to be emotionally healthy (Fromme, 1984). At all ages, the absence of satisfying relationships can cause both psychological and physical illnesses (Duck, 1991).

Individuals who have healthy relationships feel affirmed, and their self-esteem levels increase. Even a friendly hello can lift spirits and spark a feeling of "I matter." Growth can occur as you interact with others. "I learned a lot from that relationship," "My co-workers have taught me so much," and "I'm a better person because of her" are

Figure III-1 Mother-in-law Lorane Hanna and son-in-law Bob Dinkel found that a positive relationship is a source of joy.

statements of growth. "I may not have gone to college if it hadn't been for my friends' influence" shows how relationships can motivate.

Finally, besides being motivating, human contact has the power to increase your energy.

> Human beings need contact with other human beings the way a lamp needs electricity. Contact energizes people. It turns them on. When people are out of contact with other people, they get tired, depressed, anxious. Contact can relieve stress, because it increases energy (Tubesing, 1981, p. 85).

Those with an extraverted preference particularly are energized by interaction. Introverts prefer fewer episodes of contact, especially casual ones. Regardless of personality type, well adjusted people are nourished by healthy relationships.

It is clear that we need human contact, and knowing how to build nourishing relationships guarantees that this need is satisfied and the benefits of relating are realized. Additionally, in both personal and professional walks of life, being able to interact and get along with others are invaluable. John D. Rockefeller once stated, "The ability to deal with people is as purchasable as sugar or coffee and I will pay more for that ability than any other under the sun" (Donaldson and Scannell, 1986, p. 42).

Besides increasing our success in the career world, relating skills are needed to develop and enrich love relationships and help build strong families that contribute immeasurably to human development. Parents have the awesome responsibility of shaping human lives. Just as you aren't wise to drive an automobile merely by turning on the engine, pushing the accelerator, and letting the car go on its own, you will have difficulty relating without paying attention and exerting more control (Duck, 1991). Learning everything possible about relationships is essential if you are to achieve success in your own life. The rest of the book focuses on healthy relationships. After acquiring the knowledge and skills and demonstrating them, you can be a positive role model for those you know and love.

Joy comes to those who succeed in their human relationships.

—Sharon Hanna

9

Building Positive Relationships

OBJECTIVES

After completing this chapter, you will be able to

- Name and explain features of healthy relationships.
- Realize that a relationship is only as healthy as its participants.
- Define codependency and recognize that it is not healthy.
- Explain the relationship of self-esteem to positive relationships.
- Discuss positive behaviors in relationships.
- Discuss different types of relationships, including friendships.
- Define stereotyping, prejudice, and discrimination and explain ways to rid yourself of each.
- Know how to look for approachability cues and how to initiate and maintain a conversation.
- Identify factors related to attraction and liking.
- Improve your own relationships.

Humans are conceived within relationships, born into relationships, and live their lives within relationships with others. All human society has a stake in the nature of people's close relationships. We all benefit from the existence of successful relationships and share, at least indirectly, the costs of relationship deficiencies.

—Ellen Berscheid and Letitia Peplau

Well-adjusted human beings need and desire positive relationships. The social self cannot develop without interactions. To live in the world is to relate. "We are relating beings. Indeed, for our species we may almost say that to be is to relate. We relate because we must" (Rubin, 1983, p. viii). Without self-knowledge, self-love, and positive communication skills, you will encounter difficulty and disappointment in human relations; with them, you are ready to become even more skilled in the art of relating.

HEALTHY RELATIONSHIPS

Not all relationships are good for us. The ability to recognize characteristics of a healthy relationship is a first step in minimizing the possibility of becoming involved in interactions and relationships that aren't nourishing.

Social Exchange

One way to check the health of a relationship is to ask yourself honestly, "Is it good for me?" If you believe that you are receiving benefits, you will answer in the affirmative. *Social exchange theory* suggests that relationships can be assessed by their outcomes, or what the participants are receiving compared to what they are giving. In other words, you look at benefits versus costs. Receiving more pleasure than pain from associating with another person is the cornerstone of interpersonal attraction and affiliation (Hendrick and Hendrick, 1992).

Close relationships depend on social exchange. Think about your friendships. What do you receive and give? Did you once experience a friendship that you no longer have? Relationships frequently end because one or both are no longer receiving enough from the other. Elizabeth and Joyce lived in apartments in the same building. Both were single and pursuing careers. Joyce received a job transfer to a nearby city. "We'll still be close friends," said Joyce. "Oh, yes, it's not that far," agreed Elizabeth. For awhile the two remained in touch. Later, contact gradually decreased, and within 2 years, the relationship had essentially ended. What the two hadn't realized is that their relationship was based on enjoyable daily contact, so when this was no longer possible, neither received enough. The costs exceeded the benefits.

One of the basic principles of the behavioristic approach to psychology is that most people seek pleasure and avoid pain. Although relationships will have elements of displeasure, positive ones provide more pleasure. Rewards either outnumber or are more powerful than punishments. Evaluating a relationship on its rewards is practical and healthful.

Features of a Healthy Relationship

A relationship is only as healthy as its participants. In order for a relationship to be satisfying and nourishing, the people involved must exhibit certain traits. *Love for self* is a primary one. As pointed out, self-love is healthy and allows an individual to reach out positively to others. Both people are in or are committed to achieving an I'm OK, You're OK life position, and they feel and act as equals. Individuals with high self-esteem tend to be accepting of others. They will not need to manipulate people and can easily affirm them (Lauer and Lauer, 1988).

Closely related to love for self is *freedom from enabling behavior and codependency*. Enabling occurs when a person's actions directly, yet inadvertently, allow irresponsible, dysfunctional, or destructive actions of another to continue. It is usually well intentioned. Codependence is a form of enabling that originally was related to substance abuse and is now used in describing various relationships (Mastrich and Birnes, 1990). In a study *codependency* was defined as "any suffering and/or dysfunction that is associated with or results from focusing on the needs and behavior of others" (O'Brien and Gaborit, 1992, p. 19).

Codependency is sometimes considered a disease because it is progressive and habitual (Beattie, 1987). *Codependents are responsive to the needs of the world to the exclusion of their own needs.* Codependents want to be of service, and they usually are helpful, yet they never think they have done enough, and they continue to sacrifice. Codependents believe that the quality of their lives depends upon the lives of other people (Whitfield, 1989).

A codependent person feels compelled to help and control others and do for them what they could be doing for themselves. In the process, a codependent's needs are seldom met. People often do not recognize the condition because it is second nature to them, and codependency has "its roots in nurturing and caring behavior" (Mastrich and Birnes, 1990, p. 3).

Joanna is one of the kindest individuals in the world. She remembers friends' and clients' birthdays and anniversaries, she is the first one to visit someone in the hospital, and she does regular favors. She used to dote on her two grown sons and grandchildren to the exclusion of her own best interests. She reacted to all their problems and was always there for them as well as everyone else she knew. Stress-related symptoms led her to a therapist, who identified her as a codependent. After several therapy sessions, extensive reading, and soul searching, she is well again.

Generally, codependency and low self-esteem coexist. Among high school students, those who were codependent had low self-esteem. Girls showed more codependent characteristics than boys (Fisher and Beer, 1990), and the traditional feminine gender role is at fault in many cases. Perhaps, that explains why the market for codependency books and resources is 85 percent female (Kaminer, 1992). Self-worth for a codependent comes through others. They are people who "give power to others to define themselves" (Chopich and Paul, 1990, p. 41). Healthy relationships demand responsibility for one's own happiness, empowerment, and high self-esteem on the part of both participants. The ensuing positive relationship then increases self-esteem, which, in turn, continues to nourish the relationship.

What can be done about codependency? Identifying it and increasing one's level of self-esteem, if necessary, are key elements. Healing the "inner child" as discussed in Chapter 1 may be basic. Many books about enabling behaviors and codependency are available. For people who spend most of their time helping others while their own needs are pushed to the side, called the "messiah trap," Berry (1988) recommends a combination of individual counseling and a peer support group. Finally, developing an androgynous personality and assertiveness training accompanied by daily use of affirmations are especially beneficial (Mastrich and Birnes, 1990). If codependent, it helps to remind yourself that you are not only making these changes for yourself; other people will also benefit. Then you can arrive at a place in which you can say as did Jean, one of my middle-aged students: "I have been so many things to so many people. It's time to be someone for me."

Besides love for self, androgyny, and assertiveness which help to eliminate codependency, Carl Rogers (1978; 1980) identifies features of a healthy therapist–client relationship, applicable for all types of relationships. *Genuineness* creates trust in the relationship. Honesty between people is more than the absence of lying; openness and authenticity are intrinsic facets. Participants in the relationship feel comfortable showing their true selves. Game playing is unnecessary, and individuals can express what they think and feel. This means that hurt is likely; however, healthy relationships can tolerate some pain.

Warmth is another feature which Rogers refers to as *unconditional positive regard* or warm acceptance of each other. Conditional regard means that conditions are attached to the relationship: "I like you when you do me favors" and "I expect you to be there every time I call" are examples. A healthy relationship doesn't put such demands on the participants, although realistic expectations and constructive criticism are possible. If you have unconditional regard for another person, you are able to describe facts and make recommendations without judging. Animals can teach us about unconditional love which is dependable and consistent (Chopich and Paul, 1990). Unconditional positive regard amounts to acceptance which means that two people appreciate each others' unique personalities and allow for human flaws.

Empathy, a key element in healthy relationships, is the ability to experience another person's perspective. You are able to participate in another's feelings and ideas even if you haven't had a direct experience. Empathic listening, described in Chapter 6, depends on this trait. Empathy seems to be related to a high feeling preference on the Myers–Briggs Type Indicator and with higher grade point averages, according to a study (Jenkins et al., 1992).

> Empathetic men become co-beings. They don't talk at you, don't interrupt, don't give advice. They listen and stand beside you, and in their presence, you have an uncanny feeling that you have been given permission to be yourself (Keen, 1991, p. 157).

Understanding others and being empathic are challenging. What can help is to first recognize that differences in how people think and feel do not have to be translated into right and wrong. Then you can use your adult ego state to process from the other's point of view. "If another person's behavior seems illogical to us, the reason is that we do not understand it, not that he (or she) is illogical" (Lecky, 1951, p. 136). Emotionally, you may not have experienced the same feeling in a similar situation yet can still empathize.

Being empathic involves comprehending the underlying meanings of what people say. Bob talked about his hospital stay and the results of his laboratory tests and complained about his doctors to his co-workers. Dave realized that down deep Bob was scared that there was something seriously wrong. He recognized that the nervous chatter and griping was a coverup for some anxious feelings. He empathized and encouraged Bob to talk about his fear. After the feeling was released, Bob's discussions about his health became fewer.

Self-disclosure, another of Rogers's features of a healthy relationship, is necessary in developing and enlivening a relationship. As discussed in Chapter 8, all relationships require some level of disclosure. In the initial stages, only basic data and preferences are usually disclosed, and with acquaintances, this continues to be appropriate. In order to develop deeper ties, people express on deeper levels. As they reveal more of their hidden selves, a powerful basis for trust and closeness can be formed.

In some cases, further self-disclosure will indicate that this relationship is not one you want to pursue.

> There are some people who we do not feel are nutritious for us. It doesn't mean they are bad; it only means there isn't a fit. I see no problem with deciding someone is not to your taste once you have explored. This is a continuing experience of meeting, exploring, and choosing (Satir, 1978, p. 99).

In addition to the four features identified by Carl Rogers, other ingredients contribute to long-term healthy relationships. *Enjoyment* is one. Human beings relish enjoyable experiences that occur among and with other people. "I love movies," said one woman, "and I'll go to one alone. But it's so much more enjoyable to go with someone and share the experience." A healthy relationship will have times of displeasure, yet the overall vibrations will be those of joy.

Encouragement is part of a positive relationship. Healthy relationships are supportive and affirming. Positive or negative tones are determined by the participants.

> There are those who feel obligated to tell us all the things that can go wrong as we set out over the uncharted waters of our unique lives. "Wait till you get out into the cold, cruel world, my friend. Take it from me." Then there are those who stand at the end of the pier, cheering us on, exuding a contagious confidence: "Bon Voyage!" (Powell, 1976, p. 18).

Individuals within a healthy relationship encourage positive experiences for each other and provide support and affirmation.

Fairness and dependability are closely related. In a healthy relationship you can count on the other to treat you fairly, and this is reciprocated. Dependability means that each of you will do what you say unless circumstances prevent it. Trust develops between individuals who can rely on each other to be fair and dependable.

Energizing feelings are evident in healthy relationships. Being energized means that you leave an interaction feeling "up." Think about your relationships. Do you have some that leave you tired and depleted because they drain your energy? In positive relationships, individuals feel fulfilled because each provides sparks of energy. Sue has been a close friend of mine since college days, and she and I agree that one reason we enjoy interacting is that when we leave each other, we feel more energized than when we first come together. "The most important thing you can ever do for other people is to leave them feeling better emotionally after being in your presence" (Ellsworth, 1988, p. 115). Be cautious if energy flows out of you and is not restored by the relationship.

Demonstrated mutual interest in each other is essential. I asked students one day why they no longer had certain relationships. One woman replied, "She just didn't ever seem interested in me. I asked about her life; mine never seemed important to her." You show interest by asking questions such as: "What's new in your life?" "What plans do you have for the holidays?" "How are your children doing?" People who show little or no interest in others seem self-absorbed while positive individuals enjoy sharing with others, and they love to be asked about their lives!

Positive Interactive Behaviors

Think of anyone with whom you interact. What distinguishes one interaction from another? What behaviors are positive? These questions were asked of college psychology students. Following is a list of common responses.

- Acknowledgment (i.e., calling me by my name when greeting)
- Active interest shown in me
- Concern for my feelings
- Willingness to offer help; often before being asked
- Enjoyment of my company; we have fun together
- Good sense of humor
- Willingness to admit mistakes
- Interesting conversation
- Giving, but not overly so
- Ability and willingness to make decisions; doesn't always depend on me to choose activities
- Sharing; will pay their share and contribute in other ways
- Listening skills; will listen openly
- Positive attitude
- Trust; the other will not put me down or embarrass me in front of people
- Ability to keep confidences and secrets
- Willingness to stand up for me, if necessary

How many of these do you demonstrate in your relationships? How about the other people involved? Can you add to the list?

Knowing what characteristics and behaviors are desirable can help you see what you have to offer and, perhaps, what still needs to be developed. Unless people are aware of what contributes to healthy relationships, they ruin potentially positive relationships or accept less than nourishing ones.

TYPES OF RELATIONSHIPS

Relationships vary in depth from casual or informal to close and intimate. They also differ in their *interactions*, those exchanged acts that occur in face-to-face situations (Hendrick and Hendrick, 1992). You may pass a person on the street, exchange smiles and greetings, and continue on your way, possibly not realizing that you have just interacted. You may see someone on a daily basis for a period of time and then not again for months. Because of these variances, several types of relationships emerge.

Acquaintances

Ties with acquaintances are important. Social interactions give people a psychological sense of belonging. Familiar strangers are acquaintances whom you may not know by name but who have a regular place in your life—a waitress in a restaurant where you eat, the postal carrier or mail clerk, a cashier at the grocery store, or a neighbor you occasionally see. You and the other person may just smile or chat briefly. Even though such interactions seem inconsequential, their contribution to positive feelings and self-esteem levels are measurable (Montgomery and Trower, 1988).

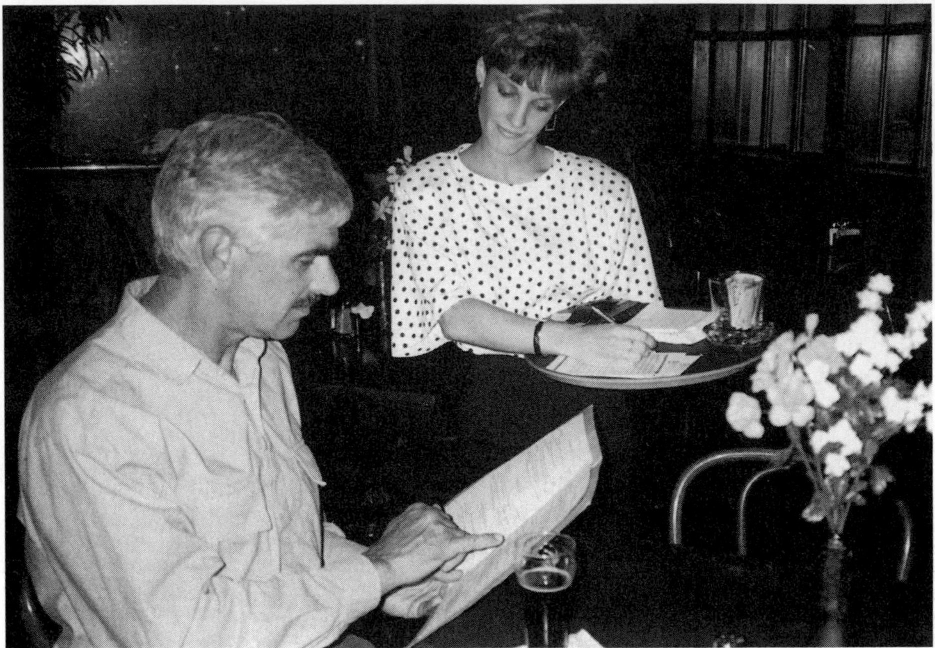

Figure 9-1 An ordinary interaction is more pleasant when individuals are friendly and positive.

Friendships

A special type of relationship is friendship. A friend is a person whom you know well and for whom you have fond feelings. Friends are valued. "I don't know what I would do if it weren't for my friends. I'd be lost," said a student. When asked to identify what is valued in life, most people mention their friends. Human beings look to friends to satisfy a number of needs, and the benefits of friendships are well documented. Friends provide support in buffering the strains of life (Jackson, 1992). In fact, the hallmark of friendship is giving and receiving of social support (Hendrick and Hendrick, 1992). Especially during adolescence, they are also important in the socialization process (Clark and Ayers, 1992).

A study at the University of Nebraska School of Medicine found that those with confiding relationships had better immune functions and lower levels of cholesterol and uric acid in their blood. Other studies show that people who have friends they can turn to for affirmation, empathy, advice, and assistance as well as affection are more likely to survive health challenges and are less likely to develop certain diseases (Brody, 1992). "Only with best friends can we get off the stage, stop the show, quit performing, and allow ourselves to be seen as we are" (Keen, 1991, p. 175).

The characteristics and features of healthy relationships, covered earlier, are common in friendships. Friends, in contrast to acquaintances, have mutual interests and provide companionship and support. A good friendship is like a marriage requiring tolerance, humor, nurturing, and time; if taken for granted, a friendship will be diminished (Brody, 1992). Take advantage of a chance to enrich a friendship by doing the activity in REFLECTIONS AND APPLICATIONS.

Stages of a friendship. Friendships begin with initial contact. You were born into a family, not into a friendship. How does one move an acquaintance relationship to a friendship? Following a first meeting, further encounters are positive and affirming. You enjoy each other's company as you plan and engage in mutually satisfying activities. Self-disclosure at deeper levels occurs, and trust is developed. "Progressive stages of increasing openness can peel off layers of our outer selves like the skins of an onion" (McCarthy, 1988, p. 169). As in all relationships, you may experience conflict and have moments of doubt in the friendship; however, if the social exchange factors are strong enough, differences get resolved. As the relationship progresses, it is easily distinguishable from an acquaintanceship.

Cycles of importance. Friends are important during all stages of life, yet the extent of significance varies. Friendships become meaningful when an individual enters school and participates in activities outside the family. During junior high and high school, friends typically dominate most aspects of life. Parents aren't far from wrong when they say, "Your friends are your whole world."

As men and women form intimate relationships with each other, they usually drift away from reliance on friendships. In fact, a common complaint is, "She doesn't have anything to do with me or her other friends any more since she's involved with him." Even though this is a normal course, most people realize that friendships are still important. Marriage and parenthood take precedence over friendships in most people's lives; a study of older individuals found that siblings, children, and other family members took precedence over friends (Connidis et al., 1992). Friends typically remain important as social companions and confidants.

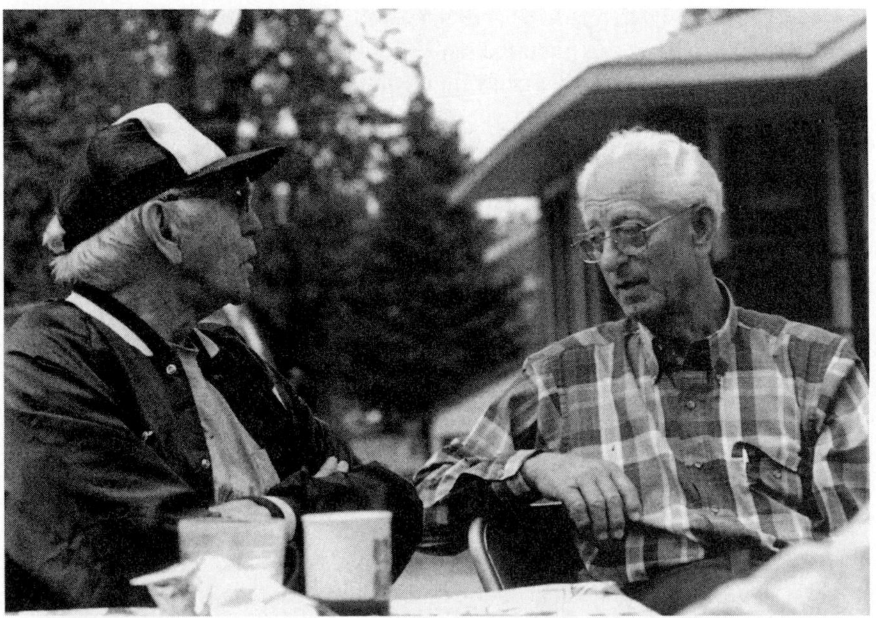

Figure 9-2 Friendship has rewards throughout a lifetime.

Types and dilemmas. The word friendship indicates a wide range of closeness. A friend can be a best friend or just a "buddy." Between these two extremes are dimensions and types of friendships. One gauge of friendship, closeness, is more than frequency of contact. A friend–confidant is a person with whom you can be totally open and who contributes to your personal growth (Powell, 1976).

Physical closeness may not be a factor as long-distance friends can be as emotionally close as ones you see regularly. When you connect, there is a feeling of comfort. I had not seen Ellen, a good friend–confidant, for 6 years, and during that time we had been in contact only about 3 times a year by telephone or letter. Yet, when we came together for a weekend, the experience was delightful, and we felt as if we had not been apart, a typical reaction in long-distance deep friendships. The same is true for my husband and a close high school friend Dan who lives 400 miles away. They pick up as if they have never been separated. "The cadence of friendship is measured in decade-long rhythms" (Keen, 1991, p. 174). It's a wonderful feeling to know that I can telephone a number of precious, long-distance friends right now and feel quite connected.

A friendship dilemma caused when degrees of closeness are not identified has to do with recognition. Best friends, "just friends," and casual acquaintances are frequently not distinguished from one another at special events. A researcher recalled the tragic death of a dear friend. At the funeral she sat far to the back of a filled church and, in the middle of her grief, had a thought that even though she was one of the deceased's closest friends, she was being treated no differently than a casual acquaintance (Rubin, 1985). American society and the English language provide specific distinctions for family relationships, yet not for friendships.

Gender differences in friendships. Same-sex friendships, female–female and male–male, tend to have different characteristics. Among adolescents, girls more than boys tended to have friends who were similar to them (Clark and Ayers, 1992). When seventh and eighth graders were surveyed, girls expected more than boys from their close friendships and reported more intimacy and self-disclosing (Clark and Ayers, 1993). Women generally spend more time talking and seem to disclose more deeply. Men are generally more active and engage in mutually enjoyable activities, many of which are sports related. One study on coping had an unexpected finding. When major stress was being experienced, women took time for themselves and tended to exercise as a way of coping, while men did seek support or advice from close friends (Gadzella et al., 1991).

Because men generally do not engage in deeper levels of self-disclosure, their friendships may not seem emotionally close. In fact, one male author maintains that most men over 30 don't have real friends. They are limited to colleagues, work buddies, and golf partners largely because the American culture discourages male friendships. He wrote that maintaining the lawn was usually seen as more important than maintaining friendships (Letich, 1991). A class discussion on this subject brought forth different opinions. Steve said his male friendships were marked by deep self-disclosing. Glenn remarked that closeness can be defined in different ways. Men, he said, are more apt to be fishing together, and one may comment, "I'm getting divorced." When he said that this could be perceived as close, the females in the class looked doubtful!

Being deprived of a same-sex confidant can be problematic. Sue and Marc had been married for 13 years and, together, had several couple friends. When they decided to divorce, both were depressed. Sue suggested that Marc talk with a male friend. "I

Figure 9-3 Male friendships often focus on shared activities.

don't have anyone I can talk to about this," he replied. "I don't feel comfortable talking about my personal life with the guys I know." Sadly, this has been the case for men in general. Because friendships offer significant benefits for everyone, both men and women are wise to cultivate them. Younger men today seem more determined to develop and keep same-sex friendships, so the future is likely to be different.

SUPPORT SYSTEMS

A major purpose of relationships is to provide support. An individual or a group can offer solace, encouragement, and advice.

Support Groups

Relationships can be typed according to the quality of support they provide. A close-knit group is made up of "the priceless people in our lives who help us realize the meaning of our existence. They know the 'real' you; they understand where we've been; and they help us grow" (H. Johnson, 1986, p. 68). They are your primary support system and contribute immeasurably to self-esteem.

Some people are neutral in terms of support; they serve other purposes. Others are prospective friends whose degree of support you do not yet know. A secondary support system is composed of groups at work, school, church, and within neighborhoods and organizations. Self-help groups are becoming increasingly popular and are recommended as a way of dealing with challenges to our physical, mental, emotional, and social selves. During crises and tragedies, a self-help group can be invaluable. In a 1993 survey by *Self* magazine, 74 percent said they had been in a self-help group. Eating disorders, alcohol or drug addiction, relationship conflicts, and depression made up the largest specific categories of reasons. Did they help? "Yes," said 71 percent with 38 percent responding, "It changed my life."

Being aware of your support systems and how each group affects your self-esteem is important. Any type of relationship that genuinely affirms you is precious.

Caregiving

Of particular importance is the special support provided by a person in a caregiving role. When individuals are unable to care for themselves, either they are placed in nursing homes or rehabilitation centers for long-term care or someone, a family member or friend, voluntarily assumes the responsibility. The task, even if rewarding, can be overwhelming. "Faced with the task of providing for a dependent loved one, caregivers are often unprepared to cope with the myriad of physical and emotional effects that accompany long-term illness" (Cole, 1991, pp. 12–13).

Caregivers need help themselves. Those who tend toward codependency are particularly at risk. A study showed that friends, not siblings as expected, provided the most emotional support for caregivers (*Modern Maturity*, 1993). If you or somebody you know is in a caregiving role, some of the suggested books in the references section can make a dramatic difference in the quality of your life.

INITIATING INTERACTIONS

In order for a relationship to begin, someone has to act. Initiating interactions is a valuable human relations skill. Your personality will play an important role. If you have an extraverted preference, you are more motivated to reach out to a new person; however, those favoring introversion can be just as skillful. Whatever your personality type, particular attitudes and behaviors are necessary in order to initiate.

Open-Mindedness

First impressions, those immediate judgments, cannot be avoided. Brief observations of the way people move, talk, and gesture as well as their posture, facial expressions, and speech provide a great deal of information, and all contribute to the formation of impressions (Ambady and Rosenthal, 1992). Inward deviance is frequently assumed from an outwardly deviant appearance, and this can be unfortunate (Duck, 1991). A way to overcome this effectively is to be open when you first meet someone and challenge negative first impressions that form after just "one slice of time."

Initial judgments are generally based on physical appearance. For example, place yourself in a classroom the first day of a new class. A grossly overweight and sloppy-looking woman makes her way to the front of the room and introduces herself as the instructor. Examine what your impression would be. How would it change if the person were overweight and neat? Although it is impossible to avoid an initial judgment, try not to allow what you first think to dictate the course of the relationship.

Ideas expressed by others also can influence your impression. In a classic experiment on expectations and first impressions (Kelley, 1950), students received short differing descriptions about a substitute instructor. Some sketches described the new instructor as "rather cold" while others used the words "very warm." The substitute led the class, and someone else recorded the frequency of participation for each student. Afterwards, the students were asked to write descriptions and ratings of the instructor. A clear difference was evident. Those who had read that the man was "very warm" participated more freely and gave him a higher rating than those who had been given the "rather cold" description.

Another study adds to the evidence that impressions are formed from factors other than face-to-face encounters (Natale, 1987). Students were asked to rate fictitious people with different courtesy titles (Ms., Miss, Mrs., or Mr.). The women who used the title "Ms." were perceived as more achievement oriented, socially assertive, and dynamic than the other women and even the men. They also believed that a "Ms." would be less likely than the other women to be happily married, to have children and to be popular and warm. It seems that regardless of the reason for a woman's choice of title, impressions of her are affected.

Any time you form a first impression, analyze it. Whatever the judgment is, allow time and involvement to determine how realistic it is. Expectations, like impressions, are powerful. A student once told me that he had heard that I was a lot of fun in the classroom, and he was looking forward to a positive learning experience. In fact, I was more humorous and livelier in his class than in others, and he and I both had a great time. What we expect of others frequently becomes a reality. At the end of the quarter, I wrote him a thank-you note for setting the stage for an enjoyable experience.

Acceptance and Tolerance

Entire books have been written on acceptance and tolerance of people who are different. This brief coverage of the subject can help you examine your attitudes and commit to any necessary positive change. Try to approach this discussion with an open mind and be ready to challenge any preconceived ideas.

Stereotyping is thinking in generalities. A major problem with stereotyping is that it typically focuses upon negative similarities among people of one group when, in fact, all people within a group are not the same. Labeling individuals before you get to know them results from stereotyping. Labels are limiting to both the person being labeled and the one who is stereotyping. A loving individual, according to Leo Buscaglia (1982), does not label others. As a child, Buscaglia himself was bothered by the distancing effect of his label regarding his Italian ancestry.

> But they didn't know who I was by calling me a "dago" and a "wop." If you want to know about me, you've got to get into my head, and if I want to know about you, I can't say, 'She is fat. She is thin. She is a Jew. She is a Catholic.' She is more than that (p. 25).

When labels stick, they become tatoos and, if negative, can damage self-esteem (Hyatt, 1991). "It is offensive and misleading to reduce an individual to a category" (Tannen, 1990, p. 16).

Actor and comedian Eddie Murphy described a stereotyping experience.

> I was walking out of the grocery store once, and I had my head down. Some kids went by, and they said "nigger, nigger." They didn't see it was me. And that tripped me out

> because if my head had been up, they would have screamed, "Hey, Eddie! All right, Eddie!"

Labeling based on what the eye can see limits perceptions. The eye can be the "most inaccurate, most inconsistent, and the most prejudicial organ we have in the body. What is truly essential is invisible to the eye" (Buscaglia, 1982, p. 94).

People also label loved ones. Assigning values or labels to family members is common: "That's my good-for-nothing brother." "I have an old-fashioned dad." "He's my lazy kid." These ideas put human beings into boxes; then they usually act out the label. The positive part is that if you have labeled someone or been labeled, you can also remove it and start anew.

Negative stereotyping and labeling usually lead to a *prejudice*, an attitude that others are inferior or less than you in some way. What results is a feeling of dislike or hatred. Prejudice is *learned* either from others or by generalizing from experiences. Jodi discovered that prejudice has many targets as she acknowledged: "Prejudice is not limited to just race and sex. I've been judging people on looks, clothing, body size, and age. I've now learned that what is inside is what's important."

Historically, the American society has experienced a myriad of problems caused by prejudice. Countless numbers of individuals have suffered because of labeling. Hope that prejudice was a thing of the past abounded for some time after the Civil Rights Movement in the sixties. That hope has not become reality. Hate crime is increasing. In 1992 there were 1730 anti-Semitic incidents, attacks against homosexuals showed an increase of 172 percent over the past 5 years, and Klanwatch reported that 1992 was the deadliest year for bias-related events in more than 10 years (Birnbaum, 1993). Research added a positive note revealing that many people have embraced nonprejudiced beliefs and standards and appear to be in the process of prejudice reduction (DeVine et al., 1991).

To continue to harbor prejudices is insensitive and illogical. In some cases, the stereotypes have a factual basis because a majority of a group conform to a particular behavior. You can accept a factual basis and still not apply it to all members of a group. People who feel and act upon prejudice are limiting themselves in terms of human relationships. Ira, an African-American, volunteered her personal feelings about prejudice in a psychology class. She said, "Prejudice causes people to miss out on the spice of life. To be influenced by prejudice is hogwash. It keeps you from being free within." I would add a challenging question: *Can anyone offer one good reason for a continuation of prejudice*? Everyone is eventually harmed.

Discrimination is treating people unfairly. Because discrimination is usually observable behavior, a society can adopt laws against it; this has been the case in recent years. Covert discrimination is still widely practiced and is commonly based on prejudice. Perceiving others to be evil or inferior often leads to treating them as such. Both prejudice and discrimination cause personal and societal problems, and neither individuals nor societies can be secure when hatred and violence prevail. "We can never achieve peace of mind and love as long as we attack others" (Jampolsky and Cirincione, 1990, p. 68).

Because prejudice is learned, it can be unlearned, and education is a strong foe of prejudice. A study showed that educated respondents were less prejudiced than others (D'Alessio and Stolzenberg, 1991). Becki shared insight in a class when she said: "Ignorance begets fear. Fear begets hatred. Hatred begets violence." What else besides lack of education contributes to prejudice? Self-esteem seems to play a part. Studies in the United States and Canada indicated that people who feel, or are made to feel, insecure or unworthy will often reestablish their self-worth by putting others down (Myers, 1992).

Figure 9-4

This doesn't mean that self-esteem leads to or keeps one from prejudice; however, it can be a factor.

Research shows some age and gender difference. In one study women were less prejudiced than men, and young Americans less than older ones (D'Alessio and Stolzenberg, 1991). In another study men were significantly less likely to help a man who was wearing a shirt with a pro-gay slogan; this was not true for women (Russell and Gray, 1992). Having an *authoritarian personality*, a belief that one's ideas are right and others are wrong, is related to prejudice. In a Canadian study, authoritarianism predicted prejudice and homophobia, an irrational hatred or fear of homosexuals, as well as punitiveness (Wylie and Forest, 1992). Homophobia seems to be connected to more authoritarian thinking and greater gender-role rigidity (Raymond, 1992). Another study showed that those with high prejudice also reported higher levels of anger toward others (DeVine et al., 1991).

What can be done about prejudice? To begin, a person must decide to challenge the rigid thinking that feeds prejudicial attitudes. Becoming more educated, fostering an androgynous personality, building self-esteem, and ridding oneself of anger and an "always right" attitude would help. Deciding that differences are not frightening or wrong is necessary and leads to feeling enlightened as you learn about multiculturism and *minority groups*, those who are disadvantaged in a society. For example, do you know that homosexuality is not considered a psychological or physical disorder and that homosexual relationships are quite similar to heterosexual ones in terms of caring and commitment? Studies reveal that except for sexual orientation there are few differences between homosexuals and heterosexuals. In fact, one even showed some advantages to being homosexual. Heterosexuals in the study had less confidence, less independence, and were less able to make decisions (Finlay and Scheltema, 1991).

Asking the following questions can challenge prejudice.

> Is my thinking reasonable and rational? If you take pride in your mental abilities, it seems likely that you would want to quit thinking in inaccurate and unreasonable stereotypes. Refuse to accept the idea that all blacks or whites, Catholics or Protestants, old people or young people, and heterosexuals or homosexuals are one way.

> Am I being fair? How would I feel if I were the victim of prejudice? Most human beings are concerned with justice and fairness. Discrimination is unfair, and even the thinking that leads to it can be challenged as unjust.

> Am I basing my impressions on a knowledge of an individual as a person or only as a representative of a group? Labeling often keeps us from getting to know the "real" person. Moving from a collective analysis which is a stereotype to an individual analysis is the key. Being free of prejudice means that you may like or dislike, but your feelings will not be based on an external factor or label. I was delighted when Jennifer, a young white female student said to me, "I have never been around blacks before because I grew up in a small rural community. Glenn (another student in the class) is the first black I've gotten to know. I'm so glad my first experience was such a positive one!"

In a study of hundreds of inner city high school and college students representing four different races, the changes that occurred as a result of continuous contact between distinct cultures led to both the desire to maintain one's own culture and to integrate in a positive way with others (Phinney et al., 1992). Most of us could increase our interactions with different groups. A study showed that only one fourth of white junior high students had a cross-race friend compared to half of the blacks (Clark and Ayers, 1992). More effort is needed.

One of the most effective ways to combat personal prejudices is to use your brain to seriously question and challenge. During a class, I threw out a question: "Where does prejudice come from?" A white student volunteered his story: "I can tell you why I'm prejudiced. When I was a kid, three black kids came into my yard and beat me up. I hated them for it, and I've hated all black people since then." Obviously, he had suffered from a bad experience and had generalized from it. I suggested that he use his imagination and pretend that the three boys had been white. I asked, "Would you now hate all white people because three white boys beat you up?" Critical thinking such as this can help people challenge the generalizations that create and maintain prejudice.

Jim, a good friend of mine in graduate school, indirectly taught my children to rid themselves of prejudice. Jim was witty, considerate, and fun. He was always available if someone needed some help–"a great guy," the children said. Jim was like many of our friends except that he was a homosexual. At the time he was still "in the closet," so his sexual orientation wasn't even discussed. Later, the reaction of the children was, "So what? It doesn't matter to us. He's still Jim." I appreciated that they based their opinions on what is truly important–*personhood.*

Donald Kaul, columnist, minces no words as he decries prejudice.

> The movement toward the full acceptance of gay rights in our society is inexorable. It's time to get with it or get out of the way. Religious groups have done their best to cast the issue in moral terms; they quote the Bible. That's the thing about the Bible. You can quote it to support just about anything, including polygamy. They called upon it to give moral authority to the institution of slavery. That was garbage and so are today's religious bleatings. That's why they call it the Good Book; it is not meant to serve evil. I've never fully understood the deep prejudice against homosexuals. I suppose a lot of people don't know any homosexuals, or think they don't. Ignorance is always bigotry's best ally. It's been my experience that gay people are remarkably like straight people—smart, dumb, kind, vicious, greedy, and generous. Even glum. Ultimately, my position is that human sexuality is so complex and diverse, what's ok with consenting adults is ok by me (*Lincoln Journal*, January, 1, 1993, p. 6B).

In a homophobic society, heterosexuals who don't conform to stereotypic gender roles can also be hurt by name calling, violence, and damaging myths (Blumenfeld, 1992;

Elze, 1992). "We are all diminished when anyone of us is demeaned" (Blumenfeld, 1992, p. 13).

Besides ridding yourself of any prejudices, you can help the victims of prejudice and society by asserting yourself in the face of demeaning words and behaviors. A study showed that hearing someone else express strong opinions against prejudice led students to have similar thoughts. The researchers concluded that a few outspoken people who are vigorously antiracist can establish a positive social climate that discourages prejudice (Goleman, 1991). As with any subject, silence is usually interpreted as agreement. Suggestions for responding to prejudicial comments were given in Chapter 8. Taking a stand can increase self-esteem. Rose spoke up loudly and clearly in class, "I don't understand why all the hate toward homosexuals. Of what are we afraid? Why don't people just leave others alone?" Yes, why don't they? Any *good* person would avoid inflicting unnecessary harm on others (Raymond, 1992).

Lack of prejudice does not mean blindness to differences; you simply do not let differences stop you from relating. You can still take them into account, adjust to them, and learn from them (Tannen, 1990). A positive practice is to view differences as gifts and opportunities. In encouraging this, Schulz (1988) writes:

> to embrace the many-splendored colors, to revel in the wisdom and the power of a different race and culture; to invite it to spill over us and to know that, if our invitation is accepted, it is we who are recipients of an honor (p. 2).

As mentioned earlier, intolerance of differences can be based on more than color of skin. Religion, ethnicity, age, sex, social class, and sexual orientation are categories on which prejudice and discrimination are based. One can even be intolerant of personality differences. An important outcome of understanding the Myers-Briggs personality types is to see differences as potential gifts and use them to benefit relationships.

Getting to know people who are different provides learning experiences. It broadens our perspectives and enriches our lives. This growth then allows us to appreciate human diversity. Sameness can be boring. In comparing the words variation and differentness, Satir (1978) makes an excellent point.

> When we see a garden of flowers and notice that there are differences among them, it is easy for us to think of them as variations. When we do this, we experience good feelings. Variation and variety are thought of as positive. When we see a group of people together and notice that they, like the flowers, are different from each other, we have an inclination to think of these as differences. Different somehow brings to mind difficulties and fear, and it is easy to prepare defenses. If we were to think of people as having variation to each other and then have the good feelings that come with that, we could get our interest and discovery buttons turned on (p. 97).

Would anyone want a large garden of flowers of just one color especially if they were all white? Human beings of various colors interacting together can be as appealing as a garden of multicolored flowers. All kinds of diversity provide opportunities for expansion of self. Multiculturism benefits individuals as well as societies.

Overcoming Shyness

After a person gets beyond obstacles created by negative first impressions or intolerance, individual traits can block attempts to get to know others. Shyness is a disadvantage in interacting. If change is desired, a shy person has to confront the problem. Stating that inaction is the most common feature of shyness, Zimbardo (1977), who conducted classic studies on the subject, emphasizes the need to change behavior. He suggests making a contract, outlining objectives and action steps.

Being realistic about what is possible to achieve is critical, and dividing a goal into smaller, manageable parts, as recommended in Chapter 5, is part of any sensible behavioral plan. Saying hello to four new people in a week's time might be a practical goal. Using the behavior modification techniques of monitoring progress and setting up rewards for successes is helpful. Support groups are beneficial, and for severe cases of shyness, therapy is suggested.

Approaching People

Even if you aren't shy, you may, in some situations, hesitate to approach. You may fear rejection or embarrassment. It can help to ask yourself, "What's the worst thing that can happen if I'm rejected?" Usually, there is no terrible outcome. Any social encounter can become embarrassing to a participant. Realizing that embarrassment isn't the worst thing in the world can be useful. Letting fears stop you from potentially satisfying interactions is certainly worse! When you do approach, you may be doing so at an inappropriate time or in an undesirable manner. *Approachability* is a combination of circumstances under which initiating contact is likely to be positively received.

Looking for approachability cues. Being observant and looking for cues are helpful in initiating conversation. Begin by realizing that unapproachable situations are best avoided. Can you think of times and situations when people would not be at all approachable or when approachability would probably be diminished? Consider individual moods, physical states, and activities: "I'm a grouch in the early morning, so people know to avoid me." "I hate being disturbed when I'm watching a football game on TV." "When I first get home from work, I want to unwind and don't like conversation for awhile." "Look out when I'm tired or hungry. I just don't want to be bothered." If you want to initiate contact, your best bet is to wait if the other person is otherwise in a hurry, involved, or preoccupied.

Conversely, approachable situations are those in which a person is not preoccupied or absorbed. Such situations are usually indicated by body language. Sitting alone and looking open are good indicators. When people are in waiting situations, such as waiting for a bus, for a class to start, or in a line, they are likely to be approachable. Social activities are certainly approachable situations.

Checking for approachability. Knowledge of a person will give you an advantage; yet, you still may be uncertain. In these cases, it is better to not act immediately. Instead, check for approachability. For example, going up to a person and asking, "Do you have some time to talk?" or "Are you busy right now?" or "Do you have 5 minutes?" are ways to check. By the way, don't ask for a second or a minute of time when you know you want more!

The checking technique is especially appreciated when the telephone is being used. Has this happened to you? Your favorite television show is on, and you are engrossed. The telephone rings; you answer. Incidentally, you don't have to answer a ringing telephone, yet most people do. A friend, seemingly assuming that because you said hello, you are ready and willing to visit, begins to talk. The person barely pauses for a breath.

You are now in an awkward position of either saying you don't want to talk at this time (whenever you can get a word in, that is) or suffering through the conversation feeling deprived and resentful. Do you realize that an assertive person would not allow this suffering? To avoid being inconsiderate when you make a telephone call, check approachability with, "Do you have time to talk?" or even "What are you doing?" And, be sure to thank people who extend you this courtesy.

Beginning the conversation. With people you know, beginning a conversation is usually not difficult. But what about people you don't know and would like to meet? You may be one who has no trouble thinking of just the right thing to say to start a conversation. For a number of people, however, thinking of something to say can be mind boggling. "I was tongue-tied," is how one young man described it. "I had wanted to meet her for months, and here she was sitting next to me in class the first day of the quarter. I couldn't think of one intelligent thing to say, so I kept quiet." Either keeping quiet or saying something "off the wall" puts a damper on interactions.

To initiate conversation in difficult situations, you can use a technique called *search the situation for topics* (Glaser, 1986). Based on the idea that you and the other person share a common environment, you make a comment based on an awareness of what is going on around you. What could the young man in the preceding paragraph have said? The two students had in common the fact that they were sitting next to each other in a class on the first day. Here are some possibilities:

"Have you heard anything about this class?"
"I heard this instructor was a lot of fun."
"What book do we need for this class?"
"Have you ever taken a psychology class before?"
"What year of school are you in?"
"What are you majoring in?"

Searching the situation is quite simple; in fact, you probably have already used this technique without realizing it.

Changing to other topics. Keeping the conversation going is sometimes challenging. Using a bridge or transition to another related topic is sensible and usually simple. In the classroom situation are ample opportunities. Talking about one class or instructor can lead to questions and comments about others. A question about the textbook can be a transition to a comment about the high cost of books and other college expenses. A question about a college major could begin a discussion of future careers. One transition can lead to another, paving the way for numerous conversational possibilities.

Giving and using free information. What seems to be wrong in this conversation between two students?

BOB: Have you heard anything about this instructor?
JOAN: No.
BOB: How about the class?
JOAN: Not much.

BOB: Is this your first quarter here?
JOAN: Yes.
BOB: What's your major?
JOAN: Business.

Like pulling teeth, right? Perhaps, Joan is just not interested in talking to Bob. However, she might not know about giving *free information*—related additional data. Let's try the conversation again, with Joan giving free information.

BOB: Have you heard anything about this instructor?

JOAN: No, I haven't because I'm in my first quarter here. I did hear a little about the class from my advisor. He said that it would really help in my major.

BOB: What is your major?

JOAN: I'm in the business department with an emphasis on marketing.

BOB: So am I. Do you have any idea what you are going to do with your degree?

The conversation is livelier and more interesting. The two people are getting to know each other better. In job interviews, providing appropriate free information increases possibilities of job offers. Of course, too much free information monopolizes the conversation. Combining free information and questions creates a positive interactive climate.

Asking questions. An impressive behavior in positive human relations is asking questions. Questioning is an excellent way to keep conversations going, to learn more about the people you meet, and to make people feel that you are truly interested in what they are saying as well as in them. Failing to ask questions could indicate self-centeredness or lack of interest. Ann recounts a lunch date.

> I met Jim for lunch. We didn't know each other well, and I was looking forward to an opportunity for us to get to know each other and then see if this might develop into a deeper relationship. We were together for two hours. Afterwards I thought, "I know almost everything about him, and he knows nothing about me except that I ask questions and am an excellent listener! I don't know if he's stuck on himself or just not interested in me, or both. I don't want to spend another two hours like that.

Self-preoccupation is a major problem in boring conversations (Duck, 1991). Successful conversations are two-way, which means that both participants ask questions and provide information. Different types of questions can be asked.

- Open-ended questions are ones that cannot be answered with one word. Instead of, "What is your major?" ask, "What are your career plans?"
- Focused questions are those that are not too broad to be answered. Instead of, "Tell me all about you," ask, "How did you decide to go into teaching?"
- Specific questions are those that ask for additional details, specific examples, or particular impressions. Examples are, "What did you think of the psychology course?" or "Tell me about the rest of your trip after you left Denver."

The importance of asking questions is difficult to overemphasize. If you think about people you enjoy, chances are that their interest in you and what is going on in your life is a major factor. Very few people resent questions. As long as your questions aren't too probing or inappropriately personal, your relationships can be enhanced by developing and using this skill.

CONTACT: CONNECTING WITH OTHERS

After an interaction takes place, people can choose to build a closer relationship. Why does this happen in some cases and not in others?

Attraction and Liking

If you grow to like another person, you will feel affection or respect or both. These feelings are two fundamental dimensions of liking. *Affection* is based on the way another person relates to you personally and is a feeling of warmth and closeness. *Respect* is liking based on the person's admirable characteristics or actions and is a cooler, more distant kind of liking (Rubin, 1973).

Why do you like some people and not others? *Attraction*, a force that draws people together or a positive attitude toward another, has been the focus of psychological research. Social psychologists have found that attraction and liking are closely linked to certain factors. As you read about each, relate it to your relationships.

Proximity. How many friends are from your hometown? Do most of your friends live near you? *Proximity* is physical occupation of the same geographic area. Obviously, in order to meet, two people must share proximity. In terms of attraction, physical sharing of space is the means by which you get to know a person. Becoming more familiar could lead to a dislike of the person. More often, though, getting to know someone leads to deeper understanding and liking.

Similarities. "Birds of a feather flock together" is an axiom with merit. Differences can be interesting and, as we've discussed, can be positive. Yet, for years social psychologists have realized that similarities are strong predictors of attraction (Byrne, 1971) and that people with little in common can repel each other (Rosenbaum, 1986). *Similarities* in attitudes, interests, degree of intelligence, religion, age, and personality are generally bonding and promote liking. Attitudinal similarity strengthens both friendships and love relationships (Rathus, 1993). Closely related is the attraction we feel toward behaviors of others that confirm our values and beliefs. For example, if equal rights are important, seeing a person actively participate in a rally increases positive feelings. In fact, I recommend to people wanting to meet potential love mates that they participate in causes and activities near and dear to their hearts.

Perhaps the most important force that attracts individuals is agreement. When people agree, it is likely that shared activities will be mutually pleasurable, and engaging in shared interests builds relationships. Also, agreement bolsters self-confidence, and individuals enjoy being affirmed. Whether or not it's accurate, people assume that anyone who shares their views must be worthy and sensible. Finally, agreement means less bickering and arguing, which is preferable to most people (Rubin, 1973).

Complementarity. An opposite characteristic which is lacking in you can be attractive in another person. This is *complementarity*. And, for practical reasons, it can benefit a relationship. Margaret, one of my college roommates, loved to clean. My interest wasn't keen in that area, so I offered to do needed errands, and she kept our room immaculate. You may also notice opposite personality traits in two friends. Kent was outgoing and loved to tell jokes. His friend Pat was quiet, except when he was laughing loudly at Kent's stories.

Reciprocity. Imagine that you have just met Sally. You feel neutral toward her; you don't necessarily like or dislike her. As time goes by, Sally demonstrates a genuine interest in and liking for you. The chances are that you will reciprocate; your feelings will become positive. *Reciprocity* is a tendency to like people who like you. As Rathus (1993) puts it, "If you like me, you must have excellent judgment." This may sound conceited; however, if you genuinely like yourself, you are likely to be attracted to others who share your feelings. When we are liked and admired, we are inclined to return those feelings and behaviors. Conversely, have you ever experienced the realization that another person does not like you? You probably tended to reciprocate and found yourself disliking that person.

Attraction and liking factors contribute to the onset of a relationship and continue to enhance its growth. Wanting to approach someone and then beginning to like that person isn't caused by a mysterious force. Rather, it is fairly easy to predict who will relate to whom and why.

IMPROVING RELATIONSHIPS

You have a choice in the types and quantity of relationships you develop and maintain, and you influence their quality, as well. Certain attitudes and behaviors deserve special attention.

Realistic Expectations of Relationships

Expecting a relationship to be 100 percent harmonious and believing that individuals will always act in certain ways is unrealistic.

> Just as no human being is perfect, neither are relationships. We are none of us ever perfect husbands, wives, children, professionals, teachers, students, employees, employers, fathers, mothers, or friends. We are humanly limited in all these social human roles. Therefore, all relationships are limited (Rubin, 1975, p. 239).

Having unrealistic ideas leads to frustration and disappointment, and usually to withdrawal and an end to the relationship. Even with acquaintances, having realistic expectations is helpful. If you're a renter, what is realistic to expect from the property owner? If you own property, are you expecting too much from your tenants?

In all types of relationships, open communication is helpful; in certain cases, written agreements about expectations are appropriate. A common tale of woe concerns roommates. Nancy describes her roommate as a "slob," one who doesn't do her share and leaves the apartment a mess. I asked her, "Did you have any kind of agreement before you became roommates about how you were going to manage living together?" Nothing had ever been discussed. Discussing expectations and agreeing to policies, preferably in writing, are more likely to achieve desired objectives than simply expecting things to work out.

Sensitivity and Cooperation

Sensitivity is having an awareness or sense about the perceptions and perspectives of others. Empathy, the ability to feel with others, is not essential; however, an understanding of the other's viewpoint is. In the work place being sensitive to the needs and desires of others creates a positive atmosphere. In a classroom setting, sensitivity is conducive to learning. When instructors and students understand each other's perspectives, and students are sensitive to one another, the atmosphere is positive. Two older students shared with me that figuring out how to fit in was their biggest challenge. Younger students' sensitivity to their different perspectives was greatly appreciated. Pondering how they would feel coming back to school after several years helped young students be sensitive.

Cooperation means working with others toward a common goal. It can occur without sensitivity, yet teamwork is enhanced in the presence of both. A printing company had to deliver a large order within a week. The owner called the employees together to discuss how the objective could be accomplished. One person's child was in the hospital awaiting surgery. Awareness and sensitivity to this personal situation led to offers from others to work longer hours to compensate for his time away from the job. The job was accomplished.

Learning activities are often based on competition rather than teamwork so wise parents and teachers incorporate cooperation in the successful completion of tasks and games. "Joy involves connecting with other people, not defeating them, outracing them, or getting the best of them" (Pearsall, 1988, p. 51).

Little Acts of Kindness

As human beings rush through busy days, little acts of kindness can mean so much. Because these are not time-consuming favors or dramatic gestures, their impact may be overlooked. I received the following suggestions when I asked my students, "What small positive act might you be a part of, either as a 'doer' or as a receiver, that would brighten your day or lighten your load?"

- When driving, if possible, stop and wait for another car to pull out onto a busy street ahead of you.
- When driving in an area that allows right turns on a red light, pull ahead in the right lane enough so that a car behind you can pull alongside you and make the turn.
- In a checkout line, when you have several purchases, allow a person behind you with just a few items to go ahead.
- In a restroom line, let a parent with a fussy child go ahead of you.
- Offer to help someone who is having difficulty carrying a package or crossing the street.
- Hold a door for another person.
- Send a note or card to someone who is not well. In fact, send more than one if the illness is prolonged.
- Use the words thank you and please with clerks, cashiers, cafeteria servers, and others.

- If you smoke, show courtesy to others around you.
- Offer your seat on a bus or in a waiting room to someone who looks as if he or she needs to sit more than you do.
- Smile and greet people, even those you don't know.

The power of smiles and greetings is often overlooked. A therapist told a story of a client. The young man was despondent, believed that nobody cared, and had the intention of driving into the base of an overpass on the interstate and ending his life. He stopped at a traffic light, looked over at a woman in the car next to him. She smiled brightly. At the next corner, he turned around and came back to the therapist's office. He is now living a seemingly happy life.

A minor event changed a dreary Monday morning. As usual, bus passengers weren't paying any attention to each other as they endured the ride. Suddenly, the driver told them to put their newspapers down and face the person next to them and repeat after him, "Good morning, neighbor." Timidly, they did so.

> We smile reflexively. We cannot help it. There is the faint sense of unleashing a common civility long repressed. The barrier has been broken. It was not so hard after all. Some of us shake hands. Many laugh. Not a single newspaper goes back up. The bus hums with conversation. I hear laughter, a warm, bubbly sound I have never heard before on bus No. 151. The driver gives no sign that he's just pulled off a Monday morning miracle (Wigand, 1988).

Making the world a better place can be accomplished in many ways. Giving a little of yourself is a rewarding experience. Volunteers are greatly needed. Nursing homes are full of opportunities to reach out. Rewarding feelings and meaningful relationships are probable results.

Assertiveness

As valuable as sensitivity, cooperation, and kindness are, honest, healthy relationships thrive on *assertiveness*—maintaining legitimate rights. When one person is passive and allows another to dominate, the eventual outcome is undesirable. Neither the dominator nor the whatever-you-say person feels satisfied after a period of time. As pointed out in Chapter 2, assertiveness helps individuals and improves relationships.

An important part of assertiveness in relationships is the ability to assertively say "no." "Saying yes to life means saying no a good deal of the time" (Ryan and Travis, 1991, p. 93). Individuals undergo tremendous stress when they don't say "no" when that's what they feel, and relationships ultimately suffer. "I never could tell my friend 'no,' and I did so many favors for her. Eventually, I found myself hating her for it, and I made excuses not to be around her," was how one woman described a past friendship. "I realize now it wasn't her fault, but mine."

Deciding that saying "no" is healthy is a primary step in making a change. Other cognitive techniques are also helpful. Ask yourself, "What's the worst thing that will happen if I say 'no?' How does that compare to what happens to me when I say 'yes' and resent it?" Then, continue to think, "What if the person is angry with me because I say 'no?' How bad will that be?" Keep telling yourself that you have the right to say "no."

Once you have decided to learn to say "no," behavioral techniques are useful. Practice how you will say it. Of course, you can just say the two-letter word, but most people feel more comfortable with other kinds of statements such as one of these possibilities.

- I have decided not to take on any more obligations.
- I would like to say yes; however, this time I'm not going to.
- I want to spend more time with my family, so I'm not going to get involved with any more outside activities right now.
- I've been doing some time management work and prioritizing, and right now other things are more important to me.
- Thanks for asking; however, I'm not going to participate now.
- Believe it or not, I'm going to say "no."

Note that you aren't using the word "can't" which, as pointed out earlier, is usually inaccurate. Making up an excuse is generally not as convincing as the truth. It's your choice as to how much to explain. You don't owe anyone a reason, although offering a statement of fact can make saying "no" easier. "I haven't felt well lately, and I'm not taking on any additional responsibilities" is brief and clear. By speaking the truth—saying that you don't want to or you won't—you are being assertive. A primary key to assertiveness is the use of "I" statements. Do you see how each way of saying "no" clearly speaks for self and is not hostile nor aggressive? Effective assertiveness is usually courteous, kind, and gentle. At times saying "no" can be the greatest act of love (Buscaglia, 1992).

You can decide to give an indefinite or a limited "no." Limited means that you are saying "no" now and might reconsider in the future. "I don't want to have any responsibility in the fall fund-raiser; however, I may help out next spring." If possible, anticipate the other person's response. You probably know some people who will accept your reason without argument. On the other hand, you may have relationships with people who have a hard time accepting "no" for an answer. With this latter group, you are wise to fortify yourself. One idea is to acknowledge their persuasive abilities and still be firm. "I know you're a hard person to say 'no' to, yet I'm going to do it this time." If you've spent a lifetime of saying "yes," you will surprise people, and some may find the "new you" less appealing (Ryan and Travis, 1991). Keep in mind that those who don't appreciate assertiveness may not be capable of building healthy relationships, and you deserve better.

Negotiation Skills

Positive negotiation skills are well worth cultivating because conflict is inherent in all relationships. *Conflict* means that disagreement or a difference in thinking is present. A major problem in conflict situations is that most people have been taught that being right is essential. However, individuals who rate high in human relations skills are well aware that needing to be right can damage relationships. "You can insist on being right or have a relationship that works, but you can't have both. And the addiction to being right about inaccurate beliefs will destroy any relationship" (Ellsworth, 1988, p. 19).

Once you realize that conflict is not a matter of who's right and who's wrong and that it is caused by differences of opinion, you are setting the stage for negotiation. Conflict management is an art like other human relations skills. Handling conflict in intimate relationships will be covered in Chapter 11; the negotiation skills described in this section are useful, as well.

Not recommended in any relationship is a behavior described as *gunnysacking*. When you "gunnysack," you keep your grievances suppressed or bottled up (Bach and Wyden, 1968). People who hide their grievances do so because of nonassertiveness, fear, and a desire to preserve peace at any cost. Because a fear of criticizing anyone else encourages gunnysacking, the methods for delivering criticism suggested in Chapter 8 are worth learning and using. A gunnysack stuffed to its limits is potentially harmful. Suppressing annoyances is stressful and can be damaging to health. Keeping quiet about grievances can diminish self-esteem, and relationships suffer terribly. "When complaints are toted along quietly in a gunny sack for any length of time they make a dreadful mess when the sack finally bursts" (Bach and Wyden, 1968, p. 19).

An aggressive style of conflict management is as damaging as gunnysacking. Closed communication is the norm. An aggressive person tries to dominate and control all issues and will use any steam-rolling method available. He or she will turn conflicts into competition and may "win" on the surface, but the relationship loses. In long-term relationships this is particularly dangerous.

The key is to learn and use conflict-management techniques. Managing conflict is essentially problem solving. First, the individuals decide to work on a problem. Of benefit is to pick a time and place most conducive to positive results. An agreement can be made that the discussion can be postponed at any time. Conflict is more easily resolved when the participants use open communication and avoid dogmatic, forcing, and grandiose expressions. "I" statements and receptive listening are highly recommended. The following steps can resolve an issue.

1. Define and describe the issue or problem and all common goals. During the process it's important that individuals define how they see the conflict and know how others are defining it (Cochrane, 1992). Discussion continues until agreement is reached on the specific issue to be resolved with the understanding that related topics can be discussed later.
2. Brainstorm to generate all possible solutions. Creativity and openness are key ingredients at this stage. All ideas are accepted with no judgments.
3. Evaluate each possible solution. Each person has the right to eliminate an idea if it is completely unacceptable. The number of solutions is usually narrowed to two or three.

Figure 9-5

4. Decide on the best solution at this time. This would be the one that achieves the goals. Flexibility is imperative. You may all agree on one choice or concede to another's point of view in order to test its effectiveness.
5. Agree to test the agreed-upon solution and meet again to evaluate. This last step is especially valuable, as agreeing to treat a solution as tentative will make it easier to gain a consensus to take action. If the solution doesn't work, the issue isn't resolved, and the process begins with the now redefined problem (Beach, 1993).

During the third and fourth steps, a positive communicator will use certain questions and phrases that express openness and encourage participation of all.

- How would you put that plan into effect?
- I understand your reasoning, and I'd like to hear how you would go about it.
- What do you think about
- I agree. Have you also considered
- Another possibility that ties in with your idea is
- I liked your first idea; however I have a few reservations about
- Another approach might be

The idea is to be nonthreatening, receptive, and tentative. This method has been called *collaboration* (Cochrane, 1992) and differs from compromise which means giving up something and ends up being win-lose. Collaboration or resolution is when shared goals are achieved, and everyone wins.

Let's follow the process through a conflict among roommates. Carol, Heather, and Laura have roomed together for 2 months. They have experienced some problems over task management in the apartment; however, the main issue has to do with Carol's fiancé, Brad, and other friends who visit the apartment. Carol and Laura share a bedroom.

1. Defining the issue and finding common goals

   LAURA: I'm upset because Brad is over here so often, and when you go into the bedroom and shut the door, I don't feel like I should come in, and it's my room, too.

   CAROL: Well, I don't like doing all the dishes around here.

   HEATHER: I'd suggest we stay on just the one topic for now. We can talk about dishes later. Can we agree that we want to remain roommates and get along? (After affirmation from both) Then I suggest we discuss and, hopefully, resolve what to do about people who come to visit. Is that agreeable?

2. Generating possible solutions

   HEATHER: Let's suggest some ideas. Remember, no comments from anyone else yet.

   LAURA: I suggest that the bedroom be off limits to guests.

   HEATHER: My idea is to have certain hours established—some for when guests are to leave and others for when we could be in any of the rooms.

   CAROL: I prefer that we have the right to have people in any room when we want, and if another person doesn't like it, she can say so—the same with asking guests to go home.

   HEATHER: Any other ideas? If not, let's talk about these.

3. Evaluating each possible solution

   CAROL: I don't like the one about off-limits at all. I have my stereo in the bedroom, and sometimes it's nice to get away from the TV in the living room.

   LAURA: I guess that off-limits is too much. I think having a reasonable time limit or set hours is a good idea. I know I can tell you that I'm upset, but that's hard to do sometimes.

   CAROL: How about if I asked you whether it's okay with you before we go in there? And if it's not, I'd understand.

   LAURA: I like that idea, and we could do the same with other guests. If one of us wants to go to bed or study, we would just agree to do that.

4. Agreeing on a tentative solution

   HEATHER: Do we agree that we will check about others being here at all and also being in other rooms?

5. Setting a testing period

   CAROL: Fine. How about trying it for 2 weeks and then seeing how we feel about it?

   LAURA: Sounds fine. In the meantime, I'm ready to tackle the dishes problem.

The described resolution occurred because the individuals followed the negotiation steps. This discussion progressed ideally—which is not usually the case. Even with some digression, having a method is far better than no discussion or pettiness and dead-ended arguments. Incidentally, this situation is based on an actual one described to me by a student who was frustrated, anguished, and sick from an ulcer because she didn't think she could say anything to a roommate who entertained her boyfriend in the bedroom for hours on end. Because of her lack of assertiveness and both roommates' lack of training in the art of negotiation, my student suffered, and the friendship between the two was destroyed.

Even when people want to settle conflict, negotiations break down when the intent of participants is to convince the others to see it their way. Instead, with a goal of solving a problem for everyone or improving a relationship, negotiation is likely to end in resolution. Of help is for participants to see conflict as an opportunity to learn and grow. Be sure to check how you have improved your relationships (Chapter 9 activity in REFLECTIONS AND APPLICATIONS).

Dealing with Difficult People

Despite your best attempts, success may seem an illusive dream. "No matter what I do or say, nothing makes any difference. I work for the most difficult person in the world" and "Nobody can get along with her" are descriptions of difficult people. They may be hostile customers, irritable co-workers, passive-aggressive supervisors, or nitpicky neighbors. Because he couldn't find another book on the subject, Bramson (1981) wrote *Coping with Difficult People*. He identifies seven patterns of difficult behavior.

1. Hostile–aggressives: People who try to bully and overwhelm others.
2. Complainers: Individuals who gripe incessantly but do not act to improve the situation.
3. Silent and unresponsives: People who respond as little as possible so aren't helpful.

4. Super-agreeables: People who are reasonable but who either don't produce or act differently when not in your presence.
5. Negativists: Pessimists whose favorite reaction is, "No, that won't work."
6. Know-it-all experts: People who seem to think that they know much more than you do on every subject.
7. Indecisives: People who don't seem to be able to make up their minds and stall all decisions, as well as perfectionists who don't complete tasks.

In order to improve your relationships, you can think about whether you fit into any of these categories and then seek to change your behavior. Bramson's book and others suggested in the reference section at the end of the book can help you deal with difficult people, as well. In the meantime, try any of the following.

Avoiding a difficult person is probably the best solution. This may not be completely possible; however, you might be able to decrease your contact time. Secondly, you can use empathy and try to see a situation from the other's perspective. Most people have a reason for being nasty, and if you can figure out underlying causes, your reaction to them will be less negative. Then, be careful not to jump to a conclusion about another's motivation. People are more complicated than what appears on the surface and having patience is invaluable (Keating, 1984).

Putting into practice what you know about personality preferences can be quite useful. For example, I used to become quite frustrated with a staff member who absolutely would not leave the matter at hand. "Don't bother me right now. I'm busy," was a common reply. At first, I thought this was rude and showed inflexibility until I realized the person's strong preference was undoubtedly sensing, and being sidetracked was especially bothersome. I now wait with as much patience as I can muster until I get full attention. We are often uncomfortable with the opposite preference, and, in some cases, it may include behaviors we could utilize (Keating, 1984).

Cognitive techniques can be beneficial when confronted with a difficult person. Keeping in mind that other people do not control you and aren't able to make you feel, think, or do anything, you can adjust your thinking in various ways. "Just because she was short tempered (and often is) doesn't mean it's going to ruin my day," changes your reality. The positive responses to criticism from Chapter 8 can help you deal with an aggressive or hostile person who comes off as a critic.

Challenging our assumptions and then using behavioral techniques also can work. We tend to see others' behaviors as absolute facets of personality. "Gary is sexist and rude," we might think after he tells a crude joke that demeans women. Yet, Gary may be engaging in what he considers humor or he could be reacting to a feeling of anxiety regarding assertive women. A suggestion is to give people more than one chance. Sometimes what is most powerful is to change your behavior and reactions toward a difficult person. When one person in a relationship changes, whatever has been going on will also change (Tannen, 1986). To help you assess your involvement with difficult people as well as unload your gunnysack, use the Chapter 9 activity in REFLECTIONS AND APPLICATIONS. Then, when confronted with a difficult person and resentments, use ideas suggested in this book with an optimistic attitude.

> Difficulties are like ocean froth; they can demand your total attention or you can choose to look beyond, to the vast tranquility of the sea. The further view does not do away with the froth, but it places it in perspective (Keating, 1984, p. 1).

Supportiveness

Picture a roomful of people. One individual is carrying a large weighty pack on her back, so big and burdensome that it's difficult not to notice. Yet, the others mingle about as if they don't see the pack. "How are you?" "Fine." "What do you think of the weather?" Cliche conversation fills the room. They talk about their families and work. They speak of many things but not the pack on the person's back. Everyone knows that it's there, and it's on each person's mind. Nobody says a thing. Even though the woman sags from the weight and looks as if she could fall, they ignore the heavy pack. We won't discuss it, they think. The woman thinks to herself,

> Oh, please talk. Why won't you say his name? I want you to say "Paul." I want for us to talk about his death and his life. Can I say "Paul" and not have you look away and ignore it. For if we don't talk, you are leaving me alone with this dreadfully heavy pack on my back.

People we know will experience crises and tragedies, and they will carry a figurative pack on their backs. If you care, you will want to know how to react at these times. Consider these possibilities.

> Marge, a co-worker, is diagnosed with cancer.
>
> Fred, a next door neighbor, dies suddenly. His wife and children are the survivors.
>
> Clara and Richard, a couple you know from an organization, are in an accident. She is badly injured.

Are you inclined to do nothing? Do you ignore the pack on the back? If so, you are not alone even though a strong recommendation is to show your concern. Completely ignoring another's tragedy sends the message, "I don't care." On a rational level, this may be unfounded. "Of course I care," said one man, "I just don't know what to do." On an emotional level, however, saying and doing nothing is hurtful.

People seem to be afraid of a griever's feelings so they try to ignore or change the subject, or they intellectualize attempting to explain away the grief. Some just may not want to be bothered. I was reminded of this one spring evening when I noticed a baby bird in our yard. It couldn't fly and was moving in a wobbly fashion while it plaintively chirped. I caught myself thinking, "I hope it can get to the neighbor's yard so I won't feel pressured to do something." Then later when it was gone, I felt guilty. My initial reaction, which I think is most often the norm, resulted from a combination of not wanting to be involved, hoping someone else would take care of it, and the most commonly given reason for not being supportive: "I just don't know what to do." Closely related is the fear that what is done or said will be wrong. Giving support is another area in which little training is offered. Yet enough has been written on the subject that "I don't know what to do" can be seen as an excuse. Being effective in human relations means that you do respond. It's helpful to be aware of what research has identified as not helpful.

- Implied total awareness: "I understand exactly what you're going through." "I know just how you feel," or "I know" used over and over.
- Supplied solutions and reasons for acceptance: "It's better this way." "You'll recover faster than you think." "It'll be just fine." "Just give it time." "He lived

a long life; he was ready to go." "Be grateful for-" "It was meant to be." "Life is for the living." "It was God's will." One author mentioned that she had never met anyone who was comforted by this last statement (Edwards, 1989).

- One-upping comments: "I know what it's like because my grandmother died last year." "You think you've got problems? Wait until you hear mine." "Not only did my sister's husband divorce her, but then—"

What you say and do will depend upon the closeness of the relationship. Showing concern even to acquaintances is a positive human relations trait. A study showed that the cause of death influenced whether remarks were helpful or not. More unhelpful remarks were reported when suicide was involved (Range et al., 1992). A listening attitude is most beneficial to victims of suicide. Instead of trying to answer the impossible question of "why," paraphrase what you are hearing and what you think the person is feeling such as, "It's so difficult to understand and hard on you not knowing." (Lukas and Seiden, 1987).

Ideally in any situation, we can verbally express caring feelings. Simplicity and sincerity are the key ingredients. Comments such as "I care" and "I'm concerned" are fine. Other possibilities are: "I love you," "I want to do something," and "I remember—" recalling a fond memory of the deceased. If people would realize that they aren't expected to solve the problem, take away the pain, or other such dramatic behaviors, they might be more inclined to express their feelings. Research indicates that the most helpful comments are expressions of personal willingness to help or listen while any behaviors that suppress grief or force disclosure are not recommended (Range et al., 1992). Besides talking with the bereaved, offering comfort and support, and listening, just being present or "there" with the bereaved is considered quite helpful (Vickio et al., 1990).

Sometimes an honest expression of your perception of the situation is best. A comforting comment given to writer Max Wylie after his daughter had been savagely murdered was, "This did not happen for the best; it happened for the worst." I remember so well a scene in a hospital room at Mayo Clinic before my surgery. I spent a few minutes alone looking into a mirror, realizing that this was the last time I would ever see my left eye. As I was being wheeled into the operating room to have the eye removed, my sister Connie leaned down to give me a loving hug and whispered in my ear, "I love you, and you don't deserve this." My keen thought was, "She knows exactly how I feel right now."

Verbal expression can open a door of relief for a suffering person. Relief can be found in talking. You don't have to have the answers; just listening will help (Buckman, 1988; Engram, 1990). Usually, people don't remain silent long enough for the griever to fully express thoughts and feelings (James and Cherry, 1988). Remember to use receptive listening techniques covered in Chapter 6 which are invaluable as you support others. A wise suggestion is to let the grieved person be the only one to make evaluative comments such as, "It was a blessing."

This is one argument you may hear against talking about the "pack on the person's back": "Maybe they are trying to forget the tragedy or not think about their situation. If I say something, it will just remind them of it." Ask yourself whether you believe that people in anguish have forgotten. If you are thinking about their tragedy or problem, don't you believe that they are, too? In situations of anxiety, studies show that conversations do not create new fears. In fact, not talking about a fear makes it bigger (Buckman, 1988).

A few years ago I went to the hospital to see a woman who had been told she was in the final stages of death from leukemia. Somewhat apprehensive, I thought about what to say. Drawing on my experience with cancer and all I had read, I expressed my concern and then asked a question about her treatment. With a look of relief on her face, she disclosed thoughts and feelings. Before I left, she said with a twinkle in her eye, "Thanks, Sharon. I really get tired of talking about the weather. It's not exactly the main thing on my mind."

As was indicated in the scenario at the beginning of this section, usually, one of the greatest gifts you can possibly give to a grieving person is to mention the name of their loved one and add some memory you have of him or her.

> Most widows want their loss acknowledged, not glossed over, and the name of their dead husband spoken, not avoided. They would like to tell callers not to bother if they are going to talk about the weather or how terribly funny their new poodle puppy is. And later on, when they meet, they wish friends and acquaintances wouldn't try so hard to avoid mentioning the subject. The omission is glaring (Ginsburg, 1987, p. 53).

Writing a note or sending a card can replace verbal expression. Supportive acts are also greatly appreciated. Don't just say, "If you need anything, call." Often, a person won't seek help; in many cases, you can either say what you want to do or just take action. A list of specific offers of help is given by Vail (1982). A few of these follow.

- In the case of a death, address thank-you-for-sympathy cards for the person.
- In any crisis, do errands, such as shopping.
- Clean house.
- Mow the yard or shovel snow.
- Take the person out for dinner or to a movie.
- Take care of the children, if any.

Promising to help and then not following through is frustrating, so refrain from idle offers. Don't overlook the supportive impact of your presence. "People don't have to say a word. If they're here, I know they care," commented a widow. "Of course I'd love a little hug or squeeze on my arm if they could," she added with a tear in her eye. Sharing your sad feelings, also, can be of comfort. Tears are a by-product of our love and compassion (Edwards, 1989).

When you show support, another human being is helped, and you, too, benefit. Listening, talking, touching, and doing are what a grieving person probably needs, according to an excellent resource on supportiveness, the book *I Never Know What to Say* (Donnelley, 1987). It and others suggested in the references section can help you help others. Genuine supportiveness strengthens relationships. A poem by Mary Bailey, described by Vail (1982) as "a lovely lady whose cherished teenage daughter was killed in an accident," eloquently expresses what a person in pain wants.

A Plea from Someone Who Has Been There

Please dear friend
Don't say to me the old clichés
Time heals all wounds
God only gives you as much as you can bear

Life is for the living
Just say the thoughts of your heart
I'm sorry, I love you, I'm here, I care
Hug me and squeeze my hand
I need your warmth and strength.
Please don't drop your eyes when I am near
I feel so rejected now by God and man
Just look in my eyes and let me know that you are with me.
Don't think you must always be strong for me
It's okay to cry
It tells me how much you care
Let me cry, too
It's so lonely to always cry alone.
Please keep coming by even after many weeks have passed
When the numbness wears off the pain of grief is unbearable.
Don't ever expect me to be quite the same
How can I be when part of my being is here no more.
But please know, dear friend, with your love, support and understanding
I will live and love again and be grateful everyday that I have you-dear friend.

—Mary Bailey

Sincere Expression

Willingness to express all sincere emotions can greatly improve your relationships. Besides sorrow, others can be difficult.

Forgiveness. Are you one who has difficulty forgiving? Do you know people who bear grudges over long periods of time? Forgiveness, especially in cases when you were truly wronged, is among the most difficult of human undertakings, and most of us have no idea how or even if to forgive (Flanigan, 1992). The benefits of forgiving are worth the difficulties. Harboring grudges, resentments, and other bitter feelings requires energy and ends up diminishing self-esteem. The inability to forgive can lead to increased blood pressure, loss of sleep, and other physical problems. The injured party who forgives is released from inner anger and resentment and freed from any psychological hold the injurer may have had (Enright et al., 1989).

Thinking about forgiveness as simply *letting go of the past* may make it more acceptable. To "forgive and forget" is not necessary; you can forgive without forgetting. Erasing a wrong-doing from memory is unrealistic and usually impossible. Neither is forgiving the same as condoning or pardoning (Calhoun, 1992; Flanigan, 1992). "Forgiveness doesn't mean forgetting, nor does it mean whitewashing what has happened. Forgiveness means letting go, moving on, and favoring the positive" (Bloomfield and Felder, 1985, p. 53).

If you have high self-esteem, forgiveness is easier because you are able to forgive yourself, too. In considering that someone else has wronged you, ask, "Am I perfect? Have I ever hurt somebody else?" The answer to the latter question will likely be that you have. The next question is, "Have I forgiven myself?" If you forgive yourself for hurting another and learn from the mistake, you will probably find yourself willing to extend the same to another. You may not resume the relationship at all, or perhaps, it will not be as it was before.

To help you forgive, *Forgiving the Unforgivable* (Flanigan, 1992) is an excellent resource. The author reminds us that family members and friends knowingly and frequently without legitimate reason cause each other to suffer. To never forgive means living a life of unending resentment. "The most intimate of injuries are often left festering and unresolved-either unforgiven or unforgivable" (p. 5). Calling forgiveness the "accomplishment of mastery over a wound" (p. 71), she outlines and describes steps to forgiveness. Since so little has been written about forgiveness, most of us need encouragement and guidance in what Flanigan calls "a gift given to the self" and the "ultimate liberator" (p. 71). When you forgive, you decide to move forward with your life. True forgiveness means putting aside thoughts of getting even. The alternative is not desirable. "The deeply wounded can either change or slowly drown in a deep pool of hatred" (Flanigan, 1992, p. 68). The choice is yours.

Warmth and demonstrated affection. These particular feelings and behaviors deserve special attention. Touch is the first sense to develop; in order to develop normally, a baby needs to be warmly and lovingly touched. Adults deprived of physical stroking in childhood often develop compulsive, destructive habits such as nail biting, overeating, or smoking. Some speculate that violent behavior may be a result of touch deprivation (Ryan and Travis, 1991). A study revealed that adults who had experienced parental warmth and affection as children felt generally happier and less stressed (Franz et al., 1991). As people age, touching generally declines, and touch deprivation has serious repercussions including a feeling of isolation (Richmond et al., 1991). The warmth of body contact and the sensation of strong arms holding us are fundamental and necessary ways of connecting with others. "From the first moments of our life to the last, we need to be held-or we fall" (Josselson, 1992, p. 29). Because touch is so critical, if you don't receive it regularly, self or professional massage is recommended. "As a form of nurturance and rebalancing, and as an aid to healing, massage is hard to beat" (Ryan and Travis, 1991, p. 59).

Reluctance to behave warmly and affectionately is apparent even in close relationships. Individuals who withhold affection can be filled with regret.

> A good friend called me one night and said he needed to talk. I lied and told him I was too busy and said I'd get back to him later. The next day I "spaced" it. That night he shot himself. I feel so guilty.

A letter to Ann Landers told of a 13-year-old girl who wanted desperately to "belong" but had few friends. Left out by others, she was extremely lonely. She tried to reach out and was rejected. She committed suicide, and the students from her school turned out in droves for her funeral. Several put a single flower on the casket. The letter ended: "Sally left this world believing she didn't have a single friend. If just one of those kids who passed her casket had taken the time and trouble to show her a little kindness, that dear girl might be alive today." Ann's response was to tell people to reach out. Do you know someone you could befriend?

In expressing affection and warmth to a friend or loved one, a word to be emphasized is *now*. Because life is tenuous, you can be too late to tell or show someone that you care. Awareness of this can provide the motivation you need. Why not call or write someone for no other reason than just to say, "I love you."

Appropriateness is a key element in demonstrating any emotion. Within close relationships you have more leeway, and warmth and affection can be shown by hugging, kissing, and other physical acts. Among acquaintances, societal guidelines usually direct

Figure 9-6

behaviors. Touch is a gesture of warmth and concern; however, it can also be perceived as seductive, impertinent, annoying, or degrading. When used appropriately, professionals can use touch to be more effective and supportive. In one study, therapists who touched their clients were judged to be more expert than those who did not (Thayer, 1988a). Nurses can use two types of touching. One is task-oriented used routinely as part of the job duties; the other is affective intended to just show concern or affection. This can be expressed through a pat on the hand or shoulder (not a patronizing pat on the head), a squeeze of the arm, or a hug (Brady and Nesbitt, 1991).

Touching is influenced by culture and gender. American society has a low-touch culture, which affects the behaviors of its citizens. In particular situations, touching is even risky. Teachers are concerned that touching a student might be misinterpreted. Following court action against a male elementary-school teacher, a parent in one of my classes expressed this thoughtful opinion.

> I hope that we don't get to the point where people are afraid to touch each other. I have taught my son and daughter to express genuine affection with appropriate touches, pats on the shoulder or back, and hugs. I hate to think that they will go to school and model after human robots fearful of physical contact. Besides, a lot of kids need affirming touches.

As pointed out in the discussion of gender roles, men generally touch others less frequently and in different ways from women. Research showed that a nurse's touch before surgery lowered blood pressure and decreased levels of anxiety in female patients while men had upsetting reactions (Thayer, 1988a). One study found a relationship between homophobia and same-sex touching in men (Roese et al., 1992). As gender roles become less stereotypic and people rid themselves of intolerance, this reaction is likely to change.

Regardless of culture and gender, a study found that people who were comfortable with touching were "more talkative, cheerful, socially dominant and nonconforming; those discomforted by touch tended to be more emotionally unstable and socially withdrawn" (Thayer, 1988a, p. 33). Touching behaviors, then, seem to be linked to positive personal characteristics. As people become more aware of the benefits of demonstrating feelings described in Chapter 4, they may touch more freely. "Without the social vocabulary of touch, life would be cold, mechanical, distant, rational, verbal. Deprived of those gestures and their meanings, the world would be far more frightening, hostile, and chilly" (Thayer, 1988a, p. 36). Examining the ways in which you express warmth and affection and making an effort to show your feelings appropriately and genuinely will improve your relationships. Do so now.

THE CHALLENGE OF RELATIONSHIPS

Are you willing to risk? All relationships involve risks. Besides the pleasures derived from connecting and interacting, you can expect disappointment and pain. "I just want to be left alone because I never want to be hurt again" can be heard from individuals who have been bruised badly by others. Being left alone isn't a positive way to live a life. When you exist only to avoid pain, you forfeit all opportunities for the joys of relationships.

Are you committed to spending time, energy, and effort in building positive relationships? Close friendships are few in number for any one person because each friendship takes a great deal of time and attention. Wanting to relate means sacrificing time alone as well as solitary pursuit of your own pleasures. Giving up the extremes of independence and dependence for the nurturance of interdependence is healthy in all close relationships. *Interdependence* means that two people can stand alone yet prefer to have a relationship with each other and strive to do what's best for both. Education in relating skills can show people how to be interdependent.

> Young people start out without the foggiest notion of how to live in human, personal interaction. I wonder if it would truly be too much to ask of our educational system that it include one goal; I wonder if they would be willing not only to believe, but to prove by their actions that one goal of education is to assist the young person to live as a person with other persons (Rogers, 1972, pp. 214–215).

Those words are challenging. Although some strides have been made since they were written, most of us are left to seek out relationship training for ourselves. Learning from this book is a major step in the process. Also, check the "Future Intentions" list in REFLECTIONS AND APPLICATIONS. The future holds more opportunities to learn and act so that you can be enriched by interactions and relationships.

SUMMARY

Because we are human, we relate. Social relationships are needed for self-development. Healthy relationships are characterized by social exchange. Participants remain in relationships because they receive as well as give, and the benefits outweigh the costs. Features of a healthy relationship include love for self, absence of codependency, genuineness, warmth with unconditional positive regard, empathy, self-disclosure, enjoyment, encouragement, fairness, dependability, energizing feelings, and mutual interests.

Various types of relationships exist. Acquaintances are not as close as friendships; however, they contribute to life satisfaction. Friendships can have both dilemmas and benefits. Although women and men generally differ in the nature of their friendships, the future holds the promise of deep, nourishing relationships for both. Besides friendships, a variety of support systems are available.

Relationships begin when one person initiates an interaction. Open-mindedness, acceptance, and tolerance promote a healthy beginning. Prejudice and intolerance are not beneficial to individuals or to societies. In order to connect, shyness needs to be overcome. When initiating an interaction, approachability is an important consideration. You can learn to check approachability and then in a positive way initiate and continue conversation.

Connecting with others is a process. Factors related to attraction and liking such as proximity, similarities, complementarity, and reciprocity affect the development of relationships. Relationships benefit when the participants have realistic, agreeable expectations of the relationship along with sensitivity, a cooperative attitude, and assertiveness.

Conflict will occur among people. Neither gunnysacking nor aggressiveness is recommended. Learning how to negotiate will help you in all walks of life. Additional techniques may be needed in dealing with difficult people. Little acts of kindness can be major ingredients of positive interactions.

Among the most awkward and difficult behaviors for most people are those of supportiveness. Ignoring another person's crisis or tragedy is commonplace yet not recommended. Showing that you care in verbal and nonverbal ways is important. Sincere expressions of forgiveness, warmth, and affection significantly improve relationships. Waiting to demonstrate these in the future is unwise. Learning individual preferences and societal meanings of touch is helpful, as appropriate touches can improve relationships.

All relationships involve risks and commitment. A major challenge in relationships is based on the fact that human beings are rarely trained in relating skills. If you want to enjoy the joy and benefits that come from healthy, nourishing relationships, you must be willing to risk, commit, and learn.

> *The singular life experience I would wish every human being before they die is to feel love for, and be loved by, another. All human beings biologically need to be healthily attached, connected with others. This powerful yearning colors our whole existence with joy or sadness.*
>
> —Teresa Adams

RESOURCES

- Codependents Anonymous, P.O. Box 33577, Phoenix, AZ 85067-3577, (602) 277–7991
- Parents and Friends of Lesbians and Gays (PFLAG), P. O. Box 27605, Washington, DC 20038

10

Succeeding in Your Career

OBJECTIVES

After completing this chapter, you will be able to

- Explain why work is a significant part of life.
- Differentiate between a career and a job.
- Discuss the aspects of self related to career and job satisfaction.
- Identify work orientations and relate them to career satisfaction.
- Recognize the importance of wise choices of career and jobs.
- Name several characteristics of a valued employee.
- Understand why perfectionism is not related to career success.
- Recognize the many choices you have regarding career.
- Identify ways you can improve your job search.
- Decrease the negative effects of rejection.
- Discuss choices you may have along your career path.
- Identify the possible work relationships you can have.
- Describe behaviors that lead to positive work relationships.
- Define and give several symptoms of burnout.
- Use a measure to determine the extent of burnout.
- Explain possible ways of preventing or overcoming burnout.
- Plan and know how to execute a successful career.

We are responsible to ourselves for the quality of our own lives. We can be friends or enemies to ourselves by the choices we make, which in turn make up the lives we lead. Real caring about ourselves is the first step in caring for others and in solving global concerns. May your career choice contribute to your dream of the future.

—Betty Neville Michelozzi

"What do you want to be when you grow up?" is a challenging question to answer when you are 3 years old. At age 18, or sometimes earlier, there comes another one: "Have you decided what you are going to do with your life?" Then be prepared for an inquiry heard over and over before retirement: "What do you do for a living?" Our self-identities are linked to career choice and current jobs, and the work place serves as the source of much of life's satisfaction or dissatisfaction. A positive professional experience is of prime importance.

Time spent on work-related activities is substantial. A 40-hour-a-week job means an average work life of about 10,000 days (Jackson, 1993). The 40-hour week has expanded. Adults now spend far more time working and commuting than they did in the past. The amount of leisure time has shrunk 37 percent since 1973, and the average work week including commuting time has increased from 41 to 47 hours, according to a 1989 Harris survey (Mallinger and DeWyze, 1992). Why are we working longer and harder? One answer is that individuals try to satisfy human needs through their careers. According to Yankelovich, a leading researcher on changing American values, people now look upon work as a means of self-expression and self-enhancement (Harris and Trotter, 1989). Commitment to work appears to be one of the creative channels that a *self-actualizing person* uses. The truly happy people whom Abraham Maslow encountered when developing the hierarchy of needs were working hard at something that they considered important and worthwhile (Schott, 1992).

Because work is so significant and the relationship between job satisfaction and personal well-being is so well documented, this chapter will focus on how to achieve success in career decisions and work interactions.

SEEKING SATISFACTION IN CAREER AND JOB

How do you differentiate between a career and a job? Did you have a job before you selected a career? Most of us did. Maybe you have a job now and either you haven't decided on a career or the job isn't related to what you eventually plan to do. Think of a *career* as a category of possibilities, a field of endeavor. A career includes a series of work experiences that represent a progression in a field. A person plans, is trained for, and dedicates time and talent to a career (Michelozzi, 1991). Within each career field are numerous job possibilities. A *job* is what a person does for several hours a day and consists of tasks or duties.

Satisfaction at work is important to personal happiness, and having satisfied workers is beneficial to an employer. A study of 13,808 teachers showed that employee satisfaction and attitudes were related to performance (Ostroff, 1992). A comparison study of American and Japanese employees indicated that American management seemed to be more "in tune" with employees' needs. In a Louis Harris survey, just 17 percent of Japanese workers reported being very satisfied with jobs compared to 43 percent in the United States (Arthur, 1992). Numerous studies reveal what is satisfying. A 1988 Gallup survey identified security and good chances for promotion as essential for most. Good health plans and other benefits ranked higher than high income which was rated eleventh on a list of important aspects. Interesting work, job security, opportunity to learn new skills, annual vacations, being able to work independently, and recognition from co-workers were factors important to over 60 percent of the respondents (Braus, 1992). Other studies identify fairness in pay and promotions (Witt and Nye, 1992) and control over one's own work (Ross and Reskin, 1992). Any of these would be wise for you to consider as you make career decisions.

Choosing Careers and Jobs

When you think about satisfaction, consider career and job separately. Most people select a category or field of interest either before or during college and then seek a job within their career area. Giving serious thought to career choice is the first step in achieving satisfaction. In the past, many individuals gave little consideration to career choice. For example, Carl farms because his father and grandfather were farmers. Chuck wanted to remain in his home town, so he took a job in a bank and made it a career. Toni chose hairdressing because there was a school near her home, and she didn't have other aspirations. As for myself, my own limitations were based on societal stereotypes. I considered only nursing, secretarial work, or teaching. By a process of elimination and because I thought it would be nice to have my summers free, I chose teaching! I'm one of the few fortunate ones who gave little thought to the decision and ended up happy with my choice. People today seem to be more concerned with career selection; however, they can still limit themselves.

As was pointed out in Chapter 2, women, in general, still sell themselves short and opt for lower paying, lower status career fields. Young men continue to feel forced to be financially successful and thus choose higher paid fields even if they have little interest. Many other men feel pressured to take over a family business. Both sexes can limit or shortchange themselves by not considering all possibilities.

Before you choose a career, a wise suggestion is to know yourself. If you have read and applied the material in this book, you have added to your self-knowledge. Now, focus on specific career-related aspects of self. The widely read book *What Color Is Your Parachute*? (Bolles, 1994) can lead you through a series of exercises to identify skills you enjoy and those you do best. "The key to our happiness, to our being able to find pleasure in our work, is the sense that we are using our abilities, not wasting them, and that we are being appreciated for it" (Kushner, 1986, p. 149).

Most people reply to the question, "What do you want to be?" by naming a title or position; this doesn't tell you what is required in a job. The critical challenge, instead, is, "What do you want to *do*?" Does your choice afford you opportunities to do what you enjoy? Having job responsibilities that are exciting, fulfilling, enjoyable and that allow personal growth and *enjoyment* of actual tasks will lead to satisfaction and higher levels of performance (Hendlin, 1992; Strasser and Sena, 1992). Teachers who are boring, unenthusiastic, or fearful may be that way because they do not enjoy doing what exciting teaching demands-being a vital speaker as well as a performer or even a "ham"! An activity in REFLECTIONS AND APPLICATIONS can help you link enjoyment and job duties.

Your values also play a part in the process of choosing a satisfying career. If you highly value money or what it can buy, you cannot expect career satisfaction in lower paid fields no matter how much you enjoy the work. Ethics are more difficult to maintain in some career fields. People with a strong moral code are likely to become frustrated and experience depressing times if confronted with frequent ethical dilemmas. Is prestige important to you? Sociologists have studied prestige statuses of various career fields, and, if this is of concern, you would be wise to acquaint yourself with the status ranking of your career choice. Maybe you value advancement and upward mobility. There is a vast difference between opportunities in the current child care field and a business management career.

Personality type and emotional coping skills are important. Some career fields allow for flexibility and imaginative processing; others are more rigid and matter-of-fact.

Figure 10-1 Enjoyment of work is priceless.

Do you tend to be more extraverted or introverted? Ask yourself how many interactions you will have on a regular basis. The Myers-Briggs Type Indicator, described in Chapter 2, provides insight into preferred work situations for each personality type. Certain careers are more stressful than others. Jon was a laid-back individual who didn't like pressure and externally imposed deadlines. His initial career choice of printing proved to be the wrong one for him. He developed stress-related migraine headaches and ulcers before he realized that he didn't want to cope with the high-speed world of printing technology.

All of this may sound complicated—and it is! However, wise decisions in the beginning can save you years of wasted energy. Even after starting a career, people may realize they have made a poor choice and change directions. Relatively few decisions are as influential in determining the course of our lives as our choice of a career path. Occupational choices have an impact on several aspects of your life including standard of living, life style, friendships, intimate relationships, how you dress each day, and where you live. For example, my younger daughter Lyn recently graduated and decided to begin her career in California. Even though I think it's a wise choice, I realize her decision influences how often we will see each other as well as the other factors mentioned earlier. A chief of a fire department caused a few eyes to widen in a class when he said that a firefighting career means spending one third of your life away from your family. Career decisions are choices about the way we live.

After a wise career choice, a specific job selection takes the spotlight. You may liken making a career selection to deciding that you want an ice cream cone. After choosing ice cream over other possibilities, you realize that you don't want to limit a selection to vanilla, chocolate, or strawberry, so you go to a specialty store. Now your choice is among any number of flavors! Within a career field are many possible jobs, and an individual who is looking for the ultimate in satisfaction doesn't just settle for the basic choices. For example, the majority of psychology majors become counselors. Many other possibilities—teaching, research, consulting, training and development, personnel work, and marketing—exist. Take advantage of the library resources available. Directories have listings of thousands of jobs; some may be unfamiliar, yet appealing.

The ego states identified in transactional analysis (TA), are involved in career and job selection. Your child ego state may be tempted by glamorous choices or those that seem "fun": "I want to be a truck driver so I can just get behind the wheel and travel and be free as the breeze" is an example of the "child" at work. The student who made this statement, by the way, soon realized that truck driving wasn't that simple! From your parent ego state, you might hear, "Get a job—any job—just so you're not being a bum" or "Get a job that pays well" or "Be a doctor because your father is one." Career and job satisfaction are too complicated to blindly follow "parent" messages or "child" feelings. As in most of life's decisions, the adult ego state plays a major role. After becoming aware of the wants and feelings of the "child" and analyzing the "parent" messages, the "adult" rationally selects both a career and a job.

Have you ever had a job you didn't like? Do you know why it wasn't desirable so you can avoid a similar situation? What have you enjoyed in previous or present jobs? Being aware of past and present satisfying factors can be helpful. Using more than your own experiences to make decisions is even more advantageous.

In terms of both career and job choices, you might consider your own work orientation. In contrast to a past belief that everyone wanted to move up the career ladder so that only the orientation of upward mobility was important, four other orientations have been identified (Derr, 1986). If you are interested in "getting ahead" or *upward mobility*, be sure to consider advancement possibilities in both career and job selections. One or more of the other four could also be significant to you.

- Being *secure* means you want job security in a stable industry with an established firm.
- Being *free* indicates that you enjoy independence and flexibility to "do your own thing" at work.
- Being *high* signifies that you want excitement and challenge in your career and job, and risks are welcomed.
- Being *balanced* is harmony between personal and professional life, and you would want a career and job that allows time for family and other interests.

The latter is typically gender related. One study showed that women rated family relationships, personal fulfillment, and security as more important and status and wealth as less important than their male counterparts did (Chusmir and Parker, 1992). Picturing yourself in careers and jobs related to the five identified orientations makes sense. Where do you feel most comfortable? Which have little appeal? You may be able to have more than one. For example, my instructor position is generally secure and affords a measure of freedom, although my class schedule is set for me, vacation time is determined by the school calendar, and school policies regulate me to an extent. And even though I attempt to balance work and home, I spend many evenings on paperwork from my job. I do get "high" when I realize the impact I have on the lives of some of my favorite people—the students! Not being especially interested in upward mobility, I am satisfied that my professional position and orientations are compatible. Similarly, if you know yourself and your preferences, you can make personal career and job satisfaction a reality.

Other ideas can be used to explain satisfaction in the work place. You may want to apply Maslow's hierarchy of needs from Chapter 3. For example, if you are struggling with survival needs, money is a critical factor, and you may opt to postpone other ingredients for satisfaction until this basic need is met. Because many individuals are on the self-esteem level, a job that enhances feelings of self-worth would be important.

Considering how many other life choices are influenced by career and job selection, the relationship between professional and personal satisfaction, and the actual time spent at work, your attention to these choices is imperative. How much satisfaction you get from your career and job will directly influence all other aspects of your life. Choose wisely!

POSITIVE PERSONAL QUALITIES AND WORK HABITS

Pretend you own a business, and you need employees. What qualities would you seek? Certain jobs demand special qualities or abilities, yet a common thread of desirable traits runs through most positions. If you have achieved the objectives presented in this book, then you possess several of the positive qualities listed in Table 10–1.

Check to see how many of these qualities honestly describe you. If you lack any, go back through the book and seek to develop them. Do you see the close relationship between the recommendations for personal satisfaction and those for professional satisfaction?

Of utmost importance is the emphasis on human relations skills. Workers are fired more often for negative personal characteristics and poor "people" skills than for any other reasons. An employer remarked, "I can help them improve technical skills; however, I don't know how to change a negative attitude and lack of 'people' skills." From discussions with a variety of employers, a profile of the ideal employee has emerged. As expected, education, training, and experience related to the job are included. Other profile characteristics are *transferable skills*, defined as desirable traits valuable in all career fields and useful in almost every job. The positive human relations attributes are essential transferable skills. In addition to the qualities in Table 10–1, owners and managers have identified ten characteristics of valued employees.

Enthusiasm is a quick response. "During an interview, if I don't pick up on some interest and enthusiasm, I won't hire the person no matter what the other skills are," said an owner of an automotive service business. Demonstrating enthusiasm about the career field and the job itself is recommended.

Desire to exert effort is another. During an employers' panel discussion, a young child development student mentioned that she had detassled corn on a farm (a tedious task on a hot summer day). A director of a day care center shrieked, "Great! When I have applicants who have stuck with that job, I'm convinced that they can work hard—which day care requires." Being a hard worker is a winning quality. Even if you initially lack desired skills, your zest for hard work will compensate, and your efforts will be rewarded.

TABLE 10-1 Positive Personal Qualities and Work Habits

High self-esteem
Positive attitude
Self-efficacy
Realistic expectations about self and others
Sense of responsibility and control
Ability to see alternatives
Orientation to positive action
Ability to meet deadlines
Spirit of contributing
Zest for life
Understanding of self, including personality traits and thought-processing strengths
I'm OK, You're OK life position
Willingness to give positive strokes
Freedom from stereotypes
Ability to feel and to manage emotions, including ability to cope with stress and crises
Ethical character
Goal orientation and desire to improve
Interpersonal communication skills
Ability to give and receive criticism
Positive interactive skills

> Work hard, not only because it will bring you rewards and promotions but because it will give you the sense of being a competent person. Some jobs can afford to be done poorly and no one will be hurt, but none of us can afford the internal spiritual cost of being sloppy in our work. It teaches us contempt for ourselves and our skills (Kushner, 1986, p. 147).

Likability or congeniality, the ability to get along with others, is highly desired. The work environment is greatly influenced by the climate produced by the personnel. Conflicts will occur; however, people who are congenial and who like others will manage them effectively. Having an appropriate sense of humor is a plus. Qualities such as sensitivity, cooperativeness, and fairness (described in Chapter 9) contribute to a positive work place.

Dependability is invariably a necessity. The fundamental responsibility is getting to work on time on a regular basis. "I have to be able to count on my employees," says a business owner. "My company has a responsibility to the customers, and they can't be served if people don't show up." If you have a positive record of attendance and punctuality, be sure to maintain it and use it to your advantage. Dependability goes beyond physical presence, however. When you are given a job, can your employer count on you to perform? Productivity is the key to success in businesses and organizations, and hard-working employees who are responsible are almost always productive. Your employer will expect you to do your share, and if you are interested in advancement, you are wise to do even more.

Three additional qualities go hand in hand and are popular with most employers in today's job market. Creativity, innovation, and initiative are sought in many positions. *Creativity* is the ability to develop good ideas that can be put into action and is not confined to artistic pursuits. *Innovation* means change and is closely related to creativity. Being imaginative at work could result in a better product or idea, an easier way to perform a task, or a more spontaneous environment. My husband, a business owner, sees a major contrast between employees who can figure out a way to solve a problem and those who seem to have little ingenuity. Regardless of job category, employees are expected to be able to reason and solve problems. You may be thinking that creativity and innovation are rare talents. Keep in mind that everyone has a degree of both, that you can employ each in any job, and that many creative, innovative ideas are simple ones. Critical and creative thinking abilities are a definite plus. Individuals who are ambitious and motivated show *initiative*. Instead of standing around waiting to be told what to do next, they seek productive activity. When I directed an early childhood development center, I was amazed at the differences among my employees in this regard. A few sought new tasks; however, the majority would finish an activity and pause until they received instructions. At times, caution in going ahead is advisable; however, chronic lack of initiative is not appreciated. With almost any job, you can usually find more to do if you look!

Flexibility is like a breath of fresh air. In many work situations, adaptation or adjustment is practical. Rigidity in habits, behaviors, and thinking can set up obstacles. Jo was considered one of the most valuable employees in an accounting firm, and her flexibility was a major strength. She could adjust her demanding schedule when necessary. During busy times she offered to work overtime or come in early. When new ideas were suggested, she exhibited an open attitude, which made others like her. Being able to "go with the flow" creates possibilities!

"It may seem old fashioned, but I expect my employees to be loyal," stated a man who headed a large corporation. *Loyalty* does not necessarily mean that you will never leave a company; however, it does imply that while employed, the employer's best interests will be of concern to you. Speaking negatively about a current or past employer, even if it's deserved, isn't recommended.

In contrast to the work world of years ago, when employees were expected to be "seen and not heard," today's employers want *assertiveness*. In Chapter 9, assertiveness was identified as a desirable characteristic in all kinds of relationships. At work, you gain little by being overly aggressive or passive. Jan was determined and ambitious. In business meetings she frequently and loudly interrupted. She was intense and hostile whenever she felt challenged. Her aggressive attitude and behavior made her unpopular and, ironically, blocked the advancement she desired so much. On the other hand, Tim was a "yes" person who was meek and humble. His supervisor and co-workers took advantage of him. At his yearly evaluation he was told he wasn't ready to move to the management level.

Assertiveness training would have helped both Jan and Tim. On the job, being able to say "no" to unreasonable requests, as discussed in Chapter 9, is important. Otherwise, you hurt yourself by stretching to the point that you feel overloaded, taken advantage of, and irritable (Smith, 1992). Being assertive during an interview can enhance your chances of being hired. Employers share the belief that behaviors during an interview indicate actions on the job.

Keeping in mind these characteristics of valued employees, a practical way of preparing for an interview is to note the qualities and work habits you possess and emphasize them in resumes, cover letters, and interviews. If you can also document when you have displayed them, you stand an even better change of being the top applicant. For example, your confidence and assertiveness will probably show in an interview, yet dependability is not likely to be evident (except in your being prompt). Be sure to mention that you are responsible, and then specifically describe your attendance and punctuality record from your last job or from school.

The more positive qualities you possess, the more likely you are to achieve career success. Because individuals differ in their perceptions, success is difficult to define. A common error is to equate succeeding with perfection. Understanding the meaning of perfectionism and the research findings on perfectionistic individuals will reveal why perfectionism is not included on the list of desired qualities.

Striving for realistic goals and pursuing your potential are positive and are *not* what perfectionism means. Instead, *perfectionism* is a belief that anything short of perfection in performance is unacceptable (Hendlin, 1992). A study of insurance agents found that perfectionists earned an average of $15,000 a year less than nonperfectionists (Burns, 1980b). One reason is that perfectionists tend to pay too much attention to details and spend time and energy getting everything just right while sacrificing worthier activities. Also, they are often indecisive for fear of making mistakes and usually afraid to take risks. Perfectionists are motivated by fear of failure and measure their own worth in terms of unachievable goals (Hendlin, 1992). Needless to say, creativity and innovation would be neglected as a result of the perfectionist's preoccupation with detail and accuracy, and the stress of not being perfect could be overwhelming. Instead, striving for excellence is recommended. This means that you accept less-than-perfect performances without feeling inadequate, are motivated by joy and challenge rather than fear, and are able to appreciate and enjoy steps toward a goal (Hendlin, 1992).

If you're a positive person who wants to realize your potential, who sets realistic goals, who takes responsibility for self, who is nonperfectionistic and strives for excellence, you can be successful at whatever job you choose. Success can mean a feeling of having done as well as you could and can be seen as a process, not as a final destination. Demonstrating the recommended personal qualities and work habits will help you achieve career success.

CHOICES: FROM THE JOB SEARCH TO RETIREMENT

As in all areas of life, you have, and will continue to have, any number of choices regarding career and jobs. Specific choices are related to the stage of your career.

The Search Itself

You may not recognize that you have a choice about how you will go about the job search itself. The majority of job hunters simply look. They do not prepare and seemingly give little thought to the process. The first step is to know yourself and what you have to offer. To help you now or in the future, complete the "Assets and Liabilities" exercise in REFLECTIONS AND APPLICATIONS. Years ago I designed and taught a course focusing on career development which is a requirement for several majors. Convincing students that the course is worthwhile was sometimes a challenge. Yet, does it seem sensible to spend 2 or more years gaining knowledge in order to get the job you want and then fail to do so because your job-seeking skills are inadequate? For example, most individuals who are looking for jobs confine their search to the classified ads in a newspaper. Would it surprise you to know that most available jobs on any given day are not advertised? If you only answer ads, you are tapping into a small share of the job market.

According to Pat Sims, a personnel specialist, several job applicants are totally unprepared. They don't have any idea of what job they want, know nothing about the business, lack the information needed to fill out an application, and don't even bring a pen. "Several bring their babies, and a few even have pets with them!" Their choice, seemingly, has been to approach the job hunt in a lackadaisical way. Employers will be inclined to believe they will handle their jobs similarly.

Most never actually *learn* how to interview. Being unprepared for a job interview can lead to a stressful situation in which you give a less than positive impression of yourself. A common problem has to do with responses that negate or qualify the interviewee.

> Jane was nervous. The minute she sat down with the interviewer, she began to wish that she had prepared better. When asked what her work experiences had been, she replied, "Well, uh, I haven't done much except work in a restaurant—really nothing in the secretarial field." The final question was, "Why should we hire you over the other applicants?" She blushed and stammered, "Well, I don't think—you know—I'm better than others so I don't really know—uh, I feel I could do a good job, I guess."

Contrast this poor performance with a well-prepared job applicant.

> Jane faced the interviewer with a smile and a look of confidence. When asked about work experience, she replied, "I have worked for 2 years in a busy restaurant. I developed many human relations skills as I greeted and waited on customers. I think these skills will be valuable in secretarial work. During college I had simulated office experience, which I really enjoyed." In response to the final question, she replied, "I have my secretarial degree and had many hands-on experiences during my training. My work experience has helped me develop many "people" skills. I am dependable, positive, friendly, enthusiastic about my career, and very interested in this job."

Figure 10-2

This impressive interview would not have occurred if Jane had not prepared by anticipating the questions and rehearsing her answers. Going to a job interview with no preparation can be as disastrous as jumping into deep water not knowing how to swim. If you have an opportunity to take a course to help you build confidence, write a better application, prepare a résumé, and learn to interview, take advantage of it. Or, read any book pertaining to the job search listed in the references section. You will already be ahead of most other applicants. Shyness can be a major obstacle in an interview. Using ideas from Chapter 9 to decrease shyness is advisable as is rehearsing the interview ahead of time.

Because rejection is an inevitable part of most job searches, it is wise to decide how you will handle it. Rejection shock, as Bolles (1994) calls it, happens to about 95 percent of all job seekers. A picture of the job search as a series of "no's" finally followed by a "yes" is realistic. Important to remember is that a "no" is not a rejection of you personally but merely an opinion of how well matched you and the position are. Also, keep in mind that rejection, like failure, is part of any successful person's experience (Strasser and Sena, 1992). Thought-changing can do wonders. Rather than think, "Something is wrong with me that they didn't want to hire me," restructure it: "Just because they didn't hire me doesn't mean something is wrong with me. They sure missed an opportunity to have a first-rate employee. It's their loss!" Then choose to move forward to a better job selection.

Your Career Path

Worth thinking about before you accept a job is where it may lead. Several decisions will be made during your work life that will dramatically influence the direction of your career path.

Career goals. Just as you couldn't plan a trip without knowing the desired destination, you are unwise to map out a career track unless you know your objective. This decision doesn't have to be made immediately, yet thinking about it can be beneficial. Young people may have aspirations of owning their own business or being the head of a company yet haven't seriously considered what is required to get there and whether they would like what they will find upon arriving. Ask yourself whether you enjoy being in charge and making final decisions. Are you willing to give the time and effort required to achieve higher positions? Advancement is rewarding, yet sometimes the status you achieve isn't worth the price.

Many overlook the need to integrate career and personal plans. Jack started his own business thinking that he would now be his own boss, be in charge of his life, and not have to work so many hours. He soon discovered that he had many bosses—his customers! He had a successful marriage and was a devoted father to two children. He found little time to spend with family. Both his business and his personal life began to suffer. He made a difficult decision to sell the business he had recently established and accept a position that didn't interfere with his family life.

Another sound reason to establish career goals is that this is frequently asked in a job interview. Your answer will influence your getting hired. Having no goals or poorly-defined ones is a liability. Also important is to have goals compatible with what the interviewing employer can offer. "I want to travel on the job, have relocation possibilities, and then eventually start my own business," could be the "kiss-of-death."

Advancement. If you decide that you want to advance into different positions, planning becomes significant. First, select employment where promotional possibilities exist. Then,

- do the best job you can,
- take advantage of learning and growth opportunities especially those that will help you at the next level,
- display professionalism by joining organizations in your field and demonstrating a high degree of ethics,
- document your accomplishments and keep your résumé updated,
- use networking and learning from those above you,
- research carefully.

The latter is important because promotion just for advancement's sake may lead to job dissatisfaction. Most of us have been convinced that upward mobility is essential and find ourselves in jobs we either don't like or don't do well. Granted you may be required to take a position with responsibilities that aren't satisfying on the way to one that is. Be sure that your final goal is where you want to be.

Having a contingency plan is also a good idea. For example, Hank decided that if he weren't promoted to a supervisory position within 2 years, he would return to school and take courses that would help him learn about the latest trends in marketing. The goal-setting techniques outlined in Chapter 5 work well in charting your career path. Action steps are a necessity. Some students write expansive career goals such as, "I plan to make a million dollars and retire within 5 years." I write in return, "Good luck and HOW are you going to do this?" The "how" is critical.

Keeping records. Maintaining a personal career file is one of the most practical and worthwhile things you can do, yet many neglect this. One day a frantic former student called me: "Did you keep our résumés on file?" My "no" reply resulted in a plaintive outburst, "I threw all my stuff from the class away, and I need a résumé right now!" Few individuals are as well organized as they could be, and poor organization makes the job search more time consuming and stressful. Keep the following items in your career file so that you can access them easily.

- All data usually requested on an application, including record of all previous employment
- Current résumé
- Education records, including grade transcripts
- Certificates, diplomas, and degrees
- Current job description plus any from the past
- Summary of all achievements and list of honors
- Any news clippings about your career, job, or yourself in a positive situation
- Any of your publications and, when appropriate, a portfolio of your work
- Letters of recommendations from past employers, educators, clients, and others
- Names, addresses, and phone numbers of contacts and past and present references

- All job evaluations and performance reviews
- Brochures about seminars and workshops you have attended

Making contacts. *Networking*, establishing contacts who may be helpful, can be invaluable. Networking can help you get a desired job, advance in your career, and change your job or career. Whom you know does make a difference. Occasionally, a job seeker will balk at the idea of getting a job through contacts. "I don't want to be hired because of whom I know but on the basis of my abilities," a young, earnest man said. He was assured that even Albert Einstein found a job after graduation only through the father of one of his classmates (Fisher et al., 1977)—a classic example of whom you know being, perhaps, as important as what you know. Besides, you probably won't be hired, even with the best contact, if you aren't qualified. Contacts who can be used as references, sources of job leads, and influential sponsors are tremendous resources throughout your career. Begin building your network immediately. A good idea is to exchange business cards with people and keep them in a file. Almost everyone likes to help others.

Continued learning. Advancement and upward mobility depend on such factors as determination, hard work, time spent, opportunity, and timing. Taking advantage of all types of educational possibilities and skills-building opportunities is highly recommended. Some students are surprised to realize that their education isn't over when they earn a degree. In order to succeed, a recommendation is to continue to learn by reading in your career field at least 4 hours a week (Strasser and Sena, 1992). Lifelong learners are invariably career-success winners.

A worthwhile question to ask in an employment interview is what further educational opportunities are encouraged or provided. Even if the employer doesn't pay for these, show that you are determined to continue to learn and grow and then do so. Also, emphasize how important learning is to you. Students invariably wonder whether an employer favors education or experience. A vice president of communications in a large insurance company suggested that successful applicants demonstrate that they have experience from their education and education from their experiences. Both are important!

Leadership. Training to become a leader will help in several ways. You may decide that you really don't want to lead, or you may acquire the skills that differentiate effective leaders from poor ones. Before you seek training, look at the traits of leadership and see whether you demonstrate most of them. Based on interviews with both executives and employees, the characteristics that were found to be important are in Table 10–2.

Being an effective leader is an art that goes beyond successful job performance. The list in Table 10–2 might look ideal; however, an excellent leader possesses even more characteristics. Effective communicating, organizing, delegating, seeing that responsibilities are carried out, giving and receiving constructive criticism, and promoting teamwork are others. One invaluable trait is a willingness to give positive strokes. "Appreciation and recognition of employees and their accomplishments are vital for maintaining an emotionally healthy and productive workplace" (Strasser and Sena, 1992, p. 30). You might want to lead; however, being an able leader requires much more than desire. The rewards can certainly be worth the effort.

TABLE 10-2 Leadership Characteristics

Energy	Intelligence	Creativity and initiative
Perseverance	Good judgment	Objectivity and balance
Personality	Stature	Enthusiasm and optimism
Self-confidence		Education and scholarship

Source: Bittel, Lester R. (1984). *Leadership: The Key to Management Success*. New York: Franklin Watts.

Challenges at work. On the job you will periodically face challenges not directly related to the work you do. Prejudice and discrimination based on such factors as age, sex, race, ethnicity, and disability are possible. *Sexual harassment*—any uninvited and undesired verbal or physical behavior related to sexuality—is of concern in today's work environment. Actions that constitute harassment range from offensive sexually tinged jokes or language to physical assault (Butler, 1992). At least 50 percent of women and a smaller percentage of men have been harassed on the job or on campus. After reading figures, it is important, however, to realize that even though most harassers are men, *most men are not harassers* (Bravo and Cassedy, 1992). Sexual harassment has come out of the closet in recent years (Butler, 1992), and people are learning what to do.

To avoid being a harasser, assume that off-color jokes and sexual advances are not welcomed, recognize that a "no" means just that, and ask how you'd feel if you or someone you cared for was harassed. To handle harassment, be assertive and let the person know the behaviors are not acceptable, talk to someone about any incident, document both the harassment and your own job performance, seek witnesses, go through appropriate channels, and use the legal system, if necessary (Bravo and Cassedy, 1992).

Knowing what to do if you are confronted and then making wise choices can lessen the trauma. Being sensitive to others in the work environment so that you don't unwittingly create problems is most advisable. Refraining from sexist or racist comments and language may require effort, yet it is the fair and decent way to behave. Challenging your own stereotypes and eliminating personal prejudice, as recommended in Chapter 9, will make this easier. Acceptance and equal treatment of others are keystones of positive human relations. Getting accurate information can defuse a potentially emotion-laden situation. For example, the word had spread that the city fire department was helping minorities by boosting their entrance-test scores. I assigned a student to check on this, and I also called the city official in charge of hiring. Both of us found that this was not the case and that it was, in fact, the result of a misinterpretation that had become a vicious rumor. Valued employees don't believe everything they hear; they take the time to check the facts.

Equity concerns such as equal pay for equal work, comparable worth, maternity and paternity leave, and quality child care have arisen and will continue to be consequential. Controversial issues such as drug testing, disease screening, and smoking policies will necessitate difficult organizational and personal decisions. Stay abreast of new developments, be objective, and remain aware of the concerns and open to possible solutions.

Career and job changes. If you are unhappy at work or if a better opportunity arises, you will probably consider a change. Changing jobs is common, and even switching careers is not unusual. Statistics reveal that Americans change jobs every 3 to 4 years (Breidenbach, 1989). A career change demands more thought and planning than a job change and is usually riskier. You are wise to do as much research as possible before contemplating a career switch. Look objectively at your present situation and note the costs of a career move as compared with the benefits. Critical thinking is helpful. As with any change, stress is a by-product, and any resulting satisfaction and pleasure are well deserved.

In some circumstances, your career path may be disrupted by events beyond your control. For example, a large company relocated and terminated most of its employees. Several of them enrolled in my courses as part of retraining programs. The general reaction has been positive. "I never would have had the nerve to make a switch like this if I hadn't been forced to do it," said one middle-aged man. "I feel like a kid again!" As is often the case, a positive result followed a period of adversity.

Retirement. The end of a career seems far away for most people; however, the most effective and productive planning for retirement is started years before a career ends. Those who don't are financially handicapped. Women, especially, are at risk. Low income early in life follows women into retirement and old age. Women have a 60 percent chance of being poor in old age mainly because they don't look ahead (Perkins, 1992). In fact, only 30 percent of American working women, ages 25 to 64, save for retirement, according to a 1993 survey by Merrill Lynch. Rather than a planned course, women are more likely than men to retire in response to life events such as illness of a loved one frequently before they are financially ready (Szinovacz and Washo, 1992). Both sexes often avoid planning for a retirement life style that can bring similar rewards to those gained from work. Thoughtful decisions will make the transition from a career orientation to retirement a positive experience. If a person wants to continue to live a happy, satisfying life, this appears to be critical. A Louis Harris poll showed that 81 percent of 65 to 69 year-olds don't look forward to retirement with pleasure (Bortz, 1991). Using the same guidelines for positive aging as those suggested in Chapter 5 can make a significant difference.

From the initial career and job selections to retirement, your career path will bring both joy and sorrow, elation and disappointment. Each stage requires choices, and because a smooth path is preferable, you owe it to yourself to consider all possibilities and make thoughtful decisions about this significant part of your life.

RELATIONSHIPS IN THE WORK ENVIRONMENT

To whom will you relate as you pursue your career? With whom will you interact on the job? Countless possibilities exist. Let's follow Rick, a surgical technologist, through part of his work day.

> The parking lot was filling as Rick left his car. He smiled and said hello to three other employees as he entered the building. In the elevator he exchanged small talk with others. He met briefly with his supervisor, a nurse, and one of the surgeons. He offered a reassuring word to a nervous patient. Later in the morning he had coffee in the employees' lounge with two co-workers. At lunch he complimented a cafeteria worker on the tempting array of fresh fruit. During the afternoon he met with other mem-

bers of the surgical team. Before the day was over, he had interacted with approximately 40 people.

In almost any job you will have relationships with co-workers, supervisors, people from other departments or work areas, and customers, clients, or patients. In addition, you may be in a position where you have subordinates or people you supervise. These relationships are enhanced by your positive behaviors.

Personality Types at Work

From an understanding of personality preferences from the Myers-Briggs Type Indicator, discussed in Chapter 2, you can use what is called typewatching. There are no good or bad types, only different ones. Each of the different personality types is profiled in the book *Type Talk at Work* (Kroeger and Thuesen, 1992), and you can learn a great deal about yourself and others in your workplace.

Each of the 16 preferences provides insight; however, by knowing more than one preference and sometimes combining them, you can get a broader picture. Four temperament types have been identified (Keirsey and Bates, 1978) and can be understood as work styles. Combining your preference for taking in information (second letter of your personality type, either *S*ensing or i*N*tuitive) with either the third or fourth letter is how to determine temperament. If your preference is sensing, combine it with your fourth letter (either *J*udging or *P*erceiving); if intuitive, match it with your third letter (either *F*eeling of *T*hinking). A few characteristics of each temperament type in the work environment follow (Kroeger and Thuesen, 1992).

NF (intuitive–feeling) is empathic, highly responsive to interpersonal transactions, keeps in close contact with others, sees possibilities, searches for meaning and authenticity, and gives and needs strokes.

NT (intuitive–thinking) is responsive to new ideas, hungers for competency and knowledge, works well with ideas and concepts, is not always aware of others' feelings, likes to start projects but may not follow through, and focuses on possibilities through nonpersonal analysis.

SJ (sensing–judging) is orderly, dependable, realistic, understands and conserves institutional values, expects others to be realistic, can be critical of mistakes more easily than rewarding expected duties, strives to belong and contribute, and prizes harmony and service.

SP (sensing–perceiving) is flexible and open-minded, willing to take risks, highly negotiable, can be perceived as indecisive, hungers for freedom and action, and best at verbal planning and short-range projects.

The more you understand and accept differences in personality, the more likely you are to be satisfied.

Promoting Positive Relations

If you possess most of the positive qualities of a valued employee described in this chapter and are practicing the skills outlined in previous ones, you will be able to cultivate positive relationships with those in your work environment. Some specific behaviors are especially important.

Give positive strokes. Appropriate affirmations can create a warm atmosphere and be rewarding to you in return. People generally react favorably to a sincere positive stroke. Even if the response isn't evident, you can be almost certain the individual enjoyed the feeling. As discussed in Chapter 2, we miss many stroking opportunities, and the work place provides several. You can give verbal or nonverbal strokes. A thank you, congratulations, or an acknowledgment note are fine ways to affirm another person.

Praise is recognized as a powerful motivator and is certainly inexpensive. "A boss who gives spontaneous praise for good work may get more work from employees than one who pays well but never praises" (Glasser, 1984, p. 169). Employees in a research study gave a higher rating to full appreciation of their work than to good pay as a morale-building factor; ironically, the managers rated pay as the top factor and appreciation as a much less important factor than the employees did (Kovach, 1980). If employees enjoy praise, wouldn't it seem sensible that employers would, too? Because of fear that positive strokes could be misinterpreted, employees may hesitate to praise their supervisors. Remember that they are human, too, and if you are sincere, the stroke will be appreciated.

Be helpful and supportive. Think of situations in which you were in need of help or support. Opportunities abound to provide both to others. Little actions mean a lot. Marge was in a hurry to get to a meeting and wanted to make one copy of a report to take with her. Jack was ahead of her and offered to make the copy before he finished his. Ted knew that his supervisor's daughter had been ill. He left a cheering note on her desk and sent a brightly colored balloon to the hospital. Rod offered to give Tom a ride to the bus stop on a rainy day.

In some cases, more is demanded. If a co-worker is ill, handling additional tasks may be in order. Helping new employees learn their duties may take time but will be appreciated. Patti had received some training in family counseling and had excellent listening skills. She spent some lunch hours with Alicia, who was going through a divorce.

Helpfulness and supportiveness are hallmarks of effective relationships with customers, clients, and patients. If you can mentally switch places with a customer, for example, you will probably be able to identify immediately what the individual wants from you. Several personal experiences with health care employees before and after cancer surgery convinced me of the impact they have on a patient.

> The nurse at the University of Illinois Medical Center in Chicago gave me a reassuring smile, and said, "Don't worry. We see many patients with these tumors, and we know what we're doing!"
>
> (This was such a relief after being told that mine was a rare cancer.)
>
> The world-renown specialist muttered to himself and to the medical students who were observing the scan of my eye, "Melanoma, melanoma—doesn't look like it, but I don't know what else it could be. Hmmm."
>
> (My stress level was at an all-time high. I knew what melanoma cancer was. I kept thinking, "Doesn't he know that I can hear him?")
>
> The young radiologist at Mayo Clinic chatted in a friendly fashion. "You're from Nebraska? I've never been there. What is it like?" Before the scans, she calmly explained to me what she was doing and what would happen.

(I thought that she was wise beyond her years and seemed to be aware of the psychological studies that show that the impact of stress is lessened when people know what to expect.)

The last thing I remember as I was being wheeled into surgery at Mayo Clinic to have my left eye removed was the confident voice of the surgical aide who had brought me there. "Wow, we have the 'A team' doing this surgery!"

(My response was a sincere, "Thanks for telling me." I felt as at ease as possible.)

The young doctor in residency said a brief hello and then sat behind a desk and looked at what appeared to be my medical records. I was there for a postoperative visit with the surgeon. For 10 long minutes he didn't look at me or say anything except an occasional "Hmmm" as he read and cracked his knuckles!

(Another stressful situation in which behaviors of a specialist created more tension.)

One of the most positive and dearest people I met is Wolfgang Kuss, owner of Midwest Eye Laboratory in Minneapolis—my eye designer, I call him. When I went to have an artificial eye made, I felt uncomfortable to say the least. Wolfgang, who had fled East Germany before the Iron Curtain, immediately set both my husband and me at ease. I laughed more and felt more positive during that hour than I had for months.

(His attitude made all the difference in the world. I continue to look forward to my checkups with Wolfgang.)

This story is somewhat humorous now, but at the time nothing about the situation was funny. I was having a uterine scan a few years after my cancer surgery. The radiology technician was unsmiling and unfriendly. The only thing she said during the 15-minute ordeal was a question: "Did anyone ever tell you that you have two uteruses? It sure looks strange." Then she left the examining room and didn't return for another 15 minutes. I lay there fighting terror, knowing that I didn't have two uteruses but wondering what she was seeing.

(A case of poor judgment and an uncalled-for comment. The ending was happy: What she saw was nothing strange.)

Were you able to recognize the helpful and unhelpful, supportive and nonsupportive behaviors in each of the situations? If your job brings you into contact with people in stressful situations, be aware that what you say and don't say and how you behave will make the situation better or worse. These interactions are significant to those who need help and support. An enlightening study demonstrated that patients who had been treated in a warm and sympathetic manner asked for half as much painkilling medication as another group. Also, those who had enjoyed a warm doctor-patient relationship were discharged from the hospital an average of 2.7 days sooner than others (Benson, 1987).

Be friendly and considerate. Congeniality and regard for others create a more positive work environment and usually bring rewards to the employee. The simple act of greeting may have an impact. Calling a person by name is an added positive behavior because it signifies that the person is important to you. If remembering names is difficult, you might want to try mental association. One of the easiest names for me to remember was that of a young man named John who had a punctuality problem. Associating him with "Johnny Come Lately" was a simple trick! Another technique is to repeat the person's name as often as you can. When introduced, say, "I'm happy to meet you, Bob." During the time you are together, call Bob by name as often as practical and use it again when you say good-bye. When you are new in a job, you will probably meet several people during a short period of time. In addition to repetition and association, you might write the names, check their names on a company list or directory, and rehearse them mentally. Don't be afraid to ask them to say their names for you again.

In addition to greetings, several other friendly, considerate gestures are possible. Ask questions about hobbies and vacation plans. Expressing interest in other people is

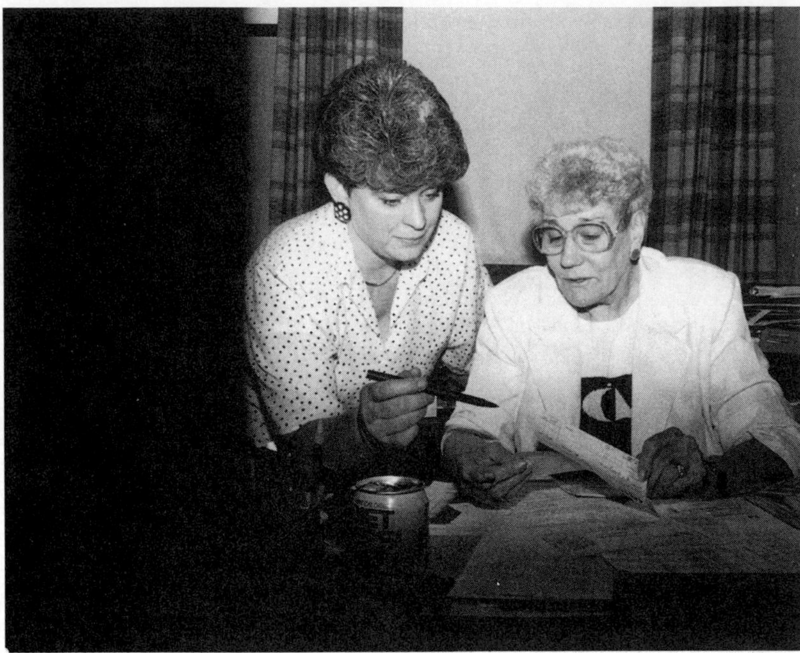

Figure 10-3 Positive relationships enhance the workplace.

affirming. Just be sure you don't go beyond what are sensible inquiries. Consideration means you will be careful to avoid irritating others. In a small office area that housed several desks, Jeff had his radio set on a loud rock-and-roll station. Four employees shared one phone extension, and Ruth spent several minutes at a time making personal calls. To make matters worse, she rarely answered the phone. Neither worker was considerate. Approachability checking, recommended in Chapter 9, is appreciated in the work environment. Because time is a valuable commodity, a considerate person does not assume that a co-worker or supervisor is available at all times. Instead, you can ask whether the person has time to spend with you.

As well as improving the work atmosphere, friendliness and consideration can pay off in tangible ways. Earnings for a waitress in California in 1978 topped $80,000. She was efficient; however, she earned large tips more for her friendly and considerate behaviors. She had a marvelous talent for remembering her customers' names, their favorite drinks and meals, and personal stories about them. She carried on lively conversations while serving in a seemingly effortless way. Not all employees are rewarded with tips; if you are, put your best foot forward! Even if you aren't, realize that positive customer relations, achieved in large part through friendliness and consideration will make you a valued employee.

Customer relations are considered the "bottom line" by business owners. Employees who turn customers away or even create negative impressions are usually fired. Being a positive salesperson or company representative isn't easy and requires determination, patience, and an understanding of human behavior. As an example, do you like to stand in line for service and then have another customer who just arrived be taken care of first? A sensitive employee would note who was there first or, if necessary, ask. As much as possible, the best employees avoid letting customers wait.

Other tips include treating the customer as if your roles were reversed, greeting individuals with a smile, listening attentively and actively to their request or complaint, handling complaints in an accommodating and cheerful manner, and asking whether your service was satisfactory. All this may sound difficult, and customer relations is definitely a challenge. Remember that you will be rewarded for your efforts. The reward may come not from others but from your own inner self saying, "Great job!"

Interactions with customers or clients may be face to face or handled on the telephone. Modern technology has created some devices that can be helpful yet can also diminish positive impressions. For example, do you recall being put on hold without even being asked whether you wanted to be? Effective telephone skills can be learned and deserve attention. No matter how or when a customer feels slighted or demeaned, the company or organization suffers. A young man named Dave at an eyeglass store made a particularly positive impression on me. After a cheerful, positive greeting, his response to my inquiry was, "I will need to check on that. Are you calling long distance?" I wasn't; however, I certainly appreciated his consideration and told him so. He continued to be friendly and most helpful. In contrast, a conversation with a legal secretary was disturbing. Her manner was brusque and defensive, and she sounded annoyed that any questions were being asked. Be aware of how you come across to any customer or client, keeping in mind that what is good for the business is beneficial to you!

Do your fair share as well as you can. In most jobs, you are part of a team, and your contribution is vital to the total effort. Lazy workers are looked down upon by co-workers and supervisors, and an inefficient team member sets up obstacles to the completion of a task. While you are at work, your responsibility is to the job at hand. Mary worked in a law office as a clerk and word-processing specialist. When the attorneys were gone, she used her time to read magazines and polish her fingernails. She was surprised when another employee told her how offensive her behavior was. Be sure not to cheat your employer and yourself in the long run by just getting by.

Be positive and realize the contributions of others. Employees with positive attitudes, as pointed out earlier in this book, are greatly appreciated. Seeing the bright side of a situation helps everyone. In every company or organization, some times are busier and more stressful than others. You may be tempted to think that your job is most demanding. Picture this scenario: Marv, Janet, and Kent are on their break in the cafeteria. Let's listen to their conversation.

KENT: I'm so busy I don't know heads from tails. All the quarterly reports I have to do are really getting to me.

MARV: Just be glad you don't have to fill all the orders that are coming in now. I probably won't even have time to take a break later.

JANET: You think you guys have it rough. If I have to field one more irate phone call, I think I'll find an easier job.

As they're busily trying to "one-up" each other, another employee walks by the cafeteria and thinks, "I don't see how those three have time to take a break. They must not have nearly as much work to do as I do!"

Did you recognize the "one-upping" comments? Realizing that you aren't the only one with a heavy load and acknowledging others' workloads would be a refreshing change from this scene. Receptive listening is as important at work as it is in other situations.

Manage conflict effectively. Despite your best attempts to create positive relationships, disagreement will occur. Knowing how to handle it will determine the lasting effects on a relationship. You have choices. In several situations, your best bet is to ignore the irritation. Most work environments have at least one annoying employee, and even those who aren't disagreeable will occasionally rub you the wrong way. Keep in mind that your behavior is not at the mercy of another person's. Nobody else can determine your actions. Using techniques to defuse your frustration and anger can turn potentially hostile situations into harmless ones.

At other times, avoiding an irritant isn't advisable. Your anger and frustration may be well spent in starting a process of conflict resolution (Strasser and Sena, 1992). Familiarize yourself with the "chain of command" in the business and know how it flows. Be honest and address legitimate concerns with your immediate supervisor first. Complaining without suggesting alternatives is not advised, although voicing a concern may be advantageous. Just be sure you aren't bringing too many problems to this person. If perceived mistreatment comes from a supervisor, you are wise to address it; however, don't let your anger control the situation. All that may be needed is an "I" statement describing your annoyance or the perception-checking technique that was explained in Chapter 8. The difference between what one person intended to mean and another's perception creates most of the problems in the work environment (Van Oosting, 1992). If criticized, using the suggested responses from Chapter 8 can keep the level of conflict manageable. The key is open communication. If more efforts are required, a negotiation strategy, as described in Chapter 9, can create a positive outcome.

Conflict-management techniques, discussed elsewhere in this book, can be applied to work situations. Of value are explanations and justifications that are sincere and adequate, delivered in a timely fashion (Sitkin and Bies, 1993). When Dan and Travis experienced conflict, they, along with their supervisor, discussed past incidents. Both employees explained their thinking, behaviors, and feelings and were able to understand each other. Understanding is more likely if people recognize personality differences. A chapter called "Conflict Resolution" in the book *Type Talk at Work* (Kroeger and Tuesen, 1992) is well worth your attention. According to the authors, different types define conflict differently and definitely address conflict management with diverse ideas and behaviors. No type excels at handling conflict; in fact, disagreeable situations can magnify our preferences and bring out the worst. I recall having to patiently explain to a strong ESTJ type that what she had said to a co-worker whose type was ESFP had indeed been insensitive. "Why would anyone be hurt by that?" she asked. Even after accepting that it could have hurt, she considered it a sign of weakness and illogical for her to apologize. The ESFP, in turn, had difficulty accepting that the lack of apology wasn't just a sign of dislike and rudeness.

The section in Chapter 9 on dealing with difficult people can also be helpful. What if the difficult person is your boss or supervisor? How to recognize, understand, and cope with a difficult boss is covered in the book *Coping with Difficult Bosses* (Bramson, 1992). By resolving problems as they arise, you could be benefiting not only yourself and the difficult boss but the business itself. "Difficult bosses reduce initiative and innovation and frequently start a selective emigration of valuable employees to more supportive work environments" (p. 3). Griping with fellow employees is not recommended as it can be hazardous. Asking yourself what does the person *do* that is bothersome, how have we acted, reacted, and interacted in the past, what are your specific goals or objectives, and what other people might need to be involved are suggested.

Then, deciding on an action plan is the next step. You are wise to weigh all you do using a cost versus benefits approach. If you determine after a reasonable period of time that your supervisor is intolerable and you have done all you can to improve the relationship, seek other employment possibilities.

Your degree of satisfaction on the job is greatly influenced by the quality of relationships. The time and effort you spend improving them are well worth it!

DEALING WITH BURNOUT

Ron, a computer analyst, groaned as the alarm clock sounded. He had slept poorly and had awakened with a throbbing in his head that he was sure would worsen as the day progressed. He was still recovering from a cold that had plagued him for weeks. He barely talked to his wife before she left for work, and he became increasingly depressed as he drove through the city to his office. He thought about the new program he was to develop and how he had postponed working on it. "I just can't concentrate," he said aloud. "I don't seem to have the ability I once had." Later at work, he responded abruptly to a co-worker's question and snapped at one of the secretaries. "What's wrong with me?" he asked himself.

Ron is the victim of *burnout*, a state of mental, emotional, social, and physical exhaustion characterized by a lack of interest and enthusiasm for one's job. Stress is the culprit. Burnout occurs when work loses its meaning, and stress is more prevalent than rewards. Unfortunately, people who need and want to feel useful and important are most likely to experience it (Leatz and Stolar, 1993). An imbalance between investments and outcomes plays a critical role in burnout, according to a study of 194 nurses (Yperen et al., 1992). Another study of health care providers pointed to inadequate communication among administration and staff, conflicts with and lack of support from co-workers, and unrealistic expectations from administration, patients, and other staff members as sources of burnout (Riordan and Saltzer, 1992).

Symptoms and Effects of Burnout

Signs of burnout are inflexible or indecisive points of view and a negative, defeatist attitude. People who are suffering from burnout begin to doubt their abilities and are quick to find fault in others. Emotionally, a burnout victim can feel depressed, helpless, hopeless, and frustrated; the physical effects include fatigue and lack of energy (Leatz and Stolar, 1993). Social exchanges are marked by irritability and hostility, or they may be almost nonexistent as burnout victims tend to isolate themselves.

An employee with burnout may be chronically late or miss work frequently, withdraw from others, and accomplish little. Sluggish is a good word to describe burnout victims like Ron. "Probably the first symptom most sufferers notice is a general malaise, an ennui with no apparent cause" (Leatz and Stolar, 1993, p. 117). In a study of teachers, burnout was related to emotional exhaustion and lack of personal accomplishment (Nagy and Nagy, 1992). A Swedish study contained an alarming statistic: workers with serious work-related problems and job stress were five times as likely to develop colon cancer (*Time*, 1993b).

Adverse effects reach beyond the work place. White-collar husbands under increased distress at work were less likely to respond with humor, enthusiasm, or

Figure 10-4

positiveness to wives or to attempts to bring humor into their lives. Both partners agreed that conversations were less intimate and enjoyable (Krokoff, 1991). Because burnout is so dreadful, preventing or remedying it becomes crucial.

Overcoming Burnout

Burnout can be prevented or alleviated by employing stress-management techniques on an everyday basis, yet sometimes burnout occurs despite one's best efforts to deal with stressors. Recognizing that you have symptoms of burnout and knowing that you can reverse your condition are essential. Ask yourself the following questions:

- Do I dread going to work more times than not?
- Am I more rigid than usual in my thinking?
- Am I thinking unrealistically about my job?
- Am I having difficulty making the types of decisions that were once relatively simple?
- Is my attitude less positive than normal?
- Do I doubt my work abilities and often feel defeated?
- Do I feel pessimistic about my career?
- Do I feel as if I am not in control of my life?
- Do I more often than usual feel depressed? Helpless? Hopeless? Frustrated? Annoyed?
- Am I more irritable than I usually am?

- Have I displayed more hostility than I usually do?
- Is my sense of humor less evident?
- Am I choosing to be alone more at work than usual?
- Do I feel less energetic?
- Am I tired more often than normal?
- Recently, have I had any of the following?

headache	nausea	gastric problems
backache	colds	complexion problems
change in eating habits	insomnia	muscle tension and aches

- Have I been late to work more frequently?
- Have I missed more work than usual?
- Is my productivity at work lower than normal?
- Do I feel less zest for life than I used to?

The more "yes" answers you gave, the more burnout is indicated. By the way, student burnout is also possible! In order to prevent serious burnout, be aware of any symptom when it first occurs and take steps to counteract it.

Seeing burnout as a surmountable challenge may be difficult while you are experiencing it. Your self-efficacy is important at this point, and realistic expectations of yourself are necessary. During a burnout period, lowering your expectations is a wise course. Rewarding yourself for any achievement is important. Positive self-talk, thought stopping, and cognitive restructuring, presented earlier, can be invaluable. Social support from supervisors is quite beneficial in lessening job-related tension (Houston et al., 1992). Another study showed that communication, increased participation in decision-making, and social support were related to reducing burnout (Miller et al., 1990). As with most problems, realizing that you are not alone in your thoughts and feelings can help.

Advocates of "mental health days" believe that staying away from work a day or so, when appropriate, is a way of preventing or overcoming burnout. Companies and organizations that realize the costs of employee stress have instituted types of personal leave for purposes such as this. Other businesses have attempted to introduce fun into the work environment (Abramis, 1989). Laughter, jokes, and joy are ways of reducing tension and making work more productive and creative and are beneficial in lowering burnout rates.

You are wise to understand that the root cause of burnout does not lie within the victim; the biggest cause is a dysfunctional work environment so an effective step is to seek changes in your present position or, if necessary, change jobs (Leatz and Stolar, 1993). Before you accept a position, find out the philosophy, attitudes, and policies of the workplace regarding stress-related concerns. Control over burnout is up to you.

SUMMARY

Human beings are typically identified by their career and job choices. The hours you spend at work will amount to a significant portion of your life. Career and job satisfaction have a tremendous impact, and thoughtful decisions influence the quality of life. Try not to limit your choices then begin your search by knowing yourself well.

Identify your interests, likes, abilities, values, personality, coping skills, and career and job orientations.

After career and job choices have been made, possessing the personal qualities and work habits desired by employers can ensure success. Experts have identified several characteristics of valued employees. Throughout your career you will have choices. Whether and how you prepare for the job search is one of the first ones. A well-prepared job seeker has a much better chance of landing a desired position. As you proceed along your career path, you will be faced with decisions about goals, advancement, making contacts and networking, continued education and training, leadership opportunities, specific challenges and concerns, career and job changes, and, eventually, retirement.

Opportunities to build relationships with co-workers, supervisors or bosses, subordinates, and customers, clients, or patients abound. Several behaviors can promote positive relations. Burnout, as the result of stress, can surface and create difficulties. You can be aware of the symptoms of burnout and learn ways to prevent or overcome it. As in all walks of life, if you know yourself well, have a high regard for yourself, demonstrate a positive attitude, gather information, use thought processing, are open and flexible, and can recognize and deal with adversity, you will direct your career path to success.

> *That which distinguishes the good teachers from the mediocre teachers is primarily not method, style, or personality-but attitude. They consistently project a positive attitude toward each student as an individual and toward the subject being taught. From such teachers, students intuitively receive the message: You are important, and it's important to me that you learn.*
>
> —Bob Resz

RESOURCES

Career planning centers and libraries at colleges and universities

Chambers of Commerce

Employee Assistance Programs

11

Developing and Enriching Intimate Relationships

OBJECTIVES

After completing this chapter, you will be able to

- Explain why love can be called an art.
- Recognize obstacles to love and addictive, compulsive behaviors.
- Name and contrast romantic and intimate love.
- Describe components and dimensions of intimate love.
- Explain the relationship growth and needs fulfillment theory, noting how it is related to intimate love.
- Identify barriers to intimacy.
- Discuss how androgyny can contribute to intimacy.
- Identify ideas for sexual fulfillment.
- Name and describe three different types of marriage.
- Tell how couples can prepare for marriage.
- Explain several factors related to marital success.
- Recognize marital myths.
- Describe positive conflict management.
- Define cohabitation and explain how it is used as well as how it can provide insight into future success.
- Discuss barriers to marriage enrichment and tell what couples can do to enhance their relationships.
- Realize that divorce occurs and explain how couples can end relationships in a way that will benefit both parties.
- List some possible benefits of divorce.

> *From "I" and "me" to "us" and "we." Your relationships will be as vital and alive as you are. I'm really convinced that if you were to define love, the only word big enough to engulf it would be "life." Love is life in all of its aspects. And if you miss love, you miss life. Please don't.*
>
> —Leo Buscaglia

"I love you" is a statement that is responsible for experiences of joy as well as despair. To love and be loved is desired by well-adjusted human beings. To achieve intimacy within a relationship is to realize the deepest meaning of love. How much do you know about love and intimacy? If you had little education in these areas, you're not alone. Intimacy has been either ignored or assumed to be so natural that thinking or talking about it was unnecessary. Or, it's been incorrectly defined as sexual relations. Consequently, most people have difficulty with their intimate relationships. This chapter will delve into love, intimacy, marriage, and divorce. You can use it as a springboard to education in what, for most people, are the most important aspects of their lives.

WHAT IS LOVE?

In writing, music, painting, and the performing arts, love is a major theme. "Love is one of the most intense and desirable of human emotions. People may lie, cheat, steal, and even kill in its name and wish to die when they lose it" (Sternberg, 1987, p. 3). In recent years, research has contributed to our understanding of love. Books and courses are available to help people make wise decisions about love and intimacy. Does studying love take away from a relationship? "This doesn't seem very romantic to me," grumbled a young woman when she was asked to answer questions about her love relationship. Regardless of one's perception of what is romantic, knowledge and understanding of love and intimacy build a strong foundation for a meaningful relationship.

Love is an art just as living is (Fromm, 1956). If you want to have a fulfilling love relationship, first, acquire information about what love is and then practice. "Learning to love doesn't just happen if we meet the right person. Feeling love may come naturally, but to be effective in an intimate relationship, loving feelings must go hand-in-hand with loving behavior. If we want to learn to love, we must proceed as if we want to learn a skill such as accounting, carpentry, typing, and so on" (Wegscheider-Cruse, 1988, p. 9).

Besides knowledge and practice, another necessary factor is priority. "The mastery of the art must be a matter of ultimate concern; there must be nothing more important than the art" (Fromm, 1956, p. 5). While reading Fromm's words, I shook my head. In 1956 when the book was published, I was "in love." I experienced love a few more times before marriage 6 years later. Did I ever read his book or, for that matter, study anything about love? Certainly not; I wasn't aware that I could be educated in this area, and, besides who needed it? "Love will conquer all," I thought along with thousands who believed that the sensation of love was enough.

"What is love?" is an important question. Because love varies from one culture to another, changes in meaning from one era to another, and even shifts within a single relationship as we and it mature (Nathanson, 1992), definitive answers may be impossible. However, we can identify obstacles, types of love, components of a loving relationship, and important elements of intimate love. Guidance in understanding love and intimacy is available.

OBSTACLES TO LOVE AND INTIMACY

Individuals can want to love and be loved and still fail miserably in the attempt. At times, they believe that they are in love, and the results are disappointing and painful. You can shift the odds in the favor of success if you know the potential obstacles.

Low Self-Esteem

The foundation for all love relationships is self-love. Human beings learn to love by being loved. The eloquent expressions of other writers concerning the relationship between self-esteem and healthy love for another can benefit anyone who desires a love relationship.

> A positive self-image, a sturdy self-esteem, and a love of self sets us free to love others (Viorst, 1986, p. 55).
>
> Learning to like and love yourself is the key to intimacy (Burns, 1985a).
>
> The first love affair we must consummate successfully is the love affair with ourselves. Only then are we ready for other relationships. Without respect for who I am and enjoyment in what I am, I have very little to give. If I do not feel that I am lovable, it is very difficult to believe that anyone else loves me. If I feel lovable as a human being, I have a surplus of life within me, an emotional "wealth" that I can channel into loving (Branden and Branden, 1982, p. 40).
>
> One who seeks in another the sense of worth one cannot find in oneself is likely to be disappointed. We cannot find salvation in a relationship (Sternberg, 1987, p. 275).

Why is low self-esteem detrimental to love relationships? First, people who don't value themselves tend to create relationships that don't succeed, thus diminishing self-worth even further. Deprived of self-acceptance, a person is more helpless in the grips of romantic love (Bell, 1991) and feels needy. "True intimacy eludes people who doubt their own worth" (Porat, 1988, p. 161).

Another problem is that those with low self-esteem generally find themselves paired with partners who also feel worthless, and intimacy is impossible. The tendency for people with low self-worth to devalue their partners is common. Elizabeth described low self-esteem problems as follows:

> My relationship with my ex-husband could easily be described as "walking on eggshells." I analyzed my thoughts before speaking and was not negative about anything (due to his low self-esteem). I felt my self-worth being dragged down to his level day to day. This is ironic considering he told me it was my optimism and strong sense of self that drew him to me. I finally realized I had to get out to save "me."

Finally, low self-esteem sets the stage for unhealthy behaviors, including manipulation, unfair fighting, extreme negative reactions to criticism, extended periods of silence, temper tantrums, and the withholding of sex. "Ultimately, people with low self-esteem feel unworthy of love. They believe that sooner or later, they will lose their lover. Because of their inordinate fear of rejection, they frequently bring about the very situation they dread. Their lives become self-fulfilling prophecies" (Porat, 1986, pp. 162–163).

In contrast, high self-esteem creates an attitude that you deserve the finest. This belief influences your behavior and the outcome. Mark confided: "I always said I could never live without her, but I have found that I can, and that bothers her. This class has helped me a lot because it has taught me that I deserve better than her." Margaret had a similar experience.

> I used to hate myself. I was told that I wasn't good enough, was stupid, and would never amount to anything. In 6 years my ex-husband gave me 27 fractures, killed my second baby in utero, and then started on my daughter when she was less than 2 years of age. In order for him to feel powerful, he would bring me down to his level or lower. Then a "feeling" came over me. It wasn't me who was all these things; it was him. I finally realized I was a worthwhile person. I loved and trusted myself enough not to need his sick love, and I sneaked out with baby in arms.

Both had learned an essential lesson—that they deserved more than they were receiving. You can eliminate a major barrier to a healthy love relationship by raising your self-esteem level and choosing a partner who values herself or himself.

Extensive Giving and Addiction

"If you love, you give and give and give" is a past belief which persists. "Sacrifice is what love is all about," is the resigned explanation of a 56-year-old woman who doesn't appear to be loved or loving. Love has even been equated with taking care of others as if that's all it is (Bepko and Krestan, 1990). Although the idea of love-giving was known by almost everyone in the past, women accepted and lived the sacrificial role more than men.

The past influences the present, and in spite of women's quest for equality and independence, the tendency among women is to give more than men do. A woman still tends to believe that if a relationship doesn't work, it's her fault and something is wrong with her (Bepko and Krestan, 1990). These thoughts are reflected in comments from young female students during the past few years.

> LISA: "I found myself constantly building him and reassuring him of my love at my expense."
>
> STACY: "The part of me that attracted him to me in the beginning I unknowingly gave up. That was ME, my personality, my independence, my self-security. I was, I thought, so much in love, and to show it, I tried to be everything I thought he wanted me to be. In doing so, I was no longer ME, the person he was attracted to."

In recent years, addictive and codependent relationships have been recognized, and the focus has been on women who give too much. Two reasons that women continue to love too much and give too freely have been suggested (Cowan and Kinder, 1987). One is the "marriage crunch"—a compelling pressure to find a man, marry, and have a family. The second, for married women, is the anxiety that the marriage may not last. Women who have these feelings often give too much in the belief that this will help them keep a man. Men, however, do not necessarily equate this endless giving to love and often grow to resent it. "When women give too much, men don't simply feel grateful; they feel suffocated" (Cowan and Kinder, 1987, p. 120).

An unhealthy type of love is characterized by either addiction or obsession. Characteristics of obsessive love are a painful, all-consuming preoccupation with another, insatiable longing, and self-defeating behaviors (Forward and Buck, 1991). Although the obsessed person may call their addiction "love," those who give too freely may not be loving at all. Instead, excessive giving may be a disguised way of satisfying deeper needs such as insecurity stemming from unresolved childhood conflicts (Cowan and Kinder, 1987). "Obsessive love has little to do with love at all; it has to do with longing. Longing is wanting something you don't have" (Forward and Buck, 1991, p. 9). One of the greatest stress producers is the feeling of subservience and lack of control (Podell, 1992) both of which are found in obsessive love.

Giving too much and being a victim in an obsessive relationship are characteristic of codependency (discussed in Chapter 9). In a case that captured the headlines for weeks, the combination of low self-esteem, love addiction, and giving too much contributed to a tragedy. New York attorney Joel Steinberg killed his illegally adopted daughter Lisa, a first-grader. Her adoptive mother, Hedda Nussbaum, was a classic case of a love-addicted woman who allowed herself and her children to be regularly beaten. She wrote on her office stationery:

> I must have Joel's love and approval to survive. I'm worthless and helpless. I don't want to take care of anyone else. I want to be taken care of. I don't want to take the responsibility for really living. I want someone to do it for me. I don't want to take the responsibility for dying, but maybe if I'm lucky, I'll get hit by a truck. I'm hopeless (Brownmiller, 1989, p. 59).

Relationships that are based on these misconceptions of love take their toll. The deadly signs of what has been called a toxic relationship (Braiker, 1992) are: helplessness, frustration, anxiety, hostility, cynicism, hopelessness, and loss of self-esteem. In addition to psychological costs, a pressing concern in the American society is physical and verbal abuse, both of which are found in addictive and obsessive relationships. The O.J. Simpson case in 1994 monopolized the media and is a tragic example of ugly behaviors in the name of love.

Verbal aggression, defined as verbal or nonverbal communication intended to cause psychological pain to another person or perceived as having that intent, was delivered in about equal amounts by both women and men in a study of 5232 American couples (Straus and Sweet, 1992). Even though obsessive love was not identified as a causal factor, those who tolerate long-term verbal abuse probably do so because of misconceptions about love. Usually, the following are present in a relationship characterized by verbal abuse: inequality, competition, manipulation, hostility, control, and negation (Evans, 1992). These also describe an obsessive love relationship. Until obsession and addiction are no longer considered love, this horrible trend will continue. The challenge is for both women and men to recognize the difference and to resist behaviors that spawn these unhealthy relationships.

A common question is why would anyone remain in an abusive relationship? The answers are not simple. Some experts believe that women can suffer from what is called *battered woman syndrome*, a type of posttraumatic stress disorder. Women who suffer from this typically put the man's needs before their own, behave passively in the face of physical and verbal harm, and act in a dependent manner. Many who were abused as children are almost stricken with fear in their present relationships (Walker, 1991; Young and Gerson, 1991). Debra described her experience as follows:

> I gave, and he took. I became his "mother," someone to take care of him and solve his problems. I thought that was what love truly meant, that I would only be important if I was needed by and doing for someone else. My needs or wants never entered my

> mind. I just plain did not exist. He didn't want me to work, and he "hit on" every female I brought to the house so I stopped associating with my friends. I didn't trust him to care for the boys for even an hour on his own so I stayed home. He kept me where he wanted me, and I let him. I despised the fact that even when he hurt me to the point I couldn't see because my eyes were swollen shut or couldn't talk because my jaw was broken, I still didn't have enough courage to move out. It seems now that I never blamed him—only me—which was fine with him. He got fired from one of many jobs, slammed me against a wall, and I packed his bags. He left, and later the hospital called. He had tried to kill himself. I remember going to see him, and the first words I spoke were, "What have *I* done?" I let Debra be destroyed.

Fortunately, Debra became strong enough to leave, return to school, and begin a new life.

Attention usually focuses on women's recognition and avoidance of addictive behaviors. However, men can change the pronoun and also answer the following questions (Forward and Torres, 1986, p. 10):

- Does he assume the right to control how you live and behave?
- Have you given up important activities or people in your life in order to keep him happy?
- Does he devalue your opinions, your feelings, and your accomplishments?
- Does he yell, threaten, or withdraw into angry silence when you displease him?
- Do you "walk on eggs," rehearsing what you will say so as not to set him off?
- Does he bewilder you by switching from charm to rage without warning?
- Do you often feel confused, off-balance, or inadequate?
- Is he extremely jealous and possessive?
- Does he blame you for everything that goes wrong in the relationship?

If you answered yes to any of these questions, analyze the relationship carefully. If you answered yes to most of the questions, you are in an unhealthy relationship. Sadly, people often harbor the misguided belief that the other will change which usually doesn't happen.

Trying to love someone else before you have yourself in tune is as potentially disastrous as beginning a long journey in a poorly equipped, rundown automobile. Healthy relationships include high self-esteem and lack of dependency and addiction. Unless you are completely committed to making your own life work, you can't be positively committed to a relationship (Ellsworth, 1988). When Chad described a past relationship, I exclaimed, "Maybe this will help obsessive love victims to realize the common outcome."

> I ended a relationship because she wasn't independent at all. She couldn't make decisions without my advice. She would sit home waiting for me to call while I went out with my friends. She just put her friends out of the picture. Then when I called, she tried to make me feel guilty for having fun without her. She complained that we didn't spend enough time together. She also called me at all hours of the night because she said she just wanted to hear my voice. I wanted to get some sleep! If she hadn't been so obsessive, things might have worked out.

He wrote about his needs in any future relationship: "She must be able to live for herself and not become a person who lives for me. I don't want a person who thinks the world revolves around me."

Fear of Risks

Any relationship is risky. Love and commitment entail even more risks because individuals invest more of themselves. In love relationships, deep self-disclosure leaves a person vulnerable. Fear of exposing the self can either prevent loving altogether or interfere with honest expression within the relationship.

Pain is inevitable in relationships, and accepting this reality is healthy. In positive relationships the benefits of loving and being loved will far outweigh the pain, and knowing this makes the risk acceptable. Without risk, individuals reduce their hurts, yet they also decrease potential for happiness. I could decide to stay indoors for the rest of my life because there are risks of getting hurt outside. Wouldn't you question this decision? Resisting a potentially happy relationship because of the possibility of hurt is equally debatable. Instead, you can learn from past hurt thereby limiting the risks.

Risks of pain are less if you keep self-esteem independent of the relationship. "When our sense of worth—whether we feel lovable or not—depends on the response of some other person to us, we are off balance. We can do nothing but fall" (Kennedy, 1975, p. 94). With self-love, you can separate the ending of a relationship from a rejection of self. The idea that you are unlovable because someone no longer wants to continue a love relationship with you is false. When you refuse to accept this fallacy, the risk of rejection is no longer an obstacle.

Lack of Knowledge

Despite all that's been expressed about love, human beings are woefully ignorant. The assumption that you don't need to know about love, that "it just happens" and then all is well, has pervaded people's thinking. "An individual can get a college degree today without ever having learned anything about how to communicate, how to resolve conflict, and what to do with anger and other negative feelings. Basic, to my mind, is the need for learning to be partners" (Rogers, 1972, p. 216).

Only in recent years have researchers studied love. Difficulty in defining the term was one of the obstacles. "Love is a difficult construct to operationalize; there are almost as many definitions of love as people willing to research it" (Coleman and Ganong, 1985, p. 174). Defining love in terms of behaviors rather than just feelings increased the number of studies. Yet, most people are unaware of research findings. Until education about love and intimacy is emphasized (which could even mean required training), many people will flounder. On the basis of their perceptions of love, they will build weak, unhealthy relationships. Instead, individuals can seek education on their own and then practice what they learn.

Internal barriers can prevent the development of healthy love. The key is to realize that love is obstructed by low self-esteem, giving too much and other obsessive, addictive behaviors, fear of risks, and lack of knowledge. Then you can remove these obstacles and proceed in the development of a loving relationship.

TYPES OF LOVE

Love comes in variations. Types can be distinguished, as can variants within each type. Keeping love as simple as possible, we will focus on two general types: romantic love and intimate love. Realize that other researchers and writers may use different words in describing types such as mature love and immature love (not referring to the age of the lovers) used by Gordon (1988b). "Mature love is energizing; immature love is exhausting" (p. 30).

Romantic Love

The sensations and all the romantic notions of love are at the heart of romantic love, or what Gordon (1988b) calls immature love. Human beings at early ages become aware of this type and then define love in terms of sensations: "Love is the feeling of being swept off your feet." "Love is when your heart pounds hard, and you just can't take your eyes off the person." "Love is feeling all mushy inside." "I love him or her so much I think my heart will burst." "I'm so in love I could just die." Is this love? The individuals sound slightly paralyzed and almost unable to function (Gordon, 1988b).

Do you remember the image of love in fairy tales? Love is an overpowering force between an attractive man and woman. He is bold, fearless, and capable of overcoming any obstacle to win her. She is frail, helpless, and simpering and, of course, extremely beautiful. He rescues her, and together they go forth to live happily ever after. Most of us grow up believing in the magic of 'chemistry' between lovers. Love feels exquisite and beyond our control (Cowan and Kinder, 1987).

Although the media and literature today do express more realistic versions of love relationships, cultural sources including novelists, poets, songwriters, and movie and television producers still portray myths and unrealistic pictures of love (Nathanson, 1992). Even products use an image of love to entice consumers. Obsession and other aspects of romantic love are packaged as perfumes and sexy lingerie. Compared to obsession, all other love seems humdrum and mundane while romanticized versions appear sultry, seductive, and the ultimate in emotionality and sensuality (Forward and Buck, 1991).

A few years ago a publishing company sent me guidelines for writing a novel. In order for it to be acceptable, the editor wrote: "The author must create a heartwarming and exciting love story. The writer's job is to get the heroine and hero together, keep them together, make sparks fly, put obstacles in the path of true love, and finally resolve the complications on a high note with a satisfying ending." The guide provided a description of characters as being quite attractive and close to ideal, including a "Mr. Right" who had to be successful in whatever he did. Plenty of sensuous description was to be a part of the novel, and most vital was that sexual attraction to the hero must be recognized early on and should be drawn out to maximum effect. In short, the piece of fiction would be a twentieth-century fairy tale. (Incidentally, I chose to write this book instead!)

Love in the American society was examined by a Hungarian researcher (Kovecses, 1991). What he did was analyze the meaning of love just from the language, and he has some interesting points. Here are some of his definitions of love based on the descriptive statements following them.

- Love means increase in body heat. "I felt hot all over when I saw her." "You really have the hots for her."
- Love means increase in heart rate. "She makes my heart race."
- Dizziness is love. "I get dizzy when I think of him."
- Love is inability to breathe. "You take my breath away."
- Love means inability to think. "He can't think straight when he's around her."

- Desire for physical closeness is love. "Don't ever let me go. I want to hold you in my arms forever."
- Sex and love are the same. "They made love."
- When in love, vision is affected. "She's starry eyed." "He can't take his eyes off her."

It's easy to see why someone from another society would be quite confused about the American version of love.

TABLE 11-1 Romantic Love Descriptors

Survival
"I can't live without you."
"I'm nothing without you."
"I just can't get enough of you."
"If you ever leave me, I'll die."
Physical sensations
Walking on air or clouds
Palpitating heart, shortness of breath
Weak knees, dizziness
Can't eat, sleep, think
Passionate, lustful with a pure sexual emphasis
"I just melt when you look at me."
"I know it's love because of the way he kisses me."
Perfection
"No one has ever loved like this before."
"It's perfect. You're perfect."
"I want to look and be my best for you."
"Nothing will ever go wrong."
Exaggerated promises
"Love conquers all."
"I don't need anyone or anything else."
"I'd do anything for you."
"We'll always be happy (and won't have to even work on it)."
"I'll never look at another man (or woman)."
Exclusivity and possessiveness
"You're the only one for me."
"You're mine."
"You belong to me, and I belong to you."
"I'm jealous and you're jealous, and that means we're in love."
"I don't need anything or anyone else."
"Just the two of us. Nothing else matters."

Descriptors of romantic love. If you were to write an all-consuming romantic novel, what images of love would you present? Hundreds of students have contributed to class discussion their descriptors of romantic love, or what I call "fluff stuff." Among the most clever ones: "I thought it was going to be an everlasting tingle." "It happens instantly in a flash like a Certs encounter." "Love feels zingy, and you get dingy." The responses are grouped into categories (Table 11–1).

One way to know that these notions are still promoted is to pay attention to music lyrics. Songs from decades ago were full of messages such as, "You belong to me" or "Our love is here to stay." "Smoke Gets in Your Eyes" is a song that equates love to a feeling of not being able to see or think clearly. Popular songs today still express an idealized, unrealistic version of love. And just listen to expressive individuals in the throes of infatuation: "It's a real high." "I feel like I'm on cloud nine."

Dilemmas of romantic love. So what is the matter with romantic love? The body, in fact, is producing chemicals that contribute to the physical sensations. However, intense sensations aren't enough. Sadly, a song from the past tells us, "Love and marriage go together like a horse and carriage," and individuals with mistaken notions of love do get married in the heat of their passion. "Falling in love is like a space launch, full of flame and fire. Getting married in the fire and flame of the blast-off stage of the relationship is extremely dangerous" (Crowther, 1986, p. 123). Typical dilemmas of romantic love are loving the feeling of being in love more than you do the other person and allowing passions to become destructive.

> Mostly love just makes people act silly, but sometimes the afflicted turn violent. Lovers have been known to kill those they love, particularly if the object of their affection is not similarly stricken. If it doesn't work, they either kill themselves or look for another victim (Chance, 1988b, p. 22).

Romantic love is not conducive to long-term individual happiness. Being responsible and in control of yourself are hallmarks of well-being. In contrast, romantic love means giving control to the other person. "Ernie always *makes me feel* terribly alone," wrote a 53-year-old student. "He wants to get married, so he *causes me to feel* so guilty when I say not now." Love that puts someone else in the "driver's seat" has unhappy prospects. "Head over heels is an uncomfortable position for human beings" (Chance, 1988b, p. 22).

Lovers become disillusioned when they finally realize that this type of love doesn't last. Women who fall in love tend to impute almost magical qualities to the object of their adoration (Cowan and Kinder, 1987) as is often the case with men. When reality sets in, lovers are then disappointed.

> No matter whom we fall in love with, we sooner or later fall out of love if the relationship continues long enough. This is not to say that we invariably cease loving the person . . . but it is to say that the feeling of ecstatic lovingness that characterizes the experience of falling in love always passes. The honeymoon always ends. The bloom of romance always fades (Peck, 1978, pp. 84–85).

This may sound depressing, yet it doesn't have to be. Most experts believe that the end of the "falling-in-love period" signals the start of a realistic stage when true love can develop. "You can certainly form a good relationship in spite of your romantic feel-

Figure 11-1

ings—but rarely because of them. The most that romance can do is to draw two people together initially, but these feelings tend not to last, and they don't guarantee a satisfying long-term relationship" (Burns, 1985a, p. 182).

Do you remember when you bought your first new car? Can you recall the thrill and joy you experienced driving or just looking at it? Later, you still enjoyed the car, yet in a different way. The newness wore off, so you didn't feel the same "high." The car was familiar, and you felt comfortable and secure with it. Your feelings, including pride, were deep and sure. This experience is similar to the evolution of long-term relationships. The glow is still there; however, it's a different, deeper glow.

Jealousy: a major challenge. Common to romantic love is jealous behavior. "Obsessive love is dominated by fear, possessiveness, and jealousy. Obsessive love is volatile and sometimes even dangerous. Ultimately, it never satisfies, it never nourishes, and it rarely feels good" (Forward and Buck, 1991, p. 9). *Jealousy* is a combination of emotions, thoughts, and actions that follow loss of or threat to self-esteem or the existence or quality of a romantic relationship (White, 1991). Emotionally, jealousy is generally a blend of fear, anger, and sadness (Hansen, 1991; Sharpsteen, 1991). Insecurity and hurt can also be involved (Parrott, 1991). Jealousy includes a triangle made up of a jealous person, a partner, and a rival (Parrott, 1991). The word stems from the Greek word jeal, which suggests that a valued possession is in danger and that some action must be taken (Buscaglia, 1984).

Jealous thoughts are influenced by culture (Salovey and Rothman, 1991). Interestingly, jealousy is considered more acceptable in romantic relationships than in friendships because relationship rules call for interdependence for friends and exclusivity for lovers. Also, because friends perceive its expression to be inappropriate, they express it less (Aune and Comstock, 1991). Related to jealousy is a person's sex; men rated higher on a jealousy scale in one study (Mathes, 1991). In another study in 5 different countries jealous men were higher on aggression while women had higher emotional reactions and more displays of feelings (Bryson, 1991).

Jealousy may be associated with sexual orientation in that homosexuals showed less jealousy than heterosexuals (Hawkins, 1990). Higher levels of prestige and attractiveness of a perceived rival led to increased jealousy (McIntosh and Tate, 1990). The intensity may be more when the other appears to be better or has characteristics we lack (Salovey and Rothman, 1991). All cases of jealousy involve insecurity about self and the relationship.

Possessiveness flames the fires of jealousy. "You are mine, and I am yours," a part of romantic-love thinking, usually leads to: "Because you are mine, you will do what I want you to do." This can mean not even looking at another attractive person. Remember the nursery rhyme character "Peter Peter Pumpkin-Eater," who put his wife into a pumpkin shell? In extreme forms of possessiveness, a lover may insist that the other not pursue any outside interests. Violence and abuse are common outcomes of possessiveness. "Absolute control over another person is neither possible, desirable, nor loving. Instead it destroys what it sets out to protect" (Buscaglia, 1992, p. 142).

Does love mean ownership of your lover? Hopefully, you can answer with no. "A love that inhibits is not love. Love is only love when it liberates" (Buscaglia, 1992, p. 100). Are your expectations unrealistic? It is silly to expect a partner to become blind to others and to react angrily if a "third party" admires one's lover. An affirmative response to a mate finding others attractive is, "I don't mind at all that Bob notices other women. In fact, realizing that he does and still prefers me is a great feeling." What Buscaglia (1984) writes is also healthy: "What a grand feeling to have a relationship with someone who is loved not only by you, but by many. That means you've made a good choice" (p. 164).

In addition to damaging a relationship, jealous feelings and behaviors have the potential to end it. "Jealousy is sometimes the surest way to get rid of the very person you are afraid of losing" (Bloomfield and Felder, 1985, p. 47). Jackie was irrationally jealous of her fiancé, Troy. She couldn't bear his talking to other women, especially when they were apart. Because Troy's job brought him into contact with both sexes, jealousy became a major problem. Jackie nagged, yelled, and cried and became suspicious and clinging. Troy's love for her declined. He felt stifled, and the intensity of their conflicts became unbearable. Eventually, he broke their engagement. "All I did was love you so much!" cried Jackie, not acknowledging that she had done far more than that. "Love is not expressed by strangulation" (Branden and Branden, 1982, p. 127).

Recognizing the presence of jealousy is the first step in controlling it. Some people are "trait jealous," in that they are chronically jealous (Mathes, 1991). Low self-esteem is usually the culprit in these cases. Individuals with high self-esteem, an inner locus of control, and less involvement in, yet more satisfied with, the relationship are generally less jealous and handle it more effectively. *Self-actualizing persons* report less jealousy (Hawkins, 1990) probably because love and self-esteem needs have been met. So raising self-esteem and reducing dependent attitudes make jealousy less likely.

In any relationship, occasional twinges of jealousy can be experienced without damage. These usually occur when, for some reason, the relationship doesn't feel secure or, perhaps, you are suffering from a feeling of insecurity. What can you do then? Analyzing your emotions by recognizing the underlying thoughts is helpful because jealousy is related to cognitive appraisals and the meaning attached to an incident. For example, your partner is dancing with an attractive person. Instead of letting jealousy take over, examine your thoughts. If you feel jealous, you are thinking: "She or he prefers that person to me," "This is a threat to our relationship." Then, use rational-emotive-therapy to change irrational thoughts.

Even though suppressing jealous feelings based on rational thoughts isn't recommended, avoiding annoying and negative behaviors such as pouting, nagging, threatening, and clinging is wise. Although most people don't like to feel jealous, denying it can allow it to cause damage. Much like stress, whether or not you acknowledge its presence, jealousy can wreak havoc on you and the relationship. Instead, expressing yourself by means of the awareness wheel helps the other person understand your perspective. You will find that your jealousy is warranted in some cases and at other times is unfounded. If the relationship is healthy, your partner will understand and help eliminate the reasons for the jealousy.

Jealousy can actually have a positive outcome (Bringle, 1991). It can be used to stabilize or change a relationship (White, 1991) and to clarify personal differences in expectations (Mathes, 1991). When your thoughts are reasonable and your jealousy is legitimate, different coping options are possible. First, through communication you can suggest changes in your partner's behaviors. Two other choices are to change your perception of the person's behaviors or change your perception of the value of the relationship. Finally, you can decide to end the relationship. Usually, jealousy lessens as two people become more mature in their relationship. Creating the kind of relationship in which jealousy will have a low survival rate is well worth the effort.

> Everyone who cares and loves feels jealous at one time or another. The essential decision is whether you will allow your jealousy to become an all-consuming monster, capable of destroying you and those you love, or become a challenge for you to grow in self-respect and personal knowledge. The challenge will rest with you (Buscaglia, 1984, p. 129).

Intimate Love

Unlike the "fluff stuff" of romantic love, intimate love is a total experience and the foundation of a long term, mutually satisfying relationship. "Love is a process, not just a feeling, of discovery, of development, of growing together" (Solomon, 1988, p. 82). Intimate love consists of feelings, thoughts, and behaviors with the behavioral aspects being significant indicators. Saying "I love you" and experiencing the sensations are meaningless without actions. Love encompasses attitudes and behaviors such as responsibility, respect, knowledge, giving, and caring. "Love is an activity, not a 'passive affect'; it is a 'standing in,' not a 'falling for.' Love is the active concern for the life and the growth of that which we love" (Fromm, 1956, pp. 22, 26). True love doesn't happen to you; you make it happen (Katz and Aimee, 1988).

The adult ego state is necessary in intimate love. One of its roles is to assess the parent and child ego states. The "adult" encourages the nourishing, loving feelings, the spontaneous delight, and the playful behaviors from the child ego state. It rejects unwise "parent" messages of "You can't be happy unless you have someone," "As a woman, you should cater to the man," or "A real man doesn't let another man approach his woman" and accepts those that suggest a wait-and-see and look-before-you-leap attitude. The "adult's" most important role is in considering all factors related to successful rela-

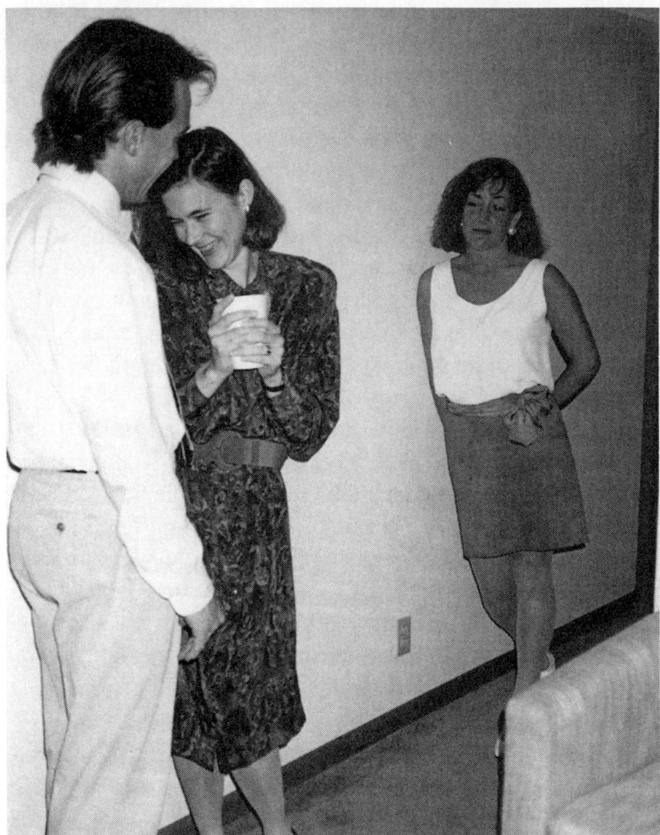

Figure 11-2 Jealousy isn't a friend to intimate relationships

tionships. It collects data and makes decisions that affect the happiness and well-being of individuals within love relationships.

Intimate love has been studied, and researchers have identified components and factors that contribute to success. You can use these findings to help determine whether what you are experiencing is intimate love. Focusing on behaviors is a good way to assess the quality of the relationship.

Rubin's components of love. Believing that social psychologists had neglected the study of love, Rubin (1970) developed a scale to measure liking and loving. He was focusing on love between unmarried opposite-sex peers that could possibly lead to marriage. The scale featured three components of love: attachment, caring, and intimacy (Rubin, 1973, 1985).

Attachment has to do with the desire for the physical presence and emotional support of the other person. It can be expanded to include a general preference for each other's company. In contrast to the stifling total togetherness of romantic love, healthy attachment means enjoyment and involvement in mutually rewarding activities. Enjoying being with each other is the glue that bonds a couple. Connie, after her divorce, insightfully commented: "A clue I didn't recognize was that Dan and I didn't enjoy activities apart from others. We always double-dated, and after we were married, our social life included other couples. The two of us didn't have fun just being together."

In a marriage-preparation class, a lack of attachment was apparent. A young woman enrolled in the class alone even though she was engaged. Her fiancé bowled on the nights of class. After a discussion of Rubin's components, she said, "I wonder about that. He isn't here tonight because of bowling, last night was Monday night football, on Wednesday nights he shoots pool, Thursday and Saturday nights he goes out with his friends. We're together on Friday nights and usually on Sunday when he isn't at a drag race." After I expressed my concern, she remarked, "Well, that's one reason I want to get married. Either he'll change, or at least I'll have more leverage to nag him about it." My expression, I'm sure, was of doubt. I encouraged her to talk with her fiancé about this. I didn't find out what he said because she didn't come to class again. I hoped she had decided to wait; however, she probably just didn't want to hear reasons to be concerned. Not facing potential problems is another facet of romantic love.

The second component, *caring*, consists of feelings of concern and responsibility for another's welfare. Caring is seen as both the source and the result of other behaviors. Tenderness, which includes awareness of the other's needs and desires (May, 1969), is related to caring. Empathy, discussed earlier, is of utmost importance if one is to care. Since caring is concern, you will share stressors and experience anxiety because you love. Caring is a basic bond of love (Solomon, 1988).

Irrational possessiveness is the enemy of caring. Consider these examples:

> Patti was excited when her friend asked her to come to work in a new business. She could finally pursue a career that she had given up 4 years ago. Her husband, Todd, said, "You aren't going to work. The kids and I need you at home."
>
> Ken received word that his scholarship request had been approved. Although it would mean sacrificing, this was his chance to complete his degree. Sally, his fiancé, protested, "I won't see you much if you have to study and work. And you won't earn as much, so we won't be able to get married as soon."

How caring were Todd and Sally? For whom did they care? Genuine concern means that you consider another's welfare. Blocking personal growth is uncaring behavior. Warm, caring behavior is like unconditional positive regard (Rogers, 1961), not the "I'll love you if . . ." ingredient of romantic love.

Intimacy, the third component, is a desire for confidential, close communication. Rubin's concept of intimacy reflects sharing and disclosing on all levels. This makes a love relationship resemble a deep friendship. Without intimacy, two people don't truly connect. The term "emotionally divorced" is often used to describe marriages lacking in intimacy. Vulnerability is necessary for intimacy, and individuals often fear the risk. I remember Teresa Adams, therapist and author, saying, "The crowd thins when it comes to intimacy." This component deserves to be developed and treasured and is discussed in a later section.

Sternberg's love triangle. Picture a triangle with three equal sides of balanced love composed of emotion, thought, and motivation. Based on his research, Sternberg identified three active ingredients of love: intimacy, commitment, and passion (1987).

Intimacy is the emotional part of love and includes closeness, sharing, communication, and support. *Commitment* indicates thinking because individuals decide to maintain a relationship. As a behavior, commitment is expressed in faithfulness to each other. *Passion* is the motivational side which leads to physiological arousal and an intense desire to be united with the loved one. Unlike intimacy, passion generally develops quickly. Interestingly, relationships can have one, two, or all three of the components.

One component:

Intimacy: Have you had an opposite-sex friendship? If you like a person of the opposite sex, and communication and support are present, the relationship is liking. Liking is often long term.

Passion: Have you experienced a strong physical attraction to another? If only sexual desire is present, the relationship is infatuation, is usually all-consuming, and fades quickly.

Commitment: Do you know anyone who is in a long-term relationship that seems to have nothing else except its longevity? Empty love, the name given for this, is seen in marriages that have endured just because neither person left.

In discussing the three, Sternberg emphasized that passion and intimacy tend to interact strongly and often fuel each other. He doesn't limit passion to sexual desire as he believes that any psycho-physiological arousal can generate passion. Commitment can be short-term meaning a commitment to love or long-term which is a commitment to maintaining that love.

All three present in a relationship is called *consummate* love and, according to Sternberg, is ideal. Two people have a strong attraction and sexual desire for each other; they are close, communicative, and supportive; and, because of a strong mutual commitment, the relationship is of high priority. Considering these ingredients, do you recognize any of your relationships? Sternberg, who has also researched intelligence, urges people to emphasize relationship intelligence (R.I.) as much as academic institutions do intelligence (Sternberg and Whitney, 1991).

Examine any love relationship in terms of the various elements from both Rubin's and Sternberg's research. If some dimensions you want are missing, express this to your partner. The more open you can be about love, the greater the possibility of achieving a satisfying relationship. Even with all the components present, love can be strengthened by paying attention to other factors.

Relationship growth and fulfillment of needs. Healthy individuals grow in a positive direction. So do healthy relationships. Individual and relationship growth are associated. If individual growth is stunted, so is the relationship. In order for growth to be positive, individuals have to be free to achieve their potential. Ultimately, putting one partner into a pumpkin shell stifles the relationship. When two people are committed to their own and each other's positive growth, wonderful things can happen. Each experiences satisfaction in life, and the relationship is vitalized. Conversely, a person who is deprived of growth has little, or nothing, to offer the relationship except frustration.

> Woe be it unto you if you give yourself totally to another. You're lost forever. Maintain yourself as the others maintain themselves. Then you put "They" together and form "Us." Then work on that "Us," and that "Us" gets bigger and bigger while the "You" and the "I" get bigger and bigger and form these enormous concentric circles that grow forever! And if, by chance, you lose that special "Us"—you still have an "I" and loving memories to build with (Buscaglia, 1982, p. 162).

Intimate love will reflect a balance between partners as individuals and as a unified couple (Katz and Aimee, 1988).

A possible area of concern is the course of individual growth. Individuals can grow, contribute to the relationship, and become closer to each other. Or, they can grow apart. A reason why teenage marriages fail at higher rates could be the tremendous surge of individual growth that takes place between adolescence and the late twenties or thirties. "Individual change and stretching have effects so be aware!" (Kinder and Cowan, 1989, p. 57). Couples who do not experience harmonious growth often find themselves worlds apart after a number of years. Being mindful that change will occur and taking care to direct the course of growth is the key. Love flourishes in an environment of positive growth. When you choose to commit to a relationship, be sure she or he is one with whom you can *live and grow*.

Based on social-exchange theory, which was covered in Chapter 9, love can be examined in terms of *fulfillment of needs*. A major function of any relationship is to satisfy individual needs. In fact, a predictor of happiness has to do with the degree of difference between what you want and what you think you are getting from a relationship (Sternberg and Whitney, 1991). One relationship cannot fulfill all of your needs. However, a love relationship, especially one that leads to marriage, is primary and must satisfy a number of important ones. "Having your emotional needs met is one of the most important payoffs your relationship can provide" (Braiker, 1992, p. 192). If you know yourself well, then you know what you need from a relationship. Think about some of these:

Need for human companionship
Need for stimulation and excitement
Need to feel valued, cared for, and nurtured
Need for sexual fulfillment
Need for emotional support
Need for self-awareness and discovery
Need to experience yourself fully and to enjoy life (Branden and Branden, 1982).

Other needs might be: equality, partnership, mutuality, good will, intimacy, validation, loyalty, fidelity, shared dreams, companionship, tenderness, and sexuality. A specific one identified by a single parent in one of my classes was the need to have a relationship in which the partner would also be a caring stepparent for her children.

After identifying your needs, you are ready for the next step. Deborah has needs for deep communication, demonstrated affection, and honesty. Can you see what would likely happen if Deborah feels a strong attraction that she calls love for Kurt, who is honest, extremely quiet, and emotionally inexpressive? People who know him describe him as somewhat reclusive and cold.

Strange as it may seem, people often fall in love with those who would have difficulty satisfying important needs. "Silent Sam or Sally" won't likely turn into a great communicator overnight. "Boring Bill or Billie" isn't apt to be much fun, and people who are "cold fish" won't find it easy to be affectionate. Some find out in time as Andrea did: "He showed little caring and didn't share with me. I did 95 percent of the caring. He was jealous and showed it in strange ways. I have learned in this class that I'm glad I got out of it and that there is still hope for me."

Fulfillment of needs requires that you match your needs with a partner who can satisfy them because it is that person who gives to the relationship what you need (see

Fig. 11–3). "It's almost like writing a job description," I explained to my class one day. The true "romantics" cringed. I hastened to add that relationships have a better chance of remaining romantic if individuals aren't frustrated by unfulfilled needs. The needs fulfillment activity at the end of this book can be used for mate selection, premarital assessment, and enrichment of marriages. One student commented that she and her husband loved each other very much; however, the activity had shown her how to make their relationship stronger and even more fulfilling. Ron, a middle-aged man, descriptively identified two of his as follows:

Support: I need cheer when I'm down, encouragement when I'm doubtful, befriending when I'm engulfed with self-doubt, and chastisement when I stray from my ideals. The "someone" will be self-reliant and think my ideas are worthy, my path has worth, and who will walk the path with me.

Insight, wisdom: I need knowledge from having been down the road and over the mountain, forgiveness, perspective. The "someone" will be open-minded, have had experience in life yet has not become embittered. She will have been hurt and learned to forgive. She will know that we each are sometimes glorious, warm, and compassionate and sometimes mean-spirited, self-centered, and thoughtless. She will have done some hard traveling and still be trucking on.

Notice that his behaviorally based words leave little, or no, doubt what he wants. The key is to communicate personal needs to each other keeping in mind that the two lists most likely won't be exactly the same.

> Imagine yourself as a plant in need of sun and water. Your partner gives you lots of sun, and you love the wonderfully warm feelings that you get, but he or she offers you little water. Although you can get water from other sources, this relationship limits you because it lacks a vital nutrient. You do not feel loved and understandably do not feel loving toward your partner nor appreciative of what is given you (Paul and Paul, 1983, p. 108).

When needs aren't satisfied, what happens? A sad possibility is that people will just settle trying to be content within relationships which aren't nourishing. Unfortunately, this "settling" is quite common and is one cause of what are called "empty-shell marriages." "Far too many succumb to a form of apathy or dull-but-tolerable coexistence: a kind of death-in-life" (Barbach and Geisinger, 1991, p. xviii). These marriages may be long-term ones; yet, the value of a relationship lies in the joy it offers, not in its longevity (Branden and Branden, 1982). Another possibility is an outside relationship. Almost every extramarital affair can be traced to an important need not being met in the marriage. An affair is often the culmination of a search for something missing (Barbach and Geisinger, 1991). The nature of the need determines the person who will be sought, the length and depth of the affair, and whether it will be disclosed to the partner (Kinder and Cowan,

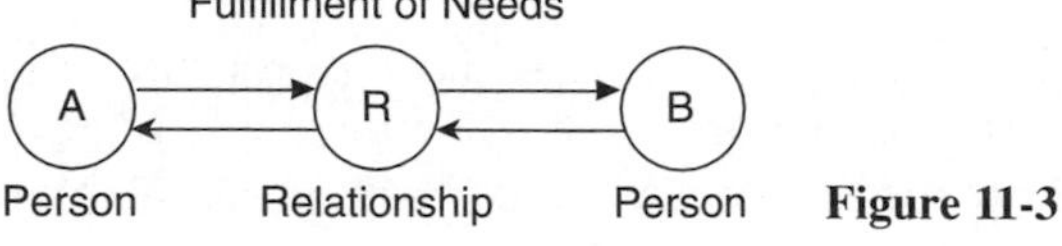

Figure 11-3

1989). In today's society the third likelihood is ending the relationship. Most divorces reflect unfulfilled needs.

How do you know that a person can or will satisfy you? Even though no guarantee is possible, you can significantly increase your chances by doing the following:

- Use the activity in REFLECTIONS AND APPLICATIONS to identify what you want trying to prioritize as much as possible. What is essential? What, if missing, would cause you to be unhappy and possibly end the relationship? Try to specifically describe what an abstract word such as "honesty" means. To just say that you want "trust" isn't explaining well. Besides the possibility of two partners' different meanings, if you aren't sure what trust means, you won't know if it's present or not.
- Communicate your needs to your partner. If not married, use the needs description to become acquainted with each other and to clarify what is important to you. If married, you can express what you presently need.
- Observe the person you love in the company of others. If you need demonstrated affection, is he or she warm around other people? Affection is difficult to assess in terms of how you are treated in the early stages of a relationship. Even "cold fish" will show passion based on sexual desires. If you're looking for everyday types of affection, the person's behavior with others is a clue. Take note of how your partner's biological family behaves. My husband is a hugger, typical of his entire family. Watching him hug them and others assured me that this was his genuine behavior.
- Be willing to do what is necessary to satisfy the other person's legitimate needs. This may mean behavior changes on your part, which then motivates the other to change, too. Keep in mind that the two of you may not have all of the same needs. You're lucky if yours are compatible.
- Don't assume that the other will change after marriage or just because time passes. Behavioral change is possible yet requires self-motivation. You can only suggest and encourage. The only one you can be assured of changing is yourself. However, a change in one does change the relationship

Having compatible needs helps. For example, if Jane wants a high degree of togetherness and Matt prefers personal space, they will have difficulty satisfying each other. This is one reason that similarities are an important attraction factor. In most cases, your needs won't be 100 percent identical; however, equality is of concern. Exchange theory indicates that relationships are more satisfying and stable when outcomes for each partner are more or less equal and when benefits far outweigh costs (Buunk, 1991).

If you find that your needs are unfulfilled and changes on the part of a partner aren't likely, you are hurting yourself, and probably the other person as well, by remaining. Relationships aren't successful if participants don't contribute what is most needed. Frustration mounts, which creates friction between the partners. Unhappy situations can have happy endings. A former student wrote me the following note:

> I want to tell you the consequences of the assignment on needs fulfillment. I was engaged at the time and ended up talking to my fiancé about our relationship. It was obvious that my needs weren't being satisfied, and he really didn't seem to care enough to change. I gave back the ring and went through a depressing period. Then I met Matt, and the two relationships are like night and day. We really clicked and are getting married next month. How sad it would have been if I had remained in that earlier relationship.

Behaviors of love. Social scientists are now directing attention to how people act when they love. What are the behaviors of love? "Joe loves me. I know because he beats up on anyone who looks at me." Is this love or is it an uncontrollable temper fired by irrational possessiveness? "She loves me because she'll do everything I want." This sounds more like servitude than love.

Be aware of how you are treated by a lover. Is it loving behavior? In any love relationship, individuals will occasionally demonstrate some less-than-loving actions. The key is the number, reasons, and aftermath. If hurtful behaviors are frequent or occur for poor reasons, and the aggressor feels no remorse and does not act to rectify the situation, you are not being loved. Ask yourself, "Do I feel loved?" If you can honestly answer in the affirmative most of the time, then the relationship is probably positive. "Do I feel affirmed?" is another essential question. Intimate love enhances self-esteem.

Love is complicated and mysterious, as anyone who has loved knows. Being able to differentiate between romantic and intimate love is a first step in understanding love relationships. Taking a close look at intimate love, its components, its potential for contributing to relationship growth and fulfillment of needs, and its behaviors reduces the possibility of the mistakes and pain that can accompany complexity. After you have examined love, you may still wonder whether what you feel is love. In a frank way, Branden and Branden (1982) state: "We suspect that people who ask this question are not in love. In our observation and experience, love reaches a critical point where it tends to generate a clarity of its own" (p. 24).

BUILDING INTIMACY

"The 2:00 A.M. knowledge that you are not alone" is the litmus test of intimacy, according to author and therapist Teresa Adams (1987, p. 95). She and other experts realize that intimacy is the pulse of the closest relationships as well as being conducive to physical and mental health (Moss and Schwebel, 1993). Both Rubin's and Sternberg's love theories identify intimacy as necessary. What exactly is intimacy, and how do two people create it?

Understanding Intimacy

Definitions of intimacy, like those of abstract words, vary. To many, intimacy is equated with sexuality. When you consider that retail stores have "intimate departments" which sell lingerie and negligees, it is little wonder that the mind focuses on bedroom scenes. The sexual relationship is only one facet of intimate love. "The most literal meaning of 'intimate' is to really know another" (Rubin, 1973, p. 160). This is an important aspect within intimacy, yet more is involved. Intimacy frees and encourages you to be your own true self and to be accepted and loved because of who you are. Intimacy means we can be who we are in a relationship and allow the other to do the same (Lerner, 1989).

In distinguishing between intimacy and closeness in *The Art of Intimacy*, Malone and Malone (1987) write:

> When I am close, I know you; when I am intimate, I know myself. When I am close, I know you in your presence; when I am intimate, I know myself in your presence. Intimacy is a remarkable experience . . . to feel and know myself in the presence of another is enlivening, enlightening, joyful, and, most of all, freeing (p. 29).

If two individuals perceive their relationship as close and intimate, they experience their togetherness, and they share and are their genuine selves with each other.

Intimacy has several key elements (Sternberg, 1987).

1. Desire to promote each other's welfare.
2. Experiencing happiness with each other.
3. Holding each other in high regard.
4. Being able to count on each other in times of need.
5. Having mutual understanding.
6. Sharing of self and possessions with each other.
7. Receiving emotional support from the other.
8. Giving emotional support to the other.
9. Communicating intimately with each other.
10. Valuing each other.

These elements promote closeness, bondedness, and connectedness essential for long-term love relationships. Check your own love relationship to see how many of the ten elements are present. If yours, as mine, contains all ten, you are indeed fortunate.

Development of Intimacy

Building intimacy requires dedication and effort. Individuals have to be willing to rid themselves of personal postures that prohibit intimacy (Malone and Malone, 1987).

- Withdrawal, which amounts to retreating from another and possibly becoming overly involved with interests outside the relationship or emotionally isolating the self.
- Personal rigidity, or lack of willingness to compromise and to allow differences.
- Overt self-righteousness, which occurs when the need to be right is more important than love.
- Lack of trustworthiness is detrimental. Trust including predictability, dependability, faithfulness, loyalty, and honesty is essential. The essence of trust is emotional safety. "Trust enables you to put your deepest feelings and fears in the palm of your partner's hand, knowing they will be handled with care" (Avery, 1989, p. 27).

Power struggles can get in the way of intimacy. Couples who have achieved trust may still not have intimacy because of controversy over power. Power can be distributed unequally, with either the man or the woman having more control, or power can see-saw back and forth in a continuous struggle. The healthiest type of power structure is shared power. "Unequal power blocks us from intimacy. No one expects a 50–50 arrangement. Instead, each person has spheres of control with both sharing power over time and issues. What we surrender in unequal power patterns, we gain in intimacy" (Adams, 1987, p. 107).

Power in a relationship is directly related to perceived equality. Equality means that no preestablished hierarchy exists or is allowed to continue. Equal attention and seriousness is extended to the emotions, needs, desires, and roles of both. When equality goes out of a relationship, love follows (Solomon, 1988). In an intimate relationship neither person silences, sacrifices, or betrays the self. Instead, each one expresses strength and vulnerability, weakness and competence in balance (Lerner, 1989). Possessing and stifling are also enemies of intimacy. Within an intimate relationship partners relish their times together, and intimacy creates a desire for closeness. If the togetherness becomes exclusive, possessive, and stifling, intimacy is weakened.

A serious obstacle that has frustrated lovers for a long time is stereotypic masculine behavior. Power, discussed earlier, is stereotypically held by the man, which destroys the potential for intimacy. Furthermore, intimacy requires expression of emotions and self-disclosure on all levels. The classic male image denies these behaviors and sets up roadblocks to intimacy (Branden and Branden, 1982; Goldberg, 1987; Jourard, 1971; Naifeh and Smith, 1984). Even though many men are changing as they learn the value of intimacy, those who continue in a stereotypic masculine role will face unsurmountable hardships.

Other dilemmas related to gender roles have been identified. First, some suggest that women and men tend to define intimacy and express love differently (Tavris, 1992). For most men, love is action and doing things for the love object; for a woman, love is talking and acknowledging how much she feels love. Women generally equate intimacy to talk and demand a particular type of talk centering on personal matters. The two sexes can also differ on the purpose for talk. For many men, the purpose is to solve problems; for women, it's likely to be simply to release feelings. Until men and women view intimacy similarly, they will have difficulty achieving it.

Second, stereotypic expectations make intimacy unlikely. Traditionally, men expressed love by providing security and through performance. Today, men continue to be romanticized as protectors like the Rock of Gibraltar which causes a dilemma. A family therapist once said, "Some women want men hard as rocks and wind up in marriages cold as stone" (Osherson, 1992, p. 20). Modifying these expectations is necessary. Sex differences are covered in the best-selling book *Men Are From Mars, Women Are From Venus* (Gray, 1992). Regardless of its less-than-wholehearted endorsement from the psychological community (Goldman, 1994), thousands seem to identify with its message. While accepting key points, my hope is that readers realize what the author acknowledges—that he generalizes about men and women. Even though gender influences personality, differences within each sex can be as dramatic as those between women and men.

Realizing that stereotypes have weakened in recent years, experts have positive expectations concerning intimacy. "Men can open up. There are no easy solutions, no foolproof formulas. In a man's struggle to discover emotional intimacy, he needs a woman's help" (Naifeh and Smith, 1984, p. 12). Over several years of getting to know students, I see a positive change taking place; yet, obstacles and dilemmas still exist. If both women and men put forth an effort to be honest, clear, and consistent, to mutually define and describe intimacy, and to have realistic expectations so that intimacy doesn't become sidetracked, they can succeed.

Androgynous behaviors, described earlier, are related to higher levels of intimacy in both sexes (Schiedel and Marcia, 1985). Expression of genuine emotions, even unpleasant ones, by men and women is androgynous and can lead to intimacy. During a seminar, Teresa Adams noted that, "Frozen anger blocks intimacy; thawed anger enhances intimacy." Empathic and nurturing behaviors build intimacy.

Intimacy is endangered by boredom and the tendency to take each other for granted. Intimacy demands quality interacting time. If, because of relationship longevity or familiarity or both, couples choose to engage in other activities or they simply ignore their relationship, intimacy can be canceled for lack of interest. "To have a long-lasting relationship, we must avoid complacency. More love has been lost on the island of contentment than in any sea of torment" (Buscaglia, 1992, p. 166).

In contrast, paying attention to each other and spending enjoyable time in interactive experiences increase the potential for intimacy. High levels of intimacy have been positively related to high levels of humor (Hampes, 1992). Communication is the single most important tool to create and sustain intimacy (Kinder and Cowan, 1989), so couples are wise to polish their skills and to clarify differences in communication styles and purposes. Because intimacy is measured by degree of self-disclosure rather than by sexual or physical actions (Braiker, 1992), couples are advised to spend more time disclosing than in pure physical demonstrations.

Building intimacy is one of the most difficult and challenging tasks within a relationship. The rewards are significant. If a relationship doesn't have intimacy, the partners may not realize what they are missing. If two human beings are truly intimate, their potential for joy is infinite.

Intimacy demands the highest risk but yields the richest reward. Intimacy is the driving force which makes the painful grit of life worthwhile. Intimacy is the life-giving beam of light, whereby we discover each other from the inside out, never quite fully, never entirely, but enough to find an exquisite inner oasis that replenishes us on our life's journey.

—Teresa Adams

SEXUAL FULFILLMENT

"Oh, great, this book has some dirty stuff in it," was the comment of one young student as he looked through his psychology text. The equation of sex to dirtiness still exists. Accompanying it are other attitudes that can interfere with sexual fulfillment. Many people seemingly have difficulty conversing about sex without resorting to euphemisms such as "doing it," "balling," "screwing," "scoring," and "getting laid." Discussions about sexuality are frequently filled with jokes (described as "dirty"), innuendos, and insinuating remarks. "There's something wrong with a country that says, 'Sex is dirty, save it for someone you love,' " said sex educator and author Sol Gordon (Gibbs, 1993, p. 62). It's ironic that even though most people think that violence is bad and sex is good, parents often do not insist that a child turn off a violent television program. Yet, if that same child were watching sex on Saturday morning, most parents would label it "gross" or immoral and write a letter in protest (Farrell, 1986). That individuals do succeed in their sexual relationships amid such a negative environment is amazing.

Sexuality is a part of being human, and lovemaking has special meaning within an intimate love relationship. Finding ways to enhance one's own sexuality and to maintain a fulfilling relationship are vital. Because most of our sexual behaviors are learned (Nathanson, 1992), possibilities abound. This section will not offer a quick "how-to" course. Fortunately, in today's society, anyone who wants to learn about the sexual act can do so. Excellent books on being sensual, handling sexual problems and dysfunctions, and enriching a sexual relationship as well as sex therapy are available, and highly recommended, for individuals and couples. Within this limited space, the importance of one's sex life will be emphasized, and general guidelines will be offered.

Sexual Behaviors

If you don't realize that sexual intercourse is occurring at an all-time high, you haven't been paying attention. For a sociology course project, Connie Chambers surveyed 90 men and women, most of whom were college students in Lincoln, Nebraska, and found that 69 percent approved of premarital sex. In a traditional fashion, 99 percent believed that sexual fidelity within marriage was important. Premarital sex statistics are at an all-time high with 90 percent of men and 80 percent of women engaging in sexual intercourse prior to marriage (Rosellini, 1992). In a survey for *Time* magazine, 74 percent of teenagers 17 years and younger said they were sexually experienced (Gibbs, 1993). That sex is occurring outside of marriage and that it influences the course of relationships are facts. Within marriages, sexual fulfillment is a major contributor or deterrent to satisfaction.

Sexual Enrichment

Therapists are quick to point out that sexual dissatisfaction within marriage is common, and usually, the underlying cause is not a sexual one. Mark Schwartz, a sex therapist, contends that when clients come to him seeking help for sexual problems, he spends 80 percent of the time in marital therapy and only 20 percent on sexual behaviors. In most cases, he says, each "I" must be fixed before any work can be done on the "we." Others agree with him and pinpoint incomplete self-disclosure as a factor. Sex deteriorates when a person is seemingly incapable of establishing a close, mutually disclosing, nonsexual relationship with another person (Jourard, 1971). Engaging in self-actualizing behaviors including having a worthwhile purpose in life was related to greater levels of sexual satisfaction in a study of nonfaculty staff members (McCann and Biaggio, 1989). Lack of self-esteem creates obstacles in sexual relationships, as well. "To the extent that we aren't yet at home with ourselves and in the world, we will inhibit our sexual feelings" (Bell, 1991, p. 166).

The best way to keep the sexual relationship healthy is to keep the rest of the relationship healthy (Barbach and Geisinger, 1991). Sexual satisfaction is positively related to marital satisfaction (Delamater, 1991). Research reveals that women's reports of open communication and an overall satisfying relationship were associated with an increase in their sexual participation (Wyatt and Lyons-Rowe, 1990). Sexual problems stem either from an individual's negative attitudes and expectations or from other difficulties within a couple relationship. Sexual frustration can complicate relationships as it becomes a source of added friction. The key is to solve underlying problems.

Even without serious complications, most couples' sexual relationships need attention and nourishment and can be improved. First, even though you think you know all there is to know about sex, you can learn more! Sexual education is an ongoing process. Despite efforts to eliminate misconceptions, they continue to influence sexual behavior. Early learning accounts for these.

> The early sexual learning we get from our parents is mostly negative, usually consisting of "don't." We have very little opportunity of being exposed to and picking up truly accurate information until we are much older, but by then our attitudes to sex and sexual behavior are rigidly fixed, and like all early established beliefs, difficult to change (Williams, 1988, p. 17).

The challenge for couples is to unlearn and relearn.

Getting rid of sexual myths is part of the education. One myth is that sex and love are the same. You are wise to think of sex and love as separate. "You can have an active, relatively satisfying sex life without having true love, and you can have true love without the fireworks of a sizzling sexual attraction" (Katz and Aimee, 1988, p. 333). This would prevent some, like Kate, from erroneously believing she was loved because "he couldn't keep his hands off me and wanted to have sex every time we were together."

Another myth is that passion and sex are most important at the beginning of a relationship. Actually, the importance of a healthy sex life increases in importance during the middle years of a marriage (Sternberg and Whitney, 1991). Unfortunately, when people don't understand this, they are apt to let the sexual relationship wane. A study of 500 couples found that men were more likely to initiate touch during the courtship and women more after marriage. However, couples who had been married for 1 year or more were less likely to touch each other at all (Willis and Briggs, 1992).

A third myth is that the sexual relationship will always stay the same. Just as you, your partner, and your relationship will change over time, so will your sexual relationship. That doesn't mean it becomes less enjoyable. Early in a relationship sex is mostly about excitement while later it's more about contentment (Nathanson, 1992). Finally, a common myth is that as people age, their sexual interests and activities die. Is this true and inevitable? No, say the experts, unless you choose this course. Take a look at these figures from the National Survey of Families and Households of 807 people 60 years of age and older (Marsiglio and Donnelly, 1991):

- 53 percent reported sexual relations within the past month.
- 24 percent of those 76 years old and older were engaging in sexual relations about four times a month with 7.4 percent reporting at least ten times.

What made a difference was the person's sense of self-worth and competence and her or his partner's health status. "In health and in the presence of favorable circumstances, a desire for sexual expression persists into advanced old age" (Williams, 1988, p. 15). Another study of Americans between the ages of 50 and 93 indicated an interest in and openness about sexual activity. In fact, the respondents were sexually active in as wide a variety of ways as young people (Duck, 1988).

Biological changes occur with age and will alter some aspects of lovemaking. Most important are cultural attitudes that can convert into self-fulfilling prophecies. "It's all over," they say, and it is. "It's not all over," they say, and it isn't. Some even suggest that lovemaking can be better with age. "Actually, it's easier to improve the quality of sex when we're past 60. What we may lack in physical robustness is made up for in tender feelings and love" (Fromm, 1984, p. 69). In the sexual education process, clearing up misconceptions is necessary.

A second cardinal rule, rather than a guideline, is to communicate openly and honestly with each other. "We don't talk about it . . . we just do it," mumbled a husband in a marriage counseling session. Not talking about such a vital part of a love relationship will diminish sexual fulfillment. When you openly communicate, you learn about each other's likes, dislikes, needs, and wants. "Men and women must teach each other how to understand and accept the nature of their own sexual systems" (Nathanson, 1992, p. 281). A frank, regularly occurring discussion of your sexual relationship, even if no problems are apparent, is highly recommended. "Good communication is fundamental to sexual competence" (Cupach and Metts, 1991, p. 105). A word of caution is in order. Communicating doesn't mean to just complain about what you don't like or how dissatisfied you are. Put the emphasis on the positive and use communication as a means of enhancing.

A third guideline is to view sexual intercourse as just one important aspect of the broad scope of love and to enjoy a process of loving each other which is more than a physical act. Mental and emotional parts of the selves are also deeply involved. In fact, one common myth is that sexual intercourse even has to be a part of lovemaking. "Lovemaking means literally that—interacting physically and emotionally with someone you care about. Arousal, intercourse, and orgasm or ejaculation are nonessential, and simply possible lovemaking options" (Williams, 1988, p. 19). Typically, all the emphasis in lovemaking is placed on the climax phase. I laughed when Mark Schwartz said, "Even foreplay is sometimes seen as unimportant. The word 'foreplay' makes it sound as if all the good stuff is still to come."

Lovemaking, in its entirety, is best seen as an ongoing interaction between two loving people.

> "Having sex" implies that something happens to you, like having a toothache or a flat tire. It sounds passive and lifeless. "Making love," on the other hand, is creative, not passive. It suggests an ongoing process, not a static situation. Making love focuses on the sensual expression of closeness between two trusting souls who like as well as love one another, not just the plug-in connection between sex organs (Castleman, 1989, p. 19).

What is quite positive is research indicating how healthy sexual relations can be. Sex can bolster the immune system, relieve pain, help regulate hormones, and be valuable therapy for psychological problems. Long-term lovemaking is especially beneficial. Regular intercourse is also good for mental health. People with active sex lives are less anxious, violent, hostile, and not as likely to blame others for their misfortunes (Von Kreisler, 1993).

Probably the most powerful enemy of sexual fulfillment is routine and boredom, and the fourth recommendation is to add variety and zest to your sexual relationship. Sameness in time, place, and technique is dull. Couples in the early stages of a relationship are generally more innovative and willing to experiment. Later, they tend to settle into predictable routines. "With mutual knowledge, unfortunately, often comes boredom and contempt which impede arousal, excitement, and enjoyment" (Nathanson, 1992, p. 285). Even in this enlightened society, contemporary marriages seem to suffer from apathy and boredom more than ever before (Kinder and Cowan, 1989). Can you determine reasons for boredom in the following:

> SHE: He wants to have sex about 3 times a week, usually on Tuesday, Thursday, and Saturday.
>
> HE: I wish she'd wear something to bed besides that old flannel nightgown. It's hard to feel desire even 3 nights a week.
>
> SHE: He doesn't seem to care about my sexual needs. Our sex is always the same.
>
> HE: Another problem is that sometimes I'm tired after watching the late-night talk show.

Was it apparent that their sexual relations predictably took place on Tuesday, Thursday, and Saturday nights at about the same time (after television) and in the same place (bed)? The flannel nightgown added to the doldrums of their sex life.

This situation points out another common problem. If you were asked, "When do most married couples make love?" your answer would probably be, "Before they go to sleep at night." For most couples, after a long, busy day, "before sleep" equates to fatigue. The "I'm too tired" excuse is probably not really an excuse. It's fact! Couples benefit by assessing the priority of lovemaking and not always relegating it to the last event of the day. Nor is it wise to let sameness ruin your sexual relationship. Being in different environments can trigger a renewed interest. The key is to involve yourselves in new and stimulating situations on a regular basis at home (Kinder and Cowan, 1989).

In most long-term relationships, enrichment of the sexual relationship is essential. Couples over time face hassles, stress, knowledge of each other's irritating qualities, disagreement, and a secret pessimism that nothing will help that leads to disenchantment. Developing a new perspective is important. A chapter called "Reawakening Sexual Desire" is included in the book *Husbands and Wives* (Kinder and Cowan, 1989) and can motivate and instruct couples on how to do this. The authors contend that sexual disinterest is a normal part of marriages, and blame is not an effective antidote. Breaking old patterns, shaking up the system, and then coming together in a new way are recommended. Other ideas are to keep in good shape, care about appearance, learn how to delight each other, and be spontaneous (Barbach and Geisinger, 1991).

A few final guidelines have to do with misinterpretations about sexual behaviors and manipulative uses of sexuality. Interpreting an occasional lack of interest in sexual intercourse as nonlove isn't unusual. Yet, the myth that love means a constant sexual "turn-on" damages relationships. Other silly misinterpretations are common. For example, you may attach a meaning to a behavior that isn't shared by the other, as in the case of this couple:

SUSAN (sobbing): Here we are n-n-newly married, and you're already tired of me.

MARK (surprised): What gave you that idea?

SUSAN: You usually make a sexual advance, and tonight you turned over and started reading.

Figure 11-4

MARK: I was planning to hug you and give you a kiss in a minute because I was close to the end of this book. I noticed that you put on your old sloppy pajamas instead of one of your gowns, so I assumed you weren't interested in lovemaking tonight.

SUSAN: What does what I wear have to do with it?

Several inaccurate assumptions can be detected in this one experience. Did you note that her expectation seemed to be that he would be the initiator of lovemaking? The myth that only men are interested in lovemaking and should make the first advance decreases spontaneity and freedom within sexual relationships.

"We'll make love if . . ." or "I won't have sex with you if . . ." are manipulative techniques that reduce lovemaking to a game. If the relationship is troubled, you can rightfully refrain from lovemaking. Saying, "I don't want to make love because I don't feel loved (or loving)" is direct and honest. To use sex as a leverage is to demean yourself and the relationship.

Sexual fulfillment is a choice. To achieve satisfaction requires commitment, time, energy, and a great deal of communication. This may sound serious; yet, rewarding sex relationships are playful, pleasurable, and fun. "The goal of lovemaking, if there is one, is simply to relax and enjoy being in close contact with your lover" (Castleman, 1989, p. 46). Keeping this in mind can motivate you to devote attention to sexual fulfillment.

MARRIAGE: A LOVING COMMITMENT

Do love and marriage go together like a horse and carriage? Not necessarily. Should everyone marry? That question is rarely answered incorrectly on a class examination. Yet, despite a consensus of opinion that marriage isn't for everyone, people generally assume that they will marry. A higher percentage of people in the United States marry than in other modern societies. Approximately 95 percent of Americans will marry (Schwartz and Scott, 1994). Occasionally, marriage is entered into under pressure. Some people do not want partners, but have been brainwashed into thinking that they should want them (Goulding and Goulding, 1989). Or, they worry that if they don't marry, something will be missing from their lives. Getting rid of these notions will be beneficial in choosing a happy life for yourself, married or not.

A commitment to marry, ideally, is a free choice. If a person likes living alone, this life style can be "glorious, lovely, and completely fulfilling" (Goulding and Goulding, 1989, p. 123). The option to remain single is more viable than ever. Having a bona fide choice is healthy for everyone. With no pressure driving individuals to marry, they can be either satisfied with single life or free to decide to marry for positive reasons. If the choice is to marry, thoughtful preparation and knowledge can set the stage for a successful union.

Understanding Marriage

Before you begin a trip, do you usually like to know where you're going and what it might be like? Too often, couples embark on a marital journey with little or no information except what their own images supply.

What is marriage? Agreement on a general definition, as well as on expectations, is a first step in understanding. In its simplest sense, marriage is a legal institution; however, this definition doesn't reveal much. Although necessary for satisfying long-term relationships, marriage is more than love and intimacy. One positive definition of a fulfilling marriage is "a state of interdependence in which the partners lose neither their identities nor their sense of autonomy" (Lauer and Lauer, 1988, p. 125). Sociologically, marriage is a socially approved mating arrangement, usually involving sexual activity and economic cooperation. In the United States, marriage is based on *monogamy*, having one mate at a time.

Commitment is a central issue in marriage and is often used in defining what marriage is. Commitment includes mutuality of purpose, a willingness to put forth effort, and a pledge of fidelity. It is a declaration of loyalty, loving conduct, ethics, and honor. Two people who share this idea of commitment are likely to exert effort and succeed in a marriage.

Types of marriages. Marriages vary in a number of ways, yet general types are identifiable. Knowing what type satisfies you is important. The idea of categorizing marriage on the basis of roles and responsibilities is relatively new. In the past, rules for who did what within a marriage were predetermined and inflexible. The *traditional marriage*, which is no longer common yet remains a choice, is one in which the husband is dominant. Roles are determined on the basis of being male or female. He is the breadwinner, and she is the homemaker. She is responsible for most of the child care and other "women's work" and defers to him. She makes decisions about the home management and the children while he retains final control over family decisions. This "father knows best" type of arrangement was more suited to the society of yesteryear. Although I don't recommend traditional marriages, this is an option if couples can afford to have only one wage earner.

In order for it to work, agreement that this is what both individuals want and an acceptance of the risks are critical. Among the risks are the limitations that sharply defined roles and responsibilities impose on human beings, pressures put on a sole breadwinner, the possibility of low self-esteem if the homemaker role is not positively recognized, and the frustrations that come from being under someone else's control.

The most critical risk for women in a traditional marriage is financial. In the event of divorce or the death of the breadwinner, the risk becomes a stark reality. Consider Rita's story:

> Rita and Jim had been in a traditional marriage for 13 years. He had not wanted her to work outside the home. "I want you at home taking care of my two boys," he said. She was agreeable, and his business brought them a more-than-adequate livelihood. Suddenly, Jim left, deserting the family and moving to another state. He left neither a forwarding address nor money. Rita, who had never worked before, was fortunate enough to find a job, but she earned only minimum wage. She had to move from her townhouse because she couldn't make the payments. "I never dreamed that this would happen to me," she said.

Widows can also experience hardship. A 56-year-old woman told of her husband's job being eliminated and, along with it, the medical benefits and company-paid life insurance. He died 6 months later, before he had found other insurance. She was left penniless, with no means of supporting herself. Even if a couple remains married and both are living, financial risks are present.

> Fred and Susie were in their late forties, their children were raised, and they were living in a nice condominium when Fred made a job change. Susie had a high school education, and even though she had earned income during their marriage, she had not pursued a career full-time. Soon after the job change, Fred was terminated because of a company down-sizing. He diligently sought a professional job with no luck. Without income, they moved in with one of their children for a time. When Fred started work as a security truck driver and Susie took a job at the local hospital, they found a small apartment. For about two years they struggled until Fred found a job more in line with his education and experience.

Couples who choose a traditional marriage are wise to be aware of the potential hazards.

Another type of marriage, the complete opposite of the traditional marriage, is called *egalitarian or shared*. Partners share equally in power, and roles and responsibilities are completely gender-free. Usually, both engage in full-time careers, and equal weight is given to considerations of promotions, job transfers, and other changes. Neither is considered as *the* wage earner. The idea that one partner "helps" the other with responsibilities is replaced with the concept of *sharing* all tasks.

In such a marriage, the question arises of who does what. A simple answer is: either or both. The couple uses communication and negotiation in the designation of tasks. A number of criteria can be used. For example, who cooks? The two can share responsibilities, either taking turns or working together in the kitchen. Other possibilities take into account preference, ability, and convenience. Who cleans the toilet bowls? That's a harder one. I have tried to convince my husband that he does it better. No? That he likes to do it more. No? That it is more convenient for him to do it. Still no? So we share!

A shared marriage is fair and sensible and fits our current economy and society. Most families today need or want two incomes. Even more important, research indicates that two thirds of women rated paid work as equal to or more important and enjoyable than housework (Carlson and Videka-Sherman, 1990) while a male's family roles were found to be as important as his work in contributing to mental health. In fact, the quality of the marital and parental roles buffered men from work-related stress (Barnett et al., 1992). A study on marital success found that husbands who did housework were far healthier four years later than those who did not (Gottmann, 1991). Shared marriages also appear to strengthen communication skills as couples negotiate new roles and workable arrangements (Hawkins and Robert, 1992) and encourage closer family relationships.

With all its advantages, actually practicing a shared marriage is challenging because of past patterns of thinking and behaving. As is the case of most categorization methods, the lines are finely drawn. Couples today may describe themselves as being in an egalitarian marriage and still engage in behaviors based only on their sex. For example, most women correspond with relatives and send greeting cards. Why? The honest answer is: just because they are women. Most husbands drive the automobile, and the wife rides. Why? Again, most often, just because they are men. And, couples can forget their commitment to a shared marriage on special occasions. At a holiday dinner in most homes, do you see equal distribution of labor? If it exists, the couple is achieving egalitarianism against the odds.

Even though many young couples say they prefer a shared marriage, and the majority of women work outside the home, research substantiates that division of labor is not shared equally in most households. In the late 1980s American couples exhibited highly sex-segregated family work patterns. Even when a husband contributed to house-

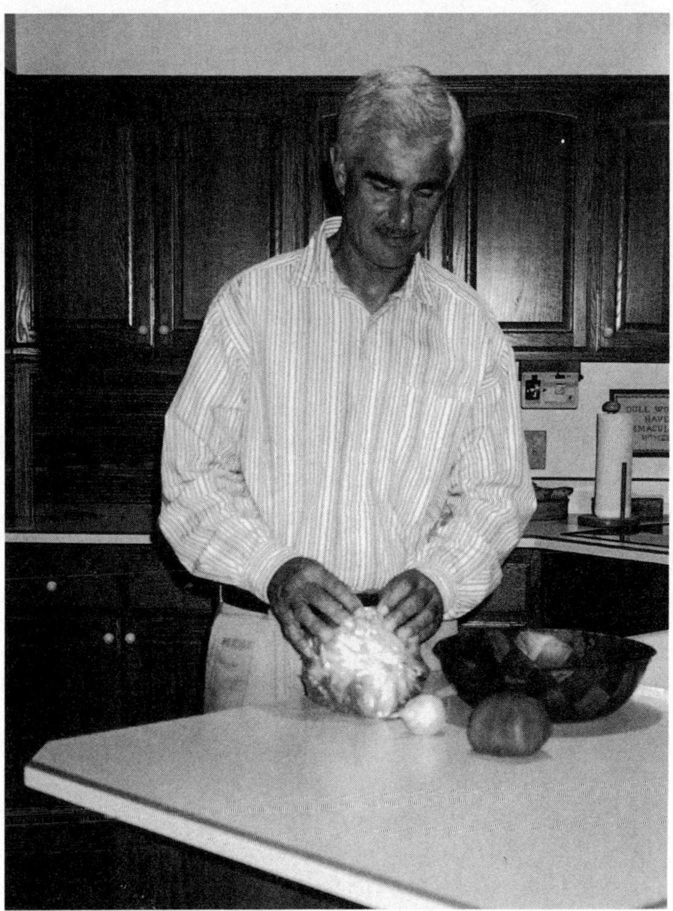

Figure 11-5 In shared marriages, the kitchen is no longer the woman's domain.

work, the tasks were traditionally segregated (Blair and Lichter, 1991). A sample of 778 households from the National Survey of Families and Households was used to compute hours per week of household labor (meal preparation, dishes, cleaning, laundry, outdoor tasks, shopping, bills, and auto maintenance). In households in which women were employed, wives averaged 31.06 hours per week of total labor while husbands averaged only about 15.28. Only 10 percent of the husbands did as much household labor as their wives, and the tasks were still largely sex-segregated (Blair and Johnson, 1992). Another study showed that women who worked outside the home did about 70 percent of the housework and put in three times as many hours around the house as their husbands did (Grant, 1988). Times are changing, yet roles and responsibilities seem quite resistant to modification.

What makes a difference in the amount and type of shared tasks? One study showed that time availability and the wife's attitudes were consistent predictors of the husband's sharing (Coltrane and Ishii-Kuntz, 1992). Reaching agreement about household tasks before making a commitment is recommended because subtle sexism among young men is still evident. When asked if they intended to be married to a woman who worked outside the home, the typical answer was, "She *can* work if she wants." However, few envisioned themselves doing housework. One male said he would participate in housework and child care depending on how much he liked his wife and how she went about asking him (Crosby, 1991). In a national poll, teenage boys, more than girls, favored a traditional marriage; 19 percent said they expected a wife to stay home contrasted with only 7 percent of the girls (*Lincoln Journal*, July 11, 1994).

> Women often demand surprisingly little in relationships with men, whether the issue at hand is emotional nurturance or who cleans up the kitchen. We may settle for small change with a lover or husband and tolerate behaviors and living arrangements that we would not find acceptable or deem fair in a close female friendship (Lerner, 1987, p. 7).

From my own experiences and knowledge of other marriages, I believe that what women expect, and in some cases, demand, usually happens. Perhaps, women discourage sharing because of learned patterns of giving and because they feel the home is their domain and source of pride as Julie wrote:

> When I first got married, I cooked and did housework to impress my spouse. Look at all the wonderful things I can do! As the years went by, these things were just expected by me to be done by me, and he expected it, too. Now I don't think impressing someone is the way to go.

The type of family may make a difference in terms of shared roles. Husbands in remarried families contributed significantly more to household tasks than those in first marriages (Ishii-Kuntz and Coltrane, 1992).

What will the future hold? A survey showed that the number of men and women who favor a traditional marriage has decreased significantly. However, men were twice as likely as women to want one (Bachman, 1987). Obviously, communication about such a vital part of marriage is in order. Problems are inevitable when people marry without forethought or discussion about marriage type. Denise captured the essence of this dilemma.

> My present relationship is far from perfect or even good. Most of what is heard about teenage marriages is true, as mine shows. Marriage vows do not give possession of one person to another. My husband doesn't realize this, but he was born too late to live the life style he would like in which men are bosses and women follow along.

A marriage works better when both feel that division of labor and authority is fair (Johnson, 1992). When responsibilities are shared, couples have the potential for intimacy, sexual energy, and increased respect for each other (Farrell, 1986).

Another way of typing a marriage is to look at its quality, rated by perceived satisfaction. Several dimensions are possible. For clarity, let's look at two basic groups identified in *Coupleship* (Wegscheider-Cruse, 1988).

- The spirited or centered couple express satisfaction about the relationship. Each feels happy and fulfilled. The relationship not only works, it thrives.
- The spiritually dead or estranged couple express dissatisfaction about the relationship. The partners feel lonely, hurt, and angry. Their relationship is unfulfilled.

Although several marriages could be categorized into one of the two, a third is possibly more common than the other two. This couple would be what I call an "in-limbo couple," whose relationship fluctuates between feelings of satisfaction and dissatisfaction. The partners in such relationships may be happy in several respects and miserable in others. Consider this relationship:

> Carol and Nick had been married for 10 years. To the outside world their relationship looked ideal. They had two children whom they adored and for whom they shared responsibility. They enjoyed sharing interests and participated in social, church, and community activities. They rarely fought, nor did they deeply self-disclose. Carol, at times, expressed, "I wish we were closer and talked and shared more." Nick reassured her, "I'm just not that way, honey. I love you, and look at how great our relationship is. We get along well. Don't worry." The bottom fell out of their relationship when they discovered that each was engaged in an extramarital affair. He said he needed to feel admired, and she found someone with whom to communicate and share. The crisis rejuvenated their marriage, and for some time they succeeded in building some intimacy. A few years later Nick said he wanted a divorce because he wanted deep self-disclosure and believed that happiness and self-revelation were only possible elsewhere.

Their "in-limbo" relationship had a happy ending for Carol who discovered new aspects of herself and developed a "spirited or centered couple" relationship with a new partner. Nick is still searching. Without a doubt, a high-quality couple relationship is what individuals want. The question is how to get it.

Preparation for Marriage

The time to ask serious questions about marriage is before the wedding ceremony. The potential for success is increased when careful examination is followed by a thoughtful decision. The adult ego state must function. Your child ego state feels love and has a desire to marry because of perceived future happiness and the prospect of pleasure. The parent ego state can deliver several possible messages, ranging from, "Don't get married. You're not ready" to "You'd better get married soon, or you may never have another chance." Neither "child" nor "parent" is a wise choice for this decision. The "adult" can help you prepare and then, ultimately, decides based on reason.

Sadly, lack of any formalized preparation is the norm. Most religious groups either require or offer premarital counseling; however, the value of it lies in the skill of the counseling clergymember. Sound, practical advice based on research may be missing. Premarital counseling by therapists is available yet not commonly sought. The educational system offers some help. Most high schools offer coursework regarding relationships. Specific classes on marriage preparation may be offered, and almost every college and university has a course in marriage and family.

How widespread these course offerings are and how many students take advantage of them are key questions. Unless all students are required to learn how to succeed in marriage, large numbers of young people will remain uneducated. This society demands that you study and pass driving tests before you are given a driver's license. In contrast, a marriage license requires no certainty that individuals know anything about relating. The damage to adults and children that results from unhappy marriages may not be as apparent as damage from careless driving, but the repercussions take an emotional and financial toll.

How to prepare. Preparation for marriage begins within the self. Chronological age is definitely a factor. Teenage marriages are riskier than those entered into at later ages. A study conducted by Teti and Lamb (1989) associated adolescent marriage with reductions in both socioeconomic status and marital success. A 1990 Census Report stated that women who marry young and those who bear a child before a first marriage increase their likelihood of divorce (Usdansky, 1992).

In recent years, age at first marriage has increased. In 1991 the median age at first marriage for women was 24.1 years nearly four years later than for their mothers (Popenoe, 1993a) and for men 26.1 years (Popenoe, 1993b). The older one's age at marriage, the lower the chances of eventual divorce, at least until about age 30 (Popenoe, 1993a) so this is a positive trend. Teenage marriage is associated with both marital instability (Teti and Lamb, 1989) and divorce (Schwartz and Scott, 1994). A young adult is more likely than an adolescent to have achieved independence, identity, maturity, and experience. When individuals marry without having had other close relationships, they may wonder what they have missed and are likely to feel restless and dissatisfied. "Experience cannot guarantee your choosing wisely, but lack of experience endangers your chances of choosing wisely and well" (Branden and Branden, 1982, p. 57).

Do you recall Erikson's psychosocial stages? Regardless of age, establishing identity is needed before intimacy is likely to be successful (Kahn et al., 1986). Even people who are divorced or widowed are wise to think about this. Identity is easily "lost" after a major life change. Related to identity is independence. Are you able to live on your own? Strong marriages are formed by two strong, independent individuals who choose to live together. Any healthy relationship is only as strong as its two individual parts. Partners must have a strong sense of "I" to form a successful "we." The symbolism about "two becoming one" may seem romantic; however, a strong "I" and another strong "I" are more likely than an enamored "we" to sustain the stressors of a long-term relationship. Love thrives when two people are quite capable of living without each other but choose to live with each other (Peck, 1978).

Clearing away personal litter from past relationships and experiences is important. Bonnie, a friend of mine since grade school, is a clinical psychologist. She reflected on the trauma and unresolved issues that ensued from being raped when she was 16 years old. "Nobody thought then of a need for counseling. I was, I guess, just expected to recover over time. I realize now that unresolved issues related to the rape contributed to unhappiness in marriage and then to my subsequent divorce."

Other personal factors related to success in marriage are healthy self-esteem, an androgynous personality, and self-created happiness. Desirable behavioral characteristics such as control of temper and other emotional responses, assertiveness, and open communication lead to better marriages. In a study designed to predict marital success, the male's physiological calm and women's assertiveness were related to later success. "When wives were only agreeable and compliant, the marriage would deteriorate over time" (Gottmann, 1991, p. 4). Also, stonewalling or presenting a "wall" to the other by the husband and verbal expressions of contempt from the wife predicted divorce. Better communication skills would have made a difference. Obviously, a well-adjusted person has a much better chance of having a successful marriage than one who is struggling with personal issues. "You want a partner, not a private nurse, caretaker, or entertainer. You'll want a partner who is also happy, so that you are not burdened with the impossible responsibility of trying to change someone else" (Goulding and Goulding, 1989, p. 124). Finally, maturity and an understanding of commitment are essential. Each person's "self" determines the success of a marriage. "Your relationships travel the same course that you travel" (Dyer, 1992, p. 114).

Singleness is an important transitional period. Those who wait to marry until later in their twenties still have many years of marriage ahead of them and definite advantages. You can use this time to "try on the world," explore yourself, develop a career, and learn about relationships (Hendrix, 1992). When people are emotionally healthy and relatively content with their lives, they are ready to move from being single to coupled (Katz and Aimee, 1988).

After personal readiness has been achieved, formal education is recommended to learn about marriage. Premarital programs can help couples and reduce divorce rates (O'Leary and Smith, 1991). One study found that premarital education in problem-solving and communication was associated with greater marital satisfaction at both 1.5 and 3 years postmarriage compared to control subjects who did not receive the education. Also, only 5 percent of the educated couples were likely to dissolve the relationship compared to 24 percent for the others (Markman et al., 1988). Rated quite positively by participants was a premarital program that explored family of origin, finances, communication, family and friends, roles, conflict resolution, parenting, sexuality, and spirituality (Russell and Lyster, 1992).

Personality and marriage-readiness tests are also beneficial as is reading about and openly discussing issues. A practical, easy-to-understand book that I highly recommend for all couples considering marriage is *Why Love Is Not Enough* (Gordon, 1988b).

MARITAL SUCCESS FACTORS

A thorough discussion of identified success factors can spell the difference between happiness and success in marriage or misery and failure. A couple is also advised to consider the opinions of others. Remember the romantic tale of Romeo and Juliet? That story leads us to believe that they were absolutely right and their families were wrong. Be careful that you don't go into a marriage blinded by this belief. If your family and friends do not think you are making a good choice, at least listen to their objections and use your "adult" to decide. Obviously, the more people who are concerned, the more you would benefit by paying attention. In a sample of 100 couples, 97 had the approval of families and friends. Among the couples who didn't, two had gone through a great deal of conflict and unhappiness and were on the verge of divorce (Johnson, 1992).

Additionally, keep in mind that exceptions aren't the rule. For example, you may know a happily married couple who wed in spite of the objection of their families. Using only one couple or even a few as justification for what you do is probably a mistake. Instead, couples are wise to draw upon research in preparing for marriage.

Recommendations for Success

Either in a premarital program, counseling setting, or by themselves, answering questions can serve an evaluative purpose. If married, you can use many of the questions to assess your relationship. Following each question are reasons for their importance as well as recommendations.

- *Have we known each other well for a long enough period?*

Length of acquaintance. Knowing each other well for at least a year is recommended. This does not mean that you are definitely ready to marry after a year's time; however, giving yourself that amount of time so that you experience the four seasons and all the holidays is revealing. One student remarked, "You need at least a year just to discuss all the marriage-readiness questions!"

- *Why do we want to marry?*

Reasons for marriage. Marriage counselors believe that the answer to "Why do we want to marry?" is one of the best predictors of marital success. Think of all the possible reasons for marriage. You are likely to come up with a number of poor reasons. Pressure is one. This can come from a lover, family, friends, or society itself. Even age exerts pressure. "I'm almost 26 years old, and I feel like I should be thinking about marriage," said a young man. If you feel any kind of pressure, force yourself to resist. Janeen, a student, wrote about her experience:

> We did not look at the "marriage," but listened to the pressure of being married and starting a family. He was a closed person and a loner. They say opposites attract, but we were too opposite. I also was filling my need of thinking I had to have someone and not looking at that "someone."

Other reasons come from the child ego state: "Oh, marriage seems like such fun." "It'll be like playing house." "We can sleep together legally." "The wedding and honeymoon will be so much fun." "I'm so in love." Even love is not a sufficient reason to marry. Although love is certainly of great importance, intimate relationships and successful marriages require even more. A need to have someone to feel fulfilled as Janeen expressed comes from our "child" and is a deficiency-based reason for marrying. "A quality love relationship is not made up of half-full partners trying to rescue each other and become whole by merging" (Bloomfield and Felder, 1985, p. 150).

Looking at the advantages and disadvantages of marriage can help you identify the "why" and evaluate costs versus benefits. Some advantages, according to Burns (1985a), are: communication, companionship, caring, sex, convenience, learning from and helping each other, financial sharing, having someone to fight with when you feel annoyed, and raising a family. Several of the advantages are possible without getting married; however, in this society, marriage is the recognized and legal way of achieving them. Another advantage is that more than 130 research studies have found that married men and women are generally happier and less stressed than unmarried people (Coombs, 1991). Disadvantages include relinquishing personal freedom to a certain extent, added stressors, having to share resources, and the risk of divorce.

Eliminating all the poor reasons still leaves the question: What is a positive reason for marrying? A couple whose marriage has great potential for success might say, "We are marrying because we are sure that we share an intimate love, we have carefully prepared and considered all known factors, we believe we have an excellent chance of succeeding in marriage, and we want to make a legal and deep commitment to this relationship." Commitment is the foundation of any genuinely loving relationship (Peck, 1978).

- *What do we expect from marriage?*

Expectations about marriage. The question about expectations can yield some intriguing answers. If two partners have opposite, incompatible, or unreasonable expectations, a red light should begin to flash. "I expect you to be there for me always. I expect you to satisfy all my needs. I don't expect that we will fight." Even if the two agree on these expectations, they are being extremely unrealistic. The gap between expectation and perceived performance produces disappointment, discouragement, and finally, disillusionment (Lingren, 1981).

Myths about marriage abound. An instrument called the "marriage quiz" was developed and administered to single, never-married undergraduates (Larson, 1988). Generally, students scored poorly; men missed more items than women. Having fewer romantic ideas and completing a marriage and family course led to much higher scores.

Some of the more widely held marital myths include thinking that you will live happily ever after without any relationship work, believing that your spouse will stay the same, assuming that fighting is always destructive, thinking that outside forces will have no effect on the marriage, and expecting that the marriage will always proceed smoothly (Fensterheim and Baer, 1988). Too often, individuals will look upon marriage as either "a bed or roses" or "a bed of thorns," and neither extreme yields a positive outcome. A couple would benefit from dispelling the myths.

Based on a general societal attitude, an underlying expectation, usually quite subtle, is that marriage will be fantastic for a brief period and then downhill after that. "The honeymoon is over" is a phrase used to describe a marital relationship after the initial stage. How many times have you heard people describe marriage in the following ways?

"They've settled down." (Doesn't this sound inviting?)

"They're an old married couple now." (Probably because they have actually "settled down.")

"You can tell they're married." (This, if a couple appears bored or uninterested in each other.)

Figure 11-6

"They must not be married." (This, if a couple is holding hands or showing affection.)

"They tied the knot." (ouch!)

Sometimes, these expectations are in place before the ceremony. I mentioned his upcoming marriage to a young man. He replied, "Yeah, I'm going to bite the dust this weekend." He evidently did just that, and in less than a year was divorced. The "ball and chain" stereotype and the idea that freedom is surrendered are apt to lead to unhappy outcomes. Also, if you begin to take each other for granted, either or both partners suffer. Then negative images can become reality. Checking expectations is essential. If yours are unrealistic, dismal, or incompatible with your partner's, either change your thoughts or postpone marriage.

- *What type of marriage do we want and how will we achieve it? What obstacles can get in the way?*

Possible types of marriage. As discussed earlier, the type of marriage you want related to quality, roles, and responsibilities will affect success. When one partner desires an egalitarian marriage and the other favors traditionalism, opportunities for conflict are greatly increased. In this transitional time, this issue deserves a great deal of time and attention not only before marriage but on a continuing basis. Periodically, checking with each other concerning perceptions of fairness will keep either from becoming resentful.

- *Are we both going to pursue careers and, if so, how will we handle such aspects as work schedules, relocation, and conflict between career and relationship?*

Careers and jobs. If you opt for a shared marriage, you will probably both be contributing income, and this is common today. Dual-earner couples make up 60 percent of all married couples (Schwartz and Scott, 1994). Men and women work not only for incomes; often, they prefer having careers. Of the 65.8 percent of working women from both black and white racial groups, 46.5 percent wanted to work. Blacks were substantially more likely to be working and, more than whites, because of economic necessity (Herring and Wilson-Sadverry, 1993).

Dual career couples can find that choices related to relocation and career advancement cause conflict. How the decision is made is critical. If couples believe in equality and comparable levels of power, decisions will be made jointly using a costs versus benefits method. The best interests of both will be considered, and either may be expected to sacrifice. Careers generally span 5 decades so altering the timing of career changes for the sake of the relationship isn't an extreme personal sacrifice (Trafford, 1993).

- *What are our career and personal goals? Are they compatible?*

Goals. All goals, if compatible, have positive effects on a relationship. Two people striving in similar directions can share excitement and challenges. As mentioned before, discussing and negotiating career goals is important, and doing so with a flexible attitude is essential. Personal goals such as home ownership, further education, and travel are equally important to share. Total honesty is imperative. Joyce sadly mentioned how Royce, before marriage, had talked about his desire to travel. "Since we've been married, all he wants to do is stay home."

- *Have we explored our financial situation? Do we know each other's present income and potential, debts, and past financial history? Will we budget? How will we manage our finances? What are our feelings and attitudes about money?*

Financial issues. Financial incompatibility and struggles can bring even the strongest relationship to its knees. Even with a more-than-adequate income, couples can face problems if they disagree on how money is to be used and have different attitudes about money. Karen was a saver and would spend money only for essentials. Luxuries weren't important. "The money is better in the bank" was her philosophy. Rod believed in using money and living for today without much thought of tomorrow. "You can't take it to your grave" was his motto. They argued regularly and bitterly about money. The handling of finances covers many areas. Will you keep your incomes separate? Will one or both of you pay bills? These are practical and necessary issues to resolve.

Another valuable exercise is to assess financial independence so that one isn't overly dependent on the other. Farrell (1986) in his enlightening book *Why Men Are the Way They Are* recommends that both ask themselves:

- Are we committed to sharing all expenses equally? If not, for what reason? (Hopefully, this doesn't indicate a future of financial dependency).
- Am I able to support myself in the style I prefer?
- If my partner worked half-time or less than I did, am I comfortable with that?
- If I worked half-time or less than my partner, am I comfortable with that?

A frank discussion of finances reveals a great deal about both people and the quality of the relationship.

- *How similar are our values? Religious beliefs? How similar are we in important aspects of life? How will we handle conflicts in these areas?*

Similarities. Differences are interesting and can be positive; however, relationships are strengthened when partners share similar values and attitudes, have some of the same interests, and share a common life style. Even though religion may not be as generally important as it once was, a similarity in this area is quite beneficial. Couples who share compatible philosophies find it easier to be intimate (Sternberg and Whitney, 1991). Strong values and attitudes, if unshared, are especially troublesome. For example, if you are opposed to prejudice and committed to human rights and equality, a partner's bigotry would pose a serious threat to a relationship. Minor differences, which lend spark and variety to a relationship, are beneficial. Major differences, especially in sensitive areas, are disruptive.

Differences in socioeconomic backgrounds also are good to examine. Do you feel comfortable in each other's worlds? Do you view the differences as positive or potentially negative? A question for many in today's society has to do with interracial and interethnic marriages. Understanding the special challenges you face in a world that is still prejudiced and discriminatory is critical. Having several other similarities and a strong intimate love will be instrumental. Realistically, you will be contending with additional obstacles because of your differences. That doesn't preclude you from being successful and, if so, deservedly, with a deep sense of pride.

- *Do we have common interests? How do we like to spend vacations? How will we use leisure time? How important are our hobbies? How will we spend holidays, in general?*

Interests and leisure time. People seek enjoyment within an intimate relationship. Even though it isn't necessary to have exactly the same interests and hobbies, sharing several and being open to others lead to mutual pleasure. Showing an interest indicates a liking and respect for the other person. If both agree about vacations and holidays in general and keep an open mind when these are being discussed, the relationship benefits.

- *Are our life styles compatible? Do we have some of the same friends? Do we like each other's friends?*

Life styles and friends. "Margie really likes to 'party,' and when we first started going out, I found her wild ways attractive. As time went by, I realized that I didn't like the drinking scene, the late hours, and all the running around. We fight about this a lot," said Greg. Compatibility of life styles impacts on long-term happiness, and if neither is willing to change, marriage is not the answer. Life style is also reflected in how you demonstrate your socioeconomic status (i.e., large, showy home versus small, average-looking residence, buying expensive new cars) and time allocation (i.e., work before play or fun comes first).

Even though you don't necessarily have to like all the friends of each other, not liking *any or few* is a "red flag." It's important to explore reasons for liking and disliking; in the process, you will learn more about the other person. Although maintaining friendships throughout life is important, putting friends ahead of a significant other is asking for trouble.

- *Are we independent of our families? What role will our families play in our lives?*

Extended family ties. Strong ties to one's biological family can cause frustrating conflict within a marriage. If one partner or the other has not physically and psychologically separated from home, the probability of marital success is low. "He spends more time with his parents than he does with me," complained a young woman. "It seems like they are always wanting him to help them, and he just picks up and goes." Families will remain important, and successful couples usually have positive relationships with extended family members, yet these relationships are to be secondary to the marriage.

What about not liking or not getting along with each other's families? Again, caution is in order. For what reasons don't you like or get along? Are your feelings similar to your partner's? "I don't really get along with two of my brothers so I don't expect her to like them," said one man. Premarital danger signs arise when low self-esteem, poor communication, and rigidity are characteristic of family members (Bilofsky and Sacharow, 1991).

"But, I'm not marrying his family. I'm marrying him." Keep in mind that this person spent many years in the family and has certainly been influenced. Individuals are wise to assess what you don't like about family members and whether your partner is similar in those areas. Upbringing, while significant, is not necessarily an accurate predictor of the future. What individuals have learned from their family experiences is most important. "People are only victims of the past when they choose to be" (Sternberg and Whitney, 1991, p. 14).

- *Do we want children? If we do, have we talked about the possibilities related to how many, when, child raising, and birth control? Have we agreed about responsibilities for child care?*

Having children. Before marriage, couples are remiss if they don't discuss whether they want to have children. A bizarre case was related by a miserable woman who had suggested to her husband of 3 years that she was ready to become pregnant. He looked surprised and said, "I don't want to have kids." Such cases are rare, yet to avoid any surprises, talk about desire for children. Essential is to discuss parenting and all aspects of raising children which are covered in the next chapter including any stereotypic ideas regarding child care. I enjoyed reading a comment in a study of dual-earner couples: "If fathers want to romp with their children on the living room carpet, it is important that they be willing to vacuum it regularly" (Hawking and Robert, 1991, p. 170). Also, a father would share in caring for the romping children.

- *Have we been open with each other about sexuality? Do we have any attitudes that may cause problems?*

Sexuality. Couples may or may not have sexual experience before they marry. If current statistics are any indication, most will. Whether or not a couple is sexually experienced, communication about sexual attitudes and desires is highly recommended. This important area is not to be avoided because both just expect that things will work out fine on their own. Dissatisfaction is likely if two people do not share similar attitudes about their sexual relationship. Reading together the earlier section on sexual fulfillment as well as other books on the subject is certainly worthwhile.

- *Do we really know each other, including our habits, faults, and idiosyncrasies?*

Knowing each other. Spending time together under all kinds of circumstances gives each partner an opportunity to truly get to know the other. How well you really know each other depends upon the absence of game playing and romantic-love facades. Annoying habits can seem "cute" at first, yet over a long period of time, they erode the relationship. The use of drugs is one behavior that must be evaluated. "I realized that he drank a lot when we went out, but I never dreamed he depended on it so much. Now his drinking is ruining our marriage." People are not apt to change their habits after marriage. In a lively public address, Jim Kern, a professional speaker, told of a young woman who bemoaned her fiancé's drinking. "I'm sure he will change after we get married," she said. Kern asked, "How many of you believe that he will?" No hands were raised. "And how many of you think he will find more reasons to drink and blame them all on her?" was the next question. The raised hands and laughter demonstrated that people know that automatic postmarital changes for the better are rare.

- *Do we have personality differences that may cause difficulties? Do we like each other's personalities and recognize positive traits?*

Personality traits. Polar opposites are not likely to remain happy together for long. You are wise to avoid extreme opposites in some areas and to recognize the reasons for your attraction (Johnson, 1992). An extravert and an introvert, as classified on the Myers-Briggs type indicator (MBTI), are likely to report significantly more problems than two who are matched in this preference category (Sherman, 1981). Creative solutions are in order. One couple decided that they would drive two cars to social events. She, an introvert, wanted to limit her time at such events to only a few hours, while he, an extravert, liked to be a part of the action for the duration. Each returned home at a different time, and both were happy. Personality differences do not necessarily create problems; rather, unawareness of the differences causes difficulty. Frequently, a person marries an opposite and then is annoyed when the partner doesn't think and act in a similar way.

Couples who are too much alike can also run into difficulty. If neither has strength in the MBTI sensing preference, for example, the couple will be at a disadvantage in matters such as budgeting and income-tax figuring. Either may have skills yet not enjoy using them. Two individuals with strong judging preferences are likely to "bat heads" when personal plans and schedules do not coincide. Deciding how to manage these areas could prevent serious problems.

Certain personality traits such as caring, warm, understanding, humorous, and unselfish are desirable for individuals and serve to create a positive environment. Husbands with sensitive personalities experienced higher quality marriages and produced higher quality marriages for their wives, according to one study (Vannoy and Philliber, 1992). Liking and appreciating each other's personalities makes a significant difference in both the success of the marriage and the happiness of each person.

- *Are we flexible and do we communicate in positive and effective ways?*

Positive communication and flexibility. "Communication is the lifeblood of any relationship, and the love relationship demands communication if it is to flourish" (Branden and Branden, 1982, p. 63). Marriages without positive communication are unhappy and prone to eventual dissolution. Listening may be considered "love in action, and nowhere is it more appropriate than in marriage" (Peck, 1978, p. 128). The factor that most strongly affects marital quality appears to be the ability to give and receive support (Vannoy and Philliber, 1992) which is accomplished through open communication.

Because communication is a primary predictor of marital satisfaction (Gottmann, 1991), learn and practice positive communication before marriage or decide not to marry. Don't make the mistake of believing that communication will improve after marriage. Over and over I hear individuals say: "We don't self-disclose deeply now, but I'm sure it will get better after we marry." I cringe remembering that I had the same thoughts before my first marriage, and it didn't get better. If communication and trust aren't established early in the relationship, they won't develop later when the stakes are much higher (Sternberg and Whitney, 1991). Taking an interpersonal communication course is one of the best possible action steps. Also, recognize that communication, even within an intimate relationship with the best intentions, isn't easy.

> As you try to hear the other person, you are, at the very least, in a three-ring circus. You are paying attention to the sound of the other person's voice, experiencing past and future fears concerning both of you, becoming aware of your own freedom to say what you are feeling, and finally concentrating on efforts to get the meaning from your partner's words (Satir, 1988, p. 70).

A personality trait that influences communication and all other aspects of a relationship is flexibility. Two rigid persons will not bend, and the marriage is what will break. Similarly, the need to be right is the greatest cause of difficulties and deterioration in relationships (Dyer, 1992). Inflexibility and a controlling personality go hand-in-hand. Controllers want to have power over others (Jones and Schechter, 1992). They go to great lengths to make sure they come out on top and generally do not consider others' feelings or wishes. Controlling methods include criticism, moodiness, anger, threats, and even overprotection. The person may also deny your perception. For example, if you object to a hurtful remark, he or she is likely to say, "You just can't take a joke," even though you are sure it wasn't a joke. Individuals with extreme negative personality traits don't make good marital partners. As with communication, don't believe the myth that the person will change for the better after marriage.

- *Do we enjoy being together and are we good friends?*

Togetherness and pleasure. Enjoyment of each other's company is essential. Long-term relationships thrive on mutual pleasures. A study of married couples showed that greater amounts of togetherness produced more satisfying marriages. Certain shared activities including eating, playing, and conversing added to satisfaction, while time spent on child care, housework, television watching, or community service had no significant effects (Bozzi, 1988). Can the two of you be alone happily while engaging in a variety of pleasurable activities? Can you be alone doing "nothing" and be content? These are important to consider.

Friendship. Being friends and not just lovers is closely related to marital satisfaction (Cowan and Kinder, 1987; Solomon, 1988). In a survey entitled "What Keeps a Marriage Going?" (Lauer and Lauer, 1985), both women and men listed, "My spouse is my best friend" as their top reason, with, "I like my spouse as a person" second. All the ingredients of friendship are necessary in intimate love. "We were friends first and then became sexually attracted to each other. I think that's why our relationship is so successful," said one woman. Friendship is a much better model for what you need in marriage than the media images of romantic love (Bell, 1991).

Friendship does not have to be present in the beginning. You can be physically attracted and then become friends. The key is that at some time friendship must develop. "Is friendship essential to love? No, but it is essential to love's lasting for it is the foundation of love" (Solomon, 1988, p. 315). Individuals who can honestly say that their marital partners are their best friends are quite fortunate.

The regrettable irony is that individuals often treat loved ones with less regard and consideration than they do their friends. "Oh, Jack doesn't care that I criticize him. He knows I love him" is a common attitude.

> The more we care, the more we seem to hurt, compare, and judge. In our zeal to make our loved ones perfect or protect them from pain, we devalue them as human beings.

> We are certainly not as trusting, tolerant or thoughtful with them as we are with friends. Still that is what is needed in loving each other (Buscaglia, 1984, p. 183).

Friendship is the glue that holds marriages together and makes them so fulfilling. Without friendship, intimate love dies.

- *How will we help each other during periods of crisis?*

Support during crises. From firsthand experiences I realize how significant this question is. If you have encountered such crises as a death in the family, a personal health problem, or a family disruption, you already know how the two of you will react. If you haven't, you are wise to discuss possibilities and make some type of commitment to each other. Being "there" for each other is a reasonable expectation and crucial to success in marriage.

You would also be wise to know how the potential partner shows support and if that way will be helpful to you. A strong thinking preference on the MBTI will immediately begin to problem-solve in a logical way while the feeling type will empathize. Certainly, individuals can offer both types of support although some offer little. Spending a long time with this person means that you are likely to go through rough times together. A high degree of emotional supportiveness that I have found in my present marriage makes all the difference in the world.

- *How well do we manage conflict?*

Last on the list of questions, certainly not because of least importance, is ***management of conflict***. In fact, the ability to handle disagreement is a pivotal skill in marriage. This important topic is covered extensively in the next section.

Other questions related to your specific relationship may also be in order. The actual discussion of all questions can reveal potential problems. For example, consider the following:

> HE: I'm Catholic, and you're Protestant. Do you think that will be a problem?
>
> SHE: I hope not, but I won't consider changing.
>
> HE: I would like to eventually live on the West Coast.
>
> SHE: Oh, no, I'd never live there.
>
> HE: I like to spend vacations just loafing.
>
> SHE: It's not a vacation if you don't travel. We're not going to just sit around.

Disregarding content, did you notice the woman's inflexibility? What style of verbalizing was she using? Her closed attitude and communication style were evident. He would be wise to take heed.

After you read this chapter and think about the success factors, a wise recommendation is to remember that no person or relationship is perfect. Again, you can use a costs versus benefits analysis taking the advice of two authors (Katz and Aimee, 1988): If your partner meets your basic requirements for love in general, if both of you have experienced other relationships, and if the two of you are willing to accept equality, then apply the 90:10 rule. In considering all factors, if the relationship is 90 percent positive, go for it! I would add to be sure that the factors in the unfavorable 10 percent aren't the most potentially destructive ones.

Managing Conflict Successfully

The ways in which couples handle disagreements are apparent before marriage. A just-kiss-and-make-up philosophy may carry people through the courtship stage, and they probably won't realize the negative impacts of their behavior until later. Learning to manage conflict, or handle disagreement, successfully from the beginning is preferable. Years ago, conflict management was not a consideration. The widely held belief was that loving couples did not fight. A disagreement was a sign of weakness in the relationship, so you hurried to "patch things up." Important conflict issues were often "glossed over" for fear that they would spell the end of the relationship. When couples did disagree, they usually did so in an unpleasant, aggressive manner. Then, making up was a relief. The crux of the problem was often left untouched. What do the experts say?

> Love rarely remains all flowers and sweetness. Disagreements, arguments, and fighting are natural when two people are trying to put together two approaches to life. More important than what you fight about is how you fight together (Wegscheider-Cruse, 1988, p. 109).
>
> One of the first tests we can apply to the health of a relationship is not so much whether there are conflicts, but whether those conflicts are addressed and resolved. Conflict can serve useful purposes (Crowther, 1986, p. 151).
>
> A fair fight can clear the air and relieve a lot of stress. Don't be afraid to fight with ones you love. Love and anger usually go together. If you didn't care about each other, you wouldn't bother to fight (Tubesing, 1981, p. 92).

One of the first and still best-known books for laypersons on the subject of conflict management is *The Intimate Enemy: How to Fight Fair in Love and Marriage* (Bach and Wyden, 1968). My copy is well-worn, and I regard the book as required reading for preparation and enrichment of marriage. The premise is that verbal conflict, defined as disagreement, between intimates is not only inevitable and acceptable but can be constructive and desirable. The book provides insight into how to fight. You may inwardly shudder at the word fight. Thinking of *fighting* as a way of handling disagreement may make it more palatable.

Two opposite types of *fighting styles* are identified. Fight evaders, nonfighters, are "doves." For any number of reasons, these people are fight-phobic and resist fighting. Gunnysacking, described in Chapter 9, is a common behavior. Two "doves" don't level with each other and often pay the price of emotional divorce. Most would not recognize this as a type of fighting; however, keep in mind the definition of fighting as a way of handling conflict. The opposite are "hawks," or aggressive fighters. They are usually loud, observably angry, and hostile. They use unfair, hurtful tactics and damage their relationship with their conflicts.

Both types experience anger which is inevitable within an intimate relationship. So when partners don't fight, according to Bach and Wyden, their anger isn't being expressed, and they aren't experiencing true intimacy. Anger is a signal worth listening to. If a person asks, "What am I angry about, what is the problem, and whose problem is it," anger is potentially constructive. Women, more than men, have been instructed to avoid conflict and anger so may be more inclined to use complaining and blaming instead of openly expressing anger. Or, they might go along with what the partner wants which results in a build-up of anger (Lerner, 1985). Believing that the "inability to manage personal conflicts is at the root of the crisis that threatens the structure of the American family" (p. 31), Bach and Wyden (1968) contend that learning the art of fair fighting is essential. Unfair fighting comes from either the "hawk" or "dove" style and is the way most of us fight. *How conflict is resolved or how the couple fights is what determines the health of the couple and the relationship*. What is recommended?

Most experts suggest that, if possible, couples carefully choose the best time, place, and conditions for resolving conflict. Too often, individuals fight when they are tired, under inordinate stress, or after drinking alcohol. Inevitably, these conditions set the stage for unfair fighting. The old adage, "Don't let the sun set on a quarrel," interpreted as, "Don't go to bed angry," is not wise advice. When tired, couples can create added problems, or, as often happens, one person "gives up" in order to get some rest.

The concept of "giving up" and "giving in" places fighting on the level of a wrestling match. Usually, the one who concedes, or "gives in," is left with resentment. Fair fighters can call a time-out, a halt in their discussion, and resume under more positive conditions. Neither competitive nor avoidant styles are beneficial (Scott, 1990). Here are a few other criteria by which to determine the extent of fairness.

Winning—losing: If either person "wins," the relationship loses. Getting rid of the win-loss notion is important. The key to win-win is to recognize and satisfy as best as possible each person's highest priorities or most important needs (Scott, 1990). A collaborative negotiation style described in Chapter 9 leads to win-win. "Happy couples care more about the health of their relationship than winning arguments" (Johnson, 1992, p. 67).

Involvement: Have you ever been engaged in a fight that was a monologue? Too often, one person does most, if not all, the talking, and the other simply absorbs or ignores. Keep in mind that as frustrating as it can be, silence is power (Tavris, 1992). In what Braiker (1992) calls destructive conflict, the amount of information exchanged is decreased with tactics such as the silent treatment and "I don't want to discuss it" approaches. In a fair fight both individuals are to be involved in the exchange and take turns verbalizing and listening.

Communication: Use of "I," not "you," statements, active, receptive listening, direct, honest, and clear messages from both partners, and no game playing nor manipulative techniques are essential guidelines. In constructive conflict the amount of information exchanged is increased, and the communication is open, flexible, and noncoercive (Braiker, 1992).

Injury: Being careful to direct criticism to behaviors, to avoid personal attacks and name calling, and to maintain consideration for the other is necessary. We all have our "Achilles Heels," and unfair fighters hit "below the belt" in areas of vulnerability.

Directness: Remaining focused in the present and on the subject at hand is difficult to do, yet significant. If a new topic is presented, the issue can get sidetracked. Promising to handle the new topic later is recommended.

Specificity: Clarity, not vagueness, and description of behaviors are needed. Using perception checking and the awareness wheel is a way of being clear. Be sure that you aren't arguing simply because of unshared meanings.

Feelings: Sharing emotions during conflict is beneficial. Frequently, when partners know each other's feelings, they experience empathy and understanding. Focusing on feelings, not actions, is beneficial as is empathizing before criticizing (Podell, 1992).

Responsibility: Both people take a share of the responsibility for the conflict itself and for the process required to resolve it. Try to consider "fault" a dirty word (Podell, 1992). Conflict is usually a two-way street. If each takes 100 percent responsibility for what happens to the relationship, this means a 200 percent commitment (Bloomfield, Vettese, and Kory, 1989).

Humor: As strange as it may seem, if in some way, positive humor creeps into a fight, the mood of both will probably lighten. Obviously, any use of sarcasm or nasty humor would

> only hurt. One time in the middle of a somewhat heated discussion, I said, "I'm so angry I've decided to quit doing the cooking." My husband laughed immediately since I do so little of it anyway. We found it hard to remain upset in the joy of laughter.

Of importance, too, is to examine the effects of the fight. Has either partner's self-esteem been diminished? If so, the fight wasn't fair. Do you feel closer, as caring, more intimate? Has the relationship been strengthened or weakened?

> Fair fighting is not a sport like boxing. It is an art and a skill like dancing. It takes cooperation and style. In fact, the style of a fight is more important than what you actually fight about. Several days after a fight, you may remember only about 10 percent of the content, but you will probably have almost total recall for the style: whether the fight was fair, how hurt you felt, how strong the emotions were, how satisfied or upset you felt afterward (McKay et al., 1983, p. 136).

Fair fighting leads partners along the path of increased closeness and intimacy. Conflict is constructive if it includes affection, humor, problem-solving, agreement, assent, empathy, and active nondefensive listening (Gottmann, 1991).

Do I Have to Give Up Me to Be Loved by You? (Paul and Paul, 1983) is another recommended book. Understandable guidelines are outlined in the section "From Conflict to Intimacy." The authors recommend viewing conflict as an opportunity to learn about self and others and to grow. When both assume responsibility for feelings, behaviors, and consequences, the relationship is enhanced. Aaron Beck (1988), eminent psychologist and founder of cognitive therapy, made a major contribution to the field of conflict management with his book *Love Is Never Enough*. Regularly scheduled discussions, which Beck calls "troubleshooting sessions," are helpful. Couples then do not

Figure 11-7 Fair fighting demands the finest communication skills.

bring up each troublesome incident when it happens; instead, they wait for the session and empty their "gunnysacks." This eliminates the common practice of nagging.

Susan Borkin, a friend and therapist in California, recommends a 20-minute period for cooling off and digesting the message after one person has expressed anger and displeasure. "Agreement is easier after feelings are vented and allowed to dissipate," Borkin maintains in her fair fighting workshops. Fair fighting is likelier if both individuals learn to feel anger coming. If you aren't able to manage the anger, you are better off calling for a time-out and refusing to continue the fight (Podell, 1992). A unique idea is to tape record the fight so each person can see what they did to escalate the conflict and how they could improve (Farrell, 1986).

Despite the best intentions, lovers do lose control at times and angrily erupt. The value of knowing how to positively manage conflict is that you know and can admit when unfair tactics were used. Apologizing and committing to try harder the next time are signs of maturity. If either person has been hurtful, listening to the other's pain, apologizing, and trying to change will help love grow. When people absolutely refuse to attempt positive change, it may be better to end the relationship. Openness and flexibility are key ingredients in positive conflict management. Have fun as you learn to assess an unfair fight described in REFLECTIONS AND APPLICATIONS.

Cohabitation as a Prelude to Marriage

Cohabitation, two partners living together as if married, has increased as a result of a more permissive societal attitude and liberalization of laws. In the United States cohabitation before first marriages has increased from 11 percent in the early 1970s to about 50 percent in the early 1990s (Bumpass, 1990). This does not represent the thousands of couples cohabiting prior to other than first marriages. Almost half of recently marrieds and those in their early 30s have cohabited (Bumpass and Sweet, 1989). Cohabitation is accepted by most and is "no longer a deviant life style alternative nor a clandestine arrangement apart from the larger context of courtship and marriage" (Spanier, 1989, p. 7).

Cohabitation can serve as a replacement for marriage; usually, however, couples cohabit as a testing ground or as preparation for marriage. Approximately 50 to 65 percent use cohabitation as a prelude to marriage (Thompson and Colella, 1992). Because 40 percent of cohabiting households include children, it is sometimes described as family status with a degree of uncertainty (Bumpass et al., 1991). If either or both is morally opposed to it, cohabitation is not advisable. A hindrance to effectiveness exists if couples "play house" while cohabiting or have stereotypic attitudes about marriage, as indicated earlier. For example, Sean and Terri lived together happily for 4 years. They married, then divorced 2 years later. Their counselor discovered that Sean had been especially attentive during the cohabitation period and lost interest after marriage. He saw marriage as a bleak life style.

Whether cohabitation can enhance chances for marital success is questionable. Results of studies of cohabitation prior to first marriages have varied; some indicate no effects while others suggest that cohabitation may have an adverse effect. Recent research paints a negative picture. Cohabitation is associated with higher marital dissolution in Canada (Trussell and Rao, 1989), Sweden (Bennett et al., 1988), and the United States (Axinn and Thornton, 1992; Bumpass et al., 1991; DeMaris and Rao, 1992). Couples who cohabited reported lower quality marriages, lower commitment to the institution of marriage, and a greater likelihood of divorce than couples who did not (Thompson and Colella, 1992). Even though figures show that cohabitation has not improved marriages, the reasons remain elusive. Speculations range from cohabitors tending to be less committed to permanent relationships (Schoen, 1992) to cohabitation weakening commitment because it demonstrates alternatives to marriage (Thompson and Colella, 1992). Other suggestions are that cohabitors may be less traditional and more independent in their thinking.

Cohabitation may have a favorable aspect that seems to get overlooked. Because 40 percent of those who cohabit end their relationship (Bumpass et al., 1991), it appears that living together does serve to screen out potentially troubled marriages. This, undoubtedly, has contained the divorce rate and kept people from suffering through unhappy unions. Also beneficial is that living together has led to a postponement of marriage until later ages (Bumpass et al., 1991) which can create better unions.

Few studies concern cohabitation prior to remarriages. I conducted such a study in Lincoln, Nebraska (Hanna and Knaub, 1981). Of 80 remarried couples in the sample, 40 had lived together for at least a month prior to their remarriages while 40 others had not. Unlike studies prior to first marriage, the cohabiting group scored higher on three measures of marital success including family strength, marital satisfaction, and their own perception of adjustment. Another study on courtship before remarriage (Montgomery et al., 1992) showed that children whose mother cohabited appeared to be more socially competent throughout the 2 years after remarriage while experiencing less negative family relationships.

If couples choose to cohabit, they would be wise to do so in a realistic manner. "Playing house" and viewing this situation as quite different from marriage will only obscure the facts. If cohabitation has any benefits in terms of preparation, the attitudes and conditions must be realistic.

Enrichment of Marriage

Pretend you have planted a garden of vegetables and flowers. You pay little attention to the garden. You never fertilize, rarely water, and you don't weed. What will happen? The garden will have little chance of thriving, and even survival is in jeopardy. Couples who don't take care of their marriages face the same risks. A relationship is in a constant state of change. Compare marriage to a highway that needs to be upgraded, maintained, and even rebuilt; the process is never finished (Sternberg and Whitney, 1991). Because the probability of attaining marriage success in a first marriage, or at all, has declined in recent years measured by numbers of intact marriages and reported levels of satisfaction (Glenn, 1991), *marriage enrichment*, the process of making a good marriage better, deserves priority.

Barriers in marriage enrichment. A realization that neglect can lead to unhappiness and even the death of a marriage can motivate couples to pay attention. Unfortunately, most individuals aren't even aware of the threat. An assumption in the past was that if you didn't fight much and life was progressing smoothly, your marriage was in good shape. That is not necessarily true.

> Relationships do not typically unravel because of major conflicts. Most relationships die slowly and without the conscious awareness of either party. There is a fine line between a relationship that moves in a positive direction and one that slips silently into apathy or the slow accumulation of disappointments and resentment (Cowan and Kinder, 1987, p. 5).

Within marriage, the sexual relationship is definitely an area of benign neglect. Sex therapist Dagmar O'Connor (1985) contrasts lovemaking attitudes and behaviors before and after marriage. Before marriage people describe themselves as being "swept away" by passion and relate the sex act to an "accident that just happened." For most individuals, these feelings add to the allure of lovemaking. Over years of marriage, couples make sex a conscious act that should happen, and then they blame the lack of excitement on being married. "That's how it is. After you're married awhile, the thrill is gone."

> We devise ways to avoid sex in marriage altogether-or at least to avoid exciting sex. Now instead of sex "just happening," "it just doesn't happen." We are not responsible for our sexual infrequency or apathy. The "chemistry" is gone; we are not "swept away" anymore; we are too "busy" for sex. It is not our fault. But it is (O'Connor, 1985, p. 6).

The thrill in making love does not have to disappear like a puff of smoke. Maintaining a fulfilling sexual relationship (using ideas covered earlier in this chapter) is a vital part of marriage enrichment.

In other areas, too, married couples have a tendency to "settle down." Rather than engage in pleasurable activities such as dancing, eating out, walking in the park, and going on picnics as they once did, a couple will often "settle down" in front of the television set night after night. They develop other predictable patterns of behaving and exhibit a "lack of individual artistry and creativity which leads to the most destructive of the 'four horsemen of the apocalypse' of marriage—boredom" (Lingren, 1981).

Boredom is the result of getting to know each other so well that couples prejudge. "I know exactly what his reaction will be" or "She always reacts like that" is what is called the "already known" syndrome (Malone and Malone, 1987). Intimacy means finding the new in the familiar and seeking creative possibilities rather than prejudging. The

Figure 11-8

unfamiliar, the risk, the unpredictability liberates human beings from boredom and enlivens relationships (Buscaglia, 1984).

Another barrier is the destructive habit of criticism. Marriage seems to give individuals license to be critical. "We love others because of what they are—then expect, even demand from them what they are not" (Resz, 1984, p. 17). Instead of appreciating the differences they were attracted to in the first place, most partners set out to change the other (Kinder and Cowan, 1989). Criticism is often used as a tool. Lovers often treat each other less kindly than they do friends. Here are some common inaccurate assumptions.

Criticizing is a way of helping another improve, so by delivering critical comments, a person is showing love.

Love can withstand the onslaught of negativism, so criticism won't hurt.

Criticism is humorous ("I'm only kidding" is a typical explanation for being critical).

Criticism, at least the way most people deliver it, is not a sign of love. Criticism does hurt, and "only kidding" is almost always only a justification. Using sarcasm or ridicule to make a critical point is harmful to the relationship. Pointing out that good relationships employ minimum criticism, Glasser (1984) writes, "The more intimate the relationship—and marriage starts out as the most intimate of all relationships—the more destructive criticism is to its success" (p. 159).

Self-righteousness usually precedes criticism, and the need to be "right" can chip away at love. "Being right is an empty victory, for even if you are right, your rightness is irrelevant to any positive change in the marriage. Your being right isn't going to change your mate for the better; it will simply make him or her feel deficient" (Kinder and Cowan, 1989, p. 83).

In addition to boredom, criticism, and self-righteousness, ten ways to invade, stifle, or kill a marriage follow (Wegscheider-Cruse, 1988):

1. Give your mother, father, friend, boss, or child more credence and respect than you give your mate.
2. Schedule your partner's time without first asking.
3. Put your own insecurities and inadequacies on your mate and expect them to be fixed.
4. Insult or put down your mate in public (or private).
5. Add "old" data or anger to a new and current fight, and resurrect old battles and ancient hurts.
6. Talk frequently about an ex-anything.
7. Withhold the sharing of true feelings.
8. Be indecisive.
9. Act fragile, helpless, or inept.
10. Tell partial truths.

Each can block enrichment of marriage. Too many will likely kill a relationship.

Picture an intimate love relationship as a large rock. No matter how solid the rock (or the relationship), erosion can take place, and the mass is weakened by a wearing-away process. Keeping your "gunnysack" full and unfair fighting can erode the rock. So can burnout which occurs in relationships just as it does in the work environment. How does one know when burnout is in process?

> Intimacy burnout becomes apparent when increasing boredom, depression, and resignation settle like lunar dust over an intimate relationship that once was vibrant, exhilarating, pulsating with energy, and so much fun that it crackled with the laughter of the young at heart no matter how old in years. In intimacy burnout, the draining energy of anxiety replaces the charging energy of discovery (Crowther, 1986, p. 50).

Becoming familiar with each other and maintaining the relationship are worthy objectives if they don't negate new experiences. When new experiences are avoided, the relationship becomes stagnant and unexciting. Familiarity and predictability can be positive as long as they don't equate to dullness in the marriage. If marital neglect has already led to apathy and boredom, or if chronic criticism and self-righteousness have taken their toll, a couple can revitalize their relationship. Couples benefit from deciding that enrichment has a high priority and then committing themselves to achieving it.

Enriching attitudes and behaviors. As in all aspects of life, focusing more on the positive than on the negative enhances a relationship. One way to do this is to record and rate each other's pleasing behaviors. Of the couples who tried this, 70 percent reported an improvement in their relationship. Nothing had changed except their awareness. Before keeping track, they had underestimated the positives in their marriage (Beck, 1988).

Improving in the vital areas of communication and conflict management is enriching. In addition, Robert Sternberg, who developed the triangular picture of love described earlier in this chapter, included ten rules for success in his book (1987).

1. Don't take the relationship for granted.
2. Make the relationship your first priority.
3. Actively seek to meet each other's needs.
4. Know when and when not to change in response to the other. Be flexible.
5. Value yourself. (Sternberg referred to what Maslow (1962) called deficiency—love in which one seeks out another in order to remedy a lack in the self contrasted with being—love where one seeks another in order to enhance an already adequate self).
6. Love each other, not the idealization of each other.
7. Tolerate what you cannot change.
8. Be open with each other.
9. Make good times together and grow through bad ones.
10. Treat the other as you want to be treated.

Besides Sternberg's recommendations, couples can decide to *do* marriage rather than just be married (Spezzano, 1992) and use any of the following ideas to enhance their marriage.

- Set aside a special time to communicate each day. This is "alone" time. Ideally, you focus on positives, and not use it as a "dumping ground" for negatives. Use this time to tell each other about positive behaviors and to self-disclose.

- Verbally and nonverbally express an interest in each other.
- Give positive strokes each day. Compliment each other. Demonstrate affection by physical contact, words, and deeds. Hug and kiss daily, yet don't necessarily do it as a routine. "We kiss each other good-bye each day" is nice, but don't allow this to replace unpredictable moments.
- Be considerate. Say good-bye when you leave and hello when you come together again. Let each other know where you are and be dependable. Empathize with each other.
- Tell each other "thank you" each day, either for a particular behavior or just to express appreciation for each other and for the relationship.
- Surprise each other with little notes, cards, gifts, and unusual plans. Spontaneity brings delight into a relationship. Create feelings of delight and amusement.
- Affirm each other privately and in front of others. Hearing a partner deliver praise about you in the presence of others is like a ray of sunshine on a cloudy day.
- Develop rituals and traditions. Celebrate special days and make everyday events more pleasurable. Institute "caring days" in which you provide treats for each other and do things you did while you were courting. *Re*romanticize the relationship (Hendrix, 1988).
- Spend time together away from everyday hassles. In spite of best intentions, you may find it difficult to forget the nitty-gritty of daily life if you remain at home. Going away for a weekend or even overnight can be a refreshing and relaxing experience. Even going out for an evening gets you away from the demands of the immediate environment.
- Increase the number and frequency of pleasurable events. Find mutually enjoyable activities and engage in them on a regular basis. High energy activities are healthy.
- Express all genuine emotions, the pleasant and unpleasant ones. Sharing true feelings is an enriching experience.
- Laugh with each other at least once a day (more than once is better)! A survey found that couples spent only about ten minutes a week on the average playing and laughing together (Hendrix, 1988).
- Talk about your early relationship and what attracted you to each other in the first place. Share other positive memories from your mutual past.
- Share your hopes and dreams. "Dreams elevate us beyond the mundane. To dream together adds an element of wonder to our relationship and gives us something to look forward to" (Buscaglia, 1984, p. 186).
- Share enrichment ideas with each other. Even if some don't seem feasible, the shared joy in dreaming is enriching.
- Give each other massages and use other types of loving non-sexual touch everyday.

Enrichment vitalizes relationships. A song from the past, "Little Things Mean a Lot," delivers an important message. In our kitchen is a mug inscribed, "I love you." Invariably, when my husband brings me coffee, it comes in that mug—a little "thing" whose meaning is far from small.

You and your partner can help each other acquire loving behaviors. Demonstrativeness, for example, is difficult for some. If you want demonstrated affection, say so. Don't be like Ann, who said, "I know Dave loves me, but he just can't show it." Yes, he can! Learning new behaviors may be necessary. Knowing that hugging and other forms of touching are healthy for individuals and that they also benefit the relationship is motivating.

An enriching behavior may be to seek counseling. Enrichment is used within a good marriage; however, the process may uncover areas where professional help could be beneficial. Two intimates are often so close to their situation that they are blinded to underlying problems. In one study marital therapy increased marital satisfaction and, in the process, decreased levels of mild to moderate depression (O'Leary and Beach, 1990). If you decide to see a counselor, try to find one recommended by people you trust. As in every field, marriage and family counselors vary in their abilities. Even after you have made your selection, if one of you feels uncomfortable with the therapist, find another one. It's important that each of you feels respected, acknowledged, and valued by the therapist (Weiner-Davis, 1992). What you are trying to achieve is of the utmost value. A helpful attitude is to think of the relationship as the client rather than either of you (Forward and Torres, 1986). This relieves anxieties of either individual concerning exposure of personal weaknesses. Cheri, a student, writes of a successful counseling outcome.

> Our early relationship was classic romantic love, as we discussed in class. It was all-consuming, insecure, out of control, and smothering. It took months of our working together with a counselor to help us see what direction we were headed—toward disaster. That has been 6 years ago. We have both grown and matured since then and continue to grow in a compatible direction. I think our greatest accomplishment has been in not taking each other for granted. I know every couple doesn't take the opportunity we did to turn our lives around, and I feel very lucky that we did.

Think of a marriage as an investment. What makes an investment portfolio valuable is having more assets than liabilities. Enrichment adds to the assets. A sad commentary on contemporary life is that people will spend more time maintaining houses, automobiles, and other machines than they do caring for their relationships. This extremely vital part of life demands and deserves tender, loving care. An attitude that "Our relationship is precious, and we want to keep it that way" can bring a dream of an enriched marriage to reality. Together, couples can choose how rewarding and successful their relationship will be.

ENDING RELATIONSHIPS

"Till death us do part" is no longer a reality. Statistics vary; however, the generally accepted prediction is that 50 percent of today's first marriages will end in divorce (O'Leary and Smith, 1991). In an interview, researcher Larry L. Bumpass noted an under reporting of divorce and separation and estimated that about two thirds of all first marriages are likely to dissolve. The United States has the highest divorce rate among major industrialized countries (O'Leary and Smith, 1991; Popenoe, 1993). Since 1970 the divorce rate has increased 71 percent (DeWitt, 1992a). The figures are unsettling for individuals and the society. No matter how disquieting the idea of divorce, thousands of people yearly find themselves faced with a legal ending to their relationship.

Reasons for Divorce

"We loved each other so much. I don't know what happened," isn't an unusual statement when a marriage ends. Frequently, the reasons are obvious. Understanding the "why" can help individuals learn from a painful experience.

An inappropriate or poor choice of a partner is a possibility. An understanding of the fulfillment-of-needs theory, described earlier, may reveal that one or both were not willing to fulfill what was needed. Lack of social exchange apparent when one or both partners decide that the benefits of marriage are outweighed by the costs is a factor. In several cases, another person is "in the picture." As one who does not believe that anyone else "breaks up" a couple, a recommendation is to examine the weakness in the relationship. Or perhaps, one individual in the marriage is simply not committed and engages in repeated self-indulgent outside relationships. In that case, the other is better off divorced.

Couples can have unrealistic expectations, and disappointment is the likely result. Or, realistic expectations may not have been met. "He's almost never home. If he isn't working, he's involved in some community service or leisure-time activity. It's as if I don't exist" is a description of a relationship that falls far short of meeting either a person's legitimate needs or realistic expectations of a marriage. Stephanie explained the ending of her marriage:

> I kept thinking he would change and things would get better. He is so irresponsible and uncaring that I don't even trust him to stay with the children. Now that I'm back in school, I feel like I've seen the light. It's not easy though . . . much like "digging myself out of a swamp." I feel like a consumer trying hard to get rid of a bad product . . . my husband!

Poor communication and conflict-management skills are common causes of divorce. Over a period of time, problems left unexpressed or poorly expressed become insurmountable. Unfair fighting tears couples apart. Finally, if one partner engages in repetitive destructive behaviors and is unwilling to change, leaving is probably the best course of action. Being ignored, neglected, or constantly criticized diminishes self-esteem. Attempts by one to control the life of the other are despicable. A decision to end such a relationship is the first step to personal freedom. Charmaine describes her experience:

> I let my husband totally rule my life and take care of everything. How belittling it was. I am a very strong-minded and strong-willed person naturally, and I saw the life being squeezed out of me. Then I decided to be "me" again. In a nutshell, he needed someone he could control. I blame myself for letting that person be myself. I let him take control from the start so he fell in love with some little wimp, which is definitely not me. I fell in love with a man who has no empathy. I want to raise our children in a caring and loving atmosphere. I want them to be the best they can be and to learn to care for and feel for others, not only for themselves. I think they will be fine. I'm fine. I'm getting "me" back, and I like her!

"A relationship that you know is destructive for you can be much more painful in the long run than the temporary pain of leaving, for a destructive relationship is like an open wound—it just continues to fester without ever healing" (Forward and Torres, 1986, p.

249). A particularly hateful behavior is abuse, either verbal or nonverbal. Habitual serious physical abuse gives separation a green light.

> Remember that you teach him how to behave by what you do. If you stay when he is physically violent, you are teaching him that you will accept more violence. It is a sign of courage and strength to seek help when you need it (Forward and Torres, 1986, p. 233).

Men can also be victims of abuse, and a refusal to allow the behavior is also in order.

Although ending a relationship can be the best solution, seeking divorce isn't always advisable. The acceptance of divorce has helped decrease the commitment to build successful marriages and has made it easy to "call it quits." Either extreme—"never divorce, no matter what" or "no problem; just divorce when the going gets tough"—is an insult to the dignity and value of nourishing relationships. Before making the serious decision to divorce, be sure that the reasons are sound and that all possible has been done to revitalize the marriage.

Of great help in doing this is counseling. In a helpful book, *Divorce Busting: A Revolutionary and Rapid Program for Staying Together*, Weiner-Davis (1992) contends that most unhappy marriages can be changed and are worth changing. Rather than hashing over past hurts and injustices, she advocates a type of Brief Therapy that emphasizes solutions rather than explanations for problems. Counselors who specialize in short-term, task-oriented therapy techniques take an active role (Zois, 1992) and help a couple develop a plan believing that minor shifts in behavior lead to major changes in relationships. As in goal-setting discussed in Chapter 5, the emphasis is on behavior changes and specific action steps. Instead of a vague "be less selfish," the two would agree to consult about weekend activities, check with each other before making plans, and share in household tasks. "Relationships change one step at a time" (Weiner-Davis, 1992, p. 111), and positively recognizing each action success motivates individuals to keep trying. Divorcing the present marriage, *not* the individual you chose, may be the best solution.

Letting Go

Divorce is painful. Even if you are the one who initiates the ending of a marriage, you can expect to experience unpleasant feelings. If you are the one who doesn't want the divorce, you will sink into one of the "dips" of life. A full gamut of emotions may be experienced, depending on the circumstances. (Helping children through divorce will be covered in the next chapter. The emphasis here is on the divorcing adult.)

You will likely feel lonely; remember that you are not alone. In response to the increasing incidence of divorce, books have been written, classes and seminars have been developed, and support groups have been formed. If you divorce, numerous resources are available. One that was especially helpful to me is *How to Survive the Loss of a Love* (Colgrove et al., 1991). Picturing the "healing process as more like a lightning bolt full of ups and downs, progressions and regression, dramatic leaps and depressing backslides" (p. 36) helped me to remain hopeful in the worst of times. Another book, *Rebuilding: When Your Relationship Ends* (Fisher, 1992), is one that Roz, a student, said "saved my life." Fifteen building blocks are described, and the final one is freedom.

One key point to remember is that you are embarking on a well-worn path over which millions have successfully passed, and you can take advantage of all that is now known about divorce. An important step is to change the typical thought that divorce is proof of individual maladjustment and the common feeling of regret that your marriage didn't last forever.

> The value of a relationship lies in the joy it affords, not in its longevity. (There is nothing admirable about two people remaining together, thoroughly frustrated and miserable, for 50 years.) The ending of a relationship does not mean that someone has failed. It means only that someone has changed, perhaps for the better (Branden and Branden, 1982, p. 206).

The divorce process, like the grief process, is a series of stages. Six are identified by Gullo and Church (1988).

- Shock, usually ranging in duration from 1 day to 1 month and characterized by numbness, disorientation, and disbelief.
- Grief or a feeling of depression of varying duration.
- Setting blame, generally accompanied by anger.
- Resignation, or the good-bye stage, when you decide to let go which can be either relieving or draining.
- Rebuilding, when you feel like life is good again (akin to the feeling of when you leave the hospital after major surgery with a clean bill of health).
- Resolution, when peace with the pain is acknowledged and you can look back and see evidence of personal growth.

You can gain strength from seeing where you are in these steps and, after time, how far you have come. Because these stages have been experienced by almost every divorcing person, you can feel assured that you, too, will eventually reach the resolution stage. The "traveling time" for most is about 1 year.

Following are some recommendations for coping with divorce.

- Use this book and others to discover means of coping and behaviors to create happiness and raise self-esteem.
- If you aren't helping yourself, seek counseling.
- Draw upon your support system. You need people. Ideally, talk to people who have divorced and feel just fine. Support groups are in almost every community.
- Find a skilled attorney. The legal aspects of divorce require expertise. Learn about current divorce laws so you have input regarding legal decisions. Your future is at stake.
- Pay special attention to your own health and needs.
- Allow yourself all your feelings without getting stuck with any. Prolonged depression and unresolved anger, for example, indicate a need for counseling.
- Resist the temptation to think of yourself as a failure. Instead, realize that the relationship failed. Do, however, examine yourself and make positive changes.
- Let go of any magical quality you assigned to the marriage and recognize that the relationship no longer exists.
- Seek new relationships with both sexes; however, do not try to build an intimate one right away. Keep in mind Erikson's identity stage, which is best to establish again before you are ready for a new relationship. This recommenda-

tion is difficult to follow because divorcing people usually relish positive attention from the opposite sex. Friendships, at this point, are nourishing. Beyond that, you reduce the potential for success in a future intimate relationship.

- Begin to dream, plan, and live. See divorce as an opportunity, not as a death sentence.

Think of these suggestions as a basic divorce "survival kit." You can add ideas by reading, experiencing, and learning. Self-support and self-respect can be developed by going back to school or taking a course, starting a new project, expanding your network of friends, and joining a worthwhile organization (Adler and Archambault, 1990).

How could anything positive come of divorce? During the initial stages, most find it hard to conceive of this possibility; however, almost every divorced person can point out several benefits. One is heightened self-esteem after, and often as a direct result of, the divorce. Expanding of horizons and becoming independent are boosters to confidence and add to the excitement of life.

New opportunities present themselves and, if taken advantage of, can lead to positive results. Advanced academic degrees, exciting careers, new or renewed hobbies and interests, and exciting interpersonal relationships can be treasures along the way. If the marriage was painful, the relief from stress and misery is a reward in itself. After their divorces Tammy, a young adult, and Shirley, a middle-aged woman, expressed their rewards and joy.

> Now that I have a chance to go to school, I'm learning about myself as well as preparing for a profession. I needed this more than words can say. My grandma used to say, "Every dark cloud has a silver lining." Now I understand. Losing a husband is hard, but finding yourself is wonderful.
>
> From divorce I have learned: to love myself, to not forget me and to think of myself, to live for today, to be an independent person, to make my own happiness, to accept my mistakes, to make my own choices, and, most importantly, that life is up to me. In my marriage I gave all of me. I didn't even know who I was. I am now a happier, wiser person and am still growing. I realize I have so much to learn . . . so many miles to travel before I sleep.

All relationships end at some time. Divorce is an ending that was precipitated by a decision. Whether one person likes the decision or not, understanding the divorce process and electing to move toward a positive ending are beneficial.

Divorce is not a failure of self; usually, it just indicates unwise choices. Objectively, divorced people can accept a share of the responsibility and resolve to be wiser in the future. They can become optimistic about future relationships and willing to risk new experiences. If they value themselves as individuals, they know that they deserve a better partner (Porat, 1988). The ability to let go and say good-bye is a sign of a well-adjusted person. A quote from Dale Carnegie is apt here: "When fate hands us a lemon, let's try to make lemonade."

SUMMARY

Love, intimacy, and marriage are important in most people's lives. Although education would be so beneficial in the areas of loving, marrying, and divorcing, unfortunately, it is not required. Love as an art requires attention, skill, practice, and priority.

Romantic love is the "fluff stuff" of which dreams may be made yet usually not realized. Several problems materialize in a romantic-love relationship; a major challenge is jealousy. In contrast, intimate love is renewing and rewarding and can serve as a strong foundation for a long term, mutually satisfying relationship. Components of intimate love have been identified. Examination of relationship growth and needs fulfillment reveals a great deal about a relationship. Intimate love expands as the individuals grow in compatible directions and as the relationship fulfills primary needs.

Intimacy includes the freedom to be one's genuine self within a relationship and the development of psychological closeness with another person. Building intimacy is challenging. Removing barriers is the first step. An androgynous personality, time, energy, and risk taking enhance intimacy. The rewards are well worth all efforts.

Lack of education is apparent in the area of sexual behavior. Despite an increase in numbers of sexually active individuals, people can be woefully ignorant about healthy sexual behaviors. Marriage does not solve the problem; in fact, sexual dissatisfaction is common. Enrichment makes the differences.

Although many people choose to marry, remaining single is a viable alternative. If one chooses to marry, an understanding of marriage helps foster a positive commitment. Shared and traditional types of marriage based on roles and responsibilities are possible, and individuals are wise to agree on the type they prefer. Marriages can also be typed according to quality.

Couples can benefit from marriage preparation. Self-examination comes first. Marital success factors, as identified by research, can be the basis of relevant, important questions. The discussion of the answers may reveal personal characteristics that are damaging to relationships. For marital partners, the questions can serve as guideposts for improving the relationship. Conflict management deserves special attention because the harm caused by mishandled conflict is a major source of marital dissatisfaction and dissolution. Conflict or disagreement is inevitable in intimate relationships. The key to marital success lies in how the conflict is managed.

Cohabitation, common in today's society, is used by many as a testing period prior to marriage, as well as an opportunity to prepare. Whether cohabitation influences the probability of marital success is questionable. Marriage enrichment is the exception, not the rule. Without attention and priority, love and intimacy can gradually erode. Enriching attitudes and behaviors are essential for long-term successful marriages.

In spite of the best intentions, marriage can end in divorce. Divorce rates are high. Time and energy spent in building and enriching marriages would reduce the number of divorces. For those who divorce, resources are available, and people can learn how to end relationships in less hurtful ways. Pain is inevitable as one passes through predictable stages, yet divorce can lead to personal growth, happiness, and an extremely satisfying future.

Intimate love is manifested by giving, receiving, sharing, and growing—two vital individuals forming a strong "We."

—Sharon Hanna

RESOURCES

- The American Society of Sex Educators, Counselors, and Therapists, 11 Dupont Circle N.W., Suite 220, Washington, DC 20005

- American Association of Marriage and Family Therapists Referrals, 1100 17th Street N.W., 10th Floor, Washington, DC 20036, (800) 374-2638
- The Hudson Center for Brief Therapy, 11926 Arbor Street, Omaha, NE 68144, (402) 330-1144
- Couple Communication Program, 7201 South Broadway, Littleton, CO 80122
- Classes and workshops on marriage preparation, marriage enrichment, and divorce adjustment offered through community colleges and university continuing-education programs.

12

Strengthening Family Relationships

OBJECTIVES

After completing this chapter, you will be able to

- Define family and realize that there are several types of families in today's society.
- Recognize the significance of parenting as well as the lack of formal required training.
- Make thoughtful decisions about parenting and preparation.
- Describe areas in which education is beneficial and know that resources are available.
- Discuss parenting responsibilities.
- Define discipline and explain the three styles.
- Give reasons that democratic discipline is recommended.
- Describe positive parenting behaviors.
- Understand ways to help a child cope with parents' divorce.
- Explain changes in the family.
- Describe the challenges and benefits of single-parent families, binuclear families, and stepfamilies.

When "I-other" relationships work, then families work. When families work, societies work; when societies work, nations work; when nations work, nature works; and when nature works, the universe works.

—Thomas and Patrick Malone

Take a moment and reflect on the momentous influences a family has on a person's life. Your family gave you a name, a geographic home, and a societal position, and most important, family members contributed to your self-concept, learned attitudes, values, behaviors, and personality. The family remains one of the most significant contributors to individuals' feelings about the quality of their lives (Mills et al., 1992). Family in the field of sociology is called a *primary group*. Such a group is typically small, intimate, and enduring.

What is a family? Responses from college sociology students range from the traditional, biological definition of "a mother, father, and child(ren)" to the all-encompassing "a group of people who love each other." You can check your own idea of family by completing the "Family Picture" in REFLECTIONS AND APPLICATIONS. In recent years the concept of family among professionals has broadened to include various types beyond the traditional definition. Most sociologists agree that a family is a relatively small domestic group of kin (related by biology, marriage, or adoption) who function as a cooperative unit. Some include any group of people in a kinlike relationship if they cooperate for economic, psychological, and sociological purposes (Popenoe, 1993). Families are expected to provide financial support, affection, companionship, and the important task of *socialization*, teaching a child the culture.

FAMILY STRENGTHS AND WEAKNESSES

In order to strengthen a family, people have to know what to do. Researchers focusing on family strengths are discovering common threads. A healthy family contributes to the well-being of all members. Vital and nurturing families are ones in which self-worth is high, there is direct, clear, specific, and honest communication, rules are flexible, appropriate, and changeable, and the link to society is open, hopeful, and based on choice (Satir, 1988).

A strong family, according to 551 family-life specialists surveyed by Curran (1983):

communicates and listens,
affirms and supports its members,
teaches respect for others,
develops a sense of trust,
has a sense of play and humor,
exhibits a sense of shared responsibility,
teaches a sense of right and wrong,
has a strong sense of family in which rituals and traditions abound,
has a balance of interaction among members,
has a shared religious core,
respects the privacy of one another,
values service to others,
fosters family table time and conversation,
shares leisure time,
admits to and seeks help with problems.

How many of these describe your family?

Unhealthy or Dysfunctional Families

Comparing strong, healthy, and functional families with chaotic, chronically anxious, and dysfunctional ones has occupied many researchers and authors in recent years. Research has concentrated on adult children of alcoholics because families with an alcoholic parent tend to be dysfunctional. A study at Duke University revealed higher rates of anxiety disorders and significantly more antisocial symptoms among adult children of alcoholics although the exact reasons were unclear (*The Menninger Letter*, 1993). Other studies are more optimistic. One showed no differences in college students with an alcoholic parent in terms of problem-solving, social support, shame, suicidal ideation, and substance use (Wright and Heppner, 1991). Another suggested that we stop advertising certain problems and characteristics as though they go hand in hand with being a child in a troubled family (Seefeldt and Lyon, 1992). Individual and family strategies seem to make a difference (Easley and Epstein, 1991).

Even though children can overcome family patterns, they are better off not having to do so. Characteristics of dysfunctional families include: inconsistency, unpredictability, mistreatment, chaos, denial of feelings and reality, and arbitrariness. The latter means that mistreatment occurs for no apparent reasons (Whitfield, 1987). Parental behaviors that create such families will be discussed later.

For what reasons are professionals concerned about unhealthy families? First, the effects on individuals can be profound. Growing up in a troubled or dysfunctional family nearly always is associated with shame and low self-esteem (Whitfield, 1987). A turbulent family history is a risk factor for later delinquency (Marquis, 1992). Men who demonstrated self-defeating behaviors said that their families had discouraged emotional expressiveness, were unconcerned about school and work accomplishments, and provided no ethical or religious values (Schill et al., 1991). A positive finding is that the parents' marital situation (intact-happy, intact-unhappy, death-disrupted, and divorce-disrupted) did not make a difference in the quality of intimate relationships formed later in life (Lauer and Lauer, 1991). This indicates that one is not destined to be adversely affected from family backgrounds.

Healthy or Functional Families

In contrast to dysfunctional ones, healthy families are open and flexible. Family members respect and allow fulfillment of one another's needs and rights, support the mental, emotional, and spiritual growth of each individual, and allow and encourage personal growth (Whitfield, 1987). Within functional families, problems are acknowledged and resolved, personal freedoms and individual freedoms are respected, individuals are treated with dignity and equality, roles are chosen and flexible, mistakes are forgiven and viewed as learning tools, and family members get their needs met (Bradshaw, 1988). An invaluable benefit of achieving the objectives of this book is that you will be capable of developing such families!

Hillary Rodham Clinton has an abiding interest in families. "One of the great consistencies in her life has been her concern for the American family, its children in particular" (Rader, 1993, p. 4). In an interview she asserted that "there is not a more important task for any of us than to focus our energies to give our children the right combination of love, discipline, and attention. As adults, this is our primary responsibility" (p. 16).

Grandparenting

Among the special family relationships are those of grandparents and grandchildren. Research shows that children maintain feelings of trust generated by loving grandparents throughout their lifetimes (Kornhaber and Woodward, 1981). A study on racial comparisons of the grandmother role showed higher levels of help given and received by black grandmothers and grandchildren than by whites. Proximity to a grandchild and the cultural emphasis on extended family networks were suggested as reasons (Kivett, 1993). Grandparents of all races are in a special position to provide understanding, love, and warmth to children. In a study grandparents identified unconditional love as the most important gift they could give. Grandchildren need grandparents who will listen without criticizing and accept them as they are (Orr and Van Zandt, 1987).

Regardless of definition or type, all families have a tremendous impact on the lives of human beings. Grandparents, parents, and siblings contribute immeasurably to an individual's quality of life. Children in various types of families will be the focus of this chapter.

POSITIVE PARENTING

The job of parent is one of the few things we expect people to be good at without having any training.

—New York Times

"The biggest responsibility in the world." "The hardest job you could imagine." "Stressful, joyful, and challenging . . . I wouldn't trade it for the world." These are a few of the responses I have received to the question, "What is parenting?" A consensus of opinion is that parenting is a difficult task although some perceive it as easy. A few erroneously believe that the hardest part is giving birth. After that, they think, it will be a "piece of cake" because raising a child will just come naturally. "I know what to do. I was a kid once," said a young parent. You may be able to "parent;" however, positive parenting doesn't come naturally. *Positive parenting* means doing everything possible to learn about and raise a child with a goal of *optimum development*. This includes the best possible prenatal and postnatal environments. Love, nurturance, and commitment are required. Raising children deserves priority and training.

The effects of inadequate parenting are profound. In a book of fiction (Conroy, 1986), the main character describes his parents as follows: "They began as lovers and ended up as the most dangerous and unutterable of enemies. As lovers, they begat children; as enemies, they created damaged, endangered children" (p. 294). Nonfictionally, Alvy (1987) identified several tragic results of poor parenting.

Emotionally disturbed human beings,
Poor academic performance,
Poor social and school adjustment,
Substance abuse,
Delinquency and crime,
Neglected and abused children.

Effective parenting can promote the opposite positive results. Parental conditions that create dysfunctional families are:

- Alcoholism or other chemical dependency.
- Codependency.
- Chronic mental illness or disability.
- Extreme rigidity and punitiveness.
- Judgmental, non-loving, perfectionistic attitudes.
- Feelings of extreme inadequacy and unmet needs.
- Child abuse of any kind (Whitfield, 1987).

Children who live with such conditions are at risk, and adults who foster them are not deserving of a parental role. One point is clear: Parenting is truly an awesome responsibility.

The scope of parenting cannot be covered in one chapter, or even in an entire book. In presenting a brief treatment of the subject of positive parenting, I take comfort in the realization that everything you have learned and gained thus far from this book will make you a better parent. For example, if your self-esteem is high, you will be more successful. In learning how to create happiness, express feelings, manage stress, cope with crisis, transmit values, communicate, manage conflict, and give and receive criticism, you have developed strategies for positive parenting. If you have a desire to learn more, you can seek resources and formal training. When you look at the lists of family-strength characteristics and descriptions of healthy families in the previous section, one obvious observation is that human relations training increases one's ability to strengthen a family. This chapter will simply open the door to positive parenting and helpful strategies for success in different types of families. The rest is up to you.

The Decision to Parent

You did not select your parents; however, you can choose whether or not to become a parent. This decision will probably be the most important one you will ever make. If you are already a parent and didn't give it a great deal of forethought, you are not alone and certainly are not wise to berate yourself. Your choice now is to learn how to be a positive parent. And, you can encourage others to make thoughtful decisions.

Again, the ego states from transactional analysis (TA) are applicable. The "child" will emotionally want a baby and will, perhaps, see raising a child as pure pleasure. The "child" could also react selfishly and not want to parent responsibly. Your parent ego state may be receiving messages such as, "You'd better have a baby soon. Your biological clock is ticking" or "You can't be truly fulfilled if you don't have a child." A 19-year-old student told me that her grandmother wanted her to get married and then quickly have a baby so that she could be a great-grandmother before she died. Ideally, whether to parent is a decision for your "adult." One suggestion is to read books about becoming a parent and child-raising before you decide. One, *When Partners Become Parents* (Cowan and Cowan, 1992), was written not so much as a "how-to" but rather as a "why-it's-so-hard-to" book and suggests new ways of achieving balance in contemporary families.

Factors to consider. Before having children, it is best if a couple's relationship is stable and time-tested. Bringing a baby into a new marriage isn't advisable, and having a baby to strengthen a weak marriage is one of the poorest reasons imaginable. A baby doesn't deserve the responsibility of saving a marriage; furthermore, this repair attempt invariably doesn't work. If you didn't do so before, take a close look at your partner as a potential parent. Angela explained why she had made a painful decision to end a relationship: "I concluded that I didn't want him to father my children."

Keeping the marriage healthy continues to be important. Research found that fathers who were distressed with their marriage tended to react toward a child in an authoritarian, irritable, cold, and angry manner. This was more extreme in cases of female children. Mothers were also more demanding and authoritarian when the marriage was distressed (Cowan and Cowan, 1992).

A critical question to answer is, "Why do we want to have a child?" A list identifying advantages and disadvantages usually reveals more "cons" than "pros." Among couples with no children men rated the importance of having children as higher than women. The researcher suggested men are more socially rewarded by being regarded as stable and as a "family man" and usually have fewer costs in terms of taking time away from job or career. The reasons given by both men and women in this study appeared to be self-serving and indicate some potential problems: having someone to care for me when I'm old, someone to love, having something to do, being able to have grandchildren (Secombe, 1991). Can you think of more positive reasons?

Couples are realistic when they acknowledge that time, energy, a great deal of effort, and money are required. The minimum cost of raising a child born in 1990 until he or she is 17 will top $150,000 for low income families. Middle income families can expect to spend $210,000 and a child of affluent parents (defined as $48,300 income) a little over $290,000 (Exter, 1991). Positive parenting requires sacrifices in all areas of self. Additional stress is inevitable.

On the other hand, parenting can be one of the most rewarding of human experiences. When asked the benefits of having children, adults mentioned adding interest to life, increasing the enjoyment of interpersonal relationships, an opening of avenues of pleasure and relating, and experiencing love and life's fuller meaning (Gerson, Berman, and Morris, 1991). An advantage recognized by a group of parents was that playing with or even thinking about their children helped lift their spirits (*Redbook*, April, 1993).

Having a realistic picture of parenting and family life will hopefully cause one to think and hesitate. You may choose to be among the 17 percent childfree couples in the United States today, a figure comparable to the decade of the 1940s, and significantly higher than the mere 7 percent in the 1970s (Secombe, 1991). Because of the importance of the decision, you owe it to yourself and to a child to be careful and deliberate. After a thoughtful decision has been made, make another one—to educate yourself.

Parent Education

In the movie *Parenthood*, a teenage boy talks about the irony of requiring fishing licenses to fish, hunting licenses to hunt, and driving licenses to drive, yet having no licensing requirement to become a parent. Society requires less to become a parent than to take on other statuses. Even marriage usually requires a blood test.

Concerns about parent education are expressed by Burton White (1975), an authority on infants and toddlers.

Figure 12-1

> I now believe that not more than one child in ten gets off to as good a start as he could. From close observations of children developing both well and poorly, I am convinced that most families, given a little help, are potentially capable of doing a good job of raising their children. Unfortunately, adequate preparation and assistance for parenthood are not currently available for most families (p. xi).

He adds that if young couples were better informed about child raising, they would find more pleasure in family life. Since White's book was published in 1975, parent education has become widely available. Classes and workshops are offered, organizations and support groups focus on family issues, and books and audiovisual aids are available. Importantly, these resources do work. A parent training program led to significant improvements for all which were maintained in a three-month follow-up (Thompson et al., 1993). Even with the number of offerings and the reported successes, the tragedy is that parents do not avail themselves of the educational opportunities they have.

"Canceled for lack of registrants" is a common frustration among continuing education departments and other groups offering parent courses. The assumption may be that such classes are canceled for lack of interest. Actually, the reason is more complex. Most parents are interested, yet are either unaware of how helpful education can be or don't think that they need training. Most of today's parents-to-be take childbirth classes. But then where do they go? They don't usually reappear for child-raising courses.

What specifically is good for parents to learn? First, education about children at all stages of development beginning with the extremely vulnerable prenatal period is highly recommended. When you learn about what is normal, what to expect, and what to do or not do, you can encourage optimum development. White (1975) is one of many who emphasize the importance of the early years and believes that a parent's first priority is to help a child reach a maximum level of competence by structuring experiences and opportunities. Without education, most people have no idea what these experiences would be.

Children have certain needs at various stages. A well-known Swiss psychologist and expert on cognitive development and early childhood experiences Jean Piaget (1969) recommends allowing infants and toddlers to explore a child-safe environment in order to develop motor skills and stimulate the senses. If a parent knows when specific motor skills normally develop, developmental delays and problems can be identified and, hopefully, a baby will not be pushed beyond reason. Other important information includes: Erikson's developmental stages, self-esteem development, and child-raising techniques. This knowledge will not only help the child but will also make parenting less burdensome and more enjoyable. If you practice open communication and handle conflict positively, you will, by example, teach priceless skills. As you continue to learn about love and marriage, you can teach positive lessons of life. Children often model their relationships after yours. Simply stated, *whatever you learn and live will be gleaned by your children.* Another advantage is that the more you know, the more secure you can be as a parent. This sense of security passes to the child. "The security of the parent about being a parent will eventually become the source of the child's feeling secure about self" (Bettelheim, 1987, p. 13).

Goals of Child Raising

One of the most valuable lessons I learned about parenting was from Deanna Eversoll, a University of Nebraska professor. "What do you want your child to be like at the age of 21?" she asked our class. After receiving several answers—responsible, honest, loving, happy, confident, independent—she challenged us: "Do you know what to do, and what not to do, to help bring these about?" A serious question to ponder is: "What makes the difference between the dreams we have for our children and the lives they end up leading?" (Helmstetter, 1989, p. 10). Parents are certainly not the only influence, yet they contribute more than any other single force to the future of their offspring.

In thinking about what you want, general ideas are preferable. Think "I want my child to be satisfied in a career," rather than "I want my child to be a doctor." This allows for flexibility and uniqueness. "As soon as we try to push our children to become the specific people that they may be in our heads, we become less effective as parents" (Glasser, 1984, p. 183).

Enabling children to discover who they want to be and then helping them become people who are satisfied with life is a worthy goal (Bettelheim, 1987). This may not be what you plan for a child. "I always wanted my child to go to a university and get a 4-year degree," one of my students said, "But he seems perfectly happy learning automotive technology at a community college. He says he wants to start his own business, so I'm happy for him."

In contrast to parents 60 or 70 years ago, modern parents are more likely to want youngsters to think for themselves, accept responsibility, show initiative, and be tolerant of opposing views. These characteristics replace such traits as obedience, conformity, and respect for home and church from earlier studies. Equating the change to better-educated parents who value the ability to think, researchers found that independence and tolerance were seen as desirable goals by parents in the United States, West Germany, Italy, England, and Japan (Remly, 1988). A study that traced nearly 400 people from age 8 through age 30 shows that children raised by supportive, accepting parents with whom they can identify are likely to develop into self-aware adults who are capable of forming long-term goals, engaging in constructive criticism, and cherishing their relationships with others (Chollar, 1987).

One student, in reply to the question about desired qualities in a child, said, "I want for us to be friends." Because parenting is a life-long commitment, developing a deep friendship with an adult child is rewarding. Being friends with a child means helping him or her develop qualities that lead to positive interactions and relationships. Liking a child for the person he or she has become is a wonderful feeling. One of my cherished possessions is a framed verse from my daughter: "How lucky we are, how fortunate I've been—that you are my mother and also my friend!"

Responsibilities of Parenting

If you were to write a job description for parenting, what would you include? One rather weary-looking mother in a parenting workshop answered, "Drive them here and there and everywhere." Transportation is only one responsibility. The number of tasks expected of mothers and fathers is nearly overwhelming with some responsibilities being more important than others.

Developing love and trust. If a child perceives the world as unloving, positive development is impossible. According to Erikson's developmental theory, trust precedes the other stages, and the early years are critical. No matter what else, love and trust must develop to form a strong foundation for the rest of life. The most valuable parenting behavior during the first year is to demonstrate loving behaviors by being responsive, warm, and nurturing. Most of the time an untouched child will die; a child not touched enough will not develop properly; a child touched in a disturbed way will suffer. Adults who were maltreated as children include John Wilkes Booth, Lee Harvey Oswald, James Earle Ray, and Sirhan Sirhan, all convicted of assassinations (Older, 1982).

A convincing 36-year study, beginning when the subjects were kindergartners and ending when they were 41 years old, showed that those who'd been raised with the most parental warmth and affection were more likely to have long and relatively happy marriages and close friendships and report greater happiness and less stress (Franz, McClelland, and Weinberger, 1991). Cuddling is a strong nonverbal message, and affectionate physical contact is meaningful at all ages (Gibson, 1992).

Love continues to be the foundation of positive parenting. As with intimate love, behaviors are the focus. Loving behaviors are those which foster positive personal growth and promote personal responsibility. Love has as its goal to enhance, not control, a child's life. Children need solace much more than control (Nathanson, 1992). Nothing is better than love, care, and training from birth on (Comer and Poussaint, 1992).

Building self-esteem and self-efficacy. Of no surprise is that two all-important responsibilities are the encouragement of children's high self-esteem and the fostering of self-efficacy. At least most parents recognize the importance of having self-esteem. In a Gallup survey 89 percent of adults said that self-esteem was important in motivating a person to work hard and succeed (Adler, 1992). "Helping your child grow up with strong self-esteem is the most important task of parenthood" (McKay and Fanning, 1987, p. 225). In the course of constructing the two strong pillars of esteem and efficacy, a child is likely to develop an inner locus of control and the other positive behaviors discussed earlier in this book.

Building self-esteem is accomplished in a number of ways. Chapter 1 provides information on your own self-esteem development and can suggest ways to enhance a child's, too. Your own high self-esteem is necessary if you want to be a positive parent. Adults are teachers of and models for self-esteem, and they can't teach or model what

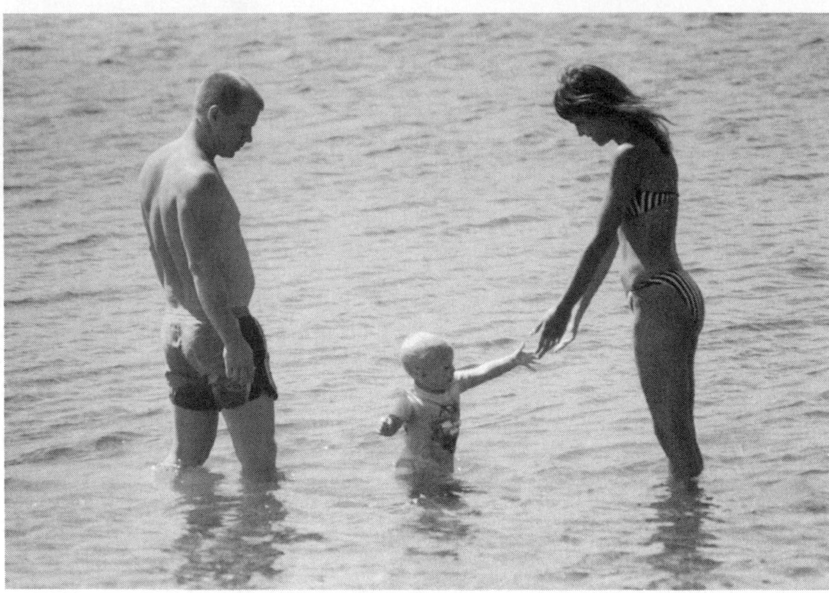

Figure 12-2 Trust develops through experiences.

they don't know. If you became a parent before your own self-esteem was high, do all you can to elevate it. The rewards will benefit both you and your children.

Also important are your parenting behaviors. Attitudes that parents have about parenting are likely to influence children's self-esteem (Anderson and Hughes, 1989). Parenting behaviors, especially support and control, were found to be significantly related to self-esteem in adolescents in the United States. The language and nonverbal behaviors you use with a child are building blocks of self-image and self-worth. "Every day, in the hundreds of interactions you have with your children, you mirror back to them who they are. Like a sculptor's tools on soft clay, your words and tone of voice shape their sense of self" (McKay and Fanning, 1987, p. 238). Children are so responsive to being celebrated and having their progress recognized (Glenn and Nelsen, 1989).

Offering positive comments for being capable and for doing well helps to build self-esteem (Clarke, 1982; Hyatt, 1991) as well as self-efficacy. In the TA framework, giving positive strokes in heavy doses is a primary parenting behavior. The "how" of praising is important. Haim Ginott, a widely recognized authority on child raising, recommends praising by describing, not evaluating. "Our words should be like a magic canvas upon which a child cannot help but paint a positive picture of self" (Ginott, 1965, p. 42).

In a book focusing on adolescents, Ginott (1969) describes descriptive recognition and contrasts it with evaluative praise. The words used in descriptive recognition tell about a specific event and the parent's specific feelings; the teenager can then draw a general conclusion about personality and character. Here is an example of descriptive recognition: "I really appreciate your helping clean house. I especially like the job you did in your own room. I'm relieved that such a big job is done." An example of evaluative praise, which is not recommended, is, "You're an angel. I couldn't ask for a sweeter daughter. I don't know what I would do without you." When you allow the child to infer positives from your descriptions, the message is stronger. Global messages that give the child a label are much less helpful than comments about specific behaviors (Cushman, 1993).

Praise does not have to be present-oriented. If a child isn't doing much now to deserve descriptive recognition, recall past situations. Parents are in the best position to raise self-esteem because they have a storehouse of memories (Faber and Mazlish, 1974). Parents are wise to remind teenagers that they are worthy human beings and that this belief is not just a reflection of parental adoration. Adolescents tend to be extremely hard on themselves so parents can help them put mistakes and shortcomings in perspective (Elkind, 1991). Positive offerings just for being alive are rare. As such, they are precious gifts of unconditional positive regard and deep love. Expressing joy for a child's birth and existence is like giving a gift for no special reason. And aren't those gifts among the finest? Priceless is the assurance that what a child *is* counts more than what he or she does.

"What can I do to help my son rid himself of 'can'ts'?" I was asked. As discussed in Chapter 3, a "can't" is extremely limiting and an enemy to the development of self-efficacy. First, model and encourage children to resist using the word "can't." Then, provide opportunities for them to demonstrate what they can do and praise appropriately. Erikson's stages play an important part. If young children have developed autonomy and initiative, they will be working on industry. During all three stages, a parent can foster the belief that a child is capable, and self-efficacy will serve her or him well throughout life. Helping children discover their uniquenesses is conducive to building self-esteem. Calling attention to a child's differentness in a positive way is as important as complimenting sameness or similarity. Guiding a child to master necessary skills builds self-esteem (Satir, 1988).

As valuable as praise generally is, unrealistic and lavish praise can be detrimental. Overpraising is often uncomfortable for children and may put pressure on them to try to live up to an unrealistic standard (McKay and Fanning, 1987). Telling children over and over that they are perfect, wonderful, and angelic will probably be rejected and may even be behaviorally refuted later. Lillian Katz of the National Association for the Education of Young Children suggests that self-esteem follows, not precedes, real accomplishment (Adler, 1992).

A strong recommendation is to avoid backhanded compliments which are ones that mix praise with insult (McKay and Fanning, 1987). Examples are, "I like the way you cleaned your room . . . for a change" or "I can't believe you did so well on your math test." Like adults, children can be hurt by the implied criticism and sarcasm and are better off without any praise at all.

Parents can do much to encourage self-esteem in children. They can also be a child's greatest enemy in developing feelings of self-worth. Some parents seem to believe that they best serve a child by being critical, yet positive parenting recommends small quantities of criticism given in nonhurtful ways. As discussed earlier, criticism delivered with "I" statements and within a framework such as the awareness wheel will get a better reception and, more importantly, does not damage self-esteem. Constructive criticism points out improvement possibilities and omits any negative remarks about the child's personality (Ginott, 1965). Larry, age 10, inadvertently spills a glass of milk. His parents' reactions are an example of criticism that is not constructive.

MOTHER: You are old enough to know how to hold a glass! How many times have I told you to be careful!

FATHER: He can't help it—he's so clumsy. He always was and always will be.

Figure 12-3 Copyright © 1993. Garfield reprinted by permission of UFS, Inc.

As Ginott (1965) points out, "Larry spilled 5 cents' worth of milk, but the caustic ridicule that followed the accident may cost much more in terms of loss of confidence" (p. 44). Instead, milk spilling and other accidents can be handled by a calm, "Accidents happen. Use the sponge on the sink to clean the table."

Children who are spoken to abusively learn to verbally abuse others. Therefore, these four steps should be followed in correcting a child (McKay and Fanning, (1987):

1. Describe the situation or behavior in nonjudgmental language. ("I notice that you haven't cleaned your room yet.")
2. Give a reason for wanting behavior to change. ("I'm frustrated when you procrastinate.")
3. Acknowledge the child's feelings and thoughts. ("I know how busy you have been" or "I realize that schoolwork has been stressful lately.")
4. State a clear expectation. ("I want the room cleaned before you go out tonight.")

Negative strokes and hurtful criticism are damaging to self-esteem. Destructive language styles are those that include generalizations (the grandiose type of closed communication) and vague or violent threats such as, "Try that again and you'll find out how mad I can get" or "If you do that one more time, I'll spank you so hard you won't be able to sit down." When criticizing, body language and paralanguage are also potentially damaging. Involuntary facial expressions of disgust and sarcastic tones of voice, among others, carry powerful messages (Cushman, 1993). Not addressing issues of concern and playing the "silent game" are also not recommended (McKay and Fanning, 1987).

Sometimes parental behaviors are subtle and hard to specify. A lovely young woman wrote years later about negative feelings she had as a child.

> I thought I was ugly. I felt inferior and detached (not emotionally detached . . . it hurt . . . but detached from any enjoyment). I got these messages subtly from home. My mother was physically very beautiful and hated aging. I think she was jealous of me although I didn't feel pretty at the time. My father was always working hard, and my mother seemed extremely jealous of any time he spent with me. I became a suicidal, anorexic, battered wife and am only now emerging from the self-esteem beating I received.

One well-intentioned parental behavior is to place unrealistic expectations on a child which can ignite a lifetime of self-criticism (Ashner and Meyerson, 1990). "I know you can do better," a parent says looking at a report card with mostly "Bs". Maybe a "B" is the best a child can do. Hundreds of my students have mentioned that whatever they did just wasn't enough, and lower levels of self-esteem and self-efficacy are often the result.

Unrealistic expectations, especially about behavior, are frequently the result of what is called "adultism" which occurs when adults forget what it is like to be a child. They then expect and require a child, who has never been an adult, to think, act, understand, and do things as an adult (Glenn and Nelson, 1989). My guess is that most heads will nod as they read this either from childhood experience or one's own "adultism." David Elkind (1988), an authority on childhood and adolescence, expressed concerns about a hurried childhood. He believes that hurrying children to grow up and treating them as adults does them harm. "Children need time to grow, to learn, and to develop" (p. 21).

Encouraging self-worth and self-efficacy is a critical parental responsibility with many rewards. When children develop high self-esteem and a sense of competence, the other responsibilities of parenting are easier. In addition, a parent has served a child well. "A belief in one's personal capabilities is an essential building block for successful adulthood" (Glenn and Nelsen, 1989, p. 71).

Developing emotional well-being. An entire chapter of this book is devoted to the emotional self. The value of teaching children how to feel and express is obvious. Once a parent has developed a positive emotional self, he or she will be able to teach and model healthy emotionality. In addition to using the material presented earlier, a few specific points can be beneficial.

Wise parents are attuned to the immense influence of their own feelings and behaviors. Frequently, and sometimes as a result of unawareness, parents use the common emotional weapons of guilt and intimidation. These can have grave psychological consequences (Bloomfield, 1983). The *martyr parent* seeks to instill guilt in children: "How could you do this to me?" "I don't deserve this kind of treatment." "I've given you everything." "I went without so you could have all the nice things." "Just go on with your busy life. I realize you don't have much time for me." If you recognize any of these messages because you once received them or because you now give them, realize that the child translates the message as, "Being who I am hurts my parent" and "I'm not good or nice enough." A revealing book, *When Parents Love Too Much* (Ashner and Meyerson, 1990), describes parents who "overparent." A potentially damaging behavior is the compulsion to help and control others and do for them what they could be doing for themselves. The parent's needs are usually unmet as all energy is focused on the child. Such codependent behavior is modeled, and children learn to feel overly responsible and guilty. In adulthood, they find it difficult to strike a balance between living their lives and loving their parents. A similar parenting style is described as emotional incest (Love and Robinson, 1990). Parents turn to their children, not to their partners, for emotional support. Even though a parent appears loving and devoted, their love is really an unconscious way to satisfy their own unmet emotional needs.

The *dictator parent* has the same motive as the martyr parent: to control the child's life even after the child is an adult. The method is intimidation. Fear-inducing statements and temper outbursts are common: "I'm the boss around here, and you do what I say." "Don't you dare talk back to me. You're supposed to show respect." "You do that again, and I'll smack you hard." "Do it or else. Remember, I'm your mother." The child remembers quite well. The reason given for the threats and abuse is that the parent knows what's best and is acting in the child's interests; however, the parent is actually inflicting great harm. Trying to produce fear in order to control is the parent's objective, and "in such an environment, a child lives on guard rather than at rest" (Nathanson, 1992, p. 410). Acting either the martyr or dictator role or overparenting are not positive parenting practices.

Worrying is a learned behavior. "I'm a worry-wart just like my mom" may be true. How sad that a parent taught a child to worry. To avoid this, ideally, you, as a parent, won't be such a worrier. If you are, let children know that they didn't cause it. Messages like, "I can't help worrying. That's what parents do," "I love you so much, and you cause me so much worry" are hard on young people. Even though they feel loved, these children live with anxiety, guilt, and dependency that often becomes a codependency (Ashner and Meyerson, 1990). Children placed in this position almost always grow up to be worriers. The truth is that the adults undoubtedly worried before the child was born and are now using the child as a scapegoat. Instead, a positive parent teaches a child to look critically at worries and to challenge them. He or she teaches the joy of problem solving rather than the anguish of fretting. "Teach your children, by example, to look into the future with excitement rather than with anxiety" (Goulding and Goulding, 1989, p. 232).

Emotions and ways of expressing them are acquired through the family. Cold, unemotional children and young adults frequently come from families of the same ilk. If children are raised in a "sick" emotional climate, they become victims of victims. Such a climate means that "people feel one way and act another, straight, honest, and discernible expressions are scarce, and superficial, hysterical, manipulative outbursts are turned on and off like summer showers" (Rubin, 1969, p. 24). Such a climate exists in dysfunctional families.

Adults described as "toxic parents" in a book by that name (Forward and Buck, 1989) also harm a child. "Like a chemical toxin, the emotional damage inflicted by these parents spreads throughout a child's being, and as the child grows, so does the pain" (p. 6). The book describes how to deal with the effects of toxic parenting; however, current parents can use it to remind them of damaging actions and to encourage loving behaviors that don't grind children down, keep them off balance, or create feelings of self-hatred.

> Love doesn't hurt, it feels good. Loving behavior nourishes your emotional well-being. When someone is being loving to you, you feel accepted, cared for, valued, and respected. Genuine love creates feelings of warmth, pleasure, safety, stability, and inner peace (p. 324).

Developing positive social relationships. Social development begins when life does. As pointed out before, trust, the cornerstone of psychosocial development, is the basic task. In the stages that follow, parents play significant roles. Knowing what and how to encourage is beneficial. The identity stage is one of the most challenging stages for both adults and children. It usually begins and is in "full bloom" during adolescence. The more you know about typical adolescent behavior the better your parenting skills will be and the more you will enjoy your teenager. The book *You and Your Adolescent* (Steinberg and Levine, 1990) is a good resource. The authors assure us that the horror stories about adolescence are false and point out that nine out of ten teenagers do not get into trouble. "Your relationship with your child will not change for the worse in adolescence, but it will change" (p. 3). The book is full of accurate information about adolescent development plus enjoyable ways to enhance the relationship. Trusting children by assuming the best, not the worst, and treating them with the same respect parents extend to total strangers are worthy recommendations.

Other authors (Glenn and Nelsen, 1989) offer insight into guiding adolescents toward identity. Helping them achieve independence is important; however, parents put children in a double bind when they steer them towards independence and then object to how they do things. Adolescence is a time for self-discovery. Parents are wise to realize that friendship is much more important than a tidy bedroom and that "finding an identity and sorting through feelings are infinitely more critical than getting the laundry done right after school" (p. 91).

Children of all ages learn from their families how to be social creatures. Even though families are not as potent in the socialization process as they once were (Fine, 1992), we still develop much of our social selves at home. Children are fortunate if they acquire what are called the "Three Cs:" to feel connected, to feel capable and competent, and to count (Bettner and Lew, 1992). In terms of relationships, intimacy is taught or not taught in the family. Parents have a tremendous responsibility to model intimate adult relationships and marital roles.

Showing an active interest. Parents who are involved, concerned, and supportive, no matter how busy they are, provide a critical link between children and the educational process (Haug and Wright, 1991). In addition, being actively interested in whatever your child does shows love and respect. This responsibility seems so obvious that I didn't think to include it in the first edition. However, quite often I hear students comment on their parents' indifference or what seems like a lack of interest in what they do. "My folks never came to school events," said Shelly. "Even when I was a homecoming queen finalist, they weren't there." I listened in astonishment recalling the endless numbers of piano recitals and band concerts my father, who had no interest in music, endured. He and my mother were always there showing their interest and support. When I taught sixth grade years ago, parents usually had perfect attendance at important school events. Times may have changed; however, the need for demonstrated interest and support remains as strong as ever. With increasing numbers of career responsibilities and other activities and interests, parents who make the time and effort are to be commended.

A Special Word to Fathers

"Please devote more space in your next edition to the father's role," said a male student who is one of a growing number of single fathers with custody; however, all fathers deserve a special mention. Because of traditional marriages, mothers in the past were charged with child-raising responsibilities while the dad was often seen as someone who came and went. Or he was the heavy disciplinarian. That has changed for many, and both young and middle-aged men in a study of androgyny reported being highly invested in their families and significantly satisfied with parenting and family life (Carlson and Videka-Sherman, 1990).

The emotional importance of the father's role was shown in another study (Snary and Pleck, 1988). The more nurturance given to sons by their fathers, the more giving and caring these offspring were at middle age. Fathers appear to be as important as mothers in this traditionally feminine role of nurturance. They're important in all other aspects, as well. Children whose fathers are involved in their early rearing tend to have higher IQs, perform better in school, and even have a better sense of humor (Gibbs, 1993).

The benefits of being fathered, as well as mothered, are well documented. Sadly, more children will go to sleep now in a fatherless home than ever before (Gibbs, 1993). Today, fatherhood is replete with confusion and challenges. What fathers, too often, hear from society and sometimes even from their own wives is a devastating message: "We don't really trust men to be parents, and we don't really need them to be. And so every day, everywhere, their children are growing up without them" (p. 53).

Society is apt to ignore fathers. The Census Bureau reports that there are 70 million mothers age 15 or older in the United States yet has little idea of how many fathers there are. Men get confusing messages. Women say they need them to be more active parents then fear that they aren't reliable enough and jealously guard their exclusive parental role (Gibbs, 1993). This was demonstrated in class when a woman commented that her husband was home babysitting. She was asked if her husband was the children's father. He was. "Then why call it babysitting?" asked another student. "Do you call it babysitting when you stay home with them?"

Men who were raised stereotypically may have difficulties realizing that fathering isn't the same as commanding a military unit. A father may want to speak of love to a son yet finds it hard to communicate. Most boys then only show love for their fathers through performance, hard work, and accomplishment (Osherson, 1992). Ron, a middle-aged student, wrote of his father:

> The only time I heard my father say, "I love you" was when I was a teenager, and he was inebriated. We didn't communicate well then. If our opinions differed, the veins

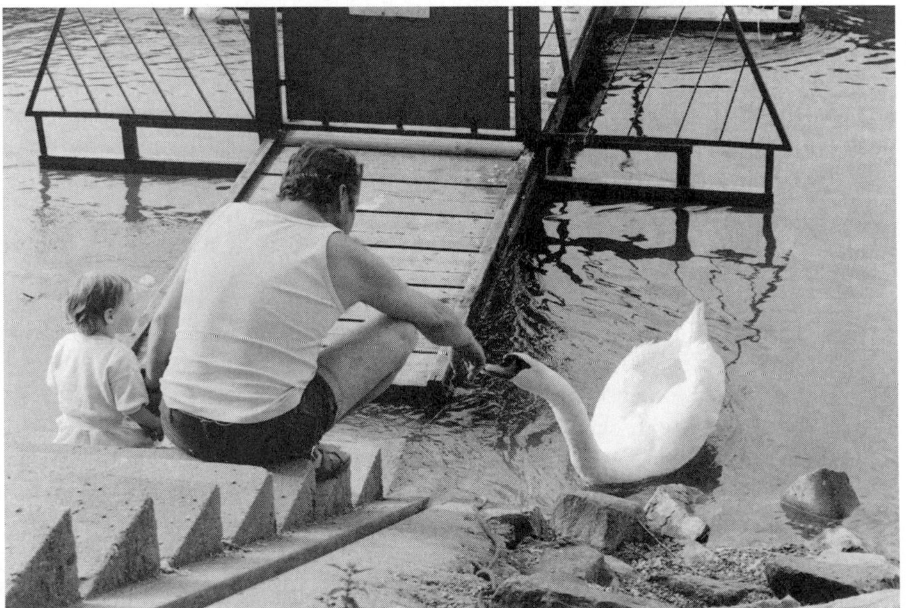

Figure 12-4 Fathers play an invaluable parenting role.

> on his temples would stand out, his fists would clench, and I would fear he might lose control. Discussion was not an option. My father's father was from the Old Country. He tells me that if he were a few minutes late, he had to kneel on dried peas on a hardwood floor for an hour or more. My father would make me feel totally inadequate if I let a wrench slip or didn't hold something steady while he tried to fasten a bolt. He is generous, intelligent, opinionated, and insensitive. Emotionally he is like some dumb animal only expressing anger. He communicates his love through his loyalty and steadfastness and through generosity with material things. He was a victim of his culture and family indoctrination. I made it my goal to be better at communicating, expressing love and empathy, and not hurting my children. I still have a way to go.

Fathers have great impact on future lives. A study showed that abuse by his father predicted a man's violent behavior (Alexander et al., 1991). Societal attitudes that support the importance of men in the lives of children need strengthening while fathers who want to be involved in an affirmative way are advised to learn as much about positive parenting as they can.

> The degree to which the father as well as the mother is nurturant, caring, and accepting is highly related to the successful development of the child. Children develop best when given opportunity to form a basic relationship with both a positively involved father and mother. Fathers are as important as mothers in the overall development of children (Alexander et al., p. 222).

For the most part, fathers today want more involvement and are taking parental responsibilities seriously. Two parenting workshop leaders report that one-third of their participants are men compared to only 10 percent ten years ago (Glenn and Nelsen, 1989). In a book of optimism, hope, and success that tries to lift the cloak of invisibility surrounding black fathers, Hutchison (1992) sums it up quite well: "Black fathers want their sons to smile into the camera on the sidelines of football games, wave, and say, 'Hi, Dad' " (p. 17). A positive example was set by FBI Director Louis Freech. When his son was sick, he left work early, and he took time off to go with his two oldest children on their first day of school (*Time*, 1993d).

Beginning at the earliest stages of life, a child's entire being is in the hands of the caregiving adults. Each child deserves and profits from the love, warmth, and support of both of his or her parents. An area in which a parent plays a primary role and one in which education is sorely needed is discipline.

Discipline and Its Multifaceted Dimensions

Ask adults to define discipline, and you get answers such as: "making a child mind you," "correcting a child," and "teaching a child right from wrong." Ask children, and you are likely to hear: "getting punished," or "not being allowed to watch TV." Sadly, parents often use only punishment to accomplish what they think discipline is.

A broader definition of *discipline* is the entire process of teaching and guiding children from infancy to adulthood. An optimistic view sees discipline as a process of helping and teaching a child to behave in desirable ways (Ames, 1992). The parent has a role of leader and teacher, while the children are learners. Thus, discipline is multifaceted, and parents use a variety of child raising techniques to guide children. What you want your child to be like are the goals of discipline. Most young adults benefit from an ability to communicate, good judgment, responsibility, courage, cooperation, and self-discipline (Bettner and Lew, 1992).

When people think about discipline, they don't usually picture anything positive. This broader concept is affirmative rather than negative. Punishment may be used, but if so, then sparingly and as a last resort. If you picture discipline as a pie, punishment is the smallest possible slice. Keep in mind that the need to punish may be due to faulty discipline and leadership on a parent's part or, in some cases, the result of first using an inappropriate method of discipline (Helmstetter, 1989).

Child-rearing practices influence all aspects of a child's life. In one study, children's loneliness was related to how they were raised. Being lonely and rejected by peers put these children at greater risk for personal and school adjustment as well as lower self-esteem (Bullock, 1993). Contrast this with a major positive facet of discipline—nurturance. Giving affection, providing encouragement, building self-esteem, and focusing on what's good and positive are nurturing behaviors. "Nurturance is the 1001 ways a parent says, 'I love you' " (Albert and Einstein, 1983, p. 6). What potential this concept of discipline has!

Styles of discipline. An understandable model describes three styles of raising a child (Albert and Einstein, 1983). The *authoritarian* style, the norm of yesteryear, puts the parent in total control as "boss." As such, a parent is dictatorial, strict, and inflexible. The child is to obey or else. Harsh punishments are commonly used. The home atmosphere is tense, rigid, and feels restrictive. The parent-child relationship is characterized by fear, distance, coldness, and rigidity. The closed communication style is used; values are moralized. The dictator parent (described earlier) is in charge.

Exactly the opposite is the *permissive* style, in which the parent is a bystander and servant while the child is powerful and in control. The parent is indecisive, yielding, inconsistent, and weak. The atmosphere is uncontrollable, wild, and chaotic with distant, tentative, and manipulative relationships. In several families, discipline shifts chaotically between the two extremes. In dysfunctional families, either or both are found.

The *democratic* style fits the broader definition of discipline and is used in positive parenting. The parent is a leader, guide, and teacher. As such, she or he is approachable, reasonable, flexible, and affirming. A child is encouraged to think, contribute, and cooperate. Power is not a major issue and is shared as much as possible. Each person has a voice and feels empowered. Open communication is the norm. The atmosphere is relaxed and consistent, and the parent-child relationship is close, open, and sharing. Democratic discipline emphasizes positiveness. Can you think of affirmative ways to guide a child? How about praise and positive strokes? Most children respond readily to praise and encouragement. Too often, instead of giving positive strokes, many parents don't comment on behavior until they reprimand. "No" in most households is said louder and more often than "yes." In fact, during the first 18 years of life the average person is told "no" or what one cannot do about 148,000 times (Helmstetter, 1989).

Positiveness is helped by a change in vocabulary. Rules is one of the "bummer" words identified in Chapter 3. Using the terms *guidelines or policies* instead sounds more positive. Who establishes these guidelines? The most powerful aspect of democratic discipline and why it is so effective is that *input regarding guidelines and consequences comes from all who are able to contribute*. There is a world of difference between the way youngsters react to limits imposed by an adult and their reactions when they have had a voice (Gordon, 1989). If you are an employee, aren't you more likely to comply with policies if you have been involved in their formation? Children react similarly in usually cooperative ways. Periodically, the family can evaluate the guidelines and the consequences. Some may be obsolete or need up-dating. Specific democratic methods follow.

Openly communicate. Open communication is one of the most powerful tools of discipline. How strange that parents forget to use it! Verbalizing openly and listening actively and receptively may be all that is required in changing a child's behavior. Thomas Gordon, famous for the book *Parent Effectiveness Training* has written *Teaching Children Self-Discipline at Home and at School* (1989). He strongly recommends both the use of "I" messages and what he calls the all-purpose people skill of active listening. When our children were asked about discipline on a television program, I was heartened to hear them say, "We were hardly ever grounded or punished. Instead we talked things out."

Model the behavior you want. Realizing that parents will have adult privileges that children do not have, discipline includes the positive examples you set. As in transmitting values, your actions will speak louder than words. Social learning theory in psychology emphasizes observational learning. Children are quite susceptible to watching and then doing. For example, the amount of tobacco used by mothers was significantly related to adolescent tobacco use in a study of seventh graders (Melby et al., 1993). Parents model how to express feelings (Bradshaw, 1988). In fact, a parent disciplines simply by the way he or she lives (Ames, 1992).

Apply behavior modification techniques. Learning theory offers a variety of tools. The ones that will be effective depend on the age and personality of a child. With young children, changing the environment by *redirecting* their attention is often sufficient. For example, a 2-year-old is naturally curious (and stubborn!) and will likely attempt to open a cupboard door against your wishes. You can simply get the child involved elsewhere. If a child isn't in danger and not likely to be harmed or hurt others, *ignoring* misbehavior can be effective because children do misbehave to get attention.

Time-out includes moving a misbehaving child to a neutral (nonentertaining) location for a brief period of time. It's recommended that this only be done after you have talked with the child and tried other methods of changing behavior. The suggested amount of time is 1 minute per year of age. Explain to the child why you are removing her or him from the scene. Continue to use time-out until the undesirable behavior stops or you decide to try another method. Time-out doesn't work all of the time with all children, and it can be overused. And, some children enjoy it. "My nephew loves time-out. He sits with his head down and hums, whistles, and smiles." In this case, the method doesn't deter misbehavior.

Rewarding desired behavior is recommended and can work miracles. Adults relish rewards; so do children. After reading a book on behavior modification, a mother shared a success story.

> My 4-year-old girl misplaced her shoes daily. When we got ready to go somewhere, we had to look for shoes. I scolded and even spanked occasionally with no luck. From a book, I got a new idea. I put a large box in her room and told her that this was her special shoe box. Each night I counted the number of shoes in the box, and she received stickers for each shoes, which she could later use for treats. She has not misplaced a shoe for a month.

Unfortunately, parents forget to apply an important principle of learning theory: Human beings generally seek pleasure or rewards. Verbal awards, according to one study, may be more beneficial than material ones. Over-doing concrete rewards can lead children to becoming motivated only by external factors (Gussman and Harder, 1990). Large doses of verbal praise are preferable.

As children get older, different behavior-modification methods are more effective. The use of *contracting* for specific behaviors and then *reinforcing* the behaviors you like works well with older children. A *negotiating* process is effective with adolescents.

Use logical consequences. In order to be prepared for adulthood and responsibility, it's important that a child experience consequences. For a child who is old enough to understand, the use of logical consequences as a method of discipline is amazingly effective. The consequences can be natural ones. If a child carelessly breaks a toy, it is no longer available. As in values development, allowing natural consequences to occur is hard on a loving parent, yet invaluable in developing responsibility.

Consequences can also be created. A key element is including the child in formulating consequences. Some descriptions of effective and fair consequences follow (McKay and Fanning, 1987).

Reasonable: If a child is 45 minutes late coming home after a movie, an earlier time could be set the next time. Grounding someone for a week is not reasonable. In fact, grounding is a consequence (sometimes a punishment for unrelated misbehavior) that can be overused. And it is often as hard on the parents as it is on the child!

Related: If children are careless in completing tasks, they are expected to do it over rather than have television privileges suspended, for example. Making the consequences relate to the misbehavior makes sense.

Timely: If grades are unusually low, and the consequence is imposed study time, the time to start is that day. Waiting too long to impose consequences makes them irrelevant.

Consistent: How many times have you heard a parent say, "If you do that one more time . . . ," and the behavior continues several more times? If the consequence for hitting a sibling is "time out," then a parent imposes the consequence until the behavior is changed. If "time out" isn't working, change the consequence.

Understandable in advance: If children have input, they will know the consequences before they misbehave. If a bicycle left outside is stolen, the child will already know that money will have to be earned to replace it. Unforeseen situations may occur; a parent can then impose reasonable consequences or involve the child in the process.

One of my favorite consequence stories concerns my stepson Greg, who was quite even tempered. However, a phone conversation with a girl evidently got the best of him. He hit the stairwell wall, making a hole in it. "The wall has to be fixed," was our reaction. He paid for, patched, and even painted the entire stairwell! Greg assures me that he hasn't used his fist on a wall since.

The use of consequences teaches responsibility and prevents parents from having to nag, scold, and use other punitive measures. A child's self-esteem usually remains intact, and the feeling of responsibility can even give it a boost.

Provide structure. Planning with children how the household will operate is highly recommended. Having an established system and designated tasks decreases the number of times a parent feels a need to intervene. Erikson's description of the developmental stage of industry indicates that children, especially preteens, will generally be responsive to successful completion of tasks.

A family meeting is a good forum to use. A parent can introduce the idea by saying, "I want to include everyone in deciding how our household is going to function. A family is a team; a home requires care and maintenance. Let's first decide what needs to be done and how often, and then how it will be accomplished." For excellent tips on family meetings, read *Positive Discipline* (Nelsen, 1987), a book written for both parents and teachers. School class meetings are also included. Meetings are best if used for positive reasons more than "problem" ones. Try beginning the routine of regular meetings by planning a family outing or trip. Regarding tasks, my stepfamily used a system in which the children had daily and weekly duties designated by number. I still smile when I think of the neighbors' reaction to one child's yelling to another, "Come on in. It's time for you to do number 2!" The system was not fool-proof, and consequences were a part of it. However, it saved hours of complaining and nagging.

Performing tasks and assuming responsibility help children develop autonomy, or independence, and industry; however, most parents build in their own obstacles: "She's too young to do that." "I couldn't let her iron her clothes; she won't do a good job." Is she really too young? My younger daughter, Lyn, started doing her own laundry when she was 7 years old. That came from my personal rebellion after the remarriage. There was not only laundry from three females, but what seemed like an avalanche of dirty clothes from three males. "I quit!" I exclaimed. "From now on we can all do our own laundry." Lyn was probably the most enthusiastic of the group. Years later, a reward was in store for me. Both Lyn and Greg said that doing their own laundry all those years was a "good deal" because they were self-sufficient in that area. As for quality, whether a child does as good a job as you can do is only as important as you make it. Self-discipline comes from children learning to set their own standards.

Advantages of the democratic style. Contrast the style with the other two. In considering what parents want children to be like as adults, what is probable with permissive discipline? Most picture a spoiled, irresponsible, and demanding individual. What about the authoritarian style? Several possibilities exist. A young adult may be fearful, obedient, and yielding to any authority figure. Frequently, however, a rebellious, aggressive attitude is the result.

Research reveals several negative effects of authoritarian discipline. Frequent use of punishment is associated with undesirable personality traits such as pessimism, suspiciousness, and a belief that life is meaningless (Gussman and Harder, 1990). Authoritarian discipline appeared to affect self-concepts in a negative way when 4100 teenagers were studied (Lamborn et al., 1991). Children from authoritarian homes appear to lack social competence with peers, to withdraw, and not take social initiative (Barber, 1992).

A series of studies suggest that harsh punitive discipline increases the probability of aggressive behavior (Patterson et al., 1989) and contributes independently to the development of adult psychological disorders. Among 200 adults, 56 percent of depressives and 43 percent of alcoholics reported being beaten with a stick compared to only 18 percent of healthy adults (Jordan, 1989). A 22-year study shows that children whose parents are overly critical, harsh, or authoritarian often turn into self-absorbed adults whose impulsiveness can lead them to violence and substance abuse (Chollar, 1987).

Other research links harsh corporal punishment in childhood with later physical abuse in a marriage (Downs et al., 1992). A study showed that women subjected to abusive parenting tend to be hostile and rebellious and are likely to affiliate with and marry men with similar characteristics (Simons et al., 1993). Finally, authoritarian discipline like moralizing of values, its accomplice, usually doesn't work. Punitive discipline may cause disobedience rather than cure it (Gordon, 1989). Avoiding its use seems to be in everyone's best interests. The adage "We reap what we sow" is usually true.

Permissive discipline has its sad effects, as well. Children with indulgent parents had higher frequencies of substance abuse, school misconduct, and less engagement in school (Lamborn et al., 1991). Permissiveness often produces insecurity and the belief that there is little cause and effect. Pampering amounts to an unloving act (Glenn and Nelsen, 1989).

Few desirable qualities are developed through permissiveness and authoritarianism, and the probability of encouraging negative traits is likely. Most parents do not want their children to be dishonest. Yet, wouldn't you learn to be a good liar if you knew that any infraction would be harshly punished? A parent may be fooled into thinking that authoritarian methods work because especially at young ages, children can be forced to mind a parent. Long-term consequences, however, are frightening. Permissiveness isn't likely to lead to responsible adult behavior and probably encourages selfishness and self-indulgence.

You may be thinking, as did one young man, "My parents were authoritarian, and I turned out okay." Certainly individuals survive harshness, just as children who are raised in a permissive atmosphere can turn out fine. Ask yourself whether the present "you" could have been improved and whether life wouldn't have been happier if you had been raised in a democratic-style home.

Although it is not commonly used, experts recommend the democratic style, and research shows a number of benefits. Raising children democratically decreases the likelihood of their developing negative traits and sets up a fertile field for positive traits and behaviors. A study showed that children who had limits and imposed logical consequences and whose parents elicited ideas from them and explained what they wanted were more independent and engaged in less disruptive behaviors than did children of parents who used physical punishment, threats, and belittling remarks (Hart et al., 1992). A style almost identical to democratic, *authoritative*, generally promotes high self-esteem, good reasoning ability, responsibility, and independence (Duck, 1991). A study in the Netherlands showed that children from authoritative discipline families were better liked at school because they had learned behavior patterns that appealed to their peers (*Psychology Today*, 1993b). Finally, democratic discipline is more enjoyable and is likely to lead to harmony and cooperation. No matter how long you have parented, you can switch to democratic discipline. A recommendation is to bring the family together and discuss the new approach.

Positive Parenting Behaviors

Obviously, what a parent does and doesn't do plays an important role in a child's development yet parents often forget to focus on their own actions. Family professionals recognize that "warm, supportive parents express interest in their children's activities, provide assistance with everyday problems, express encouragement and support in the face of challenges, and display enthusiasm and praise over accomplishments" (Simons et al., 1992, p. 824). Positive parents practice the following.

Admitting a mistake. You may wish to be an ideal parent, yet perfection isn't possible. A stress-reducing aspect of positive parenting is that parents are allowed to make mistakes. Those who are able to admit an error and apologize to their children are to be commended, because children then learn a valuable lesson. "I never heard either of my parents apologize—to each other or to us kids. I would have respected them so much more if they had. I find that I have difficulty saying, 'I'm sorry,' but I'm working on it," said one young man. When you apologize to your children, you teach them to trust their feelings and perceptions. "You are right. I did act unfairly." Then, taking responsibility for your mistakes puts the "icing on the cake." By apologizing, you are truly modeling loving behavior (Forward and Buck, 1989).

Spending quality time with children. I'd love to have a dollar for the number of times I've heard people say, "I wish I had spent more time with my children. The years went by so fast." Wouldn't it be wonderful if nobody had those regrets? Parents and children can engage in projects and other mutually enjoyable activities. Being entertained together is a common pastime; however, viewing television and movies is passive and does not usually involve close interaction. Unless it does, other activities are more beneficial. As mentioned before, positive parents also demonstrate an interest in their child's activities by attendance and active involvement. Positive parenting means you have fun with children. Laughing together is stress-reducing and bonding. "Appreciate the child within you and each other. Especially in families, let the child in each of you romp. Your kids don't need to have all the fun. Having fun together is positive bonding" (Satir, 1988, p. 330).

Communicating openly. Most important are communicating with and showing genuine interest in children as individuals. Talking and listening to your child are probably the most positive and rewarding parenting experiences of all. In order for the process to work, open communication is a necessity. The effects of not doing so may be severe. Frequent use of corporal punishment and poor communication may increase antisocial aggressiveness toward parents (Larzelere et al., 1989). Families identified as clinical or problem families had significantly poorer communication skills than nonclinical families (Thomas and Olson, 1993). Moving beyond just family, a child's social skills and peer acceptance appears to be influenced by maternal communication (Burleson et al., 1992).

As discussed previously, a poor communication habit is to ask "why" questions especially those that concern personal feelings and motivations. Interestingly, parents feel justified asking a child, "Why were you late?" and resent the same question asked of them by a child. "Why did you break that dish?" is a poor question unless you honestly believe a child did so deliberately which usually isn't the case. Children, and adults alike, feel defensive or uncomfortable when asked why (Plutchik and Plutchik, 1990). Communication is as important in parent-child relationships as in any other. Open communication is a hallmark of positive parenting!

Demonstrating warmth and affection. Positive parents are warm and affectionate. They express feelings nonverbally and verbally. The importance of demonstrativeness has been repeatedly pointed out in this book and deserves special emphasis between parents and children. A longitudinal study showed that preteens whose parents demonstrated higher levels of warmth and affection throughout their childhood had higher self-esteem and, as young adults, were capable of more congenial relationships (Franz et al., 1991). Children whose parents are physically affectionate and warm have a definite advantage.

Yet, in the United States, more than most other countries, parents tend to refrain from physical expressions of love especially with older children (Gibson, 1992). "I knew my dad loved me, but I would have loved to hear him say it—just once," said a student. Men generally have more difficulty touching their child affectionately although one study reported that fathers and sons touched frequently and thought that it was important at least in preadolescent years (Salt, 1991). Generally, when peers become important, a child shuns demonstrated affection from parents especially big hugs and kisses. Parents can still hug children in private as well as finding any of hundreds of other ways to demonstrate love (Gibson, 1992). If demonstrating warm feelings is personally difficult for you, attack the problem. In order to develop a jogging regimen, an adult may have to say, "I will run 5 miles each day." The same adult can say, "I will hug my child at least once today."

Showing appreciation and consideration. Being polite, saying "thank you," and showing appreciation in other ways seem simple, yet many of us don't practice these within the family. Parents and children alike may take for granted the kind deeds of family members and neglect courtesies they extend to other people. A positive parent makes a point of expressing gratitude on a regular basis. Children then learn from observation. Being polite to a child may do as much as the elaborate parenting strategies because it shows that their feelings are valued (Elkind, 1988).

Figure 12-5 A warm hug is positive parenting at its finest.

Exhibiting fairness and equality. After a presentation, I was asked by a woman, "What can be done about my children's fighting with each other?" No easy answer was forthcoming. I recommended books on the subject and an excellent chapter in *Raising Good Kids* (Ames, 1992). In most cases, children benefit from settling their own disputes. When a parent intervenes, fairness and an explanation of the "why" of decisions are desirable. A mother wanted to be fair with her young daughters, Nicole and Cindy. To her, fairness was keeping everything equal. When one received anything, so did the other. Their needs varied because Nicole was three years older. Yet, she was expected to wait until Cindy was ready for such things as a bicycle. This led to extreme resentment against Cindy. Communicating about reasons for buying for one and not for the other would have solved the problems. Equal does not necessarily mean "same." Making one child overly responsible for another can also lead to resentment. "I had to take my little brother everywhere. It got so I hated him."

As mentioned in Chapter 1, parents frequently compare siblings and set up undesirable competitive feelings. Comments such as, "I wish you'd be more like your sister" and "Your brother never gives us any trouble" cultivate rivalry and resentment which can damage both a child and the sibling relationship. "Upon hearing these 'loving' comments, there is a desire to drop-kick a sibling into the next century" (Lang, 1990, p. 116). A positive parent treats children democratically and instills a cooperative, not competitive, attitude.

Emphasizing uniqueness and freedom from stereotypic restrictions. Each child is unique. Focusing on special qualities and giving unconditional positive regard to children are especially worthy behaviors. Unconditional love means loving children for who they *are*, not for what they do. This doesn't mean you accept or like all behaviors; you love them no matter what.

As discussed earlier, stereotypic gender-role restrictions and expectations are limiting and unwise. "I expect the woman to wait on me. My mom always waited on my dad" and "I'll get married and have him support me like my dad did my mom" are unrealistic ideas. Parents in one study engaged in highly sex-segregated activities, and even though the children appeared to be less stereotypic, modeling was still at work (Hilton and Haldeman, 1991). In a study of dual earner families, sons spent 2.7 hours a week on housework compared to 10.2 hours for daughters (Exter, 1990). Girls, much more than their brothers, were doing what traditional women have always done. If you recall all the benefits of an androgynous personality, parents who model and teach androgyny are helping their children and preparing them for a satisfying life. Resilient children, those able to handle adversity, are likely to be androgynous (Gelman, 1991).

Young people in today's world do not benefit from the locked-in mentality of bigotry nor does a society. Even if parents aren't free from prejudice, they do a child and the world a service by keeping these attitudes to themselves. Those who model acceptance of all races and cultures are preparing a child to live peacefully in today's world.

Applying reality therapy and predictive parenting especially regarding choices. Parenting behaviors suggested by reality therapy (Glasser, 1965) and predictive parenting (Helmstetter, 1989) are highly recommended in positive parenting. One suggestion is to laugh and have fun with a child and avoid any criticism during play times. If parent and child are playing tennis for enjoyment, this isn't the time for the parent to be a critic. The world doesn't end if a mistake is made, and helping a child learn this is positive (Glasser, 1965). Use the most positive comment possible in all situations (Helmstetter, 1989). I would add a postscript: as long as you are being sincere and realistic. I recall playing golf with my dear mother when I was a preteen. I hit the ball about two feet; Mom said, "Good, honey, it went straight!" Somehow that wasn't comforting.

Both reality therapy and predictive parenting emphasize choices and responsibility for one's own actions. A positive parent offers realistic choices in contrast to no choices under authoritarian discipline and unlimited choices with permissive discipline (Nelsen, 1987). Giving young children choices, such as selecting among three different wearing apparels for the day, helps them learn to choose within limits. Later, choices become more numerous and frequently more challenging for both child and parent. Courage is in order. Children need practice with decision making, yet parents are apt to be impatient or unwilling to allow the pain of seeing them fall on their face (Spezzano, 1992).

However tempting it is to just say "no," try the "yes" method Glasser (1965) used as a parent.

> Ordinarily, under most circumstances, if they asked me something, I said yes. It meant that they had lots of privileges and lots of freedom, but they also had the responsibility that goes along with those. The kids learned that getting a yes wasn't the whole ballgame. I have a daughter who asked, when she was 15, if she could go to Japan to visit a pen pal. I said yes. I could have said, "No. How ridiculous! Going to Japan when you're 15 years old." But I said yes. Then the complications started. She asked how you go to Japan. I said, "Well, you just asked me if you could go. This is an entirely different matter. Most people go to Japan by airplane." She said, "Where will I get the money? Will you pay for it?" And then I had to say no. "I don't think I want to pay for a trip to Japan for a 15-year-old." "In other words," she said, "you won't let me go." "Oh, no. I won't stop you from going. I just won't come up with the bucks" (p. 21–22).

Glasser's daughter learned that a "yes" answer can mean the beginning of problems to be solved. The choices were there, and so were the costs or consequences.

Punishment is rarely used in positive parenting for good reasons. Under the threat of punishment, people don't make choices in true freedom, they often become devious to avoid pain, and, lacking in true choices, they tend to use violence when confronted with problems. Reality therapy also suggests not to accept excuses and not to hurt others. Giving up and making excuses are closely related, and both impair life effectiveness. Teaching a child that excuses don't solve problems and are only temporary forms of relief, as discussed in Chapter 3, is important. Hurting others includes yelling, hitting, and imposing excessive restrictions. Engaging in such behaviors is modeling. "Don't yell at me," the mother screams. "But you've been yelling at me," protests the child. The usual response is, "I'm the parent, so I can yell." Does that honestly make sense?

Managing conflict successfully. All families experience conflict. If a child doesn't disagree with a parent, something is wrong. The child is either fearful or incapable of independent thought. The conflict-management recommendations from previous chapters work well in the parent-child relationship as well. An excellent book that focuses on moving from conflict to closeness in parent-child relationships is *If You Really Loved Me* (Paul and Paul, 1987). The book's definition of conflict is "any situation which creates upsetting feelings" (p. 15). Does that leave any doubt that conflict will occur? How it is handled is the key.

Conflict over power and control are especially prevalent during adolescence. As mentioned earlier, a teenager is striving for self-identity, independence, and separation from home. A normal adolescent will disagree, sometimes unrealistically, with a parent. Agreeing with their perception while maintaining your own is recommended for parents (Elkind, 1988). Saying, "I can see why you think that" or "You have a good point" show respect and affirmation. Adolescents still care about their parents and want to be cared about so conflict can be managed positively. Adopting a "win-win" attitude about conflict rather than a "win-lose" one means teaching creative thinking and negotiation in a caring atmosphere (Satir, 1988).

In the parent-child relationship, as in any relationship, giving in is not healthy. When children become angry and resentful, a loving parent sometimes "caves in" to stop these negative feelings or for the sake of peace. Sometimes it's much better to suffer painful emotions if you, as a parent, believe that the chosen course of action is heading in a positive direction. If conflict is managed fairly, emotional outbursts will be minimized in both number and intensity. Allowing children to interact with you in dignity is positive conflict management. It's important to guide children, not to make them feel wrong (Dyer, 1992) and to see them as individuals of worth who have valid opinions.

Even when children leave home, there is potential for conflict. This could be a carry-over from unresolved hurts or newly emerging areas of disagreement. "My mom still thinks that everything I do is wrong including how I handle my children," said a young woman. "We just don't get along," said a mother of an adult child. Breaking the cycle of negative patterns of behavior, opening up lines of communication, and forgiveness are discussed in the books *Making Peace with Your Adult Children* (Smith, 1991) and *Making Peace with Your Parents* (Bloomfield and Felder, 1983).

Positive parenting is a challenge and a commitment. Education, love, and dedication are required. A realization that you are not only parenting, but also, in essence, *training the next generation of parents* is sobering and motivating. If you are or plan to be a parent, be sure to do the activity on "Parenting Behaviors" in REFLECTIONS AND APPLICATIONS. The choice of learning and practicing positive parenting behaviors is among the most significant, and potentially rewarding, ones you will ever make.

CHANGES IN THE FAMILY

Families change, as do all relationships. Although a concept of family may be "father who works, mother who is a housewife, and children," this represents less than 11 percent of families today (Schwartz and Scott, 1994). Families have and probably will become more complicated.

> It is now possible for a child to have five parents at birth: a sperm donor, an egg donor, the woman providing the womb for gestation, the man expecting to raise the child, and the woman expecting to raise the child. When one considers the added parental possibilities that emerge from divorce, remarriage, stepparenting, foster care, and other guardianship arrangements, we discover that family trees increasingly resemble inextricably intertwined vines of ivy. Yet, we must not forget that many children have only one sociological parent, and some have none at all (Spanier, 1989, p. 5).

Figure 12-6 Families have certainly changed!

Dual-Career Families

A change affecting most families is the reality of dual careers. In 1990 59 percent of married women with children under 6 were in the labor market compared to just 19 percent in 1960 (Popenoe, 1993a). Child care is one of the largest work-related costs and challenges. Even though research shows that young children develop nicely under a variety of circumstances and don't require a parent at home with them all day (Crosby, 1991), social scientists recommend that societal institutions and employers take a serious look at providing support.

All changes are significant and worthy of concern. This section will discuss other changes that affect a majority of children today—those specifically related to the parents' divorce.

The Pain of Divorce

Divorce is a process of family change, and some have suggested the term *binuclear family* to describe the structure of a family that has experienced marital separation (Ahrons and Rodgers, 1987). One reason for a new term to describe this situation is to lessen the social stigma and deviant view. The phrase "child of a broken home," in contrast, is a negative label that conjures images of something that is faulty, unworkable, and unable to be fixed. Using the term binuclear family also shows that even though a marriage ends, a family consisting of two biological parents continues.

Divorce occurs regularly in the United States which has the highest rate among industrialized societies. The figure almost tripled from 1970 to 1990. Over a million children each year are involved in their parents' divorce (Popenoe, 1993b; Smith, 1990). No matter how positive the end results may be, parents' divorce is one of the most painful experiences children will ever face. Perhaps no greater human relations challenge exists than helping children cope with their parents' divorce.

> I held my 10-year-old in my arms as she wept. "I just miss Daddy so much," she cried. This was 2 hours after he had left following a weekend visit. Who knows how much pent-up agony had finally been expelled. It was probably not enough because I knew she would continue to hurt. I assured her it was okay to miss him . . . that it showed how much she loved him . . . that I was sure Daddy was very sad, too. I suggested she write to him and make a tape recording. I told her she could call him that night. It's easy to forget how terrible it must be for a 10-year-old or any child who loves both divorced parents especially when one leaves to go home 500 miles away with 13 long weeks before the next visit.

The tightness in my throat reminds me that these are exact lines from my journal describing my daughter, Lisa, in 1977. Lyn, 4 years younger, experienced her painful reaction a few years later.

Divorce is a different experience for children than it is for adults because children lose the family structure that has been fundamental to their development. Children feel rejected, angry, powerless, lonely, and guilty.

> Loyalty conflicts, sometimes flipping from one parent to the other and back again, are a common experience for children of divorce. Children often conceptualize divorce as a fight between two teams with the more powerful side winning the home turf, and will root for different teams at different times (Wallerstein and Blakeslee, 1989, p. 13).

Despite the pain of which I am personally and professionally aware, I am convinced that divorce is still a better alternative than raising children within an unloving marriage.

> There is no evidence that children need two parents in order to grow into healthy adults. But there is a great deal of evidence that children raised in an environment of tension, conflict, and abuse either reenact these behaviors in adulthood or become withdrawn and depressed and take on the role of the victim (Forward and Torres, 1986, p. 260).

Even if tension, conflict, and abuse do not exist, an environment lacking an intimate love relationship between two parents isn't an optimum one for children. They learn about relationships and marriages within a family, and those who witness an emotionally dead marriage aren't gaining healthy messages about love.

If divorce occurs, a challenge for all loving parents is to do everything possible to ensure that children do not suffer any more than necessary. A positive memory from my divorce is Lisa and Lyn's father saying, "We had a good marriage. I'd like to see us have an even better divorce." He, too, was committed to the goal of lessening the children's pain as much as possible.

> Divorces are difficult for everyone, but children can and do survive, provided they have the guidance and continued presence of at least one loving adult. Children benefit from your strength and your ability to make decisions based on reality (Forward and Torres, 1986, p. 260).

Children are also helped by realizing that self-esteem isn't based on someone else's love for you; instead, it comes from within. Watching parents cope positively with divorce teaches valuable lessons.

Figure 12-7 Children feel a sense of loss when parents divorce.

Just as people are not trained to be married, they have little or no education in divorce. Society is making some efforts to correct this deficit by requiring postdivorce counseling and offering classes and seminars for divorcing parents and children. I try to rarely use "should;" however, the following statement deserves it: Divorcing parents *should* be required to learn how to help children cope. Ideally, individuals would seek all available resources. In reality, they don't, and the damage inflicted on children of divorce is enormous. A well-handled divorce alleviates much of a child's pain.

Children of divorce. How well children coped during a 5-year postdivorce period was related, in large part, to behaviors of the parents. Had they been able to resolve and put aside their conflicts and anger? What was the quality of parenting in the child's household? Had the relationship with the noncustodial parent continued in a positive way? The children's well-being was similar to that of their parents (Wallerstein and Kelly, 1980).

After a 10-year period the divorce experience was described by the same families (Wallerstein and Blakeslee, 1989). Some pertinent findings follow.

- Almost all regard their childhood and adolescence as having taken place in the shadow of divorce. They feel that they suffered, although most agreed that their parents were wise to have divorced.

- Children of divorce come to adulthood eager for enduring love and marriage, and they don't take divorce lightly.
- Half the children studied saw one of their parents get a second divorce in the 10-year period.
- Half had parents who stayed angry at each other.
- Three in five felt rejected by at least one parent.
- Very few were helped financially with college educations even though they continued to visit their fathers regularly. But because their fathers were relatively well off, they were ineligible for scholarships.
- Those who entered adolescence in the immediate wake of their parents' divorce had a particularly hard time.
- Almost half of the children entered adulthood as worried, underachieving, self-deprecating, and sometimes angry young men and women. Some felt used in a battle that was never their own.
- Most important, many children emerged in young adulthood as compassionate, courageous, and competent people. Those who did well were helped along the way by a combination of their own inner resources and supportive relationships with one or both parents, grandparents, stepparents, siblings, or mentors.

Of importance to parents is that most of those who did well were helped greatly by parents who had successfully rebuilt their own lives. Others were able to deliberately turn away from the examples set by parents. A smaller number were fortunate in that their parents cooperated in the task of child rearing in a positive way.

Divorce is no easier today in spite of children's realization that they are far from alone. "Each and every child cries out, 'Why me?' " (Wallerstein and Blakeslee, 1989, p. 303). Left-over hurt from divorce stems largely from parental attitudes and behaviors. Children whose parents are committed to doing a better job with their divorce than they did with their marriage are fortunate. They are unlikely to suffer developmental interference or enduring psychological distress; instead, they may "grow in their capacity for compassion and psychological understanding" (Wallerstein and Kelly, 1980, p. 316).

While not denying the pain, more recent studies have been positive and have suggested that problems typically assigned to divorce are just as likely to be related to other factors. Enlightening longitudinal studies in the United States and Great Britain revealed that much of the effect of divorce on children was the result of conditions that existed well before the parental separation occurred especially for boys (Cherlin et al., 1991). In one study academic achievement was not affected by parental divorce (Smith, 1990). Another study found that divorce per se did not cause antisocial behavior in boys. Instead, antisocial qualities of the single mothers and socioeconomic disadvantages were implicated (Bank et al., 1993). Authoritative, not authoritarian or permissive, discipline and divorced mothers' inner locus of control seems to make a positive difference in how children fare (Machida and Holloway, 1991).

Important Positive Recommendations

Leveling. Divorcing parents can make the crisis easier for children by talking with them about the divorce. The child's age will influence the content of the discussion. Preferably, both parents will participate. Children then feel that both will continue to act as parents, and they aren't as likely to take sides. At this time, and on a regular basis thereafter, children need reassurance that parental love continues and that the divorce, while painful to them, is the result of an adult relationship that didn't work. The "R" in the CPR of helping children of divorce is reassurance (Gold, 1992). Make sure that the message is clear that the children are not in any way at fault. The needs-fulfillment theory, discussed in Chapter 11, can be used with children old enough to understand. The marriage failed to meet individual needs, and neither parent is seen as the entire cause of the divorce.

Expressing. Intense feelings surrounding divorce are best vented. No matter how much it hurts parents to experience a child's pain and anger, such disclosures are to be freely encouraged. Divorce leads to a feeling of loss, and grieving is in order. A study revealed that children who experienced lower levels of mourning behaviors when parents divorced were lonelier as adults (Murphy, 1991). Parents may feel a need to repress their own emotions in front of a child. Being out of control is not recommended; however, an honest, "I'm scared sometimes, too" or "I hurt, too" can be beneficial.

Normalizing. Trying to keep life as normal as possible and avoiding other major changes are recommended. Both parents can help by keeping children involved in activities and continuing to show an active interest. If a change is in order, you can make it easier by informing the children about it and listening to their input. You may need to be strong enough to hold fast against their objections. Eight months after my separation, I decided to leave Illinois and return to Nebraska to attend graduate school. Lisa, a strong-willed 10-year-old, protested, "I won't go. I'll stay here and live with Dad." Fortunately, I was able to tell her that her father and I had discussed the decision, and even though I cared about her feelings, we were moving. Within a few months she felt fine about her new home.

A positive parenting coalition. Developing a "temporary alliance for the purpose of accomplishing a project" is how my good friends Emily and John Visher (1988) describe a parenting coalition. The Vishers, who are authors, therapists, and stepfamily adults, are founders of Stepfamily Association of America, an organization dedicated to educating and supporting stepfamilies. A coalition involves both divorced parents cooperating and staying involved in raising the children; later, it can also include stepparents. Even though a coalition approach is challenging and often frustrating, loving parents who want to serve their children best find that it is a wise investment of their time, energy, and efforts. In fact, it may be central to the welfare of a child. "Learning to work *with* rather than against a spouse is central to a healthier divorce process" (Gold, 1992, p. xiv). If you're thinking that this is impossible with your particular former spouse, reconsider. With their permission, following is a story of my husband and his former wife's journey along an extremely rocky road to a positive parenting coalition.

> It was a bitter divorce, characterized by animosity and hostility. Two boys (ages 13 and 11) felt the wrath of both parents. The boys lived with Bob, their father. Karen, their mother, was in Minnesota. Arranging visits was a nightmare. Jeff and Greg overheard the telephone screaming matches on a regular basis. Five years after their divorce, in the middle of a particularly hateful time, producers of the television show "Good Morning America" invited six of us adults who were biological and/or stepparents and the four children (the boys and my two daughters) to appear on the show and partici-

> pate in stepfamily counseling. We came together in New York City for several intense sessions before the cameras. Sixteen-year-old Greg said, "It's the hardest thing in the world when your parents hate each other." Eighteen-year-old Jeff, in what the therapist said was the most vivid description of divorce she had ever heard, recalled the early stage: "I just wanted to crawl into a hole and pull the dirt over my head. There's nothing you can do, nowhere to go; you're helpless when your parents don't get along." Tears flowed and long-buried feelings emerged. Barbara Levy, the therapist, said to Bob and Karen, "Listen to what they are saying because you two will always be parents to these two boys . . . forever and forever." Realizing the intense suffering of two children loved by both parents, a miracle occurred between Karen and Bob and, ultimately, among the stepparents and the boys' stepsiblings, Lisa and Lyn, as well. Karen and I, the boys' stepmother, hugged as we left for home. "We can do much better," was a comment. And we have.

What has happened since "Good Morning America" is a heartening human relations story told by Claire Berman in *McCall's* (November 1989) and included in a highly recommended book *Families Apart: Ten Keys to Successful Co-Parenting* (Blau, 1993). Karen, Jerry (her husband), Bob, and I now parent as a coalition in addition to being friends who enjoy each other's company. We visit each other and conduct workshops in an attempt to guide other divorced families toward peace and cooperation. As I was working on this edition, I received a birthday gift in the mail from Karen and Jerry. It was a copy of the book *Love and Friendship*. We have come such a long way. Did any of us think it would ever be possible? For years we did not. Remember self-fulfilling prophecies? They are as powerful in predicting the course of relationships as they are in terms of individual behaviors. A positive prophecy about your parenting coalition can light the way.

Children are the real winners when their parents get along. Research revealed that everyone involved is satisfied when adults can separate parental functions from the former marriage and have a cooperative, communicative relationship with respect to their children (Maccoby et al., 1990). A basic step divorced parents can take is to agree on a general "want" for the children, such as "We want the children to be spared as much pain as possible" and "We want to do what is best for the children." My own daughters benefited greatly because their father and I were able to do this. When a child's whole sense of well-being is at stake and you know there is pain, parents need to take positive action. To begin the process, one person can write a goodwill letter expressing a hope and desire to improve the situation for everyone's sake, especially children. In developing a working relationship as co-parents, use the following steps from the book *Between Love and Hate: A Guide to Civilized Divorce* (Gold, 1992).

1. Be businesslike and relate to each other as people do in the workplace. Adjust expectations using the workplace as a model. Seldom does one person get everything desired. Focus on solutions and use teamwork to reach objectives. Use businesslike communications throughout the process.
2. Separate how you feel about your ex-spouse from how you relate to the person as a parent.
3. Focus on what the children need.

Other recommendations are to use open communication, describe desired behavioral changes, and don't assume. "Your interpretation has no more corner on the truth than your spouse's" (p. 159). A skeleton of emotional connection with an "ex" will always be there, and even though it doesn't have life, it doesn't disappear. "A deep connection exists even as you create a healthy emotional distance, because no one else shares with you the depth of feeling for your children as does the other parent" (p. 18).

What not to do. Parents can help children by eliminating all-too-common negative behaviors.

- Don't criticize the personhood of the other parent. Keep negative comments to yourself. Children perceive themselves as half of each parent, so berating your former spouse is hurtful and damaging to the child. "It feels like an arrow going right through me," said one child. If you are critical, direct your comment to the behavior of the person, as recommended for all criticism. A good idea is to state it as a wish such as, "I wish your mother would be here on time to get you."
- Don't place a child in the middle of two warring camps. Children of divorce often speak of feeling "torn." Parents add to the burden by setting up situations in which children are pulled in different directions: "Whom would you rather live with?" "Do you want to spend the holidays here or with your dad?" You may wish to offer a child alternatives, but be aware that having to make such decisions is difficult.
- Don't pump a child for information: "Who is your mom dating?" "How much money did your dad spend on you?" Putting a child on the spot is cruel.
- Don't use a child as a messenger. Closely related to pumping for information is to ask a youngster to relay a message: "Tell your dad that the child support check is late." "Ask your mom if she wants you to come this summer." The adults can communicate for themselves in an "adult" manner. If this seems impossible, communicate through the mail or through another person, not through the child.
- Don't add to a child's already weakened emotional state: "I'm so unhappy. If only you lived with me, I'd be much better" will only burden a child more. Or, if a child is angry at the other parent, don't increase the pain level. Instead, encourage the child to talk the problem over with the person. If the other parent hurts the child by not being in contact or forgetting special days, listen to the pain and confine your comments to: "I don't understand why this happens. Someday he or she is likely to regret missing being a part of your life." You may inwardly feel justified by a child's resentment; however, don't feed the unpleasant emotional fire. Children don't benefit from feeling unloved and unwanted by either parent.
- Don't create more stress for the child. If finances are worrisome, for example, find a friend in whom to confide.

Parents who work together to set up custody arrangements and a reasonable, flexible schedule of visits are helping a child. A key guideline is to do what is in the best interests of the child. A father asked me once, "What do you think of this idea? My wife and I have joint custody, and we're thinking of having our 3-year-old live with her for 1 year in Montana and then a year with me in Nebraska and just keep trading off." My negative reaction was honest. Designed to make parents happy, it would likely make the child miserable.

Children typically appreciate being consulted about moving back and forth between households. The best course of action is to provide them with a number of choices that are acceptable to both parents and that do not indicate a preference for one or the other. The child's input should be neither judged nor criticized. Keeping in mind that parental conflict is the single most significant factor associated with poor adjustment (Gold, 1992), flexibility, congeniality, and cooperation are key elements in doing the best you can for a child.

Ideally, both parents will remain actively involved in a child's life. Consistency and dependability about spending quality time with a youngster are essential to well-being. If one parent has custody and the child spends the most time there, that person can keep the other parent informed about the child's school progress, activities, health, and so on. Custody battles and manipulative game playing with child support are certain to hurt children. Both the person who sends and the one who receives support can deprive and damage children.

If parents have difficulty in this area, a third party is the answer, and mediation is highly recommended. Mediation is a neutral forum in which a trained person serves as mediator and helps the family make the transition in the child's best interests (Gold, 1992). Mediation reduced frequency of custody hearings, allowed settlements in half the time, and substantially improved the father's satisfaction with arrangements in one study (Emery et al., 1992). For children, regularity of visitation predicts adjustment. Because children of divorce need functioning parents, counseling may be needed for an adult or child who is emotionally unstable or severely depressed. A good suggestion is to opt for family counseling instead of sending just the children as they may think they are "wrong" or the cause (Elkind, 1988). Most family service agencies provide help on a sliding fee scale. The choice for divorcing parents is clear. Divorce can be handled badly and cause injuries to children. Or, parents can learn and apply strategies that not only help children survive divorce; they also contribute to their positive growth.

In recent years researchers have paid attention to adult children of divorce. Interviews with hundreds of adults whose parents divorced when they were children are contained in the book *Adult Children of Divorce Speak Out* (Berman, 1991). The author found what she called "echoes" and concluded that divorce has lifelong repercussions in areas of trust, commitment, and self-esteem. Several of the adult children focus on financial security, control, success, and stability. Many are highly empathic and fiercely independent. Several problems seemed to be related to unresolved emotions. Those who felt unloved by a parent had scars. Berman recommends that these adult children let go of the anger and go back to their parents to resolve remaining conflicts.

Other authors (Beal and Hochman, 1991) believe that the family style, not the divorce per se, results in adult problems. They contend that "divorce does not have to carry a life sentence" (p. 8). Because present relationship problems can stem from unresolved issues with a family of origin, the solution is in resolution. Hopefully, reading this will motivate adult children to make the effort to heal any old hurts.

Beginning Again: Developing New Families

Families come in different sizes and ages and varieties and colors. What families have in common the world around is that they are the place where people learn who they are and how to be that way. Families don't have to look any certain way. Any of the people in any of the families can improve the quality of the living experiences they are offering to each other (Clarke, 1982, p. 1).

With no intention of slighting adoptive, foster, and never-married single parent families who contribute significantly to the well-being of children, this section will concentrate on families that form after the death of a parent or parental divorce.

Single or binuclear family. The most common type of *single-parent family* is one in which a divorced parent has the children in his or her care. This type is also known as a *binuclear family*. Depending upon custody arrangements, this may be all the time or shared with the other parent. Joint custody is becoming more prevalent. Terms such as custodial and noncustodial parents are used to identify physical, and usually, legal custody.

The total of binuclear, never-married single-parent, and widowed families accounts for 27 percent of all households that have children under the age of 18. The numbers have doubled since 1970 (Jayakody et al., 1993). Most parents with custody are women; however, the numbers of custodial fathers are increasing. Traditional gender roles are responsible for the vast difference between the numbers of custodial fathers and mothers. A father may not even think of having custody if he shares a societal belief that children are better off with a mother. Many courts still award custody on the basis of tradition. Regardless, more fathers today are seeking their full parental rights in either joint or single custody.

Still unique is the mother in a noncustodial role. Negative societal attitudes make the role difficult. Noncustodial mothers in a study pointed out emotional and financial insecurities and concerns for their children which led them to relinquish custody. The women reported feeling alienated, powerless, helpless, and without support (Arditti and Madden-Derdich, 1993).

Karen, the mother of my stepsons, led a workshop for mothers without custody. Her objective was to encourage people to accept and empathize with women in this difficult role. "I have suffered because of others' opinions of me," she admits, "and I have some regrets. I do know that my relationship with my sons is loving and close, and I honestly don't think it could have worked out as well if all this had not happened the way it did." The acceptance of mothers as loving noncustodial parents will be a major step forward. Perhaps a simple statement made by Irene, a student, will help put this in perspective: "I did not give up my child. She simply lives with her father more than with me."

Regardless of whether the custodial parent is female or male, single parenting is a challenge. "It's the hardest job in the world, no doubt about it" and "I feel I have to be all things to all people" are typical thoughts. Deciding to be the custodial parent requires objectivity and a great deal of thought. Too often, mothers assume custody just because society expects them to do so. An individual is wise to honestly assess what is in the best interests of the children. Of course, in cases of death or in which no marriage has ever occurred, a parent has no choice.

Difficulties include the inordinate stress of trying to assume multiple roles and attempting to handle all the children's pain; one's own feelings of guilt, anger, and depression; finances; and time management. A study revealed differences between male and female single parents. The middle-class women had far more financial problems with 78 percent facing money problems compared to less than 20 percent of the men. When asked to name her three main problems, one woman replied, "Money, money, and money." Women also reported more problems with role and task overload, and developing a social life. Men experienced more problems with an ex-spouse. Strength-wise, both sexes were more similar identifying satisfaction with: parenting skills, managing a family without help, communication, the ability to provide financial support, and personal growth. All said that single parenting became easier over time (Richards and Schmiege, 1993).

Single parents may believe that their children won't fare as well as they would with two parents. Having another caring adult to share the load is helpful; however, democratic discipline and other positive parenting strategies can be used effectively by one as well as by two. Support groups are major sources of help. Classes and seminars can offer practical advice and encouragement to parents floundering in their new (or old) role.

The benefits and rewards of single parenting can diminish the impact of the problems. In addition to ones already identified, most single parents proudly acknowledge:

- Heightened self-esteem and feelings of pride in all the accomplishments of single parenting.
- Close, meaningful relationships based on shared coping, emotional expression, and deep communication.
- Self-respect and the pride of being self-sufficient.
- Freedom to make solitary decisions on child raising.

A study of young adolescents uncovered another benefit. Youths in single-parent families perceived both parents as more friendly than did youngsters in married-parent families (Asmussen and Larson, 1991). Attributing negative outcomes to economic hardships and parental conflict, research found more benefits than costs. A divorced family can promote competence, independence, a greater sense of responsibility, and high self-esteem, and children acquire special skills and coping strategies (Barber and Eccles, 1992).

Contrary to what is implied by the stigma of single-parent families, children can do extremely well. Ryan, a former Stanford University athletic and academic scholarship student, was described by a high school counselor as an outstanding scholar, athlete, and all-around student—one of the most well-liked kids in his large California high school. He said, "I know of no other student, past or present, whom I would most like to have as my own child than Ryan." His college baseball coach, Mark Marquess of Stanford in a letter of recommendation, also praised Ryan.

> I have never had a student athlete that I have been more impressed with than Ryan Turner. He has an enthusiasm for everything he does that is contagious. He proved to be one of the most, if not the most, exceptional young men I have ever been associated with in my 21 years of collegiate coaching. Ryan is first class in every respect!

This young man, who could be described as the "product of a broken home," was raised since age five by his single-parent mother, who is my sister, Connie. Both Ryan and Connie deserve a great deal of credit. Incidentally, Ryan added to his laurels by being the first player signed by the Colorado Rockies!

Parents without custody also play a significant role in a child's life. As indicated earlier, children want and profit from a positive relationship with both parents. Successful noncustodial parents make parenting a high priority. Letting children know of your love and concern is essential while resisting a temptation to spoil them. The ones who do an excellent job get to know their children even better and often develop a closer relationship than they had before. They don't cause problems for the other parent; instead, they are cooperative and flexible and attempt to make the most of their special

Figure 12-8 Proud single-parent mom Connie and son Ryan after College World Series game victory.

role. When noncustodial parents do not work on relationships with children, long-term effects are sad. A study showed that divorce negatively affected interactions with adult children. Fathers had lower rates of contact with biological children which occurred more often when children were younger at the time of divorce (Bulcroft and Bulcroft, 1991). This doesn't have to happen.

Noncustodial parenting can be frustrating. "I want to be involved, but she won't allow it," said one father in reference to his former spouse. "I have no idea what's going on with my two children except what they tell me every other weekend. I can't get information from their father or their school," said a frustrated mother. In an effort to help all divorced parents Susan Diamond, dean of students at Scarsdale High School in New York, wrote an excellent book, *Helping Children of Divorce: A Handbook for Parents and Teachers* (1985). The book fills a void by up-dating schools and society on positive management of divorced families and has a special chapter on noncustodial parents' rights related to a child's school. Even without positive involvement by a noncustodial parent, children can do quite well. "Every child needs to feel that at least one adult is crazy about him or her" (Spezzano, 1992, p. 72). The love of both biological parents is even better.

With all of its challenges and frustrations, single-parenting is special and rewarding. Growing up in a binuclear family or with one surviving parent has its difficulties, yet the benefits can outweigh the costs. As with all of life's challenges, individuals can create their own realities.

Stepfamily. The stepfamily is rapidly becoming the family of the near future. This trend will continue as long as divorce and death rates remain stable. More than 40 percent (Coleman and Ganong, 1990) up to 46 percent (DeWitt, 1992b) of marriages in a given year are remarriages for at least one person. About one-third of all families in the United States are stepfamilies (Glick, 1991; Larson, 1992). By the year 2000, 50 percent of all Americans are likely to be involved in a stepfamily (Glick, 1991). Even with the numbers, social science textbooks generally contain only a statement or, in several cases, nothing about stepfamilies.

What is a stepfamily? Definitions vary even among the families themselves. The broadest concept of a *stepfamily* is any family consisting of an adult couple with at least one of them having a child from a previous relationship. The children may or may not live in the household with the couple. Usually, one or both of the adults have been married before. Divorce is the typical reason for the end of the former relationship, although stepfamilies also form after the death of a parent.

Both adults may have custody of children; one parent can have custody and the other can be a noncustodial parent; both can be noncustodial parents; or a stepparent may not have any biological children. The couple may add their own biological child to the existing stepfamily. Stepfamilies come in many varieties, and the situation can be complicated. As one who is familiar with the configurations, I would speculate that the reason stepfamilies aren't adequately covered in a number of textbooks is that the complex possibilities are too difficult to explain!

Studies comparing stepfamily types provide insight. One found that biological mothers had more optimistic perspectives than the stepfathers who agreed with several myths of stepfamilies (Kurdeck and Fine, 1991). Another revealed that adolescents living with stepfathers had higher self-esteem and fewer social problems than those living with stepmothers (Fine and Kurdek, 1992).

If you are not yet married, you could join increasing numbers of people who become stepparents in their first marriages. "Instant parent" is what they are sometimes called. Glen, a former student, wrote me a note from Kansas: "Would you believe that I'm marrying a woman with two children? After hearing you talk about stepfamilies, now I'm going to be in one!"

Men and women form stepfamilies for the same reasons they marry. They love each other, and they want to commit to a lasting relationship. For anyone considering stepfamily living, what is important is to take the time to "stop, look, listen, and learn." Preparing for a first marriage is important, and if you're going into a stepfamily: prepare, prepare, and prepare.

A stepfamily is somewhat like a Cecil B. DeMille production, with a cast of thousands (Westoff, 1977). "Both the numbers of people which may be involved and the subsequent myriad of relationships that are created contribute to the complexity of this family form" (Knaub, Hanna, and Stinnett, 1984, p. 42). A key word for stepfamilies is challenge; another is reward. "Being in a stepfamily ends one's fear of living a dull life. Stepfamilies are born in pain and can grow into joy" (Adams, 1987, p. 36).

In order to grow in joy, certain tasks are essential. A major challenge lies in overcoming society's image of a stepfamily which spills over into how individuals perceive their family. What do you think of when you hear the word stepmother? Most think of Cinderella or the wicked stepmother in the story of Sleeping Beauty. The image is powerful, and stepfamily stereotypes form early (Visher and Visher, 1988). A 3-year-old who had an excellent relationship with her soon-to-be stepmother asked on the day of the wedding, "As soon as you get to be my stepmother, will you beat me?" People presume that the stepfather will be cruel, the stepmother wicked, and that the stepchildren are poor maligned waifs. "To interact in the middle of such a dark cloud is crippling to many stepfamilies" (Visher and Visher, 1979, p. 6).

Figure 12-9

In one of the first major studies of remarriage, *attitudinal environment*, perceived support from the general society as well as specific people, was identified as a contributing factor to the success or failure of stepfamilies (Bernard, 1956). If individuals perceive a negative attitudinal environment, success can be more difficult. Conversely, a favorable environment is significantly related to family strength (Knaub, Hanna, and Stinnett, 1984). My stepson Greg pinpointed it well in a video program: "If you feel accepted from the outside, it helps you to accept yourself and the stepfamily from the inside." Support and involvement are needed from the extended family, including grandparents. Research shows that stepgrandparenting has its rewards (Orr and VanZandt, 1987) and that they can hurt or help stepfamilies. "Grandparents are in an excellent position to build bridges or build walls between stepfamily members" (Visher and Visher, 1982, p. 120).

Attitudes have become more accepting, and research has shown that many adults and children perceive their stepfamilies as positive (Duncan and Brown, 1992; Kelley, 1992; Knaub and Hanna, 1984; Knaub, Hanna, and Stinnett, 1984). Family pride and being less vulnerable to negative stereotypes and myths contributed to family strength in one study (Kelley, 1992). Gratifying is that researchers are paying more attention to strengths. In 1989 only 4 of more than 50 self-help books contained specific mention of potential strengths (Coleman and Ganong, 1989); earlier, most research emphasized only problems (Ganong and Coleman, 1986). My graduate thesis (1980) and subsequent articles (Hanna and Knaub, 1981; Knaub and Hanna, 1984; Knaub, Hanna, and Stinnett, 1984) were among the first to concentrate on what's positive about remarriage and stepfamilies.

Stepfamilies are strengthened in the same ways as other families are: communicating, showing appreciation, doing things together, handling conflict effectively, and perceived support (Knaub, Hanna, and Stinnett, 1984). An Australian study (Schultz et al., 1991) concurred with Knaub, Hanna, and Stinnett (1984) in identifying affection and sexual intimacy as a source of strength. Common strength themes are: flexibility, respect, patience, support systems, communication, and fun and humor (Kelley, 1992).

> The stepfamily is a courageous and positive new family unit. It is not second-class. We are a different kind of family and we face different kinds of problems than other families. But we will survive and provide a second chance of happiness for millions of adults and children (Getzoff and McClenahan, 1984, p. 142).

Because of stepfamily uniquenesses, special challenges are best handled before they lead to insurmountable problems.

Expectations must be closely examined. People entering into stepfamilies may have unrealistic expectations representing opposite ends of a continuum. Some adults believe that because they love, the stepfamily will automatically succeed. "I love you, and you love me, and I know the children and we will love each other, too." Being realistic, love, if it develops at all between stepparent and stepchild, takes time and effort. Both may have to settle for a feeling of care and concern.

> The belief that parents should love all their children equally and that children should love both parents equally is not a reasonable expectation for stepfamilies. In fact, such injunctions can produce guilt and may inhibit the development of a caring relationship (Kelley, 1992, p. 585).

Stepparents are advised to stop worrying about whether or not they love their stepchild and focus on establishing caring, openly communicative relationships. "In this environment, love can grow" (Bloomfield and Kory, 1993, p. 49).

The opposite expectation is a sour idea that stepfamily life will be the pits. Some parents begin by thinking, "I just know it's going to be a terrible struggle," and it's not unusual for children to say, "I know I'll hate my stepparent." Neither is realistic. Stepfamily success is clearly possible, but not guaranteed.

A common mistake is expecting a stepfamily to be like a biological one. A stepfamily is different, and "different" doesn't mean deficient. In a workshop the question was asked, "How are stepfamilies different?" A loud male voice boomed, "Blood!" He meant that the biological basis is missing for the stepparent and stepchild. When this is acknowledged and not considered negative, a positive relationship can develop. Other expectations include "shoulditis." For example, "Mike, you should love the kids; after all, they're mine," or "Mary, you need to be a real mother to my kids," and "Son, you should respect Mike because he's my husband and your stepfather." As with all forcing words, the reaction is usually negative. Expressing a realistic expectation as a "want" is healthier.

What is realistic is to realize that stepparenting is not like being a biological parent; nor is it equivalent to adopting a child (Gordon, 1988b). Realistically, the stepparent is likely to be resented at first, be somewhat feared, and be compared, usually unfavorably, to the biological parent. Stepchildren are apt to be jealous of a stepparent's place of affection in their parent's life. A jealous former spouse can magnify these feelings and make the situation even more uncomfortable.

A stepparent can expect to hear, "You're not my parent, and I don't have to love you." A suggested reply is, "I know I'm not your biological parent, and you don't have to love me. I am your stepmom (or stepdad), and I would like to have a positive relationship with you." It's best to contain negative reactions and continue to let the child know that you are concerned and that you care. An entire chapter of *Making Peace in Your Stepfamily* (Bloomfield and Kory, 1993) is devoted to excellent tips on how to be a good stepparent.

Within a stepfamily, each person assumes new *roles* or behaviors within a status. The *status* or position of stepparent is considered by sociologists to be an achieved one because it is earned by individual effort. "Stepparents aren't treated like parents automatically; their parental status must be earned" (Furstenberg and Cherlin, 1991, p. 83). Lack of training for biological parents is still the norm, and only recently have the roles of stepfather, stepmother, stepchild, and stepsibling been examined. This lack of role definition is positive in a sense, because it allows the development of a role that fits the particular situation. If you are the stepparent of a 2-year-old whose biological father is dead, you will play a different part in the child's life than you would if you were the stepparent of a child whose biological parents are divorced. In the former case, your role will be similar to that of the typical father. In the latter case, your role would be as an additional significant adult in the child's life. Trying to replace the other biological parent is not recommended. "Children need to maintain a separate tie with their biological parent that stands outside their relationship with the stepparent" (Kelley, 1992, p. 585).

The stepparent's role will vary, too, depending upon the living arrangements. Noncustodial stepparents can act more like just a friend, while a stepparent in the home will assume a parental role. Roles also differ depending upon the age of the stepchild, his or her personality, and individuals' preference. For example, a 6-year-old who is a little insecure may want a strong parental figure, while a strong-willed 16-year-old will prefer one who is flexible and friendly. A recommendation is to move slowly into a certain role. Stepparents who "come on like gangbusters" are usually resented. Almost always, shared or egalitarian marital roles work best. Resentment is likely when individuals feel that inequities exist. "In well-functioning stepfamilies, both parents earned money, wrote checks, did housework, and took care of children" (Kelley, 1992, p. 585).

Emotions are generally more intense, and often confusing, in a stepfamily. A full range of feelings is probable as people progress through stages of stepfamily life. "People in stepfamilies tend to have more than their share of hurt, disappointment, jealousy, fear, and anger" (Getzoff and McClenahan, 1984, p. 10). Freedom in expression and open communication are especially helpful. Empathy is sorely needed. Of utmost importance, as revealed in research, is the presence of warm and nurturing behaviors on the part of stepparents (Crosbie-Burnett and Giles-Sims, 1993).

For a biological parent outside the stepfamily, acceptance of a new significant adult in your child's life is difficult. "When I heard my sons talking about their stepmother," one divorced parent said, "I wanted to scream that she isn't any kind of mother to you. She's just the one who married your dad!" Stepparents, too, may have jealous or resentful feelings of the children's other parent. Keeping in mind what is best for the children is critical. Additional love and caring adults in their lives are bonuses. "No healthy stepcouple blocks a child from loving a natural parent" (Adams, 1987, p. 46). I would add that no healthy parent blocks a child from loving a stepparent.

Jealousy and resentment related to a spouse's former mate are common. "I wish she would just go away," one stepparent said of her husband's ex-wife. "She calls and monopolizes his time, and what is so maddening is that he allows it!" Positive communication skills can enable marital partners to express these feelings in noncombative ways. And learning effective, businesslike ways of parenting with a former spouse, as discussed in a previous section, could alleviate these problems.

In a number of stepfamilies, as noted before, one person is not remarried. In a workshop conducted by my husband and me, a young woman raised her hand and said, "I would like a different term instead of 'remarriage.' This is my first marriage." She has a lot of company. In almost half of what are called remarriages, one person has not been married before (DeWitt, 1992b). First-marrieds in the stepfamily face some different challenges from those that confront remarried persons. Their emotional concerns may be acute as they deal with the role of stepparenting someone else's children when they have never parented before. Education and support are definitely advised.

A number of potentially stressful *issues* confront stepfamilies. Discipline and finances topped the list of identified problems for 80 stepfamilies (Knaub, Hanna, and Stinnett, 1984). Strongly recommended is to begin a new family system based on positive parenting principles and the style of democratic discipline described earlier. The authoritarian style isn't healthy in biological families, and in stepfamilies it becomes a time bomb. Stepchildren do not usually accept a stepparent as an enforcer of limits. Since "discipline cannot be enforced without the consent of the disciplinee, stepparents cannot wield much power except through force—which is, of course, destructive psychologically if not physically" (Visher and Visher, 1988, p. 213). Having the biological parent take the lead at first is another suggestion (Kelley, 1992). Both adults working together and being supportive of each other are highly desirable.

If children move back and forth between households, binuclear family issues, identified in a previous section, need attention. The extended family becomes more extended in that stepfamilies have additional sets of grandparents and other relatives involved. How and where a stepfamily will spend holidays is an issue that has to be faced. Flexibility and compromise are necessary. In stepfamilies, people learn that holidays are not dates; instead, they are special times when family members can be together, regardless of the date. Other issues include who pays for what, for whom and what are resources such as child support used, and, of utmost importance, estate planning (Moreau, 1993). Developing a parenting coalition that includes stepparents is a wise investment of time and energy. Advantages are more resources and people to deal with issues and events, less tension, more information about the children, less manipulation, and positive feelings for all concerned (Bloomfield and Kory, 1993).

A major challenge for stepfamilies is the higher divorce rate for second marriages than for first marriages. Census Bureau figures reveal that more than 62 percent of remarriages among women under age 40 end in divorce. The more children involved, the higher the redivorce rate (*Psychology Today*, 1993c). Various reasons have been suggested. "Dealing with stepchildren and ex-spouses, complex finances, the demands of two careers, and the need to meld two distinctive ways of doing things can create stresses that challenge the best of relationships" (Stuart and Jacobson, 1985, p. 230). Because of all the challenges, the human relations suggestions contained in this book are highly recommended.

One reason for lack of success is at the heart of all the others. When people in stepfamilies are neither educated nor prepared to meet the challenges, they find themselves hopelessly frustrated. "Stepfamilies must be built with more than good intentions, dreams, and hopes. Awareness, skills, and realistic expectations can provide a stable structure that permits the stepfamily to achieve its potential" (Einstein, 1982, p. 2). Recognizing that the necessary foundation to stepfamily success is a strong couple relationship will encourage the adults to make enrichment of the marriage a high priority. "Healthy stepmarriages require mini-honeymoons every few months" (Adams, 1987, p. 44).

In order to succeed, stepfamily members are urged to learn about this unique family type. Knowing that stepfamily adjustment comes in stages and recognizing what these stages are is important (Keshet, 1987). Stepfamily integration takes time-enough to become familiar with each other and to develop trust, and this knowledge can encourage patience. Books, workshops, classes, and programs about remarriage and stepfamilies are valuable educational resources (Duncan and Brown, 1992; Nelson and Levant, 1991).

The Stepfamily Association of America, which was organized to provide education and support and foster a positive image of stepfamilies, has local chapters throughout the United States. A step-by-step program manual for stepfamilies titled *Stepfamilies Stepping Ahead* (Burt, 1988) is an invaluable help as are numerous other books and tapes available through the organization (see end of this chapter under resources).

Are the benefits worth the challenges? Thousands of stepfamily members would say they are.

> Stress does not necessarily signal dysfunction, and pain does not necessarily lead to psychological damage. Both can facilitate growth and an appreciation of the importance of caring relationships (Visher and Visher, 1988, p. 8).

The benefits can include the following:

- Additional caring relationships within the stepfamily and the extended family.
- Opportunities for learning and growing derived from other role models and from challenging situations.
- Diversity of people and interesting situations.
- Emphasis on deep communication and problem solving.
- Focus on "give-and-take," compromise, and sharing.
- Living within intimate love relationships and happy marriages.
- Satisfaction from succeeding in spite of challenges.
- Joy from being cared for (and maybe even loved) by people who are not biologically related.

Contrary to the stereotypic image, many stepfamilies are doing quite well. Family strength, marital satisfaction, and positive perceptions of family adjustment were found in a study of 80 stepfamilies (Knaub, Hanna, and Stinnett, 1984). The National Survey of Children found that most members of stepfamilies described life in quite positive terms that were not very different from how nuclear families described themselves. Reporting close relations were 78 percent of the parents and 66 percent of the children (Furstenberg and Cherlin, 1991). Marianne wrote about her remarriage.

> When I met my husband, I found that he came from a family that was all male except for his mother, who did, and still does, wait on them all hand and foot (gag!). His thinking on male-female roles underwent great changes as he found that little girls didn't just play with dolls—they fished and got dirty, they climbed trees and even wrapped dead snakes around the handlebars of their bikes. Putting two families together made all of us learn patience, tolerance, and that none of us had a set role. We lived and got through by everyone doing a little of everything. My husband just bought an eleventh-year anniversary present for the whole family. We've always considered it a "family anniversary" rather than a "wedding" one. He bought us all a cocker puppy—a family gift with family responsibility. Any wonder I love my husband?

With no biological "buffer of love," individuals can learn to care. Susie, a student, wrote that she had a stepfather and then added, "He's several *steps* above what I had." She describes their relationship as very loving.

As wonderful young adults, the four children in our stepfamily have often sent beautiful cards and notes of appreciation. From Jeff I received the business world's better-late-than-never acknowledgment of stepfamilies—a card actually designed for a stepmother. One of Greg's cards was humorous ("Remember all of the aggravation I used to cause you? I'm almost done"), but his personal note was meaningful:

> I've never regretted the addition you've been to my life. It's always been positive no matter how hard I tried to convince myself it wasn't at times. I've adopted many of your ideas into my way of life, and those are good qualities in me. You are very special. Thanks.

The verse in one of Lyn's cards to Bob said that he really knew how to be a great friend and a special stepfather (she inserted step in front of father, something they all learned to do from the beginning). Her note read: "I appreciate all you do for me. It's great having such a great friend in the same house as my stepfather. You have been, and continue to be, such a special part of my life. I feel lucky to have you."

Lisa once found a card that described Bob's relationship with her perfectly: "Thanks for the right answers, for help when I needed it, for always being on my side, for bringing joy to life, and for being just great." She signed it, "To the most wonderful stepfather and friend." Her most recent card to him featured aircraft on the front (aviation is a peak experience for him) and in the blank inside, she wrote:

> I hope you realize how lucky I consider myself to have you as a stepfather. You are a very cool person and a great friend. Thanks so much for all you are and all you do for me. You're the greatest.

The absolute joy of being affirmed and loved by children who were not born to you is worth all the stressors along the way.

A painful loss and ending can herald the beginning of a new family. The first one is a single-parent or binuclear family. Life can be stressful and challenging, yet full of potential rewards. A stepfamily is possibly the next family type. Complexities and challenges are hallmarks of stepfamily life. Education and support can be of great help.

If you know and value yourself, you are well equipped to meet the multiple challenges involved in parenting and developing strong families. The rewards are bountiful. Unique types of families who succeed illustrate excellent human relations. Successful stepfamilies prove that human beings are capable of reaching out and developing long-term nurturing and loving family relationships which are not based on biology. Such nourishing relationships are among the finest expressions of the art of relating.

SUMMARY

A family is a primary social group and has tremendous influence on the lives of its members. A family can be defined as a relatively small domestic group (related by biology, marriage, or adoption) who function as a cooperative unit. For some, any kinlike, cooperative group can be a family. Today's society includes several types of families. Identified family strengths are helpful in showing how to build successful relationships.

Parenting is a major responsibility for which no formal training is mandated. Even though educational resources are available, adults do not typically take advantage of them. Ideally, adults will become educated and make a thoughtful decision about becoming parents. The responsibilities are numerous. Love and trust are basic to a child's healthy development. Other primary tasks are encouragement of self-esteem, emotional well-being, and social development. Fathers are becoming more involved in caregiving.

Discipline, defined broadly as the entire process of guiding and teaching a child from infancy to adulthood, has many dimensions. Two styles, authoritarian and permissive, are not recommended. Families are best served by democratic discipline. Featured in this style are open communication, role modeling, behavior modification, guidelines with input from adults and children, logical consequences, and structure. Positive parenting behaviors such as admitting mistakes, spending quality time with children, demonstrating warmth and affection, showing appreciation, emphasizing uniqueness and freeing children from the restrictions of stereotypes, allowing choices, and managing conflict successfully lead to rewarding results.

A major challenge faced by numbers of parents is helping their children cope with divorce. Recommendations, if followed, can make divorce easier on children. If two biological parents are alive, children are better served by positive experiences with both. Developing a positive parenting coalition with a former spouse is often difficult, yet definitely in the children's best interests.

Today's typical family is no longer the "Father Knows Best" variety of the 1950s. Dual careers characterize the majority of families today. A single-parenting family, the result of parental divorce or death, or a never-married parent, is challenging and stressful. One in which children have two parents in different households is a binuclear family. Regardless of custody arrangement, both parents have responsibilities. Children who are single-parented can adjust positively, and adults can enjoy a myriad of rewards.

A stepfamily consists of an adult couple and at least one child from a prior relationship. Stepfamilies are rapidly increasing in numbers. Usually formed as a result of death or divorce, they can be complex and challenging. Education and support help. Overcoming a negative societal image, having realistic expectations, developing new roles and relationships, handling all kinds of emotions, and dealing with unique issues are major tasks of stepfamily members. The higher divorce rate for remarried couples might be reduced if education about and preparation for stepfamily life were the norm. Successful stepfamily relationships develop through application of personal and interactive skills and exemplify what this book emphasizes: positive human relations.

The family has a special place in thinking about close relationships. Family relationships are central to human existence, health, and happiness.

—Elaine Berscheid and Letitia Peplau

RESOURCES

- Family Service Association of America, 44 East 23rd Street, New York, NY 10017 (Local agencies in most communities)
- The Brief Family Therapy Center, 6815 W. Capitol Dr., Suite 300, Milwaukee, WI 53216, (414) 464-7775
- The Hudson Center for Brief Therapy, 11926 Arbor St., Omaha, NE 68144, (402) 330-1144

- Parents Without Partners, 7910 Woodmont Avenue, Washington, DC 20014 (local chapters in many communities)
- Stepfamily Association of America, Inc., 215 S. Centennial Mall, Suite 212, Lincoln, NE 68508, (800) 735-0329 or (402) 477-7837 (provides education and support with local chapters in many communities)
- Parenting classes and help available through:
  American Red Cross
  YWCA
  Community colleges/university continuing-education programs
  Cooperative Extension
  Parent Effectiveness Training (PET)
  Systematic Training for Effective Parenting (STEP)
  Active Parenting (a video-based program from American Guidance Service)

References

The publications marked with an asterisk (*) are recommended for additional reading.

ABOOD, DORIS A., and TERRY L. CONWAY (1992). "Health Value and Self-Esteem as Predictors of Wellness Behavior." *Health Values*, 16 (3), 20–26.

ABRAMIS, DAVID J. (1989). "Finding the Fun at Work." *Psychology Today*, March, 36–38.

*ADAMS, TERESA (1987). *Living From the Inside Out.* Self-published. 1331 Philip St., New Orleans, LA 70130.

ADESSA, MIA (1989). "Gut Emotions." *Psychology Today*, 72–74.

*ADLER, ALLAN J., and CHRISTINE ARCHAMBAULT (1990). *Divorce Recovery.* Washington DC: The PIA Press.

ADLER, JERRY (1992). "Hey, I'm Terrific!" *Newsweek*, February 17, 46–51.

ADLER, RONALD B. and NEIL TOWNE (1993). *Looking Out/Looking In.* New York: Holt, Rinehart & Winston.

ADULT PERSPECTIVE (1992). "How Good Are Your Questions?" 12 (4), December.

*AHRONS, CONSTANCE, and ROY RODGERS (1987). *Divorced Families.* Markham, Ontario: Penguin.

*ALBERT, LINDA, and ELIZABETH EINSTEIN (1983). *Dealing With Discipline.* Self-published. (Stepfamily Association of America, Inc., 215 S. Centennial Mall, Lincoln, NE: 68508).

*ALBERTI, ROBERT, and MICHAEL EMMONS. (1975). *Stand Up, Speak Up, Talk Back.* New York: Pocket Books.

*______ (1986). *Your Perfect Right: A Guide to Assertive Living.* San Luis Obispo: Impact.

ALBRECHT, KARL (1979). *Stress and the Manager.* Englewood Cliffs, NJ: Prentice Hall.

*ALESSANDRA, TONY, and PHIL HUNSAKER (1993). *Communicating at Work.* New York: Simon & Schuster.

ALEXANDER, PAMELA C., SHARON MOORE, and ELMORE R. ALEXANDER, III (1991). "What Is Transmitted in the Intergenerational Transmission of Violence?" *Journal of Marriage and the Family* 53, August, 657–688.

ALVY, KERBY (1987). *Parent Training: A Social Necessity.* Studio City, CA: Center for Improvement of Child Caring.

AMATO, PAUL R. (1993). "Children's Adjustment to Divorce: Theories, Hypotheses, and Empirical Support." *Journal of Marriage and the Family* 55, February, 23–38.

AMATO, PAUL R., and ALAN BOOTH (1991). "Consequences of Parental Divorce and Marital Unhappiness for Adult Well-Being." *Social Forces* 69, March, 895–914.

AMBADY, NALINI, and ROBERT ROSENTHAL (1992). "Thin Slices of Expressive Behavior as Predictors of Interpersonal Consequences: A Meta-Analysis." *Psychological Bulletin* 111, March, 256–274.

THE AMERICAN ASSOCIATION OF UNIVERSITY WOMEN (1993). "Hostile Hallways: The AAUW Survey on Sexual Harassment in America's Schools."

THE AMERICAN ASSOCIATION OF UNIVERSITY WOMEN EDUCATIONAL FOUNDATION (1992). "How Schools Shortchange Girls."

*AMES, LOUISE BATES (1992). *Raising Good Kids: A Developmental Approach to Discipline.* Rosemont, NJ: Modern Learning Press.

ANDERSON, MERRILEE, and HONORE M. HUGHES (1989). "Parenting Attitudes and the Self-Esteem of Young Children." *The Journal of Genetic Psychology* 150, December, 463–465.

ARDITTI, JOYCE A., DEBORAH D. GODWIN, and JOHN SCANZONI (1991). "Perceptions of Parenting Behavior and Young Women's Gender Role Traits and References." *Sex Roles* 25 (3–4), 195–211.

ARDITTI, JOYCE A., and DEBRA A. MADDEN-DERDICH (1993). "Noncustodial Mothers: Developing Strategies of Support." *Family Relations* 42, 305–314.

ARMSTRONG, BEN G., ALISON D. MCDONALD, and MARGARET SLOAN (1992). "Cigarette, Alcohol, and Coffee Consumption and Spontaneous Abortion." *American Journal of Public Health* 82 (1), 85–87.

ARTHUR, CAROLINE (1992). "Working is Worse in Japan." *American Demographics* 14, May, 16.

*ASHNER, LAURIE, and MITCH MEYERSON (1990). *When Parents Love Too Much.* New York: Avon Books.

ASMUSSEN, LINDA, and REED LARSON (1991). "The Quality of Family Time Among Young Adolescents in Single-Parent and Married-Parent Families." *Journal of Marriage and the Family* 53, November, 1021–1030.

AUNE, KRYSTYNA STRZYZEWSKI, and JAMIE COMSTOCK (1991). "Experience and Expression of Jealousy: Comparison Between Friends and Romantics." *Psychological Reports* 69, August, 315–319.

AVERY, CARL S. (1989). "How Do You Build Intimacy in an Age of Divorce?" *Psychology Today* May, pp. 27–31.

AXINN, WILLIAM G., and ARLAND THORNTON (1992). "The Relationship Between Cohabitation and Divorce: Selectivity or Causal Influence?" *Demography* 29, August, 357–374.

*BACH, GEORGE, and PETER WYDEN (1968). *The Intimate Enemy: How to Fight Fair in Love and Marriage.* New York: Avon.

BACHMAN, JERALD (1987). "An Eye on the Future." *Psychology Today,* July, pp. 6–8.

BAKER, KARLA, JOE BEER, and JOHN BEER (1991). "Self-esteem, Alcoholism, Sensation Seeking, GPA, and Differential Aptitude Test Scores of High School Students in an Honor Society." *Psychological Reports* 69, December, 1147–1150.

*BANDLER, RICHARD (1985). *Using Your Brain—For a Change.* Moab, UT: Real People Press.

BANDURA, ALBERT (1977). *Social Learning Theory.* Englewood Cliffs, NJ: Prentice Hall.

BANK, LEW, MARION S. FORGATCH, GERALD R. PATTERSON, and REBECCA A. FETROW (1993). "Parenting Practices of Single Mothers: Mediators of Negative Contextual Factors." *Journal of Marriage and the Family* 55, May, 371–384.

BARAK, AZY, SHOSHANA FELDMAN, and AYELET NOY (1991). "Traditionality of Children's Interests as Related to Their Parents' Gender Stereotypes and Traditionality of Occupations." *Sex Roles* 24, April, 511–524.

*Barbach, Lonnie, and David L. Geisinger (1991). *Going the Distance: Secrets to Lifelong Love*. New York: Doubleday.

Barber, Bonnie, and Jacquelynne S. Eccles (1992). "Long-Term Influence of Divorce and Single Parenting on Adolescent Family and Work-Related Values, Behaviors, and Aspirations." *Psychological Bulletin* 111, January, 108–126.

Barber, Brian K. (1992). "Family, Personality, and Adolescent Problem Behaviors." *Journal of Marriage and the Family* 54, February, 69–79.

Barker, Larry, Karen Gladney, Renee Edwards, Frances Holley, and Connie Gaines (1980). "An Investigation of Proportional Time Spent in Various Communication Activities by College Students." *Journal of Applied Communications Research* (8), 101–109.

Barnett, Rosalind C., Nancy L. Marshall, and Joseph H. Pleck (1992). "Men's Multiple Roles and Their Relationship to Men's Psychological Distress." *Journal of Marriage and the Family* 54, May, 358–367.

Baron, Robert A. (1985). *Understanding Human Relations: A Practical Guide to People at Work*. Boston: Allyn & Bacon.

______ (1990). *Understanding Human Relations: A Practical Guide to People at Work*. Boston: Allyn & Bacon.

Baron, Robert S., Mary L. Burgess, and Chuan Feng Kao (1991). "Detecting and Labeling Prejudice: Do Female Perpetrators Go Undetected?" *Personality and Social Psychology Bulletin* 17, April, 115–123.

Barr, Helen M., Ann Pytkowicz Streissguth, Betty L. Darby, and Paul D. Sampson (1990). "Prenatal Exposure to Alcohol, Caffeine, Tobacco, and Aspirin: Effects on Fine and Gross Motor Performance in 4-year-old Children." *Developmental Psychology* 26, May, 339–349.

Beach, Lee Roy (1993). *Making the Right Decision*. Englewood Cliffs, NJ: Organizational Culture, Vision, & Planning.

*Beal, Edward W., and Gloria Hochman (1991). *Adult Children of Divorce*. New York: Delacorte Press.

*Beattie, Melody (1987). *Co-Dependent No More*. New York: Harper/Hazelden.

*______ (1991). *A Reason to Live*. Wheaton, IL: Tyndale House Pub. Inc.

Beck, Aaron (1976). *Cognitive Therapy and the Emotional Disorders*. New York: International Universities Press.

*______ (1988). *Love Is Never Enough*. New York: Harper & Row.

Becker-Fritz, Terry, and Mary Ann Barbee (1993). "What Are the Warning Signs for Suicidal Adolescents?" *Journal of Psychosocial Nursing* 31 (2), 37–41.

*Beisser, Arnold R. (1989). *Flying Without Wings: Personal Reflections on Being Disabled*. New York: Doubleday.

*Bell, Inge (1991). *This Book Is Not Required*. Fort Bragg, CA: The Small Press.

*Belsky, Janet K. (1988). *Here Tomorrow: Making the Most of Life after Fifty*. Baltimore: Johns Hopkins University Press.

Bem, Sandra L. (1974). "The Measurement of Psychological Androgyny." *Journal of Consulting and Clinical Psychology* 42 (2), 155–162.

______ (1975). "Fluffy Women and Chesty Men." *Psychology Today*, September, pp. 60–62.

Bennett, N. G., A. K. Blanc, and D. E. Bloom (1988). "Commitment and the Modern Union: Assessing the Link between Premarital Cohabitation and Subsequent Marital Stability." *American Sociological Review* 53, 127–138.

*Benson, Herbert (1975). *The Relaxation Response*. New York: Avon.

______ (1987). *Your Maximum Mind*. New York: Random House.

*Bepko, Claudia, and Jo Ann Krestan (1990). *Too Good for Her Own Good: Searching for Self and Intimacy in Important Relationships*. New York: Harper Collins.

BERENBAUM, HOWARD, and ANN ROTTER (1992). "The Relationship Between Spontaneous Facial Expressions of Emotion and Voluntary Control of Facial Muscles." *Journal of Nonverbal Behavior* 16, Fall, 179–190.

BERMAN, CLAIRE (1989). "Stepparenting: How to Make It Work." *McCall's*, November, 97–100.

*______ (1991). *Adult Children of Divorce Speak Out*. New York: Simon & Schuster.

BERNARD, JESSIE (1956). *Remarriage: A Study in Marriage*. New York: Russell and Russell.

BERNE, ERIC (1962). "Classification of Positions." *Transactional Analysis Bulletin* 1, 23.

______ (1972). *What Do You Say After You Say Hello*? New York: Bantam.

*BERRY, CARMEN RENEE (1988). *When Helping You Is Hurting Me*. New York: Harper & Row.

BERSCHEID, ELLEN, MARK SNYDER, and ALLEN M. OMOTO (1989). "Conceptualizing and Measuring Closeness," in *Close Relationships*. ed. Clyde Hendrick. Newbury Park: Sage Publications.

*BETTELHEIM, BRUNO (1987). *A Good Enough Parent*. New York: Random House.

*BETTNER, BETTY LOU, and AMY LEW (1992). *Raising Kids Who Can*. New York: Harper Collins.

BEZJAK, JOHN E., and JERRY W. LEE (1990). "Relationship of Self-Efficacy and Locus of Control Constructs in Predicting College Students' Physical Fitness Behaviors." *Perceptual and Motor Skills* 71, October, 499–508.

*BILOFSKY, PENNY, and FREDDA SACHAROW (1991). *In-Laws/Outlaws: How to Make Peace with His Family and Yours*. New York: Fawcett Crest.

BIRNBAUM, JESSE (1993). "When Hate Makes a Fist." *Time*, April 26, pp. 30–31.

BITTEL, LESTER R. (1984). *Leadership: The Key to Management Success*. New York: Franklin Watts.

BLAIR, SAMPSON LEE, and MICHAEL P. JOHNSON (1992). "Wives' Perceptions of the Fairness of the Division of Household Labor: The Intersection of Housework and Ideology." *Journal of Marriage and the Family* 54, August, 570–581.

BLAIR, SAMPSON LEE, and DANIEL T. LICHTER (1991). "Measuring the Division of Household Labor: Gender Segregation of Housework Among American Couples." *Journal of Family Issues* 12, March, 91–113.

BLAKESLEE, SANDRA (1991). "How You See Yourself: Potential for Big Problems." *New York Times*, February 7.

BLAU, MELINDA (1991). "Recovery Fever." *New York Times*, September 9, pp. 30–37.

*______ (1994). *Families Apart: Ten Keys to Successful Co-parenting*. New York: G.P. Putnam's Sons.

BLIER, MICHAEL J., and LINDA A. BLIER-WILSON (1989). "Gender Differences in Self-Rated Emotional Expressiveness." *Sex Roles* 21 (3–4), 287–295.

BLOCK, J. (1981). "Some Enduring and Consequential Structures of Personality," in *Further Explorations in Personality*, ed. A. I. Robin et al. New York: John Wiley.

BLOOM, H. (1989). "The Importance of Hugging." *Omni*, 11.

*BLOOMFIELD, HAROLD, SIRAH VETTESE, with ROBERT KORY (1989). *Life-Mates: The Love Fitness Program for a Lasting Relationship*. New York: Penguin Books.

*BLOOMFIELD, HAROLD H., with LEONARD FELDER (1985). *Making Peace with Yourself*. New York: Ballantine Books.

*______ (1983). *Making Peace With Your Parents*. New York: Ballantine Books.

*BLOOMFIELD, HAROLD H., with ROBERT B. KORY (1978). *The Holistic Way to Health and Happiness*. New York: Simon & Schuster.

*______ (1980). *Inner Joy: New Strategies for Adding (More) Pleasure to Your Life*. New York: Wyden Books.

*______ (1993). *Making Peace in Your Stepfamily.* New York: Hyperion.

*BLUMENFELD, WARREN J. (1992). *Homophobia: How We All Pay the Price.* Boston: Beacon Press.

BOLGER, NIALL, ANITA DELONGIS, RONALD KESSLER, and ELAINE WETHINGTON (1989). "The Contagion of Stress Across Multiple Roles." *Journal of Marriage and the Family* 51 (1), 175–183.

*BOLLES, RICHARD NELSON (1994). *What Color Is Your Parachute?* Berkeley, CA: Ten Speed Press.

BOOTH, RICHARD, DAVID BARTLETT, and JOEL BOHNSACK (1992). "An Examination of the Relationship Between Happiness, Loneliness, and Shyness in College Students." *Journal of College Student Development* 33, March, 157–162.

*BORTZ, WALTER M. (1991). *We Live Too Short and Die Too Long.* New York: Bantam Books.

*BORYSENKO, JOAN (1990). *Guilt Is the Teacher, Love Is the Lesson.* New York: Warner Books, Inc.

BOUFFARD-BOUCHARD, THERESE (1990). "Influence of Self-efficacy on Performance in a Cognitive Task." *The Journal of Social Psychology* 130, June, 353–363.

BOWER, BRUCE (1992a). "Truth Aches." *Science News*, Aug. 15, 110–111.

______ (1992b). "Same Family, Different Lives." *Science News*, Dec. 7, 376–378.

*BOWER, SHARON ANTHONY, and GORDON H. BOWER (1991). *Asserting Yourself: A Practical Guide for Positive Change.* Reading, MA: Addison-Wesley Publishing Company.

BOYCE-BEAMAN, JONI, KENNETH E. LEONARD, and MARILYN SENCHAK (1993). "Male Premarital Aggression and Gender Identity Among Black and White Newlywed Couples," *Journal of Marriage and the Family* 55, 303–313.

BOYLE, EDMUND J., MARSHALL A. GEIGER, and JEFFREY K. PINTO (1991). "Empirical Note on Creativity as a Covariate of Learning Style Preference." *Perceptual and Motor Skills* 73, August, 265–266.

BOZZI, VINCENT (1988). "Time and Togetherness." *Psychology Today*, January, p. 10.

BRACKNEY, BARBARA E., and ALDA S. WESTMAN (1992). "Relationships Among Hope, Psychosocial Development, and Locus of Control." *Psychological Reports* 70, June, 864–866.

*BRADSHAW, JOHN (1988). *Healing the Shame That Binds You.* Deerfield Beach, FL: Health Communications.

*______ (1988). *Bradshaw On—The Family.* Deerfield Beach, FL: Health Communications.

*______ (1992). *Creating Love: The Next Great Stage of Growth.* New York: Bantam Books.

BRADY, BARBARA A., and SUE N. NESBITT (1991). "Using the Right Touch." *Nursing* 91, May, 46–47.

*BRAIKER, HARRIET B. (1988). *Getting Up When You're Feeling Down: A Woman's Guide to Overcoming and Preventing Depression.* New York: G.P. Putnam's Sons.

*______ (1992). *Lethal Lovers and Poisonous People: How to Protect Your Health from Relationships That Make You Sick.* New York: Pocket Books.

*BRAMSON, ROBERT M. (1988). *Coping With Difficult People.* Garden City, NY: Anchor Press/Doubleday.

*______ (1992). *Coping With Difficult Bosses.* New York: Carol Publishing Group.

BRANDEN, NATHANIEL (1969). *The Psychology of Self-Esteem.* New York: Bantam.

*______ (1983). *Honoring the Self.* Los Angeles: Tarcher.

*______ (1987). *How to Raise Your Self-Esteem.* New York: Bantam.

*______ (1992). *The Power of Self-Esteem.* Deerfield Beach, FL: Health Communications.

*BRANDEN, NATHANIEL, and E. DEVERS BRANDEN (1982). *The Romantic Love Question and Answer Book.* Los Angeles: Tarcher.

BRAUS, PATRICIA (1992). "What Workers Want." *American Demographics*, August, p. 34.

*BRAVO, ELLEN, and ELLEN CASSEDY (1992). *The 9 to 5 Guide to Combating Sexual Harassment.* New York: John Wiley & Sons.

BRAZELTON, T. BERRY (1989). "First Steps: Working Through the Lives of Children." *The World* 3 (2), 10–11.

BREIDENBACH, MONICA E. (1992). *Career Development: Taking Charge of Your Career.* Englewood Cliffs, NJ: Prentice Hall.

BRICKLIN, MARK (1993a). "Let's Declare War on Breast Cancer!" *Prevention*, September, pp. 39–40, 42.

______ (1993b). "Good News: Dieting Is Dead." *Prevention*, October, pp. 39–40, 113.

*BRIGGS, DOROTHY CORKVILLE (1970). *Your Child's Self-Esteem.* Garden City, NY: Doubleday.

______ (1977). *Celebrate Yourself: Enhancing Your Own Self-Esteem.* New York: Doubleday.

*BRIGHT, DEBORAH (1988). *Criticism in Your Life: How to Give It—How to Take It—How to Make It Work for You.* New York: Master Media.

*BRIM, GILBERT (1992). *Ambition: How We Manage Success and Failure Throughout Our Lives.* New York: Basic Books.

BRINGLE, ROBERT G. (1991). *The Psychology of Jealousy and Envy*, ed. Peter Salovey. New York: The Guilford Press.

BRODY, JANE E. (1992). "Studies Find Friendship 'Very Powerful Medicine.' " *Lincoln Journal*, February 7, pp. 9, 10.

*BRODZINSKY, DAVID M., MARSHALL D. SCHECHTER, and ROBIN MARANTZ HENIG (1992). *Being Adopted: The Lifelong Search for Self.* New York: Doubleday.

BROWNE, M. NEIL, AND STUART M. KEELEY (1990). *Asking the Right Questions: A Guide to Critical Thinking.* Englewood Cliffs, NJ: Prentice Hall.

BROWNELL, KELLY (1988). "Yo-yo Dieting." *Psychology Today*, January, pp. 20–23.

BROWNMILLER, SUSAN (1989). "Madly in Love." *Ms.*, April, pp. 56–64.

BROWNSON, ROSS C., MICHAEL C. ALAVANJA, EDWARD T. HOCK, and TIMOTHY S. LOY (1992). "Passive Smoking and Lung Cancer in Nonsmoking Women." *American Journal of Public Health* 82, November, 1525–1530.

BROWNSON, ROSS C., JEANNETTE JACKSON-THOMPSON, and JOAN C. WILKERSON (1992). "Demographic and Socioeconomic Differences in Beliefs About the Health Effects of Smoking." *American Journal of Public Health* 82, January, 99–103.

BRYSON, JEFF B. (1991). in *The Psychology of Jealousy and Envy*, ed. Peter Salovey. New York: The Guilford Press.

BRZOWSKY, SARA (1984). "Don't Dry Those Tears." *Parade*, November 18, pp. 11–13.

*BUCKMAN, ROBERT (1988). *I Don't Know What to Say: How to Help and Support Someone Who Is Dying.* Cheektowaga, NY: Key Porter Books/University of Toronto Press.

BULCROFT, KRIS, and RICHARD A. BULCROFT (1991). "The Timing of Divorce: Effects on Parent-Child Relationships in Later Life." *Research on Aging* 13, June, 226–243.

BULL, PETER E. (1988). "Noticing Posture," in *Eye to Eye: How People Interact*, ed. Peter Marsh. Topsfield, MA: Salem House.

BULLOCK, JANIS R. (1993). "Children's Loneliness and Their Relationships with Family and Peers." *Family Relations* 42, January, 46–49.

BUMPASS, L. L., T. C. MARTIN, and J. A. SWEET (1991). "The Impact of Family Background and Early Marital Factors on Marital Disruption." *Journal of Family Issues* 12, 22–42.

BUMPASS, LARRY (1990). "What's Happening to the Family? Interactions Between Demographic and Institutional Change." Presidential Address, Annual meeting of the Population Association of America Demography 27, 483–498.

BUMPASS, LARRY, and JAMES A. SWEET (1989). National Estimates of Cohabitation. *Demography*, 26 (4), November, 615–625.

BUMPASS, LARRY L., JAMES A. SWEET, and ANDREW CHERLIN (1991). "The Role of Cohabitation in Declining Rates of Marriage." *Journal of Marriage and the Family* 53, November, 913–927.

*BURKA, JANE B., AND LENORA M. YUEN (1983). *Procrastination: Why You Do It, What to Do about It.* Reading, MA: Addison-Wesley.

BURLESON, BRANT R., JESSE G. DELLA, and JAMES L. APPLEGATE (1992). "Effects of Maternal Communication and Children's Social-Cognitive and Communication Skills on Children's Acceptance by the Peer Group." *Family Relations* 41, July, 264–272.

*BURNS, DAVID D. (1980a). *Feeling Good: The New Mood Therapy.* New York: New American Library.

______ (1980b). "The Perfectionist's Script for Self-defeat." *Psychology Today*, November, pp. 34–52.

*______ (1985). *Intimate Connections.* New York: Morrow.

*______ (1989). *The Feeling Good Handbook.* New York: William Morrow and Company, Inc.

*BURT, MALA (1988). *Stepfamilies Stepping Ahead: An Eight-Step Program for Successful Stepfamily Living.* Self-published. (Available from Stepfamily Association of America, Inc., 215 S. Centennial Mall, Lincoln, NE: 68508).

*BUSCAGLIA, LEO (1982). *Living, Loving, and Learning.* New York: Ballantine.

*______ (1984). *Loving Each Other.* Thorofare, NJ: Slack.

*______ (1992). *Born for Love: Reflections on Loving.* Thorofare, NJ: Slack, Inc.

*BUTLER, PAMELA E. (1992). *Self-Assertion for Women.* New York: Harper Collins Publishers.

BUUNK, BRAM P. (1991). *The Psychology of Jealousy and Envy*, ed. Peter Salovey. New York: The Guilford Press.

BYRNE, DONN (1971). *The Attraction Paradigm.* New York: Academic Press.

CAIN, ROY (1991). "Relational Contexts and Information Management Among Gay Men." *Families in Society* 72, June, 344–352.

CALHOUN, CHESHIRE (1992). "Changing One's Heart." *Ethics* 103, October, 76–96.

CAMPBELL, JANE, PAUL SWANK, and KEN VINCENT (1991). "The Role of Hardiness in the Resolution of Grief." *Omega* 23 (1), 53–65.

CAMPBELL, KEITH E., DAVID M. KLEIM, and KENNETH R. OLSON (1992). "Conversational Activity and Interruptions Among Men and Women." *The Journal of Social Psychology* 132, June, 419–421.

*CANFIELD, JACK, and FRANK SICCONE (1993). *101 Ways to Develop Student Self-Esteem and Responsibility.* Boston: Allyn and Bacon.

CARL, HELEN (1980). "Nonverbal Communication During the Employment Interview." *ABCA Bulletin*, December, pp. 14–18.

*CARLSON, BOB, and O. J. SEIDEN (1988). *Healthwalk.* Golden, CO: Fulcrum.

CARLSON, BONNIE E., and LYNN VIDEKA-SHERMAN (1990). "An Empirical Test of Androgyny in the Middle Years: Evidence from a National Survey." *Sex Roles* 23, September, 305–324.

CARON, MARK D., SUSAN KRAUSS WHITBOURNE, and RICHARD P. HALGIN (1992). "Fraudulent Excuse Making Among College Students." *Teaching of Psychology* 19 (2), 90–92.

CARR, JACQUELYN B. (1991). *Communicating and Relating.* Dubuque, IA: Wm. C. Brown.

*CARTER-SCOTT, CHERIE (1989). *Negaholism: How to Recover From Your Addiction to Negativity and Turn Your Life Around.* New York: Villard.

CASSIDY, JUDE, and STEVEN R. ASHER (1992). "Loneliness and Peer Relations in Young Children." *Child Development* 63, April, 350–365.

*CASTLEMAN, MICHAEL (1989). *Sexual Solutions.* New York: Simon & Schuster.

CHANCE, PAUL (1988a). "Personality's Part and Parcel." *Psychology Today*, April, pp. 18–19.

______ (1988b). "The Trouble with Love." *Psychology Today*, February, pp. 22–23.

*CHAPMAN, ELWOOD N. (1993). *Your Attitude Is Showing.* Chicago: Science Research Associates.

*CHELLIS, MARCIA (1992). *Ordinary Women, Extraordinary Lives.* New York: Penguin Books.

CHERLIN, ANDREW J., FRANK F. FURSTENBERG JR., P. LINDSAY CHASE-LANSDALE, KATHLEEN E. KIERNAN, PHILIP K. ROBINS, DONNA RUANE MORRISON, and JULIEN O. TEITLER (1991). "Longitudinal Studies of Effects of Divorce on Children in Great Britain and the United States." *Science* 252, June, 1386–1389.

CHIPUER, H. M., ROBERT PLOMIN, NANCY L. PEDERSEN, GERALD E. MCCLEARN, and JOHN R. NESSELROADE (1993). "Genetic Influence on Family Environment: The Role of Personality." *Developmental Psychology* 29 (1), 110–118.

CHIU, LIAN-HWANG (1990). "The Relationship of Career Goal and Self-Esteem Among Adolescents." *Adolescence* 25, Fall, 593–597.

CHOLLAR, SUSAN (1987). "We Reap What We Sow." *Psychology Today*, December, p. 12.

______ (1988). "Alcohol in Their Blood." *Psychology Today*, March, p. 18.

*CHOPICH, ERIKA J., and MARGARET PAUL (1990). *Healing Your Aloneness: Finding Love and Wholeness Through Your Inner Child.* New York: Harper Collins Publishers.

CHUSMIR, LEONARD H., and BARBARA PARKER (1992). "Success Striving and Their Relationship to Affective Work Behaviors: Gender Differences." *The Journal of Social Psychology* 132, February, 87–99.

*CLAPP, GENEVIEVE (1992). *Divorce and New Beginnings: An Authoritative Guide to Recovery and Growth, Solo Parenting, and Stepfamilies.* New York: John Wiley & Sons.

CLARK, M. L., and MARLA AYERS (1992). "Friendship Similarity During Early Adolescence: Gender and Racial Patterns." *The Journal of Psychology* 126, July, 393–405.

______ (1993). "Friendship Expectations and Friendship Evaluations: Reciprocity and Gender Effects." *Youth & Society* 24, March, 299–313.

*CLARKE, JEAN ILLSLEY (1982). *Self-Esteem: A Family Affair.* Minneapolis: Winston Press.

CLARKSON, PETRUSKA (1992). *Transactional Analysis Psychotherapy: An Integrated Approach.* London: Tavistock/Routledge.

COCHRANE, DIANE L. (1992). *Work-Related Conflict Can Be Productive.* Chicago: Dartnell Corporation.

*COCOLA, NANCY WASSERMAN, and ARLENE MODICA MATTHEWS (1992). *How to Manage Your Mother: Skills and Strategies to Improve Mother-Daughter Relationships.* New York: Simon & Schuster.

COLE, DEBRA E., HOWARD O. PROTINSKY, and LAWRENCE H. CROSS (1992). "An Empirical Investigation of Adolescent Suicidal Ideation." *Adolescence* 27, Winter, 813–818.

COLE, DIANE (1988). "Grief's Lessons: His and Hers." *Psychology Today*, December, pp. 60–61.

COLE, GALEN, LARRY TUCKER, and GLENN M. FRIEDMAN (1990). "Relationships Among Measures of Alcohol Drinking Behavior, Life-Events and Perceived Stress." *Psychological Reports* 67, October, 587–591.

*COLE, HARRY A. (1991). *Helpmates.* Louisville, KY: Westminster/John Knox Press.

COLEMAN, MARILYN, and LAWRENCE H. GANONG (1985). "Love and Sex Role Stereotypes: Do Macho Men and Feminine Women Make Better Lovers?" *Journal of Personality and Social Psychology* 49 (1), 170–176.

______ (1989). "Stepfamily Self-Help Books: Brief Annotations and Ratings." *Family Relations* 38, 91–96.

______ (1990). "Remarriage and Stepfamily Research in the 1980's: Increased Interest in an Old Family Form." *Journal of Marriage and the Family* 52, 583–589.

*COLGROVE, MELBA, HAROLD H. BLOOMFIELD, and PETER MCWILLIAMS (1991). *How to Survive the Loss of a Love.* Los Angeles: Prelude Press.

COLTON, HELEN (1983). *The Gift of Touch.* New York: Seaview/Putnam.

COLTRANE, SCOTT, and MASAKO ISHII-KUNTZ (1992). "Men's Housework: A Life Course Perspective." *Journal of Marriage and the Family* 54, February 6, 43–57.

CONGER, JOHN J., and ANNE C. PETERSON (1984). *Adolescence and Youth: Psychological Development in a Changing World.* New York: Harper & Row.

CONNIDIS, INGRID ARNET, and LORRAINE DAVIES (1992). "Confidants and Companions: Choices in Later Life." *Journals of Gerontology* 47, May, 115–122.

CONROY, PAT (1986). *Prince of Tides.* Boston: Houghton Mifflin.

COOKLIN, ALAN I., and GILL GORELL BARNES (1988). "Parents and Children," in *Eye to Eye: How People Interact*, ed. Peter Marsh. Topsfield, MA: Salem House.

COOMBS, ROBERT H. (1991). "Marital Status and Personal Well-Being: A Literature Review." *Family Relations* 40, January, 97–102.

COOPER, KENNETH H. (1982). *The Aerobic Program for Total Well-Being: Exercise, Diet, Emotional Balance.* New York: Bantam.

COOPERSMITH, STANLEY (1967). *The Antecedents of Self-Esteem.* San Francisco: W. H. Freeman & Company Publishers.

*COREY, GERALD, and MARIANNE SCHNEIDER COREY (1993). *I Never Knew I Had a Choice.* Pacific Grove, CA: Brooks/Cole.

COSTA, P. T., and R. R. MCCRAE (1980). "Still Stable after All These Years: Personality as a Key to Some Issues in Adulthood and Old Age," in *Lifespan Development and Behavior*, vol. 3, ed. P. B. Baltes and O. G. Brim. New York: Academic Press.

*COUSINS, NORMAN (1979). *Anatomy of an Illness.* New York: Bantam.

*______ (1983). *The Healing Heart.* New York: Avon.

*______ (1989). *Head First.* New York: Penguin Books.

*______ (1991). *The Celebration of Life.* New York: Bantam Books.

*COWAN, CAROLYN PAPE, and PHILIP A. COWAN (1992). *When Partners Become Parents.* New York: Basic Books.

*COWAN, CONNELL, and MELVYN KINDER (1985). *Smart Women Foolish Choices.* New York: Penguin, Inc.

*______ (1987). *Women Men Love, Women Men Leave.* New York: Clarkson N. Potter.

CRAMER, ROBERT ERVIN, MARGUERITE DRAGNA, and ROBERT G. CUPP (1991). "Contrast Effects in the Evaluation of the Male Sex Role." *Sex Roles* 24, February, 181–193.

CRISPELL, DIANE (1993). "Sex Surveys: Does Anyone Tell the Truth?" *American Demographics*, July, pp. 9–10.

CROSBIE-BURNETT, MARGARET, and JEAN GILES-SIMS (1993). "Stepparenting Styles and Adolescents' Adjustment." Paper presented at Annual Conference of the National Council on Family Relations.

CROSBY, FAYE J. (1991). *Juggling: The Unexpected Advantage of Balancing Career and Home for Women and Their Families.* New York: The Free Press.

*CROWTHER, C. EDWARD (1986). *Intimacy: Strategies for Successful Relationships.* Santa Barbara: Capra.

CUPACH, WILLIAM, and SANDRA METTS (1991). "Sexuality and Communication in Relationships." in *Sexuality in Close Relationships* ed. Kathleen McKinney and Susan Sprecher, Hillsdale, NJ: Lawrence Erlbaum Associates.

CURRAN, DOLORES (1983). *Traits of a Healthy Family.* New York: Ballantine.

CUSHMAN, KATHLEEN (1993). "Why Shame Hurts So Much." *Parents Magazine*, April, pp. 106–108, 110.

CUTLER, BLAYNE (1989). "Are You an Average Person?" *Reader's Digest*, September, pp. 189–195.

D'ALESSIO, STEWART J., and LISA STOLZENBERG (1991). "Anti-Semitism in America: The Dynamics of Prejudice." *Sociological Inquiry* 61, Summer, 359–366.

*DALEY, DENNIS C. (1991). *Kicking Addictive Habits Once and For All.* Lexington, MA: Lexington Books.

DARLEY, JOHN M., SAM GLUCKSBERG, and RONALD A. KINCHLA (1991). *Psychology.* Englewood Cliffs, NJ: Prentice Hall.

DAUBMAN, KIMBERLY A., LAURIE HEATHERINGTON, and ALICIA AHN (1992). "Gender and the Self-Presentation of Academic Achievement." *Sex Roles* 27, August, 187–204.

*DAVIS, DEBORAH L. (1991). *Empty Cradle, Broken Heart.* Golden, CO: Fulcrum Publishing.

DELAMATER, JOHN D. (1991). "Emotions and Sexuality." in *Sexuality in Close Relationships* ed. Kathleen McKinney and Susan Sprecher, Hillsdale, NJ: Lawrence Erlbaum Associates.

DELANEY, LISA (1993a). "Top Fat Burners." *Prevention*, April, pp. 65–69.

______ (1993b). "The 'No-Hunger' Weight Loss Plan." *Prevention*, September, pp. 43–46.

DEMARIS, ALFRED, and K. VANINADHARAO (1992). "Premarital Cohabitation and Subsequent Marital Stability in the United States: A Reassessment." *Journal of Marriage and the Family* 54, 178–190.

DENTON, KATHY, and DENNIS KREBS (1990). "From the Scene to the Crime: The Effect of Alcohol and Social Context on Moral Judgment." *Journal of Personality and Social Psychology* 59, August, 242–248.

*DEPAULO, J. RAYMOND, and KEITH RUSSELL ABLOW (1989). *How to Cope with Depression.* New York: Fawcett Crest.

DERR, C. BROOKLYN (1988). *Managing the New Careerists: The Diverse Career Success Orientations of Today's Workers.* San Francisco: Jossey-Bass.

DEVINE, PATRICIA G., MARGO J. MONTEITH, JULIA R. ZUWERINK, and ANDREW J. ELLIOT (1991). "Prejudice With and Without Compunction." *Journal of Personality and Social Psychology* 60, June, 817–830.

DEVITO, JOSEPH A. (1989). *The Interpersonal Communication Book.* New York: Harper & Row.

DEWITT, PAULA MERGENHAGEN (1992a). "Breaking Up Is Hard to Do." *American Demographics* 14, October, pp. 52–55.

______ (1992b). "The Second Time Around." *American Demographics* 14, November, pp. 60–63.

*DIAMOND, SUSAN ARMSTRONG (1985). *Helping Children of Divorce: A Handbook for Parents and Teachers.* New York: Schocken.

*DIGIULIO, ROBERT C. (1989). *Beyond Widowhood: From Bereavement to Emergence and Hope.* New York: Free Press.

DINDIA, KATHRYN, and MIKE ALLEN (1992). "Sex Differences in Self-Disclosure: A Meta-Analysis." *Psychological Bulletin* 112, July, 106–124.

DOLGIN, KIM G., LESLIE MEYER, and JANET SCHWARTZ (1991). "Effects of Gender, Target's Gender, Topic, and Self-Esteem on Disclosure to Best and Midling Friends." *Sex Roles* 25, September, 311–329.

DONALDSON, LES, and EDWARD E. SCANNELL (1986). *Human Resource Development: The New Trainer's Guide.* Reading, MA: Addison-Wesley Publishing Company.

DONNELLY, DENISE, and DAVID FINKELHOR (1992). "Does Equality in Custody Arrangement Improve the Parent-Child Relationship?" *Journal of Marriage and the Family* 54, November, 837–845.

*DONNELLEY, NINA HERRMANN (1987). *I Never Know What to Say.* New York: Ballantine Books.

*DOWLING, COLETTE (1991). *You Mean I Don't Have to Feel This Way?* New York: Charles Scribner's Sons.

DOWNS, W. R., B. A. MILLER, M. TESTA, and D. PANEK (1992). "Long-Term Effects of Parent-To-Child Violence for Women." *Journal of Interpersonal Violence* 7, 365–382.

DOYLE, JAMES A. (1985). *Sex and Gender: The Human Experience.* Dubuque: IA: Wm. C. Brown.

DUCK, STEVEN, (1988). "Enjoying a Sexual Relationship," in *Eye to Eye: How People Interact*, ed. Peter Marsh. Topsfield, MA: Salem House.

______ (1991). *Understanding Relationships.* New York: The Guilford Press.

DUNCAN, STEPHEN F., and GENEVA BROWN (1992). "RENEW: A Program for Building Remarried Family Strengths." *Families in Society* 73, March, 149–158.

DURNING, ALAN THEIN (1993). "Are We Happy Yet? How the Pursuit of Happiness is Failing." *The Futurist* 27, January/February, 20–24.

*DYER, WAYNE (1976). *Your Erroneous Zones.* New York: Funk & Wagnalls.

*______ (1980). *The Sky's the Limit.* New York: Pocket Books.

*______ (1989). *You'll See It When You Believe It.* New York: Avon Books.

*______ (1992). *Real Magic.* New York: Harper Collins.

EASLEY, MARGARET, and NORMAN EPSTEIN (1991). "Coping with Stress in a Family with an Alcoholic Parent." *Family Relations* 40 (2), 218–224.

THE ECONOMIST (1992). "Ashes in Their Mouths." 323 (7761), May 30, 86–87.

EDWARDS, DEANNA (1989). *Grieving: The Pain and the Promise.* Salt Lake City: Covenant.

*EINSTEIN, ELIZABETH (1982). *The Stepfamily: Living, Loving, and Learning.* Boston: Shambhala.

EKMAN, PAUL (1992). "Are There Basic Emotions? (Comment on A. Ortony and T. J. Turner)." *Psychological Review* 99, July, 550–553.

EKMAN, PAUL, RICHARD J. DAVIDSON, and WALLACE V. FRIESEN (1990). "The Duchenne Smile: Emotional Expression and Brain Physiology." *Journal of Personality and Social Psychology* 58, February, 342–353.

ELIOT, ROBERT S., and DENNIS L. BREO (1984). *Is It Worth Dying For?* New York: Bantam.

ELKIND, DAVID (1988). *The Hurried Child.* Reading, MA: Addison-Wesley Publishing Company.

______ (1991). "Boosting Self-Esteem." *Parents' Magazine*, March, p. 195.

ELLIS, ALBERT (1984). "The Essence of RET." *Journal of Rational-Emotive Therapy* 2, 19–25.

*ELLSWORTH, BARRY A. (1988). *Living in Love With Yourself.* Salt Lake City: Breakthrough.

ELMER-DEWITT, PHILIP (1986). "Extra Years for Extra Effort." *Time*, March 17, p. 66.

______ (1992). "Depression: The Growing Role of Drug Therapies." *Time*, July 6, pp. 57–59.

ELSON, JOHN (1991). "Drink Until You Finally Drop." *Time*, December 16, pp. 64–66.

*ELZE, DIANE (1992). "It Has Nothing to Do with Me," in *Homophobia: How We All Pay the Price.* ed. Warren J. Blumenfeld. Boston: Beacon Press.

EMERY, ROBERT E., SHEILA G. MATTHEWS, and MELISSA M. WYER (1992). "Child Custody Mediation and Litigation: Further Evidence on the Differing Views of Mothers and Fathers." *Journal of Consulting and Clinical Psychology* 59, June, 410–418.

*ENGRAM, SARA (1990). *Mortal Matters: When a Loved One Dies.* Kansas City: Andrews and McMeel.

ENRIGHT, ROBERT D., MARIA J. D. SANTOS, and RADHI AL-MABUK (1989). "The Adolescent as Forgiver." *Journal of Adolescence* 12, March, 95–110.

EPSTEIN, SEYMOUR (1976). "Anxiety, Arousal, and the Self-Concept," in *Stress and Anxiety*, vol. 3, ed. Irwin Sarason and Charles Spielberger. Washington, DC: Hemisphere.

ERIKSON, ERIK (1963). *The Challenge of Youth.* New York: Anchor.

ERNST, FRANKLIN H. (1973). *Who's Listening*? Vallejo, CA: Addresso'set.

EUSTER, GERALD L. (1991). "Memorial Contributions: Remembering the Elderly Deceased and Supporting the Bereaved." *Omega: Journal of Death and Dying* 23 (3), 169–179.

*EVANS, PATRICIA (1992). *The Verbally Abusive Relationship: How to Recognize It and How to Respond.* Holbrook, MA: Bob Adams, Inc.

EXTER, THOMAS (1991). "Everybody Works Hard Except Junior." *American Demographics* 13, May, p. 14.

______ (1991). "The Costs of Growing Up." *American Demographics* 13, August, p. 59.

EYSENCK, H. J. (1990). "Genetic and Environmental Individual Differences: The Three Major Dimensions of Personality." *Journal of Personality*, 58 (1).

EYSENCK, HANS J. (1988). "Health's Character." *Psychology Today*, December, pp. 23–35.

*FABER, ADELE, and ELAINE MAZLISH (1974). *Liberated Parents, Liberated Children*. New York: Grossett & Dunlap.

FACKELMANN, KATHY A. (1990). "More Evidence Ties Smoke to Artery Disease." *Science News* 137 (21), May 26, p. 326.

FADERMAN, LILLIAN (1991). *Odd Girls and Twilight Lovers*. New York: Columbia University Press.

FAGOT, BEVERLY I., MARY D. LEINBACH, and CHERIE O'BOYLE (1992). "Gender Labeling, Gender Stereotyping, and Parenting Behaviors." *Developmental Psychology* 28, March, 225–230.

FARBEROW, NORMAN L., DOLORES GALLAGHER-THOMPSON, MICHAEL GILEWOSKI, and LARRY THOMPSON (1992). "The Role of Social Support in the Bereavement Process of Surviving Spouses of Suicide and Natural Deaths." *Suicide and Life-Threatening Behavior* 22 (1), 107 124.

*FARRELL, WARREN (1986). *Why Men Are the Way They Are: The Male-Female Dynamic*. New York: McGraw-Hill.

*FAST, JULIUS (1970). *Body Language*. New York: M. Evans.

FEHR, B. and J. A. RUSSELL (1984). "Concept of Emotion Viewed from a Prototype Perspective." *Journal of Experimental Psychology: General*, 113, 464–486.

FELSTEN, GARY, and KATHY WILCOX (1992). "Influences of Stress and Situation-Specific Mastery Beliefs and Satisfaction with Social Support on Well-Being and Academic Performance." *Psychological Reports* 70, February, 291–303.

*FENSTERHEIM, HERBERT, and JEAN BAER (1988). *Making Life Right When It Feels All Wrong*. New York: Macmillan.

FERRARI, JOSEPH R. (1991). "Compulsive Procrastination: Some Self-Reported Characteristics." *Psychological Reports* 68, April, 455–458.

*FIEVE, RONALD R. (1989). *Moodswing*. New York: William Morrow and Company.

FINE, MARK A. (1992). "Families in the United States: Their Current Status and Future Prospects." *Family Relations* 41, October, 430–435.

FINE, MARK A., and LAWRENCE A. KURDEK (1992). "The Adjustment of Adolescents in Stepfather and Stepmother Families." *Journal of Marriage and the Family* 54, November, 725–736.

FINLAY, BARBARA, and KAREN E. SCHELTEMA (1991). "The Relation of Gender and Sexual Orientation to Measures of Masculinity, Femininity, and Androgyny: A Further Analysis." *Journal of Homosexuality*, 21 (3), 71–85.

FISCHMAN, JOSHUA (1988). "Exercise: Getting Your Head in Shape." *Psychology Today*, January, p. 14.

*FISHER, BRUCE (1992). *Rebuilding: When Your Relationship Ends*. San Luis Obispo, CA: Impact.

FISHER, CLAUDE S., ROBERT M. JACKSON, C. ANN STUEVE, KATHLEEN GERSON, LYNN M. JONES, and MARK BALDASSARE (1977). *Networks and Places: Social Relations in the Urban Setting*. New York: Free Press.

FISHER, DEENA, and JOHN BEER (1990). "Codependency and Self-Esteem Among High School Students." *Psychological Reports* 66, June, 1001–1002.

*FLANIGAN, BEVERLY (1992). *Forgiving the Unforgivable*. New York: Macmillan.

*FORWARD, SUSAN, with CRAIG BUCK (1986). *Toxic Parents: Overcoming Their Hurtful Legacy and Reclaiming Your Life*. New York: Bantam Books.

*______ (1991). *Obsessive Love*. New York: Bantam Books.

*FORWARD, SUSAN, and JEAN TORRES (1986). *Men Who Hate Women and the Women Who Love Them*. Toronto: Bantam.

Foshee, Vangie, and Karl Bauman (1992). "Gender Stereotyping and Adolescent Sexual Behavior: A Test of Temporal Order." *Journal of Applied Social Psychology* 22, October, 1561–1579.

Franklin, Deborah (1989). "What a Child Is Given." *New York Times Magazine*, September 3, pp. 36–41.

Franz, Carol E., David C. McClelland, and Joel Weinberger (1991). "Childhood Antecedents of Conventional Social Accomplishment in Midlife Adults: A 36-Year Prospective Study." *Journal of Personality and Social Psychology* 60, April, 586–595.

*Friedan, Betty (1993). *The Fountain of Age*. New York: Simon & Schuster.

Fromm, Erich (1956). *The Art of Loving*. New York: Harper & Row.

Fromme, Allan (1984). *60+: Planning It, Living It, Loving It*. Toronto: Bantam.

Frost, Jan (1990). "Do We Mean the Same by the Concept of Family?" *Communication Research* 17, August, 431–443.

Fuenning, S. I. (1981). *Physical Fitness and Mental Health*. Lincoln, NE: University of Nebraska Foundation.

Fullen, James D., and John C. Tabor (1984). *One Plus One: An Integrated Approach to Communications*. Dubuque, IA: Kendall/Hunt.

Furstenberg, Frank F., Jr., and Andrew J. Cherlin (1991). *Divided Families*. Cambridge, MA: Harvard University Press.

Gadzella, Bernadette M., Dean W. Ginther, and Maryjane Tomcala (1991). "Differences Between Men and Women on Stress Producers and Coping Strategies." *Psychological Reports* 69 (2), 561–562.

Gadzella, Bernadette M., Kent Hartsoe, and James Harper (1989). "Critical Thinking and Mental Ability Groups." *Psychological Reports* 65, December, 1019–1026.

Gallois, Cynthia (1993). "The Language and Communication of Emotion: Universal, Interpersonal, or Intergroup? (Part of a Special Issue on: Using and Abusing Language)." *The American Behavioral Scientist* 36, January/February, 309–338.

Ganong, L. H., and M. Coleman (1986). "A Comparison of Clinical and Empirical Literature on Children in Stepfamilies." *Journal of Marriage and the Family* 48, 309–318.

Garcia, Manuel E., Joy M. Schmitz, and Leonard A. Doerfler (1990). "A Fine-Grained Analysis of the Role of Self-Efficacy in Self-Initiated Attempts to Quit Smoking." *Journal of Consulting and Clinical Psychology* 58, June, 317–322.

Gardner, Howard (1983). *Frames of Mind: The Theory of Multiple Intelligences*. New York: Basic Books.

Gastil, John (1990). "Generic Pronouns and Sexist Language: The Oxymoronic Character of Masculine Generics." *Sex Roles* 23, December, 629–643.

Gelman, David (1991). "The Miracle of Resiliency." *Newsweek*, Summer, pp. 44–47.

Gentry, Deborah B., and Wayne A. Benenson (1993). "School-to-home Transfer of Conflict Management Skills Among School-age Children." *Families in Society* 74, February, 67–73.

Gerlach, Jeanne, and Betty L. Hart (1992). "Gender Equity in the Classroom: An Inventory." *Teaching English in the Two Year College* 19 (1), 49–54.

Gerson, Mary-Joan, Linda S. Berman, and Anne M. Morris (1991). "The Value of Having Children as an Aspect of Adult Development." *The Journal of Genetic Psychology* 152, September, 327–339.

*Getzoff, Ann, and Carolyn McClenahan (1984). *Stepkids: A Survival Guide for Teenagers in Stepfamilies*. New York: Walker.

Gibbs, Nancy R. (1988). "All Fired Up Over Smoking." *Time*, April 18, pp. 64–71.

______ (1993). "How Should We Teach Our Children About Sex?" *Time*, May 24, pp. 60–66.

______ (1993). "Bringing Up Father." *Time*, June 28, pp. 53–61.

______ (1993). "Laying Down the Law." *Time*, August 23, pp. 22–26.

GIBSON, JANICE T. (1992). "Your Loving Touch." *Parents* 67, March, pp. 65–69.

*GINOTT, HAIM (1965). *Between Parent and Child.* New York: Macmillan.

*______ (1969). *Between Parent and Teenager.* Toronto: Macmillan.

*GINSBURG, GENEVIEVE DAVIS (1987). *To Live Again: Rebuilding Your Life After You've Become a Widow.* Los Angeles: Tarcher.

GIORDANO, PEGGY C., STEPHEN A. CERNKOVICH, and ALFRED DEMARIS (1993). "The Family and Peer Relations of Black Adolescents." *Journal of Marriage and the Family* 55 (2), 277–287.

GLASER, SUSAN (1986). *Toward Communication Competency.* New York: Holt, Rinehart and Winston.

GLASSER, WILLIAM (1965). *Reality Therapy: A New Approach to Psychiatry.* New York: Harper & Row.

*______ (1984). *Control Theory: A New Explanation of How We Control Our Lives.* New York: Harper & Row.

*GLENN, H. STEPHEN and JANE NELSEN (1989). *Raising Self-Reliant Children in a Self-Indulgent World.* Rocklin, CA: Prima Publishing & Communications.

GLENN, NORVAL D. (1991). "The Recent Trend in Marital Success in the United States." *Journal of Marriage and the Family* 53, May, 261–270.

GLICK, PAUL C. (1991). "Parents with Young Stepchildren and with Adult Stepchildren: A Demographic Profile." Paper presented at Stepfamily Association of America National Conference.

GOFFMAN, ERVING (1959). *Presentation of Self in Everyday Life.* New York: Anchor Books.

______ (1963). *Behavior in Public Places.* New York: Free Press.

______ (1967). *Interaction Ritual.* Garden City, NY: Doubleday.

*GOLD, LOIS (1992). *Between Love and Hate: A Guide to Civilized Divorce.* New York: Plenum Press.

GOLDBERG, HERB (1979). *The New Male.* New York: Signet.

*______ (1987). *The Inner Male.* New York: Signet.

GOLDMAN, ABIGAL (1994). "Popularity Orbits Relationship Author." *Lincoln Journal*, September 26, p. 5.

GOLEMAN, DANIEL (1987). "Personality: Major Traits Found Stable Through Life." *New York Times*, June 9, pp. C1, C5.

______ (1988). "Keeping Stiff Upper Lip May Risk Health." *New York Times*, reprinted in *Lincoln Journal*, March 7, p. 7.

______ (1991a). "New Way to Battle Bias: Fight Acts, Not Feelings," *New York Times*, July 16, pp. 1, 3.

______ (1991b). "Doctors Find Comfort Is a Potent Medicine." *New York Times*, Nov. 26, pp. C1, C8.

GOODPASTER, SHONA and JAY HEWITT (1992). "Anticipated Reaction of Others to Intimate vs. Nonintimate Self-Disclosure." *Perceptual and Motor Skills* 74, April, 433–434.

*GORDON, SOL (1988a). *When Living Hurts.* New York: Dell.

*______ (1988b). *Why Love Is Not Enough.* Boston: Bob Adams.

*GORDON, THOMAS (1989). *Teaching Children Self-Discipline.* New York: Random House.

GORMAN, CHRISTINE (1988). "Why It's So Hard to Quit Smoking" *Time*, May 30, p. 56.

GOTTMAN, JOHN M. (1991). "Predicting the Longitudinal Course of Marriages." *Journal of Marital and Family Therapy* 17, January, 3–7.

*GOULDING, MARY MCCLURE, and ROBERT L. GOULDING (1989). *Not to Worry.* New York: Morrow.

GRANT, ELEANOR (1988). "The Housework Gap." *Psychology Today*, January, p. 10.

GRAY, JOHN (1992). *Men Are From Mars, Women Are From Venus.* New York: HarperCollins.

GRAY, LIZBETH A., and MARIE SARACINO (1991). "College Students' Attitudes, Beliefs, and Behaviors About AIDS: Implications for Family Life Educators." *Family Relations* 40, July, 258–263.

GREENBURG, MELANIE A., and ARTHUR A. STONE (1992). "Emotional Disclosure about Traumas and its Relation to Health: Effects of Previous Disclosure and Trauma Severity." *Journal of Personality and Social Psychology* 64, July, 75–84.

GREENWALD, JOHN (1993). "The Board Vs. the 'Babe.'" *Time*, August 30, p. 39.

*GROLLMAN, EARL A., and GERRI L. SWEDER (1986). *The Working Parent Dilemma: How to Balance the Responsibilities of Children and Careers.* Boston: Beacon.

*GULLO, STEPHEN, and CONNIE CHURCH (1988). *Loveshock: How to Recover From a Broken Heart and Love Again.* New York: Simon & Schuster.

GUSSMAN, KATHERINE, and DAVID W. HARDER (1990). "Offspring Personality and Perceptions of Parental Use of Reward and Punishment." *Psychological Reports* 67, December, 923–930.

HAGGA, DAVID A., and BONNIE L. STEWART (1992). "Self-Efficacy for Recovery From a Lapse After Smoking Cessation." *Journal of Consulting and Clinical Psychology* 60, February, 24–28.

HAI, DOROTHY M., ANDRIS ZIEMELIS, and JANICE ROSSI (1986). "Personality Types: Comparison of Job Applications and Applicants." *Psychological Reports* 59, December, 1119–1125.

HALBERSTAM, JOSHUA (1993). "You're So Vain." *Self*, July, pp. 116–119, 136.

HALE, RAY, ROBERT M. NEVELS, CHRIS LOTT, and THOMAS TITUS (1990). "Cultural Insensitivity to Sexist Language Toward Men." *Journal of Social Psychology* 130, October, 697–698.

HALL, EDWARD T. (1969). *The Hidden Dimension.* New York: Anchor/Doubleday.

______ (1973). *The Silent Language.* New York: Doubleday.

HALLORAN, JACK, and DOUGLAS BENTON (1987). *Applied Human Relations: An Organizational Approach.* Englewood Cliffs, NJ: Prentice Hall.

HAMPES, WILLIAM P. (1992). "Relation Between Intimacy and Humor." *Psychological Reports* 71, August, 127–130.

*HANDLY, JANE, and ROBERT W. HANDLY, with PAULINE NEFF (1990). *Why Women Worry and How to Stop.* New York: Fawcett Crest.

HANNA, SHARON L. (1980). "The Strengths Within Families of Remarriage: A Descriptive Study." Lincoln, NE: Master's Thesis.

HANNA, SHARON L., and PATRICIA KAIN KNAUB (1981). "Cohabitation Before Remarriage: Its Relationship to Family Strengths." *Alternative Lifestyles* 4 (4), 507–522.

HANSEN, GARY L. (1991). *The Psychology of Jealousy and Envy*, ed. Peter Salovey. New York: The Guilford Press.

HARDESTY, CONSTANCE, and JANET BOKEMEIER (1989). "Finding Time and Making Do: Distribution of Household Labor in Nonmetropolitan Marriages." *Journal of Marriage and the Family* 51 (1), 253–267.

HARMAN, MARSHA J., and CONSUELO ARBONA (1991). "Psychological Adjustment Among Adult Children of Alcoholics: A Cross-Cultural Study." *The Journal of Psychology* 125, November, 641–648.

HARRIS, SYDNEY (1982). "When Your Leading Role Models Are Entertainers, What Kind of a Society Will You Have?" *Lincoln Journal*, April 3, p. 6.

HARRIS, T. GEORGE, and ROBERT J. TROTTER (1989). "Work Smarter, Not Harder." *Psychology Today*, March, p. 33.

*HARRIS, THOMAS (1969) *I'm OK, You're OK.* New York: Harper & Row.

*HARRIS, THOMAS A., and AMY BJORK HARRIS (1985). *Staying OK.* New York: Harper & Row.

HARRISON, ALLEN F., and ROBERT M. BRAMSON (1982). *The Art of Thinking.* New York: Berkley Books.

HART, CRAIG H., MICHELE D. DEWOLF, PATRICIA WOZNIAK, and DIANE C. BURTS (1992). "Maternal and Paternal Disciplinary Styles: Relations with Preschoolers' Playground Behavioral Orientations and Peer Status." *Child Development* 63, August, 879–892.

HATFIELD, ELAINE, and RICHARD L. RAPSON (1992). "Similarity and Attraction in Close Relationships," *Communication Monographs* 59, June, 209–213.

*HAUG, NANCY, and NANCY D. WRIGHT (1991). *Erasing the Guilt: Play an Active Role in Your Child's Education No Matter How Busy You Are.* Hawthorne, NJ: The Career Press.

HAVARI, HALLGEIR (1991). "Perception of Goal Proximity, Latency and Duration of Action Plans, and Worry in Relation to Goal Distance in Time and Personality Characteristics." *Perceptual and Motor Skills* 72, June, 707–741.

HAWKINS, ALAN J., and TOMI-ANN ROBERTS (1992). "Designing a Primary Intervention to Help Dual-Earner Couples Share Housework and Child Care." *Family Relations* 41, April, 169–177.

HAWKINS, ROBERT O. (1990). "The Relationship Between Culture, Personality, and Sexual Jealousy in Men in Heterosexual and Homosexual Relationships." *Journal of Homosexuality* 19 (3), 67–84.

*HAY, LOUISE L. (1991). *The Power Is Within You.* Carson, CA: Hay House Inc.

HAZELL, PHILIP, and TERRY LEWIN (1993). "Friends of Adolescent Suicide Attempters and Completers." *Journal of the American Academy of Child and Adolescent Psychiatry* 32 (1), 76–81.

*HEATH, DOUGLAS H. (1991). *Fulfilling Lives: Paths to Maturity and Success.* San Francisco: Jossey-Bass, Inc. Publishers.

*HELDMANN, MARY LYNNE (1988). *When Words Hurt: How to Keep Criticism from Undermining Your Self-Esteem.* New York: Ballantine Books.

*HELMSTETTER, SHAD (1989). *Predictive Parenting: What to Say When You Talk to Your Kids.* New York: Pocket Books.

*______ (1991). *You Can Excel in Times of Change.* New York: Pocket Books.

HEMENWAY, DAVID, SARA J. SOLNICK, and GRAHAM A. COLDITZ (1993). "Smoking and Suicide Among Nurses." *The American Journal of Public Health* 83 (2), 249–251.

*HENDLIN, STEVEN J. (1992). *When Good Enough Is Never Enough.* New York: G. P. Putnam's Sons.

HENDRICK, SUSAN S., and CLYDE HENDRICK (1992). *Liking, Loving, and Relating.* Pacific Grove, CA: Brooks/Cole Publishing Company.

*HENDRIX, HARVILLE (1988). *Getting the Love You Want: A Guide for Couples.* New York: Henry Holt & Company.

*______ (1992). *Keeping the Love You Find.* New York: Pocket Books.

HENRY, WILLIAM A. (1993). "Born Gay?" *Time*, July 26, pp. 36–39.

HERRING, CEDRIC, and KAREN ROSE WILSON-SADBERRY (1993). "Preference or Necessity? Changing Work Roles of Black and White Women, 1973–1990." *Journal of Marriage and the Family* 55, May, 314–325.

HILTON, JEANNE M., and VIRGINIA A. HALDEMAN (1991). "Gender Differences in the Performance of Household Tasks by Adults and Children in Single-Parent and Two-Parent, Two-Earner Families." *Journal of Family Issues* 12, March, 114–130.

HIRSH, SANDRA (1985). *Using the Myers-Briggs Type Indicator in Organizations.* Palo Alto, CA: Consulting Psychologists Press.

*HIRSCH, SANDRA, and JEAN KUMMEROW (1989). *Life Types.* New York: Warner Communications Company.

HODGSON, THOMAS A. (1992). "Cigarette Smoking and Lifetime Medical Expenditures." *The Milbank Quarterly* 70 (1), 81.

HOFFMAN, LOIS WLADIS (1991). "The Influence of the Family Environment on Personality: Accounting for Sibling Differences." *Psychological Bulletin* 110 (2), 187–203.

HOLMES, THOMAS H., and RICHARD H. RAHE (1967). "The Social Readjustment Rating Scale." *Journal of Psychosomatic Research* 11, 213–218.

*HOPSON, DARLENE POWELL, and DEREK S. HOPSON (1990). *Different and Wonderful.* New York: Simon & Schuster.

HOPSON, JANET L. (1988). "A Pleasurable Chemistry." *Psychology Today*, July/August, pp. 29–30, 32–33.

HOUSTON, B. KENT, DAVID S. CATES, and KAREN E. KELLY (1992). "Job Stress, Psychosocial Strain, and Physical Health Problems in Women Employed Full-Time Outside the Home and Homemakers." *Women & Health* 19 (1), 1–26.

HULKA, BARBARA (1986). "Environmental Tobacco Smoke Proves Harmful to Kids' Health." *Lincoln Journal*, November 21, p. 8.

HULL, JON D. (1993). "A Boy and His Gun." *Time*, August 2, pp. 21–27.

HUMBLE, CHARLES, JANET CROFT, ANN GERBER, MICHELE CASPER, CURTIS G. HAMES, and HERMAN A. TYROLER (1990). "Passive Smoking and 20-Year Cardiovascular Disease Mortality Among Nonsmoking Wives, Evans County, Georgia." *American Journal of Public Health* 80 (5), 599–601.

*HUTCHINSON, EARL OFARI (1992). *Black Fatherhood: The Guide to Male Parenting.* Los Angeles: Impact! Publications.

HYATT, RANDY (1991). "Self-esteem: The Key to Happiness." *USA Today*, March, pp. 86–87.

HYDE, J. S., E. FENEMA, and S. J. LAMON (1990). "Gender Differences in Mathematics Performance: A Meta-Analysis." *Psychological Bulletin* 107 (11), 139–155.

HYDE, J. S, and M. C. LINN (1988). "Gender Differences in Verbal Ability: A Meta-Analysis." *Psychological Bulletin* 104 (11), 53–69.

HYMES, ROBERT W., and MICHAEL M. AKIYAMA (1991). "Depression and Self-Enhancement Among Japanese and American Students." *The Journal of Social Psychology* 131, June, 321–334.

*INLANDER, CHARLES B., and MARIE HODGE (1992). *100 Ways to Live to 100.* Allentown, PA: People's Medical Society, Inc.

ISHII-KUNTZ, MASAKO, and SCOTT COLTRANE (1992). "Remarriage, Stepparenting, and Household Labor (Part of a Symposium on: Remarriage)." *Journal of Family Issues* 13, June, 215–233.

JABS, CAROLYN (1991). "Are You Raising An Optimist?" *Working Mother*, September, pp. 42, 44–46.

JACKSON, JUDY, and SUSAN D. COCHRAN (1991). "Loneliness and Psychological Distress." *The Journal of Psychology* 125, May, 257–262.

JACKSON, PAMELA BRABOY (1992). "Specifying the Buffering Hypothesis: Support, Strain, and Depression." *Social Psychological Quarterly* 55, December, 363–378.

JACKSON, STANLEY W. (1992). "The Listening Healer in the History of Psychological Healing." *The American Journal of Psychiatry* 149, December, 1623–1632.

*JACKSON, TOM (1993). *Guerrilla Tactics in the New Job Market.* New York: Bantam.

*JAMES, JOHN W., and FRANK CHERRY (1988). *The Grief Recovery Handbook.* New York: Harper & Row.

*JAMES, MURIEL, and JOHN JAMES (1991). *Passion For Life.* New York: Penguin Group.

JAMES, WILLIAM (1923). *The Principles of Psychology.* New York: H. Holt & Co.

*JAMPOLSKY, GERALD G. (1979). *Love Is Letting Go of Fear.* Millbrae, CA: Celestial Arts.

*______ (1990). *One Person Can Make a Difference.* New York: Bantam.

*JAMPOLSKY, GERALD G., and DIANE V. CIRINCIONE (1990). *Love is The Answer: Creating Positive Relationships.* New York: Bantam Books.

JANKO, EDMUND (1989). "Knowing Is Not Thinking." *Phi Delta Kappan*, March, pp. 543–544.

JAYAKODY, RUKMALIE, LINDA M. CHATTERS, and ROBERT JOSEPH TAYLOR (1993). "Family Support to Single and Married African American Mothers: The Provision of Financial, Emotional, and Child Care Assistance." *Journal of Marriage and the Family* 55, May, 261–276.

*JEFFERS, SUSAN (1987). *Feel the Fear and Do It Anyway.* New York: Fawcett Columbine.

*JEFFRIES, WILLIAM C. (1991). *True to Type.* Norfolk, VA: Hampton Roads Publishing Co.

JENKINS, STEPHEN J., JAMES C. STEPHENS, ALEXANDER L. CHEW, and ELIZABETH DOWNS (1992). "Examination of the Relationship Between the Myer-Briggs Type Indicator and Empathetic Response." *Perceptual and Motor Skills* 74, June, 1003–1009.

*JOHNSON, CATHERINE (1992). *Lucky in Love: The Secrets of Happy Couples and How Their Marriages Thrive.* New York: Viking.

*JOHNSON, HELEN M. (1986). *How Do I Love Thee*? Salem, WI: Sheffield.

JOINER, THOMAS E., MARK S. ALFANO, and GERALD I. METALSKY (1992). "When Depression Breeds Contempt: Reassurance Seeking, Self-Esteem, and Rejection of Depressed College Students by Their Roommates." *Journal of Abnormal Psychology* 101, February, 165–173.

*JONES, ANN, and SUSAN SCHECHTER (1992). *When Love Goes Wrong: What to Do When You Can't Do Anything Right.* New York: Harper Collins.

JORDAN, NICK (1989). "Spare the Rod, Spoil the Child." *Psychology Today*, June, p. 16.

JOSSELSON, RUTHELLEN (1992). *The Space Between Us.* San Francisco: Jossey-Bass Publishers.

JOUBERT, CHARLES E. (1990). "Relationship Among Self-esteem, Psychological Reactance, and Other Personality Variables." *Psychological Reports* 66, June, 1147–1151.

JOURARD, SIDNEY M. (1971). *The Transparent Self.* New York: Van Nostrand Reinhold.

JOURNAL OF THE AMERICAN MEDICAL ASSOCIATION (1991). "Alcohol and Other Drug Use Among High School Students—United States." vol. 266 (23), 3266–3267.

______ (1992). "Tobacco, Alcohol, and Other Drug Use Among High School Students—United States." vol. 269 (14), 1841–1842.

JUNG, C. G. (1968). *Analytical Psychology, Its Theory and Practice.* New York: Vintage Books.

JUNG, CARL (1923). *Psychological Types.* New York: Harcourt, Brace.

KABAT-ZINN, JON, ANN O. MASSION, JEAN KRISTELLER, LINDA G. PETERSON, KENNETH E. FLETCHER, LORI PHERT, WILLIAM R. LENDERKING, and SAKI F. SANTORELLI (1992). "Effectiveness of a Meditation-Based Reduction Program in the Treatment of Anxiety Disorders. (Annual Meeting of the Society of Behavioral Medicine 1990, Chicago, Illinois)." *American Journal of Psychiatry* 149 (7), 936–943.

KAFKA, RANDY R., and PERRY LONDON "Communication in Relationships and Adolescent Substance Use: The Influence of Parents and Friends." *Adolescence* 26, Fall, 587–598.

KAHN, STEPHEN, GARY ZIMMERMAN, MIHALY CSIKSZENTMEHALYI, and JACOB W. GETZELS (1986). "Relations Between Identity in Young Adulthood and Intimacy at Midlife." *Journal of Personality and Social Psychology,* May, pp. 1316–1322.

KAMBERG, MARY-LANE (1989). "A Sad State of Mind." *Current Health* 2, December, pp. 17–19.

*KAMINER, WENDY (1992). *I'm Dysfunctional, You're Dysfunctional.* Reading, MA: Addison-Wesley Publishing Company.

KANTROWITZ, BARBARA (1986). "Three's a Crowd." *Newsweek*, September 1, pp. 68–76.

KAPLAN, JANICE (1993). "You Can Win the Fat Wars." *Redbook*, April, pp. 88–91.

KAPLAN, ROBERT M., DEBORAH L. WINGARD, and JANICE B. MCPHILLIPS (1992). "Cigarette Smoking, Mortality, Institutional and Community-Based Care Utilization in an Adult Community." *Journal of Community Health* 17, February, 53–60.

KAPRIO, JAAKKO, MARKKU KOSKENVUO, and HELI RITA (1987). "A Prospective Study of 95,647 Widowed Persons." *American Journal of Public Health* 77 (3), 283–287.

*KATZ, STAN J., and AIMEE E. LIU (1988). *False Love and Other Romantic Illusions.* New York: Ticknor & Fields.

KAUL, DONALD (1993). "Gen. Powell's Stand Disappointing." *Lincoln Journal*, January 1, p. 6B.

——— (1993). "Foster's Fate Could Happen to Anyone." *Lincoln Journal*, August 19, p. 18.

*KEATING, CHARLES J. (1984). *Dealing with Difficult People*. Ramsey, NJ: Paulist Press.

*KEATING, KATHLEEN (1983). *The Hug Therapy Book*. Minneapolis: CompCare.

*KEEN, SAM (1991). *Fire in the Belly: On Being a Man*. New York: Bantam Books.

*KEIRSEY, DAVID, and MARILYN BATES (1978). *Please Understand Me*. Del Mar, CA: Prometheus Nemesis.

KELLEY, HAROLD H. (1950). "The Warm-Cold Variable in First Impressions of Persons." *Journal of Personality* 18, 431–439.

KELLEY, PATRICIA (1992). "Healthy Stepfamily Functioning." *Families in Society* 73, December, 579–587.

*KENNEDY, ALEXANDRA (1991). *Losing a Parent: Passage to a New Way of Living*. New York: Harper Collins.

*KENNEDY, EUGENE (1975). *If You Really Knew Me, Would You Still Like Me*? Niles, IL: Argus.

KERNIS, MICHAEL H., BRUCE D. GRANNEMANN, and LYNDA C. MATHIS (1991). "Stability of Self-esteem as a Moderator of the Relation Between Level of Self-esteem and Depression." *Journal of Personality and Social Psychology*. 61, July, 80–84.

*KESHET, JAMIE K. (1987). *Love and Power in the Stepfamily*. New York: McGraw-Hill.

——— (1990). "Cognitive Remodeling of the Family: How Remarried People View Stepfamilies." *American Journal of Orthopsychiatry* 60, April, 196–203.

KESTENBAUM, ROBERTA (1992). "Feeling Happy Versus Feeling Good: The Processing of Discrete and Global Categories of Emotional Expressions by Children and Adults." *Developmental Psychology* 28, November, 1132–1142.

KETTERLINUS, ROBERT D., MICHAEL E. LAMB, and KATHERINE NITZ (1991). "Developmental and Ecological Sources of Stress Among Adolescent Parents." *Family Relations* 40, October, 435–441.

KEYES, KEN (1975). *Handbook to Higher Consciousness*. Coos Bay, OR: Living Love.

*KILEY, DAN (1989). *Living Together Feeling Alone*. New York: Prentice Hall.

*KINDER, MELVYN, and CONNELL COWAN (1989). *Husbands and Wives*. New York: Penguin Books.

KIVETT, VIRA R. (1993). "Racial Comparisons of the Grandmother Role: Implications for Strengthening the Family Support System of Older Black Women." *Family Relations* 42, April, 165–172.

KNAUB, PATRICIA KAIN, and SHARON L. HANNA (1984). "Children of Remarriage: Perceptions of Family Strength." *Journal of Divorce* 7 (4), 73–90.

KNAUB, PATRICIA KAIN, SHARON L. HANNA and NICK STINNETT (1984). "Strengths of Remarried Families." *Journal of Divorce* 7 (3), 41–55.

KOBASA, SUZANNE C. (1979). "Stressful Life Events, Personality, and Health: An Inquiry Into Hardiness." *Journal of Personality and Social Psychology* 37 (1), 1–11.

KOHLBERG, LAWRENCE (1963). "The Development of Children's Orientations Toward a Moral Order I: Sequence in the Development of Moral Thought." *Vita Humana* 6, 11–35.

KOLATA, GINA (1991a). "The Aging Brain: The Mind Is Resilient, It's the Body That Fails." *The New York Times*, April 16, pp. C1, C10.

——— (1991b). "Mental Gymnastics." *New York Times Magazine*, October 6, pp. 15–17, 42, 44.

KOONTZ, KATHY (1988). "Eight Reasons Why You Should Exercise." *McCall's*, July, p. 89.

KOPPER, BEVERLY A., and DOUGLAS L. EPPERSON (1991). "Women and Anger: Sex and Sex-Role Comparisons in the Expression of Anger." *Psychology of Women Quarterly* 15, March, 7–14.

KORNHABER, A., and K. L. WOODWARD (1981). *Grandparents/Grandchildren: The Vital Connection*. Garden City, NY: Anchor.

KOVACH, KENNETH (1980). "Why Motivational Theories Don't Work." *S.A.M. Advanced Management Journal*, Spring, p. 46.

KOVECSES, ZOLTAN (1991). "A Linguist's Quest for Love." *Journal of Social and Personal Relationships* 8 (1), 77–97.

*KROEGER, OTTO, and JANET M. THUESEN (1992). *Type Talk at Work.* New York: Delacorte Press.

KROKOFF, LOWELL J. (1991). "Job Distress Is No Laughing Matter on Marriage, or Is It?" *Journal of Social and Personal Relationships* 8, 5–25.

KUBANY, EDWARD S., DAVID C. RICHARD, GORDON B. BAUER, and MILES Y. MURAOKA (1992). "Verbalized Anger and Accusatory 'You' Messages as Cues for Anger and Antagonism Among Adolescents." *Adolescence* 27, Fall, 505–516.

*KUBLER-ROSS, ELISABETH (1969). *On Death and Dying.* New York: Macmillan.

KURDEK, LAWRENCE A., and MARK A. FINE (1991). "Cognitive Correlates of Satisfaction for Mothers and Stepfathers in Stepfather Families." *Journal of Marriage and the Family* 53, August, 565–571.

KURTZ, THEODORE (1991). "Dynamic Listening: Unlocking Your Communication Potential." *Public Management* 73, August, 26–28.

*KUSHNER, HAROLD (1986). *When All You've Ever Wanted Isn't Enough.* New York: Pocket Books.

LAGRAND, LOUIS E. (1991). "United We Cope: Support Groups for the Dying and Bereaved." *Death Studies* 15 (2), 207–230.

LALIBERTE, RICHARD (1993). "Boosting Immunity." *Self*, June, pp. 132–135, 166.

LAMBORN, SUSIE D., NINA S. MOUNTS, LAURENCE STEINBERG, and SANFORD M. DORNBUSCH (1991). "Patterns of Competence and Adjustment Among Adolescents from Authoritative, Authoritarian, Indulgent, and Neglectful Families." *Child Development* 62, October, 1049–1065.

*LANG, DENISE (1990). *Family Harmony.* New York: Prentice Hall.

LARSON, JAN (1992). "Understanding Stepfamilies." *American Demographics* 14, July, pp. 36–38.

LARSON, JEFFRY H. (1988). "The Marriage Quiz: College Students' Beliefs in Selected Myths about Marriage." *Family Relations* 37 (1), 3–11.

LARZELERE, ROBERT E., MICHAEL KLEIN, WALTER R. SCHUMM, and SAMUEL A. ALIBRANDO JR. (1989). "Relations of Spanking and Other Parenting Characteristics to Self-Esteem and Perceived Fairness of Parental Discipline." *Psychological Reports* 64, June, 1140–1142.

LASZLO, JOHN (1987). *Understanding Cancer.* New York: Harper & Row.

LAU, S., and GERALD E. GRUEN (1992). "The Social Stigma of Loneliness: Effect of Target Person's and Perceiver's Sex." *Personality and Social Psychology Bulletin* 18, April 182–189.

LAUER, JEANETTE, and ROBERT LAUER (1985). "Marriages Made to Last." *Psychology Today*, June, pp. 22–26.

*LAUER, ROBERT H., and JEANETTE C. LAUER (1988). *Watersheds: Mastering Life's Unpredictable Crises.* Boston: Little, Brown.

______ (1991). "The Long-Term Relational Consequences of Problematic Family Backgrounds." *Family Relations* 40, July, 286–290.

LAZARUS, RICHARD S. (1966). *Psychological Stress and the Coping Process.* New York: McGraw-Hill.

______ (1981). "Little Hassles Can Be Hazardous to Your Health." *Psychology Today*, July, pp. 58–62.

*LEATZ, CHRISTINE A., and MARK W. STOLAR (1993). *Career Success/Personal Stress: How to Stay Healthy in a High-Stress Environment.* New York: McGraw-Hill.

LEBOEUF, MICHAEL (1979). *Working Smart: How to Accomplish More in Half the Time.* New York: McGraw-Hill.

Lecky, Prescott (1951). *Self-Consistency: A Theory of Personality.* Garden City, NY: Anchor.

Lee, G. R. (1977). "Age at Marriage and Marital Satisfaction: A Multi-variate Analysis with Implications for Marital Stability." *Journal of Marriage and the Family* 39, 493–504.

*Lerner, Harriet Goldhor (1985). *The Dance of Anger.* New York: Harper & Row.

*______ (1989). *The Dance of Intimacy.* New York: Harper & Row.

*______ (1992). *The Dance of Deception: Pretending and Truth-Telling in Women's Lives.* New York: Harper Collins.

*Leshan, Eda (1990). *It's Better to Be Over the Hill Than Under It.* New York: Newmarket Press.

Letich, Larry (1991). "Do You Know Who Your Friends Are?" *Utne Reader*, May/June, pp. 85–87.

Levin, Irene (1993). "Family as Mapped Realities." *Journal of Family Issues* 14, March, 82–91.

Levine, Marvin (1988). *Effective Problem Solving.* Englewood Cliffs, NJ: Prentice Hall.

Levoy, Gregg (1988). "Tears That Speak." *Psychology Today*, July/August, pp. 8–10.

Lewis, Jerry M. (1979). *How's Your Family?* New York: Brunner/Mazel.

Lilly, Catherine (1984). "Taking Your Own Name." *New Directions for Women* 13 (6), 11.

Lincoln Journal (1990). "Heart Study: Thinner Is Better." March 29, p. 13.

______ (1990). "Parents' Smoke Raises Cancer Risk." September 6, p. 2.

______ (1991). "Passive Smoke Kills 53,000 Annually." January 10, p. 1.

______ (1993). "Experts: HIV Is Spreading Among Teens." June 6, p. 3A.

______ (1993). "AIDS No. 1 Killer of Men in 64 Cities." June 16, pp. 1, 7.

______ (1993). "Losing the Battle of the Bulge." June 24, p. 7.

______ (1994). "Binge Drinking Seen as Epidemic on College Campuses." June 7, p. 16.

______ (1994). "Teens Having Sex Earlier, but Pregnancy Rates Lower." June 7, p. 1.

______ (1994). "Boys Value Way It Was While Girls Break Away." July 11, p. 5.

Lindberg, Anne Morrow (1955). *Gift from the Sea.* New York: Pantheon Books, a division of Random House.

Lingren, Herbert G. (1981). "Strengthening the Couple Relationship." March. NebGuide F-2. Lincoln, NE: Cooperative Extension Service Institute of Agriculture and Resources.

Livingston, Kathryn E. (1992). "Are You Touching Your Child Enough?" *Redbook*, October, pp. 190, 192, 200.

Livson, F. (1976). "Patterns of Personality Development in Middle-aged Women: A Longitudinal Study," *International Journal of Aging and Human Development* 1, 107–115.

Lobdell, Judith, and Daniel Perlman (1986). "The Intergenerational Transmission of Loneliness: A Study of College Females and Their Parents." *Journal of Marriage and the Family* 48 (3), 589–595.

Loehlin, John C., Joseph M. Horn, and Lee Willerman (1990). "Heredity, Environment, and Personality Change: Evidence From the Texas Adoption Project." *Journal of Personality* 58, March, 221–243.

Long, Patricia (1987). "Laugh and Be Well?" *Psychology Today*, October, pp. 28–29.

*Love, Patricia, with Jo Robinson (1990). *The Emotional Incest Syndrome: What to Do When a Parent's Love Rules Your Life.* New York: Banatam Books.

Luft, Joseph (1969). *Of Human Interaction.* Palo Alto, CA: Mayfield.

*Lukas, Christopher, and Henry M. Seiden (1987). *Silent Grief: Living in the Wake of Suicide.* New York: Bantam Books.

Lund, Dale A., and Michael S. Caserta (1992). "Older Bereaved Spouses' Participation in Self-Help Groups." *Omega: Journal of Death and Dying* 25 (1), 47–61.

Maccoby, Eleanor, and Caroline Jacklin (1974). *The Psychology of Sex Differences.* Stanford, CA: Stanford University Press.

MACCOBY, ELEANOR E., CHARLENE E. DEPNER, and ROBERT H. MNOOKIN (1990). "Coparenting in the Second Year after Divorce." *Journal of Marriage and the Family* 52, February, 141–155.

MACHIDA, SANDRA, and SUSAN D. HOLLOWAY (1991). "The Relationship Between Divorced Mothers' Perceived Control Over Child Rearing and Children's Post-Divorce Development." *Family Relations* 40, July, 272–278.

MACIONIS, JOHN J. (1994). *Society: The Basics.* Englewood Cliffs, NJ: Prentice Hall.

*MALLINGER, ALLAN E., and JEANNETTE DEWYZE (1992). *Too Perfect: When Being in Control Gets Out of Control.* New York: Clarkson Potter/Publishers.

*MALONE, THOMAS PATRICK, and PATRICK THOMAS MALONE (1987). *The Art of Intimacy.* New York: Prentice Hall.

MALTZ, MAXWELL (1960). *Psycho-cybernetics.* New York: Pocket Books.

MARKMAN, H., F. FLOYD, S. STANLEY, and R. STORASSI (1988). "Prevention of Marital Distress: A Longitudinal Investigation." *Journal of Consulting Clinical Psychology* 56, 210–217.

MARQUIS, PETER (1992). "Family Dysfunction as a Risk Factor in the Development of Antisocial Behavior." *Psychological Reports* 71, October, 468–470.

MARSH, PETER (1988). "Making Eye Contact," in *Eye to Eye: How People Interact*, ed. Peter Marsh. Topsfield, MA: Salem House.

MARSIGLIO, WILLIAM, and DENISE DONNELLY (1991). "Sexual Relations in Later Life: A National Study of Married Persons." *Journal of Gerontology* 46, November, 338–344.

*MARTSON, STEPHANIE (1990). *The Magic of Encouragement: Nurturing Your Child's Self-Esteem.* New York: Pocket Books.

MASLOW, ABRAHAM (1968). *Toward a Psychology of Being.* New York: D. Van Nostrand.

*MASTRICH, JIM, with BILL BIRNES (1990). *Strong Enough For Two: How to Overcome Codependence and Other Enabling Behavior and Take Control of Your Life.* New York: Macmillan.

MATHES, EUGENE W. (1991). "Dealing with Romantic Jealousy by Finding a Replacement Relationship." *Psychological Reports* 69, October, 535–538.

______ (1991). *The Psychology of Jealousy and Envy*, ed. Peter Salovey. New York: The Guilford Press.

MAY, ROLLO (1953). *Man's Search for Himself.* New York: Dell.

______ (1969). *Love and Will.* New York: W. W. Norton & Co.

MCAULEY, EDWARD, and KERRY S. COURNEYA (1992). "Self-efficacy Relationships with Affective and Exertion Responses to Exercise." *Journal of Applied Social Psychology* 22, February, 312–326.

MCAULEY, EDWARD, KERRY S. COURNEYA, and JANICE LETTUNICH (1991). "Effects of Acute and Long-Term Exercise on Self-efficacy Responses in Sedentary, Middle-aged Males and Females." *The Gerontologist* 31, August, 534–542.

MCAULEY, EDWARD, SUSAN WRAITH, and TERRY E. DUNCAN (1991). "Self-Efficacy, Perceptions of Success and Intrinsic Motivation for Exercise." *Journal of Applied Social Psychology* 21, January, 139–155.

MCCANN, JOSEPH T., and MARY KAY BIAGGIO (1989). "Sexual Satisfaction in Marriage as a Function of Life Meaning." *Archives of Sexual Behavior* 18, February, 59–72.

MCCARTHY, BARRY (1988). "Friends and Acquaintances," in *Eye to Eye: How People Interact*, ed. Peter Marsh. Topsfield, MA: Salem House.

MCCUSKER, JANE, ANNE M. STODDARD, and JANE G. ZAPKA (1992). "AIDS Education for Drug Abusers: Evaluation of Short-Term Effectiveness." *American Journal of Public Health* 82, April, 533–540.

MCINTOSH, EVERTON G., and DOUGLASS T. TATE (1990). "Correlates of Jealous Behaviors." *Psychological Reports* 66, April, 601–602.

______ (1992). "Characteristics of the Rival and the Experience of Jealousy." *Perceptual and Motor Skills* 74, April, 369–370.

*McKay, Matthew, Marth Davis, and Patrick Fanning (1983). *Messages: The Communication Book.* Oakland, CA: New Harbinger.

*McKay, Matthew, and Patrick Fanning (1987). *Self-Esteem.* Oakland, CA: New Harbinger.

McLeod, Beverly (1986). "Rx for Health: A Dose of Self-Confidence." *Psychology Today*, October, pp. 46–50.

McMinn, Mark R., Shannan F. Lindsay, Laurel E. Hannum, and Pamela K. Troyer (1990). "Does Sexist Language Reflect Personal Characteristics?" *Sex Roles* 23, October, 389–396.

Mead, George H. (1934). *Mind, Self, and Society.* Chicago: University of Chicago Press.

Mehrabian, Albert (1968). "Communication without Words." *Psychology Today*, September, pp. 53–55.

______ (1981). *Silent Messages.* Belmont, CA: Wadsworth.

Melby, Janet N., Rand D. Conger, Katherine J. Conger, and Frederick O. Lorenz (1993). "Effects of Parental Behavior on Tobacco Use by Young Male Adolescents." *Journal of Marriage and the Family* 55, May, 439–454.

The Menninger Letter (1993a). "Risks to Adult Children of Alcoholics." August, p. 6.

______ (1993b). "Perfectionists May Be Prone to Depression." September, p. 5.

______ (1994a). "Low Self-esteem May Fuel Depression." May, p. 5.

______ (1994b). "Steroids Influence Moods, Actions." July, p. 7.

______ (1994c). "Trust in Supervisors Fueled by Communication." July, p. 1.

Messina, James J. (1982). *Basic Communication Skills Handbook.* Tampa, FL: Advanced Development Series.

Michaels, Joseph (1983). *Prime of Your Life: A Practical Guide to Your Mature Years.* Boston: Little, Brown.

*Michelozzi, Betty Neville (1991). *Coming Alive from Nine to Five.* Palo Alto, CA: Mayfield.

Miles, Margaret-Shandor, and Alice Sterner-Demi (1992). "A Comparison of Guilt in Bereaved Parents Whose Children Died by Suicide, Accident, or Chronic Disease." *Omega: Journal of Death and Dying* 24 (3), 203–215.

Milgram, Norman A., Weizman Dangour, and Amiram Raviv (1992). "Situational and Personal Determinants of Academic Procrastination." *The Journal of General Psychology* 119, April, 123–133.

*Miller, Emmett E. (1978). *Feeling Good: How to Stay Healthy.* Englewood Cliffs, NJ: Prentice Hall.

Miller, Katherine I., Beth Hartman Ellis, Eric G. Zook, and Judith S. Lyles (1990). "An Integrated Model of Communication, Stress, and Burnout in the Workplace." *Communication Research* 17, June, 300–326.

Miller, Neil (1989). *In Search of Gay America.* New York: The Atlantic Monthly Press.

*Miller, Sherod, Phyllis A. Miller, Elam W. Nunnally, and Daniel B. Wackman (1991). *Talking and Listening Together.* Littleton, CO: Interpersonal Communication Programs.

*Miller, Sherod, Elam W. Nunnally, and Daniel B. Wackman (1979). *Talking Together.* Littleton, CO: Interpersonal Communication Programs.

*Miller, Sherod, Daniel B. Wackman, Elam W. Nunnally, and Phyllis A. Miller (1988). *Connecting with Self and Others.* Littleton, CO: Interpersonal Communication Programs.

Mills, Robert John, Harold G. Grasmick, Carolyn Stout Morgan, and Deeann Wenk (1992). "The Effects of Gender, Family Satisfaction, and Economic Strain on Psychological Well-Being." *Family Relations* 41, October, 440–445.

Minton, Lynn (1993). "Gay Sensitivity Sessions: Readers Speak Out." *Parade*, March 7, p. 12.

MODERN MATURITY (1993). "With a Little Help from My Friends." June-July, p. 8.

MONTAGU, ASHLEY (1990). "Reaching the Child Within Us." *Utne Reader*, January/February, pp. 87–90.

MONTGOMERY, BARBARA M., and PETER TROWER (1988). "Friends and Acquaintances," in *Eye to Eye: How People Interact*, ed. Peter Marsh. Topsfield, MA: Salem House.

MONTGOMERY, MARILYN J., EDWARD R. ANDERSON, E. MAVIS HETHERINGTON, and W. GLENN CLINGEMPEEL (1992). "Patterns of Courtship for Remarriage: Implications for Child Adjustment and Parent-Child Relationships." *Journal of Marriage and the Family* 54, 686–698.

MOORE-EDE, MARTIN (1993). *The Twenty Four Hour Society.* Reading, MA: Addison-Wesley Publishing Company.

MOREAU, DAN (1993). "Yours, Mine and Ours." *Kiplinger's Personal Finance Magazine*, August, pp. 71–75.

MORROW, LANCE (1993). "The Strange Burden of a Name." *Time*, March 8, p. 76.

MOSS, BARRY F., and ANDREW I. SCHWEBEL (1993). "Defining Intimacy in Romantic Relationships." *Family Relations*, 42 (1), 31–37.

MOSS, RUTH J. (1988). "Write Off Your Ills." *Psychology Today*, November, p. 13.

*MOYERS, BILL (1993). *Healing and the Mind.* New York: Doubleday.

MULINS, LARRY C., and MARY MUSHEL (1992). "The Existence and Emotional Closeness of Relationships with Children, Friends, and Spouses: The Effect on Loneliness Among Older Persons." *Research on Aging* 14, December, 448–470.

MURPHY, PATRICIA A. (1991). "Parental Divorce in Childhood and Loneliness in Young Adults." *Omega* 23 (1), 25–35.

MURRAY, JOHN B. (1990). "Review of Research on the Myers-Briggs Type Indicator." *Perceptual and Motor Skills* 70, June, 1187–1202.

*MYERS, DAVID (1992). *Pursuit of Happiness.* Dresden, TN: Avon Books.

MYERS, ISABEL BRIGGS (1980a). *Introduction to Type.* Palo Alto, CA: Consulting Psychologists Press.

*______ (1980b). *Gifts Differing.* Palo Alto, CA: Consulting Psychologists Press.

NAGY, STEPHEN, and CHRISTINE M. NAGY (1992). "Longitudinal Examination of Teachers' Burnout in a School District." *Psychological Reports* 71, October, 523–531.

*NAIFEH, STEVEN, and GREGORY WHITE SMITH (1984). *Why Can't Men Open Up?* New York: Clarkson N. Potter.

*NARCISO, JOHN, and DAVID BURKETT (1992). *Relating Redefined.* Houston, TX: Redman Wright.

NATALE, JO ANNA (1987). "Ms. Conceptions." *Psychology Today*, December, p. 20.

*NATHANSON, DONALD L. (1992). *Shame and Pride.* New York: W.W. Norton & Company.

NATIONAL RESEARCH COUNCIL (1987). *Risking the Future: Adolescent Sexuality, Pregnancy, and Childbearing*, vol. 1. Washington, DC: National Academy Press.

NECHAS, EILEEN (1985). "A Frown Can Get You Down," *Prevention*, November, pp. 6–7.

*NELSEN, JANE (1987). *Positive Discipline.* New York: Ballantine Books.

NELSON, WENDY P., and RONALD F. LEVANT (1991). "An Evaluation of a Skills Training Program for Parents in Stepfamilies." *Family Relations* 40, July, 291–296.

NEWMAN, LUCILE F., and STEPHEN L. BUKA (1991). "Clipped Wings." *American Educator*, Spring, 27–33, 42.

*NEWMAN, MILDRED, and BERNARD BERKOWITZ (1974). *How to Be Your Own Best Friend.* New York: Ballantine.

*NORRIS, PATRICIA A., and GARRETT PORTER (1987). *I Choose Life.* Walpole, NH: Stillpoint.

*NORWOOD, ROBIN (1985). *Women Who Love Too Much.* Los Angeles: Tarcher.

NOVELLO, ANTONIA C. (1992). "Underage Drinking: A Report from the Inspector General." *The Journal of the American Medical Association* 268 (8), August 26, p. 96.

O'BRIEN, PATRICK E., and MAURICIO GABORIT (1992). "Codependency: A Disorder Separate from Chemical Dependency." *Journal of Clinical Psychology* 48, January, 129–136.

*O'Connor, Dagmar (1985). *How to Make Love to the Same Person For the Rest of Your Life and Still Love It!* Toronto: Bantam.

Okun, Barbara F. (1992). *Effective Helping: Interviewing and Counseling Techniques.* Monterey, CA: Brooks/Cole.

Older, Jules (1982). *Touching Is Healing.* New York: Stein and Day Publishers.

O'Leary, K. Daniel, and Steven R. H. Beach (1990). "Marital Therapy: A Viable Treatment for Depression and Marital Discord." *The American Journal of Psychiatry* 147, February, 183–186.

O'Leary, K. Daniel, and David A. Smith (1991). "Marital Interactions." *Annual Review Psychology* 42, 191–212.

Orr, Clarice, and Sally Van Zandt (1987). "The Role of Grandparenting in Building Family Strengths," in *Family Strengths: Pathways to Well-Being.* Lincoln, NE: University of Nebraska Center for Family Strengths.

*Osherson, Samuel (1992). *Wrestling with Love: How Men Struggle with Intimacy with Women, Children, Parents, and Each Other.* New York: Ballantine Books.

Ostroff, Cheri (1992). "The Relationship Between Satisfaction, Attitudes, and Performance: An Organizational Level Analysis." *Journal of Applied Psychology* 77, December, 963–974.

Page, Randy M. (1991). "Indicator of Psychosocial Distress Among Adolescent Females Who Perceive Themselves as Fat. " *Child-Study Journal* 21 (3), 203–212.

Page, Randy M., and Galen E. Cole (1991). "Demographic Predictors of Self-Reported Loneliness in Adults." *Psychological Reports* 68, June, 939–945.

______ (1991). "Loneliness and Alcoholism Risk in Late Adolescence: A Comparative Study of Adults and Adolescents." *Adolescence* 26, Winter, 925–930.

Painton, Priscilla (1993). "Couch Potatoes, Arise!" *Time*, August 9, pp. 55–56.

Papini, Dennis R., Frank F. Farmer, Steven M. Clark, Jill C. Micka, and Jawanda K. Barnett (1990). "Early Adolescent Age and Gender Differences in Patterns of Emotional Self-Disclosure to Parents and Friends." *Adolescence* 25, Winter, 959–976.

*Papolos, Demitri F., and Janice Papolos (1987). *Overcoming Depression.* New York: Harper Collins.

Parade Magazine (1990). "There'll Always Be Sex." May 6, p. 19.

______ (1992). "The Change in Teenagers." September 13, p. 14.

Parker, Gordon B., Elaine A. Barrett, and Ian B. Hickie (1992). "From Nurture to Network: Examining Links Between Perceptions of Parenting Received in Childhood and Social Bonds in Adulthood." *The American Journal of Psychiatry* 149, July, 877–885.

Parrott, W. Gerrod (1991). in *The Psychology of Jealousy and Envy*, ed. Peter Salovey. New York: The Guilford Press.

Pasick, Robert (1992). *Awakening from the Deep Sleep.* New York: Harper Collins.

Patterson, G. R., B. D. DeBaryshe, and E. Ramsey (1989). "A Developmental Perspective on Antisocial Behavior." *American Psychologist* 44, 329–335.

*Paul, Jordan, and Margaret Paul (1983). *Do I Have to Give Up Me to be Loved by You?* Minneapolis: CompCare.

*______ (1987). *If You Really Loved Me.* Minneapolis: CompCare.

Payne, Thomas (1993). "Healthfront." *Prevention*, July, pp. 11–12.

Pearl, Tracy, Donald W. Klopf, and Satoshi Ishii (1990). "Loneliness Among Japanese and American College Students." *Psychological Reports* 67, August, 49–50.

*Pearsall, Paul (1988). *Super Joy.* New York: Doubleday.

Pearson, Marie, and John Beer (1990). "Self-conciousness, Self-Esteem and Depression of Gifted School Children." *Psychological Reports* 66, June, 960–962.

*Peck, M. Scott (1978). *The Road Less Traveled.* New York: Simon & Schuster.

*Pennebaker, James (1991). *Opening Up: The Healing Power of Confiding In Others.* New York: Avon Books.

PENNEBAKER, RUTH (1992). "Go Ahead, Say It!" *Parents*, June, pp. 71–77.

PERKINS, KATHLEEN (1992). "Psychosocial Implication of Women and Retirement." *Social Work* 37, November, 526–532.

PERLMAN, DANIEL (1988). "Overcoming Loneliness," in *Eye to Eye: How People Interact*, ed. Peter Marsh. Topsfield, MA: Salem House.

PETO, RICHARD, ALAN D. LOPEZ, JILLIAN BOREHAM, MICHAEL THUN, and CLARK HEATH JR. (1992). "Mortality from Tobacco in Developed Countries: Indirect Estimation from National Vital Statistics." *The Lancet*, 339 (8804), May 23, 1268–1279.

PHINNEY, JEAN S., VICTOR CHAVIRA, and LISA WILLIAMSON (1992). "Acculturation Attitudes and Self-Esteem Among High School and College Students." *Youth & Society* 23, March, 299–312.

PIAGET, JEAN (1950). *The Psychology of Intelligence.* London: Routledge and Paul.

PIAGET, JEAN, and BARBEL INHELDER (1969). *The Psychology of the Child.* New York: Basic Books.

*PIPHER, MARY (1994). *Reviving Ophelia: Saving the Selves of Adolescent Girls.* New York: G. P. Putnam's Sons.

PLOMIN, ROBERT, and JOHN R. NESSELROADE (1990). "Behavioral Genetics and Personality Change." *Journal of Personality* 58 (1), 191–220.

PLOTNIK, ROD (1993). *Introduction to Psychology.* Belmont, CA: Brooks/Cole Publishing Company.

PLUTCHIK, ROBERT (1980). *Emotion: A Psychoevolutionary Synthesis.* New York: Harper & Row.

PLUTCHIK, ROBERT, and ANITA PLUTCHIK (1990). "Communication and Coping" in *Emotions and the Family* ed. Elaine A. Bleckman. Hillsdale, NJ: Laurence Erlbaum Associates, Publishers.

*PODELL, RONALD M. (1992). *Contagious Emotions: Staying Well When Your Loved One Is Depressed.* New York: Pocket Books.

POMERLEAU, ANDREE, DANIEL BOLDUC, and GERARD MALCUIT (1990). "Pink or Blue: Environmental Gender Stereotypes in the First Two Years of Life." *Sex Roles* 22, March, 359–367.

PONZETTI, JAMES J., JR. (1992). "Bereaved Families: A Comparison of Parents' and Grandparents' Reactions to the Death of a Child." *Omega: Journal of Death and Dying* 25 (1), 63–71.

POOL, ROBERT (1993). "Evidence for Homosexuality Gene." *Science* 261, July 16, pp. 291–292.

POPENOE, DAVID (1993a). "American Family Decline, 1960–1990: A Review and Appraisal." *Journal of Marriage and the Family* 55 (3), August, pp. 527–555.

POPENOE, DAVID (1993b). *Sociology.* Englewood Cliffs, NJ: Simon & Schuster.

*PORAT, FRIEDA (1988). *Self-Esteem: The Key to Success in Work and Love.* Saratoga, CA: R & E.

*POTTER, LINDA LYTLE (1979). *When Someone You Love Dies: A Book to Share Feelings.* Self-published (Available from Tom Potter, 1800 Memorial Drive, Lincoln, NE 68502).

*POWELL, JOHN (1969). *Why Am I Afraid to Tell You Who I Am*? Niles, IL: Argus.

*______ (1976). *Fully Human, Fully Alive.* Valencia, CA: Tabor.

PREVENTION (1991). "Smoking's New Wrinkle." October, p. 12.

PSYCHOLOGY TODAY (1993). "Shuttle Diplomacy." August, p. 15.

______ (1993). "The Path to Popularity." August, p. 17.

______ (1993). "The Power of the Personal." September/October, p. 22.

RADER, DOTSON (1993). "We Are All Responsible." *Parade Magazine*, April 11, pp. 4–7.

RANGE, LILLIAN M., ANDREA S. WALSTON, and PAMELA M. POLLARD (1992). "Helpful and Unhelpful Comments after Suicide, Homicide, Accident, or Natural Death." *Omega* 25 (1), 25–31.

RATHUS, SPENCER A. (1993). *Psychology.* Fort Worth: Harcourt Brace Jovanovich.

*RATHUS, SPENCER A., and SUSAN BOUGHN (1993). *AIDS What Every Student Needs to Know.* Fort Worth: Harcourt Brace Jovanovich.

*RAYMOND, DIANE (1992). "In the Best Interests of the Child: Thoughts on Homophobia and Parenting," in *Homophobia: How We All Pay the Price.* ed. Warren J. Blumenfeld. Boston: Beacon Press.

REDBOOK (1993). "Pick-Me-Ups for Parents." April, p. 30.

REECE, BARRY L., and RHONDA BRANDT. (1993). *Effective Human Relations in Organizations.* Boston: Houghton Mifflin.

REED, MARK D., and JASON Y. GREENWALD (1991). "Survivor Victim Status, Attachment, and Sudden Death Bereavement." *Suicide and Life Threatening Behavior* 21 (4), 385–401.

REMLEY, ANNE (1988). "From Obedience to Independence." *Psychology Today*, October, pp. 57–59.

RENO, RAYMOND R., and DAVID A. KENNY (1992). "Effects of Self-Consciousness and Social Anxiety on Self-Disclosure Among Unacquainted Individuals: An Application of the Social Relations Model." *Journal of Personality* 60, March, 79–94.

RENSHAW, PETER D., and PETER J. BROWN (1992). "Loneliness in Middle Childhood (Australia and United States)." *The Journal of Social Psychology* 132, August, 545–547.

*RESZ, ROBERT (1984). *Bits and Pieces.* Lincoln, NE: Southeast Community College Press.

REYNOLDS, CHARLES F. (1992). "Treatment of Depression in Special Populations." *Journal of Clinical Psychiatry* 53 (9), 45–53.

RICHARDS, LESLIE N., and CYNTHIA J. SCHMIEGE (1993). "Problems and Strengths of Single-Parent Families: Implications for Practice and Policy," *Family Relations* 42, July, 277–286.

RICHMOND, VIRGINIA P., JAMES C. MCCROSKEY, and STEVEN K. PAYNE (1991). *Nonverbal Behavior in Interpersonal Relations.* Englewood Cliffs, NJ: Prentice Hall.

RIMM, ERIC B., JOANN E. MANSON, MEIR J. STAMPFER, GRAHAM A. COLDITZ, WALTER C. WILLETT, BERNARD ROSNER, CHARLES H. HENNEKENS, and FRANK E. SPEIZER (1993). "Cigarette Smoking and the Risk of Diabetes in Women." *The American Journal of Public Health* 83 (2), 211–215.

RIORDAN, RICHARD J., and SANDRA K. SALTZER (1992). "Burnout Prevention Among Health Care Providers Working with the Terminally Ill: A Literature Review." *Omega* 25 (1), 17–24.

RIOS, DELIA M. (1993). "Now the Blame Falls Squarely on Men." *Lincoln Journal*, August 23, p. 6.

*ROBBINS, ANTHONY (1991). *Awaken the Giant Within.* New York: Simon & Schuster.

ROBERTSON, JOAN F., and RONALD L. SIMONS (1989). "Family Factors, Self-Esteem, and Adolescent Depression." *Journal of Marriage and the Family* 51 (1), 125–138.

RODIN, JUDITH (1986). "Aging and Health: Effects of the Sense of Control." *Science* 233, 1271–1276 .

RODIN, JUDITH, CARMI SCHOOLER, and K. WARNER SCHAIE (1990). *Self-Directedness: Cause and Effects Throughout the Life Course.* Hillsdale, NJ: Lawrence Erlbaum Associates.

ROESE, NEAL J., JAMES M. OLSON, and MARIANNE N. BORENSTEIN (1992). "Same-Sex Touching Behavior: The Moderating Role of Homophobic Attitudes." *Journal of Nonverbal Behavior* 16, 249–259.

*ROGERS, CARL (1961). *On Becoming a Person.* Boston: Houghton Mifflin.

*______ (1972). *On Becoming Partners: Marriage and Its Alternatives.* New York: Delacorte Press.

______ (1978). "The Necessary and Sufficient Conditions of Therapeutic Personality Change," in *Personality Readings in Theory and Research*, ed. E. A. Southwell and M. Merbaum. Monterey, CA: Brooks/Cole.

*______ (1980). *A Way of Being.* Boston: Houghton Mifflin.

ROKACH, AMI (1990). "Surviving and Coping with Loneliness." *Journal of Psychology* 124, January, 39–54.

ROSELLINI, LYNN (1992). "Sexual Desire." *U.S. News & World Report*, July 6, pp. 61–66.

ROSENBAUM, M. E. (1986). "The Repulsion Hypothesis: On the Nondevelopment of Relationships." *Journal of Personality and Social Psychology* 51, 1156–1166.

*ROSENBERG, ELLEN (1983). *Growing Up Feeling Good.* New York: Beaufort Books.

ROSS, CATHERINE E., and BARBARA F. RESKIN (1992). "Education, Control at Work, and Job Satisfaction." *Social Science Research* 21, June, 134–148.

ROTENBERG, KEN J., and NANCY CHASE (1992). "Development of the Reciprocity of Self-Disclosure." *The Journal of Genetic Psychology* 153, March, 75–86.

ROTHERAM, MARY JANE (1987). "Children's Social and Academic Competence." *Journal of Educational Research* 80 (4), 206–211.

RUBIN, LILLIAN B. (1985). *Just Friends: The Role of Friendship in Our Lives.* New York: Harper & Row.

*RUBIN, THEODORE I. (1969). *The Angry Book.* New York: Macmillan.

______ (1975). *Compassion and Self-hate: An Alternative to Despair.* New York: Ballantine.

______ (1983). *One to One: Understanding Personal Relationships.* New York: Pinnacle.

RUBIN, ZICK (1970). "Measurement of Romantic Love." *Journal of Personality and Social Psychology* 16, 265–273.

______ (1973). *Liking and Loving.* New York: Holt, Rinehart and Winston.

RUNCK, B. (1980). *Biofeedback Issues in Treatment Assessment.* Rockville, MD: National Institutes of Health.

RUSSELL, MARY N., and ROSANNE FARNDEN LYSTER (1992). "Marriage Preparation: Factors Associated with Consumer Satisfaction." *Family Relations* 41, October, 446–451.

RUSSELL, P. A., and C. D. GRAY (1992). "Prejudice Against a Progay Man in an Everyday Situation: A Scenario Study." *Journal of Applied Social Psychology* 22, November, 1676–1687.

*RYAN, REGINA SARA, and JOHN W. TRAVIS (1991). *Wellness: Small Changes You Can Use to Make a Big Difference.* Berkeley, CA: Ten Speed Press.

RYCHTARIK, ROBERT G., DONALD M. PRUE, and STEPHEN R. RAPP (1992). "Self-efficacy, Aftercare and Relapse in a Treatment Program for Alcoholics." *Journal of Studies on Alcohol* 53, September, 435–440.

SABLE, PAT (1991). "Attachment, Loss of Spouse, and Grief in Elderly Adults." *Omega: Journal of Death and Dying* 23 (2), 129–142.

SALOVEY, PETER, and ALEXANDER J. ROTHMAN (1991). *The Psychology of Jealousy and Envy*, ed. Peter Salovey. New York: The Guilford Press.

SALT, ROBERT E. (1991). "Affectionate Touch Between Fathers and Preadolescent Sons." *Journal of Marriage and the Family* 53 (3), 545–554.

*SANDERS, CATHERINE M. (1992). *Surviving Grief and Learning to Live Again.* New York: John Wiley & Sons.

*SATIR, VIRGINIA (1972). *Peoplemaking.* Palo Alto, CA: Science and Behavior Books.

*______ (1976). *Making Contact.* Millbrae, CA: Celestial Arts.

*______ (1978). *Your Many Faces.* Millbrae, CA: Celestial Arts.

______ (1983). *Conjoint Family Therapy.* Palo Alto, CA: Science and Behavior Books.

*______ (1988). *The New Peoplemaking.* Mountain View, CA: Science and Behavior Books.

SCHACHTER, SHERRY (1992). "Adolescent Experiences with the Death of a Peer." *Omega: Journal of Death and Dying* 24 (1), 1–11.

*SCHAEFFER, BRENDA (1987). *Is It Love or Addiction?* New York: Hazelden.

SCHEFLEN, ALBERT E. (1972). *Body Language and Social Order.* Englewood Cliffs, NJ: Prentice Hall.

SCHEUBLE, LAURIE, and DAVID R. JOHNSON (1993). "Marital Name Change: Plans and Attitudes of College Students." *Journal of Marriage and the Family* 55, August, 747–754.

SCHIEDEL, DON G., and JAMES E. MARCIA, (1985). "Ego Identity, Intimacy, Sex Role Orientation, and Gender." *Developmental Psychology* 21 (1), 149–160.

SCHILL, THOMAS, JANE BEYLER, JOANN MORALES, and BONNIE EKSTROM (1991). "Self-Defeating Personality and Perceptions of Family Environment." *Psychological Reports* 69, December, 744–746.

*SCHMIDT, JERRY A. (1976). *Help Yourself: A Guide to Self-Change*. Champaign, IL: Research Press.

SCHOEN, ROBERT (1992). "First Unions and the Stability of First Marriages." *Journal of Marriage and the Family* 54, May, 281–284.

SCHOLES, DELIA, JANET R. DALING, and ANDY S. STERGACHIS (1992). "Current Cigarette Smoking and Risk of Acute Pelvic Inflammatory Disease." *American Journal of Public Health* 82, October, 1352–1355.

SCHOTT, RICHARD L. (1992). "Abraham Maslow, Humanistic Psychology, and Organization Leadership: A Jungian Perspective." *Journal of Humanistic Psychology* 32 (1), 106–120.

SCHULTZ, NOEL C., CYNTHIA L. SCHULTZ, and DAVID H. OLSON (1991). "Couple Strengths and Stressors in Complex and Simple Stepfamilies in Australia." *Journal of Marriage and the Family* 53, August, 555–564.

SCHULZ, BILL (1988). "Finding Time." *The World*, March/April pp. 2–3.

SCHWARTZ, GIL (1993). "Lighten Up!" *Self*, July, pp. 62–64.

SCHWARTZ, MARY ANN, and BARBARA MARLIENE SCOTT (1994). *Marriages and Families: Diversity and Change*. Englewood Cliffs, NJ: Prentice Hall.

*SCOTT, GINI GRAHAM (1990). *Resolving Conflict with Others and Within Yourself*. Oakland, CA: New Harbinger Publications.

SEALOCK, RICK (1993). "Menace II Society." *Psychology Today*, September/October, p. 10.

SECCOMBE, KAREN (1991). "Assessing the Costs and Benefits of Children: Gender Comparisons Among Childfree Husbands and Wives." *Journal of Marriage and the Family* 53, February, 191–202.

SEEFELDT, RICHARD, and MARK A. LYON, (1992). "Personality Characteristics of Adult Children of Alcoholics." *Journal of Counseling and Development* 70 (5), 588–593.

*SELIGMAN, MARTIN E. P. (1990). *Learned Optimism: How to Change Your Mind and Your Life*. New York: Pocket Books.

SELYE, HANS (1974). *Stress without Distress*. Philadelphia: Lippincott.

______ (1978). "On the Real Benefits of Eustress" (as interviewed by Laurence Charry), *Psychology Today*, March, pp. 60–63.

SHAFFER, DAVID R., LINDA J. PEGALIS, and DAVID P. CORNELL (1992). "Gender and Self-Disclosure Revisited: Personal and Contextual Variations in Self-Disclosure to Same-Sex Acquaintances." *The Journal of Social Psychology* 132, June, 307–315.

SHARPSTEEN, DON J. (1991). *The Psychology of Jealousy and Envy*, ed. Peter Salovey. New York: The Guilford Press.

SHAVER, PHILLIP, JUDITH SCHWARTZ, DONALD KIRSON, and CARY O'CONNOR, (1987). "Emotion Knowledge: Further Exploration of a Prototype Approach." *Journal of Personality and Social Psychology* 52 (6), 1061–1086.

SHAW, J. S. (1982). "Psychological Androgyny and Stressful Life Events." *Journal of Personality and Social Psychology* 43, 145–153.

SHELDON, AMY (1990). " 'Kings Are Royaler Than Queens': Language and Socialization." *Young Children* 45 (2), 4–9.

SHERMAN, RUTH (1981). "Typology and Problems in Intimate Relationships." *Research in Psychological Type*, 4.

*SIEGEL, BERNIE S. (1986). *Love, Medicine, and Miracles*. New York: Harper & Row.

SIMMONS, CHRISTINA M., DONALD W. KLOPF, and MYUNG-SEOK PARK (1991). "Loneliness Among Korean and American University Students." *Psychological Reports* 68, June, 754.

SIMON, SIDNEY B., LELAND W. HOWE, and HOWARD KIRSCHENBAUM (1991). *Values Clarification: A Handbook of Practical Strategies for Teachers & Students*. New York: Warner Books Incorporated.

SIMONS, RONALD L., JAY BEAMAN, RAND D. CONGER, and WEI CHAO (1992). "Gender Differences in the Intergenerational Transmission of Parenting Beliefs." *Journal of Marriage and the Family* 54, November, 823–836.

SIMONS, RONALD L., CHRISTINE JOHNSON, JAY BEAMAN, and RAND D. CONGER (1993). "Explaining Women's Double Jeopardy: Factors that Mediate the Association Between Harsh Treatment as a Child and Violence by a Husband." *Journal of Marriage and the Family* 55, August, 713–723.

*SIMONTON, O. CARL, STEPHANIE MATTHEWS-SIMONTON, and JAMES L. CREIGHTON (1978). *Getting Well Again*. New York: Bantam.

*SIMONTON, STEPHANIE MATTHEWS (1984). *The Healing Family*. New York: Bantam.

SIMS, DARCIE (1985). "The Grief Process." *The Compassionate Friends Newsletter* 8 (2), 1, 6.

SITKIN, SIM B., and ROBERT J. BIES (1993). "Social Accounts in Conflict Situations: Using Explanations to Manage Conflict." *Human Relations* 46, March, 349–370.

SKINNER, B. F. (1953). *Science and Human Behavior.* New York: Macmillan.

______ (1987). *Upon Further Reflection*. Englewood Cliffs, NJ: Prentice Hall.

SMITH, ELEANOR (1988). "Fighting Cancerous Feelings." *Psychology Today*, May, pp. 22–23.

______ (1989a). "AIDS and Personality." *Psychology Today*, March, p. 74.

______ (1989b). "The New Moral Classroom." *Psychology Today*, May, pp. 32–36.

*SMITH, MANUAL (1985). *When I Say No, I Feel Guilty.* Toronto: Bantam.

SMITH, RANDY J., DIANE B. ARNKOFF, and THOMAS L. WRIGHT (1990). "Test Anxiety and Academic Competence: A Comparison of Alternative Models." *Journal of Counseling Psychology* 37, July, 313–321.

*SMITH, SALLY (1991). *Succeeding Against the Odds*. Los Angeles: Jeremy P. Tarcher, Inc.

*SMITH, SHAUNA L. (1991). *Making Peace With Your Adult Children*. New York: Plenum Press.

SMITH, SUSAN (1992). "Refusing Unreasonable Requests." *Communications in Nursing*. St. Louis: Mosby Year Book.

SMITH, THOMAS EWIN (1990). "Parental Separation and the Academic Self-Concepts of Adolescents: An Effort to Solve the Puzzle of Separation Effects." *Journal of Marriage and the Family* 52, February, 107–118.

*SMOLIN, ANN, and JOHN GUINAN (1993). *Healing After the Suicide of a Loved One*. New York: Simon & Schuster.

SNARY, J., and PLECK, J. H. (Aug., 1988). "Fathers' Participation in Childrearing: Consequences for Fathers' Midlife Outcomes." Paper presented at 96th Annual American Psychological Association. Div. 20, Atlanta, Ga.).

*SOLOMON, ROBERT C. (1988). *Love: Reinventing Romance for Our Times*. New York: Simon & Schuster.

SPADE, JOAN Z. (1991). "Occupational Structure and Men's and Women's Parental Values." *Journal of Family Issues* 12, September, 343–360.

SPANIER, GRAHAM B. (1989). "Bequeathing Family Continuity." *Journal of Marriage and the Family* 51 (1), 3–13.

*SPEZZANO, CHARLES (1992). *What to Do Between Birth and Death: The Art of Growing Up*. New York: William Morrow and Company.

SPRECHER, S. (1987). "The Effects of Self-Disclosure Given and Received on Affection for an Intimate Partner and Stability of the Relationship." *Journal of Social and Personal Relationships* 4, 115–127.

STACY, ALAN W., STEVE SUSSMAN, and CLYDE W. DENT (1992). "Moderators of Peer Social Influence in Adolescent Smoking." *Personality and Social Psychology Bulletin* 18, April, 163–172.

*STEARNS, ANN KAISER (1984). *Living Through Personal Crisis.* Chicago: Thomas More Press.

STEEL, JENNIFER L. (1991). "Interpersonal Correlates of Trust and Self-Disclosure." *Psychological Reports* 68, June, 1319–1320.

*STEINBERG, LAURENCE, and ANN LEVINE (1990). *You and Your Adolescent.* New York: Harper Collins.

*STEINEM, GLORIA (1993). *Revolution From Within: A Book of Self-Esteem.* Boston: Little, Brown.

STEINER, CLAUDE (1974). *Scripts People Live.* New York: Bantam.

*STERNBERG ROBERT J. (1987). *The Triangle of Love: Intimacy, Passion, Commitment.* New York: Basic Books.

*STERNBERG, ROBERT, with CATHERINE WHITNEY (1991). *Love the Way You Want It.* New York: Bantam Books.

STEWART, JONATHAN W., PATRICK J. MCGRATH, and FREDERIC M. QUITKIN (1992). "Can Mildly Depressed Outpatients with Atypical Depression Benefit from Antidepressants?" *The American Journal of Psychiatry* 149, May, 615–619.

STODDARD, MARTHA (1993). "Talk Line Gives Caring Ear to Local Gay, Lesbian Youth." *Lincoln Journal Star*, January 23, p. 10.

STONE, ARTHUR A., DONALD S. COX, HEIDDIS VALDIMARSDOTTIR, LINA JANDORF, and JOHN M. NEALE (1987). "Evidence That Secretory IgA Antibody Is Associated With Daily Mood." *Journal of Personality and Social Psychology* 52 (5), 988–993,

*STONE, HAL, and SIDRA STONE (1993). *Embracing Your Inner Critic.* New York: HarperCollins.

STRACHAN, CATHERINE E., and DONALD G. DUTTON (1992). "The Role of Power and Gender in Anger Responses to Sexual Jealousy." *Journal of Applied Social Psychology* 22, November 16, 1721–1740.

*STRASSER, STEPHEN, and JOHN SENA (1992). *Work Is Not a Four Letter Word.* Homewood, IL: Business One.

STRAUS, MURRAY A., and STEPHEN SWEET (1992). "Verbal/Symbolic Aggression in Couples: Incidence Rates and Relationships to Personal Characteristics." *Journal of Marriage and the Family* 54, May, 346–357.

STRAUSS, RONALD P., INGE B. CORLESS, and JAMES W. LUCKEY (1992). "Cognitive and Attitudinal Impacts of a University AIDS Course: Interdisciplinary Education as a Public Health Intervention." *American Journal of Public Health* 82, April, 569–572.

STROBER, MICHAEL, ROBERTA FREEMAN, JOANNE RIGALI, SUSAN SCHMIDT, and ROBERT DIAMOND (1992). "The Pharmacotherapy of Depressive Illness in Adolescence: II. Effects of Lithium Augmentation in Nonresponders to Imipramine." *Journal of the American Academy of Child and Adolescent Psychiatry* 31 (1), 16–20.

STROEBE, MARGARET, and WOLFGANG STROEBE (1991). "Does 'Grief Work' Work?" *Journal of Consulting and Clinical Psychology* 59, June, 479–482.

*STUART, RICHARD, and BARBARA JACOBSON. (1985). *Second Marriage.* New York: W. W. Norton & Co.

SWARTZ, MIMI (1993). "You Are Happy! You Just Don't Know It." *Self*, October, pp. 140–143.

SWEET, JAMES A., and LARRY L. BUMPASS (1987). *American Families and Households.* New York: Russell Sage Foundation.

SZINOVACZ, MAXIMILIANE, and CHRISTINE WASHO (1992). "Gender Differences in Exposure to Life Events and Adaptation to Retirement." *Journals of Gerontology* 47, July, 191–196.

*TANNEN, DEBORAH (1986). *That's Not What I Meant! How Conversational Style Makes or Breaks Your Relations with Others.* New York: William Morrow and Company.

*______ (1990). *You Just Don't Understand: Women and Men in Conversation.* New York: Ballantine Books.

TAVRIS, CAROL (1989). "Don't Act Your Age!" *American Health*, July/August, pp. 50–52, 54, 56, 58.

*______ (1992). *The Mismeasure of Woman.* New York: Simon & Schuster.

TELLEGEN, A., D. T. LYKKEN, T. J. BOUCHARD, K. J. WILCOX, and N. L. SEGAL (1988). "Personality Similarity in Twins Reared Apart and Together." *Journal of Personality and Social Psychology* 54, 1031–1039.

TETI, DOUGLAS M., and MICHAEL E. LAMB (1989). "Socioeconomic and Marital Outcomes of Adolescent Marriage, Adolescent Childbirth, and Their Co-occurrence." *Journal of Marriage and the Family* 51 (1), 203–212.

THAYER, STEPHEN (1988a). "Close Encounters." *Psychology Today*, March, pp. 30–36.

______ (1988b). "The Language of Touch," in *Eye to Eye: How People Interact.* ed. Peter Marsh. Topsfield, MA: Salem House.

THOMAS, VOLKER, and DAVID H. OLSON (1993). "Problem Families and the Circumplex Model: Observational Assessment Using the Clinical Rating Scale (CRS)." *Journal of Marital and Family Therapy* 19, April, 159–175.

THOMPSON, KARIN E., and LILLIAN M. RANGE (1993). "Bereavement Following Suicide and Other Deaths: Why Support Attempts Fail." *Omega* 26 (1), 61–70.

THOMPSON, RONALD W., CRYSTAL R. GROW, PENNEY R. RUMA, DANIEL L. DALY, and RAYMOND V. BURKE (1993). "Evaluation of a Practical Parenting Program with Middle and Low Income Families." *Family Relations* 42, 21–25.

THOMSON, ELIZABETH, and UGO COLELLA (1992). "Cohabitation and Marital Stability: Quality or Commitment?" *Journal of Marriage and the Family* 54, May, 259–267.

Time (1994). "Health Report." July 18, p. 14.

______ (1993a). "Index of Leading Cultural Indicators." March 29, p. 18.

______ (1993b). "Health Report." August 30, p. 16.

______ (1993c). "Health Report." September 13, p. 17.

______ (1993d). "At the New FBI, the F Is for Family." September 20, p. 20.

______ (1982). " 'We're Going Down, Larry.' " January 15, p. 21.

TJOSVOLD, DEAN, VALERIE DANN, and CHOY WONG (1992). "Managing Conflict Between Departments to Serve Customers." *Human Relations* 45, October, 1035–1054.

TOBIAS, ANDREW (1992). "The Dividends for Quitters." *Time*, October 12, p. 76.

TOUFEXIS, ANASTASIS (1989). "Shortcut to the Rambo Look." *Time*, January 30, p. 78.

TRAFFORD, ABIGAIL (1993). "The New Marriage." *Self*, July, pp. 107–109, 128.

TRUSSELL, J., and K. V. RAO (1989). "Premarital Cohabitation and Marital Stability: A Reassessment of the Canadian Evidence." *Journal of Marriage and the Family* 51, 535–544.

*TUBESING, DONALD A. (1981). *Kicking Your Stress Habits: A Do-It-Yourself Guide for Coping With Stress.* New York: New American Library.

TUCKER IRVING F. (1991). "Predicting Scores on the Rathus Assertiveness Schedule from Myers-Briggs Type Indicator Categories." *Psychological Reports*, 69, October, 571–576.

TUFTS UNIVERSITY DIET AND NUTRITION LETTER (1992). "A Drug Problem Often Overlooked." January, Vol. 9, No. 11, p. 9.

TURRISI, ROBERT, and JAMES JACCARD (1991). "Judgment Processes Relevant to Drunk Driving." *Journal of Applied Social Psychology* 21, January 16, 89–118.

TYLER, AUBIN (1988). "The Tippler's Blues." *Psychology Today*, March, pp. 18–19.

UNITED STATES DEPARTMENT OF HEALTH AND HUMAN SERVICES (1993). "Depression is a Treatable Illness." April, Rockville, MD.

USDANSKY, MARGARET (1992). "1990s Wedding Bell Blues." *USA Today*, December 9, p. 12a.

*VAIL, ELAINE (1982). *A Personal Guide to Living with Loss.* New York: John Wiley.

VANNOY, DANA, and WILLIAM W. PHILLIBER (1992). "Wife's Employment and Quality of Marriage." *Journal of Marriage and the Family* 54, May, 387–398.

VAN OOSTING, JAMES (1992). *Practicing Business Communication in the Workplace.* Boston: Houghton Mifflin Company.

VAN ROOSMALEN, ERICA H., and SUSAN A. MCDANIEL (1992). "Adolescent Smoking Intentions: Gender Differences in Peer Context." *Adolescence* 27 (105), 87–106.

VARGAS, MARJORIE FINK (1986). *Louder Than Words: An Introduction to Nonverbal Communication.* Ames: Iowa State University Press.

VASEY, MICHAEL W., and THOMAS D. BORKOVEC (1992). "A Catastrophizing Assessment of Worrisome Thoughts." *Cognitive Therapy and Research* 16 (5), 505–520.

VICKIO, CRAIG J., JOHN C. CAVANAUGH, and THOMAS W. ATTIG (1990). "Perceptions of Grief Among University Students." *Death Studies* 14 (3), 231–240.

VIORST, JUDITH (1986). *Necessary Losses.* New York: Ballantine.

*VIRTUE, DOREEN (1988). *My Kids Don't Live with Me Anymore.* Minneapolis: CompCare Publishers.

*VISHER, EMILY, and JOHN VISHER (1979). *Stepfamilies: Myths and Realities.* Secaucus, NJ: Citadel.

*______ (1982). *How to Win as a Stepfamily.* Chicago: Contemporary Books.

*______ (1988). *Old Loyalties, New Ties.* New York: Brunner/Mazel.

VON KREISLER, KRISTIN (1993). "Sexual Healing." *Redbook*, April, pp. 86, 126, 128–129.

*VON OECH, ROGER (1983). *A Whack on the Side of the Head: How to Unleash Your Mind for Innovation.* New York: Warner.

*______ (1986). *A Kick in the Seat of the Pants.* New York: Harper & Row.

WAGNER, KATHARINE G., and LAWRENCE G. CALHOUN (1992). "Perceptions of Social Support by Suicide Survivors and Their Social Networks." *Omega: Journal of Death and Dying* 24 (1), 61–73.

WALDROP, JUDITH (1993). "Under the Sun." *American Demographics*, July, p. 4.

WALKER, LENORE E. (1991). "Post-Traumatic Stress Disorder in Women: Diagnosis and Treatment of Battered Woman Syndrome." *Psychotherapy* 28 (1), 21–29.

*WALKER, VELMA, and LYNN BROKAW. (1992). *Becoming Aware: A Human Relations Handbook.* Dubuque, IA: Kendall/Hunt .

WALL, MARK D., TRUDY KLECKNER, JOHN H. AMENDT, and R. DUREE BRYANT (1989). "Therapeutic Compliments: Setting the Stage for Successful Therapy." *Journal of Marital and Family Therapy* 15, April, 159–167.

WALLERSTEIN, JUDITH S., and SANDRA BLAKESLEE (1989). *Second Chances: Men, Women, and Children a Decade after Divorce.* New York: Ticknor & Fields.

WALLERSTEIN, JUDITH S., and JOAN BERLIN KELLY (1980). *Surviving the Breakup: How Children and Parents Cope With Divorce.* New York: Basic Books.

WALLIS, CLAUDIA (1983). "Stress: Can We Cope?" *Time*, June 6, pp. 48–54.

WALLIS, CLAUDIA, and JAMES WILLWERTH (1992). "Schizophrenia: A New Drug Brings Patients Back to Life." *Time*, July 6, p. 52–57.

WARD, BETTY (1989). "Grief Is an Experience." *Life Lines Magazine*, March/April, p. 17.

WEBSTER-STRATTON, CAROLYN (1990). "Stress: A Potential Disruption of Parent Perceptions and Family Interactions (Part of a Special Issue on: The Stresses of Parenting)." *Journal of Clinical Child Psychology* 19, December, 302–312 .

*WEGSCHEIDER-CRUSE, SHARON. (1985). *Choice-making.* Pompano Beach, FL: Health Communications.

*______ (1988). *Coupleship: How to Have a Relationship.* Deerfield Beach, FL: Health Communications.

*WEINER-DAVIS, MICHELE (1992). *Divorce Busting: A Revolutionary and Rapid Program for Staying Together.* New York: Simon & Schuster.

WELLBORN, STANLEY (1987). "How Genes Shape Personality." *U.S. News and World Report*, April 13, pp. 58–62.

WESTOFF, LESLIE A. (1977). *The Second Time Around.* New York: Viking.

WHITBOURNE, SUSAN KRAUSS, MICHAEL K. ZUSCHLAG, LISA B. ELLIOT, and ALAN S. WADERMAN (1992). "Psychosocial Development in Adulthood: A 22-Year Sequential Study." *Journal of Personality and Social Psychology* 63, August, 260–271.

WHITE, BURTON (1975). *The First Three Years of Life.* Englewood Cliffs, NJ: Prentice Hall.

WHITE, GREGORY L. (1991). in *The Psychology of Jealousy and Envy*, ed. Peter Salovey. New York: The Guilford Press.

*WHITFIELD, CHARLES L. (1987). *Healing the Child Within.* Deerfield Beach, FL: Health Communications.

*WHITLOCK, KATHERINE (1989). *Bridges of Respect: Creating Support for Lesbian and Gay Youth.* Philadelphia: American Friends Service Committee.

*WHOLEY, DENNIS (1988). *Becoming Your Own Parent.* New York: Doubleday.

WIEDENFELD, SUE A., ANN O'LEARY, and ALBERT BANDURA (1990). "Impact of Perceived Self-efficacy in Coping with Stressors on Components of the Immune System." *Journal of Personality and Social Psychology* 59, November, 1082–1094.

WIGAND, PATTIE (1988). "Monday Morning Miracle," as told to Philip Yancy, *Family Circle*, February 23, p. 26.

WILLIAMS, ROBERT L., and JAMES D. LONG (1983). *Toward a Self-Managed Life Style.* Boston: Houghton Mifflin.

*WILLIAMS, WARWICK (1988). *Rekindling Desire: Bringing Your Sexual Relationship Back to Life.* Oakland, CA: New Harbinger.

WILLIS, FRANK N., and LEON F. BRIGGS (1992). "Relationship and Touch in Public Settings." *Journal of Nonverbal Behavior* 16, Spring, 55–63.

WITT, ALAN L., and LENDELL G. NYE (1992). "Gender and the Relationship Between Perceived Fairness of Pay or Promotion and Job Satisfaction." *Journal of Applied Psychology* 77, December, 910–917.

WOLVIN, ANDRES, and CAROLYN GWYNN COAKLEY (1988). *Listening.* Dubuque, IA: William C. Brown.

WOOD, ROBERT E., and EDWIN A. LOCKE (1987). "The Relation of Self-Efficacy and Grade Goals to Academic Performance." *Educational and Psychological Measures* 47 (4), 1013–1024.

*WOODWARD, JOHN C. (1988). *The Solitude of Loneliness.* Lexington, MA: Heath.

WOOLLAMS, STAN, and MICHAEL BROWN (1979). *TA: The Total Handbook of Transactional Analysis.* Englewood Cliffs, NJ: Prentice Hall.

WORCHEL, STEPHEN and WAYNE SHEBILSKE (1989). *Psychology: Principles and Application.* Englewood Cliffs, NJ: Prentice Hall.

WORKMAN, MATHEW, and JOHN BEER (1989). "Self-Esteem, Depression, and Alcohol Dependency Among High School Students." *Psychological Reports* 65, October, 451–455.

WRIGHT, DEBORAH M., and P. PAUL HEPPNER (1991). "Coping Among Nonclinical College-Age Children of Alcoholics. " *Journal of Counseling Psychology* 38 (4), 465–472.

WYATT, GAIL ELIZABETH, and SANDRA LYONS-ROWE (1990). "African American Women's Sexual Satisfaction as a Dimension of Their Sex Roles." *Sex Roles* 22, April, 509–524.

WYATT, GARY (1990). "Risk-taking and Risk-avoiding Behavior: The Impact of Some Dispositional and Situational Variables." *The Journal of Psychology* 124, July, 437–447.

WYLIE, LINDA, and JAMES FOREST (1992). "Religious Fundamentalism, Right-Wing Authoritarianism and Prejudice." *Psychological Reports* 71, December, 1291–1298.

YESMONT, GEORGIA A. (1992). "The Relationship of Assertiveness to College Students' Safer Sex Behaviors." *Adolescence* 27, Summer, 253–272.

YOUNG, GEORGE H., and SAMUEL GERSON (1991). "New Psychoanalytic Perspectives on Masochism and Spouse Abuse." *Psychotherpay* 28 (1), 30–38.

YPEREN, NICO, W. VAN, BRAM P. BUUNK, and WILMAR B. SCHAUFELI (1992). "Communal Orientation and the Burnout Syndrome Among Nurses." *Journal of Applied Social Psychology* 22, February, 173–189.

ZAJONC, ROBERT (1990). "The Face as Window and Machine for the Emotions." *LSA Magazine* (University of Michigan), 14 (1). Fall, pp. 17–21.

*ZIMBARDO, PHILIP G. (1977). *Shyness: What It Is, What to Do About It.* New York: Jove/HBJ.

*ZOIS, CHRIST (1992). *Think Like a Shrink: Solve Your Problems Yourself With Short-Term Therapy Techniques.* New York: Warner Books.

REFLECTIONS AND APPLICATIONS

This section of the book is intended to get you involved in looking at yourself and your relationships. We gain more by thinking and writing than just by reading. Be honest and strive for a deeper understanding or your life—and enjoy!

SELF-APPRAISAL

Before you read the book and complete the other activities in this section, use the following scale and rate yourself honestly in these areas. Each reflects the potential benefits of learning from this book and continuing to improve your human relations skills.

5 = Perfect (couldn't improve)
4 = Very good (almost to the desired level)
3 = Average (could be improved)
2 = Below average (could be much better)
1 = Poor (needs a great deal of improvement)

1. _______ How well do I really know and understand myself?
2. _______ How much regard do I have for myself?
3. _______ What do I think about my ability to change?
4. _______ How effectively do I manage stress?
5. _______ How well do I cope with crises?
6. _______ How would I rate my personal relationships (friendships, significant other)?
7. _______ How would I rate my family relationships?
8. _______ How would I rate my work or school relationships?
9. _______ How well do I handle my emotions?
10. _______ How happy am I?

Total your scores and divide by 10 to get an average score. If you have less than a 5.0 average, this book will help you. If you scored a 5.0 (perfect), you can benefit from learning what this book has to teach about perfectionism.

Honestly reflect on what you hope to gain from this book, then write your ideas below. Be specific. After you have read the book, read this page to see what you have accomplished.

Chapter 1

SELF-CONCEPT INVENTORY

Complete the inventory about yourself (2 sides) and have at least two other people (preferably a male and a female) fill out similar inventories *about you*. One 2-sided inventory for another person is provided from which you can make copies.

Descriptors: Describe yourself in the following four areas of self using at least four words, phrases, or sentences for each:

Physical (appearance, condition of body, and health):

Mental (abilities, preferred ways of learning, attitude or mental outlook):

Emotional (usual feelings or typical ones in certain situations, mood):

Social (statuses and roles, behaviors around others, preferences of social activities):

If I were to achieve my ideal self, would these descriptors be different, and, if so, in what ways? Use other paper, if needed.

Physical:

Mental:

Emotional:

Social:

Complete the following sentences:

Some relationships that are important to me are

Two of my skills or talents are

Two characteristics or behaviors I appreciate in myself are

One thing I would like to improve about myself is

I am proud of myself for

A goal I have for myself is

What do I value? Name at least four.

For the next 3 questions, use other paper if necessary.

During an average weekday, specifically how do I spend my time?

What would I do with one million tax-free dollars?

If I were told that I had only 1 to 3 months to live, what would I do during that time?

The X on the continuum below shows how I assess my attitude.

Very negative Negative Average Positive Very positive

How do I rate my current level of self-esteem?

1 = very low 2 = low 3 = average 4 = high 5 = very high

What am I doing or what will I do to build or strengthen a positive attitude and self-esteem?

Identify one belief or thought about self:

Past behavior(s) that demonstrated this belief:

If this self-fulfilling prophecy is negative, how can you change it?

I have self-efficacy about (list 3):

SELF-CONCEPT INVENTORY

Please answer the following questions about ______________________________.

My relationship to this person is as a(an) ______________________________.

Descriptors: Describe this person in the following four areas of self using at least four words, phrases, or sentences for each.

Physical (appearance, condition of body, and health):

Mental (abilities, preferred ways of learning, attitude or mental outlook):

Emotional (usual feelings or typical ones in certain situations, mood):

Social (statuses and roles, behaviors around others, preferences or social activities):

If this person were to achieve his or her ideal self, would these descriptors be different, and, if so, in what ways?

Physical:

Mental:

Emotional:

Social:

Complete the following sentences:

Some relationships that are important to this person are

Two of this person's skills or talents are

Two characteristics or behaviors this person appreciates about him or herself are

One thing about self this person would like to improve is

One thing about self this person is proud of is

One of this person's goals is

What does this person value? Name at least four.

For the next 3 questions, use other paper if necessary.

During an average weekday, specifically how does this person spend her or his time?

What would this person do with a million tax-free dollars?

If this person had only 1 to 3 months to live, what would he or she do during that time?

Thinking of attitude as a broad outlook on life, place an X on the continuum to describe this person.

Very negative | Negative | Average | Positive | Very positive

Thinking of self-esteem as a value placed on self or genuine regard for who one is, what is this person's current level of self-esteem?

1 = very low 2 = low 3 = average 4 = high 5 = very high

THANK YOU VERY MUCH FOR YOUR HELP!

Chapter 2

PERSONALITY: THE CORE OF SELF

- Drawing from mental, emotional, and social descriptors of self as well as common behaviors, five words or more that describe your personality are:

- In what ways, if any, is your personality similar to family members? Identify the person and the characteristic. If your personality is not at all like anyone else in your family, speculate or explain why it isn't. Use other paper if necessary.

- Disregarding chronological age, in which of Erikson's stages do you think you are and why?

- What, if any, difficulties did you encounter in any of the stages?

Give an example of when you behaved from your:

(1) "parent"
(2) "child"
(3) "adult"

- Monitor both positive and negative strokes given and received for a few days. Give examples of any or all types. Describe briefly what you learned from doing this.

- Circle what you think (or know) your four MBTI preferences to be. For each preference describe some behaviors that support each one. If you have none, explain why you think you tend to be more the opposite preference.

Extraversion	Introversion
Sensing	Intuition
Thinking	Feeling
Judgment	Perception

- Identify a personality trait about yourself you especially like and one that is related to one of the preferences. Describe how it helps you and for what reason(s) you like it.

- Do the same with a personality trait about yourself you would like to change. Be sure to relate it to a preference.

- In which of the following areas would your life have been or will be different if you had been born the opposite sex? Put a check in the first blank if you believe it would have been different.

_______	Career choice	_______	Education activities	_______	Sports/other
_______	Household tasks	_______	Marriage and child raising	_______	Self-esteem
_______	Self-efficacy	_______	Independence	_______	Assertiveness
		_______	Emotions		

Pick one category you checked and explain how you think it would have been different.

Answer the following as Yes, No, or Unknown (neither yes nor no).

1. _______ I usually express my anger.
2. _______ I am generally self-sufficient and independent.
3. _______ I am a caring person.
4. _______ I often demonstrate affection.
5. _______ I am usually assertive rather than passive or aggressive.
6. _______ I want to achieve success.
7. _______ I usually show fear when I experience it.
8. _______ I let others know I love them.
9. _______ I laugh *and* cry when appropriate.
10. _______ I am capable in several areas.
11. _______ I can solve problems and take care of others.
12. _______ I can support myself.

"Yes" answers indicate an androgynous personality.

- Either list examples of recent assertive behavior or identify situations in which assertive behavior on your part would have been advantageous.

Chapter 3

HAPPINESS—IT'S UP TO ME!

On a scale of 1 to 5 (1 = very unhappy, 2 = unhappy, 3 = moderately happy, 4 = happy, 5 = very happy), currently I rate myself: _______

In order to be satisfied, I need

These needs are met by

An example of a time when life seemed especially wonderful was

An example of a time when life seemed extremely difficult was

From the rest of your life (80% for most people), describe a time when you created your own reality by making the situation happier or unhappier.

Decide to create your own happiness by:

Initiating Pleasure and "Smelling Roses"

In the first column, write a pleasurable activity and/or ways of "smelling roses" in your life. Then fill in the other columns. Continue on a sheet of paper as this can be quite an eye-opening exercise.

PLEASURE	HOW OFTEN DO I DO?	WHEN DID I LAST DO?

The last time I enjoyed the "present" or "now" was

Select yourself, someone you know, or make up an example of:

"futurizing"

"pasturizing"

Giving to Others

One way I "give to life" is

A nourishing, rewarding relationship I have is with

The last time I let her or him know how much I value this relationship was when I

Thinking and Acting Positively

Write an excuse you have either made or could have made. Then, reword it to reflect the truth.

Catch yourself using "can't/couldn't" when not literally true. Write how you used it and what is actually true. Do the same for "should/shouldn't" (or "have to," "must," "need to" or "ought").

Decrease the number of "bummer" words you use and increase the positive. Fill in the following blanks:

Instead of saying _______________, I did (or can) say _______________.

Briefly describe a situation or event in your past or present life. Show that you can consider alternatives by listing several choices you had or have. Don't evaluate a choice at this time (especially don't think "I can't do that").

Briefly describe a problem or bothersome situation from your past. List any positive action steps you took in a effort to solve or change it. If you took no action, what *could* you have done?

The last time I procrastinated was

This was an example of procrastination that was (positive or negative) because

Chapter 4

EMOTIONAL MONITORING AND LEARNING

- Over a period of a week, keep an emotional diary. Whenever you become aware of a particular feeling, list the emotion, the reason for it, your physiological arousal (if apparent), and the way you expressed the emotion (verbally, nonverbally, or both).

- List two emotions you commonly experience then describe how you express them.

- With whom do you feel most comfortable expressing these emotions? If you experience discomfort expressing them, with whom does this occur?

Finish these statements:

When I'm slightly annoyed, I usually

When I'm angry, I usually

I show my affection to ______________ by

When I'm happy, others know it because I

When I'm proud, I usually

I am afraid of

I show fear by

When I'm sad, I usually

I get sad when

I don't show affection to ______________ because

As a result of being (male or female), what idea did you receive regarding emotional expression?

From the following, list one message (verbal or nonverbal) received concerning emotional expression.

Family

Peers

Ethnic group and/or religion

RATIONAL-EMOTIVE-THERAPY

Fill in the ABC boxes regarding an event in your life.

The Way It Was

***A**ctivating Event*	***B**elief*	***C**onsequences* (emotions and behaviors)

The Way It Could Have Been Using Thought-Changing

***A**ctivating Event*	***B**elief*	***C**onsequences* (emotions and behaviors)

Practice using RET at least once a day and enjoy the results.

Identify sources of stress in your life.

A major life change

A common hassle or everyday irritant

Internal or self-imposed

What, if anything, can you do about any of these?

Coping with Stress

Try deep breathing several times during the day. Breathe in slowly and deeply through your nose, hold briefly, then exhale through your mouth. To check if you are breathing deeply, place your hands (outstretched middle fingers lightly touching each other) over your diaphragm. Inhale. Did your middle fingers separate slightly? If not, you are not breathing deeply. Deeply inhaled air will expand the diaphragm area (like a balloon), and your fingers will spread slightly. A few of these deep breaths can relieve stress and anxiety in most situations. If you want to use a relaxation technique, get into a comfortable position and use several deep breaths to lower your body's state of arousal.

Take charge of your stress by putting into practice another of the suggested stress-reducing suggestions.

The one I've selected is

When I will start is

Draw a path of life for yourself identifying major ups and downs.

Which of the coping mechanisms/behaviors recommended in this chapter have you used?

Chapter 5

VALUES, DECISIONS, GOALS

Use the same four values you identified in the Chapter 1 activity and describe as follows:

Value | *Received by Which Method(s)* | *Influence*

My 10-year-old decade was ______________.

What significant event(s) occurred at that time?

How have you been or may you become influenced by the decade?

Give any examples of values being transmitted to you by:

Moralizing

Laissez-faire or hands-off

Identify any of the recommended ways your values were developed.

As a parent, what are you doing or will you do to transmit values?

If you have already experienced either a major life change, mental unrest, or a change in needs, briefly describe what that was. If you have not yet experienced any of these, describe some likely future reasons your values could change.

A poor choice I have made regarding my health was

A wise choice I have or will make regarding my health is

An important decision I have made was

I made the decision in the following way:

I used more of my ______________________________ (thinking or feeling) preference.

Goals I have completed in the last year are

Develop a list of "wants" allowing your child ego state complete freedom. Use other paper. No matter how unrealistic they are, DREAM. Then select one and decide to make it a goal.

One of my short-term goals is ____.

Check the following if you can answer "yes."

_______ Is the goal mine, not someone else's?
_______ Is the goal in accord with my values?
_______ Is the goal a priority of mine?
_______ Is the goal realistic?
_______ Is the goal specific?

Identify specific action steps pinpointing as much as possible. Be sure to mention exactly what action you will take with a specific way to measure it as well as a date of completion for each step.

When completed, be sure to pat yourself on the back!

Chapter 6

HOW WELL DO YOU LISTEN?

Using the scale answer the following questions:

5 = Almost always	4 = Usually	3 = About half the time
	2 = Sometimes	1 = Hardly ever

1. _______ I am interested in other people.
2. _______ I ask questions about other people's interests.
3. _______ The opinions of others are of interest to me.
4. _______ I am able to focus my attention on what someone is saying.
5. _______ I put aside my thoughts and feelings and concentrate on what is being said.
6. _______ I try to create a positive listening environment by getting rid of distractions and other obstacles.
7. _______ I realize I have a psychological filter and check it periodically so that it doesn't interfere with my listening.
8. _______ I approach others with the idea that they have something of value to contribute to a conversation.
9. _______ When listening, I face the person who is talking.
10. _______ I keep an open body position.
11. _______ When listening, my body is relaxed, yet attentive.
12. _______ I maintain eye contact at least three quarters of the time. When I look away, I quickly bring my eyes back to the speaker's face.
13. _______ When listening, my facial expression registers what I am thinking and feeling.
14. _______ My facial expression changes during a typical conversation.
15. _______ When listening, I nod my head affirmatively an appropriate number of times.
16. _______ During conversation I am comfortable with appropriate touching.
17. _______ When listening, I use brief verbal responses which show interest.
18. _______ I ask encouraging questions of the speaker.
19. _______ When listening, I try to find ways to clarify the speaker's point.
20. _______ I avoid negative listening behaviors.

Total your score. Give yourself a grade as follows:

95 – 100 = A+	90 – 94 = A	85 – 89 = B+	80 – 84 = B
75 – 79 = C+	70 – 74 = C	65 – 69 = D+	60 – 64 = D

59 or below = Unsatisfactory

Most importantly, what can you do to improve your listening?

Observe two other people who are in a listening role. Briefly, describe and evaluate their listening behaviors.

Chapter 7

IDENTIFYING CLOSED COMMUNICATION

Use the following letters to identify closed types. If the statement has more than one type, use more than one letter.

D = Dogmatic C = Commando G = Grandiose

1. _______ That man has an obnoxious personality.

2. _______ He needs to listen more to other people's opinions.

3. _______ Jane always thinks of other's feelings.

4. _______ I think you should quit that job.

5. _______ It seems to me that he will never learn good money management skills unless he has his own income.

6. _______ Nobody appreciates what I do.

USING OPEN COMMUNICATION

Re-write each of the statements above in the open style.

1. ____

2. ____

3. ____

4. ____

5. ____

6. ____

Listen for any example of closed communication, write it, then reword it in the open style.

Ask someone to listen to you for any uses of fillers.

UNDERSTANDING PARALANGUAGE AND BODY LANGUAGE

While listening to a conversation, be aware of examples of paralanguage and body language. Describe some of these. Disregarding what was actually being said as much as possible, briefly explain what could be interpreted from the paralanguage and body language examples.

Pretend you are writing a script for a play. Write a short scene between two or more characters. Write the lines to be said and after each, describe briefly the paralanguage and body language you want the characters to demonstrate.

Carry on a conversation with someone and try not to vary your body language during the time (same posture, facial expression, etc.).

Chapter 8

SELF-DISCLOSURE

Using the following, identify each self-disclosing statement.

BD = Basic data   P = Preference   B = Belief   F = Feeling

_______ I was concerned when he was late coming home.

_______ I thought he might have had an accident.

_______ My opinion on that candidate is a positive one.

_______ I graduated from high school last year.

_______ I voted in the last election.

_______ I enjoyed the concert.

_______ I am disappointed because you don't want to go with me.

_______ I don't think that was a wise choice.

_______ I didn't like that restaurant.

_______ I was quite proud of my grade.

Now write one statement disclosing about yourself on each level.

BD ____

P ____

B ____

F ____

Fill in the blanks about your self-disclosure.

I enjoy sharing preference statements with ____________________ because

I am comfortable disclosing about my beliefs with ______________________________.

One person who shares beliefs with me is ______________________________ while ______________________________ seems reluctant to do so.

My feelings in most situations are easy to disclose to ______________________________ because ______________________________.

One person who discloses feelings to me is ______________________________.

A person who doesn't reveal feelings to me is ______________________________.

SENSING, INTERPRETING, OR FEELING?

Tell which is provided in the statements using the following code.

S = sensing   I = interpretation   F = feeling

_______ It seems to me that she is upset.

_______ I'm happy.

_______ I think that taking time to visit her was good for me.

_______ I heard what he said.

_______ I noticed that she didn't talk to him.

PERCEPTION CHECKING

Write what you could say in the following situations using perception checking. Because each scenario contains only sensing *or* interpretative information, you are to make up what is missing.

Your friend Jack tells you that he has seen your roommate and another person looking at apartments. Use perception checking in talking to your roommate about this.

1.

2.

3.

You think that your supervisor at work is unhappy with your performance. Use perception checking to speak to him or her about this.

1.

2.

3.

FEELING STATEMENT

Write a feeling statement about the supervisor situation described above. Remember that your feeling is related to your interpretation.

GIVING CRITICISM

Your child or roommate has not cleaned up the kitchen after using it as agreed upon. Write what you would say using recommendations for delivering criticism.

POSITIVE RESPONSES TO CRITICISM

Your employer has said to you, "You don't seem to care about your job." First, write the two-step response if you *understand the reason* for the criticism.

1.

2.

Then write the two-step response if you do *not understand the reason* for the criticism.

1.

2.

AWARENESS WHEEL

Read the scenario regarding Terri and Matt in the Fair Fighting activity in Chapter 11. Pretend you are Matt before the fight begins. Write statements of awareness he could have used in discussing the situation with Terri.

Sensing

Thinking

Feeling

Wanting

Acting

You might also try doing the same for Terri's dimensions of awareness before she spoke to Matt about the situation.

Chapter 9

FRIEND-TO-FRIEND

With a friend, talk about the following, then write a short summary of your discussion in each category.

Social Exchange

What do each of us receive from our friendship? What more, if anything, would we like to receive from this friendship?

Attraction Factors

Describe briefly how any of the following were involved in your friendship.

Proximity

Similarities

Complementarity

Reciprocity

Characteristics and Behaviors

How would each of us describe a best friend? Which of the behaviors and characteristics do we possess? What do we like about each other?

Expectations

What do we expect of each other in this friendship?

IMPROVING RELATIONSHIPS

Identify any situation in which you have or could have demonstrated the following positive characteristics:

Tolerance or acceptance

Empathy

Sensitivity

Cooperation

Assertiveness

Negotiation skills

Complete the following sentences:

To me, a person is being difficult when he or she

I usually deal with this by

An effective way to deal with it might be to

I probably am "difficult" to others when I

Unload Your Gunnysack

Using "I" statements describe a resentment, then tell how you feel and what you want.

Resentment (I resent it when you)	Feeling (When this happens, I feel)	Want (I want you to)

Future Intentions

In the future, I would like to:

_______ Call or write a note when someone needs support.
_______ Tell someone that I have been concerned about him or her and I care.
_______ Visit someone in the hospital or nursing home.
_______ Actually, do something to assist a person or family during a crisis.
_______ Be a courteous driver.
_______ Help someone by opening a door, offering to let them go ahead of me, etc.
_______ Smile and greet someone.
_______ Do a favor for another person.
_______ Say thank you and please. Show appreciation.
_______ Forgive someone.
_______ Demonstrate warm and affectionate behavior.

Of the ones checked, which *will* you do?

What have you gained (learned) so far that will help you develop healthy relationships?

Chapter 10

ASSETS AND LIABILITIES

Your assets are what you have to offer a potential employer. These are strong points that will help you get and keep a job. Your liabilities are drawbacks or limitations that could hinder you from getting or keeping a job. Consider the following categories.

Interests	Education	Work Experience	Personality
Skills	Goals	Volunteer Work	Work Habits

In each of the areas, list assets then liabilities. Use anything from the chapter to help you (i.e., the table of positive personal qualities and work habits and the characteristics employers have identified as positive).

Now select what you consider to be your top six assets and your top three liabilities. Practice discussing your assets so that you can use them to answer interview questions such as "Why should we hire you?" or "What do you have to offer?" Think about your liabilities and decide how you could discuss them if that is ever required. If you have any liabilities that can be changed before your job search, set a goal to do so.

JOB SATISFACTION

List as many as possible under the following columns.

What I Like to Do	What I Do Well

Circle any that you either *do* at your present job or those that you believe you will be *doing* at a future job.

The more you like to do and do well that you can actually *do* at work adds up to job satisfaction!

Chapter 11

NEEDS FULFILLMENT

Think of any relationship you have or want to have. In the right-hand column, name 5 needs you would like to have fulfilled in the relationship and then describe them in behavioral terms. In the left-hand column corresponding with each need, describe what the other person must be like and/or do in order to satisfy that need. Use the following example as a guide.

Need	Person
Companionship and enjoyable experiences. Both of us will have fun together on a regular basis because we enjoy each other's company and have several mutually enjoyable activities.	She (or he) will have many of the same interests as I do and enjoy several of the same activities. She (or he) will have a personality I like, and we will be able to have fun together by ourselves and in the company of others.

Need	Person
1.	**1.**
2.	**2.**
3.	**3.**
4.	**4.**
5.	**5.**

Now looking back, write about any of your needs which were not fulfilled in a past relationship. Or, do so for a present relationship. Use your own paper.

FAIR FIGHTING

Read the following scenario, then using the fair fighting criteria described in the chapter, identify all the ways in which this was an unfair fight. Jot these down in the margin.

Matt and Terri, who are engaged to be married, had attended a wedding and reception together. At the reception Terri spent a great deal of time talking with friends of hers from high school whom Matt did not know and then she danced a few times with a former boyfriend. After the reception they have the following conversation.

Terri: You're mad, I can tell.

Matt: No, I'm not.

Terri: Come on, Matt. You've been quiet since we left the reception. I know you are.

Matt: I'm surprised you even noticed.

Terri: What's that supposed to mean?

Matt: You were so busy having a great time.

Terri: What else are you supposed to do at a reception . . . sit alone and not talk to anyone like you do?

Matt: Like I do, huh? You weren't exactly the friendliest person in the world when we went to my class reunion last summer!

Terri: No wonder. They were all so boring. At least my high school friends are fun.

Matt: You looked like you were having *a lot* of fun dancing with Paul.

Terri: So that's it! You are so insecure sometimes. I can't believe you would be jealous just because I danced with him. Remember when you danced with several old girlfriends at your reunion? Did I get jealous? No!

Matt: You wouldn't ever get jealous because you think you're so much better than anyone else. Besides that, you don't show me enough affection. I give and give and don't get a lot in return unless you happen to be in the mood to really pay attention to me. You talk to your other friends more than you do to me and seem to enjoy their company more. You don't act like you're ready to get married; in fact, you don't even seem to really be in love with me. And every time we fight, you want to have the last word.

Terri: You sure seem to have a lot of complaints! And of course there's *nothing* wrong with you. Why don't you just find someone else?

Matt: Maybe I will! I hope you're satisfied that you've won another one.

Chapter 12

FAMILY PICTURE

Using any figures you want (human-like, stick figures, circles, squares, etc.), draw a diagram of your family. Label each figure with the person's name and relationship to you.

If possible, compare your diagram to others and think about how your concept of family is similar or different.

PARENTING BEHAVIORS

What do or would you like your child to be like when he or she is a young adult? First, list or describe the characteristic in the right-hand column, then describe what would be advisable for you to do or not do in terms of parenting behaviors. Use other paper if necessary. **Use this as a guide now or in the future.**

Description of Young Adult	Parenting Behaviors

Index

D

E

Q

R

S